KEY WORD®

a HEBREW WORD for the DAY

KEY WORDS from the OLD TESTAMENT

AMG

DR. J.D. WATSON

A Hebrew Word for the Day

Published by AMG Reference, an imprint of AMG Publishers, Inc.
6815 Shallowford Rd.
Chattanooga, Tennessee 37421

ISBN–13: 978-0-89957-697-8
ISBN–10: 0-89957-697-4

First printing–October 2010
Cover designed by Bright Boy Design, Chattanooga, Tennessee
Edited and Proofread by Warren Baker, Trevor Overcash, Rich Cairnes, and Rick Steele

Printed in the United States of America
15 14 13 12 11 10 –DP– 8 7 6 5 4 3 2 1

Dedication

This work is dedicated first to my dear Savior and Lord,
Jesus Christ, and also to

Mr. Roy McKee

a dear, faithful brother,
whom I have had the honor of shepherding for many
years and who has been a constant source of encouragement.

Acknowledgments

First and foremost, I want to thank my friend Dr. William D. Barrick, professor of Old Testament and director of ThD Studies at The Master's Seminary, for writing the Introduction and for his technical editing of the manuscript. His scholarship, some of which is reflected in his occasional comments in the endnotes, was invaluable.

I also want to thank my friend of many years, Bob Dasal, former editor-in-chief of *Pulpit Helps*, for "hand carrying" the idea for this book's predecessor, *A Word for the Day*, to Dan Penwell, Manager of Product Development/Acquisitions at AMG. Thanks then to Dan, and the AMG editorial committee, for asking me to write this second volume. And thanks also to Rick Steele, Dan's replacement after his retirement, for guiding the project.

Many thanks also go out to all the editors, proofreaders, and typesetters who diligently labored to make this book readable: Warren Baker, Rich Cairnes, Trevor Overcash, and Rick Steele.

Among all the other things my loving helpmeet, Debbie, does, I thank her for her proofreading and the countless hours of work she put in on the indexes.

Thanks to Cook Communications Ministries for the "Words and Speaking in Proverbs" table mentioned on July 16: Copyright 1985 Cook Communications Ministries. *The Bible Knowledge Commentary: Old Testament* by Walvoord and Zuck. Reprinted with permission. May not be further reproduced. All rights reserved.

Preface

The Old Testament is the one true revelation regarding the creation of the universe, the origin of man, the fall of mankind through Adam and Eve, Noah's ark, God's special selection of the people of Israel, personalities like Abraham, Joseph, Moses, King David and others, the Exodus, the Kingdoms of Israel and Judah, untold miracles, and the foundations of the plan of God for the salvation of those who have faith according to the Scriptures.

These themes and stories summarize the extent of Old Testament knowledge for most believers. For those students of faith and of the Bible that want more, there are commentaries to help expound on the stories, theological books to help assimilate the meanings and teachings of the Bible, special books to deal with difficult passages, and concordances to reference between passages that use the same English word or phrase.

All of these resources are a definite help in studying God's Word. But what do you do when the only way to fully understand the Bible is to study the words of the original languages? For the Old Testament this might mean signing up for classes in Hebrew and Aramaic. However, AMG has, for many years, provided tools to allow believers to dig deep into the riches of the Hebrew Old Testament and the Greek New Testament, without having to formally study Hebrew or Greek to do so.

The Key Word Study Bibles and Complete Word Study series products provide all the tools you need for the study of the meaning of the original languages. Yet, as wonderful as these works are, gleaning materials from them still requires time and effort. And in these busy times, a brief devotion on the meaning of a particular word in a particular passage might take some time. In *A Word for the Day*, "Doc" Watson already did all the work. In that book he revealed the dimensions of key words from the vocabulary of the Greek New Testament in a book of daily studies. In ***A Hebrew Word for the Day,*** "Doc" Watson does a similar set of devotionals using words from the vocabulary of the Hebrew Old Testament in similar daily studies. One day at a time, he will share the images he found in his own personal studies, and give suggestions on how using these studies can lead you into a more complete understanding of God's Word.

Dr. Warren Baker
Chattanooga, TN

Also by the author:
A Word for the Day: Key Words from the New Testament
AMG Publishers
www.AMGPublishers.com

Contents

Introduction

As I wrote in the introduction to the predecessor of this book, *A Word for the Day*,[1] words matter, so the words of the Scriptures matter most. As also noted there, since words don't seem to mean much nowadays, the need for precision in Christian doctrine and practice has never been more critical. While that book is based upon Greek words, this one is founded upon a study of Hebrew words.

When I think of the Hebrew language, I think of pictures. With broad, sweeping strokes, it paints beautiful landscapes and provides detailed descriptions. A major reason for this is the Hebrew vocabulary. So rich is it, in fact, that quite often several individual Hebrew words can be translated into a single English word. There are, for example, three words translated "salvation," four rendered "man," and four others rendered "marriage." If that does not seem significant, we see as many as thirteen Hebrew words translated "light," fourteen as "dark," eighteen as "fear," and twenty-five as "deliver." Those are just a few examples, as are "destroy," which is the translation of fifty-five Hebrew words, "bring" with sixty-six, and "take" for seventy-four. Such diversity is also seen in the many descriptive names used for God (see January 7–30), Scripture (see February 11–24), and other concepts.

Another evidence of the importance of the Hebrew Old Testament is that most New Testament doctrines have their basis in Old Testament theology. From sin, to salvation, to service, the New Testament is *enfolded* in the Old, while the Old is *unfolded* in the New. Or, as Augustine put it, "The New is in the Old *contained*, the Old is in the New *explained*." While some theological truths (such as the church) are foreign to the Old Testament, most New Testament subjects are rooted in the Old, such as: the nature of God, Creation, man, morality, sin, redemption, worship, wisdom, truth, and the list goes on. (Note the further discussion in the Forward that follows.)

To illustrate, just as we must listen to a symphony or concerto from the beginning to hear the theme (or themes) that will be developed through the various movements, we must do the same with Scripture. Themes introduced in the Old Testament are developed in the New. Further, Bible teachers often speak of fulfilled Bible prophecy or the fulfilling of the Mosaic Law in Christ (see February 9, 16), so to appreciate fully such fulfillment, it is necessary for us to understand the truths of the Old Testament, truths that are expressed, of course, by words.

The *words* of Scripture, therefore, are the *stones* used to build its structure. Without words, there can be no truth. If I may illustrate with a controversial subject, any translation approach that is not word-for-word is dangerous at best. The popular approach dubbed *dynamic equivalence* is unconcerned with the words themselves; instead, it is only the "thought of the writer" that matters. But, if we may ask, how can we know the thoughts of the writer without the exact words? Without a word-for-word approach, in which the Hebrew and Greek words are rendered as closely as possible into English, how can we expect accuracy? And if we don't have accuracy, how can we have authority? It continues to puzzle and grieve me that many Christian leaders, who profess to be concerned about biblical authority, continue to defend dynamic equivalence.

How important are the biblical languages? Having always been strong on the mastery of the biblical languages, Martin Luther wrote: "And let us be sure of this: we will not long preserve the gospel without the languages. The languages are the sheath in which this sword of the Spirit is contained; they are the casket in which this jewel is enshrined; they are the vessel in which this wine is held; they are the larder in which this food is stored; and, as the gospel itself points out, they are the baskets in which are kept these loaves and fishes and fragments. . . . Therefore, although faith and the gospel may indeed be proclaimed by simple preachers without a knowledge of languages, such preaching is flat and tame; people finally become weary and bored with it, and it falls to the ground. But where the preacher is versed in the languages, there is a freshness and vigor in his preaching, Scripture is treated in its entirety, and faith finds itself constantly renewed by a continual variety of words and illustrations."[2]

This book, therefore, is about Hebrew words. Each day of the year, we will examine a particular Hebrew word by first presenting a brief word study and then a practical application to make that word real in your life. For reinforcement, each day also includes other related verses you can study on your own ("Scriptures for Study"). Finally, we would encourage you to use each day's study to generate "promptings for prayer." Meditate on each day's study and allow the Holy Spirit to prompt you in the three basic aspects of prayer: thanksgiving, praise, and petition.

Like its predecessor, this book has been one of the greatest joys of my life and one of the most profitable exercises of my ministry for our Lord. If I may add, there is no greater flattery to a writer, not to mention humbling responsibility, than knowing that people are actually reading the words he writes. And this writer thanks you from his heart for doing so. I pray that the words you are about to read will be a source of joy and profit. Most of all I pray:

εἰς ἔπαινον δόξης τῆς χάριτος αὐτοῦ

(eis epainon doxēs tēs charitos autou)

"To the praise of (the) glory of the grace of him. . . ."—Eph. 1:6

Foreword

Why spend time becoming familiar with the words, phrases, divine titles, and concepts of the Old Testament? Often someone asks, "Shouldn't I be more interested in pursuing New Testament truths and teachings? After all, isn't the New Testament the ultimate revelation from God?" Take the time to scan through the headings of the pages in this daily devotional. How many words, phrases, or concepts do you find that are not also in the New Testament? In reality, the New Testament writers were saturated with a knowledge of the Old Testament and it poured forth from their very souls. Their blood ran "Bibline"—a description devotees have applied to Charles Haddon Spurgeon and John Bunyan. Cut them and the essence of the Bible flows from them. Paul, John, and Peter, together with all the other New Testament writers, spoke and wrote with Old Testament vocabulary, Old Testament phraseology, and Old Testament theological and spiritual concepts. "Church" is one of the few New Testament concepts not found within the Old Testament—that is why she and the age in which God established her were a mystery (Eph. 3:3–9).

Think of the key theological concepts that highlight the New Testament's teachings. The Old Testament speaks of sacrifice almost from the beginning (Gen. 4:3–5; 8:20) and develops the concept more fully in Leviticus 1–7. Substitution is the undeniable theme of Isaiah 53:4–6. Reconciliation refers to making peace with God (cf. Isa. 27:5). Psalm 49 presents redemption in a manner that is remarkably sophisticated. The "sweet savour" of the sacrifices is the Old Testament equivalent of propitiation (Exod. 29:25; Lev. 1:9). More than 200 years prior to Christ, the Greek Septuagint translated the Hebrew word for *pardon* with the Greek *hilasmos*, which the New Testament employs for *propitiate* (Ps. 24:11). Job 14, together with 19:25–27, provides readers with a sophisticated discussion of resurrection. Even the concept of everlasting life tantalizes the Old Testament reader in passages such as Psalms 16:11; 21:4; 22:26; 37:27–28; 49:10; 61:6–7; 139:24; and Ecclesiastes 12:5. The list of theological terms goes on: *salvation, forgiveness, sanctification, justification, righteousness, holiness,* and many more. All are rooted in the Old Testament. A greater understanding of the Old Testament produces a clearer understanding of the New Testament's employment of these words and their associated theological concepts. One of the examples is the concept of *divine election* (**bāchar,** April 14)—originally revealed in the Old Testament, but later developed more fully in the New Testament.

It is reported that an old prospector summed up his life in the following words: "I spent five years looking for gold and twenty years looking for my burro." Striking gold in word studies has about the same ratio. For every nugget the student finds, he can expect to spend four hours looking for it. Word studies are not for the lazy or the quitter. It is a labor of love requiring commitment and perseverance.

Sound interpretation does not come as the result of word studies alone. Indeed, an interpreter's overoccupation with word studies can be detrimental to biblical exposition. Word studies have the potential of being as inaccurate as mechanical translation. Nigel Turner put it this way:

> Just as a sentence is more revealing than a single word, so the examination of a writer's syntax and style is that much more important to a biblical commentator. It is not surprising that fewer books have been written on this subject than on vocabulary, because whereas students of vocabulary can quickly look up lists of words in concordances and indices, in the field of syntax the study is more circuitous. There is no help except in a few selective grammars and monographs, so that the worker really must work his way through all the texts in Greek (*Grammatical Insights into the New Testament* [Edinburgh: T. & T. Clark, 1965], pp. 2–3).

Bible students will learn far more about obedience, disobedience, sacrifice, and sin from the full statement of a passage such as 1 Samuel 15:22–23 than from word studies of *zeḇach, šāma', chaṭṭāṯ, and mā'as*—all of which are found in that passage. Likewise, the student finds out more about the doctrine of sin by the apostle's propositional statement that "sin is the transgression of the law" (1 John 3:4) than a detailed analysis of the Greek word hamartia.

Having decried the potential overemphasis of philology or etymology, we must, however, recognize that the choice of individual words was indeed significant to the writers of Scripture. The interpreter is thoroughly justified in asking, "Why did the writer choose this term as opposed to one of its synonyms?" The choice of word made a difference to the writer, who was superintended by the Holy Spirit (2 Pet. 1:21), so it ought to make a difference to us.

So, we ask again: Why pursue word studies? Because the Spirit-superintended writer of the Scriptures chose his words with care and purpose. It made a difference to him and to the Spirit of God. It is the reader's obligation to discover the reason for one word's choice over another. Sometimes the reason is due to a different meaning. Sometimes it is due to a need for variety to expand the scope of the concept being described. Sometimes it is due to the need for poetic assonance or the constraints of an acrostic. Whatever the word, there is at least one good reason for its choice—a reason that is key to a fuller understanding of the biblical text itself.

An American television commercial depicts a father and his young son sitting on the seashore, the father sipping a drink through a straw, and watching the sun set in all its splendor and glory. The sounds of the sipping coincide with the progressive sinking of the sun. Suddenly, the sun is gone and the drink is finished. The young lad says, "Do it again, Daddy." A similar situation involves reading *A Hebrew Word for the Day.* As each day's meditation on a Hebrew word closes, the reader will find himself or herself saying, "Do it again, Doc." Word by word each day's meditation draws the reader inexorably on to the next delightful study of God's Word in its multifaceted glory. If the taste of such flavorful morsels draws you on to a deeper and more detailed analysis of God's Word, these meditations will have accomplished their purpose.

Dr. William D. Barrick
Professor of Old Testament
Director of ThD Studies
The Master's Seminary

Conventions and Abbreviations

Akkadian – From two of the sons of Noah—Ham and Shem—came several languages spoken by their descendants. Hamitic languages included Egyptian (called Coptic after the third century AD), North African Berber, Sudanese, Bantu, Hottentot, and Bushman. In contrast, one of the languages of the Semites—who were, of course, the racial family to which Israel belonged—was Akkadian, also called Assyrian and Babylonian, and was the common language of Southwest Asia during those empires. While not used in the Old Testament, many Old Testament Hebrew words were influenced by the Akkadian. Other Semitic languages include: Aramaic, Arabic, Ethiopic, Phoenician, and Ugaritic.

AV – *Authorized King James Version* (unless noted otherwise, all Scripture quotations are taken from the AV).

Bold text – a primary word examined in a daily reading.

Classical (ancient or secular) Greek – Greek prior to New Testament times. References to that include, for example, the Greek used by Plato (ca. 435–427 BC) and the Greek of the poet Homer (eighth century BC), who is famous for his epic poems, *The Iliad* and *The Odyssey*.

ESV – *English Standard Version*

NASB – *New American Standard Bible*

NIV – *New International Version*

NT – New Testament

OT – Old Testament

Septuagint – the Greek translation of the Hebrew Old Testament; translated in the third and second centuries BC, probably in Alexandria, for the Library of Ptolemy Philadelphus, king of Egypt, by a delegation of seventy Jewish scholars; hence the name *Septuagint* (seventy), and the use of the abbreviation LXX.

Strong's Number – For easy cross-referencing to many Hebrew tools, Hebrew and Greek words in the readings also include the universally used Strong's number enclosed in parentheses. A "G" following a number indicates a Greek word.

Hebrew Pronunciation Guide

Guide to the Transliteration of Hebrew Consonants

Hebrew Name	*Transliteration*	*Phonetic Sound*	*Example*
Aleph	ʼ	Silent	Similar to *h* in honor
Beth	*B*	b	as in boy
Veth	*ḇ*	v	as in vat
Gimel	*G*	g	as in get
Gimel	*ḡ*	g	as in get
Daleth	*D*	d	as in do
Daleth	*ḏ*	d	as in do
Hē	*H*	h	as in hat
Waw	*W*	w	as in wait
Zayin	*Z*	z	as in zip
Cheth	*Ḥ*	ch	Similar to *ch* in the German *ach*
Teth	*Ṭ*	t	as in time
Yodh	*Y*	y	as in you
Kaph	*K*	k	as in kit
Chaph	*ḵ*	ch	Similar to *ch* in the German *ach*
Lamedh	*L*	l	as in lit
Mem	*M*	m	as in move
Nun	*N*	n	as in not
Samekh	*S*	s	as in see
Ayin	ʻ	Silent	Similar to *h* in honor
Pē	*P*	p	as in put
Phē	*p̄*	f	as in phone
Tsadde	*Ṣ*	ts	as in wits
Qoph	*Q*	q	as in Qatar
Resh	*R*	r	as in run
Sin	*Ś*	s	as in see
Shin	*Š*	sh	as in ship
Taw	*T*	t	as in time
Thaw	*ṯ*	th	as in this

Guide to the Transliteration of Hebrew Vowels

Name	Transliteration	Sound
Shewa (Silent)	Not transliterated or pronounced	
Shewa (Vocal)	*e*	u as in but
Pathah	*a*	a as in lad
Hateph Pathah	*a*	a as in lad
Qamets	*ā*	a as in car
Hateph Qamets	*ā*	a as in car
Sere	*ē*	ey as in prey
Sere Yodh	*ēy*	ey as in prey
Seghol	*e*	e as in set
Hateph Seghol	*e*	e as in set
Hiriq Yodh	*iy*	i as in machine
Hiriq	*i*	i as in pin
Qamets Qatan	*o*	o as in hop
Holem	*ō*	o as in go
Holem Waw	*ô*	o as in go
Qubbuts	*u*	u as in put
Shureq	*û*	u as in tune

Thy Word Have I Hid in Mine Heart Today

(A Sonnet of Prayer)

Thy Word have I hid in mine heart today,
That in nothing might I sin against Thee;
I come before Thy face without delay,
Because of my Savior at Calvary.
Thy Word have I hid in mine heart today,
Your Truth being my uttermost desire;
Because it's my pillar, my ground, and stay,
Of its proclamation I never tire.
Thy Word have I hid in mine heart today,
It is my single greatest possession;
From its sufficiency I will not stray,
For its power keeps me from transgression.
    Thy Word have I hid in mine heart today,
    That I might know Thy thoughts, Thy will, Thy way.

New Song

chādāš šiyr

We've all heard the old expression that someone is "singing a different tune" or has "changed his tune." The expression probably arose in the Middle Ages **among** wandering minstrels. As they traveled from court to court, they thought it prudent to change the words of their songs to please each baron.[3]

Long before the Middle Ages, however, God's people were **singing** a **new song**, and that **song** was of much greater **joy** and significance. **New** is the Hebrew *chādāš* (2319), which often indicates something **new** in the sense of "never seen or done before."[4] It appears in Ezekiel 18:31, for example: "Cast away from you all your transgressions, whereby ye have transgressed; and make you a new heart and a new spirit."

Song, then, is *šiyr* (7892), a type of lyrical **song** or religious **song**. It also appears several times in Ezra and Nehemiah to refer to songs of Levitical choirs. In Nehemiah 12:46, for example, Nehemiah recounts that in David's **day** music directors led "songs of praise."

Significantly, it is at times also used in a negative **way**. Amos uses it to picture the apathy of the people, as they lay around eating, drinking, strumming their musical instruments, and singing, totally oblivious to God's coming judgment (in Amos 6:5, "music" is *šiyr*). Here is a warning to the world, and even the church, concerning complacency and an insatiable desire for entertainment and leisure.

It is when we see these two words together, however, that we discover a wondrous truth. The term **new song** appears seven times in the OT, and in each case we see a **new song** being composed in response to what God has done. "Fresh mercies," writes commentator Adam Clarke, "call for new songs of praise and gratitude." The first occurrence, in fact, is Psalm 33:3, which is set in the context of the great event of Creation.

What, then, could be more appropriate as we start a **new** year than to be reminded to sing a **new song** every day? Does not each day bring **new** mercies, **new** blessings, **new** joys, **new** triumphs? It also reminds us that we do, indeed, "sing a different tune" than the world.

Scriptures for Study: Read the other OT occurrences of **new song**, noting how God is being praised for what He has done: Psalm 40:3; 96:1; 98:1; 144:9; 149:1; Isaiah 42:10. 📖 Note also the two NT occurrences of **new song**: Revelation 5:9; 14:3. **New** is the Greek *kainos* (G2537), "something new in quality," having never existed before.[5]

Psalm

mizmôr

In **light** of yesterday's **meditation** on **song** (*šiyr*, 7892), another **blessed** OT **word** concerning music is **psalm**. The Hebrew is *mizmôr* (4210), which appears fifty-nine times in the OT, only in the Psalms, and always in the title (e.g., 3–6; 8–9; 11–15; 18–41). It is derived from the verb *zamar*, "to make music primarily on stringed instruments," and oh, what music we find in the Psalms! We discover in the Psalms the very depths of theology and spiritual truth. *Mizmôr*, then, is a **praise** song accompanied by a stringed musical instrument (as **David** sang a **psalm** while playing his lyre). This is all the more significant since in fifty psalms the words "To the chief Musician" also appear.

It is instructive to compare *mizmôr* with *šiyr*. While *mizmôr* appears only in the Psalms and only in a title, *šiyr* "is not confined to the Psalter and within the Psalter itself is used both as a title and in the psalm proper."[6] Perhaps even more significantly, while *šiyr* can also refer to a secular song (e.g., Isa. 23:16), *mizmôr* always refers to a religious song,[7] which we could define as "a sacred, inspired poem of praise." It is also significant that both words occur together in Psalms 30:1 and 65:1 (literally, "A Psalm-Song"), emphasizing both the voices (*šiyr*) and the accompanying musical instruments (*mizmôr*).

Music is truly a **wonderful** gift. For millennia, music has fascinated and captivated mankind, who have invented an enormous **number** of instruments, from the complex to the simple. Far more important, however, are "songs," because they are composed of words.

We would do well to remind ourselves that the **book** of Psalms (*Sēper Tehillim*, "Book of Praises") was the *hymnbook* of Israel, a book of sacred, sound, and solemn poems of theological depth. Oh, that we would desire such depth in our churches! Let us abandon the trite and trivial and embrace what is true and tasteful.

Scriptures for Study: Read Psalm 30, meditating on both ideas of **psalm** and **song**.

Name (1)

šēm

Today we begin a study that will continue throughout the month, one which I **pray** will touch our hearts and lives like nothing else can, namely, a study of the names of **God** used in the OT. This is critically important in our **day**, for many of the problems we see in the church come from a wrong conception of God. We simply do not **know** who He is. To combat this, instead of the shallow fluff (and even heresy) that lines the shelves of many Christian bookstores, would that pastors encouraged their people to read books such as A. W. Tozer's *The Knowledge of the Holy*, or Arthur W. Pink's *The Attributes of God*. To go deeper, Puritan Steven Charnock's, *The Existence and Attributes of God*, will furnish them with a lifetime of depth and meditation.

Before plunging into the many names of God in the OT, however, let us first consider three words that will help lay a foundation: **name**, **remember** (January 5), and **meditation** (January 6). While the etymology of the root *šēm* (8034), which appears some 864 times, is uncertain, some scholars believe that it comes from "the Arabic root *wšm* 'to mark or brand,' hence an external mark to distinguish one thing or person from another."[8] Names in the Semitic world—the "Semites," descendants of Noah's son Shem, were the racial family to which Israel belonged—were much more significant than in our Western culture. A person's **name**, in fact, "often carried more significance than an identification mark; it was considered to be a description of character or conditions."[9] Nabal's **name**, for example, reflects the fact that He was a **fool** (1 Sam. 25:25); ***Eve*** means "the mother of all living" (Gen. 3:20); *Isaac* means "he laughs," a reminder of his parents' laughter at the thought they could conceive a child in their old age; and *Babel* means "confusion," hence the **name** of the tower where God confounded earthly languages.

The names of God, therefore, are extremely significant. So important are His names that some theologians **call** this "name-theology." I like that term. "Theology" is the study of God, and to know His *names* is to know *Him*. As we study "name-theology," let us seek God with a *dedication* of mind, *devotion* of **heart**, and *depth* of **soul**.

Scriptures for Study: What do Psalms 20:5 and 44:8 encourage us to do concerning God's **name**? 🕮 What, then, is our responsibility, according to Exodus 9:16? 🕮

Name (2)

šēm

The word **name** (*šēm*, 8034) raises a couple of questions. "Why does God give Himself a name?" and then, further, "Why does God give Himself *several* names?" As for the first question, a **name** is important because it is personal and enables **God** (and us) to make contact. Without names, most all communication would be practically impossible.

That second question, however, takes us far deeper. Why is God called by *many* names? Why isn't just one, such as God (*'Elōhiym*, January 7), **good** enough? We would submit that God's giving Himself multiple names serves three purposes, purposes that simply could not be served by any one **name**:

First, God's multiple names more fully reveal His *person*. No single **name** of God could come even close to expressing His full nature, character, and **work**. That is a major limitation of language. As we will see, each **name** reveals something **new**, something unique, something deeper that we have not seen before.

Second, God's multiple names more fully demonstrate His *presence*. How often do we really stop and think about the implications of the truth that God is *with* us? Second Samuel 5:10, for example, declares that "David went on, and grew great, and the LORD God of hosts was with him," and as Luke recounts, when Joseph was "sold . . . into Egypt . . . God was with him" (Acts 7:9). Without exception, every name of God speaks of His presence with us and the staggering implications of that fact.

Third, God's multiple names more fully address His *people*. *Anthropomorphism* is the ascribing of human characteristics to nonhuman things. Many of us do this with our pets. God has done this very thing, though infinitely deeper. He speaks (Gen. 1:3), hears (Exod. 16:12), and sees (Gen. 1:4). **Scripture** uses figures of speech when indicating He has a **face** (Num. 6:25), a back (Exod. 33:23), arms (Exod. 6:6; Isa. 53:1), and hands (Isa. 14:27). Why does He do this? It is for our benefit, so we, in our limited human **understanding**, can grasp a little more of who He is and how He reaches down to us. Again, every one of His names underscores His relationship with His people, and no single **name** could possibly suffice.

Oh, let us **rejoice** in how God reveals Himself through His multiple names! Without this, we could never even **hope** to **know** Him.

Scriptures for Study: What do verses such as Psalms 34:3, 69:30, and 1 Timothy 6:1 encourage us to do concerning God's **name** (and names by implication)?

Remember
zākar

The Hebrew *zākar* (2142) occurs some 238 times in the OT,[10] fifty-seven of which are in the Psalms. It is usually translated in the AV as **remember**, "remembered," or "remembrance," but a few other translations include: "mention, think, and mindful." It means not only to **remember** but also "to think of or pay attention to."

The fact that *zākar* appears so often demonstrates that *remembrance in ancient Israel was a major part of proper **worship*** (March 1). Psalm 22:27, for example, declares: "All the ends of the world shall remember and turn unto the LORD: and all the kindreds of the nations shall worship before thee." Psalm 45:17 also declares, "I will make thy name to be remembered in all generations: therefore shall the people praise thee for ever and ever," as does Psalm 63:5–6: "My mouth shall praise thee with joyful lips: When I remember thee upon my bed, and meditate on thee in the night watches." We simply cannot worship unless we are remembering.

Indeed, one of the greatest acts of worship is to **remember** what **God** has done. The psalmist again declares, "I will remember the works of the LORD: surely I will remember thy wonders of old. . . . who is so great a God as our God?" (77:11, 13; cf. 105:5; 106:7). True worship considers God *alone*, lifting up *only* Him, and one **way** to do that is to recall His great works in the universe and in the hearts of His people.

Another graphic illustration of *zākar* involves the **book** of Deuteronomy. Its **name** literally means "second law," the book in which Moses restates the **Law** that he passed down to the next generation. *Zākar* appears fourteen times, as in chapter 5 to challenge the people to **remember** and **obey** God's commands (vv. 15–21).

Of special note is Psalm 20:7: "Some trust in chariots, and some in horses: but we will remember the name of the LORD our God." **David** probably penned this **psalm** on the occasion of going to **war**, perhaps with the Ammonites and Syrians (2 Sam. 10:1–19), who boasted of their many horses and chariots. While most men **trust** in military might or other earthly **power** or ability, David trusted God alone. What motivated such trust? Just remembering God's name, pondering who He really is, meditating on His attributes, character, and reputation.

Scriptures for Study: What is the psalmist's desire in Psalm 45:17? 🕮 In Psalm 63:5–7, what are some of the results in our lives when we **remember** God?

Meditation

higgāyôn

One more **word** that will help prepare us for considering the depth of God's names, as well as ready us for the rest of the studies in this **book**, is the word **meditation**. What *is* **meditation**? Many think of it as some empty-mindedness, where one sits cross-legged on the floor, fingers making some odd shape, and then contemplating the sound of one **hand** clapping.

On the contrary, true **meditation** involves thinking, not mindlessness. The Hebrew *higgāyôn* (1902, from the verb *hāgâ* [1897], "to growl, groan, sigh, mutter") refers to the murmur or dull sound of a harp and therefore the subdued or **soft** playing of a musical instrument. Does that not tell us what **meditation** is? We can define it as *quiet and concentrated thought*. We should often quietly ponder the Word, concentrate on its **precepts**, turn it over and over in our thoughts. This word goes further to picture soft muttering, as we might repeat a verse over and over to help assimilate and even memorize it.

A **wonderful** verse here is Psalm 19:14: "Let the words of my mouth, and the meditation of my heart, be acceptable in thy sight, O LORD, my strength, and my redeemer." In his classic **work** *The Treasury of David*, Charles Spurgeon writes about this verse: "As the miser often returns to look upon his treasure, so does the devout believer by frequent meditation turn over the priceless wealth which he has discovered in the book of the Lord." In contrast to the miser who picks up handfuls of **gold** coins and allows them to sift through his fingers as he greedily gazes upon them, we handle the priceless **wealth** of the Word and **praise** God for it.

What a lack there is of that today! While **worship** is certainly vocal, many churches are places of entertainment. In contrast, God speaks in "a still small voice" (1 Kings 19:12), or literally, "a sound of soft stillness," so we must be still and listen and respond with quiet **meditation**.

Therefore, as we begin our study of the names of God, let us approach it *meditatively*, that is, thoughtfully, contemplatively, and even musingly. Let us mull these names over and over in our minds, allowing them to sink **deep** into our hearts. Let us **remember** (January 4): to truly **know** God's **name** (January 3) is to know God.

Scriptures for Study: What is the object of **meditation** in Psalm 119:97 and 99? 🕮 What is our reaction to and result of **meditation** in Psalm 104:34?

God

'Elōhiym

We reverently step into God's presence today by meditating on His primary **name—God**. The Hebrew *'Elōhiym* (430) is the plural of *'Elôach* (433). The singular occurs only in poetry (e.g., Ps. 50:22; Isa. 44:8), while the plural *'Elōhiym* appears more than 2,600 times in the OT and usually refers to the One, True **God**. Not only does it speak of **God** as the Creator (Gen. 1:1; 5:1), but also as the **King** (Ps. 47:7), the **Judge** (Ps. 50:6), the **Lord** (Ps. 86:12), and the Savior (Hosea 13:4). (See January 23 for a discussion of *'ēl.*)

A basic feature of Hebrew is that any **word** ending in *iym* is plural, thus making *'Elōhiym* plural. This fact, however, has created three views as to *why* it appears in the plural. Some regard it as an intensive to signify God's fullness of **power**, others see it as a majestic form to indicate God's kingly rule, while still others believe it is an allusion to the Trinity.[11] While the doctrine of the Trinity is not as prevalent in the Old Testament as the **New**, it is there nonetheless, and to deny that fact is one of the most serious heresies of all false teaching.[12]

Genesis 1:1, 2, for example, alludes to two members of the Trinity, as the "Spirit of God [*'Elōhiym*] moved upon the face of the waters." We then read in verses 26 and 27, "And God [*'Elōhiym*] said, Let us make man in our image, after our likeness . . . So God [*'Elōhiym*] created man in his own image." Isaiah 48:16 also declares, "Come ye near unto me, hear ye this; I have not spoken in secret from the beginning; from the time that it was, there am I: and now the Lord GOD, and his Spirit, hath sent me" (cf. 63:7–10).

Finally, while some scholars trace the origin of this amazing word to a root that means the "Strong One," others trace it to a root that denotes **fear**, which therefore creates the idea of **reverence**. Others believe, however, that it is possible for some names to be derived from two or even three roots, which means that *'Elōhiym* could be both—the Strong One, who is to be feared and revered because of who He is.[13] That is, indeed, the challenge to us, to **remember** (January 4) who *'Elōhiym* is and what He has done.

Scriptures for Study: Read Genesis 1. How many times do you see the word **God** (they are all *'Elōhiym*)? What does that say about Creation?

YHWH (Jehovah, LORD)

Yāhweh

Here is a fascinating **name** indeed. Despite years of scholarship, little is known of the **word** ***YHWH*** (*Yāhweh*, 3068) outside the text of **Scripture**. Even its original pronunciation has been lost, because for centuries Jews would not even utter it, sometimes out of **reverence** but more often out of superstition. While the true pronunciation is not known with absolute certainty, the *Encyclopedia Judaica* claims that *Yāhweh* is the most likely pronunciation.

Up until the **Middle** Ages (AD 800–900) only the consonants YHWH (called the *Tetragrammaton*) appeared in the Hebrew Bible, at which **time** the vowels from another name of **God**, *'Aḏōnāy* (136), were added with the **hope** of recovering the pronunciation. Today, some Jewish students and scholars read *'Aḏōnāy* (**Lord**) when they see the Tetragrammaton, although most of them just say *Hashshem* ("the Name"), and most traditional English translations indicate this by using the word **LORD** in small capital letters.

On the other **hand**, **YHWH** is actually more fully defined in Scripture than all God's other names and is the most significant, appearing 5,321 times in the OT.[14] It comes from the Hebrew verb meaning "to be or exist" (*hāyāh*, 1961) and therefore emphasizes God's self-existence and unchangeableness, as He revealed Himself to Moses saying, "I AM THAT I AM" (Exod. 3:14), that is, "I Am the One Who Is." It was this name, in fact, that God chose as His personal name.

Jehovah is also the name that is specifically God's "covenant name," the name He usually used when making covenants and giving promises to His people, such as **Noah** (Gen. 8:20–9:27), Abraham (Gen. 12:1–3; 13:14–17; 15:1–18), and Moses (Exod. 20:1–31:18). In those passages, in fact, we find the word **YHWH** some sixty-eight times.

One of the chief uses of this name for God relates to His **work** of **redemption**. Leviticus 26:45, for example, declares, "I will for their sakes remember the covenant of their ancestors, whom I brought forth out of the land of Egypt in the sight of the heathen, that I might be their God: I am the LORD [Jehovah]." Psalm 19:14 proclaims, "Let the words of my mouth, and the meditation of my heart, be acceptable in thy sight, O LORD [Jehovah], my strength, and my redeemer."

Oh, let us **rejoice** in the *revelation* of God this word provides and the *redemption* it represents.

Scriptures for Study: In preparation for tomorrow's reading, how many times do you find the word **LORD** (*Yāhweh*) coupled with the word God (*'Elōhiym*) in Genesis 2:4—3:24?

Lord [with] God

Yāhweh [with] 'Elōhiym

A fascinating feature of the first two chapters of Genesis is that while chapter 1 speaks exclusively of *'Elōhiym*, chapter 2 (starting in verse 4) speaks exclusively of *Yāhweh 'Elōhiym*, that is, **Lord God** (which also appears in various verses in chapter 3). Why the sudden change and what is the significance?

One explanation, from liberal scholarship, is that an author other than Moses' wrote this chapter. But the evidence of exclusive Mosaic authorship of Genesis (and all the Pentateuch) is overwhelming. Another explanation is that while Moses wrote the account, he used different documents for each chapter.

The reader who believes in the inspiration of **Scripture**, however, recognizes the better explanation, namely, that **God** revealed this sudden change to Moses for a reason. What was the reason? We submit that it is twofold:

First, as we have seen, *'Elōhiym* is used to speak of **God** as the Creator of all things, while *Yahweh* is used to indicate more of a personal relationship between **God** and **man**. For example, while as *'Elōhiym* He *created* **bread** (or the ingredients to make it), as *Yahweh* He *dispenses* that bread to the people. Further, while Genesis 1 looks at Creation *broadly*, as He deals with the whole universe, Genesis 2 looks at Creation *intimately*, as He deals with just **Adam** and **Eve** on a personal level.

Second, by using both terms, **God** reveals to us that *'Elōhiym* is *Yāhweh* and *Yāhweh* is *'Elōhiym*, that is, the two names refer to one and the same, the One, True **God** who manifests himself as both Creator and Provider. He is, therefore, the **God** of *revelation*, the **God** of *Creation*, and the **God** of ***redemption***.

Psalm 19 also dramatically demonstrates these two names. Verses 1–6 speak of **God** (*'ēl* [410], a root meaning the generic "god" or "*the* God" of Israel) as Creator—"The heavens declare the glory of God; and the firmament sheweth his handywork" (v. 1). Starting in verse 7, however, He is also **Lord** (*Yāhweh*), as He speaks of His **law** and its leading men to redemption—"The law of the Lord is perfect, converting the soul" (v. 7). **Lord** appears seven times in verses 7–14, each one revealing personal relationship (see today's "Scriptures for Study").

Take some **time** today to meditate on the **wonderful** truth that **God** not only created you, but He has a personal relationship with you through the **Lord** Jesus Christ.

Scriptures for Study: Read Psalm 19, noting the use of both **Lord** (*Yāhweh*) and **God** (*'Elōhiym*). How does each occurrence of **Lord** show a personal relationship?

Lord Will Provide [Jehovah-Jireh]

Yāhweh Yir'eh

As we have seen in the **last** two days, **YHWH** (*Yāhweh*, 3068) is the personal, **covenant**, and redemptive **name** of **God**. Of such pivotal importance is this **word** that we discover several compounds of it, each of which reveals a special **way** God deals personally with His people. Today we begin a study of eleven such OT names.

The first is **Jehovah-jireh** in Genesis 22:14. Abraham is about to **sacrifice** Isaac on Mount Moriah but God stops his **hand** and provides a ram in the thicket instead. It was then that "Abraham called the name of that place Jehovahjireh," that is, literally, the **Lord Will Provide**, or even more significant, the **Lord Will See to It**. That latter idea is the most **blessed** because of the literal meaning of *yir'eh* (from *rā'āh*, 7200), "to see." Interestingly, our English word "provide" actually comes from the Latin *providēre*, "to see ahead," implying taking precautionary measures in preparation to meet a need.

Likewise, and much more significantly, then, *rā'āh* denotes seeing with the eyes, as, "When Isaac was old, and his eyes were dim, so that he could not see" (Gen. 27:1). This word is further used to indicate prophecy—that is, seeing into the future, and is so used many times in both the Major and Minor Prophets.[15] God obviously saw the need for a sacrifice before it even arose.

The encouragement here for us is both unmistakable and wondrous. As He did then, God also sees *our* need before it arises and makes provision for it. As Paul declares, "My God shall supply all your need according to his riches in glory by Christ Jesus" (Phil. 4:19). Indeed, the **Lord** will see to it; He will take care of it.

What is easily missed in that verse, and in Genesis 22:14, however, is that obedience is the requirement for God's provision. While the scene in Genesis pictures the future substitutionary **death** of Christ, its main point is God's servant obeying God no matter what the price. Likewise, the context of Philippians 4:19 concerns obedience to God in the form of sacrificially giving to those in need. So, as also illustrated in Matthew 6:25–33, God promises He will supply all our physical needs *if we seek Him*.

Scriptures for Study: What does 2 Corinthians 9:8–11 **teach** us about God's provision? 🕮 What, then, does God challenge us to do in 1 Corinthians 16:2 and Ephesians 4:28?

LORD That Healeth [Jehovah-Rapha]

Yāhweh Rāpa'

After the Exodus and Red Sea crossing, the Israelites found themselves in the **wilderness** of Shur, where there was no water. When they finally did find water in Marah, it was too bitter to drink. After sweetening the water, **God** said, "If thou wilt diligently hearken to the voice of the LORD thy God, and wilt do that which is right in his sight, and wilt give ear to his commandments, and keep all his statutes, I will put none of these diseases upon thee, which I have brought upon the Egyptians: for I am the LORD that healeth thee" (Exod. 15:26).

The verb **healeth** is *rāpa'* (7495), which appears more than sixty times and means not only "to heal and restore health," but "to make fresh, usable, and fertile." Lepers, for example, were sometimes healed (Lev. 14:3, 48), while Abimelech, his wife, and his maidservants were restored to fertility (Gen. 20:17). In that great messianic chapter in Isaiah, we read of the spiritual healing He will bring: "With his stripes we are healed" (53:5).

We cannot help but think here of 2 Chronicles 7:14: "If my people, which are called by my name, shall humble themselves, and pray, and seek my face, and turn from their wicked ways; then will I hear from heaven, and will forgive their sin, and will heal [*Rāpa'*] their land." While *dispensationally* speaking this is a promise given specifically to Israel, *practically* speaking what would such **repentance** do for our troubled nation today? After all, Jeremiah 51:8–9 declares that even foreign cities and powers can **know** God's healing if they **repent**. How much healing would result if we called upon God, stopped our **worship** of self, put **prayer** back in our schools and God's **commandments** back in the courtroom, and turned from our unconscionable sin, such as the murder of the unborn?

It is significant that the Septuagint often translates *Rāpa'* with the Greek *iaomai* (2390G, "to cure, restore"). Peter uses this, in fact, in his partial quotation of Isaiah 53:5 in 1 Peter 2:24. Further, we must "confess [our] faults one to another, and pray one for another, that [we] may be healed" (James 5:16) both physically and spiritually. Further still, "The Spirit also helpeth our infirmities: for we know not what we should pray for as we ought: but the Spirit itself maketh intercession for us with groanings which cannot be uttered [i.e., dismayed sighs that cannot be expressed in words]" (Rom. 8:26).

Scriptures for Study: Who is being healed in Isaiah 19:22 and 57:18?

LORD My Banner [Jehovah-Nissi]

Yāhweh Nissiy

In Exodus 17:8–15, the scene is Israel's battle with the Amalekites, "when Moses held up his hand . . . Israel prevailed: and when he let down his hand, Amalek prevailed" (v. 11), so Aaron and Hur "stayed up his hands" (v. 12) and Israel was victorious. We then read, "And the LORD said unto Moses, Write this for a memorial in a book, and rehearse it in the ears of Joshua: for I will utterly put out the remembrance of Amalek from under heaven. And Moses built an altar, and called the name of it Jehovahnissi" (vv. 14–15), the **LORD My Banner**.

Nissi is obviously a transliteration of the Hebrew *nissiy*, which is from *nēs* (5251), which paints quite a picture. Imagine a great multitude of people, such as an army, rallying around a pole on which flew a standard or other ensign. Here they gather to look upon the object with **hope** and expectation. That was the *nēs* in ancient times. Besides military assembling, people would gather around a *nēs* for other common actions or announcements of important information.

Another graphic example appears in Numbers 21:4–9, where because of their murmuring and rebellion, the people were plagued by venomous snakes. Upon their **repentance**, Moses fashioned a facsimile of a snake made of bronze and placed it on a "pole" (v. 8). All that was required for healing was looking upon that symbol of **sin** judged and provided for. So graphic was this symbol that our **Lord** referred to Himself as being lifted up in like manner (John 3:14–15).

I was reminded of the raising of the American flag on Mount Suribachi on Iwo Jima in February 1945. Upon finally taking the island after three days of savage fighting, a Marine patrol hoisted a small flag, followed shortly after by a larger one, which was immortalized in the most famous photograph of the Pacific **War** and later recreated in the bronze statue that today looks out over the Potomac River. Not only was that flag an incalculably valuable morale booster when it was raised, but the statue, dedicated in 1954, became the official Marine Corps Memorial.

Far grander, however, is the believer's **banner**. Was it Israel who actually prevailed against the Amalekites? No, it was God. Likewise, God will win the victory in our spiritual war as we **trust** in His Word alone. Victory comes only with obedience, and He is our **Banner**.

Scriptures for Study: Read Isaiah 11:10–16. Who is the "banner" in this passage, and who is being drawn to Him?

LORD of Peace [Jehovah-Šālôm]

Yāhweh Šālôm

The story of Gideon is a challenging one indeed. We **remember** how he gathered his army (Judg. 7), weeding out various members until his force was a mere 300 to go against 135,000 Midianites (8:10), all to demonstrate that it was **God** who would give the ultimate victory (6:16; 7:2, 7, 20).

What is easy to miss, however, is Gideon's reaction to God's **call** to this task—and we don't mean the often-observed point of his "putting out a fleece" (Judg. 6:37–40). What we mean here is stated in 6:24–26: "Then Gideon built an altar there unto the LORD, and called it Jehovahshalom [the LORD is Peace]: . . . And it came to pass the same night, that the LORD said unto him, Take thy father's young bullock, even the second bullock of seven years old, and throw down the altar of Baal that thy father hath, and cut down the grove that is by it: And build an altar unto the LORD thy God upon the top of this rock, in the ordered place, and take the second bullock, and offer a burnt sacrifice with the wood of the grove which thou shalt cut down."

Šālôm (7965) was a common greeting, appearing some 236 times, and is translated more than 250 times in the Septuagint with the common Greek *eirēnē* (1515G). The depth of *šālôm* is that it means not so much the opposite of **war**, but the opposite of *any* disturbance in the tranquility of God's people. In general, as one authority puts it, "Implicit in *šālôm* is the idea of unimpaired relationships with others and fulfillment in one's undertakings."[16]

What is the deeper significance of Gideon's **altar**? Not only was it a symbol of **peace** that alleviated his **fear** of being in God's presence, it also resulted in Gideon tearing down the altar to the pagan fertility god Baal, including the goddess Asherah ("grove" is *'ašērāh* [842], the consort of Baal; cf. Judg. 3:7; 1 Kings 18:19; 2 Kings 23:4), that existed in his family's home.

It is a wondrous truth to **know** that through Christ we have the "peace of God, which passeth all understanding," which "[keeps our] hearts and minds" (Phil. 4:7). **Peace** in its fullest cannot come, however, as long as there are idols of any kind in our homes. Is there any you need to tear down?

Scriptures for Study: What is the only source of **peace** (Num. 6:26; Isa. 26:3)? 🕮 Compare Proverbs 3:13–17 with Isaiah 57:21 and 59:8. Who has **peace** and who does not?

Lord of Hosts [Jehovah-Ṣābā'ôt]

Yāhweh Ṣebā'ôt

The wonderfully descriptive **name Lord of Hosts** occurs some 240 times in the OT. **Hosts** is *ṣebāôt* (6635), which while sometimes referring to **work** in general (2 Kings 25:19; Jer. 52:25), usually speaks of military service or the actual "men of war" as a whole (Num. 31:21).

While this title does not first appear until 1 Samuel 1:3, the concept is clearly rooted in Genesis 2:1: "Thus the heavens and the earth were finished, and all the host of them." One commentator puts the meaning well: "It represented Jehovah as ruler over the heavenly hosts (i.e., the angels, according to Gen. 32:2, and the stars, according to Isa. 40:26), who are called the ["hosts"] of Jehovah in Ps. 103:21; Ps. 148:2. . . . It is simply applied to Jehovah as the God of the Universe, who governs all the powers of heaven, both visible and invisible, as He rules in heaven and on earth."[17]

First Samuel 17:45 tells us, "[*Yāhweh*] of hosts [is] the God of the armies of Israel." **God** is sovereign and rules all things, from the forces of nature, to the heavenly hosts, to the armies of men.

The name **Lord of Sabaoth** also appears twice in the NT, once in Romans 9:29 (a quotation of Isa. 1:9), and again in James 5:4, where James declares that this God of Hosts, this God of Armies, is not oblivious to the cries of those who have suffered injustice; He will vindicate them and **judge** the oppressor. *That* is our assurance.

This also challenges us that we are each a soldier in God's army (Eph. 6:10–20). This **war** involves many things: spiritual apathy, unholy living, doctrinal error, and much more. Sadly, however, many are not fighting against much of anything. Let us ponder a few words of Isaac Watts' hymn, *Am I a Soldier of the Cross?*:

Am I a soldier of the cross, A follower of the Lamb,
And shall I fear to own His cause, Or blush to speak His Name?
Must I be carried to the skies on flowery beds of ease,
While others fought to win the prize, And sailed through bloody seas?
Sure I must fight if I would reign; Increase my courage, Lord.
I'll bear the toil, endure the pain, Supported by Thy Word.

Scriptures for Study: Psalm 46 (historical context: 2 Kings 18–19; 2 Chron. 32; Isa. 36–37), on which Martin Luther based his famous hymn, "A Mighty Fortress Is Our God," is one of great comfort. Read it and note what we have in the **Lord of Hosts**.

LORD Is My Shepherd [Jehovah-Rō'iy]

Yāhweh Rō'iy

Psalm 23 is another great **psalm** of comfort, to many readers the greatest of all, for in it we find another "Jehovah-compound," the **LORD Is My Shepherd**. The Hebrew behind **shepherd** (*rō'iy*, or *rō'eh*, 7462) is one of many words that have a truly ancient history. It goes all the **way** back to the Akkadian (*re'û*) (an extinct Semitic language that existed in Assyria and Babylon), and is then subsequently found in Phoenician, Ugaritic, Aramaic, and Arabic.

Appearing some 170 times in the OT, *rō'iy* pictures the simplicity of ancient civilization. Shepherding was the most common occupation throughout ancient Palestine, and this common, ordinary **word** simply refers to the feeding of domestic animals. Such a mundane word, however, was transformed by biblical usage. It was used to describe the true function of the leaders of God's people. A true leader is not a despot or dictator who not only drives his sheep but sometimes even slaughters them. Rather, a true leader is a **shepherd** who leads, tends, feeds, and protects his sheep at the risk of his own **life**.

Our **Lord**, of course, is the Great **Shepherd**. As Charles Spurgeon writes in his *The Treasury of David*, "What condescension is this, that the Infinite Lord assumes towards his people the office and character of a Shepherd!" Think of it! God descended and assumed one of the lowliest occupations in the ancient world. Likewise, the true function of the **king** of Israel was to be a **shepherd** (2 Sam. 5:2; 7:7; Jer. 3:15), as was that of other leaders, although at times they did it badly (Jer. 2:8; 22:22; Ezek. 34:2, 3, 8, 10).

Coming to the NT, the word *pastor* is the direct descendant of that OT precedent. The word "pastors" in Ephesians 4:11, in fact, is a translation of the Greek *poimēn* (4166G), which means **shepherd** (*poimēn* is used to translate *rā'â* in the Septuagint). In Classical Greek, it referred to the herdsman who tended and cared for the sheep. It was also used metaphorically to refer to a leader, a ruler, or a commander. Plato, for example, compared "the rulers of the city-state to shepherds who care for their flock."[18] This meaning was carried over into the NT. A pastor leads, tends, feeds, and protects the sheep that God has entrusted to his care. What a solemn responsibility!

Scriptures for Study: Read the "Shepherd Trilogy," noting that in Psalm 22, the Great **Shepherd** *redeems* the sheep (cf. John 10:11); in Psalm 23, He *rescues* the sheep (cf. Rev. 7:17); and in Psalm 24, He *rewards* the sheep (cf. 1 Pet. 5:4).

The LORD Our Righteousness (1)

Yāhweh Ṣidqēnû

What a glorious "Jehovah-compound" we consider today! Jeremiah 23:5, 6 declares, "Behold, the days come, saith the LORD, that I will raise unto David a righteous Branch, and a King shall reign and prosper, and shall execute judgment and justice in the earth. In his days Judah shall be saved, and Israel shall dwell safely: and this is his name whereby he shall be called, The LORD Our Righteousness." This verse is a messianic prophecy. The background of it appears in 2 Kings 24:8–17. Upon his **father** Jehoiakim's **death**, Jehoiachin took the **throne** of Judah at a mere eighteen years of age, but sadly, like his father, "did that which was evil in the sight of the LORD" (v. 9). After Jehoiachin had been on the throne for only three months, however, the Babylonians invaded, destroying Jerusalem and taking the people into captivity, just as Jeremiah had foretold (Jer. 1:14, 15; 5:15; 6:22–26).

The most devastating result of the deportation of Jehoiachin (also called "Coniah" and "Jeconiah") was the ending of the Davidic dynasty (22:24–26, 30). It is in 23:5–6, however, that Jeremiah declares that **God** promises to raise up **David** again in the form of "a righteous Branch" and "a King," and this is none other than the **Lord** Jesus Christ.

Further, and most significant of all, the **name** of this coming **King** would be **THE LORD OUR RIGHTEOUSNESS**. Appearing some 117 times (most often in Psalms and Isaiah), the Hebrew noun *ṣedeq* (6664), which forms the basis of *ṣidqēnû*, primarily speaks of that which conforms to a moral, ethical standard, or norm, and is often connected to the term *justice* (Ps. 119:106; Isa. 58:2). Because of their fallen nature, men do not **want** a moral or ethical standard, as illustrated by Israel's own repeated rebellion, which caused their captivity. Why are many people today fighting to remove the Ten **Commandments** from the courtroom? It is simply because with God's moral and ethical standard plastered on the **wall**, men are condemned before court is even in session.

God is not only righteous in Himself—He lives up to His own perfect moral and ethical standard—but He also produces righteousness in those He saves through Christ. While many in pulpits today go out of their **way** to avoid mentioning **sin**, **salvation** is *about* sin and righteousness, that is, *our sin* and *Christ's righteousness,* which saves us from our sin.

Scriptures for Study: Read that great description of the coming Messiah in Isaiah 11:1–11, which speaks not only of His first coming but His second as well.

The Lord Our Righteousness (2)

Yāhweh Ṣidqēnû

Yesterday we studied the compound **Jehovah-Ṣidqēnû**, **THE Lord OUR RIGHTEOUSNESS**, in Jeremiah 23:5, 6. Based on this **name** of **God**, the beloved Scottish preacher, pastor, and poet Robert Murray M'Cheyne (1813–43), who was also a Hebrew scholar, wrote the **wonderful** hymn, "I Once Was a Stranger," (which can be sung to the melody of "My Jesus, I Love Thee" by Adoniram Gordon). It is a truly **blessed** piece of **work**:

I once was a stranger to grace and to God,
I knew not my danger, and felt not my load;
Though friends spoke in rapture of Christ on the tree,
Jehovah Tsidkenu was nothing to me.

I oft read with pleasure, to sooth or engage,
Isaiah's wild measure and John's simple page;
But e'en when they pictured the blood-sprinkled tree
Jehovah Tsidkenu seemed nothing to me.

Like tears from the daughters of Zion that roll,
I wept when the waters went over His soul;
Yet thought not that my sins had nailed to the tree
Jehovah Tsidkenu—'twas nothing to me.

When free grace awoke me, by light from on high,
Then legal fears shook me, I trembled to die;
No refuge, no safety in self could I see—
Jehovah Tsidkenu my Saviour must be.

My terrors all vanished before the sweet name;
My guilty fears banished, with boldness I came
To drink at the fountain, life-giving and free—
Jehovah Tsidkenu is all things to me.

Jehovah Tsidkenu! my treasure and boast,
Jehovah Tsidkenu! I ne'er can be lost;
In thee I shall conquer by flood and by field,
My cable, my anchor, my breast-plate and shield!

Even treading the valley, the shadow of death,
This "watchword" shall rally my faltering breath;
For while from life's fever my God sets me free,
Jehovah Tsidkenu, my death song shall be.

Scriptures for Study: What is the assurance and promise of Isaiah 41:10? Where does God **lead** us, according to Psalm 23:3?

LORD of Recompense [Jehovah-Gemûlâ]

Yāhweh Gemûlāh

Because of His perfect, absolute righteousness, **God** is also called by two names that speak of His judgment upon *un*righteousness. We find the first, for example, in Jeremiah 51:56, where He is called *Jehovah Gemûlāh.* The **prophet** foretells that God will come "upon Babylon, and her mighty men are taken, every one of their bows is broken: for the LORD God of recompences shall surely requite." The Hebrew *gemûlāh* (1578)—a derivative of *gāmal* (1580), "to deal, to recompense, to ripen"—speaks of full repayment for what is deserved.

There are many instances of this **word** (and other derivatives) that speak of recompense, both of judgment and blessing. Used positively, for example, when **David** was fleeing from Absalom, Barzillai provided him with supplies (2 Sam. 19:32), and David returned the favor (v. 36). It is even used to speak of benefits God has given (Ps. 103:2). At times, the positive and negative are actually contrasted, as in the **Virtuous Woman**, who "will do [*gāmal*] him [her husband] good and not evil all the days of her life" (Prov. 31:12).

It is the negative, however, that is truly sobering. The instance here in our text speaks of God's retribution on His enemies, as does Isaiah 59:18: "According to their deeds, accordingly he will repay, fury to his adversaries, recompence to his enemies; to the islands he will repay recompence." The psalmist calls upon this God of Recompense to "give [the wicked] according to their deeds, and according to the wickedness of their endeavours: give them after the work of their hands; render to them their desert [*gemûl*]" (Ps. 28:4).

We cannot help but make special note of Psalm 94:2: "Lift up thyself, thou judge of the earth: render a reward [*gemûl*] to the proud." As we will **observe** in a future study (March 19), **pride** is never used in a positive **way** of **man** in **Scripture**. Here we read of, in fact, its costliness; God will recompense it, judging it as harshly as He did the Babylonians. How this should show us what a serious **sin** pride is!

Scriptures for Study: On the positive side, what does Psalm 116:12 command? 🕮 On the negative side, what does Isaiah 3:9 warn?

LORD That Smiteth (Jehovah-Nāḵāh)

Yāhweh Nāḵāh

As if the title **LORD of Recompense** were not clear enough, **God** is also called *Yāhweh-Nāḵāh*, **the Lord that Smiteth**, in Ezekiel 7:9. Writing about Israel's own rebellion, the **prophet** declares that God "will recompense thee according to thy ways and thine abominations that are in the midst of thee; and ye shall know that I am the LORD that smiteth." The Hebrew *nāḵāh* (5221) means "to beat, to strike, or to wound," usually (although not always) in a nonlethal **way**. Appearing some 500 times, this root is used in a wide variety of ways.

Balaam, for example, struck his donkey (Num. 22:23, 25, 27). Moses was angered and killed an Egyptian because the **man** was beating a fellow Hebrew (Exod. 2:11). Nehemiah beat certain Hebrew men for intermarrying with pagans (Neh. 13:25), as OT **law** allowed beating for various offenses (Deut. 25:2, 3). Jeremiah was beaten and imprisoned for his **preaching** (Jer. 20:2; 37:15), and the future Messiah would give "[his] back to the smiters" (Isa. 50:6). There are instances when *nāḵāh* is also used to speak of killing. The **death** penalty was issued, for example, for a person striking another severely enough to kill him (Exod. 21:12).

Most importantly, however, is how *nāḵāh* is used in reference to God. The men of **Sodom** and Gomorrah, for example, were stricken blind by the two angels (Gen. 19:11), God struck the Egyptians with plagues (Exod. 3:20), and He brings judgment even upon His own people because of their **sin** (1 Kings 14:15; Lev. 26:24). God has even commanded that parents must discipline their children and includes the reason why (Prov. 23:13, 14).

Yes, these **last** two names we have examined are hard to **face** and seem harsh, but they are essential to a proper **understanding** of God. In a **day** when God is viewed as a tolerant grandfather who simply smiles understandingly at sin, men need to be told that God is a God of retribution and **wrath**, who will bring judgment on those who reject Him. As in the days of **Noah**, "[The LORD's] Spirit shall not always strive with man" (Gen. 6:3).

Likewise, we as believers need to be reminded that God disciplines and chastises His own people when they **rebel**: "For whom the Lord loveth he chasteneth, and scourgeth every son whom he receiveth" (Heb. 12:6; cf. vv. 7, 8).

Scriptures for Study: According to Psalm 94:12 and Proverbs 3:11, 12, what should be our attitude toward God's correction of us?

LORD That Doth Sanctify You [Jehovah-Maccaddeshcem]

Yāhweh Qāḏaš

Another dramatic "Jehovah-compound" is **Jehovah-Maccaddeshcem** (or *M'kaddesh*), **The Lord That Doth Sanctify You**. Exodus 31:13 tells us, "Speak thou also unto the children of Israel, saying, Verily my sabbaths ye shall keep: for it is a sign between me and you throughout your generations; that ye may know that I am the LORD that doth sanctify you." **Maccaddeshcem** is derived from *qāḏaš* (6942), which "signifies an act whereby, or a state wherein, people or things are set aside for use in the worship of **God**: they are consecrated or 'made sacred.'"[19] The scene in this verse, of course, is the setting aside of the **Sabbath** as holy. It was a **sign** to Israel alone of God's **covenant** with them and marked Israel out as His people. Observing the Sabbath showed that the Israelites were set apart (i.e., holy) to God.

This **word** is, in fact, one of the most striking examples of a NT doctrine that is rooted in OT doctrine. The equivalent Greek verb is *hagiazō* (37G), which appears about thirty times in the NT (the adjective *hagios* [40G] and noun *hagion* [39G] appear many more times). While in secular Greek it meant "to stand in awe of or be devoted to the gods," Paul lifted it to a **new** level of meaning: "to set apart or be separate." Words in this group are translated with such words as *holy, sanctification,* and *saint.* Particularly significant is *saint,* which refers to *every* believer, not some especially holy person. Paul uses this term some forty-two times, and in every instance he refers to one who has trusted Christ as Savior and **Lord**, one who has been set apart.

We see the title **Jehovah-Maccaddeshcem** again in Leviticus 20:8: "And ye shall keep my statutes, and do them: I am the LORD which sanctify you," a statement that couples God's setting apart Israel with their keeping of His Word. We again find the same principle even more strongly stated in the NT. Our Lord Himself declared that He will "Sanctify [God's people] through [His] truth: [His] word is truth" (John 17:17). Paul likewise writes that Christ will "sanctify and cleanse [the church] with the washing of water by the word" (Eph. 5:26). Let us be reminded moment-by-moment that **Scripture** is the source of sanctification.

Scriptures for Study: With Ephesians 5:26 in mind, what does verse 27 go on to say about the purpose of this sancification?

LORD Is There [Jehovah-Shammah]

Yāhweh Shāmmāh

The **last** verse of Ezekiel reveals one more "Jehovah-compound" (48:35). The Hebrew *shāmmāh* (8033) indicates a place "there" (Job 39:30; Gen. 2:8). *Where* is **God**? He is *there* in Jerusalem.

Scripture actually speaks of three "Jerusalems": *First,* of course, was (and is) historic Jerusalem. It (*not* the city of Rome) is the Holy City (Neh. 11:1; Isa. 52:1; Dan. 9:24; Matt. 4:5; 27:53; Rev.11:2).

Second, the Millennial Jerusalem, the restored city where Jesus will rule for 1,000 years. It will have twelve gates, three on each side, one for each of the twelve tribes of Israel, and a circumference of "eighteen thousand measures" (Ezek. 48:28–35), almost thirty-seven miles (in contrast to about four miles in the first century AD, according to Josephus, the leading Jewish historian of that **day**). What will its greatest feature be? "The name of the city from that day shall be, The LORD is there" (v. 35). So holy will the city be that even its **name** will be changed to reflect it.

This foreshadows the *third* and final Jerusalem, the **New** (or Holy) Jerusalem, the capital city of the **new heaven** and new earth (Rev. 21), the dwelling place of God's people forever. While some teachers spiritualize much of the Bible's prophetic passages, ending up with arbitrary speculation, the plain language of Scripture should be our authority. This city will **descend** out of heaven, its captivating beauty likened to a bride in the eyes the groom (v. 2). This is not some ethereal, mystical city, rather a *real* one with foundations, walls, gates, and dimensions. It is a massive cube, in fact (v. 16), not a pyramid, as some speculate—pyramids have been associated with paganism since the days of Babylon. With a "furlong" (Greek *stadion*, 4712G) being about 607 feet, the walls are 1,380 miles in each direction, roughly the area from the West Coast to the **middle** of Kansas and from Canada to Mexico. With foundation stones made of **precious** gems (vv. 18–20) and 1,200-mile high gates, each made of a single flat pearl (v. 21), human language still falls short in describing that city.

Greatest of all, God's glory will emanate from that city, illuminating the entire recreated universe (Rev. 21:23; 22:5) in unfathomable colors from the transparent **gold** and gems of the city's structure. Further, we will actually be enabled to see that blazing glory of God's **face** (22:4). Oh, the **Lord** will, indeed, be there and so shall we!

Scriptures for Study: Read Revelation 21:1–22:5 and **rejoice** in what is to come.

Lord

'Adōnāy

The Hebrew *'Adōnāy* (136) rendered **Lord** (initial cap and lowercase in contrast to initial cap and small caps for *Yāhweh,* see January 8) in most English translations, appears well over 400 times. While the singular *'adōn* is used also of men—Sarah referred to Abraham as "lord" (Gen. 18:12) and his servants called him "master" (24:9, 10), Ruth addressed Boaz as "lord" (Ruth 2:13), as did Hannah address Eli (1 Sam. 1:15), and so forth—the "plural of majesty," *'Adōnāy,* is used only of **God** and speaks of His dominion, possession, and sovereignty.

It is extremely significant that the direct NT Greek equivalent is *kurios* (2962G), which is frequently applied to the **Lord** Jesus. Again, while "lord" is sometimes used as simply a title of honor, such as rabbi, teacher, master (Matt. 10:24; cf. Luke 16:3), or even a husband (1 Pet. 3:6), *when used of Jesus in a confessional **way**, it without question refers to His divinity*. The simple, but deeply profound, confession *Kurios Iēsous* (**Lord** Jesus) is rooted in the pre-Pauline Greek Christian community and is probably the oldest of all Christian creeds. Jesus is **Lord**!

Another startling fact is that in hundreds of instances, **Lord** (*'Adōnāy*) is actually coupled with either God (*'Elōhiym*; Ps. 38:15; 86:12; Dan. 9:3, 9, 15) or "GOD" (*Yehōwāh*, instead of uppercase **LORD**; e.g., Gen. 15:2, 8; Ps. 71:5; and more than 200 times in Ezekiel). This dramatically combines the various aspects of each divine **name** to paint a more graphic picture of who God is.

While a controversial issue, I would humbly submit that *'Adōnāy* (and *kurios* by extension) being coupled with other names also further underscores the importance of emphasizing the principle of Lordship. In a **day** when the Lordship of Christ means very little in the thinking of many Christians, we must emphasize it all the more. The popular notion of "accepting Jesus as Savior but not as Lord until a later date" is foreign to the NT. Neither is it a historical position in the church; it is, in fact, a thoroughly modern invention, spawned by the relativism, pragmatism, and tolerance of our age. There is simply no **salvation** apart from Jesus as **Lord** (Rom. 10:9, 10). It is a staggering contradiction to say a person can believe in Jesus as Savior but reject Him as **Lord** simply because a change of **life** automatically results in a change of Lordship (2 Cor. 5:17).

Scriptures for Study: Read Mark 8:34–38, 12:28–34, and Luke 14:25–35, meditating on their **deep** significance.

Almighty God

'Ēl-Šadday

There has long been debate about whether or not the three terms *'ēl*, *'elōhiym*, and *'elôach* all come from the same root, and there is still no definitive conclusion. As one Hebrew authority writes, "Some hold that the two are distinct, deriving *'ēl* from the root *'wl* (strong). Others see *'elōhiym* derived from the root *'lh*, together with *'elôach*, that root meaning **fear**. Still others hold that both *'ēl* and *'elōhiym* come from *'elôach*. More probable [as we noted back on January 7] is the view that *'elōhiym* comes from *'elôach* as a unique development of the Hebrew Scriptures."[20]

Whichever is true, however, the meaning of *'ēl* (410) is unchanged. Here is the **name** by which **God** made Himself known to the patriarchs (Abram, for example, in Gen. 14:19–22). *'Ēl* is one of the most ancient (and "generic") Semitic terms for **God**, god (pagan or false), or deity, and means **strength**, mighty, mighty one, or even hero.

It is perhaps because of these questions of origin and generic meaning, that in almost every OT occurrence of *'ēl* it is coupled with a qualifier that further defines and clarifies it.[21] One such "epithet" is *Šadday* (or *Shaddai*, 7706), which means "almighty, possessing all power, all-sufficient." We find it first in Genesis 17:1: "When Abram was ninety years old and nine, the LORD appeared to Abram, and said unto him, I am the Almighty God; walk before me, and be thou perfect." *El-Šadday*, then, "is found in the passages that report God's promises of fertility, land, and abundance to them, indicating that He, the **Almighty**, could fulfill His promises (Gen. 17:1; Gen. 28:3; Gen. 35:11)."[22] The other patriarchs, Isaac and Jacob, also knew Him by this name (28:1–3), as did Joseph (48:3).

It is most significant that this name is a universal name for **God**, as is demonstrated by the non-Israelite Job and his "friends," who used it some thirty times (e.g., 5:17; 13:3; 22:25, 26; 32:8; 33:4; 37:23). So prominent is it in Job, in fact, that thirty-one of its forty-eight occurrences are here. Regardless of the age in which we live, we **rejoice** that **God** is "the same yesterday, and to day, and for ever" (Heb. 13:8) and is the **Almighty**, possessing all **power**, the only One possessing all-sufficiency.

Scriptures for Study: What is the NT assurance revealed in Matthew 19:26, Ephesians 3:20, and Philippians 4:13?

God Most High

'Ēl-'Elyôn

Another qualifier (or "epithet") that is often attached to *'Ēl* to further define and clarify it is *'Elyôn* (5945) which means "Most High, the Highest," and appears thirty-one times in the OT in reference to **God**. Not only is there no one higher but there is also no *possibility* of being higher. The most notable use of this **name** is in Genesis 14:18–20, where the non-Israelite Melchizedek, a vivid OT type of Christ, was a king-**priest** of **God Most High**. So important is this incident, that it is again referred to in Hebrews 7:1, 2: "For this Melchisedec, king of Salem, priest of the most high God, who met Abraham returning from the slaughter of the kings, and blessed him; To whom also Abraham gave a tenth part of all; first being by interpretation King of righteousness [the meaning of Melchizedek], and after that also King of Salem, which is, King of peace."

'Elyôn also appears in Isaiah's recounting of Satan's rebellion: "I will ascend above the heights of the clouds; I will be like the most High" (Isa. 14:14). This demonstrates a key aspect of this title, namely, God's omnipotence, rule, and sovereignty. *'Elyôn* is "over all the earth" (Ps. 47:2; 83:18, where it is also coupled with *Yāhweh* [see January 8]; 97:9) and is "higher than the kings of the earth" (89:27).

In the minds of many today, **God** is not the Sovereign **God** who controls all things. He's no longer a **God** who had a sovereign plan from before the foundation of the world and is now providentially executing that plan. Basically, sovereignty means that since **God** is the *Creator* of all things, He then *owns* all things and therefore *rules* all things. To say that **God** is sovereign is to say that He is supreme. To say that **God** is sovereign is to say that He is the **Most High**. To say that **God** is sovereign is to say that He does everything according to His will, His purpose. To say that **God** is sovereign is to say that He is the Ruler over all things. To say that **God** is sovereign is to say that no one can *ruin* His *plan*, *wreck* His *purpose*, or *resist* His ***power***. *In short, to say that* ***God*** *is sovereign is to say that* ***God*** *IS* ***God***! Oh, let us **hate** anything that lessens **God**!

Scriptures for Study: Read David's **prayer** of thanksgiving in 1 Chronicles 29:11, 12 (**Lord**, of course, is *Yāhweh* [January 8ff]). Have you ever prayed like that?

Holy God

'Ēl- Qāḏôš

Today we reverently step on **holy** ground. Another qualifier added to *'Ēl* is *Qāḏôš* (6918, a derivative of the verb *qāḏaš*, to be holy, to consecrate), which is not only the polar opposite of wicked, but also of just ordinary. It denotes something that is sacred and set apart from anything that is **evil** or even common. Isaiah 5:16 declares, "But the LORD of hosts shall be exalted in judgment, and God that is holy shall be sanctified in righteousness." Joshua echoes, "he is an holy God" (Josh. 24:19).

There is a fascinating truth about the use of the **word *holy*** in **Scripture**. To make the superlative in English, we add "–est" to a word (or the word "most"), such as "holiest." In Hebrew, however, the superlative may be expressed by saying something three times.

It is, therefore, interesting that when the angels exalted **God**, they didn't say, "Eternal, Eternal, Eternal," or "Faithful, faithful, faithful," or "Wise, wise, wise," or "Mighty, mighty, mighty," or "Loving, loving, loving," or even "Gracious, gracious, gracious." They said, "Holy, holy, holy, is the LORD of hosts: the whole earth is full of his glory" (Isa. 6:3). *This demonstrates that God's holiness is the crown of all that He is.*

Oh, how the Puritans were captivated by this! Thomas Watson wrote, "Holiness is the most sparkling jewel of His crown; it is the name by which God is known."[23] Stephen Charnock added, "This attribute hath excellence above His other perfections. . . . None is sounded out so loftily, with such solemnity, and so frequently by angels that stand before His throne, as this . . . [and] it is the glory of all the rest."[24] While some today elevate God's ***love*** over all else, those great Puritans understood that of all God's attributes, *holiness* is the one that most uniquely describes Him, a summation of all His other attributes, the fact that He is unlike any other being. It indicates His complete and infinite perfection. Holiness is the attribute of **God** that binds all the others together.

When properly understood, this will transform our lives and revolutionize the quality of our **worship**. In fact, why did **God** "[choose] us in [Christ] before the foundation of the world[?] That we should be holy and without blame before him in love" (Eph. 1:4). We then live **holy** because *He* is **holy** (1 Pet. 1:15, 16; Lev. 11:44, 45; cf. 19:2; 20:7, 26). Nothing characterizes the Christian more than holiness of **life**.

Scriptures for Study: What is the characteristic of the "new man" in Ephesians 4:24? 🕮 To what has **God** called the Christian (1 Thess. 4:3, 4, 7)?

God of Truth

'Ēl-'Emûnâ

Few words captivate and consume this writer more than the **word *truth*** (**grace** is another). Sadly, however, few words are under more attack than this one. We live in an age of unprecedented relativism, where **truth** is "up for grabs," is different for each person, and changes according to circumstances.

In stark contrast, **God** is the **God of truth**. As Moses sings, "He is the Rock, his work is perfect: for all his ways are judgment: a God of truth and without iniquity, just and right is he" (Deut. 32:4). The psalmist echoes in a messianic prophecy, "Into thine hand I commit my spirit: thou hast redeemed me, O LORD God of truth" (Ps. 31:5; cf. Luke 23:46). And the **prophet** Isaiah repeats, "That he who blesseth himself in the earth shall bless himself in the God of truth; and he that sweareth in the earth shall swear by the God of truth" (Isa. 65:16).

Truth is a translation of *'emeṯ* (571, or *'emûnāh*, 530, April 7), which has at its root the ideas of firmness and certainty and includes such concepts as **truth**, rightness, and faithfulness. Also inherent in the word is the idea of ***faith***, which in biblical usage "is an assurance, a certainty, in contrast with modern concepts of faith as something possible, hopefully true, but not certain."[25]

It is extremely significant that the Septuagint translates this Hebrew word with the Greek *alētheia* in some 100 instances. As one Greek authority defines it: "Etymologically *alētheia* means nonconcealment. It thus denotes what is seen, indicated, expressed, or disclosed, i.e., a thing as it really is, not as it is concealed or falsified. *Alētheia* is the real state of affairs."[26] The fundamental concept of ***truth*** is that it is absolute and certain, is incontrovertible, irrefutable, unarguable, and unchanging. If something is true, it is *always* true and can *never* be *un*true, no matter what the circumstances.

This **name** greatly helps us understand who **God** is. He is the **God** of certainty, firmness, and assurance. He *never* changes and is absolutely dependable. Again, Jesus Christ is "the same yesterday, and to day, and for ever" (Heb. 13:8, January 23). As we **rejoice** in the certainties of the **God of truth**, let our desire in turn be the pursuit of absolute **truth** in all things and in every area of **life**.

Scriptures for Study: What does John 14:6 declare? 🕮 In John 16:13, what is one ministry of the Holy Spirit? 🕮 In John 17:17 and 19, what is a result of **truth**?

Other 'Ēl Compounds

There are many other compounds of *'Ēl*, each of which reveals to us a little more of God's nature and **work**. Let us note some (but still not all) of them today and marvel even more in who **God** is. There is **Mighty God**, or even **Heroic God** (*'Ēl-Gibbôr*, 1368, Isa. 10:21), **God of Knowledge** (*'Ēl-Dē'āh*, 1844, 1 Sam. 2:3), **God of Glory** (*'Ēl-Kāḇôḏ*, 3519, Ps. 29:3), the **Everlasting God** (*'Ēl-'Ôlām*, 5769, Gen. 21:33), the **God of Seeing** (*'Ēl-Ro'iy*, 7210, Gen. 16:13), and even the **Jealous God** (*'Ēl-Qannā'*, 7067, Exod. 20:5; Deut. 4:24; 5:9; 6:15; Josh. 24:19; Nah. 1:2).

Illustrating "that there is none other God but one" (1 Cor. 8:4) and that any other "god" is a false one, we discover that He is the **Living God** (*'Ēl-Chay*, 2416, Josh. 3:10; 1 Sam. 17:26, 36; 2 Kings 19:4, 16; Ps. 42:2; 84:2; Isa. 37:4; Jer. 10:10; 23:36; Dan. 6:20, 26; Hosea 1:10) and the **One God** (*'Ēl-'Echād*, 259; Mal. 2:10).

Deeper, many *'Ēl* compounds illustrate God's personal relationship with believers. He is the **God of Bethel** (*Ēl-Bēyṯ-'ēl*, 1008; Gen. 31:13; 35:7), demonstrating that He comes to where we are. He is **God My Rock** (*'Ēl- Sela'iy*, 5553; Ps. 42:9), picturing the security and refuge we find in Him. Also, **God is My Strength and Power** or even **God Is My Fortress** (*'Ēl-Mā'ûzziy* [and] *Chayil*, 4581 and 2428, 2 Sam. 22:33), assuring us that He is with us in battle.

Deeper still, in a redemptive sense, He is the **God Who Formed Me** (*'Ēl-Chûl*, 2342, Deut. 32:18), showing us He is our true **Father**. Also, He is **God Our Savior** (*'Ēl- Yāša'*, 3467, Ps. 106:19–21), declaring that He alone is the **Deliverer**, as He delivered His people from Egypt—a truth they forgot when they made and worshipped the golden calf.

So from the first occurrence of *'Ēl* (Gen. 14:18) to the **last** (Mal. 2:10), **God** gives us glimpses into who He is and what He does. He is, indeed, the "God of gods, and Lord of lords, a great God, a mighty, and a terrible" (Deut. 10:17). "Great" is *gāḏôl* (1419), which "emphasizes the importance, size, and significance of something or someone."[27] Does that not truly sum up who He is?

Scriptures for Study: Read some of (or all) the verses mentioned in today's study and marvel in **your God** (Exod. 6:7, and some 180 other occurrences of those words).

King

melek̲

The Hebrew *melek̲* (4428) appears more than 2,500 times in the OT, about thirty-five of which refer to **God**. In general, it refers to any person with authority or **power**, such as a chief magistrate, captain, ruler, or prince, and is denoted by a lower-case "k" in our English translations, while an uppercase "K" refers to God.

To understand this **word**, however, it is necessary to examine how civil authority operated in the ancient world. While the civil authority of today operates by statutory (or case) **law**, in ancient times it operated according to common (or customary) law,[28] which ruled by long-established custom. Additionally, rule was dictated by the magistrate himself, which was actually part of the custom. Obviously, therefore, such rule could be either **good** or bad depending upon the **man**.

With that background, it is easy to see what this **image** said to the people about God. As **King**, He is the Ruler and Sovereign who possesses absolute power and authority. The first occurrence of *melek̲* in reference to God is in Psalm 5:2 and is particularly significant: "Hearken unto the voice of my cry, my King, and my God: for unto thee will I pray." As John Gill observes, "Though David was a king over others, yet the Lord, who is the King of kings, was King over him, and he owned him to be so; he was set upon the throne by him, had his kingdom from him, and was accountable to him."[29] The permanence of God's rule should also strike *us*. While politicians, presidents, and potentates come and go, "The LORD *is* King for ever and ever" (Ps. 10:16; cf. 29:10).

All this points us immediately to the **Lord** Jesus Christ, the "KING OF KINGS, AND LORD OF LORDS" (Rev.19:16; also 17:14; 1 Tim. 6:15), who will one **day** "smite the nations: and he shall rule them with a rod of iron: and he treadeth the winepress of the fierceness and wrath of Almighty God" (Rev. 19:15) and will rule from Jerusalem for a thousand years (20:1–6). As every **number** in Revelation is literal (e.g., seven churches, twenty-four elders, 144,000 from the tribes of Israel), there seems no valid exegetical reason to doubt that this number (which appears six times) is also literal, declaring the literal, earthly millennial reign of our Lord.

Dear Christian **Friend**, is He already the **King** in your **life**?

Scriptures for Study: What does Psalm 24:7–10 declare about God as **King**? 🕮 What should we do in light of God being our **King**, according to 47:6, 7?

Father

'ab̲

No examination of the names and titles of **God** would be complete without considering the title of **Father**.[30] The Hebrew *'ab̲* (1), which "apparently is derived from such baby sounds as *abab*,"[31] appears almost 1,200 times in the OT. We should also note that *'ab̲* (2) is the Aramaic form, the basis for the NT usage of *abba* (5G) that appears three times (Mark 14:36; Rom. 8:15; Gal. 4:6).[32] Obviously, *'ab̲* refers to a biological **father** (Gen. 2:24), but it also refers to the **head** of a household (24:40), a grandfather (28:13), an ancestor (10:21), or even a patron of a class (4:20). What does such fatherhood indicate when we think of God as our **Father**? Let us consider five applications.

First, our **Father** *begets* us. He gives us **life**. "Have we not all one father? hath not one God created us?" (Mal. 2:10). Spiritually then, through Christ, we are "born again, not of corruptible seed, but of incorruptible" (1 Pet. 1:23). Having thus been "born of God," we **know** God (1 John 4:7), **love** God (5:1), overcome the world (5:4), and guard our behavior (5:18, "keepeth" is *tērēō* [5083G], "keep an eye on, watch over, observe attentively, guard protectively"), and do not habitually commit **sin** (1 John 3:9).

Second, our **Father** *teaches* us. We are to "hear the instruction of [our] father" and learn doctrine, **wisdom**, and God's **law** from Him (Prov. 1:8; 4:1–4; 5:1). From where do we get our spiritual Father's instruction? From His **Word** alone.

Third, our **Father** *disciplines* us. As an earthly **father** corrects his child because of love (Prov. 3:12; Deut. 8:5), so God our **Father** "chasteneth, and scourgeth every son whom he receiveth. . . . for what son is he whom the father chasteneth not?" (Heb. 12:6, 7; cf. 2 Sam. 7:14). Yes, discipline is painful, but it brings us back to obedience.

Fourth, our **Father** *provides* for us. Why do we worry about clothing, food, and other basic needs of life? Our "Father knoweth that [we] have need of these things" and He will provide them when we seek Him (Luke 12:28–31; cf. Matt. 6:9–11).

Fifth, our **Father** ***gives us a name***. As one's family name is a **precious** thing, God has given us names that should be precious to us. Each of us is a "saint" (Phil. 4:21), a "Christian" (1 Pet. 4:16), and a believer (Acts 5:14). Let us live up to those names' lofty standards.

Scriptures for Study: How do we become children of God (Gal. 3:26)? 📖 What proves we are children of God (1 John 3:10; 5:2)? 📖

Other Names and Titles for God

Amazingly, there are more than 100 names for **God** used in the Bible. We could spend almost one-third of this **book** exploring just those names, but if we did that, we would have to ignore many other theologically significant words. We have only scratched the surface this month, but before leaving this subject, let us at least briefly note a few more of God's magnificent names. (Additionally, **tomorrow** we will consider how we can better **glorify God** and honor His **name(s)** in our Christian living.)

Exodus 3:13, for example, declares that **God** is the **God of Your Fathers**, indicating His promises to the patriarchs, as do the titles: **God of Abraham** (Gen. 28:13; 1 Chron. 29:18), **Fear of Isaac** (Gen. 31:42, 53), **Mighty [One] of Jacob** (49:24), and especially **God of Israel** (Num. 16:9; 1 Sam. 5:8; Ps. 41:13).

How varied and all-encompassing are His names! He is the **First** (*ri'šôn*, 7223) **and the Last** (*'acharôn*, 314), indicating His eternality (Isa. 44:6, 48:12). He is a **Consuming Fire** (*'ākal 'ēš*, 398/784), purifying the valuable and destroying the rubbish (Deut. 4:24). He is **Judge** (*šāpaṭ*, 8199), judging with perfect knowledge and impartiality (Ps. 50:6; Isa. 33:22). He is a **Man of War** (*'iyš milchāmāh*, 376/4421), fighting victoriously against His enemies and the enemies of His people (Exod. 15:3).

We cannot leave this grand theme without noting titles that refer to Messiah, the Savior and Redeemer who would come. In Isaiah 9:6, that amazing verse, we read: "For unto us a child is born, unto us a son is given: and the government shall be upon his shoulder: and his name shall be called Wonderful, Counsellor, The mighty God, The everlasting Father, The Prince of Peace." **Wonderful** is *pele'* (6382), which speaks of a wonder, miracle, or marvel and always appears in the context of an act of **God** (e.g., Ps. 78:12, "marvellous things"; Isa. 29:14, "wonder"). **Counsellor** is *yā'as* (3289), meaning "to advise." How much better would our government be if we heeded God's advice?

Oh, how we could go on! Dear Christian **Friend**, you **serve** the Great **God**. I **pray** you will seek to **know** Him more deeply in your Christian walk. I would again point you to the wonderful books mentioned back on January 3.

Scriptures for Study: Read the verses mentioned in today's study and take some **time** to meditate on the wonders of our **God**.

Glorify [God]

kāḇēḏ

In **light** of the **wonder** and weight of God's names and titles, we are challenged to truly **glorify** Him and honor His names. **David** prayed in Psalm 86:12, "I will praise thee, O Lord my God, with all my heart: and I will glorify thy name for evermore." **Glorify** is *kāḇēḏ* (3513), which is also translated "honour" (e.g., Prov. 3:9; 4:8) and "heavy," speaking of His judgment (e.g., Isa. 30:27).

It is that last translation, in fact, that makes this **word** interesting. This verb literally means "to be heavy or weighty." We have all heard the expression that someone's opinion "carries a lot of weight," indicating that the person is important or influential. Similarly, when we refer to someone as a "heavyweight," we mean that they possess **power**, prominence, or stature. **God,** therefore, is "heavy," that is, powerful, and is worthy of honor, glory, respect, and obedience. How, then, can we **glorify** and honor **God**?

First, by never taking His **name** in vain (Exod. 20:7; Lev. 19:12; Deut.5:11). So common is the expression, "Oh, my God!" in our **day** that we have lost sight of how truly blasphemous it is, and I have heard even many Christians using it. Any such flippant, frivolous, or false statements do not honor God's holy name. Our speech is to be "seasoned with salt" (Col. 4:6), which **among** other things means "wholesome and palatable."

Second, we honor **God** by praising His name. Psalm 50:23 declares, "Whoso offereth praise glorifieth me." By recalling and speaking God's names and attributes, we **praise** and honor Him. We can thank and praise Him for His sovereignty, providence, holiness, justice, **mercy**, **grace**, and so much more. I **pray** we will address Him using His various names to bring Him further glory.

Third, we honor **God** by living up to His name. To be a "Christian" (*Christianos*, 5546G, "of the party of Christ") means we **bear** His name and must live up to it and never do anything to dishonor it. All **God's** names, therefore, come into view through Christ, and we are to live up to each as we reflect the Son's character (cf. Gal. 5:22, 23).

Scriptures for Study: Read the verses mentioned in today's study and meditate on how you can better honor and **glorify God**.

Man [and] Adam (1)

'āḏām

"What a piece of work is a man! how noble in reason! how infinite in faculty! in form and moving how express and admirable! in action how like an angel! in apprehension how like a god! the beauty of the world! the paragon of animals!" So wrote William Shakespeare.[33] That is true, however, only because **God** alone did it all. We had nothing to do with it, regardless of the ramblings of the humanist.

A Greek **word** that perfectly illustrates this is *poiēma* (4161G, English "poem"), which Paul uses to refer to us as God's "workmanship, created in Christ Jesus" (Eph. 2:10). Another form of the word, *poiētēs*, refers to one who makes something or to a **work** of art. In ancient Greek this referred to an author or poet. So we are God's work of art, masterpiece, or poem.

The Hebrew *'āḏām* (120) appears more than 550 times in the OT, 408 of which are translated **man** ("men" 121) and thirteen as **Adam** (AV). While its origin is unsure, it seems to be linked to *'āḏōm* or *'āḏēm* (119), "to be red, ruddy, or dyed red." A related word is used, for example, of David's ruddy appearance (1 Sam. 16:12; 17:42). Another clue is the Akkadian *adamātu*, "dark red soil," which takes us immediately to Genesis 2:7: "And the LORD God formed man of the dust of the ground, and breathed into his nostrils the breath of life; and man became a living soul," picturing that **man** was created out of the very elements of the earth and is connected to it.

The word "formed" (*yāṣar*, 3335) refers to fashioning or shaping something, as a potter fashions a **vessel** from the clay. The **power** of God then gave **man** a **life** that is unique over all Creation, making **man** in His **image** and **likeness** (Gen. 1:26); while **man** is finite, he is still the reflection of such qualities as God's personality, truth, **wisdom**, **love**, holiness, and justice. Once dead "Adamites," we are now alive in Christ (1 Cor. 15:22).

Another Creation occurs when Christ enters our life. We become the "new man" (Eph. 2:15; 4:24). The Greek *kainos* (2537G) *anthropos* (444G) speaks of **man** (as a species) becoming **new** in the sense of quality and having never existed before.[34] We have truly been created new in Christ (2 Cor. 5:17), with transformed character and habits. Indeed, "What a piece of work is a [spiritual] man!"

Scriptures for Study: Read Genesis 2. What observations can you note about **man** (**Adam**)? (Note: **Man** in verse 23 is a different word, which we will examine **tomorrow**.)

Man (2)

'iyš

A second **name** for **man** in the OT is *'iyš* (376), which speaks of **man** as an individual, or the male gender, rather than the more general idea of mankind indicated by (*'āḏām*, February 1). This meaning is all the more evident in the first appearance of *'iyš*: "And Adam said, This is now bone of my bones, and flesh of my flesh: she shall be called Woman, because she was taken out of Man" (Gen. 2:23). **Adam**, who was the first representative of mankind, here refers to himself as male in contrast to female (**Woman**, *'iššāh*, from *'iyš,* February 5).

Occurring more than 1,700 times, *'iyš* is used in several ways. In addition to indicating the male gender, it is used to specify certain *types* of men, such as: a farmer ("husbandman," or "man of the earth," Gen. 9:20), a hunter ("man of the field," 25:27), an old **man** ("man of gray hairs," Deut. 32.25), a soldier (**man of war**, Josh. 17:1), a landowner ("man of wealth," Ruth 2:1), and a **prophet** ("man of God," e.g., Deut. 33:1; Josh. 14:6).

Of special application to men today, we read of an "honourable man" (1 Sam. 9:6; *kāḇēḏ,* January 31), a **man** of **integrity**, honesty, and faithfulness. Solomon then speaks of "a man of understanding" (Prov. 1:5) (*biyn*, 995, March 24), a **man** who perceives, understands, and discerns truth (Prov. 1:5; 17:28). How we need such men in a **day** when there is little personal integrity, little honesty, and very little discernment of what is right and **good**.

Another key idea in this **word** is that of a "husband," and it is so translated some 65 times, the first of which is in Genesis 3:6: "And when the woman saw that the tree was good for food, and that it was pleasant to the eyes, and a tree to be desired to make one wise, she took of the fruit thereof, and did eat, and gave also unto her husband with her; and he did eat." The far-reaching tragedy of this scene is not just the bringing of **sin** to mankind, but the destruction of God's order of the husband leading and the wife following. As the apostle Paul wrote, "For the husband is the head of the wife" (Eph. 5:23), and he is therefore to **lead** rightly according to the Word of God.

Scriptures for Study: In addition to the encouragements of today's study, what is a husband to do regarding his godly wife, according to Proverbs 31:28? 🕮 What, then, is she to him in Proverbs 12:4?

Man (3)

'enôš

Still another **word** for **man** in the OT is the Hebrew *'enôš* (582). While most Hebrew nouns derive from verbs, the source of *'enôš*, which appears about 550 times, is not absolutely certain. There seems little doubt, however, that it comes from *'naš* (605), to be feeble, weak, or sick, for this is the sense in which the word is used in many contexts. The ideas in *'enôš*, therefore, are man's weakness, mortality, and vulnerability; one authority adds the ideas of "insignificance or inferiority."[35]

All this is underscored, in fact, by the very first occurrence of this word in Genesis 6:4, which mentions "men of renown." Whether one views those as a race of giants birthed by "fallen angels" ("sons of God") cohabiting with human women (a view that is actually based exclusively in pagan myth, not biblical precedent), or as simply great warriors and men of extreme violence who were already living at that time, *'enôš* indicates their true nature. We see the same emphasis concerning the wicked men of **Sodom** (Gen. 13:13).

Of special note is the idea of man's insignificance, inferiority, and, inability. Because he is simply "mortal man" (Job 4:17), "What is man [*'enôš*], that [God is] mindful of him? and the son of man [*'āḏām*], that [God] visitest him?" (Ps. 8:4); who is he that God would even "[take] knowledge of him" at all? (144:3). All such questions are rhetorical. Compared with **God**, **man** is an insignificant speck living on a tiny ball in the **midst** of a vast universe, just a dot on a dot. Even more degradingly graphic is Job 25:6: "How much less man, that is a worm [lit. "maggot," *rimmāh*, 7415]? and the son of man, which is a worm [or "parasite," *tôlā'*, 8438]?"

Here is a wondrous paradox, however. While the first occurrence of **man** in Psalm 8:4 is *'enôš*, and the second is *'āḏām* (February 1), the reverse is the case in 144:3, showing they are practically interchangeable. While on the one **hand man** is mortal and weak, on the other God has made him immortal and strong and even given him glory through Christ. While many hymnbooks in our **day** have changed the lyrics of Isaac Watts' hymn "At the Cross" from "such a worm as I" to "sinners such as I" (as the former offends people's self-esteem), Watts was biblically correct. It should make us all the more thankful for what God accomplished through Jesus Christ our **Lord**.

Scriptures for Study: What does Psalm 8:5 go on to say that further reinforces the paradox of verse 4? 📖 What does **David pray** for in 9:19, 20?

Man (4)

geḇer

One final Hebrew **word** for **man** in the OT is *geḇer* (1397). At first glance this word seems to be a staggering contradiction to *'enôš*, which we examined **yesterday**. While *'enôš* pictures man's weakness, mortality, and vulnerability, *geḇer*, which appears sixty-six times, declares that **man** is a mighty being, a virile warrior, in fact.

So which one is it? Is **man** weak or mighty? The **answer** is *both*. As one authority so well puts it: "Man is a marvelous compound of strength and weakness . . . while he is rightly called *'enôš* by the corruption of his nature, he may also lay claim to the title of *geḇer* by virtue of the mighty energies that are capable of being exhibited in his life and character."[36] Though frail and feeble, it can still be said, "What a piece of work is a man!" Even in his weakness, he is "fearfully and wonderfully made" (Ps. 139:14).

Geḇer, then, is often used in the context of valor in **war**, as there was much of that in Israel's history. Second Samuel 23, for example, is a virtual catalog of David's mighty men, starting with David himself ("man") in verse 1. Another form of the word (*gibbôr*, 1368) appears some thirty-nine times in just 1 and 2 Chronicles, and is translated as "mighty men (1 Chron. 7:7)," "mighty men of [valour] (12:30)," and even "mighties" (11:12).

The problem comes, however, when **man** arrogantly thinks his **power** is adequate and divorces his valor and prowess from God's enabling. "A mighty man [*gibbôr*] is not delivered by much strength" (Ps. 33:16), and "the [mighty] man [*geḇer*] that [makes] not God his strength" is headed for destruction (52:1–7; "mighty man" in verse 1 is *gibbôr*). In contrast, "Blessed is the [mighty] man [*geḇer]* that trusteth in the LORD, and whose hope the LORD is" (Jer. 17:7). Further, the word for "desperately wicked" in verse 9 (*'ānaš*, 605, "to be sick, incurable") is related to yesterday's word *'enôš*.[37]

How sad are the "macho" attitudes and descriptions of manhood today! One Christian **book**, for example, even says that men should get their patterns for living from the heroes in movies such as *Braveheart, The Magnificent Seven, Die Hard,* and *Gladiator*. In dramatic contrast, the *biblical* picture is that manliness is standing for Christ and warring against the world in His **strength**. My fellow Christian brethren, I would therefore humbly encourage: Let us **strive** to be "real men."

Scriptures for Study: What prevails over the mighty man, according to Proverbs 21:22 ("mighty" is *gibbôr*)? 📖 What does that very quality then produce (24:5)?

Woman [and] Eve

'Iššāh [and] Chawwāh

Today's words will not please the militant feminists of our **day**, but **God** has done more for women than the so-called "feminist movement" could even dream of. **Adam** actually gave *two* names to the **woman** that God provided for him. The first, of course, was **Woman** (Gen. 2:23), the Hebrew *'Iššāh* (802), which Adam himself defined as "taken out of Man." She is, quite literally, a part of **man**. (See February 8 for another use of *'iššāh*.)

While Greek, Roman, and Jewish culture all held women in low regard, God and His **Word** hold them in the highest. The OT specifically teaches that women are spiritually equal to men. The Mosaic **Law** was given to all Israel, women as well as men (Deut. 1:1). Both were to **teach** it to their children (Deut. 6:4–7; Prov. 6:20). The protection of the law applied equally to women (cf. Exod. 21:28–32). Women had **inheritance** rights (Num. 36:1–12). Men and women alike participated in the Jewish religious feasts (Exod. 12:3; Deut. 16:9–15). The single greatest spiritual **vow**, the Nazirite vow, was open to both men and women (Num. 6:2). Women were involved in spiritual service (Exod. 38:8; Neh. 7:67). Nor did God hesitate to deal directly with women (Gen. 3:13; 16:7–13; Judg. 13:3).

The second **name** Adam gave this **Woman** was **Eve**, a name that should truly **bless** the **heart** of every **woman**. It is the Hebrew *Chawwāh* (2332), which is related to *chāyāh* (2421, "to be alive") and Adam expounds as "the mother of all living" (Gen. 3:20), as she gave birth (**life**) to the entire human race (4:1, 2). What a truth! Every wife is both an *'iššāh,* who is dependent on a man for her living, and a *Chawwāh,* on whom every man is dependent for his life. The warm-hearted Walt Disney movie *The Lion King* contained a **song** titled "The Circle of Life," but what we see here is the *real* circle of life. And God did (and continues to do) all this through one institution, **marriage**, which we will study beginning February 8.

To each dear, godly lady who might be reading this, may God richly bless you as you bring life into this world for His glory.

Scriptures for Study: Read the verses mentioned in today's study, meditating on the place God has given women and the implications of that truth.

Virtuous Woman

chayil

Proverbs 31:10 declares, "Who can find a virtuous woman? for her price is far above rubies." The Hebrew for **virtuous** is *chayil* (2428) and ironically is a *masculine* noun that means **strength**, force, **wealth**, and an army. Its basic idea, therefore, is strength and influence, so the picture of this type of **woman** is one of strong moral character who influences others by that strength.

The words "Who can find" do not imply that such a **woman** does not exist, but rather that such a **woman** is, indeed, quite rare and of tremendous value. How true! How many (few) women, even Christians, have such character and positive influence on other women? Many have been so affected by the world that the things spoken of here are either considered worthless or at least *worth less* than what the world says is true womanhood.

The best biblical example of this **Virtuous Woman** is Ruth, who is actually the only **woman** in **Scripture** who bears this title. For her to end up in the royal line of Christ (Matt. 1:5) is all the more amazing. Boaz said of her, "All the city of my people doth know that thou art a virtuous woman" (Ruth 3:11). Here was a pagan **woman** who abandoned the "nature-gods" of Moab after her husband died and not only turned to the only True and Living **God** but also went with the people of God when they returned to Bethlehem. No example of commitment is more graphic in Scripture than Ruth's own words: "Whither thou goest, I will go; and where thou lodgest, I will lodge: thy people shall be my people, and thy God my God" (1:16). While that verse is oddly quoted at many Christian weddings, it has nothing to do with **marriage**, rather with Ruth's total commitment to Naomi (and implied commitment to God).[38]

Solomon estimates the worth of such a **woman** as "far above rubies," which are far more **precious** than even diamonds. Today rubies are more useful than even in Solomon's **day**, being used in watches, scientific equipment, and ruby lasers. What we would **call** in our day "the high maintenance woman" is the one who *wants* rubies, but the **Virtuous Woman** is already *worth more than* rubies.

Oh, that we would see more virtuous women in our homes and churches today, and that older women would by example **teach** the younger women this very truth (Titus 2:3–5).

Scriptures for Study: What is the **Virtuous Woman** to her husband in Proverbs 12:4? 📖 What is the source of this kind of wife (Prov. 19:14)?

Help Meet

'ēzer neged

Genesis 2:18 reveals the exact reason **God** provided **Eve** for **Adam**: "The LORD God said, It is not good that the man should be alone; I will make him an help meet for him." Here is an often misunderstood (even hated) verse, but it, along with 1 Corinthians 11:9— "Neither was the man created for the woman; but the woman for the man"—could not be clearer. Before we chalk all this up to some supposed "male chauvinism," let us consider the truly incredible reason for it.

The Hebrew for **help** here is *'ēzer* (5828), which speaks of a "helper, assistant, one who aids." The most significant aspect of this **word**, however, is that most of its twenty-two occurrences indicate *divine* aid, especially in the Psalms (20:2; 33:20; 70:5; 89:19; 115:9–11; 121:1, 2; 124:8; 146:5). Think of it! A godly wife is actually divine aid. God made her specifically to aid the **man**. Why? Because he needs it! **Meet**, then, is *neged* (5048), which includes such concepts as "over against, corresponding to, and counterpart." So God made man a counterpart, a helper who complements him, an assistant who is appropriate and suitable for his needs.

I certainly identified with a **sign** in a wallpaper and paint store that read, "Husbands choosing colors must have note from wife."[39] How true that is for me! If it's not blue, then I don't really care. If it weren't for my wife's knowledge, my clothes would seldom be coordinated. And that's just *one* area in which she is a helper who is appropriate and suitable for my needs.

One writer says it well: "As a result of the Creation order, men and women are oriented to one another differently. They need one another, but they need one another *differently*. The man needs *the* help; the woman needs *to* help."[40] That says it perfectly. When we understand that principle, when we are related to our spouse as God has designed us to be, we will see our marriages transformed. That thought prepares us for tomorrow's study of **marriage**.

Scriptures for Study: Read the verses in Psalms mentioned above. How is God's help pictured in 33:20 and 115:9–11? 📖 What response does such help generate in us (146:5)?

Marriage (1)

bā'al, lāqach, yāḇam, "iššāh

Several Hebrew words are translated "married," "marry," or "**marriage**," each of which provides insight into what this relationship should be biblically. One is *bā'al* (1166), which means "to marry, have dominion, or to rule over." It is used, for example, to demonstrate political dominion (1 Chron. 4:22) as well as God's dominion over His people (Isa. 26:13), which in turn is pictured as a **marriage** (Jer. 3:14). This does not mean a husband rules like a little Napoleon over his wife, rather that he leads in a godly **way** and cherishes her as his own body (Eph. 5:25–29). It is used also in the contexts of both virginity (Isa. 62:5) and adultery (Deut. 22:22), the latter of which was punishable by **death**. These demonstrate that purity should be part of both the foundation and continuing structure of **marriage**.

Another **word** is *lāqach* (3947), which is used more than one thousand times in a variety of ways. With the basic meaning "to take, to grasp, to take hold of," it is used for **Noah** taking hold of the **dove** to bring it back into the **ark** (Gen. 8:9), taking vengeance (Isa. 47:3), or even figuratively for "taking on" commands, a metaphor for obedience (Prov. 10:8). It is, therefore, easy to see the significance of taking a wife (Gen. 25:1), as this **word** also includes the idea of keeping what one takes (Gen. 14:21).

Another word is *yāḇam* (2992), which specifically addresses the custom in the Mosaic **Law** called "levirate marriage" (Latin *levir*, "brother-in-law"), which required that upon his brother's death, if there was not already a male heir, a **man** was to marry his brother's wife so the family **name** could be passed on (Deut. 25:5–10). Obviously, we have no such custom today, but it does at least illustrate the importance of having children.

One other word is *'iššāh* (**woman** or "wife," 802, February 5). It underscores that the woman is part of the man. God has instituted **marriage** to make two people into one person (Gen. 2:24; Mark 10:6–8; Eph. 5:31; 1 Cor. 6:16) so they can function to the fullest. While God leads and empowers some Christians never to marry so they can more fully devote themselves to the Lord's **work** (Matt. 19:11, 12; 1 Cor. 7:7–9), the general rule is **marriage**.[41] Let us each cherish the one-person relationship God has given us. (We will **return** to **marriage** on February 10.)

Scriptures for Study: There was much **Scripture** mentioned in today's study. Read those verses that particularly interest you, and consider the critical importance of **marriage**.

Covenant

beriyt̲

The **covenant** is a dominant OT theme. The Hebrew always used for this concept is *beriyt̲* (1285), a broad term covering several types of agreements, including a **covenant** between friends (1 Sam. 18:3) or rulers (1 Kings 5:12, "league").

While its etymology is uncertain, it might very well be related to the Akkadian *burru*, "to establish a legal situation by testimony with an oath." This is all the more possible because of the Septuagint's use of *diathēkē* (1242G) to render *beriyt̲*, since the former also speaks of a legal transaction or testament. Similarly, the Latin *pactum* (English "pact") speaks of such a legal agreement or contract. In other words, all these words are stronger than just a general agreement, especially when we are referring to the covenants of **God**.

Simply stated, the covenants of **Scripture** are the permanent, legal transactions God made with various individuals and that extended to their descendants.[42] Scripture reveals several covenants: Noahic (Gen. 9:9–17), Abrahamic (12:1–3; 13:14–17; 17:1–22; 22:16–18; Gal. 3:8), Mosaic (Exod. 20:1–17; 21:1–31:18), Davidic (2 Sam. 7:4–17), and **New** (Jer. 31:31, 32; Heb. 7:18, 19, 22; 8:6–12).

Especially significant was the Mosaic **covenant**, a "conditional covenant" in which God **blessed** the people if they obeyed Him. Given only to *racial* Israel, the **commandments** (Exod. 20:1–6), social **judgments** (21:1–24:11), and religious ordinances (24:12–31:18) were solely intended to reveal man's **sin** (Rom. 3:20) and point him to the coming Christ, who would fulfill *all* the symbols and pictures contained in that Mosaic system (Matt. 5:17).

Of pivotal importance, the Greek *diathēkē* appears no less than fourteen times in that glorious NT **book** of Hebrews, the key **word** of which is "better." The writer declares (7:18, 19, 22) that the Mosaic **Law** (the Old **Covenant**, February 13–16) had passed its usefulness because of its own weakness, having been replaced by the "better testament" of Jesus (the New **Covenant**). He goes on in 8:6, 7 to show that while the old was *not* "faultless," the new one *is* because it is a better **covenant**. He goes on in verses 8–12 to quote Jeremiah's prophecy of the New **Covenant** and concludes in verse 13 that the Old has vanished.

So, fulfilled in Christ, the Mosaic system is no longer needed, appropriate, or even edifying. While the old only *painted pictures*, the new *presents the Person*. Once there was only *shadow*, now there is *substance*.

Soli Deo Gloria (To God alone be glory)!

Scriptures for Study: Read Hebrews 9:13–28, noting the contrast between the Old **Covenant** and the New.

Covenant (Marriage) (2)

beriyt

Today we continue our study of the scriptural use of the **word *covenant*** by noting how it relates to **marriage** (February 8). In this context, Malachi 2:14 is crucial to a proper biblical **understanding** of **marriage**: "Yet ye say, Wherefore? Because the LORD hath been witness between thee and the wife of thy youth, against whom thou hast dealt treacherously: yet is she thy companion, and the wife of thy covenant." In light of the rampant divorce rate in the ancient nation of Israel, the context speaks of the seriousness and devastation of divorce, that is, the breaking of the **covenant** (the promise, agreement, pact, commitment, even legal contract) between husband and wife.

Marriage has always been under satanic attack through the ages. While there were exceptions (Jacob and Rachel, Abraham and Sarah), the rule in Jewish culture (contrary to the Mosaic Law in **Scripture**) was that the husband and wife were far from equals. The wife was property, just like cattle. She always **walked** behind the man, never ate with him, and did much of the physical **labor**. Her husband could divorce her for any reason. The Greeks were worse. The wife was only for giving legitimate children, female and male prostitution were unbelievably rampant, and most sex was outside of **marriage**. The Romans were worse still. Divorce was extremely common and easily accomplished. Feminism (women's liberation), birth control, **marriage** contracts, and open **marriage** all developed in the empire and contributed to its downfall. Today's attitudes are merely extensions of those ancient times with a few twists being provided by advanced technology.

Biblically, however, the basic essence of **marriage** is companionship. ***Marriage* *is a formal* *covenant* *(agreement or promise) between a* *man* *and a* *woman* *to become each other's loving* *companion* *for* *life*.** A companion is one with whom we are united in goals, values, affections, and, in the case of **marriage**, even body. When the "covenant of companionship" is made, those "covenanters"[43] promise to selflessly **love** each other, take away loneliness, meet sexual needs, honor and be faithful, **bear** children as **God** dictates, and so very much more.

As **wonderful** as **marriage** is—as I **write** this, I've been married for thirty-six years, and we still feel like newlyweds—when we get to **heaven** there will be no **marriage** (Matt. 22:30), for there we will **know** far greater glories, and Jesus will be our Perfect Companion. In the meantime, let us have marriages that are all God wants them to be.

Scriptures for Study: Preferably with your spouse, review God's requirements for husbands and wives in Ephesians 5:18–33, committing yourselves anew to these truths.

Cain

Qayin

When we hear the **name** ***Cain,*** most of us probably think immediately of the first murderer and his heinous crime. But there is more here. The Hebrew is *Qayin* (7014), which as most scholars agree is a play on the verb *qānāh* (7069), "to buy, purchase, acquire, or possess." This seems all the more apparent in what **Eve** herself says of **Cain**: "I have gotten [i.e., acquired, *qānāh*] a man from the LORD" (Gen. 4:1).

It did not take long, however, for that **blessed** acquisition to take a turn for the worse, long before Cain's murder of his **brother Abel**. Jude alludes to Cain's real problem when he writes of apostates: "Woe unto them! for they have gone in the way of Cain" (v. 11). The Greek for **way** is *hodos* (3598G), which literally refers to a road, highway, or street, but metaphorically to a course of conduct or way of thinking. So what was Cain's way of thinking? That he could please **God** his own way.

What **offering**, then, did **Cain** bring, and why did God not accept it? Some teachers insist the problem was that **Cain** did not bring **blood**, as did Abel. Genesis 3:21, it is argued, reveals that God taught **Adam** and Eve that blood had to be shed for sin, so this same knowledge was undoubtedly handed down to **Cain** and Abel. While we respect this view and its defenders, that is not what the text precisely says. The Hebrew, in fact, for the offering (April 17, 20) both men brought is *minchāh* (4503), which does not refer to blood at all, rather the general idea of a gift. The offering each **man** brought, therefore, was appropriate to his vocation and could have been accepted equally.

So why was Cain's offering not accepted? We submit two reasons: *First,* the absence of a term such as "first fruits" for **Cain** (in contrast to Abel bringing the "firstlings" (Gen. 4:4)) shows that **Cain** didn't bring the best, the choice of his crop, rather whatever he could "get by on," whatever he thought would appease God. *Second,* and more importantly, Abel's offering was by ***faith*** *alone* (Heb. 11:4, April 9–11); Cain's was not.

What, then, is the way of **Cain**? *The way of religion*. Cain's way of thinking was that he could please God his own way, and *that* is religion. Christianity, however, is not a religion; it is a **life**, a life found only in Christ by **grace** through faith.

Scriptures for Study: Read Matthew 7:13, 14, noting the two **paths** Jesus outlines. 📖 What does 1 John 3:12 say about **Cain**?

Abel

Hebel

In stark contrast to **Cain**, whom we studied **yesterday**, there was his **brother Abel**, whose **name** also tells us much. The Hebrew is *Hebel* (1893), which is identical to *hebel* (1892; see also June 28) and has an interesting etymology. It literally means "wind, breath, or vapor," while another form speaks of **vanity** or emptiness, as is true thirty-eight times in Ecclesiastes alone (e.g., "vanity of vanities; all is vanity," 1:2), showing the total emptiness and utter futility of **life** without **God** (Rom. 8:20–22).

While this **word** at first seems odd when applied to **Abel**, it in reality is quite appropriate. Why that name? One commentator offers this reason: "By the time of Abel's birth, Eve had become thoroughly impressed with the impact of God's curse on the world. God had indeed made the creation 'subject to vanity.'"[44] Abel's existence itself was a vapor, that is, short-lived in comparison with the life spans of the **day**. **Adam**, for example, lived 930 years (Gen. 5:5). By the **evil** of his own brother, however, Abel's life was cut short. As vapor is present one moment and gone the next, so it was with **Abel**.

The application of this word to each of us is challenging. James writes on this very subject: "Go to now, ye that say, To day or to morrow we will go into such a city, and continue there a year, and buy and sell, and get gain: Whereas ye know not what shall be on the morrow. For what is your life? It is even a vapour, that appeareth for a little time, and then vanisheth away. For that ye ought to say, If the Lord will, we shall live, and do this, or that. But now ye rejoice in your boastings: all such rejoicing is evil" (James 4:13–16). Compared with the long life spans of people in Genesis, each of us is on this earth for a very short time. In light of eternity, it truly is only a vapor. How, then, should we live? Should we live a life of arrogance and self-determination? Or should our life be one that seeks God at every turn, whether it be in business decisions, personal living, or family life? To believe truly in the sovereignty of God is to believe He is in control of all things and that we are to bring ourselves into conformity to His will.

Scriptures for Study: Read what Job writes about the fleeting nature of life (7:6, 7; 9:25, 26; 14:1, 2). 📖 What **wonderful** encouragement do Peter and John give us (1 Pet. 1:24, 25; 1 John 2:17)?

Law (1)

Tôrāh

In addition to the fascinating study of God's many names, which formed the bulk of our readings **last** month, there is another OT subject that has many facets, namely *God's* ***Word***. There are, in fact, no less than eight different Hebrew words in Psalm 119 alone that describe the many aspects of God's Word.

The first such word is **law**, which is the most frequent of all, appearing some 219 times. The Hebrew is *tôrāh* (8451), a feminine noun meaning "direction, teaching, and instruction." Generally speaking, **law** most often refers to a body of teaching, and that is precisely what *all* **Scripture** is. While we will examine in subsequent studies the Mosaic **Law** and its bearing on NT believers, *all* Scripture provides direction and instruction. While not all Scripture was written *to* the church (NT believers), all Scripture was written *for* the church. In other words, all Scripture provides legitimate application for us in this age.

It's interesting and instructive that the very first occurrence of *tôrāh* is in Genesis 26:5, long before God gave the Mosaic **Law**: "Because that Abraham obeyed my voice, and kept my charge, my commandments, my statutes, and my laws." In other words, God has *always* had laws. This is further evident in the fact that before God gave the Mosaic **Law**, some of its basic principles already existed **among** the Babylonians, Hittites, and other civilizations. This clearly demonstrates that at the very least a basic verbal **law** had been handed down through the years. It eventually was ignored by the majority after Babel, but there were some, such as Abraham, who retained the knowledge of God's **law**. We see the same implication in Job (which predates the Mosaic Law): "Neither have I gone back from the commandment of his lips; I have esteemed the words of his mouth more than my necessary food" (Job 23:12). Again, long before Moses, there were **commandments**, that is, **law**, which while eventually replaced by the Mosaic **Law**, was nonetheless a code of behavior and a body of teaching by which **man** was bound. As we will see, this is the **law** written in man's hearts (Rom. 2:15), a **law** he cannot escape.

Scriptures for Study: What do Psalm 1:1–3 and 119:1 promise to those who **keep** God's **law**, that is, the instruction of His Word in general?

Law (2)

Tôrāh

While *tôrāh* (8451) speaks of God's **Word** in general, it is also used to refer specifically to the **Law** God gave to Israel at Sinai—the Mosaic **Law**, with all its ceremonies, sacrifices, and ordinances. Through Moses, and in the minutest detail, God gave Israel 613 commands that covered every area of **life**—moral, civil, and ceremonial.

First, there was the Ten **Commandments**, the Moral **Law**, the Decalogue, "ten words" (Exod. 20:1–17), followed by the **judgments**, directing the social and civil life of Israel (21:1–24:11), and concluding with the ordinances (24:12–31:18), dictating the religious life of Israel. What is also significant is that it was necessary that they keep *all* that **Law**. To "keep the whole law," in fact, "and yet offend in one point" meant they were guilty of breaking all 613 laws (James 2:10, from Deut. 27:26).

We will **return** to the latter two aspects of the **Law tomorrow**, but we note today that this Moral **Law** was written in the hearts of men everywhere (Rom. 2:15). This demonstrates that men **know** in their **heart** (i.e., by their mind and conscience, December 6) not to lie, steal, murder, or violate the other moral commands. Again, such moral **law** is found in legal codes of **nations** throughout history.

These moral laws (except for keeping the **Sabbath**, which was replaced by the Lord's **Day**, March 20–21) are also found restated several times in the NT: having no other gods (Exod. 20:3; Deut. 5:7; Acts 5:29); making no idols or images (Exod. 20:4–6; Deut. 5:8–10; Acts 17:29–31; 1 Cor. 8:4–6; 10:14; Col. 3:5; 1 John 5:21); not profaning God's **name** (Exod. 20:7; Deut. 5:11; James 5:12); honoring one's **father** and mother (Exod. 20:12; Deut. 5:16; Eph. 6:1–3; Col. 3:20); not murdering (Exod. 20:13; Deut. 5:17; Rom. 13:9, 10; James 2:11); not committing adultery (Exod. 20:14; Deut. 5:19; Rom. 13:9,10; 1 Cor. 6:9; Heb. 13:4; James 2:11); not stealing (Exod. 20:15; Deut. 5:19; Rom. 13:9, 10; Eph. 4:28); not lying (Exod. 20:16; Deut. 5:20; Eph. 4:25,31; Col. 3:9; Tit. 3:2); not coveting (Exod. 20:17; Deut. 5:21; Rom. 7:7; 13:9; Eph. 5:3–5; Heb. 13:5 James 4:1–3).

Let us **rejoice** in and **obey** God's **Law**.

Scriptures for Study: Read the many verses listed in today's study and apply them to your own living.

Law (3)

Tôrāh

There is some confusion about the place of the **Law** (*tôrāh*, 8451) today. Some teachers (as did the Judaizers of old: Acts 15:5; Gal. 2:11–13; 3:1, 3; 5:1) insist that Christians must **keep** the Mosaic **Law**. It is essential to a proper **understanding** of **Scripture**, however, to recognize that the recipients of the **Law** were those whom **God** "brought . . . out of the land of Egypt" (Exod. 20:2), that is, Israel *alone*. It was never meant for the church, or **Gentiles** in general. It was a **covenant** made *with* Moses *for* racial Israel.

The fourfold purpose of the **Law** is summarized in Galatians 3:19–25. *First,* it was to make **sin** known (v. 19, "added because of transgressions"), "for by the law is the knowledge of sin" (Rom. 3:20). *Second,* it demonstrates that "all [men are] under sin" (Gal. 3:22; cf. Rom. 3:23) and sin's horror (Rom. 7:7–13). *Third,* it actually imprisons men: "Before faith came, we were kept under the law, shut up unto the faith which should afterwards be revealed" (Gal. 3:23; cf. 1 Tim. 1:9). "Kept" is *phroureō* (5432G), which means "to keep inward under lock and key." The **Law** was a jailer who held in custody those subject to sin, and who kept them that **way** until Christ came to free them.

Fourth, and most significantly, because God is holy (1 Pet. 1:16), the **Law** was a schoolmaster that pointed men to Christ and His righteousness (vv. 24, 25). The end of the **Law** came when Christ was crucified. One of the most basic principles of understanding the Bible is that the Mosaic **Law** ended in Christ. If that is not recognized, the result will be enormous confusion and serious error. Paul, therefore, makes the matter absolutely clear with the **word** *schoolmaster.* The Greek is *paidagogos* (3807G), which was a person (usually a slave) assigned as a tutor and guardian for young boys. By its very definition, it was both a *temporary* and *lowly* position. When the son came of age into full sonship at about eighteen, the schoolmaster's responsibilities ended. Paul's imagery, then, is unmistakable. The Mosaic **Law** was a temporary schoolmaster that was designed to **lead** Israel to maturity, that is, *Christ.* Once Christ arrived, was crucified, and rose again, He became the controlling force in the believer's **life**.

The Mosaic **Law**, therefore, was *never* intended to be the rule in the Christian's life. As we will see **tomorrow**, the Christian is under a "new law."

Scriptures for Study: Read Galatians 5:16–26, noting the great superiority of walking in the Spirit over following "the weak and beggarly elements" of the old **law** (Gal. 4:9).

Law (4)
Tôrāh

Before moving on, let us take one more look at **law** (*tôrāh*, 8451). One school of Bible teaching is fond of saying, "We are no longer under law but under grace," which is true when we are speaking of the Mosaic system, but is not true if we conclude there is *no **law** at all*. In other words, just as **grace** existed in the OT, **law** still exists today, but just as grace was manifested differently under the Old **Covenant**, **law** is manifested differently in the **New** Covenant (February 9).

So basic is the truth that the Mosaic **Law** is passed that our **Lord** Himself declared, "Think not that I am come to destroy the law, or the prophets: I am not come to destroy, but to fulfil" (Matt. 5:17). "Fulfil" is *plēroō* (4137G), a verb that speaks of filling a container to capacity and means "to influence fully, control, or satisfy." The entire Mosaic **Law** pointed to Christ, so when He came, He "satisfied" it, so it passed away.

Even more significant, our Lord later even summarized the *entire* **law** (all 613 commands of it!) into two: **Love God** and your **neighbor**, on which "hang *all* the law and the prophets" (Matt. 22:36–40; emphasis added). What **law** is now in force that replaces and supersedes the old? *The **law** of love*. As Paul wrote, "He that loveth another hath fulfilled the law. . . . Love worketh no ill to his neighbour: therefore love is the fulfilling of the law" (Rom. 13:8, 10).

Oh, how far superior this **law** is to the old! Jesus declared, "Except your righteousness shall exceed the righteousness of the scribes and Pharisees, ye shall in no case enter into the kingdom of heaven" (Matt. 5:20), and then went on to illustrate. While the old **law** said not to murder, the **new** says not to have rash **anger** (Matt. 5:21–26; cf. Exod. 20:13). While the old said not to commit adultery, the new says to not even look with lust (Matt. 5:27, 28; cf. Exod. 20:14). While the old said not to **swear** falsely, the new says, "Swear not at all," that is, carelessly or profanely (Matt. 5:33, 34; cf. Lev. 19:12). While the old said "an eye for an eye," the new says to turn the other cheek (Matt. 5:38, 39; cf. Exod. 21:24). Let us **glorify** our Lord by keeping *His* **law**, not the one He fulfilled.

Scriptures for Study: What did Paul tell the Galatians about how the **law** is fulfilled (Gal. 5:14)? 📖 What does he **call** that **law**, in fact (6:2)?

Testimonies

'ēḏāh [and] 'ēḏût

The second **name** we note for God's **Word** is **testimonies** (or "testimony"). The Hebrew is *'ēdāh* (5713; or *'ēḏûṯ*, 5715), another feminine noun originally meaning a "testimony, witness, or even a warning sign." Of its twenty-five appearances, fourteen are in Psalm 119 (*'ēḏût* appears sixty times, with nine of those in Ps. 119). We should also interject here that all eight of the synonyms we are examining appear in the first eleven verses of that wondrous **psalm**, which is devoted to praising the virtues, merits, and sufficiency of the Word of God and demonstrates the psalmist's total commitment to it.

This word, therefore, refers to "testifying to a fact or event." It first appears, for example, in Genesis 21:30, where Abraham's gift of lambs to Abimelech bore **witness** to Abraham's statement concerning the ownership of the well at Beersheba. Even more graphic is 31:52, where Jacob used a pile of stones to **bear witness** to the agreement between him and Laban concerning land boundaries.

It eventually came to be used, then, for a solemn testimony of the will of God, a sober and serious expression of God's standards for human behavior. In other words, God's **testimonies** are not *suggestions* or *optional proposals,* rather His absolute standards. It is tremendously significant, in fact, that the stone tablets containing the Ten **Commandments** are called God's "testimony," *'ēḏût* (Exod. 25:16; 31:18; 32:15), God's "solemn divine charge or duty."[45] It was also frequently used of the **tabernacle** ("tabernacle of testimony", Exod. 38:21; Num. 1:50, 53) and even the **Ark of the Covenant** ("ark of the testimony," Exod. 25:22; 26:33, 34; 30:6, 26). Further, it is also used at times to refer to the entire **law** (February 13–16) of God (Ps. 19:7; 119:14, 31, 36, 88, 99, 111, 129, 144, 157).

The definition of *right behavior,* therefore, is not "up for grabs," as relativism maintains in our **day**. It is rather a marked-out standard from God. This standard is also what we should be proclaiming without apology to the world, just as **David** did "before kings" (Ps. 119:46); as Shadrach, Meshach, and Abednego did before the **king** of Babylon (Dan. 3:1–16); as Peter did before the religious leaders (Acts 4); as Stephen did before the council (6:15–7:54); and as Paul did before Felix (Acts 24), Festus (Acts 25), and Agrippa (Acts 26).

Scriptures for Study: What do the verses above in Psalms 19 and 119 say about the **testimonies** of God and our response to them?

Precept

piqqûḏ [and] pāqaḏ

The third **name** for God's **Word** is the term ***precept***. The Hebrew here is *piqqûḏ* (6490), a masculine noun also meaning "instruction." It's a poetic word found only in the Psalms (twenty-four times, all but three in 119), always in the plural, that speaks of injunctions and moral obligations.

Especially noteworthy is the fact that *piqqûḏ* comes from the root *pāqaḏ* (6485), a verb that means "to attend to, visit, search out, scrutinize, or make careful inspection of." One aspect of this word is the idea of paying attention to something. Joseph, for example was made the "overseer" of Potiphar's **house** (Gen. 39:1-4), paying attention to and caring for all the affairs of the house.

The word is especially significant when used of God paying attention to something. In a positive **way**, at his **death** Joseph told his brothers that God would "visit" them and bring them into the Promised Land (Gen. 50:24). Likewise, God was certainly paying attention to the plight of His people in their bondage in Egypt and said to Moses, "I have surely visited [*pāqaḏ*] you, and seen that which is done to you in Egypt" (Exod. 3:16). He went on to say He would deliver them. The negative is also true, that God pays attention to those who are doing **evil**, as when He gave the **commandment** in the Decalogue not to make any type of **image** or **idol** or bow down to any false god, for He is "a jealous God, visiting [*pāqaḏ*] the iniquity of the fathers upon the children" (Exod. 20:5).

One authority, in fact, provides a definition in this vein that should particularly strike us: "[*pāqaḏ*] expresses the idea that God is paying attention to how He wants things ordered."[46] It continues to amaze me how church leaders today, as if God isn't watching, persist in doing things the way *they* **choose**, from creating whatever methods and ministries they deem fit, to running the church as they would a corporation. Instead of opening **Scripture** to see how God wants things ordered, we do what pleases people. Psalm 119:4, for example, declares, "Thou hast commanded us to keep thy precepts diligently," underscoring that God wants things done His way. Let us commit ourselves to that principle, for God *is* paying attention.

Scriptures for Study: Read just a few of the occurrences of **precept** in Psalm 119, noting what our attitude and response should be: verses 4, 15, 27, 40, 45, 87, and 93.

Statute(s)

chōq [and] chāqaq

The fourth synonym we encounter for God's **Word** is **statute**, which is the Hebrew *chōq* (2706), a masculine noun derived from a verb (*chāqaq*, 2710) that means "to cut, scratch, inscribe, or engrave." Oh, what a word we have here! While it is used for such ideas as cutting a tomb out of rock (Isa. 22:16), its most common use is to refer to engraving or **writing**.

At one time, one of the major attacks on the authenticity of the Bible by its critics was the belief that writing did not exist in Moses' time, "proving" that Moses couldn't have written the Pentateuch, rather that it was written four centuries later by four separate authors. This was forever dispelled, however, in 1902 by one of the most important archaeological finds of all time, the Code of Hammurabi, discovered by M. J. de Morgan. Hammurabi was **king** of Babylon (ca. eighteenth century BC) and was, therefore, a contemporary of Abraham. The code, written on an eight-foot-high, two-foot-wide, and one-and-a-half-foot-thick polished block of **black** diorite stone, contains laws (some similar to the Mosaic **Law**) dealing with **worship**, justice, taxes and other money matters, building, and matters of commerce.

The existence of that code, as well as others of the ancient world—such as the Egyptian Rosetta Stone (ca. 200 BC)—wonderfully illustrate our word for today. It is used, for example, of the **statutes** God gave to Moses (Exod. 15:26; Num. 30:16, Mal. 4:4). The word *lûach* (3871) speaks of a stone slab (Exod. 34:1). God inscribed His law on such tablets; they were known as the "tables," as in the "tables of testimony [February 17], tables of stone, written with the finger of God" (Exod. 31:18).

The old expression "set in stone" also illustrates this truth. God's **statutes** (or decrees) are engraved in stone, graphically demonstrating their permanence. Turning again to Psalm 119, we find *chōq* twenty-one times, the first of which is in verse 5: "O that my ways were directed to keep thy statutes!" God's Word is not open for debate, not subject to reinterpretation for the times. God's Word is set in stone!

Scriptures for Study: Read a few of the occurrences of **statutes** in Psalm 119, noting what our attitude and response to them should be: verses 8, 23, 54, 71, 83, 112, and 117.

Commandment(s)

miṣwāh [and] ṣāwāh

The fifth term we meet in **Scripture** in reference to itself is ***commandment***. This noun's related verb is *ṣāwāh* (6680), a general **word** that denotes a superior verbally ordering or commanding a subordinate. In its first occurrence, **God** verbally "commanded" **Adam** that he could "freely eat" of every **tree** in the garden except "the tree of the knowledge of good and evil" (Gen. 2:16, 17). It is also commonly used of people commanding other people (e.g., Gen. 18:19; Exod. 1:22; Judg. 4:6; 1 Kings 5:17).

The feminine noun *miṣwāh* (4687), however, is especially significant. Appearing some 181 times, it speaks more of official edicts or decrees. While it is used at times of the commands of men (e.g., Esther 3:3; Prov. 6:20; Isa. 29:13), all sixty-three of its occurrences in the Pentateuch are of God's commands, as are all twenty-two in Psalm 119 and, of course, others throughout the OT. Further, it appears quite often in reference to the entire body of divine **law** and instruction (Gen. 26:5; Exod. 16:28; Deut. 6:2; 1 Kings 2:3).

The common expression of our **day** that someone is "searching for truth" is actually a misnomer. Truth is not hidden; it has not been lost. As Deuteronomy 30:11 declares, "This commandment which I command thee this day, it is not hidden from thee, neither is it far off." Truth, in fact, is quite easy to see if one simply opens one's eyes. As Paul declares, even nature itself declares that there is a God of Creation (Rom. 1:20), and as **David** adds, "The heavens declare the glory of God; and the firmament sheweth his handywork" (Ps. 19:1).

Let us meditate today on three attitudes we should have toward God's **commandments**. *First,* let us ***remember*** them as true. As the psalmist challenges, we will "remember his commandments to do them" (103:18) simply because His "commandments are truth" (119:151). *Second,* let us *regard* them as valuable. When we truly see their value, even "above gold; yea, above fine gold" (119:127), we will "not wander from" or "err from" them but rather "learn" them (119:10, 21, 73). *Third,* let us *revere* them as holy. "Blessed is the man that feareth the LORD, that delighteth greatly in his commandments" (112:1) and that has "respect unto all [His] commandments" (119:6).

Scriptures for Study: What should fathers do with God's **commandments** (Deut. 6:6–9)? 📖 What does 12:32 then declare (cf. Rev. 22:18, 19)?

Judgment

mišpāṭ

The sixth term we see **Scripture** using of itself is ***judgment***. The Hebrew *mišpāṭ* (4941) is a masculine noun indicating a binding judicial decision that establishes a precedent. While the structure of American government is distinctively divided into branches—executive, legislative, and judicial—this was not the case in ancient times. When we see the **word *judgment*** we tend to think of something judicial only, but *mišpāṭ* is broader than that, indicating not only judging but also ruling.

Mišpāṭ is very common in the OT, appearing 417 times. Its first occurrence is in Genesis 18:19, where **God** says of Abraham, "I know him, that he will command his children and his household after him, and they shall keep the way of the LORD, to do justice and judgment." Here is the first mention in Scripture of the importance of teaching our children. What should we be teaching them? Certainly not humanism and evolution, but rather the things of God, morality, and the precedents of Scripture.

My personal passion for Psalm 119 takes me to it often, and we find *mišpāṭ* there no less than twenty-three times. The first occurrence is in verse 7: "I will praise thee with uprightness of heart, when I shall have learned thy righteous judgments," indicating that we **praise** God only when we follow the precedents set down in His Word. It is absolutely impossible to praise God fully unless His Word is our sole authority.

So not only does God's Word give us ***precepts***, as noted on February 18, but it also provides *precedents*. Just as an attorney will **plead** based on precedents to **try** to prove his case, the greatest schooling, the greatest lessons of **life**, the most important things we can learn (and then **teach** to our children and other believers) are the precedents set down in God's Word. Tragically, many Bible interpreters ignore the precedents, the clear rulings of Scripture. One graphic example is the clear precedent in Scripture of the primacy of **preaching**. True biblical and expositional preaching (March 15) has all but vanished, being replaced by things that are "more appropriate to the modern mind," it is argued, or "more appealing to the unchurched."

Never has there been a greater need for "[declaring] all the judgments of [God's] mouth" (Ps. 119:13) than there is today, for it is only there we will find **hope** (v. 43) and comfort (v. 52) simply because those **judgments** are right (v. 75).

Scriptures for Study: What else does Psalm 119 challenge us to do concerning God's **judgments** (vv. 102, 106, 120, and 164)?

Word

dāḇār [and] 'imrāh

One of the most significant words used for **Scripture**, of course, is the term **word**, which actually is a translation of several Hebrew words. Today we examine two of the most important.

The first is *dāḇār* (1697), which means a **word** or "speech" and is a general term for God's revelation. The Ten **Commandments** are referred to in Exodus 34:28 and Deuteronomy 10:4 using *dāḇār*, which we could translate as "the ten words" because they are exactly what God said. The passion of the Christian should not be the most entertaining speaker of the **day** or the latest self-help teacher. The believer's passion should be, "God says . . ." Its first occurrence in Psalms 119, for example, is in verse 9: "Wherewithal shall a young man cleanse his way? by taking heed thereto according to thy word," a clear reference to God's moral **law** being the one and only path to right living (February 14).

Another Hebrew **word** translated ***word*** is *'imrāh* (565), a derivative of *'āmar* (559). While the latter is found often, the former is a rare poetic **word** that appears more in Psalm 119 than everywhere else combined. It is more or less a synonym for *dāḇār* and simply emphasizes not just a concept or thought but the very words of God, and is often used in the phrase "the words of my mouth"[47] (e.g., Ps. 19:14; Prov. 4:5; 5:7; 7:24; 8:8). Another form (*'ēmer*; 561) is often translated with the Greek *rhēma* (4487G) in the Septuagint (e.g., Ps. 78:1; 138:4), which usually relates to individual words and utterances.[48]

Turning once again to Psalm 119, the first occurrence of *'imrāh* there is that **wonderful** verse, "Thy word have I hid in mine heart, that I might not sin against thee" (v. 11). In a day when God's *words* are more and more being replaced by *concepts*, or what is called "dynamic equivalence," this **word** underscores that it is the individual words that are crucial. The same principle is underscored in Psalm 12:6, 7: "The words of the LORD are pure words: as silver tried in a furnace of earth, purified seven times. Thou shalt keep them, O LORD, thou shalt preserve them from this generation for ever." Let us truly desire the *words* of Scripture.

Scriptures for Study: Read a few of the occurrences of *'imrāh* in Psalm 119, noting the significance of each: verses 50, 67, 76, 103, and 117.

Way

derek [and] 'ōrach

Some Bible students consider the **word *way*** another term that refers to God's Word, and certainly we have no objection to that. Like ***word, way*** is a translation of two Hebrew words.

One is *derek* (1870), which in the literal sense speaks of a "road" or "trodden path." Metaphorically, then, it refers to a marked-out pattern of **life**, as in Proverbs 3:6: "In all thy [patterns of life] acknowledge him, and he shall direct thy paths." Deuteronomy 8:6 likewise commands, "Thou shalt keep the commandments of the LORD thy God, to walk in his [patterns of life], and to fear him." We find other verses that speak of either righteous, pleasant, or wise patterns of life (2 Sam. 22:22; Prov. 3:17; 6:6), but also patterns that are **evil** and dark (1 Kings 22:52; Prov. 2:13).

We once **walked** in iniquity, but the true believer now walks in God's **way**, that trodden path that God has made by His **law**, the trail that God Himself, through Christ, blazed through the jungle of earthly existence. It simply is not enough to just "not do *wrong*." We must do *right*. "The surest way to abstain from evil," Spurgeon wrote, "is to be fully occupied in doing good."[49] If we concentrate on doing **good**, doing wrong will not be an issue.

The second word translated **way** is similar to *derek*. It is *'ōrach* (734), which literally refers to a "path, highway, or caravan (in the plural)." Figuratively, it "describes the path of an individual or course of life (Job 6:18) or the characteristics of a lifestyle, good or evil (Ps.16:11)."[50] We hear much about "lifestyle" nowadays, including "an alternate lifestyle," a euphemism used to mask the **sin** of homosexuality (both male and female), sometimes accepted by professing Christians despite its being condemned in **Scripture**.[51]

Any lifestyle that violates Scripture is wicked, and every lifestyle is a deliberate choice, for which each of us is responsible and for which we will one **day answer** to God (Rom. 14:12). Let each of us (especially our young people as they prepare for life) **choose** to "[walk] not in the counsel of the ungodly, nor [stand] in the way of sinners, nor [sit] in the seat of the scornful" but rather make sure our "delight is in the law of the LORD" (Ps. 1:1, 2).

Scriptures for Study: In Daniel 1:8, what was the proof of that **young** man's deliberate choice (note "purposed") of a godly lifestyle? 🕮 How did Joseph demonstrate his choice of a godly lifestyle (Gen. 39:6–12)?

Scripture [Write, Writing]

keṯāḇ

Before leaving the subject of words that speak of **Scripture**, we should consider the **word *Scripture*** itself. While the word **Scripture** appears only once in our Authorized Version OT (Dan. 10:21, see below),[52] the Hebrew behind it is also translated **write** and **writing** (e.g., Esther 3:14; Ezra. 4:7).

The noun *keṯāḇ* (3791) is derived from the verb *kāṯaḇ* (3789), which appears some 223 times and is simply a common word that means to **write**. This verb oddly does not appear in Genesis; its first occurrence is in Exodus 17:14, where we read of Israel's miraculous victory over the Amalekites and **God** telling Moses to **write** it down. This is, in fact, the first **writing** that would become **Scripture**. The occurrence in Daniel 10:21 is also significant: "I will shew thee that which is noted in the scripture of truth." John Gill explains, "The decrees and purposes of God, which are sometimes signified by a book, and things written in it . . . so sure and certain [are they], and which will be most truly, infallibly, and punctually performed . . . [that they] are noted, marked, engraven, in the eternal mind of God; they are 'in writing,' and they are 'truth.'"[53]

Another writer puts the nature of *kāṯaḇ* perfectly: "This use of the word implies something more than keeping a record of something so that it will be remembered. [It] refers to the unchangeableness and binding nature of the Word of God. God has said it, it is fixed, and it will occur."[54]

The old cliché that goes, "God said it, I believe it, and that settles it," is a sad misnomer. While it is certainly stated with the deepest sincerity and the purest of motives, is it true? No, it is not. What settles a matter *forever* is what God says about it, regardless of what we believe. Some argue in defense, "Well, my believing it settles the matter *for me*." Again, not so. The matter is settled in ***heaven*** for you, not here on earth when you believe it. Realizing the truth of this principle is essential to the doctrine of biblical authority. If a matter is settled when we believe it, then what God says is not actually in effect until we put our stamp of approval upon it. We could greatly improve this cliché simply by saying, "God said it, *that* settles it, and I, by God's grace, believe it."

Scriptures for Study: What was "written" in Exodus 24:12 (cf. 31:18; Deut. 4:13)? What material was used (February 19)? 🕮 What does Joshua 1:8 declare about God's "written" Word?

Create
bārā'

Having considered several synonyms for **Scripture**, nothing could be more appropriate than examining the second truth—God's existence is the first—that Scripture declares: "In the beginning God created the heaven and the earth" (Gen. 1:1; also Isa. 45:12). "Created" (or **create**) is the Hebrew *bārā'* (1254), a **word** that appears some fifty-three times and is used of God alone.

Unlike other words that speak of making something, *bārā'* speaks of creating from nothing. The word *yāṣar* (3335), for example, means "to form, fashion, or shape," as a potter makes a **vessel** (Isa. 29:16) and as God made **man** from dust (Gen. 2:7). Similarly, *'āśāh* (6213) means "to do, to make, to accomplish," as in constructing something with existing materials (Gen. 13:4). There is also *kûn* (3559), which means "to set up, to make firm, to establish," as in founding a city (Hab. 2:12). Amazingly, all four words appear together in Isaiah 45:18: "God himself . . . formed [*yāṣar*] the earth and made [*'āśāh*] it; he hath established [*kûn*] it, he created [*bārā'*] it not in vain."

Bārā' is, therefore, unique. While the potter needs clay and the builder needs materials, God needs nothing. He merely speaks into existence whatever He chooses, as we repeatedly read "And God said" in Genesis 1. Further, God will also **create** the **New** Heavens and New Earth (Isa. 65:17; Rev. 21:1–5).

So in Genesis 1, we see the creation of all three basic elements of the physical universe: space ("heavens"), matter ("heavens and earth"), and **time** ("beginning"). God did it all, and any compromise with the idea of "millions of years" is a denial of God's unique, finished **work** of Creation and is the result of the brainwashing of people's minds by ungodly men.

Another particularly intriguing appearance of *bārā'* occurs in Psalm 51:10, where **David**, after his terrible sin, pleads, "Create in me a clean heart, O God." We are reminded here of Ephesians 2:10, which declares that the believer is "created in Christ Jesus." "Created" is *ktizō* (2936G), the word often used in the Septuagint to translate *bārā'*. God created the believer from nothing. Before Christ came into our lives, each of us was a worthless lump of clay, dead in trespasses and sins (Eph. 2:1–3). But then God created us! And to what were we created? "Unto good works, which God hath before ordained that we should walk in them" (v. 10).

Scriptures for Study: What is the purpose of God's creation of man in Isaiah 43:7? 🕮 What should be our response to that creation (Ps. 148:5)?

Day

yôm

As if the evolutionist's challenge of divine creation were not bad enough, there have been some Christians who compromise with evolution by actually allowing for "millions of years." The idea of the "geologic column" was literally invented by the God- and Bible-hating amateur geologist Charles Lyle (1797–1875). It exists nowhere except in the textbooks, and has not even the smallest shred of empirical evidence to support it, but has nevertheless become "gospel" to the evolutionist.

Inexplicably, Christian leaders became so intimidated by evolution that they concocted theories that would accommodate both the Bible and the "millions of years" of the geological ages. The "Gap Theory," for example, was created for the sole purpose of fitting the geological ages into the Bible, teaching that Genesis 1:1 indicates complete creation, while 1:2 and what follows is the *re*creation after a "gap" of millions of years between the two verses. Similarly, the **Day** Age Theory teaches that each "day" of Creation consisted of millions of years, which again allows for the geological ages.

All such God-dishonoring theories are shown to be false not only by the statement that "God created," but also by the **word *day***. While the Hebrew *yôm* (3117) at times refers to an indefinite time, such as the span of **life** (Ps. 102:3) or even a "full" year (Lev. 25:29; 1 Sam. 27:7), its most common and natural reference in its more than 2,200 appearances is to a normal twenty-four-hour period (Gen. 39:10). This is all the more clearly demonstrated in the Creation account by the qualifiers first, "second," "third," etc., being coupled with "evening and morning," which is never used in the OT in a nonliteral manner. Further, why were the **sun** and **moon** created? To distinguish between and "rule" the two parts of a solar **day** (Gen. 1:16). Further still, nonliteral usages, such as "the day of the Lord" (e.g., Isa. 2:12; Ezek. 30:3), a period that is longer than a single **day**, are always clarified by the context. This is common even in modern usage and is always clear in context. To deny such truth is not only to dishonor **God** but to show oneself foolish.

The normal use of **day** in the OT serves to encourage us not only to **praise** God as Creator "every day" (Ps. 145:2), but also to meditate on His Word "all the day" (Ps. 119:97).

Scriptures for Study: What did the psalmist do seven times a **day** and why (Ps. 119:164)? 🕮 What else should we do "from day to day" (96:2)?

Blessed

'ešer

The very first **word** we read in the **book** of Psalms is **blessed**. The Hebrew here is *'ešer* (835), a masculine noun meaning a person's state of bliss. It's never used of **God**, rather always of people, and is exclamatory in emphasis, as in "O the bliss of . . ."[55] Most of its forty-four appearances are appropriately in the poetry of Psalms and Proverbs.

It is extremely significant that the Septuagint translates *'ešer* using the Greek *makarios*, which our **Lord** used nine times in the Beatitudes (Matt. 5:3–11). Many Bible teachers say this word just means "happy," which is always circumstantial. It actually speaks of the far deeper idea of an inward contentedness not affected by circumstances (Phil. 4:11–13).[56]

Of the many occurrences of *'ešer*, one that immediately strikes us is Psalm 1:1: "Blessed is the man," where the unknown psalmist distinguishes two lifestyles (February 23), one that is **blessed** and one that is not. We find in verses 1–3 three realities that produce genuine bliss and contentment:

First, a *path* that is holy. In three distinct statements, the psalmist outlines holiness. The holy person first does not *stroll* with the "ungodly" (*rāšā'*, 7563) people. He doesn't associate with, listen to, or join those who are guilty before God and transgressors of His **Law**. Second, the holy person does not *stand* with sinners. **Way** is *derek* (February 23), a marked-out pattern of **life**, and "standeth" is *'āmaḏ* (5975), which figuratively indicates living somewhere, standing, remaining there (e.g., Exod. 8:22, **dwell**). The holy life, then, is one that does not remain in **sin** (1 John 3:9, where "commit" is present tense, to "continually habitually commit sin"). Third, the holy person does not *sit* with the "scornful" (*liyṣ*, 3887) person, that is, one who boasts, scoffs, mocks, and derides, as in showing or expressing utter contempt, in this case for the things of God.

Second, blessedness comes from a *passion* for **Scripture**. The blissful and contented person is one who takes **delight** (February 29) in God's Word and his **meditation** (January 6) on it is the rule of life and his daily priority.

Third, blessedness comes from a *prosperity* dependent upon God. The **image** of sitting by a **river** is a graphic one, picturing nourishment, growth, fruitfulness, and much more. While "prosperity teachers" promise monetary riches, true prosperity is found in the spiritual riches we have in Christ (Eph. 1:3–23).

Scriptures for Study: Read the following verses, noting what else brings bliss and true contentedness: Psalms 2:12; 32:1, 2; 112:1; 119:1, 2; 127:4, 5; Prov. 3:13 ("happy"); 8:32.

Undefiled

tāmiym

Psalm 119:1 also stands out as a verse that speaks of being **blessed**: "Blessed *are* the undefiled in the way." The Hebrew here for **undefiled** is *tāmiym* (8549), an adjective that speaks of being "blameless, complete, and without blemish."

In more than half its OT occurrences, *tāmiym* describes an animal to be sacrificed to the **Lord**, whether a ram, a bull, or a lamb, since such animals were required to be "without blemish" (e.g., Exod. 29:1; Lev. 4:3; 14:10). It is also used to refer to time, as in a "whole" **day** (Josh. 10:13), a "complete" seven Sabbaths (i.e., "weeks," Lev. 23:15), and a "full" year (Lev. 25:30). When used in a moral sense, as it is here, *tāmiym* speaks of truth, **integrity**, virtue, uprightness, and righteousness.[57] It appears, for example in Psalm 18:23, where the psalmist again declares, "I was also upright before [God], and I kept myself from mine iniquity." Solomon echoes this principle in Proverbs 11:5: "The righteousness of the perfect shall direct his way: but the wicked shall fall by his own wickedness." (See also Josh. 24:14, "sincerity", and Prov. 2:21, "perfect").

Added to this **word** is the word **way** (*derek,* February 23), once again a marked-out pattern of **life**. True bliss and contentment, then, come when our pattern of life is characterized by unblemished behavior. How ironic (and tragic) that the world looks for happiness in the exact opposite, pursuing it in lawlessness and just living their own way, but they will never find it there. Every young person should be challenged with this principle. They might think they will be happy by doing what they **want**, but they will not. Hopefully, they will not have to find out the hard way that true contentment, bliss, meaning, purpose, and **peace** will come by a life of unblemished behavior, a lifestyle that is characterized by purity. Charles Spurgeon put it well when he wrote in his classic *The Treasury of David*: "Doubtless, the more complete our sanctification the more intense our blessedness." In other words, and let us mark this down: *The holier we live, the more content we will be.*

Scriptures for Study: Who is spoken of as being **undefiled** ("perfect") in Genesis 6:9 and 17:1? 🕮 In Psalm 15:1–5, what other traits characterize those who will abide with **God** ("uprightly" is *tāmiym*)?

Delight

šāʿaʿ [and] chāp̱ēṣ

Today we meditate on a truly **wonderful word**. For our text, we look again at Psalm 1:1 and several verses in Psalm 119. In the latter, the psalmist (probably **David**[58]) uses **delight** (or "delights") no fewer than nine times to express one of his many attitudes toward **Scripture**, but he uses two different Hebrew words.

In verse 16 (also 47 and 70), he uses *šāʿaʿ* (8173), which speaks of "taking **joy** or enjoyment from something" or even "fondling." He uses *šaʿašuʿiym* (8191) in verse 24 (also 77, 92, 143, 174), another form of *šāʿaʿ* that is used figuratively, for example, in the phrase "a pleasant plant" in Isaiah 5:7 to refer to God's pleasure in the people of Judah.

It is then in Psalm 119:35, however, that the word *chāp̱ēṣ* (2654) appears, which indicates a stronger *emotional **delight*** than do the others: "Make me to go in the path of thy commandments; for therein do I delight." One authority also points out that "the object solicits favor by its own intrinsic qualities."[59] Shechem, son of Hamor, for example, had an emotional **delight** in Jacob's daughter Dinah (Gen. 34:19). *chāp̱ēṣ* also appears in Proverbs 31:13, where the **Virtuous Woman** "worketh willingly [i.e., with emotional delight] with her hands." Oh, what an encouragement to Christian ladies today!

David, therefore, declares that he takes emotional **delight** in God's clear, definite, and authoritative "commandments," as well as in God's **Law** (Ps. 1:2). At one **time** or another we've all probably thought God's commands are burdensome. I once heard a preacher put it well: "Many think God is the Great Cosmic Party Pooper." Indeed, many think God just ruins all our fun with His **commandments**. But read 1 John 5:3: "For this is the love of God, that we keep his commandments: and his commandments are not grievous [heavy and oppressive]." While the Mosaic system *was* a "yoke of bondage" (Gal. 5:1, February 9, 16), God's Moral Law, as well as the commands of Christ and words of Paul and other NT writers is not, for it exists to protect us, to **keep** us from harm and total disaster. Many people talk about "loving God" while at the same time ignoring His Word. They think His commands are oppressive so they redefine them according to modern thought. John, however, makes it clear that only those who **delight** in God's commands truly **love** Him. This attitude contributes much to a consistent Christian **life**.

Scriptures for Study: What is the object of the psalmist's **delight** (*chāp̱ēṣ*) in Psalm 40:8? 🕮 What should we desire according to Proverbs 8:11 ("desired" is *chāp̱ēṣ*)?

Worship (1)

shāchāh

We first considered **worship** back on January 5, where we observed that one of the greatest acts of **worship** is to **remember** what **God** has done. Let us go deeper into this critical subject.

Our English **word** ***worship*** appears some sixty-four times in the AV, all of which (except 1 Kings 12:30, Jer. 44:19, and eleven verses in Daniel, which we will study **March 2**) are a translation of the Hebrew *shāchāh* (7812), which itself appears about 190 times. Its primary meaning is "to bow down," as seen in its first occurrence in Genesis 18:2, when Abraham "bowed himself toward the ground" in **reverence** (March 3) to the three messengers who came to announce that Sarah would have a son.

It is quite possible that *shāchāh* derives from the Akkadian *shihû*, to wallow or **descend**, since *shāchāh* also speaks of prostrating oneself before the object of **worship**. Lot, for example, "bowed [*shāchāh*] himself with his face toward the ground" in reverence to the two angels who came to **Sodom** (Gen. 19:1), and Ruth "fell on her face, and bowed herself to the ground" before Boaz (Ruth 2:10). *Shāchāh*, therefore, indicates reverence not only for God but also for a monarch or superior.

When used in **worship** for God, of course, *shāchāh* takes on **new** depth. After all, even the earth itself worships God (Ps. 66:4). Only God deserves **worship** (Ps. 29:2; Rev. 4:11), so God should be the only one in view in **worship**. It is a sad fact that "worship," as carried on in many churches today, is based almost exclusively on man-centered methods and on the *feelings* of the worshipper. Many people's "worship" consists of what music they like and what they are going to get out of the church service. But that is far from the biblical view of **worship**. **Worship** is contemplation, **meditation**, and consideration of *God*, not **man**. It is coming before Him in reverence (March 4), emptying ourselves of "self" and what pleases us, and giving **praise** (March 5) and glory to Him alone.

We should be reminded of how the Israelites "made them a molten calf, and . . . worshipped it" (Exod. 32:8) and be challenged to rid our lives of any "golden calves" that might be there. As God's **Law** declares, "Thou shalt not bow down thyself to [any graven image]" (Exod. 20:4, 5), a principle often repeated in the NT (1 Cor. 10:14; Col. 3:5; 1 John 5:21; cf. Acts 19:26–35).

Scriptures for Study: What is one **way** we **worship** God, according to Psalms 29:2 and 96:9? 🕮 What is one reason we **worship** no other God, according to Exodus 34:14?

Worship (2)

shāchāh

Scripture is permeated with the principle of **worship**. In the OT, **worship** was the chief concern of Abraham (Gen. 22:5); at the core of the Moral **Law** (Exod. 20:3–5; 34:14); the foundation of Joshua's military service (Josh. 5:14); Eli's reaction to **God** giving him Samuel (1 Sam. 1:28); David's response to the **death** of his child (2 Sam. 12:20); Ezra and the people's response to the reading of **Scripture** (Neh. 9:3); and Job's reaction to losing his family and **wealth** (Job 1:20).

The same principle permeates the NT. **Worship** was the first concern of the Magi when they came to visit Jesus (Matthew 2:2); the central issue of the greatest spiritual battle ever fought (4:8–10); Mary of Bethany's chief desire (John 12:1–3); the theme of the **Lord** Jesus' discussion with the Samaritan **woman** immediately after telling her about **salvation** (4:20–24); and the key issue Paul emphasized to the Athenians (Acts 17:23). Further, the defining characteristic of the true Christian (Phil. 3:3) and the definitive activity in **heaven** will be **worship** (Rev. 4:10, 11).

We must, therefore, be careful *how* we **worship**. *First*, God will not tolerate the **worship** of a false god (Exod. 34:14, 15). He is absolutely intolerant of idolatry. The whole reason for both the Assyrian and Babylonian captivities was Israel's continued **worship** of pagan gods. We can do the same by elevating a job, money, fame, or anything else to "god" status.

Second, God will not accept the **worship** of Him in the wrong **way**, such as **worship** that is self-defined, as illustrated by Nadab and Abihu (Lev. 10:1, 2) and Uzzah (2 Sam. 6:1–9). This also includes "Christian symbols" we might erect.

Third, God will not accept the **worship** of the True God with the wrong attitude, such as ceremony, habit, and tradition (Mark 7:6, quoting Isa. 29:13; Amos 5:1, 21–23). Our **worship** can become just ritual, routine, and repetition with no value whatsoever and in the end be hypocrisy. Let us carefully guard our attitude in **worship**.

Scriptures for Study: Read the following passages, noting the wrong **worship** in each: Malachi 1:6–14; 3:13–15; Isaiah 1:11–20; Colossians 2:20–23.

Worship (3)

s̱eghiḏ

A fascinating contrast to *shāchāh* is the Aramaic *s̱eghiḏ* (5457), which appears in the OT only in the **book** of Daniel, where it is always translated **worship** (or similar) and always of a false god. This is noteworthy simply because it *is* Aramaic, the language of pagan Babylon, from where Daniel wrote (Aramaic was the international language of commerce and diplomacy that came with the Assyrian empire in the eighth century BC). Significantly, *s̱eghiḏ* corresponds to the Hebrew *sāgaḏ* (5456), which appears only four times, all in Isaiah (44:15, 17, 19; 46:6) and always of an **idol**.

The scene in Babylon, of course, was that Daniel and a few other nobles were forced into captivity by Nebuchadnezzar in 605 BC to **serve** in the king's court, followed by the remainder of Judah in 597 and 586 BC. It is in Daniel 3 that Nebuchadnezzar, motivated by his arrogance and sense of self-importance after his dream about being "the head of gold" (2:32, 36), built a ninety-foot-tall statue of himself (Dan. 3:1–3). He then required that at the hearing of special music, played on a variety of instruments, everyone was to "fall down and worship [*sāgaḏ*]" the **image** (vv. 5, 6) or be cast into a furnace. As we recall, Shadrach, Meshach, and Abednego refused, were thrown into the furnace, but were miraculously delivered (vv. 8–30).

The beloved J. Vernon McGee makes this smile-inducing comment: "I would like to give this orchestra a name: the Babylonian Beboppers."[60] His point is that that music was designed to appeal to the flesh and aided in forcing people to **worship**. While music is a very subjective medium—we all have our own tastes, likes, and dislikes—we still need to be very careful when it comes to the music we use in **worship**. Most importantly, the *music* should be appropriate to the *message*, that is, the lyrics.

Many people look for a church based solely on the style of music it offers. That is anything but worshipful. Let us sanctify our music in **worship**.

Scriptures for Study: Read the account in Daniel 3 and **rejoice** in the **pure worship** we can offer **God**. 🕮 Review the encouragements about music in our January 2 reading.

Reverence [and] Fear (of God)

yārē'

At times *shāchāh* is also translated **reverence** (e.g., 2 Sam. 9:6; Esther 3:2, 5). More often, however, it is *yārē'* (3372), which, along with the derivative *yir'āh* (3374), simply means "to fear, be afraid, or stand in awe."

"The fear of the LORD," Solomon wrote, "is the beginning of knowledge" (Prov. 1:7) and "the beginning of wisdom" (9:10). In other words, *true knowledge begins with a **fear of God**.* If we are to **know** anything, we must begin with the presupposition of **God**. How, for example, can an intelligent person believe (and then brag about believing it) that the universe sprang from nothing and then evolved? How can truly brilliant people say something so absurd and irrational? Because they do not start with **God**. Without Him, we can know nothing.

Such knowledge begins with the **fear of God**. While this has been softened by many to mean simply **reverence**, which *is* part of it, the primary meaning is **fear** and terror. This principle, in fact, is found many times in **Scripture**, as in Exodus 2:25: "Moreover he said, I am the God of thy father, the God of Abraham, the God of Isaac, and the God of Jacob. And Moses hid his face; for he was afraid to look upon God" (cf. Gen. 22:12; Exod. 3:6; 14:31; 20:20; Ezek. 30:13). Likewise, in the NT, lost man is spoken of as having "no fear of God before [his] eyes" (Rom. 3:18)."

The greatest evidence, however, is that every **time** we see someone in Scripture get a glimpse of **God**, even a believer, they are terrified: Isaiah (Isa. 6:5), Daniel (Dan. 10:8, 9; 8:17), Ezekiel (Ezek. 1:28; 3:23; 9:8; 43:3; 44:4), Samson's **father** Manoah (Judg. 13:22), and Job (Job 42:5, 6).

In sad contrast, there is among many today a frivolous and nonchalant attitude toward **God**—He is thought of as our buddy and pal. Many church services are casual and man-centered, where **God** is given lip service but in reality is simply a spectator. We have lost the Truth of God's holiness and man's sinfulness. We have lost what people of Scripture knew, namely, that when confronted with the blazing glory of **God**, *they were terrified in their unworthiness*. We should, therefore, "serve God acceptably with reverence and godly fear: For our God is a consuming fire" (Heb. 12:28, 29). Let us, therefore, be fearful of disobeying **God**, fearful of disobeying His **Word**.

Scriptures for Study: To what is the **fear** of **God** tied in Deuteronomy 6:2?

Praise [Hallelujah] (1)

hālal [*hālal yāh*]

Another predominant theme in **Scripture**, as well as an integral part of **worship**, is **praise**. So central is this activity that we will consider it over the next few days.

The most general Hebrew **word** for **praise** is *hālal* (1984), from which we get the English **Hallelujah**; the Greek *allēlouia* (239G) is a transliteration of *hālal* with the addition of *Yāh* (3050), a shortened form of "Yahweh" (*Yehōwāh,* 3068, January 8). *Hālal yāh*, then, means "praise ye Yah," which occurs some twenty-six times in the **book** of Psalms.[61] Except for 135:3, it always appears at the beginning or ending of a Psalm, "suggesting that it was a standardized call to praise in temple worship."[62] (We should interject, as one Hebrew authority insists, while "this word is sometimes spelled *alleluia* in modern hymnals, in imitation of the mode of spelling that found favor in medieval times . . . The letter H ought certainly to be restored at both ends."[63])

Significantly, the original picture in *hālal* was "to shine," even "the giving off of light by celestial bodies."[64] Job used it poetically, for example, as he "beheld the sun when it shined [*hālal*]" (Job 31:26). Similarly, the Greek *doxa* (1391G), which is usually translated "glory," includes the idea of "radiance" (although those concepts were added to *doxa* in the NT and are foreign to secular Greek).[65]

Hālal ultimately came to mean "to praise, celebrate, commend, or even boast." Appearing more than 160 times, it sometimes refers to praising of people, such as when the princes of Egypt "commended" Sarah's beauty (Gen. 12:15, the first occurrence of *hālal*) and when a husband praises his virtuous wife (Prov. 31:28).

It is, of course, when used of **God** (its most frequent use) that *hālal* takes on its greatest significance. Scripture is permeated with this theme. It is noteworthy that its first appearance in reference to **praise** of God is in 2 Samuel 22:4, where **David** praised God for delivering him out of the hands of Saul, also calling God his Rock, Fortress, **Deliverer**, **Shield**, **Salvation**, Tower, and Refuge (vv. 2, 3). Is that not, indeed, cause for **praise**? This **song** of **praise**, in fact, is virtually identical to Psalm 18.

Not only do men and angels **praise** and commend God, but even nature itself does so (Ps. 148). All that we do should **praise** God (1 Cor. 10:31), even the playing of musical instruments (Ps. 150), and such **praise** is therefore constant (Ps. 34:1; 35:28; 44:8).

Scriptures for Study: In preparation for the next few days' readings, read Psalm 100 and meditate on praising God in everything.

Praise [Hallelujah] (2)

tôḏāh [and] hālal [and] hālal yāh

One unknown writer submits, "How is praising God possible? Singing songs and hymns, clapping our hands, even jumping for joy. . . . the list is endless." Sadly, however, some of those things nowadays are more man-centered than spiritual. Much more to the point is what ***Scripture*** says about how to **praise God**.

It is not surprising that more than half the occurrences of *hālal* are in the Psalms. Psalms 146–150, in fact, have been dubbed the "**Hallelujah** Psalms," each beginning or ending "Praise ye the Lord" (*hālal yāh*). If there is one **psalm** that stands out as a succinct outline of how to **praise** God, it is Psalm 100. It and Psalm 145 are the only two with the specific heading, "A psalm of praise."

Praise here is actually a different Hebrew **word**, *tôḏāh* (8426), which is derived from *yāḏāh* ("to confess publicly," 3034), and expresses the idea of an **offering** or **sacrifice** of thanksgiving. "The basic difference between this verb and its synonym, *hālal*," writes one authority, "is that [*hālal*] tends to stress 'acclaim of,' 'boasting of,' or 'glorying in' an object, while *yāḏāh* emphasizes 'recognition' and 'declaration' of a fact, whether good or bad."[66] One might "acknowledge" his **sin** (Ps. 32:5), for example, or more commonly **praise** (Ps. 99:3; Isa. 38:19) and "give thanks" (Ps. 97:12; 136:1–3, 26) to God. We see no fewer than seven ways to **praise** God in Psalm 100.

First, "Make a joyful noise unto the LORD, all ye lands" (v. 1; also 98:4). "Joyful noise" is *rûaʿ* (7321), which primarily means "to shout." It appears, for example, in Joshua 6:5, where the people were to "shout with a great shout" to bring down the walls of Jericho. It often indicates a shout of joy in response to God's deliverance (Job 38:7; Ps. 95:1, 2; Zeph. 3:14; Zech. 9:9), a **war** shout (Josh. 6:16; 1 Sam. 17:20), or a shout of victory over an enemy (Jer. 50:15).

How can we "make a joyful noise"? Simply by announcing who God is, what He has done, and what He is doing. Sometimes this will have to be announced pretty loudly just to be heard over the noise of the world and the attacks of the critics. Speaking of God's attributes is a practical **way** of doing this, praising Him as the omniscient, omnipotent, omnipresent, eternal, immutable, holy, righteous, just, sovereign, loving, merciful, and gracious God. **Hallelujah**!

Scriptures for Study: Read Psalms 26:7 and 107:22. What is one **wonderful** way we can show "thanksgiving" (*tôḏāh*)?

Serve [and] Singing [and] Praise (3)

'ābad [and] rānan [and] hālal

Continuing our look at Psalm 100, we note the second and third ways to **praise God** in this **wonderful** "psalm of praise."

Second, "Serve the LORD with gladness" (v. 2). Many in modern church ministry think "**praise** and **worship"** is reserved for the church building and is comprised of **singing** and other "religious" exercises. The psalmist tells us, however, that praising God is extremely practical. **Serve** is *'ābad* (5647), a verb that appears almost 300 times, the first of which is in Genesis 2:5 ("till") and 15 ("dress"), where God gives **Adam** the task of taking care of the garden. It is found repeatedly, then, to portray **labor** on one's own behalf (e.g., 4:2; Isa. 19:9) or for another person (e.g., Gen. 29:15; Exod. 1:14).

This tells us something astounding: We can **praise** God no matter what we are doing. That is precisely what Paul meant when he wrote, "Whether therefore ye eat, or drink, or whatsoever ye do, do all to the glory of God" (1 Cor. 10:31). Dear Christian, do you dedicate each day's activities to God? Do you do everything with the attitude that you are praising Him in it? Does the outcome of all your labor give **praise** and glory to Him? Do you take "gladness" in it (*śimchāh,* 8057, "joy, rejoicing, pleasure," July 20)?

Third, "Come before his presence with singing" (v. 2). **Singing** is *renānāh* (7445), which appears only three other times (Ps.63:5, "joyful"; Job 3:7, "joyful"; 20:5, "triumphing") and literally means "cry of joy." It is derived from the verb *rānan* (7442), "to sing or shout joyfully." As one might expect, half of its some sixty occurrences are in the Psalms, but another fourteen are in Isaiah. What do we have to sing about? We "rejoice in [our] salvation" (Ps. 20:5), "sing aloud of [God's] mercy" (59:16), **rejoice** in His "help" (63:7), "sing" about His righteous judgment and government (67:4), and much more.

As Paul declares, there is nothing more indicative of the Spirit-filled **life** than the expression of **song** (Eph. 5:18, 19). Despite popular teaching, music must not be the foundation of church ministry or even the major emphasis. It's not even mentioned, in fact, in Acts 2:42, which lists the activities of the early church; the primary emphasis was doctrine. **Singing** (not just instrumental music but ***singing***) is important, however, for its purpose is to be a restatement of doctrine. Oh, that we would seek depth in our church music!

Scriptures for Study: What do we have to sing about in Proverbs 29:6? 📖 What is the object of our **singing** in Isaiah 24:14?

Know [and] Praise (4)

yāḏa‘ [and] hālal

The old Scottish (Genevan) Psalter of 1551 affectionately and respectfully refers to Psalm 100 as "Old Hundredth." The first stanza declares:

All people that on earth do dwell,
Sing to the Lord with cheerful voice.
Him serve with fear, His praise forth tell;
Come ye before Him and rejoice.

Here "is one of the every-day expressions of the Christian church," writes Charles Spurgeon in *The Treasury of David*, "and [it] will be so while men exist whose hearts are loyal to the Great **King**. Nothing can be more sublime this side of **heaven** than the **singing** of this noble **psalm** by a vast congregation." Today we consider a *fourth* way to **praise God** according to "Old Hundredth."

The words "Know . . . that the LORD he is God" (v. 3), show us that we **praise** God by increasing our knowledge of Him. **Know** is *yāḏa‘* (3045), which appears more than 900 times and has a wide range of meanings concerning knowledge acquired by the senses, "to know relationally and experientially." It is similar to the Greek *ginōskō* (1097G), "to know by experience," and often is practically synonymous with love and intimacy (Matt. 1:25), as well as the personal relationship the believer has with Christ (Phil. 3:10; 1 John 2:3, 5; cf. Matt. 7:23).

Yāḏa‘, then, first appears in Genesis 3:5, where **Satan** tells **Eve** that eating of the forbidden **tree** would enable her to **know good** and **evil**. Verse 7 goes on to say that **Adam** and Eve knew they were naked. It also speaks of sexual intimacy (4:1) and even its perversion, such as homosexuality (19:5). Spiritually, not only does *yāḏa‘* speak of God knowing us (18:19; Deut. 34:10), but also of our knowing Him. While the lost do not **know** God (Jer. 10:25; Job 18:21; John 17:25), the believer does, and that knowledge is to increase and grow. The psalmist desired to understand and **know** God's **Word** (Ps. 119:125). Solomon wanted "to know wisdom and instruction; to perceive the words of understanding" (Prov. 1:2) and then added, "Teach [*yāḏa‘*] a just man, and he will increase in learning" (Prov. 9:9). Peter likewise declares, "Grow in grace, and in the knowledge of our Lord and Saviour Jesus Christ" (2 Pet. 3:18).

Scriptures for Study: In what does true knowledge result (Ps. 9:10)? 📖 What does Psalm 44:21 declare about God?

Bless [and] Praise (5)

bārak̲ [and] yād̲a'

Psalm 100, that great "**psalm** of praise," concludes with the fifth, sixth, and seventh ways to **praise God**.

Fifth, the words, "Enter into his gates with thanksgiving, and into his courts with praise" (v. 4), provide us with a dramatic picture of **prayer**. "Gates" is *ša'ar* (8179), which while often referring to any ordinary **gate** (e.g., Exod. 20:10), also refers to the strong, fortified gates of a large, walled city (2 Chron. 26:9; Psalm 107:16), as well as the place where the civil court would gather in an Israelite town (Deut. 21:19; Josh. 20:4). Similarly, "courts" is *chāṣēr* (2691), which referred to, in an unwalled village (Josh. 15:46), the courtyard of a **house** (2 Sam. 17:18) or a **temple** (2 Kings 21:5). We **praise** God, therefore, by coming through the gates of **heaven**, His very "courtyard," and into His holy presence through prayer. We will look deeper into the **word *prayer* tomorrow**.

Sixth, "Be thankful unto him" (Ps. 100:4). "Thankful" is *yād̲a'* (3034), which as noted back on March 6 means "to confess publicly." This brings us back to the verbal **praise** we have noted before. We **praise** God by vocally and publicly reciting His attributes and great works. Psalm 107 repeatedly sings the chorus, "Oh that *men* would praise [*yād̲a'*] the LORD *for* his goodness, and *for* his wonderful works to the children of men" (vv. 8, 15, 21, 31). How this challenges us to public, corporate **worship**! "Not forsaking the assembling of ourselves together, as the manner of some is; but exhorting one another: and so much the more, as ye see the day approaching" (Heb.10:25).

Seventh, "Bless his name" (Ps. 100:4). "Bless" is the verb *bārak̲* (1288), which means "to kneel, bless, salute, greet" and is related to the noun *berek̲* (1290), "knee." It is used of men, as God **blessed** Abraham, for example (Gen. 12:3), but here we see that it is **man** who blesses God. This is best understood perhaps, as one authority tells us, in noting that "to bless in the OT means to endue with power for success, prosperity, fecundity, longevity, etc. It is frequently contrasted with *qālal* (7043), to esteem lightly, curse (cf. Deut. 30:1, 19)."[67] Obviously, we do not *give* **power** or any such thing to God, but we certainly do ***praise*** Him in those things and esteem Him as highly as we can in our human **strength**. Oh, that we would **praise** God, that we would speak well of Him in every **way**!

Scriptures for Study: Read Psalm 107, making a list of things for which you can **praise** God.

Pray [and] Prayer (1)

pālal [and] tepillāh

As noted in the Preface, we often find several Hebrew words that translate into the same English **word**. Today we have one such dramatic example, as there are no less than twelve Hebrew words that are rendered **pray** (or **prayer**) in the English. The first and foremost Hebrew word indicating the general idea of **prayer** is the verb *pālal* (6419), with the related noun *tepillāh* (8605). The Septuagint usually translates *pālal* with the Greek *proseuchomai* (4336G), itself the most common Greek word for **prayer** in the NT, appearing some eighty-five times. It's a general word that speaks of **prayer** to **God**. **Prayer** to other gods or **saints** is less than worthless; it's utter blasphemy against the One, True God.

Pālal has an interesting, although not precisely known, etymology. The higher critic Julius Wellhausen (1844–1918), for example, thought it came from the Arabic *falla*, "to notch the edge of a sword," and therefore meant cutting or wounding oneself in frenzied **worship**, as was the ancient pagan custom. That simply cannot be, however, since such a practice was forbidden in the **Law** (Deut. 14:1) and so would not have become the precedent for biblical prayer. Another view is that *pālal* comes from a stem that means "to throw oneself down," which implies that **prayer** involves prostration. Still another view is that *pālal* carries the idea of "cause to (re)assess," as in Ezekiel 16:52, where the **prophet** says (in effect) of corrupt Jerusalem, "You have caused reassessment [AV 'judged'] in favor of your sisters, Sodom and Samaria," indicating that Jerusalem is more wicked than both her "sisters."[68]

Whatever its etymology, *pālal* came to mean "to pray, intervene, or intercede." In almost all its more than eighty occurrences, the action points back to the subject,[69] as in "to cause another to intervene or arbitrate in one's case."[70] That is, indeed, what we are doing in **prayer**; we are asking God to intervene, for we can do nothing. Abraham interceded for Abimelech (Gen. 20:17) and Moses interceded for the people at Sinai, lest God **destroy** them for their idolatry with the golden calf (Deut. 9:26).

Prayer involves not only intercession but confession of **sin** (Ezra 10:1; Dan. 9:4, 20; Ps. 51:1, 2; 1 John 1:9), petitions for deliverance in **time** of trouble (2 Kings 19:15–19; Jonah 2:1; cf. James 5:13) and help in sickness (2 Kings 20:1, 2; James 5:14), and much more. As we continue meditating on this subject **tomorrow**, let us each "reassess" our own **prayer life** to ensure that it honors God alone.

Scriptures for Study: Meditate on the verses cited in today's study and "reassess" your own **prayer** life.

Pray [and] Prayer (2)

pālal [and] śiyach [and] šā'al

Prayer is, of course, a recurring theme in the Psalms. While the verb *pālal* (6419) appears only four times (5:2; 32:6; 72:15; 106:30, "to judge"), we find the noun *tep̱illāh* (8605) some thirty-two times. In its first occurrence, for example, **David** prays, "Hear me when I call, O God of my righteousness: thou hast enlarged me when I was in distress; have mercy upon me, and hear my prayer" (Ps. 4:1). *There* is a **man** who is dependent upon **God**.

Another Hebrew **word** translated ***prayer,*** however, is *śiyach* (7879), which appears fourteen times in the OT, five of which are in the Psalms, and speaks of contemplation and **meditation**. Its primary meaning, however, is actually "complaint," which might seem odd at first. The idea, however, is not complaining in the sense of blaming God, rather **deep** meditation brought on by distress and urgent need. Job, for example, used this very word in the **midst** of his suffering (Job 7:13; 9:27; 10:1; 21:4; 23:2), as did David in his distress when he **hid** in a cave from Saul (Ps. 142:2; cf. 64:1; 102:1). **Prayer** is David's "battleaxe and weapon of war," writes Charles Spurgeon; "he uses it under every pressure, whether of inward sin or outward **wrath**, foreign invasion or domestic rebellion. We shall act wisely if we make **prayer** to God our first and best trusted resource in every hour of need."[71]

Still another word for **prayer** in the OT is *šā'al* (7592), which appears about 170 times and is also found in Akkadian, Ugaritic, and even "in the Aramaic of Daniel and Ezra (Dan. 2:10, 11, 27; Ezra 5:9, 10; 7:21)."[72] It simply means "to ask something of someone," whether one is just asking a question (Gen. 32:17), making a simple request (Judg. 5:25), or even begging (Prov. 20:4).

An integral part of **prayer**, then, is inquiring of and asking God, not just for things, but for guidance, **strength**, and all else. While we no longer ask the Urim and Thummim (Exod. 28:30) for guidance, let us be like David who often "enquired of the LORD" (1 Sam. 23:2; 30:8; 2 Sam. 2:1; 5:19, 23; 1 Chron. 14:10, 14). We never *demand* anything in **prayer**; rather we "ought to say, If the Lord will, we shall live, and do this, or that" (James 4:15).

Scriptures for Study: What **wonderful** thing does the psalmist ask for in Psalm 27:4–9 ("desired" in v. 4 is *šā'al*)? 🕮 Note how Matthew 6:31–33 is illustrated in Psalm 105:40 ("asked" is *šā'al*).

Call [and] Prayer (3)

qārā'

Besides the some one dozen words rendered **prayer** in the OT, another that clearly pictures **prayer** in a few instances is the verb *qārā'* (7121), the root of which (*qr'*) is found in "Old Aramaic, Canaanite, and Ugaritic, and other Semitic languages (except Ethiopic)."[73]

Appearing more than 730 times, *qārā'* has a wide range of meanings, depending upon the context and grammar, including: "to call, declare, summon, invite, read, be called, be invoked, be named." It is used, for example, of summoning someone, as when **God** "called unto Adam" (Gen. 3:9), when God "called unto [Moses] out of the midst of the bush" (Exod. 3:4), and for **Adam** naming the animals (Gen. 2:20) and **Eve** (3:20). It is also used of reading aloud from a **book** or scroll (Exod. 24:7; Neh. 13:1; Jer. 36:6, 8). It is even used for the act of **preaching** (Neh. 6:7; Jonah 3:2, March 16).

Another significant use of *qārā'* is in men calling upon God, a use we see often and that graphically illustrates **prayer**. After the fall, some men realized the all-encompassing consequences of **sin** and began to **call** on God's **name** (Gen. 4:26; 12:8; 13:4). We are especially struck by verses such as Psalm 3:4: "I cried unto the LORD with my voice, and he heard me out of his holy hill." Also, Psalm 18:6: "In my distress I called [*qārā'*] upon the LORD, and cried [*qārā'*] unto my God." Such statements, in fact, are a recurring theme in the Psalms (18:6; 30:8; 34:6; 120:1; 130:1; 138:3).

Psalm 119:145 is particularly striking: "I cried with my whole heart; hear me, O LORD: I will keep thy statutes." Think of it! The psalmist's entire being was engaged in **prayer**. He had written in verse 10, "With my whole heart have I sought thee." We then read in verse 146: "I cried unto thee; save me, and I shall keep thy testimonies." Here is true, earnest **prayer**. And what is the goal of such earnestness? In modern teaching, the goal is ourselves, getting what we **want**. The psalmist's goal was a little different, to say the least. His aim was to "keep [God's **statutes** [February 19] and] **testimonies** [February 17]." Let us **pray** earnestly to that end.

Scriptures for Study: What is the admonition of Psalm 116:2? 🕮 What then is the promise of Psalm 145:18?

Prevented [and] Prayer (4)

qādam

There is a truly fascinating **word** used in Psalm 119:147 and 148 in the context of crying out to **God** in **prayer**: "I prevented the dawning of the morning, and cried: I hoped in thy word. Mine eyes prevent the night watches, that I might meditate in thy word."

Prevent is *qādam* (6923), which primarily means "to come before, to meet, to go before." In the procession carrying the **Ark of the Covenant** to the sanctuary in Jerusalem, for example, "the singers went before" those who played instruments (Ps. 68:25; cf. 2 Sam. 6:12–19). For this reason modern translations render Psalm 119:147, "I rise before dawn and cry for help" (NIV, NASB, ESV). In other words, **David** awoke long before dawn, hearing every change of the guard through the **night** watches.

There is another meaning of *qādam*, however, that indicates a possibly deeper significance. The other meaning is "to confront," either with a peaceful or hostile intent. David uses this word in another **prayer**, this one concerning his adversaries: "Arise, O LORD, *disappoint* him, cast him down: deliver my soul from the wicked, which is thy sword" (Ps. 17:13). The idea is confronting someone. What David might also mean, then, is that dawn is his enemy, as if he could confront it and **keep** it from rising. Yes, he rises before dawn, but he then doesn't **want** the dawn to come. Once the **sun** comes up, he must get on with the day's activities, and he would rather spend **time** in **prayer**.

Significantly, *qādam* appears again in Psalm 119:148 ("prevent"). "Night watches" (*'ašmûrāh*; 821) refers to the old Jewish division of the "night" being three watches of four hours each: the **first** (or beginning), 6 p.m. to 10 p.m. (Lam. 2:19), the second (or **middle**), 10 p.m. to 2 a.m. (Judg. 7:19), and the third (or **morning**), 2 a.m. to 6 a.m. (Exod. 14:24).[74] So what is the psalmist's possible meaning? *He doesn't want the night to end.*

In any case, we see here one of the most graphic illustrations in **Scripture** of what true **prayer** is: ***Prayer** is constant communion with God.* **Prayer** is not just asking and getting things from God; it is moment-by-moment communion. We will continue these thoughts **tomorrow**.

Scriptures for Study: At what time of day does the psalmist seek God in the following verses: Psalms 5:3; 22:2; 42:8; 55:17?

Prevented [and] Prayer (5)

qādam

Before leaving this critical subject, we should reemphasize the true nature of **prayer**. To many of us, **prayer** is what we use only when we are in need or when trouble arises. But **prayer** is *moment-by-moment communion.* Luke refers to this principle in Luke 18:1, as does the apostle Paul in Ephesians 6:18 and especially in 1 Thessalonians 5:17: "Pray without ceasing." The Greek behind "without ceasing" is *adialeiptōs* (89G), which literally means "continually, no gaps, without intermission."[75] Prayer, then, is not just those specific times when we **pray**, but also *a constant communion with* ***God****, a continuous consciousness of God's presence in which we view everything in* ***life*** *in relation to Him.* Our lives are (or should be) a living **prayer**.

Nehemiah provides a **wonderful** example of such praying without ceasing. **King** Artaxerxes noticed that Nehemiah was sad and asked him why, at which **time** Nehemiah told him of the destruction of Jerusalem. The king then asked Nehemiah to make a request of him that he might grant it. Before asking that the king send him to Judah, Nehemiah prayed a brief **prayer** (Neh. 2:4, *pālal* appears here). In the **midst** of a stressful situation, Nehemiah was conscious of God's purpose. What a contrast that is to today's popular emphasis that we should pray, "Bless me, God!" That is not what Nehemiah prayed, or, for that matter, what Paul or our **Lord** ever prayed. No, Nehemiah was concerned with what God wanted.

God doesn't just **want** us to *say prayers*, but to *pray*. Yes, we most certainly should have set aside times when we pray specifically, but at the foundation of that is that we should throughout the **day** be talking to the Lord as we go about our tasks. Another definition that sums this up is: "Living our life in God-consciousness." Day-by-day, moment-by-moment, we are aware not only of God's *existence*, but also of His very *presence* in us. Our "specific times" of **prayer** will then simply be an outworking of our "constant communion."

Finally, as we are to set our minds constantly on the things of **heaven**, "not on things on the earth" (Col. 3:2), our lives become a continual ascending **prayer**, a perpetual communion with the Lord. The continual burning of incense (Exod. 30:8) represented Israel's prayers constantly before God, but here is a far better replacement. Nor do we need the OT sacrifices, for our lives are a living **sacrifice** (Rom. 12:1).

Scriptures for Study: Meditate on the outline of **prayer** our Lord provides in His "Model Prayer" (Matt. 6:9–13): **praise**, thanksgiving, self-examination, and petition.

Preaching [and] Preach (1)

bāśar

There are two words translated **preach** (or similar) in the NT: *euangelizō* (2097G), "to proclaim good or joyful news," and *kērussō* (2784G), "to announce or to publicly herald."[76] We mention this because of the Septuagint's use of them to translate two Hebrew words.

The first **word** is *bāśar* (1319, Septuagint *euangelizō*), which means "to bring news or to bear tidings, whether good or bad," and is found in most Semitic languages. The basic idea is the announcing of a message, such as the **death** of Eli's sons (1 Sam. 4:17, the only negative use), Jeremiah's birth (Jer. 20:15), or military news (1 Sam. 31:9; 2 Sam. 1:20; 18:19, 20, 26).

Of its almost fifty occurrences, however, the idea in several is clearly what we **know** as **preaching**. Isaiah 61:1, 2, for example, declares, "The Spirit of the Lord GOD is upon me; because the LORD hath anointed me to preach good tidings [*bāśar*] unto the meek; he hath sent me to bind up the brokenhearted, to proclaim liberty to the captives, and the opening of the prison to them that are bound; To proclaim the acceptable year of the LORD." This is a clear reference to the coming Messiah, who quoted this passage, in fact, in Luke 4:16–21.

Another important occurrence appears in Psalm 40:9, 10: "I have preached righteousness in the great congregation: lo, I have not refrained my lips, O LORD, thou knowest. I have not hid thy righteousness within my heart; I have declared thy faithfulness and thy salvation: I have not concealed thy lovingkindness and thy truth from the great congregation." Many commentators agree that this is another reference to Messiah, himself a preacher, who would go "about all Galilee, teaching in their synagogues, and preaching the gospel of the kingdom" (Matt. 4:23), the "good news" (*euangelion*, 2098).

Once again we see **preaching** in Isaiah 52:7: "How beautiful upon the mountains are the feet of him that bringeth good tidings [*bāśar*], that publisheth peace; that bringeth good tidings of good, that publisheth salvation; that saith unto Zion, Thy God reigneth!" While this announces Israel's release from Babylonian captivity, it foretells the **redemption** of the world by Christ, as Paul quotes this verse in Romans 10:15.

How crucial it is that we proclaim the gospel of Christ! As we continue this theme **tomorrow**, we will see the pivotal place **preaching** should have today.

Scriptures for Study: What is the importance of the gospel according to Romans 1:16?

Preaching [and] Preach (2)

qārā'

The second Hebrew **word** translated ***preach*** is *qārā'* (7121), "to proclaim or call out." Isaiah 61:1, which we studied **yesterday**, uses this very word for **preach**. It is so translated in Nehemiah 6:7, "And thou hast also appointed prophets to preach of thee at Jerusalem," and Jonah 3:2: "Arise, go unto Nineveh, that great city, and preach unto it the preaching that I bid thee." As noted yesterday, it is rendered *kērussō* (2784G) in the Septuagint.

Nehemiah also provides us with one of the most graphic examples of **preaching** in **Scripture**. In Nehemiah 8:1–8, we read that the people gathered and stood for hours listening to the Word of **God** read and expounded. Verse 8 is pivotal: "So they read in the book in the **law** of God distinctly, and gave the sense, and caused them to understand the reading." While *qārā'* is rendered "read," the rest of the verse demonstrates more than just reading.

"Gave" is *śûm* (7760), "to set or establish," and "sense" is *śeḵel* (7922), expressing such concepts as "intelligence, knowledge, and understanding." The point was to establish the people in the knowledge of God's Word. After seventy years of Babylonian captivity, the people no longer spoke Hebrew, rather Aramaic. Ezra, therefore, had to explain the Scripture, "[Give] the sense," exposit it in much the same **way** we must today, since most people do not **know** Hebrew or Greek. In fact, *exposition is even more essential in our* ***day*** because we are far removed from Bible times in language, culture, and history. There is no doubt that expository **preaching** is the Biblical precedent and is the type of **preaching** that should be used the majority of the time. If we are not expositing Scripture, we are not handling it rightly.

In light of the importance of the *words* of Scripture (February 22), exposition of those words is absolutely essential. Today, topical, thematic, and issue-oriented "preaching" dominates in some churches, but such **preaching** does not hinge solely upon the *words* of Scripture. Only systematic exposition stays true to the words in their individual meaning and the context in which they appear. It is historical fact that the strongest, most effective **preaching** in the church's history has always been exposition. If I may be so bold, it is only the expositor who fully loves the *Word,* because he loves the *words*.

Let us **pray** for expositors, who are sorely needed in our day.

Scriptures for Study: What is the importance of **preaching** (Greek *kērussō*), according to Romans 10:14? 🕮 In 1 Corinthians 1:23, what is the attitude of unsaved people toward **preaching** (*kērussō*)?

Preaching [and] Preach (3)

qārā'

Before leaving this pivotal theme, we should note how **preaching** relates to **worship** (March 1–3). It is extremely significant that the people's response to Ezra's reading and exposition of **Scripture** (Neh. 8:8; cf. 6:7) was worship (9:3). This is the climax; everything points to this and has prepared for it. There is nothing of equal importance to the exposition of God's **Word**. Take the **time** now to read Jonah 3:2 again, as well as Psalms 80:18 and 105:1, where **call** is *qārā'*, signifying proclamation.

While lost in most churches today, **preaching** was central to the early church (note the primacy of "doctrine" in Acts 2:42) and its immediate descendants. **Writing** in the **middle** of the second century, apologist Justin Martyr described a typical worship service of his **day**: "And on the day called Sunday, all who live in cities or in the country gather together to one place, and the memoirs of the apostles or the writings of the prophets are read, as long as time permits; then, when the reader has ceased, the president verbally instructs, and exhorts to the imitation of these **good** things. Then we all rise together and pray, and, as we before said, when our prayer is ended, bread and wine and water are brought, and the president in like manner offers prayers and thanksgivings, according to his ability, and the people assent, saying Amen."[77]

Mark it down—*the reading and explanation of the Word of God was the absolute center of the worship service.* (Note that this statement also refutes the accusation made by modern "Sabbath keepers" that Sunday did not become the day of worship until the fourth century.)

Sadly, this is not the case today. Central today is music, drama, comedy, discussion, anecdotes, or anything else we can think of *except* **preaching**. But *nothing* praises God as does the proclaiming of His Word as absolute Truth.

We should be challenged by these comments by the late pastor and great expositor James Boice: "There is nothing more important for Christian growth and the health of the church than sound Bible teaching. Yet sadly, serious Bible teaching is being widely neglected in our day, even in so-called evangelical churches. Instead of Bible teaching, people are being fed a diet of superficial pop psychology, self-help therapy, feel-good stimulants, and entertainment, and the ignorance of the Bible in churches is appalling."[78]

Scriptures for Study: Note the centrality of **preaching** in the following texts: Isaiah 1:2–31; Matthew 5–7 (Jesus' sermon is the greatest model of exposition); Acts 2:14–36; 7:2–63; 15:14–21; 17:16–31.

Pulpit
migdāl

Nehemiah 8:4, 5 provides us with one other aspect of **preaching**, namely, that a **pulpit** was built for that purpose. The Hebrew *migdāl* (4026), which has forms in other Semitic languages, actually means "a tower." It's used for the Tower of Babel (Gen. 11:4), a tower built into a city **wall** (2 Chronicles 14:7), and the watchtower in a **vineyard** (Isa. 5:2).

Many old churches had high pulpits accessed only by a spiral staircase, which is the idea in the Hebrew. Scotsman Alistair Begg recounts a vivid memory from his childhood when he sat in St. George's Tron Church in Glasgow waiting for **morning worship** to begin. He writes: "At about three minutes to eleven the beadle [parish official] would climb the **pulpit** stairs and place a large Bible on the lectern. Having opened it to the appropriate passage, he would **descend**, and the minister would in turn ascend the stairs and sit in the cone-shaped **pulpit**. The beadle would complete his duties by climbing the stairs the second **time** to close the **pulpit** door and leave the pastor to his task. There was no doubt in my young mind that each part of that procedure was marked with significance. There was clearly no reason for the pastor to be in the **pulpit** apart from the Bible upon which he looked down as he read. I understood that, in contrast to his physical posture, the pastor was standing under Scripture, not over it. Similarly, we were listening not so much for *his* message but for *its* message."[79]

So central was preaching to John Calvin, that he ordered all altars (which for centuries had been the focal point of the pagan mass) removed from the churches and a **pulpit** with a Bible on it placed in the center of the building. Everything pointed to that as the center of worship. Similarly, Martin Lloyd-Jones ordered the **pulpit** to be bolted to the floor at Westminster Chapel in London.

How different it is in many churches today! If the speaker must have a lectern, it is on the same level with the congregation so as not to imply that he is "above them." *Is* the preacher better than the people? Should *he* be elevated above them? Of course not. We *do,* however, elevate the **Word** of **God** and its proclamation as absolute truth.

Dear Christian **Friend**, I **pray** that you will seek a church where the Word of God is elevated and its exposition is primary.

Scriptures for Study: Second Timothy 4:1–4 are **among** the **last** words Paul wrote. What do they say about preaching?

Pride [and] Proud

gā'āh [and] zēḏ

The English **proud** appears some forty-two times in the OT (AV) and **pride** another forty-six, both of which are a translation of several Hebrew words. One such **word** is *gā'āh* (1342), a verb primarily meaning "to rise," with the added ideas of "exalt" and "lift up." In the literal sense, for example, it pictures stream waters rising (Ezek. 47:5), the **proud** (or "frothing") waves of the sea (Job 38:11), or plants growing (8:11).

It is the figurative meaning, however, that is most significant. It is **God** *alone* who is to be exalted. Another form of the word (*gâ'ôn*, 1347), for instance, speaks of the "LORD, and for the glory of his *majesty*" (Isa. 2:10) and "the voice of his *excellency* (Job 37:4). Significantly, the Septuagint usually renders these and other related words as *doxa* (1391G), which speaks of "radiance" and "glory."

Most significantly, it is the negative use of *gâ'ôn* and related words that stands out, and such negative use is always of **man**. "I will break the pride of your power," God said to His people (Lev. 26:19), for "the fear of the LORD is to hate evil: pride, and arrogancy, and the evil way, and the froward mouth, do I hate" (Prov. 8:13), and, "Pride goeth before destruction, and an haughty spirit before a fall" (16:18).

Likewise, Isaiah 13:11 declares, "I will cause the arrogancy [*gâ'ôn*] of the proud to cease and will lay low the haughtiness of the terrible," while also introducing another word. **Proud** here is *zēḏ* (2086, from *ziyḏ*, 2102), which appears some thirteen times, most often in the Psalms. Its basic idea is "pride and a sense of self-importance, which often is exaggerated to include defiance and even rebelliousness."[80] Jeremiah 50:31, 32 is especially graphic on God's attitude toward **pride**: "Behold, I am against thee, O thou most proud [*zāḏôn*, 2087], saith the Lord GOD of hosts: for thy day is come, the time that I will visit thee. And the most proud shall stumble and fall, and none shall raise him up: and I will kindle a fire in his cities, and it shall devour all round about him."

In a **day** when pride is cloaked with high-sounding terms such as "self-esteem" and "positive pride," we do well to remind ourselves where pride will take us, as it was the ancient **sin** of **Satan** before his fall and the one that brought him down to **hell** (Isa. 14:12–15; cf. 1 Timothy 3:6). Pride is never positive.

Scriptures for Study: Note the following uses of *zēḏ*: Psalm 19:13 ("presumptuous"); 86:14; 119:21, 51, 69, 78.

Sabbath (1)

šabbāṯ

What was instituted as the **Sabbath** (*šabbāṯ*, 7676) in the Mosaic **Law** continues to be a misunderstood concept in our **day**. Some well-meaning Christians, in fact, insist on worshipping on the **Sabbath** (Saturday) instead of the Lord's Day (Sunday).

The root of *šabbāt* is the verb *šaḇaṯ* (7673), which means "to cease or rest." It first occurs in Genesis 2:2, where **God** "rested on the seventh day from all his work which he had made." That, of course, set the precedent that God desires His people to cease **work** (implying rest), but how they do so has not been the same in all ages.

Based on *šaḇat* in Genesis, some teachers conclude that the **Sabbath** *day* (*šabbāt*) is perpetual and the same in every age, but **Scripture** simply does not say that. Yes, *šabbāt* occurs in Genesis in reference to *God*, but not a single **time** to indicate a prescribed **Sabbath** day for ***man***. There is, in fact, not even an *implication* that man was required to **observe** (or ever *did* observe) the **Sabbath** day until the Mosaic Law was given after Israel came out of Egypt (Exod. 16:23–29; 20:8–11). None of the patriarchs of Genesis, for example, is said to have observed the **Sabbath**.

Job is another crucial example. Several factors date the events of Job as occurring sometime after Babel but before, or perhaps contemporaneously, with Abraham. In other words, Job lived before the Mosaic Law was given. It is, therefore, significant, as one theologian puts it, that while "Job discloses the religious life and experiences of the patriarchs, and though their various responsibilities to God are therein discussed, there is never a reference to a Sabbath-day obligation."[81] In dramatic contrast, it is clearly and distinctly stated that the **Sabbath** was given to *racial* Israel through Moses (Exod. 16:29; 20:8–10; Neh. 9:13, 14; Ezek. 20:11–13). The remainder of the OT is permeated with references to the **Sabbath**, the **word** appearing some seventy-seven times (in the other four books of the Pentateuch, 2 Kings, 1 and 2 Chronicles, Nehemiah, Psalms, Isaiah, Jeremiah, Ezekiel, and Amos). So complete was such cessation from any **labor** to be (Exod. 20:10) that the people couldn't even gather sticks for a fire (Num. 15:32–36) or **light** a fire in their homes (Exod. 35:3).

So, since God desires His people not to labor on the seventh day, does the Christian have "a day off" in this age? We will **answer** that question **tomorrow**.

Scriptures for Study: What else was the **Sabbath** for, according to Numbers 28:9, 10, Leviticus 23:3, and Deuteronomy 5:15?

Sabbath (2)

šabbāt

As noted **yesterday** (see also **Law**, February 15), the Mosaic Law, including the **Sabbath**, was given to *racial* Israel (Exod. 20:2). *None* of the Mosaic system was meant for the church or **Gentiles** in general. This includes the **Sabbath**, which was not commanded until the Mosaic system, and is never repeated in the NT, as are the other nine **commandments** that are written on men's hearts (Rom. 2:15, February 14).

While it is quite true there are sixty occurrences of the **word *Sabbath*** in the NT (*sabbaton*, 4521G), all but one are in the Gospels and Acts, where it is simply used as historical reference (e.g., as in "such-and-such a thing happening on the Sabbath," such as when Jesus went to the synagogue on the Sabbath, Mk. 1:21). The *only* occurrence in the Epistles is Colossians 2:16: "Let no man therefore judge you in meat, or in drink, or in respect of an holyday, or of the new moon, or of the sabbath days." It is beyond doubt that the **Sabbath** is not in force in the NT.

It is the **first day** of the week, the day of our Lord's resurrection, that became the church's day for public **worship**—it is the clear precedent (John 20:19; Acts 20:7; 1 Cor. 16:2; Rev. 1:10). In addition to Justin Martyr (see March 17), the writings of Barnabas and Ignatius in the first and early second centuries prove this beyond the slightest doubt.[82]

That being said, however, since God's resting in Genesis established the precedent that He wanted His people to enjoy rest, is the Lord's Day the Christian "day of rest" in this age? No, as Hebrews 4:1–11 wonderfully demonstrates. There we read of the perfect rest provided by the finished **work** of Christ. "The rest under Christ," writes one theologian, "is not for one day in the week, nor is it that Sabbath rest which was due after a six-day strain. . . . It is rather the abiding rest of faith in Another . . . It is rather the rest of Christ's imparted, resurrection life, and that life is ceaselessly active."[83]

Thanks be to God that because of **grace** through Christ, no longer do we need a prescribed *day* of rest because our Lord fulfilled the Mosaic System, including the **Sabbath**. Whenever we need rest, therefore, we take it. We live not by *legalism* but by *liberty* (Gal. 2:4; 5:1, 13).

Scriptures for Study: Read Hebrews 7:18, 19, 22 and 8:6–13, noting how the writer declares that the Mosaic Law (the Old C**ovenant**) had passed its usefulness because of its own weakness and that "a better testament" of Jesus (the **New** Covenant) replaced the Mosaic Law.

Wisdom (1)

chokmāh

The **word** most often translated ***wisdom*** in the OT of our English Bible is the Hebrew *chokmāh* (2451), which refers to "a person's ability to make the right choices at the opportune times." The Greek equivalents of *chokmāh* in the Septuagint are: *sophos* or *sophia* (4680G, 4678G, "clever, skillful, experienced," e.g., Eph. 1:8, 17; 3:10; James 1:5), *phronimos* or *phronesis* (5429G, 5428G, "sensible, thoughtful, prudent, wise," e.g., Eph. 1:8; 1 Cor. 4:10), and *suniemi* or *sunetos* (4920G, 4908G, "intelligent, sagacious, prudent, wise," e.g., Eph. 5:17; 1 Tim. 1:17). All these demonstrate the true depth of *chokmāh*.

The ability to make the right choices at the opportune times, however, is only half the issue. *How* and *where* do we get this? To get a proper biblical **understanding** of **wisdom**, it's crucial to go back in history. As one Hebrew authority recounts, the subject of **wisdom** was a chief concern in the ancient Near East. To the Mesopotamians and Sumerians, it involved human experiences, character, and **counsel** regarding practical advice. To the Egyptians, it involved the concept of *ma'at* (truth, intelligence, justice), which brought order to the whole universe. To the Greek mind, knowledge itself was virtue. According to Plato, a person could live the **good life** if he loved wisdom and knowledge. Unlike those, however, that leave the One, True **God** out of the equation, **wisdom** in the OT is distinct in that it reveals a holy and just God who demands that men live holy lives according to His character and standards. While *chokmāh* at times refers to ordinary intelligence and skill (Exod. 35:35; Dan. 1:4), divine and moral **wisdom** is still in view.[84]

Biblically, then, **wisdom** is not found in *experience* but in *revelation*; the only **way** we can have **wisdom** is if it is revealed to us. I like Dr. Roy Zuck's definition: "Wisdom means being skillful and successful in one's relationships and responsibilities . . . observing and following the Creator's principles of order in the moral universe."[85] In that definition you find most of the important elements of biblical **wisdom**. Where do we find **wisdom**? We find it in what the Creator says, which in turn is found in **Scripture** alone.

Scriptures for Study: In the following verses, what other traits does wisdom provide: Psalm 37:30, Proverbs 2:10, 3:13 (see also February 27, *'ešer*)?

Ancients [and] Wisdom (2)

zāqēn [and] choḵmāh

Concluding our study of the biblical use of **wisdom**, true **wisdom** begins with a right relationship with **God**. Unless we begin with God as our presupposition, we will fail. Unless we start with God, we will have no wisdom.

As Solomon declares, "The fear of the LORD is the beginning of knowledge: but fools despise wisdom [*choḵmāh*] and instruction." The wise person believes that there *is* a God: "The fool hath said in his heart, There is no God" (Ps. 53:1). The wise person believes that God is *the Creator and Ruler* of all things, and he believes that God has put within His Creation *a divine order* that, if obeyed, leads ultimately to blessing. Wise people also assert that there is *a Moral **Law*** operating in this world, a principle of divine justice that makes sure that eventually the wicked are judged and the righteous are rewarded. Biblical **wisdom** has no relationship to a person's IQ or education, because it is a matter of moral and spiritual **understanding**. It has to do with *character* and *values*; it means *looking at the world through the grid of God's Truth*, evaluating, discerning, and deciding everything according to the absolutes of God's **Word**.

I am always struck by Psalm 119:98–100, where **David** says that God's Word "made [him] wiser than [his] enemies" and gave him "more understanding than all [his] teachers" and "the ancients." **Ancients** is *zāqēn* (2204), which speaks of an old **man** or an **elder**, who was a civil official in Israelite society. The root concept of this word, in fact, is to be fully bearded; the marker of age and maturity was a full beard. David is saying, therefore, he has more understanding than the civil leaders and those who are considered wise by virtue of their age and **life** experience. It is possible this could refer even further back to sages and philosophers of bygone days.

Is David being arrogant? Indeed not. People of the world **pride** themselves in their knowledge and scholarship. While there is nothing wrong with scholarship—in fact, it is absolutely necessary for many endeavors and vocations (including the **pulpit** ministry)—knowledge alone is insufficient at best and totally empty at worst. Notice that David does *not* say he is *smarter* or even has more *knowledge* than those around him or those who have come before him. Rather he says he has more ***wisdom*** and ***understanding***. Let that be your desire as well.

Scriptures for Study: In the following verses, what other traits does **wisdom** provide: Proverbs 8:11; 14:8 (February 23, *derek*); and 24:3?

Understanding

biyn

The Hebrew *biyn* (995) is translated several ways in our AV Bible, including (and most often) "understand" (62) and **understanding** (32). Several other translations (e.g., "consider, perceive, discern") reflect the fact that *biyn*, which with its derivatives appears 247 times, has a wide range of meanings, also including: "to discern, perceive, observe, understand, pay attention, be intelligent, and be discreet."

Biyn is, therefore, much more than just gathering knowledge. It's about **understanding** that knowledge. As was true of Daniel, for example, a person might be able to hear words, but not understand them (Dan. 12:8). As vital as knowledge is, by itself it is virtually worthless. To illustrate, a **man** might **know** by **heart** every medical **work** that has ever been written and yet be the worst doctor in the world because he doesn't truly understand how it all works. He can *memorize* it, but he can't *apply* it.

Biyn, therefore, speaks of how we use the knowledge we acquire. I am struck often by the depth of Psalm 119. In verse 27, the psalmist (probably **David**) prays, "Make me to understand the way of thy precepts: so shall I talk of thy wondrous works," and again in verse 34, "Give me understanding, and I shall keep thy law; yea, I shall observe it with my whole heart," and still again in verse 73, "give me understanding, that I may learn thy commandments" (see also v. 100, March 23). David didn't **want** just knowledge but to know why that knowledge was important, the **way** that knowledge applied to the real world, and even the consequences that knowledge would have on everything else.

That is what is so desperately needed today. A consistent Christian life is absolutely impossible without constant learning and a growing **understanding** of what that knowledge will demand in one's Christian walk. And from where does such **understanding** come? David again answers, "Through thy precepts I get understanding: therefore I hate every false way" (Ps. 119:104). **Understanding** is not a product of rationalism or empiricism. It is comes only from **God** (Dan. 2:21) and only by diligent seeking (Prov. 2:4–5).

We will conclude our study of *biyn* **tomorrow** by noting its core concept: **discern**.

Scriptures for Study: In Proverbs 17:10, what is the difference between the wise (*biyn*) man and the **fool**? 📖 In 28:5, what do those who "seek the LORD" understand?

Discern

biyn

One Hebrew authority digs to the true depth of *biyn* (995) by noting: "The background idea of the verb is to 'discern,' and this lies behind the [derivatives, such as] . . . the preposition *bên* 'between.' The combination of these words, 'discern between,' is used in 1 Kings 3:9, 'That I may discern between good and evil.' *Biyn* includes the concept of distinguishment that leads to understanding."[86]

In simpler terms, the key idea in *biyn* is "to discern, to distinguish between." From where does **understanding** come? *From discernment.* First Kings 3:9[87] is, indeed, pivotal. If you ask most Christians, "What did Solomon ask God for?" most will **answer** immediately, "He asked God for wisdom," but that is not precise. He did not ask **God** for ***wisdom*** (*chokmâ*, March 22), rather he asked God for *discernment.* Our English **word** comes from the Latin *discernere* (*dis*, "apart," and *cernere*, "to sift"), and **Scripture** repeatedly emphasizes this principle. We are to separate, sift through, and distinguish between in order to see and understand.

Catastrophically, however, discernment has all but vanished. Many Christians are tolerant of, or even embrace, false teaching, such as: mysticism, prosperity teaching, seeker-sensitive church ministry, user-friendliness, the "emerging church" movement, unity with Islam, and the list goes on. "The simple believeth every word: but the prudent man *looketh well to* [or discerns, *biyn*] his going" (Prov. 14:15). What was the responsibility of the OT priests? To "teach [God's] people the difference between the holy and profane, and cause them to discern between the unclean and the clean" (Ezek. 44:23). That is likewise the responsibility of pastors today (Acts 20:28–31; Eph. 4:11–14).

So what does discernment mean? There is only a single principle: *What does the **Word** of God say*? It doesn't matter if some **new** idea or teaching "sounds good," but whether it's right according to Scripture. At the very **heart** of the Reformation was the concept of *sola scriptura* ("Scripture Alone"), which is to dictate all we believe and practice—not church tradition, human opinion, pragmatism, or anything else.

As **David** again pleads in Psalm 119:169, "Give me understanding [discernment, *biyn*] according to thy word." While David had very little Scripture at his disposal and so *cried* for discernment, many today don't even *care* about discernment even though they have God's completed revelation in their hands.[88]

Scriptures for Study: What did Job say about discernment (Job 6:30)? 🕮 Carefully consider just a few NT passages that speak of the critical nature of discernment (Acts 17:11; 1 Tim. 6:20, 21; Heb. 4:12; 2 Pet. 2:1, 2; 1 John 4:1).

Fool (1)

'ewiyl [and] kesiyl

Opposite those who are wise, **understanding**, and discerning is the **fool**, about whom the Bible has much to say. There are some 160 references to the **fool** (or "fools" and "foolish") in **Scripture** (AV), most of which are in the OT (only thirty-three in the NT).

One **word** translated **fool** is *'ewiyl* (191), which is derived, some scholars think, from *yā'al* ("to be foolish"), while others think it comes from "an Arabic word meaning 'be thick,' and therefore 'thick-brained' or 'stupid.'"[89] Whichever is correct, *'ewiyl* seems to be the **first** level of foolish behavior. This type of **fool** is one who seeks controversy and argument (Prov. 20:3), despises instruction because of perceived self-sufficiency (1:7; 12:15), and is basically immoral (7:21, 22; 14:9). So complete is this fool's insolence, in fact, that it is a waste of **time** to even speak to him: "The instruction of fools is folly" (16:22). Even if you ground him in a mortar with a pestle, it would do no **good** (27:22). What is this fool's end? He "shall fall" (10:8, *lāḇaṭ,* 3832, "torn down, ruined").

The next level of **fool** is *kesiyl* (3684), which appears some seventy times, more than twice as often as *'ewiyl*. It comes from the root *kāsal* (3688), which appears only in Jeremiah 10:8 in reference to **idol** worshippers. The associated Arabic **word** gives a picture of sluggishness.[90] Here then is the dull, obstinate fellow who, even if you put truth right in front of his eyes, will not see it (Prov. 17:24). He simply cannot (and would not even if he could) see what is right. And, like *'ewiyl*, it is pointless to speak to this **fool** (23:9).

This **fool** is vividly contrasted in Proverbs 1:22: "How long, ye simple ones, will ye love simplicity? and the scorners **delight** in their scorning, and fools hate knowledge?" While the "simple" **man** is *naive* about what is true, and while the "scorner" *mocks* truth as unknowable or relative, the **fool** obstinately and irrationally *refuses* truth, adamantly rejecting true knowledge, which is not only the knowledge *of* **God** but any knowledge that comes *from* God. Again, what is this fool's end? He will be shamed and dishonored (3:35) and ultimately destroyed (18:7).

How does the **fool** encourage the believer? We are reminded that while the **fool** despises **wisdom** and instruction, we **know** that it is God who is the beginning of everything (Prov. 1:7).

Scriptures for Study: Note some of the traits of *'ewiyl* in the following verses: Proverbs 12:15; 14:3, 9; 15:5. 📖 Now note a few of the traits of *kesiyl*: 14:7, 8; 15:7; 26:11; 29:11.

Fool (2)

nāḇāl

We find one other **word** for ***fool*** in the OT. This one is the third level of foolish behavior, the ultimate, consummate **fool**. We could **call** the Hebrew *nāḇāl* (5036) "the worst of both worlds," for it not only includes the characteristics of both *'ewiyl* and *kesiyl*, but adds the idea of "an arrogant bore," a totally insensitive, immoral, and ungracious person. He speaks well of nothing (Prov. 17:7), is a disgrace to all that is **good** (Ps. 74:22), and his mind is closed.

So closed is this fool's mind, in fact, that one verse sums him up in total: "The fool hath said in his **heart**, There is no God. They are corrupt, they have done abominable works, there is none that doeth good" (Ps. 14:1). Even though all Creation loudly proclaims not only God's *existence*, but also His eternal, sovereign ***power*** and even His *Godhead*, that is, His glorious character and attributes (Rom. 1:20), this depraved, obstinate wretch shakes his fist and says, "There is no God."

What does such rejection of God **create**? *First,* total corruption. The Hebrew behind "corrupt" (*shāchaṯ*, 7843) is the same word used four times in reference to the state of the earth before the Flood (Gen. 6:11, 12, 17), where "every imagination of the thoughts of his heart was only evil continually" (6:5). *Second,* such rejection of God brings abominable works. "Abominable" (*ta'aḇ*, 8581) speaks of abhorrent, repulsive things, such as "whoredoms" (Ezek. 16:25) and **idol worship** (1 Kings 21:26). *Third,* such rejection of God results in the absence of any good whatsoever, man's total depravity in thought, inclination, motive, and desire (Rom. 1:21–32; Eph. 2:1–3).

Is there any better example of this **fool** than the evolutionist? The idea that the universe made itself over billions of years is irrational, irresponsible, and irreconcilable. What are the results of such obstinacy? When existence is reduced to "survival of the fittest," **life** becomes cheap and the results are such things as the Jewish Holocaust, abortion, school violence, and the general disintegration of society.

Finally, like *'ewiyl* and *kesiyl*, what is this fool's end? Like Abner, his **death** is one of dishonor, discredit, and debasement (2 Sam. 3:33). Let us proclaim at full volume, "let God be true, but every man a liar" (Rom. 3:4).

Scriptures for Study: Note that even Israel as a nation becomes *nāḇāl* (Deut. 32:21), which serves as a solemn warning to **nations** today. 🕮 Note a few other traits of *nāḇāl*: Job 30:8; Psalm 74:18; Isaiah 32:6.

Cleave

dāḇaq

Today we meditate on a **word** of **deep** significance. The English **cleave** appears twenty-six times in the OT, all but six of which are translated from *dāḇaq* (1692), meaning "to cling to, join with, stay with." It's used, for example, in Job 19:20 for **bone** cleaving to skin, in Job 41:1, 15–17 of the great sea creature Leviathan, whose scales are tightly fastened together, in Job 38:38 for clods of earth being stuck together, and in Numbers 36:7 for someone holding on to an **inheritance**. So hard did Eleazar's **hand cleave** to his **sword** as he fought the Philistines (2 Sam. 23:10), we could say poetically that the sword became a part of his **arm**.

More significant, however, is the figurative use of *dāḇaq* in picturing relationships, especially of their closeness and loyalty. The first appearance of *dāḇaq*, in fact, pictures the devotion and intimacy of **marriage**, where "a man [leaves] his father and his mother, and shall cleave unto his wife: and they shall be one flesh" (Gen. 2:24). David's men cleaved unto him in loyalty when Sheba rebelled against the **king** (2 Sam. 20:2).

Most important, however, are the pictures we see of the loyalty and devotion of **God's** people to Him. We read several times of God commanding His people to **cleave** unto Him (Deut. 10:20; 11:22; 13:4; Josh. 22:5; 23:8), for such cleaving demonstrates true **love** for Him (Deut.30:20).

A particularly striking example of such faithfulness appears in Psalm 119:31, where the psalmist says to God, "I have stuck unto thy testimonies." "Stuck" is *dāḇaq*. In verse 25, David says, "My soul cleaveth unto the dust," that is, despair was sticking to him as though it were glued. Now, however, it is *he* who is glued, glued to God's Word (**testimonies**, February 17). "While the dust of despair is glued to me," David says in effect, "I am ever glued to God's standards." A woodworker uses glue to join boards together, and so strong is that bond that the board will **break** in another spot before it will break on that joint. That is how we are to be glued to the Word of God.

Scriptures for Study: What were God's people told not to **cleave** to in Joshua 23:12? 🕮 Read the verses in Deuteronomy and Joshua noted above and meditate on your closeness to God.

Longeth

kāmah

Psalm 63:1 is one of those verses of **Scripture** that once you read it, you can't leave it: "O God, thou art my God; early will I seek thee: my soul thirsteth for thee, my flesh longeth for thee in a dry and thirsty land, where no water is." Once **David** understood who **God** (*'Elōhiym*, January 7) is, he longed for God in a **way** that should strike all of us.

To get the full impact of this verse, we need to set the stage (2 Sam. 15). After being driven from his **throne** by the political intrigue of his own son, Absalom, David is forced to leave Jerusalem and head into some of the most desolate, dismal, and depressing land on earth, the **wilderness** of Judea, which stretches right to the banks of the Dead Sea to the east.

David, therefore, writes: "My flesh longeth for thee." **Longeth** is *kāmah* (3642), which appears only here in the OT and literally means "to faint" and is related to an Arabic **word** that means "be pale of face, gray."[91] Driven into exile, it wasn't his possessions, **power**, or position that David missed; rather it was God and the "sanctuary" (v. 2), that is, God's presence in the **tabernacle**, that place of **prayer** and public **worship**, that David longed for.

Especially striking is that *kāmah* speaks of something *physical*. David's craving for God was not some "emotional high," rather a physical need; without God's presence, his **face** was pale and he was physically ill. As the story continues, Zadok and Abiathar actually brought the **Ark of the Covenant** to David, sincerely thinking this would comfort and encourage him, but David sent them back. Why? It wasn't some *object* that David needed, no matter how sacred. It was *God* that David needed. He didn't **want** a *picture*; he needed the *Person*.

We, too, live in a "dry and thirsty land," a desolate world. While it has *amusements*, some of which we can certainly enjoy, as did David, true *pleasure* is found in God alone. Likewise, if we were driven into exile, what would we miss most? Would we long for our nice **house**, creature comforts, and possessions? Or would it be God's presence that we missed most? Would we miss the house of God, being with God's people, and being immersed in His Word?

Scriptures for Study: What does Psalm 63:1 say concerning how David began His **day**? 🕮 Compare that with the following: 5:3; 119:87, 147, 148 (March 13); Proverbs 8:17.

Backsliding[s]

mešûḇāh [and] šôḇāḇ

Jeremiah 3:6–4:2 recounts Jeremiah's second message of his **book** (the first is in 2:1–3:5). He tells the story of two sisters, Israel (the northern **kingdom**) and Judah (the southern kingdom). Israel had committed spiritual adultery against **God**, that is, the **worship** of idols—specifically, the fertility cult of the ancient world. God waited for her to **return**, but she refused to do so, so He gave "her a bill of divorce" and sent her away (v. 8), a clear reference to the Assyrian captivity in 722 BC. In spite of the object lesson this provided Judah, she did not learn from it, would not **turn away** from idolatry, becoming even worse than Israel, and was also taken into captivity by the Babylonians beginning in 605 BC.

Two words stand out in this passage. The first is the **word** ***backsliding(s),*** which appears seven times (vv. 6, 8, 11, 12, 14, 22 [twice]), and which is translated from two separate Hebrew words. Most often used is *mešûḇāh* (4878). Coming from the root *šûḇ* (7725), "to return or go back, bring back," which we will look at in more depth **tomorrow**, the literal idea is "back-turning, backsliding," and so figuratively speaks of disloyalty and faithlessness. Most of its twelve occurrences are here in Jeremiah, but its two appearances in Hosea are most significant, where the people were "bent to backsliding" (11:7), that is, *apostasy had become their* ***way of life***, but it was still possible for them to be healed (14:4). While some use the term "backslidden Christian," that is inappropriate. This is an exclusively OT term that spoke of willful, perpetual apostasy.

The other word for **backsliding** in our text is *šôḇāḇ* (7726, vv. 14, 22), which is again from the root *šûb*. In this form it is an adjective, appearing only one other place (Isa. 57:17, "frowardly"), to picture a continual unfaithfulness to God.

While this passage is OT and, of course, Jewish, it nonetheless provides a picture for the church to consider. Prior to the Reformation, the church had drifted far from God and His revelation in **Scripture**. It had become thoroughly pagan in worshipping idols, relics, and **saints**, and **salvation** was simply a matter of doing certain works (called "sacraments") to obtain God's **grace**. Disastrously, the church today is drifting back to those days, and she desperately needs to return to the truth, which we will consider tomorrow.

Scriptures for Study: The only place *mešûḇāh* is used of an individual is Proverbs 1:32. What is the end for those who "[turn] away" from knowledge (v. 29)?

Return[ed]

šûb

The other English **word** that stands out in Jeremiah's second great message (3:6–4:2) is ***return*** (or ***returned***), which appears five times (vv. 7, 12, 22, 4:1 [twice]). As mentioned **yesterday**, the Hebrew is *šûb* (7725), "to return, to restore, to go back." One of the most frequently used words in the OT, it appears well over 1,000 times, occurs in other Semitic languages (e.g., Aramaic), and branches into several other words.

The basic idea in *šûb* is "returning to one's original state,"[92] as in **man** returning to the dust of the ground in **death** (Gen. 3:19), or "movement back to the point of departure,"[93] as when Abraham's descendants in their fourth generation would **return** to Canaan (Gen. 15:16). The most significant theological use is that of God's people returning to God in **repentance**, as it is used here and elsewhere (e.g., Ezek. 14:6, **repent**). **David** also uses it when he writes, "[My shepherd] restoreth my soul" (Ps. 23:3, June 6).

Again, here is a picture for the church and a need for her **return**. At the root of the Reformation were five key truths that had been lost for 1,000 years and are lost to much of the church today. All beginning with the Latin *sola* ("alone"), they were: *sola scriptura*, the **Scripture** alone (our only *model*), *sola fide*, **faith** alone (our only *means*), *sola gratia*, **grace** alone (our only *method*), *solus Christus*, Christ alone (our only *Mediator*), and *soli Deo gloria*, to God alone be glory (our only *motive*). We can combine these into this summary of true, biblical Christianity: It is *Scripture* alone that declares that **salvation** comes by *grace* alone, through *faith* alone, in *Christ* alone, by which *God* alone is glorified.

The Reformation, and Christianity itself, can in no **way** be understood apart from these truths. They are the very core of both. Without them, Christianity does not exist, and to pervert even *one* is to **destroy** *all*, for they are one indivisible truth. They also enable us to evaluate the church as a whole, and individual churches in particular. Their existence reveals the orthodoxy of *the* church and *a* church, while their absence reveals, to use another biblical **image**, "Ichabod" (*'iy-ḵāḇôḏ*; 350), "the glory is departed" (1 Sam. 4:21).

Tragically, much of the glory of God has departed from the church (and churches) simply because these truths have all but vanished. These truths fueled the Reformation, and only a **return** to them will revive a dying evangelicalism.

Scriptures for Study: Read the following verses, noting the use of *šûb*: Psalms 19:7 ("converting"); 51:12; 119:59; Proverbs 1:23.

Sin (1)

chāṭā'

The pictorial power of the Hebrew language," writes one Hebrew authority, "is seldom exhibited more clearly than in connection with the various aspects of evil."[94] Of the four main words that indicate **sin** in the Hebrew, *chāṭā'* (2398) is used most often and means "to miss the mark." It is used in this literal sense, for example, in Judges 20:16, where Benjamin's 700 left-handed slingers "could sling stones at an hair breadth, and not miss." It also refers to breaking civil **law** (Gen. 40:1, "offended").

Human failure and sin, however, are the prominent focus of *chāṭā'*. *Sin,* therefore, means "missing the mark." Which mark? *God's mark*, the mark He sets as the standard, namely, His righteousness and commands. Just as an archer sets his sights on a specific target, it is God's righteousness at which we "shoot" our arrows, but miss every time.

It is extremely significant that the Septuagint translates *chāṭā'* using the Greek *hamartanō* (264G), which also means "to miss the mark." The pivotal NT verse, of course, is Romans 3:23: "For all have sinned, and come short of the glory of God." Again, what is the mark for which we shoot? *The glory of God*, which includes His righteousness and perfection *but we always miss*, whether deliberately or unintentionally. As Paul wrote earlier, "There is none righteous, no, not one" (Rom. 3:10, paraphrasing Ps. 14:3).

If there is one doctrine that has been diluted by modern thought, it is most certainly the doctrine of **sin**. Opinions vary from "a low self-esteem" and "psychological self-abuse" to simply "felt needs" and personal problems. Even worse, while the **word *sin*,** along with its other forms (sins, sinner, sinners, sinful), appears some 900 times in **Scripture**, many "preachers" refuse to even *mention* the term. When asked in a television interview about the gospel, one popular leader (who proudly never preaches on sin) said, "To me good news is letting people know that God loves them, Jesus came, that we can overcome any obstacle, that we can be forgiven for our mistakes. I don't see how beating people down [apparently by preaching about sin] . . . helps them grow closer to God."[95]

That, however, is *not* the gospel, as we will see. Oh, how we need to "earnestly contend for the faith which was once delivered unto the saints" (Jude 3).

Scriptures for Study: Compare Romans 3:10–18 with the following OT passages, from which Paul either quotes or paraphrases: Psalms 5:9; 10:7; 14:1–3; 36:1; 140:3; Isaiah 59:7, 8. His indictment of the Jews has the authority of Scripture behind it.

Sin (2)

šagāh [and] āwōn [and] peša'

Is the issue of **sin** really all that important? Yes—it is mentioned approximately 900 times in the Bible. In addition to the most commonly used Hebrew **word**, *chāṭā'*, we find several others used to picture the seriousness of **sin** (see July 11 for another).

One such word is *šagāh* (7686), "to go astray, to deceive, to wander, to make a mistake, to reel." It's used primarily to express the idea of straying or wandering and frequently describes a wandering or aimless flock, both figuratively and literally (Ezek. 34:6). Isaiah used this verb to suggest "swerving, meandering, or reeling in drunkenness" (Isa. 28:7, "erred"). It also describes moral corruption (Prov. 5:23, "to go astray").[96] It is also translated **sin** in Leviticus 4:13, "sin through ignorance."

Another word is *'āwāh* (5753), which is equivalent to the Arabic *'awaya*, "to bend or twist," and so reflects not only those ideas but also to "distort" and "pervert," whether intentional or not. Men pervert what is right (Job 33:27; Jer. 3:21) and commit "iniquity," which is to bend God's revelation (Ps. 106:6). The word *'āwōn* (5771), which appears more than 230 times, speaks of Israel choosing to **return** to the "iniquities of their forefathers," that is, twisting and perverting God's Word to "[go] after other gods to serve them" (Jer. 11:10). This word is also translated **sin** in 1 Kings 17:18, where a widow speaks to Elijah in **fear** that her son died because she bent or distorted some requirement.

One other word for **sin** is *peša'* (6588), which appears over ninety times to indicate "willful deviation from, and therefore rebellion against, the path of godly living"[97] (e.g., Isa. 58:1; 59:12; Amos 5:12).

Is there now any doubt as to the **answer** to the question, "Is the issue of sin really all that important?" Indeed, ***sin*** is the *problem*, ***salvation*** is the *provision*, and the *Savior* is the *path*. After salvation, however, is **sin** still a problem? *Positionally* no, but *practically* yes. While we are freed from the bondage of **sin** as the rule of **life** (Rom. 6:1–7), "the flesh" ("our selfish properties," *sarx*, 4561G) still rears its ugly **head** and wars within us (Rom. 7). Thankfully, we can have victory over this by the indwelling Holy Spirit (Rom. 8), and we have the assurance of **forgiveness** through confession when we do **sin** (1 John 1:9).[98]

Scriptures for Study: Read David's **prayer** of confession and restoration (Ps. 51). Note the words for **sin** in verses 1–4: "transgressions" (*peša'*), "iniquity" (*'āwōn*), "sin" (*chaṭṭā't*, a derivative of *chāṭā'*), and "sinned" (*chāṭā'*). **Praise** God today for His forgiveness (April 16).

Save [and] Salvation

yāša‘ [and] yešû‘āh

One of the key themes of the Bible, of course, is **salvation**. Nevertheless, despite not only the prominence of this theme but also the clarity of what it is and how it comes, there seems in our **day** to be much confusion about it. An **understanding** of these words, however, along with yesterday's study of **sin**, clears up all question.

As most Hebrew nouns come from a verb, the verb here is *yāša‘* (3467), which appears about 200 times and means "to save, help, deliver, or defend." The "underlying idea of this verb is bringing to a place of safety or broad pasture as opposed to a narrow strait."[99] This idea actually comes from the same Arabic root that means "to make wide or sufficient," since "wide" implies freedom from stress and encumbrance. Such change, however, demands deliverance, and such deliverance must come from outside the individual. The Septuagint usually renders *yāša‘* as the Greek *sōzō* (4982G), "to deliver or preserve from danger or destruction."

A vivid example of *yāša‘* is Israel's deliverance from Egypt (Exod. 14:30), accomplished, of course, solely by **God**. Even when deliverance came through some human instrumentality, it was still only by God's **power**, as when Gideon saved God's people from the Midianites only because God empowered him (Judg. 6:14–16).

From what, then, does **salvation** deliver us? What is its *substance*? **Salvation** is deliverance from spiritual **death**. Because of Adam's **sin** in the garden of Eden (Gen. 2:17), "the soul that sinneth, it shall die" (Ezek. 18:4; also Rom. 5:12). It is, therefore, Christ alone who came to "save his people from their sins" (Matt. 1:21).

Further, no verse of **Scripture** is clearer on the *source* of **salvation** (*yešû‘āh*, 3444) than is Jonah 2:9: "Salvation is of the LORD." From beginning to end, and everything in between, **salvation** is *all* from God. It is not because of our partial merit or **good** works (Titus 3:5), not because we "said a prayer," not because of our own "foreseen faith"— even the **faith** to believe the gospel is God-given (Eph. 2:8, 9; John 6:65; Phil. 1:29; Acts 18:27). Rather, "Salvation is of the Lord," writes Spurgeon. "The Lord has to apply it, to make the unwilling willing, to make the ungodly godly, and bring the vile rebel to the feet of Jesus, or else salvation will never be accomplished."[100]

Scriptures for Study: God continues to deliver us on a daily basis. Read Psalm 20, noting God's deliverance from enemies.

Filthy Rags

'iddâ beged

Addressing the ever-increasing propensity for redefining **salvation** and the gospel nowadays, no teaching is more prevalent today (or throughout history) than the one that insists that salvation is either wholly, or at least partly, the result of human merit or works. There is perhaps no more graphic verse in **Scripture** that speaks to the contrary, however, than Isaiah 64:6: "But we are all as an unclean thing, and all our righteousnesses are as filthy rags; and we all do fade as a leaf; and our iniquities, like the wind, have taken us away."

Rags is *beged* (899), which is the most common OT **word** for clothing and by itself refers simply to any kind of garment, as in its first appearance in Genesis 24:53, where a servant brought jewels and "raiment" to Rebekah. When coupled with a qualifying word, however, it is used to refer to specific types of garments, from something as common as a widow's clothing (Gen. 38:14) to the specialized, holy garments of Aaron (Exod. 28:2–4).

Our text, therefore, adds a very unique qualifying word to *beged*. (We do not wish to offend any reader's sensitivities, so we will say this as delicately as possible.) **Filthy** is *beged* (5708), which appears only here in the OT and refers to a woman's menstrual period, and therefore, the cloth that accompanies it when coupled with *beged*. Does this not clearly demonstrate what all our **good** works are, what any "righteous deed" we might perform really is? *All of them* are as filthy and repulsive as *beged*.

No truth is clearer in Scripture than that salvation is apart from any merit or works of men. Scripture repeatedly declares man's uncleanness and depravity (Job 15:14–16; 25:4; 40:4; Ps. 51:5; Rom. 1:21–32; 7:18, 24; Eph. 2:1–3) and that works cannot **save** (Job 9:20; Rom. 3:20, 28; 4:5; 9:11, 16, 30; 11:6; Gal. 2:16; 3:16–21; Eph. 2:8, 9).

Sadly, every false religion, cult, and human philosophy teaches that enough works will result in salvation, "renewal," "enlightenment," or whatever concept they **choose** as their goal. Even some today who **call** themselves evangelicals are diluting salvation by insisting that works have a part in salvation. James makes it clear that works are the *result* of salvation (James 2:14–26), but it is **grace** (April 6, 7) alone through **faith** (April 9) alone that is the *cause*. Let us **rejoice** this **day** in God's **power**, for that alone can save us.

Scriptures for Study: Read the verses cited above about depravity and the insufficiency of works, and then rejoice in God's power (and willingness) to save.

Mercy

chesed̲

Mercy is a translation of the Hebrew *chesed̲* (2617), which is "one of the most important [words] in the vocabulary of OT theology and ethics," appearing some 240 times, most frequently in the Psalms.[101] It speaks of kindness, lovingkindness, **mercy**, goodness, faithfulness, loyal **love**,[102] and acts of kindness. While the **word** is used for kindness one person might show another, such as David's kindness to Mephibosheth, the son of David's dear **friend** Jonathan (2 Sam. 9:7), it is God's **mercy** to **man** that stands out.

If there is a single word, in fact, that could summarize God's dealing with His people, it would be the word **mercy**. One example, and by far the most notable appearance of *chesed̲*, is in Psalm 136, where the psalmist declares twenty-six times of God, "His mercy endureth for ever." This **psalm** is a study in **worship**, with God's **mercy** at the forefront, displaying what wondrous works He has done. **Mercy** is at the *foundation* of His character (vv. 1–3), the *function* of His creative **work** (vv. 4–9), the *fountain* from which all His blessings flow to His people (vv. 10–25), and the *force* behind His Rulership in **heaven** (v. 26).

The greatest manifestation of God's **mercy**, of course, is that of **redemption** (April 8), His saving men from **sin** (Ps. 51:1, "lovingkindness", 86:13). We are always struck by Jonah's opposition to going to the unimaginably wicked Assyrians at Nineveh. Because he knew that God was a God of "kindness" (loyal love, committed to the objects of His love) and would **save** those pagans when they didn't (in Jonah's thinking) deserve it (Jonah 4:2).

It is also noteworthy that with few exceptions, the Septuagint translates *chesed̲* with the common Greek word *eleos* (1656G), which speaks of "kindness or **good** will towards the miserable and afflicted, joined with a desire to relieve them."[103] The whole point of **mercy**, therefore, is to relieve the affliction that man suffers because he cannot relieve it himself. **Mercy** is always to the helpless.

With God's **mercy** as our model, we are to show **mercy** to others. "Thus speaketh the LORD of hosts, saying, Execute true judgment, and show mercy [i.e., covenant loyalty manifested in love] and compassions every man to his brother" (Zech. 7:9; James 2:13–17). Judgment, in fact, is reserved for those who do not show **mercy** and kindness (Ps. 109:16).

Scriptures for Study: What does Psalm 103:8 say about God and **mercy**? 📖 What is the prerequisite for God's **mercy** in 32:10?

Grace

chānan

When we encounter the **word *grace*,** we are again on holy ground. No other word sums up biblical theology, and therefore the Christian **faith**, as does **grace**. The Hebrew verb is *chānan* (2603), and the noun is *chēn* (2580). Related to the Akkadian *enēnu* and *hanānu* ("to grant a favor"), *chānan* means "to be gracious, considerate, show favor" and "depicts a heartfelt response by someone who has something to give to one who has a need."[104] It is often used for people being gracious to each other, as when Job asked his friends to "pity" him (Job 19:21), and for people having pity on the poor (Prov. 19:17).

It is the theological use, of course, that is the most significant. Like **mercy**, **grace** is always to the spiritually helpless, those who cannot **save** themselves. The psalmist cries out to **God** because of his *solitude* (Ps. 25:16), his *suffering* (31:9), and his ***sin*** (51:1, *chānan* is "mercy"). Further, we see God's graciousness in *protection* (Gen. 6:8ff), *prosperity* (33:11), and even *progeny* (33:5). And we should not ignore that this is all according to God's sovereign will alone, as He "will be gracious to whom [He] will be gracious" (Exod. 33:19).

It's also fascinating to note that this word, and its derivatives, form the basis for the names of several people in **Scripture**, such as Hannah and Johanan, for example. Those names have in turn given us several of their own derivatives that we use today, such as Anna, Ann, and several versions of John.[105] God's people are, indeed, struck by the **power** and depth of this word.

Finally, as one authority also observes, "In many ways, *chānan* combines the meaning of the Greek *charis* (with the general classical Greek sense of 'charm' or 'graciousness') and the NT sense of 'undeserved favor' or 'mercy.'"[106] The Septuagint, in fact, often renders *chānan* as *charis* (5485G). Further, as the OT *chānan* is associated with Messiah, so, too, is the NT *charis* coupled with the person and **work** of Jesus Christ, for He is the ultimate manifestation of the **grace** of God.[107]

We will ponder a **wonderful** picture of God's mercy and **grace tomorrow**, but for today I **hope** you will meditate on just how wondrous God's **grace** is, and that it alone is why you are one of His own from "before the foundation of the world" (Eph. 1:4).

Scriptures for Study: Identify the recipient of **grace** in each of the following: Genesis 18:3; 19:19; Exodus 33:12, 13; Ezra 9:8 (*techinnāh*, 8467, from *chānan*).

Mercy [and] Grace

chese<u>d</u> [and] chānan

While not interchangeable, *chesed* (**mercy**) and *chānan* (**grace**) are closely related. While **mercy** is the *withholding* of what *is* deserved (e.g., **death** and **hell**), **grace** is the *bestowing* of what is *not* deserved (e.g., **life** and **heaven**). Second Samuel 9 gives one of the most graphic pictures in all the Bible of *both* **mercy** and **grace**, with ten startling parallels to the Savior and sinner:

First, Mephibosheth, the son of **King** David's **friend** Jonathan, was crippled by a fall (4:4), just as each of us was crippled by Adam's fall, even rendered "dead in trespasses and sins" (Eph. 2:1–3). *Second,* as David wanted to show Mephibosheth "kindness [*chesed*] for Jonathan's sake" (2 Sam. 9:1), **God** has shown us **mercy** and **grace** for the sake of the **Lord** Jesus (Eph. 4:32). *Third,* that kindness was neither deserved nor earned by Mephibosheth, who could do little for himself, much less do anything for the king of Judah and Israel. We in turn deserved nothing but death, and there are not enough works in the universe to **save** a single **soul** (Eph. 2:8, 9; Titus 3:5). *Fourth,* Mephibosheth was sought by the king (vv. 1, 5), again picturing unmerited favor. Likewise, not a single person has ever "[sought] after God" by his own **power** (Rom. 3:11). "Ye have not chosen me, but I have chosen you," Jesus declared (John 15:16). A dead **man** can do nothing, so "no man can come to [Christ], except the Father which hath sent [Him] draw him" (John 6:44; cf. v. 65; Acts 16:13, 14). *Fifth,* David ordered and empowered servants to fetch Mephibosheth (v. 5), a graphic picture of evangelism. God has likewise called and empowered each of us as witnesses (Acts 1:8; Matt. 28:19, 20).

Sixth, a result of all this was that Mephibosheth reverenced the king (2 Sam. 9:6), a challenge to us to **worship** Jesus. *Seventh,* he became a servant of the king (v. 6), as are we of Christ (e.g., Rom. 6:16). *Eighth,* he was given riches and security (v. 7), just as we have spiritual riches (Eph. 1) and security in Christ (John 10:28, 29; Rom. 8:29–39). *Ninth,* he was made a king's son (v. 11), as we are God's children (John 1:12, 13). And *tenth,* his physical condition was hidden from view when he sat at the king's **table** (v. 13). We, too, have been sanctified by Christ (Heb. 9:12–15) and "sit together in heavenly places in Christ Jesus" (Eph. 2:6).

Scriptures for Study: If you haven't already done so, read this **wonderful** account and **rejoice** in God's **mercy** and **grace**.

Redemption

pāḏāh [and] gā'al

One Hebrew authority writes, "Whatever theory one may hold as to the possibility . . . or probability of a Divine intervention in human affairs, the Bible is pledged to the fact that such an intervention has taken place."[108] That is an understatement! **God** has, indeed, intervened, and how thankful we are that He did!

No **word** underscores God's intervention more, in fact, than does **redemption**. The first important word here is *pāḏāh* (6299), which is of immense theological significance. It was originally a word of commerce for paying a price for something to transfer ownership, such as buying an animal (Exod. 13:13; 34:20) or even a slave (21:8; Lev. 19:20). Especially significant theologically is Numbers 18:15–17, where the priests received **redemption** money in place of a **firstborn** son or unclean animal, all rooted in Exodus 13:13–15, where *pāḏāh* also refers to the firstborn in Egypt. Therefore, as the psalmist writes, "Into thine hand I commit my spirit: thou hast redeemed me, O LORD God of truth" (Ps. 31:5), for He "redeem[s] my soul from the power of the grave" (49:15).

The second word we encounter is *gā'al* (1350), a specific word that is almost exclusively Hebrew[109] and means not only "to redeem" but "to act as a kinsman-redeemer." One authority well sums it up: "The word means to act as a redeemer for a deceased kinsman (Ruth 3:13); to redeem or buy back from bondage (Lev. 25:48); to redeem or buy back a kinsman's possessions (Lev. 25:26); to avenge a kinsman's murder (Num. 35:19); to redeem an object through a payment (Lev. 27:13)."[110]

Putting the two words together, then, while *pāḏāh* speaks of deliverance from bondage, *gā'al* speaks more technically of a kinsman doing the redeeming. Again, while *pāḏāh* is used for the redeeming of the Israelites out of Egyptian bondage (Exod. 13:15), *gā'al* is used of Boaz as the kinsman-redeemer (Ruth 3:12, 13; cf. "levirate marriage" in Deut. 25:5–10), a **wonderful** picture of the Savior who is to come. Christ is, indeed, our Kinsman-Redeemer (our "Elder-brother," i.e., "the firstborn among many brethren," Rom. 8:29), coming to our aid, paying our debts, and supplying our needs.

Finally, it is immensely significant that both these words are usually translated as *lutroō* (3084G) in the Septuagint, which means "to release on receipt of a ransom," for it was Christ who "came . . . to give his life a ransom for many" (Matt. 20:28).

Scriptures for Study: From what does **redemption** flow in Isaiah 54:8 and 63:9 (*gā'al*)? 📖 In view of God being our Redeemer, what should be our response (Ps. 19:14; 107:2)?

Faith (1)

'āman

Back on January 16, we mentioned the Hebrew *ṣeḏeq* (6664), which primarily speaks of conforming to a moral, ethical standard or norm, and is often connected to the term *justice*. As noted there, **God** is not only righteous in Himself—He lives up to the perfect moral and ethical standard of Himself—but He also produces righteousness in those whom He saves through Christ.

The question arises, however, how exactly does God produce this righteousness? Coupled with God's **grace** is **faith**. In the NT, in fact, these two words appear together in twelve verses (most notably, Romans 5:2 and Ephesians 2:8, 9). In contrast, the OT contains a unique **word** for ***faith***, the Hebrew *'emûnāh* (530, January 26), often also translated **truth**. This word comes from the root *'āman* (539), a verb whose core concept is "certainty," which is graphically underscored in Hebrews 11:1, which, of course, was written to Christian Jews. That verse declares that the foundation, the very essence of **faith** is an absolute confidence that while we can't see something, we still **know** that it is real and that it is ours. Pictures in the OT include the certainty of a building's "pillars" (2 Kings 18:16), building a "sure" **house** (1 Sam. 2:35), and driving "a nail in a sure place" (Isa. 22:23).

Spiritually, then, *'āman* is the believing and receiving of something as being true and sure, as Abram "believed in the LORD; and [God] counted it to him for righteousness" (Gen. 15:6; cf. Rom. 4:3–5, 9; Gal. 3:6–14). A key OT text is Habakkuk 2:4—"The just shall live by his faith [*'emûnāh*]"—the background of which is the conceit and arrogance of the Babylonians. "Lifted up" is *'āp̄al* (6075), appearing only here in the OT and literally meaning "to swell"; the Babylonians were, indeed, swollen, puffed up in their **pride** and self-sufficiency. In stark contrast, God declares that the righteous person will live by **faith**. So pivotal is this principle that it is quoted three times in the NT. By quoting this text in Romans 1:17, Paul says ***salvation*** is by **faith**, in Galatians 3:11 he emphasizes that that salvation is *not by works*, and in Hebrews 10:38[111] he adds that we now *live* by **faith** in all things. We will continue these thoughts **tomorrow**.

Scriptures for Study: What picture of certainty do we see in 2 Samuel 4:4 ("nurse" is derived from *'āman*). 🕮 What is the object of certainty in Psalm 19:7 ("sure" is derived from *'āman*)?

Faith (2)

'āman

Composer-conductor Leonard Bernstein once said, "I believe in everything, in anything that anybody believes in, because I believe in people. In other words, I believe in belief. I believe in faith."[112] But true **faith** is not vague and nebulous. **Faith** is *certainty*. This truth, in fact, brings up the key principle to **understanding faith**, namely: ***Faith** must have an object.*

Some common concepts of **faith** in our **day** include: "my faith," "my faith helped me," and "I was so troubled that I lost my faith." The obvious problem with all those, of course, is that **faith** is made to be its own object. That is not only poor grammar, but is also sadly ridiculous. What's the point in saying "I drove," for example, unless we add, "I drove my car." "Drove" is the verb; "car" is the object. Likewise, the Greek word for **faith** is a verb, so without an object, the entire concept is incomplete.

In dramatic contrast to today's "faith in faith," every **time** we see **faith** being exercised in **Scripture**, it always has an object, and that object, however manifested, is always in what **God** has said. **Noah**, for example, "being warned of God of things not seen as yet, moved with fear, prepared an ark to the saving of his house" (Heb. 11:7; cf. Gen. 6:13, 22; 7:1, 5). Indeed, Noah believed what God said. What, then, must the object of **faith** be today? Jesus Christ and Him alone (e.g., Rom. 3:22; 5:1; Gal. 2:16, 20; 3:24).

This principle also underscores another, namely, that **faith** speaks of *obedience*, as the Greek *pisteuō* (4100G) unquestionably means.[113] As one reads Hebrews 11, in fact, obedience is always, without exception, involved. Is obedience the *cause* of **salvation**? Absolutely not! It is, however, always the *result* of salvation and evidence of it. The "easy believism" of our day that says, "Just believe in Jesus"—which means whatever each person chooses it to mean—is not the gospel. Salvation, true **faith** in Jesus Christ, means that "old things are passed away; behold, all things are become new" (2 Cor. 5:17), and that our lives are now characterized by obedience. Our **Lord** made the issue clear: "If ye love me, keep my commandments. . . . If a man love me, he will keep my words . . . He that loveth me not keepeth not my sayings" (John 14:15, 23, 24; also 1 John 2:1–6).

Scriptures for Study: Read Hebrews 11, noting the action that accompanied **faith** in each instance.

Faith (3)

'āman

The great reformer Martin Luther once said, "If ever a monk could get to heaven by monkery, I would have gotten there." Luther struggled with his **sin** for years, doing every **good work**, sacrament, and penance the Roman Church specified, but still his guilt would not lift. He knew he was sinful and damned but did not **know** the **answer**. It was upon a **deep** study of Romans 1:16, 17, however, that Luther discovered, "The just shall live by faith," a re-discovery that ultimately launched the Protestant Reformation, bringing the church out of a thousand years of darkness (see March 31).

It was this doctrine of "faith alone" (*sola fide*), in fact, that became the "material principle" of the Reformation. While a "formal principle" (which was *sola scriptura*) speaks of the authority that shapes a movement, a "material principle" is the *central teaching* of a movement or system. *Sola fide*, then, encapsulates Christianity like no other term. **Salvation** does not come through *works* (which is the material principle of *Catholicism* and *all* religion); rather salvation comes through ***faith***.

What was the Reformation about? In short, the Reformation was about a repudiation of the whole idea of human effort as a **way** to commend the sinner toward **God**, coupled with the recovery of the gospel of **faith** in Christ alone. That alone, in fact, *is* the gospel, the good news, as declared in Galatians 1:8–9; 2:16; Romans 3:21, 22, 30; and many other verses. Salvation comes not by *ceremony*, but by the *cross*. It is not by the *ritual* of the *church*, but the *righteousness* of *Christ*. It is not by the *bondage* of the ***Law*** but by the ***blood*** of our ***Lord***. It is not by *our continuous works* but by *His completed work*. In short, the righteousness of God is not *gained* by *works*, but is a *gift* of ***faith***.

So much did Rome **hate** this doctrine (and still does), that the Council of Trent, which was assembled in response to the reformers, stated: "If anyone says that *by faith alone* the sinner is justified, so as to mean that nothing else is required to cooperate in order to obtain the grace of justification . . . let him be anathema."[114] We emphasize this simply because *sola fide* is under attack once again, this **time** even by professing evangelicals, who wish to undo the Reformation by diluting the gospel.

Oh, that we would all proclaim the true gospel!

Scriptures for Study: Rejoice in the true gospel by reading the following **Scripture** passages: Romans 4:3–25; 5:17–19; Ephesians 1:6,7; 2 Corinthians 5:21.

Love (1)

'āhab̲

The most often-used Hebrew **word** for **love** in the OT is *'āhab̲* (157), which speaks generally of desire, affection, or inclination, "a strong emotional attachment to and desire either to possess or to be in the presence of the object."[115] *'āhab̲* has an extremely wide range of meanings, so wide, in fact, that its some 250 occurrences cover just about everything from "God's infinite affection for his people to the carnal appetites of a lazy glutton."[116]

Unlike the Greek words *philos* (5384G, "esteem, tender affection") and *agapē* (26G, "selfless, sacrificial love"),[117] which differentiate kinds of **love**, Hebrew does not do this quite as clearly. While other words do show somewhat differing ideas—*dôd̲* (1730), for example, speaks strongly of sexual affection (Prov. 7:18; Song of Sol. 1:2, 4; 7:12)—for the most part Hebrew words for **love** are general.

Like the word **faith**, therefore, the real crux of **love** (*'āhab̲*) lies in its *object.* A **man** can **love** "pleasure" and "wine," for example, but these will bring him to poverty (Prov. 21:17). Likewise, it can refer to sexual lust, as Absalom had for his sister Tamar (2 Sam. 13:1). The prophets spoke of the wrong object of **love** when God's people committed spiritual adultery with pagan gods (Jer. 22:20, 22; Ezek. 16:36; 23:5; Hosea 2:5–13).

On the positive side, examples of **good love** and affection include: a **father** for his son, such as Abraham had for Isaac (Gen. 22:2); a husband for his wife, such as Elkanah's **love** for Hannah (1 Sam. 1:5); and one **friend** for another, as was true of **David** and Jonathan (20:17). Certainly one of the greatest objects of **love** in our lives should be **wisdom** (March 22): "Forsake her not, and she shall preserve thee: love her, and she shall keep thee" (Prov. 4:6). Another is **truth** coupled with **peace** (Zech. 8:19).

Still another, and most notably, is God's Word. *'Āhab̲* appears no less than twelve times in Psalm 119 to demonstrate the psalmist's **love** for the Word (v. 140). It was his "meditation all the day" (v. 97) because he loved its **commandments** (vv. 47, 48, 127), **law** (vv. 97, 113, 163, 165), **testimonies** (vv. 119, 167), and **precepts** (v. 159). We should also interject that He loved God's **name** (v. 132).

This should encourage us to be conscious of the objects of our **love**. We will apply these thoughts a little more deeply **tomorrow.**

Scriptures for Study: What are the objects of **love** (positive or negative) in the following verses: Psalm 4:2; 11:5; 26:8; 40:16; Proverbs 22:11?

Love (2)

'āhaḇ

As noted **yesterday**, *'āhaḇ* (157) speaks generally of desire, affection, or inclination, but the real issue is the object of that **love**, desire, affection, or inclination. Let us conclude today by examining two objects of **love**:

First, and most important, is God's **love** for His people. Several times we read of God's **love** for His **chosen** people Israel. He declared, for example, He "loved Israel for ever" (1 Kings 10:9). He loved them, in fact, in spite of their spiritual adultery and loving other gods (Hosea 3:1; cf. Mal. 1:2; 2:11). Further, what is the basis of God's choosing (or electing) Israel? "The LORD did not set his love upon you, nor choose you, because ye were more in number than any people; for ye were the fewest of all people: But because the LORD loved you" (Deut. 7:7, 8; cf.4:37). Not only did God **love** and **choose** Israel, He loved and chose His elect before the foundation of the world (Eph. 1:4, 5).

Second, let us consider carefully our **love** for God. Perhaps the key text here is Deuteronomy 6:5 (cf. Matt. 22:37–38): "Thou shalt love the LORD thy God with all thine heart, and with all thy soul, and with all thy might." **Heart** is *lēḇāḇ* (3824), referring not only to the physical organ, but figuratively to the whole of the inner person and personality. **Soul** is *nep̱eš* (5315), meaning "breath, the act of breathing, and figuratively the inner being with its thoughts and emotions." "Might," then, is *me'ōḏ* (3966), indicating might, **power**, will, or even "muchness." While the world tells us that **love** is feelings (which often amounts simply to lust), real **love** is an act of the will.

While we respect writers who maintain that these three should not be considered individually, rather as a whole,[118] as in loving God with "all that is within [us]" (Ps. 103:1), we respectfully disagree. Words mean things, and by considering each of these words, we discover the true depth of God's command. Let us each ask ourselves: *Does my heart beat with God's, does my personality reflect Him, do I live and breathe Him and His **Word**, and is all my might and will set upon Him?*

Oh, let there be no other "objects" in our lives that we **love** as we **love** Him!

Scriptures for Study: One of the great themes of Deuteronomy is our **love** of God. Read the following verses and reflect on your **love** for Him: 4:29; 10:12; 11:13; 13:4; 26:16; 30:2, 6, 10.

Choose [and] Chosen

bāchar

The doctrine of election has been one of controversy for many years. This is tragic because it, along with **grace** and other doctrines, provides **peace** and assurance. We **know** we belong to **God** simply because He chose us for Himself.[119] While more fully *developed* in the NT, the principle of election is *rooted* in OT theology.

Appearing about 170 times in Hebrew—it also appears in Aramaic and other Semitic languages, with parallels in still others—*bāchar* (977) means "to take a keen look at, to prove [rarely, as in Isa. 48:10], to choose. It denotes a choice, which is based on a thorough examination of the situation and not an arbitrary whim."[120] In fact, it "always involves a careful, well-thought-out choice (cf. 1 Sam. 17:40; 1 Kings 18:25; Isa. 1:29; 40:20)."[121] This point is extremely important, for it proves that God's election is not based on whim, as some critics accuse, but on His omniscient, sovereign will.

With few exceptions *bāchar* has **deep** theological overtones, whether it is God making a choice (Deut. 7:7; 1 Sam. 2:28; Neh. 9:7; Ps. 135:4) or **man** (Gen. 13:11; Deut. 30:19; Josh. 24:15; Judg. 10:14). God's choosing, of course, is the most significant. In Deuteronomy alone, *bāchar* appears thirty times, all but two of which refer either to God choosing Israel or something related to her **life** (e.g., Deut. 4:37; 7:6, 7; 10:15; 12:5, 11; 14:1, 2).

In each case, then, why does God **choose**? For His own well-thought-out purpose and glory. It is this **seed** doctrine that then comes to full bloom in the NT. Not only did God **choose** *Israel* because of His **love** (Deut. 7:7, 8), will, purpose, and glory, but He also chose *us* for the same reasons (Eph. 1:4–6, 9, 11, 12). A common criticism of this doctrine is that it is cold and unloving, but God's love is at the very root of His election. And what is His purpose? While we don't know it all—"who hath known the mind of the Lord?" (Rom. 11:34)—one part of the reason is that we can now be holy (Eph. 1:4; 4:24). Another is so we will be conformed to the **image** of Christ (Rom. 8:29).

One of the saddest developments of our **day** is the misunderstanding of this biblical (and consistently historical) doctrine. To miss it is to omit a basic foundation stone and weaken the entire structure of biblical theology and therefore the church itself.

Scriptures for Study: Read the Scriptures cited today and **rejoice** that you belong to God by His will and for His purpose.

Hope

yāchal

The concept of **hope** in modern thinking is that of uncertainty, a wish that something will happen the **way** we **want** it to. In **Scripture**, however, **hope** means "expectation." The Hebrew *yāchal* (3176) means "to wait, tarry, trust, and hope." It's used of **Noah**, for example, as he waited *expectantly* for the waters to recede (Gen. 8:12). The Septuagint translation is also significant, where *yāchal* is often translated with the Greek *elpizō* (1679G), "to expect with desire."[122]

Deeper, however, is that such expectant **hope** "is closely linked with 'faith [and] trust' and results in 'patient waiting.'"[123] In other words, true **faith** results in **hope**. We see people waiting with **hope** and certainty throughout the Psalms, demonstrating that we are expectantly waiting for **God** to do what He says He will do. Of special note, for example, is Psalm 42:5: "Why art thou cast down, O my soul? and why art thou disquieted in me? hope thou in God: for I shall yet praise him for the help of his countenance."

Psalm 119 is very special to this writer, one reason being this **word** *yāchal*. Assurance in modern thinking is based on feelings or psychological techniques, but only the Word of God can assure us. Verse 81 declares, "My soul fainteth for thy salvation: but I hope in thy word," and 114 adds, "Thou art my hiding place and my shield: I hope in thy word" (cf. vv. 105, 117; 130:5). It is in God's Word alone that we find **hope** and security.

Oh, that we would see this truth today! God's Word is the only certainty for growth, development, depth, solace, and victory in Christian living. If this sufficiency of Scripture (and the **preaching** of it) is not the central emphasis of ministry in our church, we simply do not have a valid church.

On the heels of Psalm 119:81 (cited above), verse 82 tells us, "Mine eyes fail for thy word, saying, When wilt thou comfort me?" Commenting on the NT cross-reference 1 Peter 1:3, 4, commentator Robert Leighton writes: "*A living hope*—living in death itself! The world dares say no more for its device, than *Dum spiro spero*—While I breathe I hope—but the children of God can add by virtue of this living hope, *Dum expiro spero*—While I breathe my last, I hope."[124] What a blessing it is to have that wondrous assurance of Christ and His Word! That does, indeed, bring **hope** to a troubled **soul**.

Scriptures for Study: What does Psalm 71:14 encourage us to do? 🕮 What other truths are coupled with **hope** in 130:7?

Forgiveness [and] Sin Offering

sālach [and] chaṭṭā't

Today's first **word** has such **deep** theological significance that its forty-six occurrences speak exclusively of God's **forgiveness** of man, never of men forgiving each another. As well as "to forgive," the Hebrew *sālach* (5545) means "to pardon or to spare." Its first occurrence, in fact, demonstrates this profound importance. After Israel's **sin** at Sinai, Moses interceded for the people, praying, "O Lord, let my Lord, I pray thee, go among us; for it is a stiffnecked people; and pardon [*sālach*] our iniquity and our sin" (Exod. 34:9).

The deepest significance of *sālach*, however, lies in the very fact that almost half its occurrences are in Leviticus and Numbers, the books that most strongly emphasize the Levitical, sacrificial laws. In Leviticus 4:1–5:13 (cf. 6:24–30), for example, we read of the **sin offering** (*chaṭṭā't*, 2403, a derivative of *chāṭā'*, April 1). This was a **blood sacrifice**—for without the shedding of blood, there is no **forgiveness** (4:20; also Heb. 9:22)—and was offered in the case of *unintentional* sin (Lev. 4:2), sin committed out of weakness (in contrast to defiant, rebellious sin, for which only judgment awaited in Numbers 15:30, 31). *Sālach* appears no less than six times in this Leviticus passage (4:20, 26, 31, 35; 5:10, 13), where it is always translated "forgiven," and underscores God's **forgiveness** of sin through His **mercy** and **grace**.

What, then, is the significance of all this to the believer today? *True, once-for-all **forgiveness** comes through Jesus Christ.* Since "it is not possible that the blood of bulls and of goats should take away sins," it was Christ alone who "offered one sacrifice for sins for ever" (Heb. 10:4, 12). The OT **sin offering** specifically prefigured the reality that Christ would be "made . . . sin for us, who knew no sin; that we might be made the righteousness of God in him" (2 Cor. 5:21). Further, as the **sin offering** was taken outside the city (Lev. 4:21; cf. Heb. 13:11), so would the **Lord** Jesus be taken outside the city (Heb. 13:12; cf. John 19:17–20).

Further still, in the very next verse in Hebrews, the believer is challenged to "go forth therefore unto [Christ] without the camp, bearing his reproach" (Heb. 13:13). In other words, we are to leave behind all false religion (which Judaism had now become) and embrace our Lord totally, even suffering for Him (Phil. 1:29; 2 Tim. 3:12; 1 Pet. 4:12–16).

Scriptures for Study: What city does Hebrews 13:14 refer to (cf. 2 Cor. 5:1)? 🕮 Then, in verse 15, what kind of sacrifice do we offer God now?

Offering

qurbān

Yesterday's reading introduced us to the OT Levitical offerings. Let us continue that examination over the next few days to see how Christ wonderfully fulfilled all those and how they practically apply to Christians. We note first the **word**, ***offering***, which is a translation of the Hebrew *qurbān* (7133), the most common word in the OT for an **offering** or gift of any kind. It appears about eighty times, seventy-seven of which are in Leviticus and Numbers. It was also familiar to readers of the NT (Mark 7:11).

Perhaps the best **way** to understand *qurbān* is to compare it with *minchāh* (4503), the word used for the **offering** both **Cain** and **Abel** brought to **God** (Gen. 4:3–4, April 20). While *minchāh* is a general word for "gift," whether to God or a **man** (Gen. 32:13), the root word from which *qurbān* is derived is *qārab* (7126), a verb that appears in almost all Semitic languages and means "to come near, to approach." While God, for example, told Moses in Exodus 3:5 "draw not nigh" because the place he was on was holy ground, through offerings the people could **draw near** (Lev. 1:14, "bring"). "It is no ordinary nearness that is represented by [*qārab*]," writes one authority, "but rather that of the closest and most intimate kind (see, e.g., Num. 16:9; Ps. 65:4; Jer. 30:21)."[125] Each **offering** (*qurbān*) God prescribed was designed to bring His people close to Him.

Is not the application to the Christian obvious? The psalmist promises us, "The LORD is nigh [*qārôḇ*, 7138, another derivative of *qārab*] unto all them that call upon him, to all that call upon him in truth" (Ps. 145:18). It is then the writer of Hebrews who elaborates on what now makes us near: "For the law made nothing perfect, but the bringing in of a better hope did; by the which we draw nigh unto God" (Heb. 7:19; also 10:22). The old Mosaic system, at the core of which were the Levitical offerings, was far from "perfect," that is, mature, full grown, complete (*teleios*, 5046G). They could bring men close to God to a certain extent, but not in the fullest, most complete sense. What is the far "better" way to draw near to God? Through the once-for-all **sacrifice** of Jesus Christ (Heb. 10:12).

Scriptures for Study: Read Hebrews 10:19–25. What did the **blood** of Christ make possible? 🕮 How do we now draw near? 🕮 What are the practical applications?

Sacrifice

zāḇach

Another crucial **word** in the context of the offerings of the OT, of course, is the word ***sacrifice***. The Hebrew is *zāḇach* (2076), which means "to slaughter, to kill, to offer, to sacrifice." While at times it refers to killing an animal simply for food (Deut. 12:21; 1 Sam. 28:24), it is used mainly for the slaughter of animals for **sacrifice**, either to the true **God** or even a false one (Judg. 16:23; 2 Chr. 28:23).

Why was **sacrifice** required? Because the result of **sin** is **death** (Rom. 6:23; James 1:15), and the only thing that can pay the price of sin is **blood**—"without shedding of blood is no remission" (Heb. 9:22; cf. Lev. 4:20). It was, therefore, the **Lord** Jesus who was the focal point of the entire sacrificial system. Everything pointed to Him, for He would be the perfect "Lamb of God, which taketh away the sin of the world" (John 1:29), it was He who would "save his people from their sins" (Matt. 1:21). It was, in fact, the OT **Passover** itself that pointed to "Christ our passover" (1 Cor. 5:7), whose "precious blood" is "as of a lamb without blemish and without spot" (1 Pet. 1:19).

What has happened to the old system? Hebrews 8:13 declares, "A new covenant, he hath made the **first** old. Now that which decayeth and waxeth old is ready to vanish away." Chapters 9 and 10 detail how the Mosaic system, from *symbols* to *sanctuaries* to *sacrifices*, vanished. In fact, that system began to decay when Israel rejected Christ (Luke 19:37–44) and finally disappeared with the destruction of the **temple** in AD 70. The Mosaic system was but a "*shadow* of good things to come" (Heb. 10:1, emphasis added), but Jesus is the *substance*.

Does all that mean there is no kind of **sacrifice** today? No, but all **sacrifice** we offer to God is *living*. No longer is there the *dead* **sacrifice** of the Old C**ovenant**, rather the *dynamic* **sacrifice** of the New. That's what Paul meant when he wrote, "Present your bodies a living sacrifice, holy, acceptable unto God" (Rom. 12:1) and what Peter referred to as he wrote to Christian Jews, As "[living] stones, [you] are built up a spiritual house, an holy priesthood, to offer up spiritual sacrifices, acceptable to God by Jesus Christ" (1 Pet. 2:5). Our entire lives now—all we do and say—are living sacrifices to God.

Scriptures for Study: Read the following verses, noting what kind of "spiritual sacrifice" each emphasizes: Romans 15:16, Ephesians 5:2, Philippians 4:10–18, Hebrews 13:15–16; Revelation 8:3.

Burnt Offering

'ōlāh

The **word** usually translated ***burnt offering*** in the OT is *'ōlāh* (5930). Interestingly, it is derived from a root (*'ālāh*, 5927) that while sometimes rendered "to burn," as in the burning of a **lamp** (Exod. 27:20), actually means "to go up, to ascend," or "to move from a lower place to an upper." Its first occurrence (Gen. 2:6) is most interesting, where were we read that in the Garden of Eden "there went up a mist from the earth, and watered the whole face of the ground." Other images include the flight of an eagle (Isa. 40:31, "mount up") and plants coming up (34:13, "come up").

The **burnt offering** is the first **offering** mentioned in the Levitical system (Lev. 1:3–17; cf. 6:8–13), no doubt because this type of **offering** is the first mentioned (excluding **Cain** and Abel's) in the biblical record (cf. Gen. 8:20; 22:2). The meaning in the Levitical system, of course, went deeper. Its purpose was "to make atonement" for the **sin** of the offerer (Lev. 1:4) and to demonstrate—as illustrated by the term "whole burnt offering" (Ps. 51:19)—his complete consecration, his total dedication to **God**.

All this demonstrates the true nature of the OT **burnt offering**, which we could even **call** the "ascending offering." As the flames consumed the animal, the offerer could watch the smoke and sparks ascend heavenward and **know** that God had accepted him as he identified himself with the sacrificed animal.

The first application we see in all this is in the **Lord** Jesus. His complete dedication is evident as He prayed in Gethsemane, "O my Father, if it be possible, let this cup pass from me: nevertheless not as I will, but as thou wilt" (Matt. 26:39). Knowing what lay ahead, namely, the ultimate **burnt offering** that He would become, our Lord was willing to be that **sacrifice** (vv. 39–44; cf. Phil. 2:5–11).

The second application is that this again illustrates for the NT believer that we each are a "living sacrifice" (Rom. 12:1), that all we do ascends heavenward to God. "By him therefore let us offer the sacrifice of praise to God continually, that is, the fruit of our lips giving thanks to his name" (Heb. 13:15).

Scriptures for Study: Read Hebrews 10:5–10, noting Christ's willingness to become the **burnt offering** for sin.

Grain Offering

minchāh

Also called the **meat offering** in the AV (as in the general sense of *food*, not the specific sense of *flesh*) and the **meal offering**, the **grain offering** (Lev. 2:1–16; cf. 6:14–18; 7:12, 13) was the only Levitical **offering** that did not involve **blood** (although for the extremely poor, the **sin offering** could also be of fine flour). The offering could be brought in a variety of forms: fine flour mixed with **oil** and frankincense (vv. 1, 2); cakes made of fine flour (with no **leaven**) mixed with oil and either baked in an oven (v. 4), on a griddle (v. 5), or in a covered pan (v. 7); or fresh heads of roasted grain, again mixed with oil and frankincense (vv. 14, 15). Its purpose was to remind the people that **God** gave them all their needs and therefore to motivate the offerer to express his thanksgiving and homage to God.

The Hebrew is *minchāh* (4503), which most OT scholars believe comes from the root verb *mnch*, "to give," and therefore refers to a gift or even tribute. In the general sense of a gift, it is used for Jacob giving "a present" (more of a bribe in reality) to Esau (Gen. 32:13–15). People also brought presents to Solomon when they came to listen to his great **wisdom** (1 Kings 10:25).

Its first occurrence, however, is actually theological (Gen. 4:3–5), where it is used for the offering both **Cain** and **Abel** brought to God (February 11). While Abel's presentation of his offering reflected true thanksgiving and homage, Cain's revealed his rebellion and self-sufficiency.

The emblems in this offering, therefore, are striking. Christ's perfect humanity is pictured in the absence of leaven, while the oil represents the Holy Spirit (cf. Luke 4:18; 1 John 2:20, 27). The frankincense added a special fragrance to the memorial part of the offering burned on the **altar** (cf. Exod. 30:34–38).

While this OT offering points us to Christ, as do all the offerings, it also challenges us to thanksgiving and homage. Not only does God give us all our physical needs (Matt. 6:25–33; Phil. 4:14–19), but He also gives "us richly *all things* to enjoy" (1 Tim. 6:17, emphasis added). What response should this motivate? "In every thing give thanks: for this is the will of God in Christ Jesus concerning you" (1 Thess. 5:18).

Scriptures for Study: What do the following verses say about giving thanks: Psalm 34:1; Ephesians 5:20; Colossians 3:17?

Peace Offering

šelem

In Leviticus 3:1–17 (cf. 7:11–36) we read about another Levitical **offering**, the **peace offering** (or **fellowship offering**). The Hebrew is *šelem* (8002), which is, of course, derived from the term *šālôm* (7965, January 13), meaning **peace** or "wholeness."

The **peace offering** first expressed not only the peace the worshipper had with **God**, but, second, that this peace actually resulted in *fellowship* with God. This fellowship is graphically indicated by the fact that this was the only **sacrifice** in which the worshipper shared, along with the **priest**, in a communal meal. This is further underscored by two other unique features: This was the only sacrifice for which a female animal was allowed and also the only sacrifice that did not have to be unblemished. Since the offering was primarily for food for the priest and offerer, such restrictions were unnecessary.

The application for the NT believer is a beautiful foreshadowing of the peace and fellowship we have with God through the **Lord** Jesus. Besides fellowship with God (1 John 1:3), the true Christian knows three types of peace that are beyond the comprehension of the unbeliever:

First, we have peace *from* God—the *source* of peace: "Grace to you and peace from God our Father, and the Lord Jesus Christ" (Rom. 1:7). "From" is the preposition *apo* (575G), which in the construction here is descriptive,[126] basically meaning the going forth or proceeding of one object from, by means of, or because of another. Peace doesn't come by **meditation** or mantras; it proceeds only from God.

Second, we have peace *with* God—the *security* of peace: "Therefore being justified by faith, we have peace with God through our Lord Jesus Christ" (Rom. 5:1). "With" is the Greek preposition *pros* (4314G), which in the construction here[127] speaks of concepts such as "toward, for the sake or purpose of, near, beside." No longer are we at **war** with God, but with Him in security.

Third, we have the peace *of* God—the *serenity* of peace: "The peace of God, which passeth all understanding, shall keep your hearts and minds through Christ Jesus" (Phil. 4:7). Here the English preposition "of" is understood in the construction of the Greek for "God,"[128] telling us that this peace belongs to God and that this same peace will **keep** (*phroureō*, 5432G, "to guard militarily") our minds and hearts.

Scriptures for Study: Read the following verses, noting what each says about the peace God has given us: John 14:27; Ephesians 2:12–18; Colossians 3:15. 📖 What kind of fellowship does Philippians 3:10 encourage us to have?

Trespass Offering

'āšām

We find one other major Levitical **offering** (Lev. 5:15–7:7; cf. 7:1–10), the **trespass offering** (also called "guilt," "reparation," or "compensation"). Like the **word** behind **sin offering** (April 16), the Hebrew here (*'āšām*, 817, "guilt, offense") is the word for *both* the offense and the **sacrifice** for the offense. Specifically, *'āšām* "is used where a sin, moral or ceremonial, has been committed through error, negligence, or ignorance."[129] Also like the sin offering, the **trespass offering** was also made to atone for sins committed unknowingly. Unlike the sin offering, however, which was offered when no restitution was possible, the **trespass offering** was offered when restitution *was* possible.

The **trespass offering** was required for two types of offenses: *First,* it was required for sins committed against "the holy things of the Lord" (Lev. 5:15). Such sins included: not paying a **tithe**, eating parts of the sacrifice that belonged to the priests, or failing to redeem the **firstborn**. Restitution involved paying a penalty equal to one-fifth of the value. *Second,* the **trespass offering** was required for sins committed against one's **neighbor** (6:1–7), such as fraud, robbery, and extortion. Restitution here also included a penalty of twenty percent (double tithe).

The pivotal characteristic of both these offerings is that unlike the other three, which were voluntary, these two were compulsory. This underscores that sin must be dealt with; it cannot be ignored. As we have noted in previous studies, sin is always the problem. While we might prefer to re-label sin as a "mistake, miscalculation, or misstep," we must **call** it what it is—*sin.*

Like the other offerings, the **trespass offering** provides an application for the NT believer. Since Christ is our once-for-all **trespass offering**—"And you, being dead in your sins and the uncircumcision of your flesh, hath he quickened together with him, having forgiven you all trespasses" (Col. 2:13)—we are now challenged to live a **life** that exemplifies Christ. While the Mosaic **Law** defined the *letter* of the law, passages such as Ephesians 4:24–32 display the *spirit* of the law and far exceed its limitations and legalism. Because we are made **new** in Christ, no longer do we lie, steal, cheat, or otherwise grieve the Spirit of **God** within us.

Scriptures for Study: Read Ephesians 4:24–32, noting the characteristics of the new **man**.

Altar

mizbēach

Integrally attached to the OT offerings was the **altar**, the raised structure on which **blood** was sprinkled and the fat of animals was burned. The Hebrew *mizbēach* (4196) is derived from *zāḇach* (2076), the **word** for **sacrifice** (April 18). *Mizbēach* appears about 400 times, about half of which are in the Pentateuch.

Early altars were made of earth and stone (Exod. 20:25), but **God** later commanded the people to **build** altars of better materials, such as wood and metal (27:1–8; 30:1–10). This impressed upon the people that they must **worship** in God's prescribed **way** and that such worship demanded quality. It's noteworthy that *mizbēach* is also used to refer to pagan altars, which must be torn down and destroyed (34:13).

One of the most vivid examples of an **altar** is the one on which Abraham placed his only son Isaac in readiness to sacrifice him according to God's command. (Isaac's place was taken by the ram that God provided [Gen. 22:1–19, January 10]). Here is, of course, the clearest OT picture of the future substitutionary **death** of the **Lord** Jesus Christ (Matt. 20:28; John 1:29; 2 Cor. 5:21).

So is there an **altar** today? Not in the strict sense, for the "final altar" was the cross (Heb. 13:10–13). Our **sin** was laid there and paid for once by Christ (10:10). *First,* we don't lay ourselves on an **altar** for ***salvation***, for Christ was the Lamb on that final **altar**.

Second, neither must we daily place ourselves on some supposed **altar** for *sanctification*, that is, "crucify ourselves daily" for holiness, as some misinterpret Romans 6:6: "Knowing this, that our old man is crucified with him, that the body of sin might be destroyed, that henceforth we should not serve sin." In fact, every verb tense in Romans 6 that refers to our identification with Christ in His death refers to that identification as having been *completed in the past.* Our "old man," therefore, "[*was*] crucified with [Christ]" so that now "we should not serve sin." *That* is sanctification (see September 27 for more on this subject). We can now live holy because Christ died on that final **altar**.

Scriptures for Study: Read Romans 6 and **rejoice** that you have been freed from the bondage, the control, of sin.

Atonement

kāpar

Woven into the very fabric of **Scripture**, and a key to **understanding** the OT concept of **forgiveness** of sin, is the **word** ***atonement***. The Hebrew is *kāpar* (3722), from which is derived *kippūr* (3725), as used in the **name** of the well-known Jewish feast *Yôm Kippūr* ("day" of "atonement" in Leviticus 16).

The root *kāpar*, as well as its Arabic equivalent, means "to cover over or pacify," but not in the sense of simply trying to conceal something. "It suggests the imposing of something to change its appearance or nature."[130] In Isaiah 28:18, for example, it refers to a **covenant** being "disannulled" (i.e., "written over"). It also appears in Genesis 6:14, where it is translated "pitch," a substance put over wood to make it waterproof, that is, to change the appearance and nature of the wood. To illustrate further, painters often paint over an existing picture they no longer want and **create** a **new** one. The old picture is still there, but has been covered over in such a **way** as to change its appearance.

This fundamental meaning tells us the true nature of OT **atonement**: It was a covering for **sin** not simply to conceal it but to change its appearance and nature. It didn't *remove* the sin totally, as Christ's **sacrifice** would do, but it did "paint over it." As mentioned earlier, that is exactly what it means in Genesis 6:14 (which actually is the very first occurrence of *kāpar*). While it's rendered "pitch," this is not the usual word for this bituminous substance. Moses' infant basket, for example, was waterproofed with "pitch," which is *zepet̲* (2203), what we think of today as "tar" (Exod. 2:3). "Whatever the exact nature of this pitch [in Genesis]," writes Henry Morris, "(probably a resinous substance of some kind, rather than a bituminous material), it sufficed as a perfect covering for the Ark, to keep out the waters of judgment, just as the blood of the Lamb provides a perfect atonement for the soul."[131]

So while "it is not possible that the blood of bulls and of goats should take away sins" (Heb. 10:4; cf. v. 10), which was only an **atonement**, our Lord's sacrifice on the cross did just that. "This man, after he had offered one sacrifice for sins for ever, sat down on the right hand of God" (10:12). While the OT priests never sat down, since the **work** of sacrifice was never complete, our Lord was the **Last** Lamb.

Scriptures for Study: Read the following verses, noting what Christ's sacrifice accomplished: 1 John 1:7; 2:1, 2; 4:10.

Scapegoat

'azā'zēl

The origin of *'azā'zēl* (5799) is uncertain. Some scholars think it combines the two Hebrew words *'ēz*, "goat," and *'āzal* (not used in the OT), "to send away," or *'āzēl*, "to go away." Others think it comes from the Arabic *'azāla*, "to banish" or "to remove." Whichever is correct, *'azā'zēl* is a vivid illustration of God's **forgiveness**, appearing only four times in the OT, all in Leviticus 16 (vv. 8, 10 [twice], 26). (The concept of a **scapegoat** [short for "escape-goat"] is still used today to refer to someone taking the blame for someone else.)

On the **Day** of Atonement (Yom Kippur), the most sacred day in the Jewish community, the high **priest** selected two unblemished goats, one of which he killed and sprinkled its **blood** on the **mercy** seat. He took the other, laid his hands on it, confessed the sins of the nation, and then sent it into the **wilderness**.

Some scholars speculate, based on certain Jewish interpreters, that *'azā'zēl* is actually the proper **name** Azazel, which probably referred to a demon. Since one goat was "for God," it is argued, the other was "released for Azazel." Such a pagan concept, however, based on the mythology of the OT pseudepigraphal ("false writings") *Book of Enoch*, is clearly unacceptable. Rather, the true picture of the **scapegoat** is that the sins of the people were carried away into the wilderness, never to be heard from again or held against them by God. "As far as the east is from the west," **David** writes, "so far hath [God] removed our transgressions from us" (Ps. 103:12).

As beautiful as that symbol was, however, it was still just that, a *symbol*. While it *pictured* taking away **sin**, it could not actually *perform* it. It would take something else to accomplish the miracle of taking away sin forever. What miracle? Isaiah alluded to it when he wrote, "And the LORD has laid on [Messiah] the iniquity of us all" (Isa. 53:6). Then, John the Baptist declared it openly on the day he saw Jesus approaching: "Behold the Lamb of God, which taketh away the sin of the world" (John 1:29). Our **Lord**, therefore, was not only the perfect *sacrificial lamb*, but He was also the perfect ***scapegoat***. He not only *redeemed* His people with His blood, but He also *removed* their sin forever.

Scriptures for Study: Read Isaiah 53:4–6, 9–12, noting what Messiah would accomplish. 🕮 What does 2 Corinthians 5:21 also declare about the Lord Jesus?

Passover

pāsach

No discussion of the OT offerings and sacrifices would be complete without an examination of **Passover**. Appearing only seven times, the Hebrew verb *pāsach* (6452) is actually quite ordinary, meaning "to leap, pass over, halt, limp," and perhaps even "to protect."[132] In the confrontation between Elijah and the prophets of Baal, for example, the prophets "leaped upon" the **altar** in their attempt to get their god to respond; this was undoubtedly some kind of ritual dance (1 Kings 18:26). Just before this (v. 21), Elijah had asked the people, "How long halt [i.e., dance or bounce back and forth] ye between [the] two opinions?" of **God** and Baal. It is also used of Mephibosheth, who at five years old fell and "became lame" (2 Sam. 4:4).

By far the most significant use of *pāsach* (and the derivative noun *pesach*, 6453) appears in Exodus, its first occurrence, in fact. We first read in Exodus 12:13, 23, and 27 that when God saw the **blood** properly placed on the door posts and lintel, He would "pass over" (or "leap over") that household and the plague of the **death** of the **firstborn** would not touch it. One authority suggests that in light of Isaiah 31:5—"As birds flying, so will the LORD of hosts defend Jerusalem; defending also he will deliver it; and passing over he will preserve it"—*pāsach* also carries the idea of "to defend or protect." At that first **Passover**, therefore, the **Lord** protectively covered the houses of the Israelites and would not allow the death **angel** to enter.[133]

The **Passover** is, indeed, the most vivid, dramatic, and powerful OT foreshadowing of the **atonement** the Lord Jesus would accomplish on the cross once for all (Heb. 10:10). No NT passage, therefore, is clearer than 1 Corinthians 5:7, 8: "Purge out therefore the old leaven, that ye may be a new lump, as ye are unleavened. For even Christ our p**assover** is sacrificed for us. Therefore let us keep the feast, not with old leaven, neither with the leaven of malice and wickedness; but with the unleavened bread of sincerity and truth." This declares not only the *reality* of the **Passover** Lamb, but the practical *result* of His atonement, namely, holiness of **life**. As the OT **Passover** clearly separated the godly from the pagans, God's NT people are saved to be holy (Eph. 1:4; 1 Pet. 1:15, 16) and separate from the world (2 Cor. 6.14–18).

Scriptures for Study: What does 1 Corinthians 5:9–11 **teach** about separation?

Wilderness

midbār

The most common Hebrew **word** translated **wilderness** is *midbār* (4057), which appears about 250 times. The literal idea, of course, is that of a desert, or other such uninhabited wasteland (Deut. 32:10; Job 38:26), such as the great Sinai **wilderness** (Deut. 2:7; cf. Exod. 19:1, 2; Lev. 7:38), or sometimes even vast pastureland (Joel 2:22; Ps. 65:12). Besides Sinai, many other tracts of **wilderness** are referred to including Beersheba (Gen. 21:14), Sin (Exod. 16:1; 17:1), Judah (Judg. 1:16; Ps. 63:1 title), Damascus (1 Kings 19:15), Shur (Exod. 15:22; 16:1), and Egypt (Ezek. 20:35).

The figurative ideas behind *midbār*, however, provide **deep** application. One of the concepts represented by **wilderness** is that of *trial and testing*. A dominant theme throughout the Pentateuch, for example, is Israel's presence in the **wilderness** on their **way** to the Promised Land. Deuteronomy 8:2, in fact, explicitly states that the desert was a place to prove whether Israel would **obey** God's **commandments**. Sadly, she repeatedly failed, from grumbling about food (Exod. 16:2, 3) and water (17:1–3), to her idolatry at Mount Sinai (Exod. 32), to her ultimate failure in "the wilderness of Paran, to Kadesh" (Num. 13:26; see Num. 13–14)), where the people were afraid to enter the Promised Land. This resulted in their having to wander in the **wilderness** for forty years, demonstrating that *judgment* is also represented by **wilderness**.

Two other ideas pictured in a **wilderness**, however, are positive, namely, *solitude* and *preparation*. **David** felt he could be at rest in the **wilderness** away from people (Ps. 55:6, 7) and had the opportunity to seek God early in the **morning** while in the **wilderness** (63:1). God took Moses into the **wilderness** to prepare him for what he would face (Exod. 2:15ff, Midian was located either in Arabia, east of the Gulf of Aqaba, or in the Sinai Peninsula). Likewise, John the Baptist was prepared in the **wilderness** (Matt. 3:1–4), and our **Lord** Himself spent forty days and nights in the **wilderness**, where he experienced all the above (4:1, 2). Further, on at least one other occasion He "withdrew himself into the wilderness, and prayed" (Luke 5:16).

Dear Christian **Friend**, even if you live in a city of a million people, you live in a **wilderness**—it is called the *world*. Your **faith** will be tried and tested every **day**, but God is using the trials and testing to prepare you and to prove He is there with you.

Scriptures for Study: What does Philippians 2:14 command? 📖 Read 2 Corinthians 11:23–30. Besides "perils in the wilderness," what else did Paul suffer, and what was his attitude?

Mountain

har

Mountains have throughout **time** been symbols. To the ancient Incas of Peru, for example, the gods of the **mountain** peaks governed wild plants and animals, crops, herds, waters, and people. Some of those beliefs still exist today **among** natives. Centuries earlier, peoples of Mesopotamia and Syria-Palestine worshipped the mountains. The pagan fertility god Baal, which is mentioned often in the OT, was viewed as living in "the high places of Baal" (Num. 22:41, *Bamoth-Ba'al*, 1116/1167), probably a mountaintop overlooking the plains of Moab (21:19, 20).

The usual Hebrew **word** for **mountain** is *har* (2022), which appears about 550 times, often with profound theological significance. Mountains symbolized several things, two of the most outstanding being a person's nearness to **God** and a place for receiving **truth**. Elijah, for example, prayed fervently for rain on top of Mount Carmel (1 Kings 18:41–46) and spent forty days on Mount Horeb (Sinai) getting refreshment and **strength** (1 Kings 19:8, 9). Abraham took Isaac to **worship** and **sacrifice** on Mount Moriah (Gen. 22), which would one **day** stand in the midst of Jerusalem, and where Solomon would **build** the **temple** (2 Chron. 3:1). Most dramatic of all, it was at Sinai that God revealed His **Law** (Exod. 19–20).

Indeed, the **majesty**, **power**, and sheer mass of mountains draw us to their heights like a magnet draws iron filings, whether we just want to drive through them on the highway or climb them on foot. Since New Zealand mountaineer Sir Edmund Hillary, for example, first reached the summit of Mount Everest in 1953 on the ninth British expedition, many more have followed, risking a terrible **death** just to stand on its 29,035-foot summit. But while such feats are exciting, no one lives at such an altitude or anywhere even close to it. Why? For many reasons, of course, such as paralyzing cold, little oxygen, and no food.

Similarly, some Christians today want to "live on the mountaintop." They are constantly seeking the next **new** revelation or emotional high. Such living, however, will always fail them in the end because the mountaintop simply cannot sustain them. Yes, it's **wonderful** to go up on the **mountain** for refreshment and renewal, but like those who did so in **Scripture**, one must always come back down. As we will study in the next few days, it is in the **valley** that we learn the greatest lessons and find what we need to sustain us.

Scriptures for Study: Read the following verses, noting in each how God is spoken of as being greater than the mountains: Psalm 90:2; Isaiah 40:12; Habakkuk 3:6; Deuteronomy 32:22; Job 9:5.

Valley of Achor (1)

'ēmeq 'aḵôr

A common Hebrew **word** denoting a **valley**, vale, or lowland is *'ēmeq* (6010). Unlike the mountaintop, it is in the **valley** that we really live, where we can **build** homes (Num. 14:25), grow food (1 Sam. 6:13), and pasture our animals (Ps. 65:13). Significantly, however, because we live in the **valley**, it is also there we learn the lessons of **life**.

One such lesson is illustrated by the **Valley of Achor** in Joshua 7, located in the Judean desert about a mile south of Jericho. It was actually a barren **wilderness** (Isa. 65:10), which is understandable as the story unfolds. During the conquest of Canaan, **God** told the people to **destroy** everything in Jericho, except **silver**, **gold**, iron, and bronze, which were to be brought into God's treasury. **Achan**, however, took some of the booty for himself, resulting in Israel's defeat at Ai, which resulted in the execution of Achan and his family in that **valley** (vv. 24, 26). **Achor** is *'aḵôr* (5911) and means "pain or trouble," as does the **name** Achan (*'āḵān*, 5912), which are truly the result of **sin**.

There are really two reasons for Israel's defeat at Ai: *First*, of course, it was because of Achan's sin. He disobeyed the direct command of God in Joshua 6:17–19. Of special note, however, are Achan's own words in 7:21: "When I saw among the spoils a goodly Babylonish garment, and two hundred shekels of silver, and a wedge of gold of fifty shekels weight, then I coveted them, and took them; and, behold, they are hid in the earth in the midst of my tent, and the silver under it." Do you see the four stages of sin? He *saw*, he *coveted*, he *took*, and he ***hid***. What he forgot, however, was, "Be sure your sin will find you out" (Num. 32:23).

Second, a point that is sometimes missed, is that the people were defeated also because they failed to consult God on the matter of Ai. As Joshua 7:2, 3 indicates, they relied solely on their own reconnaissance and decided that since Ai was small, it would be an easy conquest. Oh, how often that mistake is made today! We rely on our own **understanding** and perceived self-sufficiency. Tragically, we see this also in Christian ministry in the form of manmade methods.

Yes, we learn much by looking at the V**alley of Achor**. We will continue our look **tomorrow**.

Scriptures for Study: Read the stories of Eve's sin (Gen. 3:1–8) and David's sin (2 Sam. 11), noting the similarity of their steps to those that Achan took.

Valley of Achor (2)

'ēmeq 'akôr

Yesterday we considered the **Valley of Achor** (Josh. 7), the "valley of pain and trouble." We conclude today by noting that not only does its history demonstrate how **sin** subtly overtakes us, but it also shows us sin's results.

First, sin defeats us. As noted **yesterday**, Israel relied not on **God** but on her own **understanding** of the situation and so took only a small army of "about three thousand men" to Ai (v. 4). The result of that *attitude* of self-sufficiency, along with Achan's *action* of disobedience, was not only Israel's *defeat*—her men "fled before the men of Ai" (v. 4)—but also her *disgrace*, as the army of Ai "chased [her]" as she retreated (v. 5, 12). Indeed, sin destroys, dishonors, and debases us.

Second, sin hinders fellowship with God. As God Himself declared, "Neither will I be with you any more, except ye destroy the accursed from among you. Up, sanctify the people" (vv. 12, 13). **Accursed** appears six times in verses 11–15. The Hebrew is *chērem* (2764), which speaks here of "devoted to destruction." While Jericho itself was "accursed" (6:17–18), Israel had permitted that accursed thing to enter the **camp**, so God demanded that it be purged before she could **know** full fellowship again. While God "will never leave thee, nor forsake thee" (Heb. 13:5), and while the true believer does not *lose* fellowship with God, since such fellowship is part of **salvation** (1 John 1:3),[134] fellowship and communion are certainly *hindered* by **sin**.

Third, even with confession, the results of sin remain. While Achan admitted his sin (7:20, 21), he and his family were still put to **death** (vv. 23–25). While this might seem harsh to some today, it is a consistent principle. Even though God forgives us, the "wages of sin is death" (Rom. 6:23), which is why Jesus had to die for sin. While God can certainly forgive, each sin can still have consequences.

Fourth, sin affects others. Achan's sin affected his entire family (who were probably accomplices, see Deut. 24:16), as he led them astray into sin. Even his innocent livestock and possessions were destroyed (v. 24). One of Satan's most effective **lies** is reflected in the often-used phrase, "My sin only affects me." Families, churches, and entire nations are affected by the sin of individuals. Let us steer clear of the **Valley of Achor**.

Scriptures for Study: Read the following, noting what each says about sin: Jeremiah 17:9, 10; 23:24; Amos 9:3. 🕮 What is our provision for sin in those times it does overtake us (1 John 1:9)?

Valley of Berachah

ʿēmeq berāḵāh

A biblical **valley** that provides us with great encouragement is the **Valley of Berachah** (about six miles southwest of Bethlehem) referenced in 2 Chronicles 20. God's people find themselves once again in peril, this **time** from a horde comprised of Moabites, Ammonites, and others attacking from the northern and eastern coasts of the Red Sea (vv. 1–2). **King** Jehoshaphat, as he should have, turned to God, "proclaim[ing] a fast throughout all Judah" and encouraging the people "to seek the LORD" (vv. 3–4).

It is then in verse 15 that God, through His **prophet** Jahaziel, uttered the key words of the story: "Be not afraid nor dismayed by reason of this great multitude; for the battle is not yours, but God's." In the verses that follow, He commanded that they were simply to go into the **valley**, stand still, and not fight. When they did so the next **day**, God miraculously turned the enemy soldiers against one another and they slaughtered each other to the last man.

Verses 25–27 record the response of the people to what God had done. As they went down to collect the spoils of the battle, they "assembled themselves in the valley of Berachah; for there they blessed the LORD: therefore the name of the same place was called, The valley of Berachah." **Berachah** is a transliteration of the Hebrew *berāḵāh* (1294), a proper **name** from the feminine noun *berāḵāh* (1293), "blessing, the bestowment of favor." As one authority writes, "To bless in the OT means 'to endue with power for success, prosperity, fecundity, longevity, etc." (Mar. 9).[135] In the present context, then, blessing God's name takes the form of praising Him for what He has done (vv. 21, 22, 28).

In today's atmosphere of "self," we tend to think that we have to "do it all." We perceive a "need" and immediately found a new organization, invent a new method, or start a new ministry. Much of our apologetics is simply arguing the evidence instead of proclaiming the truth. It seems we just don't think God can accomplish His **work**.

Yes, He uses us, but He wants to use us *His* **way**, not ours. It has been said, when God's *people* do God's *work* in God's *way*, they will receive God's *results* in God's *time*. How thrilling it is to **trust** the **Lord** and His **Word**, and what blessing and **praise** result when we do!

Scriptures for Study: Read and meditate on Psalm 103 today. **Bless** appears five times and is the Hebrew *bārak̲* (1288), the root of *berāḵāh*, and means "to kneel, bless, praise, salute."

Valley of Vision

gay' chizzāyôn

The Hebrew *gay'* (1516) is another common **word** for **valley**. At times it also refers to a gorge or ravine with steep sides enclosing it, such as the Valley of Hinnom outside Jerusalem, where child **sacrifice** took place in Judah in her idolatrous days before captivity (Jer. 7:31, 32; 19:2; 32:35). The same Hebrew word for "valley" is also used in Psalm 23:4, which conjures up the picture of a dark, narrow gorge that hides dangers around every corner (June 8).

The **valley of vision** is mentioned only twice, both in the same passage (Isa. 22:1, 5)—"The burden of the valley of vision" (v. 1). This is an interesting valley because it's actually not a typical valley. While Jerusalem itself was built on several hills, it also was (and still is) surrounded by higher mountains. It is in relation to those mountains, therefore, that Jerusalem appears to be in a **valley**.

It is the word **vision**, however, that is the key to **understanding** the reference. This is the Hebrew *chizzāyôn* (2384, from the root *chāzāh*, 2372, "to see, behold, prophesy") and refers to a dream, **vision**, or revelation. **God** came to Abram, for example, in a **vision** (Gen. 15:1). Most of its nine occurrences, as here in Isaiah, speak of revelation or prophecy. Jerusalem, therefore, is the **valley of vision** because she is the center of prophetic activity.

Inseparably tied to this is the word **burden** (*maśśā'*, 4853, December 18), which literally refers to a **load** or weight (Exod. 23:5; Ps. 38:4) and figuratively speaks of a burdensome message that must be delivered. Isaiah's message was, indeed, a burdensome one of coming judgments (Isa. 13:1; 14:28; 15:1; 17:1; 19:1; Nah. 1:1; Hab. 1:1; Zech. 12:1; Mal. 1:1). God's people should have heeded the **vision**, should have listened and obeyed God's revelation. But, alas, they did not.

Herein **lies** a crucial truth. When many today see the word ***vision,*** they immediately interpret this to mean seeking God through dreams and other such "revelations." But the only place God has revealed Himself is in His Word. The only "vision" we need is what God has revealed in **Scripture**. It is that *alone* we need to see.

Scriptures for Study: Read all the often-quoted verse Proverbs 29:18 (**vision** is *chāzôn*, 2377, derived from *chāzāh*). Is this talking about "far-sighted thinking" or being "imaginative in ministry" as is commonly taught today? What really changes people's lives?

Tabernacle

'ōhel

Before Solomon built the **temple** in about 960 BC, the **tabernacle** was the center of the **worship** of **Jehovah** for God's people. The first area was the court, which was simply a fenced area measuring 150 feet long and 75 feet wide. The fence was seven-and-one-half feet high, consisting of fine linens that hung on hooks of **silver** attached to pillars of brass.

At the far end of the court stood the **tabernacle** itself (Exod. 25–31; 35–40). The Hebrew *'ōhel* (168), which means "tent," is used in this literal sense as the home of nomadic peoples, such as the patriarchs of Genesis (Gen. 4:20; 9:21; 13:5; 25:27), and soldiers (1 Sam. 17:54). It figuratively refers to a dwelling in general (Ps. 91:10; 132:3). So the **tabernacle** was an ornate tent, a dwelling place for God's presence **among** His people.

Measuring about forty-five feet long and fifteen feet both wide and high, the tabernacle's framework was made of acacia wood, and then roofed with four coverings: linen, goat's hair cloth, rams' skins dyed red, and badgers' skins. Inside were two chambers, the Holy Place for the first thirty feet and then the Holy of Holies in the final fifteen, separated by a veil made of blue, purple, and scarlet linen magnificently embroidered with cherubs. It was in the Holy of Holies that the **Ark of the Covenant** stood, and into which only the High **Priest** could go once a year on the **Day** of Atonement (Yom Kippur).

While many teachers explain what all the furnishings, materials, and even the colors represent, our main concern here is the *purpose* of the **tabernacle**: *to provide a dwelling place for God among His people*. It graciously provided a place where His people could come to commune with Him *personally* and worship Him *properly*. While ancient peoples viewed their temples as the dwelling place of their gods, the people of the One, True God understood that their God was not confined to that place, as He fills the entire universe (1 Kings 8:27; Isa. 66:1, 2),

What of the NT believer? "The Word was made flesh, and dwelt among us, (and we beheld his glory, the glory as of the only begotten of the Father,) full of grace and truth" (John 1:14). "Dwelt" is from the Greek *skēnoō* (4637G), which means "to encamp or pitch a tent" and is usually used in the Septuagint to translate *'ōhel*. And what is God's "tent" now? *You*.

Scriptures for Study: What do Hebrews 9:11 and 2 Corinthians 5:1 tell us about the present **tabernacle**?

Temple

hēyḵāl

The Hebrew behind **temple**, *hēyḵāl* (1964), does not in itself imply anything sacred. It refers simply to any palace or **temple** and is derived from the Akkadian *ekallu*, "large house." That background clearly appears in references to the palaces of Ahab (1 Kings 21:1), the **king** of Babylon (2 Kings 20:18), and the king of Nineveh (Nah. 2:6).

Like the **tabernacle**, but replacing its impermanence, the **temple** was the more permanent dwelling place of **God** for the sake of His people. This is underscored all the more by the hundreds of references to the "house of God" (e.g., Ezra 1:4; Neh. 6:10; Dan. 5:3) and the **house of the LORD** (e.g., Ezra 1:3; Isa. 66:20; Jer. 17:26) in the "holy city" of Jerusalem (Neh. 11:1; Matt. 4:5; Rev. 11:2).

As noted **yesterday**, while others might detail the furnishings of God's **house**, we want to emphasize here God's presence in that place. There is, in fact, a unique contrast between pagan temples and God's **temple**. While pagan temples had images and idols of their gods, a practice strictly forbidden by the Moral **Law** (Exod. 20:4–5) written in men's hearts (Rom. 2:15), all the architecture and furnishings in God's **temple** were simply reminders of His actual presence in that place. Therefore, "as we are the offspring of God, we ought not to think that the Godhead is like unto gold, or silver, or stone, graven by art and man's device" (Acts 17:29).

It's noteworthy that the Greek *naos* (3485G) is usually used to render *hēyḵāl* in the Septuagint. Unlike the general **word** for the **temple** area as a whole (*hieron*, 2411G), *naos* in ancient Greek (as far back as 1600 BC) was used of the innermost sanctuary or cell of a pagan **temple** where the **image** of gold was placed. Likewise, it refers to the "inner sanctuary," the Holy of Holies, in God's **temple**, as in the tearing of the veil to show that Christ's **death** had now given **man** access to that place (Matt. 27:51).

Like the **tabernacle**, then, what is God's **temple** now? *You.* Each believer is now "the temple of the Holy Ghost" (1 Cor. 6:19) and just as no Jew would knowingly do anything to damage or desecrate the **temple**, neither should we (vv. 12–20).

Scriptures for Study: What is the believer called in each of the following verses: Ephesians 2:21, Hebrews 3:6, and 1 Peter 2:5?

Tremble (1)

chārēḏ

In our study of the **tabernacle**, we referred to Isaiah 66:1, 2 in passing, but there is a truth there that deeply affects this writer and that is well worth our serious consideration in light of our modern **day**: "Thus saith the LORD, The heaven is my throne, and the earth is my footstool: where is the house that ye build unto me? and where is the place of my rest? For all those things hath mine hand made, and all those things have been, saith the LORD: but to this man will I look, even to him that is poor and of a contrite spirit, and trembleth at my word."

Does **God** demand magnificent structures, such as the breathtaking St. Paul's Cathedral in London, to **worship** Him? Not according to Isaiah, who in this chapter continues his prophecy concerning the glorious future. He begins, however, by contrasting the attitude of the true and faithful servant of God with the apostate and worldly character of most of the nation. He declares that there are only two places where God dwells: first in ***heaven*** and second in *the contrite **heart** of the person who trembles at His **Word***. God is not looking for a **temple** made of stone or sacrifices made without thought. He is concerned rather with what is in the heart, specifically, *our attitude toward His Word.*

Paul declared the same truth: "Wherefore, my beloved, as ye have always obeyed, not as in my presence only, but now much more in my absence, work out your own salvation with fear and trembling" (Phil. 2:12). To our shame, we see little, if any, **fear** and trembling in our churches. Oh, we see much excitement, activity, and other user-oriented attitudes, but *where is the trembling before God's Word?*

Trembleth is a translation of *chārēḏ* (2730), "to shake," from which are derived the ideas of trembling and fear. God told Gideon, for example, to limit the **number** of soldiers by observing who was afraid, which sent 22,000 back home (Judg. 7:3). In 1 Samuel 4:13, Eli sat "by the wayside watching: for his heart trembled for the ark of God," because the **Ark of the Covenant** was in danger of being captured by the Philistines.

As we continue these thoughts in coming days, let us each ask ourselves, "Do I tremble before God's Word? Do I have a **deep reverence** for God's revelation and a fear in my heart of disobeying it?"

Scriptures for Study: Read the following verses, noting the emphasis on trembling at God's Word: Ezra 9:4; 10:3; Ps.119:120.

Tremble (2)

chārēḏ

Continuing our consideration of "to this man will [the LORD] look, even to him that is poor and of a contrite spirit, and trembleth at my word" (Isa. 66:1, 2), we read another graphic example in Ezra 9. Many of the Israelites had again intermarried with pagans around them, in direct violation of God's **Law** (Deut. 7:2, 3). Such intermarriage would most certainly bring idolatry into the next generation. Ezra was deeply burdened and gathered around him the godly people who remained: "Then were assembled unto me every one that trembled at the words of the God of Israel, because of the transgression of those that had been carried away; and I sat astonished" (Ezra 9:4). Oh, would to God that we were astonished at sin! Would that we were appalled at those who claim to **love** God but disregard His clear **Word**!

Ezra writes again: "Now therefore let us make a covenant with our God to put away all the wives, and such as are born of them, according to the counsel of my lord, and of those that tremble at the commandment of our God; and let it be done according to the law" (10:3). Would that we would throw out what contradicts the Word of God, that which violates the principles and **precepts** of His Truth!

With all this in mind, what does it mean to tremble at God's Word? We would submit four principles:

First, to tremble at God's Word means to take His Word seriously, especially when it speaks of judgment. Many Christians simply do not tremble at God's Word. Many pastors do not teach them to do so. **Scripture** is often taken lightly, if it is even preached at all, and we certainly don't **want** to talk about judgment and **wrath**. "Oh, those subjects are Old Testament images," it is taught; "we want to hear about the Jesus of love, peace, and unity in the New Testament." Ignored by such false teachers, of course, are the numerous NT passages about God's wrath (e.g., Rom. 1:18; 2:5–16, 1 Thess. 1:10), not to mention the entire **book** of Revelation.

Second, to tremble at God's Word means to believe without doubt that Scripture says what it means and means what it says. We don't look at Scripture allegorically, mystically, or even figuratively unless the context clearly indicates it. Rather we look at exactly what it says and **know** that that is exactly what God means. We will continue these thoughts **tomorrow**.

Scriptures for Study: In Judges 3:20, what was the immediate response of even a heathen **king** at hearing that Ehud had a message from God for him?

Contrite [and] Trembleth (3)

dāḵāh [and] chārēḏ

What does it mean to tremble at God's **Word**? The *third* principle is that our **heart** is broken and **contrite** (Isa. 66:2) before the **Almighty God** of the universe. We humble ourselves before Him and **repent** of the **sin** of violating His Word. **Contrite** is *dāḵāh* (1794), literally "to crush, break in pieces, crouch," and therefore to be crushed emotionally and spiritually, as was **David** because of sin (Ps. 51:17).

Fourth, to tremble at God's Word means that our heart is tender to His Word, that we stand in absolute awe of it and are just waiting for what He has to say so we can do it without delay. Our **Lord** could not have been clearer when He declared, "If a man love me, he will keep my words. . . . He that loveth me not keepeth not my sayings" (John 14:23, 24).

Oh, how many people there are today who say they **love** God but have nothing to do with His Word; church for them is a place to have their needs addressed, to get what they want. If I may be so blunt, to think for a single moment that the church is a place to come for *me*—that is, what I can get—is arrogant and blasphemous! Nevertheless, countless people have bought into this philosophy of ministry and church-building.

No, what God is looking for is just one **man** or **woman** who will tremble at His Word. The church is the place for us to come and sit in humble anticipation of what His Word says. Our Lord says (in effect) without any ambiguity: *Those who love Me* ***keep*** *My words; those who do not love Me do not keep My words.* He declares in 14:21: "He that hath my commandments, and keepeth them, he it is that loveth me." The only **way** to **know** God, the only way to know the Lord Jesus, is through His Word. Jesus' words struck the apostle John so profoundly that not only does he quote them here in his gospel, but he builds upon them in his first epistle: "Whoso keepeth his word, in him verily is the love of God perfected: hereby know we that we are in him" (1 John 2:5). In other words, we know we are Christians, we have assurance of **salvation**, only if we keep God's Word. Mark it down: *No one loves God who does not love and tremble at His Word.*

Scriptures for Study: For the godly believer, what goes hand in hand with "trembling" (*rāʿaḏ*, 7460) in Psalm 2:11?

Trembleth (4)

chārēḏ

Before leaving this **word**, let us ask one more question: What frame of mind (or **heart**) is involved in trembling at God's Word? Let us prayerfully ponder three attitudes that produce such trembling:

First, **reverence** for God's Word. We must approach the Bible like no other literature. While we might be amazed by a clever twist in a mystery writer's story, such a thing fades to nothing in comparison with our reverence for **Scripture**. We come before it *quietly*, in abject *silence*, because we are in truth entering the **throne** room of God, hearing the very words of the Sovereign God of the universe. In contrast to the blasphemy, if we may be so blunt, of the "Christian comedian" so popular today, we are not dealing with things that are funny, rather the serious, holy things of God. The only **way** people will understand Scripture is by humbly and reverently coming before it, not guffawing at the comedian, or the pastor who doubles as entertainer.

Second, a desire to hear the Word read and preached. No better example exists than Nehemiah 8 (March 16), where the people stood for six hours while the **Law** was read and explained (v. 3). Oh, but not today! Many churches have to have pageants and plays, music concerts, motivational talks, and ten-minute devotionals that appeal to people's feelings and stroke their sensitivities. Such people (both preachers and pew-sitters) do not tremble at God's Word.

Third, submission to God's Word. We submit to its every command, not resist, argue against, or bring frivolous questions and objections before it. To tremble before God's Word means *we are submitted to whatever it declares before we even hear the declaration*. The real issue, in fact, is always biblical *authority* and *sufficiency*. Once that is settled, we will never get "hung up" on any other issue or get upset when a preacher tells us how we should live based upon Scripture.

Theologian John Walvoord well writes, "The yielded Christian has an unusual relationship to the Word of God. As its revelation becomes known and its application becomes evident, the issue of being yielded to the truth as made known by the Holy Spirit becomes very real."[136] Amen! And what is that "unusual relationship"? *He trembles before God's Word!* Sadly, that is so unusual, in fact, that it will appear very odd in today's world, even **among** some who call themselves Christians.

Scriptures for Study: Compare Ephesians 5:18 with Colossians 3:16. What is the key to "Spirit-filling"? 🕮 You might want to review our study of reverence back on March 4.

Prophet

nāḇiy'

There has for centuries been debate as to the meaning of the Hebrew noun *nāḇiy'* (5030). The older, out-of-date *Gesenius' Hebrew and Chaldee Lexicon* (1847), edited by Samuel Tregelles, theorized that *nāḇiy'* derives from the verb *nāba'*, "to boil up or bubble forth." The **prophet** then, it is argued, was one who entered an ecstatic state and "poured forth" the words of **God**. Most have rejected this, however, because it is more a pagan idea than biblical, as pagans often practiced ecstatic, uncontrolled speech.

A more recent suggestion is that *nāḇiy'* comes from the Akkadian root *nabû*, "to call," and therefore refers to one who is called by God to announce His words.[137] While uncertain, of course, this view does have the advantage of support in biblical usage. In its second occurrence, in fact, we read: "And the LORD said unto Moses, See, I have made thee a god to Pharaoh: and Aaron thy brother shall be thy prophet. Thou shalt speak all that I command thee" (Exod. 7:1, 2). A **prophet**, then, is called by God to act in His place and pass on His words. While **Scripture** does not record God's **call** of every **prophet**, it does record several using *nāḇiy'*, including: Jeremiah (1:5; cf. vv. 1–10), Ezekiel (2:5; cf. vv. 1–4), and Haggai (1:1–3, 12).

Significantly, the Septuagint almost always translates *nābî'* using the verb *prophēteuō* (4395G) or the noun *prophētēs* (4396G). Descended directly from the OT **prophet**, the NT **prophet** was one who, along with proclaiming truth already revealed (implied in Acts 13:1), also spoke *immediately* of the Holy Spirit, that is, speaking under the direct inspiration of the Holy Spirit.[138]

While there are teachers today who claim to be prophets, such claims are in error, often indicating extremely dangerous false teachers. Before the completion of Scripture, speaking immediately of the Holy Spirit was necessary, but God's **Word** is now final. The descendant of the **prophet** today is the "pastor and teacher" (Eph. 4:11), who speaks based on his careful study of Scripture and the illumination of the Holy Spirit.[139] He, too, has been called of God to **preach** His Word. Once called, he is tested for qualification (1 Tim. 3:1–7; Titus 1:5–9), trained in doctrine and practice (1 Tim. 3:6; 2 Tim. 2:2), ordained by other leaders (Acts 14:21–25; 1 Tim. 4:14; 5:22; Titus 1:5), and then sent forth by the church (Acts 13:2, 3). Let us **pray** for more such men.

Scriptures for Study: Note the precedent of God calling men to service: Matthew 4:18–22; 10:5; Luke 9:1, 2; Hebrews 5:4.

Priest

kōhēn

While the underlying root, and therefore origin, of the Hebrew *kōhēn* (3548) has been lost in antiquity, most of its more than 740 occurrences refer to the Levitical **priest**, the official mediator between **God** and His people. Only in a few instances is it rendered differently, such as "principal officer" (1 Kings 4:5) and "chief rulers" (2 Sam. 8:18; 20:26), or at times to pagan "priests" (e.g., Gen. 47:26; 1 Sam. 6:2; 2 Kings 10:19). More than one-third of its appearances are in the Pentateuch, with some 185 in Leviticus alone, which has led to that book's being dubbed the "manual of the priests."[140]

What is important to see is that the **priest** (and priesthood), like other elements of the old Levitical system (such as **sacrifice**, the various **offerings**, and the **Sabbath**), was part of the Mosaic **Law** given to racial Israel alone. A grave error invented and propagated by Roman Catholicism is that of the priesthood, which resembles paganism more than it does the OT priesthood.[141] The first-century church had no priests, and nowhere do we read that this is an office in the church. Pivotal is the fact that neither the Greek noun *hiereus* (2409G) nor the verb *hierateuō* (2407G)—the Septuagint equivalents of *kōhēn*—appear even once in the Epistles except in Hebrews. And why the mention there? To show "the priesthood being changed, there is made of necessity a change also of the law," and that Christ alone is now our "priest for ever after the order of Melchisedec" (7:12, 17).

In addition to the **Lord** Jesus as our High **Priest**, which is repeatedly emphasized in Hebrews (3:1; 4:14, 15; 5:10; 6:20; 7:26; 8:1; 9:11; 10:21), every believer is a member of "a royal priesthood" (1 Pet. 2:9); all of us are "kings and priests unto God" (Rev. 1:6). This is why, while only priests could enter God's presence in the **tabernacle** and **temple**, we all now have "boldness to enter into the holiest by the blood of Jesus, By a new and living way, which he hath consecrated for us, through the veil, that is to say, his flesh" (Heb. 10:19, 20). We need no earthly **priest** to mediate for us, because now "there is one God, and one mediator between God and men, the man Christ Jesus" (1 Tim. 2:5). We all have direct access to the Holy of Holies because Christ alone is our Mediator. Spend some **time** today thanking God for that access.

Scriptures for Study: Besides the **Scripture** cited today, also read Hebrews 7 to prepare for tomorrow's study of **Melchizedek**.

Melchizedek

malkî ṣeḏeq

In Genesis 14:18, Psalm 110:4, and then at length in Hebrews 5–7, we read about a **man** who is puzzling to many believers, **Melchizedek** (*malkiy-ṣeḏeq*, 4442; *Melchisedek*, 3198G). In keeping with the significance of names in the Semitic world, this **name** is formed from *melek*, "king" (January 28), and *ṣeḏeq*, "righteous" (January 16), and therefore means "righteous king" or "king of righteousness." While the precise *identity* of Melchizedek is unknown, his *significance* is unmistakable.

First, we see his *personage*. Melchizedek was the **king** of Salem, that is, ancient Jerusalem, as most Jewish scholarship has always maintained (cf. Ps. 76:2). While some teachers think that Hebrews 7:3 implies that Melchizedek was some mystical character who had no parents (leading to the possibility he was actually the pre-incarnate Christ), the rendering of the ancient Syriac Version of the NT (early second century) makes it clear that he did have parents: "whose father and mother are not written in the genealogies." Some ancient Arabic writers claim that his **father** was Peleg, the descendant of **Noah** through Shem, but that, of course, cannot be verified by **Scripture**. As we will see, in fact, there is a reason his parentage is unnamed.

Second, his *priesthood*. Here is the key to **understanding** Melchizedek. While the ancient world was permeated by paganism, there were some who worshipped the true, "most high **God**," which demonstrates that the knowledge Noah and his sons had of God had not died out. While the priesthood of Aaron had a physical lineage and was hereditary, Melchizedek's was not hereditary, which is why his parentage is not specified. Here we see, then, Melchizedek's priesthood existing before the Levitical system was even revealed, thereby pointing to something deeper, something beyond that temporary system, namely, the **Lord** Jesus Himself.

Third, his *permanence*. Not only was Aaron's priesthood (the Levitical system) interrupted at times, but ultimately it ended entirely, being fulfilled and replaced by the finished **work** of Christ. In the true sense, then, the priesthood of Christ was not directly connected with Aaron's, for while the Levitical system was temporary, the priesthood of Christ, which Melchizedek foreshadowed, is everlasting (Heb. 7:15–18).

The key **word** of Hebrews is *better* (appearing thirteen times), and Jesus is, indeed, a better ***hope*** (7:19; cf. 6:18; Titus 1:1), *testament* and ***covenant*** (Heb. 7:22; 8:6), *promise* (8:6), ***sacrifice*** (9:13—10:18), and, yes, a far better *priesthood*. Let us **rejoice** again in our Great High **Priest** and His eternal, once-for-all sacrifice for our **sin**.

Scriptures for Study: What contrast does John 1:17 make? 🕮 What does Romans 8:3, 4 declare?

Elder

zāqēn

The OT term **elder** is an important one because it is also a NT term. The Hebrew *zāqēn* (2204 and 2205, March 23), which is probably a derivative of *zāqān* (2206, "beard," e.g., 2 Sam. 20:9), basically means "old or aged," which in turn developed into the idea of an older person, as were Abraham and Sarah in the first OT occurrence (Gen. 18:11). The concepts of dignity, rank, and privilege also soon developed, as pictured by Saul bowing to Samuel (1 Sam. 28:14).

Most notably, *zāqēn*, then, referred to the group of men called the "elders of Israel" (Exod. 3:16; 18:12). While the origin of this office is unknown, we do **know** it existed outside of Israel (Num. 22:7), undoubtedly coming from the tribal concept in general. In Israel's early days, seventy such tribal leaders assisted Moses in ruling (Num. 11:16; Deut. 27:1), which led to this body being the decision-making body of the people, whether locally in a city (Judg. 8:14), regionally in a tribe (11:5), or nationally in all Israel (Exod. 3:16). They judged, disciplined, and guided.

Sadly, however, the elders of Israel did not always **lead** wisely or in a godly manner. Ezekiel, for example (Ezek. 8–9), describes how corrupt the elders had become, seeing them burning incense to the animal deities of the Canaanites (8:10–12). Worse, such corrupt leadership led the people into idolatry, as Ezekiel then saw women "weeping for Tammuz" (vv. 14), a Babylonian fertility god, whose descent into Hades in the summer caused the **death** of vegetation. Led by his mother, Ishtar, worshippers wept and mourned his death for forty days (the actual origin of "Lent"), bringing his **return** in the spring and the rains with him. (In truth, virtually all our Easter traditions are rooted in paganism.) The **worship** of these fertility gods was unspeakably vile, and the damage caused by corrupt leadership was (and is), indeed, incalculable.

Coming out of that OT office, **elder** is also in the NT. The Greek *presbuteros* (4245G, English "Presbyterian"), is used to refer to the *character* of this **man** who leads in the church, picturing age, maturity, and godliness. Two other terms that refer to this same man are "bishop," which refers to his *position* as leader, that is, a ruler and guardian, as well as "pastor," referring to his *duty*, which is primarily feeding God's people.[142] Like the OT **elder**, then, the responsibilities of the NT **elder** (or pastor or bishop) are enormous. Some churches have an elder governing board that often includes the pastor but also includes men of high standing in the church that have the ability to teach. Spend some **time** today praying for your elder(s).

Scriptures for Study: Read Acts 20:13–31, noting the serious duties of NT elders.

Minister

šāraṯ

The Hebrew verb *šāraṯ* (8334) means to **minister** or **serve**. Appearing almost 100 times, it speaks either of rendering service to an important person, such as a ruler, or serving **God** through **worship**, as did the Levitical priests. Its first appearance, for example, reflects that first idea, as Joseph "served" as an overseer of Potiphar's **house** (Gen. 39:4). Such a servant was on a higher plane than the usual slave or laborer (*'āḇaḏ*, 5647). He was in royal service in an important household (1 Kings 10:5) or in government, much as we speak today of someone in "public service" (1 Chron. 27:1; Esther 1:10).

It is that second type of service, however, that we find most often. It is, in fact, usually in the context of the **tabernacle** and **temple** that we find *šāraṯ* (or noun form *šārēṯ*, 8335) referring to the service of the priests and Levites (cf. Exod. 28:35, 43; 29:30; Num. 1:50; 3:6; Deut. 10:8; 1 Kings 8:11; 2 Chron. 5:14; Ezek. 40:46; 44:11–16.). While they offered the sacrifices, serving God by representing the people and being their mediator, the Levites were their aides, taking care of the practical matters such as provision, cleaning, music, and guarding the treasury.

It is also significant that the **word** usually used in the Septuagint to translate *šārēṯ* is the Greek *leitourgos* (3011G), which also speaks of both a public servant and a servant of God. The predominant idea of *leitourgos* (also *leitourgia*, 3009G, and *leitourgeō*, 3008G) in the NT, however, is that of "priestly service" to God in one way or another. Many people make comments such as, "Our minister takes care of this or that," implying that only those in full-time service are ministers. Yes, certain service is done by those in full-time ministry, as Paul ministered to the **Gentiles** through **preaching** the gospel (Rom. 15:16), for which he was specifically called and trained. Every single believer, however, is one who serves God, and is therefore a minister.

Serving others is one specific way these words indicate that we each do "priestly service." Romans 15:27 declares that we "minister unto [each other] in carnal things," that is, temporal needs. Likewise, the emphasis of 2 Corinthians 9:12 is on the **offering** Paul was taking for the poor **saints** in Jerusalem. God's people are also to meet the temporal needs of those who are in full-time service (Phil. 2:30; 1 Tim. 5:17, 18).

Scriptures for Study: In light of 2 Corinthians 9:12 above, what does Paul first emphasize in 8:14, 15? 🕮 How does this also compare with James 2:14–16?

Manna (1)

mān

One of this writer's favorite OT incidents appears in Exodus 16:1–35, where **God** miraculously feeds His people for forty years in the **wilderness**. This is all the more significant because He did this in spite of their rebellion and complaint. The most amazing thing about the story, however, is *what* God fed them and *how* He did it.

The key, of course, lies in the **word *manna*,** which is actually a simple transliteration of the Hebrew *mān* (4478). In other words, the word is not translated, that is, its actual meaning is not rendered, rather the letters of the word are simply given English equivalents. It is because of this that verse 15 sounds very odd. When the people woke up that first **morning** of the provision, they saw "a small round thing" lying on the ground (v. 14) and then said, "It is manna: for they [knew] not what it was" (v. 15) What? How could they call it something if they didn't **know** what it was?

The answer to the oddity, of course, is in the actual meaning of *mān*, which is, "What is it?" A literal translation, therefore, is: "And the sons of Israel see, and say one unto another, 'What is it?' for they have not known what it is."[143] Moses goes on to tell them all they need to know about it—"This is the bread which the LORD hath given you to eat" (v. 15)—and that is all we, too, need to know about God's provision. While skeptics have tried to explain the **manna** by natural means, such as lichen growing on rocks or insect-excreted granules on tamarisk thickets, such unbelief rebels against the thought of God's supernatural provision.

The NT significance of **manna** is striking. We find the word five times, where it is again simply transliterated (*manna*, 3131G, for *mān*). Most significantly, after the Jews asked Jesus for a **sign** to prove He was who He claimed to be, even citing the **manna** incident as an example of what they wanted, He answered, "Moses gave you not that bread from heaven; but my Father giveth you the true bread from heaven. For the bread of God is he which cometh down from heaven, and giveth life unto the world" (John 6:32–33). Contrasting Moses with Himself, Jesus says that while the **manna** (and the entire Mosaic system) had to be provided and administered daily, Jesus is the true "bread from heaven" that satisfies forever.

Scriptures for Study: What does the rest of that John passage go on to say about Jesus (vv. 34–58)?

Manna (2)

mān

God's miraculous feeding of His people in the **wilderness** (Exod. 16:1–35) is more than just a *story*. It is, in fact, a *promise:* **God** provides for His people. Let us conclude our look at **manna**, by considering seven principles:

First, the *place* of the provision was "the wilderness of Sin" ("Sin" referring to the region of Sinai), where they "murmured against Moses" (vv. 1–2), graphically demonstrating their character. Incredibly, only a month after their miraculous deliverance from Egypt, they had already forgotten the bondage, beatings, and barrenness of their existence there and now longed for its "flesh pots" (luxuries, v. 3). How often do we think the world has something to offer?

Second, the *puzzlement* of the provision was again that question, "What is it?" One of the greatest joys of enjoying God's provision is not knowing what form it will take or where it will come from.

Third, the *person* of the provision was God alone (v. 15). We are sometimes tempted to think our salary is our provision, or that our IRA or 401(k) is our future provision, but those can be gone in a flash (or crash). God is the *true* source. As Paul asked, "What hast thou that thou didst not receive?" (1 Cor. 4:7).

Fourth, the *presentation* of the provision was that it came with (perhaps even from) the early **morning** dew and was lying on the ground. This required the people to humble themselves by stooping down to pick it up (Exod. 16:14) and to do it quickly before it was gone (v. 21). Instead of uttering common phrases as, "I am a self-made man," or, "I built this company from nothing," let us humble ourselves before God's sovereign, gracious provision before the opportunity passes.

Fifth, the *proviso* of the provision was to take only what was needed and not try to save some (vv. 16–19), emphasizing living by **faith** daily. Sadly, some of the people still tried (v. 20), and how often we also doubt!

Sixth, the *purpose* of the provision was not primarily to meet man's needs, a common attitude today, but to declare God's glory. "The glory of the LORD appeared in the cloud" (v. 10), and He commanded a **Sabbath** for rest and **worship** (v. 23).

Seventh, the *permanence* of the provision was that as long as it was needed, in this case forty years (v. 35), God's provision was always there. Should we ever doubt?

Scriptures for Study: Note God's promise of provision in each of the following: Deuteronomy 8:3 (Matt. 4:4); Psalm 23:1–5; Matthew 6:25–34; Philippians 4:19.

Death

mûṯ

The **word** generally used in the OT for **death** or dying, occurring about 800 times, is *mûṯ* (4191), which appears in all Semitic languages. The Canaanites (some of whom wrote and spoke in a language known as Ugaritic) even employed it in the **name** *Mot,* the god of **death** and the slime and filth of the netherworld. It speaks of natural **death** (Gen. 5:5, first occurrence; 25:8), putting someone to **death** through **war** or judicial execution (Josh. 10:26), and so forth.

It is also used in the figurative sense of the **death** of land (Gen. 47:19) or even **wisdom** (Job 12:2). An interesting metaphorical use occurs in 1 Samuel 25:37, 38, where Nabal's "heart died within him," indicating that when Abigail told him about her interceding for him with **David**, he was so overcome that he had a stroke and was paralyzed (figuratively died) until he literally died.

The key to understanding **death** biblically, however, is that it was not God's original intention. **Death**, in fact, did not exist in the original creation. God told **Adam** that in the day he partook of the forbidden fruit, he would *then* "surely die" (Gen. 2:17). This underscores like nothing else that, while God's intention for His Creation was unending **life** through obedience, **death** was the inevitable (and demanded) result of man's disobedience. With that one single sin, Adam died spiritually and also began to die (along with all Creation) physically. All Creation, in fact, "groaneth and travaileth in pain" as does a **woman** in childbirth (Rom. 8:22).

While this truth has been challenged several times by such heretics as Pelagius, Cassianus, and Arminius, as well as several in our own **day**, the extent of man's **death** at the Fall was complete (Eph. 2:1–3; Rom. 3:10–12). Why did Adam die spiritually? Because He disobeyed God, thereby violating God's own holiness. Tragically, many today believe that **love** is the supreme characteristic of God, but that is a fatal mistake. It is God's holiness that is supreme (January 25), and therefore, "The soul that sinneth, it shall die" (Ezek. 18:4, 20; also Rom. 6:23).

The "social gospel" of our day (the idea that our goal ought to be reforming society and solving social ills) is one of Satan's most brilliant, devious, and successful **lies**. Spiritual **death**—that is, separation from God—is the result of **sin** (April 1, 2). Only in Christ is there **salvation** (April 3).

Scriptures for Study: Read Romans 5:12–21. How did sin enter the world? 🕮 Whom does sin reign over? 🕮 What is the only answer to the offense of sin?

Hell

še'ôl

The Hebrew *še'ôl* (7585) is sometimes misunderstood. At least part of the reason for this stems from how it was treated in the original English Revised Version (1881) and therefore by several modern translations. While the AV is not perfect, one Hebrew authority observes that at least it variously translates *še'ôl* as "the grave," **hell**, and "the pit," while "the RV has unfortunately put *še'ôl* in the OT, and *hades* [86G] in the NT."[144] In other words, some modern translations have simply transliterated the words, thereby causing confusion as to what *še'ôl* refers.

In Psalm 9:17, for example, the AV and NKJV rightly read, "The wicked shall be turned into hell, and all the nations that forget God," **hell** being the place of eternal punishment. In contrast, some modern translations (e.g., ESV, NASB) read "Sheol," which is ambiguous. (Worse, the NIV seriously errs with "grave."[145])

While its original meaning is uncertain, *še'ôl* is used first to refer to the grave, that is, **death** itself. In its first occurrence, for example, Jacob is inconsolable over what he thinks has been Joseph's death: "I will go down into the grave unto my son mourning" (Gen. 37:35; cf. Job 21:13; Ps. 30:3). Most such verses, in fact, are poetic, making it possible "that *še'ôl* is just a poetic synonym for *qeber* which is used seventy-one times for 'grave' (and the verb *qābar* is used all 132 times for 'bury')."[146]

The second use of *še'ôl* seems to be that of the place for the wicked after death. Besides Psalm 9:17, we read that fornicators and adulterers "are in the depths of hell" (Prov. 9:18; cf. Rev. 21:8); "Drought and heat consume the snow waters: so doth the grave those which have sinned" (Job 24:19); and **Satan** himself is consigned to this place (Isa. 14:12–15; cf. Rev. 20:10).

While the OT mentions the reality of **hell** infrequently, the NT dispels any ambiguity. Using the words *hades* and *gehenna* (1067G)—the latter transliterates *gay-hinnōm* (1516/2011), a **valley** outside Jerusalem known for the grossest of idolatrous practices—**hell** is a place of "torment" (Luke 16:28), "everlasting fire" (Matt. 25:41; cf. Mark 9:44; Rev. 21:8), "outer darkness," "weeping," and agony (Matt. 8:12), from which there is "no rest day nor night" (Rev. 14:11).

While some today believe that **hell** is nothing more than a "low self-esteem," **hell** is a literal place, a place we proclaim to the lost as their end if they reject Christ.

Scriptures for Study: Read the verses cited today and be encouraged to be a **witness** for Christ, warning people of what is to come.

Life (To Live)

chāyāh

Today's word is a stark contrast to yesterday's (**death**). The verb *chāyāh* (2421), which has equivalents in other Semitic languages (except Akkadian) and appears about 270 times, means "to live, be alive, remain alive," and even, as we will see, "revive from sickness, discouragement, or death." **Life** is always a **good** thing, the OT reveals. A vivid illustration is in Ecclesiastes 9:4: "For to him that is joined to all the living there is hope: for a living dog is better than a dead lion." In other words, as long as there is **life**, there is **hope**, for as a **lion** was the most honored beast in that **day** and the **dog** the most despised, the live dog is better off in still having hope.

In the Psalms, especially 119, *chāyāh* is often rendered "quicken" or "quickened" in the AV. In Psalm 119:25, for example, **David** prays, "Quicken thou me according to thy word." While some modern translations reflect the basic meanings "live" and "be alive," as in "preserve my life" (NIV) and "give me life" (ESV), such renderings miss the true point. This **word** also speaks of reviving someone, as in reviving them from sickness or discouragement, and it is that idea in view in David's **prayer**. Only **God** can revive us from despair. It will not come from self-determination, will power, psychological technique, or clever cliché. It will come only from God's Word working in our **heart** and mind. Further, as *chāyāh* is used in several ways—to show that an object is safe (Num. 14:38), to indicate that something is reviving (Ezek. 37:5), and to demonstrate that something is flourishing (Ps. 22:26)—the Word of God, therefore, *brings* **life**, *sustains* **life**, and *is* our **life**.

We are reminded here of God's promise in Hebrews 13:5: "I will never leave thee, nor forsake thee." This is a quotation of Deuteronomy 31:6: "Be strong and of a good courage, fear not, nor be afraid of them: for the Lord thy God, he it is that doth go with thee; he will not fail thee, nor forsake thee." We are never alone because (1) the Holy Spirit dwells *in* us, and (2) we also always have God's Word *with* us. Whenever we faint in *despair*, **wither** in *depression*, or collapse in *despondency*, the Word of God is always there to revive us.

Scriptures for Study: Read 2 Corinthians 4:7–10. What four contrasts does Paul offer to demonstrate the true encouragement we have from God?

Heaven (1)

šāmayim

The Hebrew behind **heaven** in some 420 occurrences is *šāmayim* (8064), but can be translated as a singular or plural depending upon the context. Genesis 1:1, for example, is better rendered "heavens," while it is best to say that snow falls from **heaven** (Isa. 55:10). Equivalents are found in several Semitic languages, such as the Akkadian (*shamû*), Aramaic, and Arabic. This **word** is used in the OT to speak of no less than four areas that constitute "the heavens." (Similarly, about one-third of the 282 NT instances of the Greek *ouranos* [3772G] are plural.)

First, it is used for what we usually mean when we say "sky," that is, where the birds fly (Gen. 1:20; Deut. 4:17; Matt. 6:26), high above the ground but below the heavenly bodies. *Second,* it refers to the "upper atmosphere," from whence come clouds (Judg. 5:4; 1 Kings 18:45; Matt. 24:30), rain (Gen. 8:2; 1 Kings 18:45; Isa. 55:10; James 5:18), snow (Isa. 55:10), hail (Josh. 10:11), dew (Deut. 33:13), and frost (Job 38:29). *Third,* it speaks of "outer space," where the **sun**, **moon**, and stars are (Gen. 1:14; cf. 15:5; Judg. 5:20; Heb. 11:12). Psalm 104:2 graphically pictures the beauty and vastness of space, where the "heavens" are stretched out "like a curtain." *Fourth,* it denotes the dwelling place of **God**, as He "sitteth in the heavens" (Ps. 2:4) and "is the LORD [*Yāhweh*] . . . God [*'Elōhiym*] in heaven above" (Deut. 4:39; cf. 10:14; 26:15).

While God dwells in **heaven**, however, He is not limited to that place, nor can it, or the rest of Creation, contain Him (1 Kings 8:27). While we marvel at the vastness of the universe, the unnumbered stars—astronomers estimate there are ten trillion trillion stars—God not only *created* them (Ps. 8:3; 33:6; Amos 5:8), but He also *numbered* them (Isa. 40:26; Ps. 147:4) and even *named* them (147:4).

While the so-called scientific community prefers to believe the nonsensical notion of the "Big Bang," from whence the elementary particles of the universe supposedly sprang and then evolved into all the complex systems that now exist, **Scripture** states simply, "The heavens declare the glory of God; and the firmament sheweth his handywork" (Ps. 19:1), "and the heavens shall declare his righteousness" (Ps. 50:6). While these things are not to be worshipped (Exod. 20:4; Jer. 44:17–25), all we have to do to "see God" is to look up.

Scriptures for Study: Read and meditate on God's glory through natural revelation in Psalm 19:1–6 (cf. Rom. 1:20).

Heaven (2)

šāmayim

While "ideas of eternal life in the OT have been difficult to address," writes one OT scholar, "it is enough to point out that the OT view of **God** itself decreed the survival of those who trusted in him."[147] Similarly, while OT references to **heaven** as the abode of believers are sparse, there are allusions to it. As God promised through Isaiah, "For, behold, I create new heavens and a new earth: and the former shall not be remembered, nor come into mind" (Isa. 65:17; cf. 66:22; 2 Pet. 3:13; Rev. 21:1), clearly implying that God's people will live with Him in a totally recreated universe.

The NT, of course, is much clearer about the believer's future place of rest. At the same time, however, a question has arisen whether **heaven** is a *real place* or just a *state of mind*. While liberal theology has always denied **heaven** as a literal place, it is sad that even some evangelicals are hesitant to speak of **heaven** as a place. Clearly, however, our **Lord** ascended "into" a place called "heaven" (Acts 1:11), Stephen "looked up stedfastly into heaven [a place]" and saw "the heavens opened" (7:55, 56), and our Lord with no ambiguity declared, "I go to prepare a place for you" and "will come again, and receive you unto myself; that where I am, there ye may be also" (John 14:2, 3). Further, it certainly appears that Paul's being "caught up into paradise" refers to a real place (2 Cor. 12:1–9).

Believers, therefore, have a future (and even present) place in **heaven**. We are citizens of **heaven** right now (Phil. 3:20 "conversation" is *politeuma*, 4175G, "citizenship"), with our names already written there (Luke 10:20), and we have "a building of God, an house not made with hands, eternal in the heavens" (2 Cor. 5:1). It is there we will be perfectly conformed to Christ's **image** (Phil. 3:21; 1 John 3:1–3), and it is there we will remain for eternity (1 Thess. 4:16, 17).

What, then, will we do in **heaven**? Looking at Christianity today, one would think that **heaven** will be filled with entertainment, for that is the foundation of many churches. No, **heaven** will primarily be a place of *adoring* ***worship*** (Rev. 19:1), as well as a place of *abundant* ***life*** (1 Tim. 4:8), a place of *absolute holiness* (Rev. 21:27), a place of *active service* (Rev. 22:3), and a place of *assured rest* (Rev. 14:13). Are you preparing for that today?

Scriptures for Study: Meditate today on Psalm 73:24–26. Is that your desire?

Star

kôḵāḇ

A **friend** once invited me to look at the Orion nebula through his telescope, an act that hooked me forever on stargazing. I have since spent countless hours observing the heavens through telescopes and wide-angle binoculars. A **star** is a marvel of Creation. It is a ball of mostly hydrogen, held together by its own massive gravity. With a core the temperature of millions of degrees, a **star** releases an incomprehensible amount of energy by the nuclear fusion of hydrogen into helium.

Our **sun**, for example, is such a **star**, having a diameter of about 865,000 miles and a mass about 332,000 times that of the earth. It releases an estimated 70,000 horsepower per square *yard* of its surface and has a radiance of about 1,500,000 candlepower per square *inch*. Of the estimated ten trillion trillion stars, however, our sun is actually quite average. While it is a "yellow star" (spectral type G2) with a temperature of about 9,000 degrees (F) at the surface, "blue stars," such as Rigel (in the constellation Orion, type B8), are 50,000 degrees and above. As for size, Antares, for example, is so large that if it were in our solar system, it would encompass the orbit of Mars (obviously engulfing the earth).

While some astronomers declare with dogmatic authority that stars are "born in stellar nurseries called nebulae," that is in reality total speculation, since such a birth has never been observed. Some scientists accuse Creationists of "blind faith," but without evidence there is only theory, not **proved** science. **Scripture** not only declares that **God** made the stars, but it also mentions stellar objects by **name**. Job 9:9 names Arcturus (in Boötes), a star twenty-five times the size of our sun and the third brightest in the sky (also 38:32); Orion (also see 38:31; Amos 5:8); and the Pleiades (in Taurus), an "open star cluster."

The Hebrew *kôḵāḇ* (3556) appears about thirty-seven times (with the "morning stars" of Job 38:7 referring to angels or possibly Venus and Mercury [cf. 3:9]). Ancient pagans (as well as idolatrous Israel) worshipped the stars (Deut. 4:19), and astrologers have studied their movements for guidance (Isa. 47:13). (Even the educated evolutionist is really not much superior to such primitives.) God gave the stars for no such purpose, and no *true* stargazer can look heavenward without God's glory (Ps. 148:3) in mind.

Scriptures for Study: Read Genesis 1:16–19. Besides His glory, why did God **create** the stars? On what **day** did He create them? Can you explain why there was already **light** (v. 3)? We will explain **tomorrow**.

Light

'ôr

Psalm 119:105 is one of those gems of **Scripture** that shines with such brilliance that we are drawn to it often: "Thy word is a lamp unto my feet, and a light unto my path." There are two words here that capture our attention: **light** and **lamp**.

Light is *'ôr* (216), which is also found in Akkadian and Canaanite and refers to the actual **light** that has a source such as the **sun** (the "greater light"), the **moon** (the "lesser light"), and the "stars also" (Gen. 1:16; cf. Ps. 136:7; 148:3). **Light** was already present in verse 3 of Creation, however, for **God** Himself is **light** (1 John 1:5) and wears **light** as a garment (Ps. 104:2; Hab. 3:3, 4). Significantly, **light** "is always used as a positive symbol, such as for good fortune (Job 30:26), victory (Mic. 7:8, 9), justice and righteousness (Isa. 59:9), guidance (Psa. 119:105), and a bearer of deliverance (Isa. 49:6)."[148]

A graphic illustration is the Reformation, which brought **light** into a world that had been dominated by darkness for a thousand years. The reformers proclaimed the **light** of the gospel. While the Reformation was certainly not perfect, it did bring back the truth of **salvation** that had been lost for centuries.

David later writes in Psalm 119: "The entrance of thy words giveth light" (v. 130). Just as the entrance of **light** illuminates a room when the shades are opened, so does the **Word** of God shine into the **heart** of the believer. Two of the prominent ideas in the Hebrew are *direction,* which is illustrated by the pillar of fire that was a **light** for the wandering Israelites (Exod. 13:21), and *instruction,* as illustrated often in Scripture.

Proverbs 6:23 declares, "For the commandment is a lamp; and the law is light; and reproofs of instruction are the way of life," which deals specifically with parents' instruction. In Psalm 19:8, we also read that "the commandment of the LORD is pure, enlightening the eyes." Each of us is challenged, therefore, as was Israel, to "walk in the light of the LORD" (Isa. 2:5), for the purpose of His Word is to be "a light of the people" (51:4).

Scriptures for Study: What is the **light** referred to in John 1:7–9? 🕮 What, then, is our **light** according to 2 Peter 1:19?

Lamp

niyr

What a picture Psalm 119:105 paints for us! "Thy word is a lamp unto my feet, and a light unto my path." In view of our study of **light** yesterday, we can here picture a lone traveler walking in a forbidding **wilderness** engulfed in darkness. In his **hand**, however, he holds up a **lamp**. While its actual candlepower is quite modest, in contrast to the surrounding blackness it blazes like a tiny **sun** and can be seen by an observer who stands far in the distance. Our traveler does indeed have ample light to illuminate his **way** down the unfamiliar path.

So while **light** refers to light *itself*, not the *source* of the light, **David** still illustrates with a **lamp** because light does have a source. The light of which he speaks is not something mystical, ethereal, or theoretical. It is real and practical and has a literal source. David declares, then, that God's **Word** is the **lamp** that lights his path through this forbidding world. What kind of **lamp** does he picture? The Hebrew *niyr* (5216) refers to the small, bowl-shaped **lamp** that operated with a wick fed by **oil**. Such lamps took on various shapes as the centuries passed. What is the application for us, however, thousands of years later? Let us ponder a few types of "lamps" in our **day**.

The Bible is a *reading* **lamp**, with which we can read the very thoughts of God in the quiet hours. It is a *miner's* **lamp**, which illuminates the darkest places in the pit but also reveals the gems buried there. It is a *safety* **lamp**, which, like the one used by miners many years ago that **prevented** the **lamp** flame from igniting dangerous gases, protects us from the unseen dangers lurking around us. It is the *lighthouse* **lamp**, which lights the shore and reveals the rocks of ruin that await.[149] It is a *hurricane* **lamp**, which like its namesake can never be blown out no matter how strong the wind. It is a *street* **lamp**, which illuminates the shadows of the **night** and reveals enemies that hide there. And it is the *hand* **lamp**, the simple flashlight, that we can easily carry and point in any needed direction.

Dear Christian **Friend**, are you ever without your **lamp**?

Scriptures for Study: What is David's encouragement in Psalm 18:28? 📖 What is called a **lamp** in Proverbs 6:23?

Snare

pach

In view of the words **light** and **lamp** in Psalm 119:105, five verses later **David** mentions a specific item that light reveals: "The wicked have laid a snare for me" (v. 110; also v. 85; 140:5; 142:3). **Snare** is *pach* (6341), which is used literally of a **snare** for trapping birds (Ps. 91:3; 124:7; Prov. 7:23; Eccles. 9:12; Amos 3:5), but usually as a metaphor for moral and spiritual danger.

What immediately comes to mind whenever I encounter this **word** are the booby traps used by the Viet Cong in the Vietnam War. One of the most infamous was the "punji pit." Sharpened bamboo sticks were placed in pits that were then concealed under a mat with a covering of dirt and vegetation. Even more diabolic was coating the tips of punji sticks with poison, or even human excrement, to greatly increase **blood** poisoning. The "whip" was a larger piece of bamboo bent tight and wedged in place; when a trip wire released it, the spikes imbedded in it would impale the victim. Other trapping methods were also used by the Viet Cong.

We note those snare examples because, as David says, "The wicked have laid a snare." How we need to see this! Each one of those examples involved camouflage, making the danger blend in with the surroundings. Likewise, **Satan** hides the danger when he sets the **snare** for us and even sets it where we normally travel. Thankfully, however, just as a **good** squad leader, platoon sergeant, or other trainer would **teach** his men how to avoid such things, the **precepts** of God's Word, as David goes on to **write**, are what illuminate the far more devastating *spiritual* booby traps the wicked so diabolically set. Further, as those trained soldiers are careful not to stray from their training and multiple warnings, we must not stray from God's precepts.

Scriptures for Study: Read Psalm 124, another **psalm** of David. Who was on Israel's side? What would have happened otherwise? What was the final outcome?

Heritage (Inheritance)

nāchal

The verb *nāchal* (5157) means "to receive, to take property as a permanent possession, usually as the result of succession." Appearing some sixty times in the OT, its first occurrence is in Exodus 23:30, where **God** promises to drive the Canaanites from the land of promise, enabling His people to "be increased, and inherit the land." Interestingly, two verses before, God promised to send "hornets" to aid in this task. This divine judgment could refer to literal hornets, but could possibly be figurative language for the Egyptians, as they raided Canaan regularly and the **word** for *hornet* (*ṣir'āh*, or *zirāh*, 6880) is similar to the one for Egyptians (*miṣrayim*, 4714). We also find *nāchal* several times in Joshua (1:6; 11:23; 13:6, 7, 33; 19:9;).

A **wonderful** occurrence of *nāchal* is in Psalm 119:111: "Thy testimonies have I taken as an heritage for ever," or more literally, "I have inherited Thy testimonies." While we might get really happy when someone does leave us something valuable in their will, that is merely temporal. God's Word is the greatest **inheritance** we possess. Do we truly grasp that truth? Nothing, absolutely *nothing*, equals the value of the Word of God.

It is extremely significant that the Septuagint often translates *nāchal* as the Greek *klēronomia* (2817G), or a similar form. The NT repeatedly speaks of the **inheritance** we have as believers. There is no better place to see this emphasis, in fact, than in Ephesians 1. As the Urim and Thummim were used in the OT to discover God's will (e.g., Num. 27:21; 1 Chron. 24:5, 6) and to divide land (1 Chron. 6:54–81), the same idea is found in Classical Greek, as lots were drawn to discover the will of the gods. The root *klēros* (2819G), in fact, referred to "the fragment of stone or piece of wood which was used as a **lot** (December 22). Paul, therefore, tells us in Ephesians 1:11, "In whom also we have obtained an inheritance, being predestinated according to the purpose of him who worketh all things after the counsel of his own will." In other words, the lot of **inheritance** has fallen to us, not by chance, but by the sovereign will of God. He goes on to say that the "earnest" (literally, "first installment," *arrabōn*, 728G) of our **inheritance** is the Holy Spirit, who has sealed (*sphragizō*, 4972G) us in Christ (v. 14).[150] He then reveals the "riches of the glory of [Christ's] inheritance in the saints" (v. 18). Oh, what a **heritage** we have!

Scriptures for Study: Read Ephesians 1 today and **rejoice** in your riches!

Enlarge

rāchab̲

What an important **word** this is in our time and with some of the prevalent teachings in the church! The Hebrew *rāchab̲* (7337) means "to extend, open wide, gain living space or territory." As one authority tells us, "The root often occurs in descriptions of the spaciousness of the land of Canaan (Genesis 26:22). . . . It is repeated in reaffirmations of the extent of Israel's promised **inheritance** both during and after the conquest of Canaan (Exodus 34:24; Deut. 12:20; Isaiah 54:2)."[151]

It is also used, however, as do the psalmists, in a figurative sense. Psalm 18:36, for example, pictures giving **strength**: "Thou hast enlarged my steps under me, that my feet did not slip" (also 2 Sam. 22:37). Particularly striking is Psalm 119:32: "I will run the way of thy commandments, when thou shalt enlarge my heart." While today's ever popular prosperity teachers read such a verse and speak of **God** "increasing our borders" and making us rich, that is not David's **prayer**. Yes, used literally, *rāchab* means the increasing of land and property, but he applies it to something infinitely deeper. He prays, "enlarge my *heart*," that is, make my ***heart*** more spacious. "Heart" is *lēb̲* (3820), derived from *lēb̲āb̲* (3824, April 13), which refers not only to the physical organ, but figuratively to the whole of the inner person and personality.

Why does David **pray** like that? Why does he ask God to extend, open wide, increase the living space in his inner person? So more of God's Word will fit into it so he might, therefore, be more fit to "run the way of [God's] commandments." As Paul challenges us: "Know ye not that they which run in a race run all, but one receiveth the prize?" (1 Cor. 9:24), and again in Hebrews 12:1: "Wherefore seeing we also are compassed about with so great a cloud of witnesses, let us lay aside every weight, and the sin which doth so easily beset us, and let us run with patience the race that is set before us."

Oh, that each of us would pray with David, "Lord, make my heart bigger so I can fit more of your Word into it that I might be better equipped to run the race you have laid out for me."

Scriptures for Study: Who was the recipient of "largeness of heart" in 1 Kings 4:29? What else did he receive? 🕮 What is the promise of Isaiah 40:31?

Teach (1)

šānan [and] lāmad

As is often true of the richness of the Hebrew vocabulary, several words convey the idea of *teaching* in the OT, no less than twelve, in fact.[152] One of the more graphic ones is *šānan* (8150; Arabic, *sanna*), which means "to sharpen or whet." Appearing some ten times, it refers in the literal sense to sharpening swords and arrows (Deut. 32:41; Isa. 5:28). One figurative meaning is someone using sharp words to hurt others (Ps. 64:3; 140:3). Its very first occurrence, however, pictures teaching, where **God** says of His words, "Teach them diligently unto thy children" (Deut. 6:7). Whether we take this to mean that we are to "whet or sharpen" the words themselves as we apply them or use the words to sharpen our children, the difference is minor and the challenge the same. Parents, specifically fathers, are responsible for teaching their children the **Word** of God (Eph. 6:4), a principle that is ignored more and more in our **day**.

Also rendered **teach** is *lāmad* (3925), which appears about eighty-five times in the OT (and Akkadian) and means "to learn, study, and teach," as well as "to be taught and to be learned." Its importance is seen in its first occurrence: "Hearken, O Israel, unto the statutes and unto the judgments, which I teach you, for to do them, that ye may live" (Deut. 4:1). So foundational is this word that one of its derivatives, *talmiyd* (8527), which means "scholar" (1 Chron. 25:8), is the source of the word *Talmud,* the **name** for the commentaries written by the ancient rabbis on the Torah (**Law**). Further underscoring the pivotal place the teaching of the word of God has in the believer's **life**, *lāmad* appears nine times in Psalm 119 (vv. 12, 26, 64, 66, 68, 108, 124, 135, 171).

Finally, it's also interesting that the Septuagint renders this word using two Greek words: *didaskō* (1321G), "to teach systematically," and *manthanō* (3129G), "to learn." This is significant, as one authority puts it, because "while Greek uses two different words . . . each having its own content, goal, and methods, Hebrew uses the same root for both words because all learning and teaching is ultimately to be found in the **fear** of the **Lord** (Deut. 4:10; 14:23; 17:19; 31:12, 13). To learn this is to come to terms with the will and law of God."[153]

Is there any doubt as to the importance of teaching?

Scriptures for Study: Read the verses in Psalm 119 mentioned today. What aspects of God's Word does each command that we learn? (See also February 19 and 21.)

Teach (2)

yārāh

One other graphic **word** translated **teach** in the OT is *yārāh* (3384), a very interesting word indeed. As one authority tells us, the fundamental idea of this root is to throw or cast "with the strong sense of control by the subject." That writer goes on to say: "Lots were cast in regards to dividing the land among the various tribes (Joshua 18:6). **God** cast the Egyptian army into the Red Sea (Exodus 15:4; cf. Job 30:19). With stones it has the idea of placing them in a certain place; God laid the cornerstone of the world (Job 38:6) and Laban set up a heap of stones and a pillar as a **witness** between Jacob and himself to their **covenant** of **peace** (Genesis 31:51, 52.). The three most frequent uses of this root deal with shooting arrows, sending rain, and teaching."[154]

That creates a graphic **image** for us when we think about teaching. It is essential for a teacher to control what is taught, to place what is taught in a certain place and **way**, to **teach** principles that are foundational, as pictured by the cornerstone of a building, and to properly aim those principles as an archer aims and shoots his arrows.

What a marvelous description of teaching! Sadly, however, the general fare in churches today is a far cry from such a foundational, aimed, and systematic presentation of truth. It is appalling how many professing Christians today simply do not want, and absolutely refuse to sit under, **deep**, systematic truth. In many churches, **preaching** and substantive teaching have all but vanished, being replaced by entertainment and feelings-oriented, motivational speeches. But what the truly spiritual Christian wants (as **David** cries to be taught in Psalm 119:33) is truth.

If I may be so bold, there is, indeed, something seriously wrong when that is not the desire of the leaders and people in our churches. We repeat, *truly spiritual people want truth*. That means, however, that the reverse is also true: Those who do not want truth are not spiritual, rather they are "carnal" (1 Cor. 3:1–4), if not even the "natural man" (2:14). While that statement would be considered by many people today as being "judgmental" or "intolerant," it is biblically true. Every Christian is to "as newborn babes, desire the sincere milk of the word, that ye may grow thereby" (1 Pet. 2:2).

Scriptures for Study: What does Peter further command in 2 Peter 3:18? 📖 What is Paul's similar challenge in 1 Corinthians 14:20 and Ephesians 4:14, 15?

Keep [and] Observe

nāṣar [and] šāmar

Yesterday we made brief reference to Psalm 119:33, where **David** cries, "Teach [*yārāh*] me, O LORD, the way of thy statutes." Is it enough, however, just to learn **new** things? Is it enough just to **know** more facts about the Bible? No, for David goes on to say, "and I shall keep it unto the end" and then in the next verse, "I shall keep thy law; yea, I shall observe it with my whole heart." It's not enough to *know* truth; we must also ***obey*** truth.

While we will look specifically at the word ***obey*** **tomorrow**, there are two other words here that should strike us. **Keep** is (5341) *nāṣar*, which originally came from the Akkadian (*nasāru*) and meant "to watch over, protect." A similar Arabic word (*nazara*) means "to keep in view, look at." The idea in *nāṣar*, then, is "to guard, observe, and preserve." It's used, for example, for a watchman over his **vineyard** or garden (Job 27:18; Prov. 27:18). In this context, therefore, and numerous other verses, we are to maintain what **God** has entrusted to us, to **keep** the truths of God in both actions and mind, to guard them with all our **strength** (Ps. 105:45; 119:2, 22, 33, 34, 56, 69, 100, 115, 129, 145).

Not only are we to **keep** the Word, but we are also to **observe** it. While the idea here is similar to **keep**, there is also in this word (*šāmar*, 8104) the idea of "care," as **Adam** and **Eve** were to watch over and care for the Garden of Eden (Gen. 2:15). It also speaks of protecting something, as when David gave orders to **keep** Absalom safe (2 Sam. 18:12). Still further, one of its most frequent uses in its some 420 occurrences is to denote paying close attention to something, such as the obligations of God's Word, as in Leviticus 18:26: "Ye shall therefore keep [*šāmar*] my statutes and my judgments, and shall not commit *any* of these abominations" (also Exod. 20:6; Deut. 26:16; Ezek. 11:20).

What is our real attitude to God's Word? Do we truly care for it, protect it, and pay close attention to its obligations and demands? Or is it just "the Good Book" that we give lip service to and reinterpret to fit our lifestyle and belief system?

Scriptures for Study: In each of the following occurrences of *šāmar*, what are we to **keep** or "heed": Psalm 119:4, 5, 9, 55, 57, 60, 63, 88, 106, 146?

Obey

šāma'

Today's Hebrew **word** is one of those that permeates the OT, appearing some 1,150 times, and having equivalents in Akkadian, Aramaic, Arabic, Ugaritic, and Ethiopic. *Šāma'* (8085) basically means "to hear with the ear" with several shades of meaning derived from it that generally denote *effective* hearing, that is, truly *listening*. Ideas conveyed by *šāma'*, then, are "paying attention, regarding, and obeying."

The first occurrence of *šāma'* well illustrates the above concepts. After they sinned, **Adam** and **Eve** "heard the voice of the LORD God walking in the garden in the cool of the day" (Gen. 3:8). Here was, as many expositors believe, the preincarnate Word, the **Lord** Jesus, walking in the Garden. Adam and Eve recognized Him as such and knew fully how they had disobeyed His one and only command. We find *šāma'* again in verse 10 and still again in verse 17, where **God** told Adam that he "hearkened" (listened to, obeyed, or at least followed the lead of) his *wife* instead of His *God*.

We repeatedly find this word, therefore, in reference to obeying God. We are told to "hear the word of the LORD" (e.g., Isa. 66:5; Jer. 22:29), "hear [His] voice" (Isa. 28:23), "[hearken] unto counsel" (Prov. 12:15), and **obey** His **law** and "commandments" (Isa. 42:24; Neh. 9:16). Two passages that sum it all up are, "Hear, O Israel: The LORD our God is one LORD: And thou shalt love the LORD thy God with all thine heart, and with all thy soul, and with all thy might" (Deut. 6:4, 5), followed by the command to **keep** these words in one's **heart** and **teach** them to your children (vv. 6–9). Those verses actually comprise the "Shema," the basic confession of **faith** of Judaism recited both **morning** and **evening**.

The challenge to us today is both clear and convicting. As *šāma'* indicates "hearing with the intent to obey," so does the Greek *akouō* (191G), which is how the Septuagint renders *šāma'* here. It means not only to hear in general (e.g., Matt. 2:3), to hear with attention (e.g., Mark 4:3, "hearken"), and to understand (e.g., Mark 4:33), but also to **obey** (e.g., Luke 16:19–31).[155] In a **day** when Christ is presented as a **way** to **salvation** without Lordship, and when Christian living is viewed as not involving strict obedience to anything definitive, Scripture's emphasis on obedience has never been more critical.

Scriptures for Study: Who hears God, according to Proverbs 1:5 (cf. v. 7)? 🕮 To what should we hearken and what is the result in 1:33; 8:32–35? 🕮 What comes by "hearing" in Romans 10:17?

Vain Thoughts

sēʿēp̱

We consider today a **word** that appears in only one OT verse: "I hate vain thoughts: but thy law do I love" (Ps. 119:113). The words **vain thoughts** are only a single word in the Hebrew, *sēʿēp̱* (5588), and its meaning is very enlightening: "double-mindedness, vanity of thought. It indicates a person who engages in doublethink, a process of illogical thought, perverse thinking that distorts and reverses the truth."[156] Here is a picture of the skeptic, the doubter, the philosopher, the **perverse** "modern thinker." These are the people, as the apostle Paul words it, who in their "ungodliness and unrighteousness . . . hold [suppress] the truth in unrighteousness" (Rom. 1:18).

This word is all the more interesting when we consider that its Septuagint translation is *paranomoi*, from *para* (3844G, "against, contrary to") and *nomos* (3551G, **law**, "regulation"). The verb form (*paranomeō*, 3891G) appears in Acts 23:3 for doing what was "contrary to the law," and the noun form (*paranomia*, 3892G) is used in 2 Peter 2:16 to recall Balaam being "rebuked for his iniquity." Putting it all together, where does the modern "doublethinker" get his thoughts? From whence do his perverse thinking and distortion of the truth come? *From breaking God's law and ignoring His Word.*

Besides the opinions, philosophies, apostasies, and blasphemies of the world, what do we see even in the church? "We hear much in these days of '*men* of thought,' '*thoughtful* preachers,' and '*modern* thought,'" wrote Spurgeon in the *nineteenth* century, "[but] what is this but the old pride of the human heart?"[157] And how much worse is the *twenty-first* century? The Word of God is frequently anything but elevated. Many churches use nothing but modern marketing techniques to **build** the church. Many pastors psychologize and entertain instead of **preaching** truth. Many apologize for implying anything that might "offend." Much of theology has turned into little more than philosophical curiosity. What is all that, if not a reversal of truth and ignoring God's Word?

In stark contrast, **David** says, as he does in Psalm 119:47, 48, and 97, in effect, "Thy law do I love." There is, indeed, only one remedy to the **vain thoughts** of *men*, and that is the absolute truth of *God*. "When we love the law," Spurgeon adds, "it becomes a law of love, and we cling to it with our whole heart." We must each ask, Do I love *vain thoughts* or do I *valuable truth*?

Scriptures for Study: What does James tell us in his letter (1:8)? 🕮 What then is his **counsel** in 4:8?

David (1)

Dāwiḏ

While no more inspired than any other **Scripture**, Psalm 23 is, indeed, one of its crown jewels. "Using common ancient near-eastern images," writes one expositor, "David progressively unveils his personal relationship with the LORD."[158] **David** refers to the **LORD** as his Shepherd (*Jehovah-Rā'â,* January 15), and then in beautiful poetry speaks of what he receives from his Shepherd: *protection* (vv. 1–4), *provision* (v. 5), and *permanence* (v. 6).

Throughout much of this month, we will meditate on this **psalm** by examining many of its words. The first is **David** himself. While the etymology is uncertain, it is commonly believed that *Dāwiḏ* (1732) is derived from the root *dôḏ* (1730), meaning "beloved, loved one, and even uncle" (e.g., Lev. 20:20). Most of its fifty-eight occurrences refer to "the beloved" in Song of Solomon. As **David** prefigures Messiah (Ezek. 34:23, 24; 37:24, 25; Hosea 3:5; Jer. 30:9), who in turn was spoken of as the Father's "beloved Son" (Matt. 3:17), this etymology seems at least possible.

While there is much detail about this pivotal character—his **name** appears more than 1,000 times—we can briefly summarize **David** with seven words:

(1) *Son*. The youngest of eight brothers, **David** was the son of Jesse of Bethlehem, grandson of Ruth and Boaz, tracing his **heritage** back to Abraham and then forward to Messiah (Matt. 1:1–17). Anointed secretly by Samuel as the next **king** (1 Samuel 16:1–13), this **young man** was infused with the Spirit and destined for true greatness. (2) *Shepherd*. Oh, the lessons he learned as a shepherd! Courage, compassion, care, and much more helped mold a leader. (3) *Singer*. A musician and poet without equal, **David** penned most of the Psalms, providing unprecedented **praise** to **God**. (4) *Soldier*. Facing Goliath in his **youth** and later entire armies, **David** was a true warrior who received his **power** from God. (5) *Sovereign*. In a forty-year reign (1010–970 BC), the Hebrew nation reached the peak of its unity and power under King David's leadership. (6) S*inner*. As no one is perfect, **David** fell into sin, the most grievous of which was adultery with Bathsheba and the murder of Uriah. The consequences of **sin** are great, and untold misery came to David's household. (7) *Savior*. Not **David** himself, of course, but the "Son of David," Jesus Christ, who would **save** His people from their sins and sit on David's **throne**.

Scriptures for Study: In preparation for tomorrow's study, read Psalm 51, David's great psalm of **repentance**.

David (2)

Dāwid

Of the many events in David's **life**, few were as far-reaching as his adultery with Bathsheba. That act, along with his attempted cover-up, brought incalculable misery to David's household, just as Nathan predicted (2 Sam. 12:10, 11), starting with the **death** of the child conceived in that **sin** and then encompassing rape, rebellion, revenge, and revolt within his **house** (12:15–20:26).

Psalm 51, however, is a **light** in the darkness. While the consequences of sin were not diminished, this **psalm** records David's confession and **forgiveness**. It stands even today as a model for Christians.

First, we see David's ***repentance*** (vv. 1–6). "Acknowledge" (v. 3) is *yāḏa'* (March 8), which speaks of knowledge acquired by the senses. **David** uses personal pronouns thirteen times to underscore that only he was to blame for his sin, not Bathsheba, his parents, society, or even an aberrant gene in his DNA. His sin was *willful* ("transgressions" in v. 1 is *pesha',* April 2), and was against **God** alone. Yes, he had betrayed and hurt his family, Bathsheba, Uriah, and the entire nation, but sin is always against *God,* the breaking of *His* **law**. This passage emphasizes the broken **heart** brought on by sin, and the desire to turn from it and be forgiven.

Second, we see David's *refinement* (vv. 7–12). He prayed that God would "purge [him] with hyssop" (v. 7). Because of its stiff branches and hairy leaves, this common plant from the mint family was used for sprinkling purifying water (Lev. 14:2–7, 49–52; Num. 19:1–19). **David** also prayed that God would "wash" him (vv. 2, 7). The Hebrew *kāḇas* (3526) commonly referred to washing clothes, both the ordinary task (Gen. 49:11; 2 Sam. 19:24) and ritual cleansing (Exod. 19:10; 14; Lev. 11:25). Further, **David** wanted a "clean heart" (v. 10). **Clean** is *ṭāhôr* (2889, August 2), which speaks of the absence of impurity, filthiness, defilement, or imperfection, such as "pure gold" (Exod. 37:11) or "pure words" (Ps. 12:6). **David** did, indeed, want refinement, for only with such cleansing comes **joy**, "gladness," and "[rejoicing]" (v. 8).

Third, we see David's *restoration* (Ps. 51:13–19). Upon being *delivered* from *sin*, **David** now *declares* God's ***salvation***. He desires to proclaim to others what God will do in the repentant heart. As God recommissioned Peter for service (John 21), the restored believer is one who proclaims the gospel of Christ with **new** fervor.

Scriptures for Study: Read Psalm 32, where **David** tells of his joy after God forgave him. 📖 What does 1 John 1:9 say about God's forgiveness of His children?

Want

chāsēr

David writes in Psalm 23:1, "The LORD is my shepherd; I shall not want." After using God's **covenant name LORD** (January 8) and then picturing such a personal relationship by likening Him to a **Shepherd** (January 15), the first blessing **David** mentions receiving from his Shepherd is that he does not **want** for anything.

The Hebrew *chāsēr* (2637) means "to be lacking or needy or to decrease." The first two of its some twenty occurrences reflect that latter idea when the waters of the Flood "were abated" and "decreased" (Gen. 8:3, 5). The idea of lacking is apparent in the third occurrence when Abraham found a "lack" of righteous people in **Sodom** (18:28).

Our text, however, says that David did *not* lack for anything, that he was *not* needy, that there was no decrease of any necessary thing in his **life**. The most frequent use of *chāsēr*, in fact, is to show that God's provision is sufficient to meet the needs of His people. As one might expect, we find this very **word** in the account of God feeding His people in the **wilderness**. God's provision of **manna** was so miraculous that "he that gathered much had nothing over, and he that gathered little had no lack; they gathered every man according to his eating" (Exod. 16:18).

That is, indeed, the Shepherd's promise. If we follow Him, we will **want** for nothing. As Spurgeon writes, "I shall not lack for *temporal things.* Does he not feed the ravens, and cause the lilies to grow? How, then, can he leave his children to starve? I shall not want *for spirituals*, I **know** that his grace will be sufficient for me. Resting in him he will say to me, 'As thy day so shall thy strength be' [Deut. 33:25]. I may not possess all that I wish for, but 'I shall not *want.*'"[159]

Is there a prerequisite for such provision, or is it automatic no matter how one might live? As David makes clear elsewhere, "They that seek the LORD shall not want any good thing" (Ps. 34:10; also Matt. 6:25–34). In contrast, when God's people turned to **idol worship**, "[They] wanted all things, and [were] consumed by the sword and by the famine" (Jer. 44:18). While there are starving people in many places in the world, the problem is not a lack of *resources*, rather a wrong *response* to God, not a lack of *food*, rather a lack of ***faith***.

Scriptures for Study: Read the following passages, noting the promise of God's provision in each: Deuteronomy 8:3, 9 (also Matt. 4:4); Matthew 6:25–34; Philippians 4:19. Is there ever a reason to doubt?

Lie Down [and] Green (Pastures)

rāḇaṣ [and] deshe'

A particularly pictorial phrase found in Psalm 23:2, another provision from the Shepherd, is, "He maketh me to lie down in green pastures." The Hebrew verb behind **lie down** is *rāḇaṣ* (7257), which is equivalent to the Akkadian *rabāṣu*, meaning "a stable" or possibly "a lying place." Appearing about thirty times, the idea in the Hebrew is not so much a place to sleep, but rather a place to **lie down** to rest from exertion.

We see just such a pastoral scene in verses such as Genesis 29:2, where Jacob comes to Haran and sees a "well in the field, and, lo, there were three flocks of sheep lying by it; for out of that well they watered the flocks." While a much smaller scene, the picture of a bird's nest is no less tranquil as we watch the mother "sitting upon the young, or upon the eggs" (Deut. 22:6). But who would want to rouse a **lion** when it is resting (Gen. 49:9)?

Perhaps most **blessed** of all is a scene Isaiah paints for us of the coming Millennium, when "the wolf also shall dwell with the lamb, and the leopard shall lie down with the kid; and the calf and the young lion and the fatling together; and a little child shall lead them. And the cow and the bear shall feed; their young ones shall lie down together: and the lion shall eat straw like the ox. And the sucking child shall play on the hole of the asp, and the weaned child shall put his hand on the cockatrice' [viper's] den" (Isa. 11:6–8). What a **day** that will be!

But what about the here and now? What are the **green pastures** (literally, "pastures of tender grass") **God** provides today? (**Green** is *deše'*, 1877, "the tender first shoots of vegetation.") No one answers that question better than the beloved Puritan Matthew Henry: "God's ordinances are the green pastures in which food is provided for all believers; the word of life is the nourishment of the new man. It is milk for babes, pasture for sheep, never barren, never eaten bare, never parched, but always a green pasture for faith to feed in. God makes his saints to lie down; he gives them quiet and contentment in their own minds, what ever their lot is; their souls dwell at ease in him, and that makes every pasture green."

Dear Christian **Friend**, are you resting there today?

Scriptures for Study: Compare Ezekiel 34:13–15 with John 6:35 and Matthew 11:28. What is the promise then and now?

Lead(eth) [and] Still Waters

nāhal [and] menûchāh

The words "he leadeth me beside the still waters" in Psalm 23:2 provide us another beautiful picture and another provision from the Shepherd. It is hard to imagine, in fact, how this scene could possibly be painted in any brighter colors. Because we believe in the inspiration of **Scripture**, we **know** that no one—past, present, or future—could have written this **psalm** but **David**. Both David's *character* and God's *control* are obvious.

Leadeth is *nāhal* (5095), which not only carries the idea of leading and guiding but also the more specific concept of leading by the **hand**. In Isaiah 51:18, for example, Israel's spiritual condition is likened to one who is so drunk that if taken by the hand he could not be led. Exodus 15:13 refers to how **God** "led" His people to the Promised Land, and that is certainly illustrated as He "went before them by day in a pillar of a cloud, to lead them the way; and by night in a pillar of fire, to give them light; to go by day and night" (13:21). Additionally, while the **word** does not actually appear in Judges 16:26, the parallel there is that helpless Samson had to be led by the hand to a pillar. Likewise, the angels had to **lead** Lot and his family by the hand out of **Sodom** (Gen. 19:16).

So David says God gently leads him by the hand and brings him to the **still waters**. **Waters** is *mayim* (4325), which refers to water in many ways, such as in a well (Gen. 26:18), a sea (Amos 5:8), a spring (Gen. 16:7), rain (2 Sam. 21:10), and so forth. More significant here is the word **still**, which translates *menûchāh* (4496), "resting place, a place of peace, quiet, and trust," as Canaan was to be for Israel (1 Kings 8:56). These "waters of rest and quietness" David refers to, then, are found in the tranquil pond or slow-moving stream that draws us to it for refreshment and reflection. Just as sheep like neither fast-moving nor stagnant water to drink, so do we need to get away from the pace of the **day** and drink that cool, calm, and **clean** water of the Word of God. While the food of the pasture *restores*, the water from the stream *refreshes*.

Scriptures for Study: What is accomplished by "the washing of water by the word" in Ephesians 5:25–27?

(Restoreth) Soul

nep̱eš

Psalm 23:3 provides us with another provision from the Shepherd: "He restoreth my soul." **Restoreth** is a translation of *šûḇ* (7725, March 31). Its basic concept is "returning to one's original state" or "movement back to the point of departure."

The pivotal question now is, "What is the **soul**?" This is the Hebrew *nep̱eš* (5315), which appears some 753 times in the OT and has an incredibly broad range of meanings. As one authority observes, in fact, "It is virtually untranslatable by any one English word."[160] The AV uses sixteen different words that appear more than once, and forty-seven more miscellaneous words.[161] Its literal meaning comes from the rarely used root verb *nāp̱aš* (5314, Exod. 23:12; 31:17; 2 Sam. 16:14: "to take breath or refresh oneself"). The literal idea in the noun, therefore, is the act of breathing or, more to the point, the essence of **life**.

It is "from that concrete concept," however, writes another authority, "a number of more abstract meanings were developed."[162] Perhaps the most succinct definition of this abstract concept is, "In relation to people, the underlying essence of *nāp̱aš* may be described as that quality which lends to human beings their distinctive individuality as creatures made in the image of God."[163] In other words, it relates to a person's being, what makes a person a person, one's own unique essence in the **image** of **God**. While animals are said to have *nāp̱aš*, that is, life and breath (Gen. 1:20), humans have the unique, personal qualities of intellect, emotion, and will, which are the essence of personality and reflect being created in God's image—God "breathed into his nostrils the breath of life; and man became a living soul" (2:7).

What, then, does **David** tell us? He declares that the Shepherd restores his **soul**—his essence, all that he is in his thinking, feeling, and willing—to what it should be. He brings it back to the point at which it wandered away. No characteristic of a sheep is more definitive than its tendency to wander and get lost (Ps. 119:176). As that old hymn well puts it: "Prone to wander—Lord I feel it—prone to leave the God I love; / Here's my heart, O take and seal it, seal it for Thy courts above."

Let us **pray** with David each **day**, "[The Shepherd] restoreth my soul."

Scriptures for Study: Read Psalm 19:7 ("converting" is *šûb*, and **soul** is *nāp̱aš*). What is the key ingredient here? 📖 Read the following verses, noting in each what we should do with all our **heart**, **soul**, and mind: Deuteronomy 4:29; 6:5; 10:12.

Paths

ma'gāl

The next provision from the Shepherd that **David** lists in Psalm 23:3 is, "He leadeth me in the paths of righteousness for his name's sake." **Righteousness** is *ṣeḏeq* (6664, January 16, "conforming to a moral or ethical standard or norm"), which is often connected to the term *justice* (Ps. 119:106; Isa.58:2). **Leadeth** is again *nāhal* (5095, June 5, "leading and guiding by the hand"). What, then, are the **paths** of righteousness?

Paths is *ma'gāl* (4570), which appears sixteen times in the OT. While it is used to refer to the circle of a **camp** (1 Sam. 17:20; 26:5, 7), which might actually refer to wagons and chariots arranged in a circle to form a protective perimeter, the primary concept is a track, a well-worn path, or even a rut.

In the context of sheep, therefore, it is in their nature to wander away, to get off the well-worn path and follow any curious object they see or run with any whim they might feel. How often we do the same! We are enticed into some unholy conduct (James1:14, 15). We are lured off the path of truth and follow "strange doctrines" (Heb. 13:9; also Eph. 4:14). So David reminds us we must once again allow the Shepherd to lead us by the hand down the well-defined path of God's moral and ethical standards and norms, to allow His **Word** alone to rule our coming and going, to dictate where we go and how we get there.

We should not leave this subject without noting that David adds a motive for our desire to be led "in the paths of righteousness," namely, "for [God's] name's sake." Not only are the **paths** of righteousness for ***our good***, but more important for *His glory*. Just as **salvation** is not *primarily* for our good but His glory (Eph. 1:4–6, 11–14), so is a **life** of righteousness to be first and foremost for His honor and glory. As Asaph writes, "Help us, O God of our salvation, for the glory of thy name: and deliver us, and purge away our sins, for thy name's sake" (Ps. 79:9).

Scriptures for Study: What is David's **prayer** in Psalm 17:5? 🕮 What does Proverbs 4:26 **counsel** us to do?

Shadow of Death

ṣalmāwet

Psalm 23:4 declares, "Yea, though I walk through the valley of the shadow of death, I will fear no evil: for thou art with me," providing us with still another provision from the Shepherd. This provision is that of ***peace*** in the face of *peril*.

The phrase **shadow of death** translates a single **word** in the Hebrew, *ṣalmāwet* (6757), and what a word it is! It is actually a compound, comprised of *ṣēl* or *ṣēlel* (6738/6752, **shadow**) and *māweṯ* (4194, **death**). This obviously yields the quite literal translation we find in our beloved AV and several other versions. We find this translation, in fact, in all the other thirteen occurrences of the word. Not only does it sometimes refer to **death** itself (Job 38:17; Ps. 107:10, 14), but also to physical darkness (Job 24:17; Amos 5:8) and figuratively to spiritual darkness (Isa. 9:2).

While some commentators view David's reference solely to physical **death** and the peace he knows (or will **know** then), that does not seem to be the primary emphasis. More to the point, the picture seems to be that of a dark, narrow gorge (**valley**, May 2) that hides dangers around every corner. As another commentator submits, "The idea is that of death casting his gloomy shadow over that valley—the valley of the dead. Hence, the word is applicable to any path of gloom or sadness; any scene of trouble or sorrow; any dark and dangerous way. Thus understood, it is applicable not merely to death itself—though it embraces that—but to any or all the dark, the dangerous, and the gloomy paths which we tread in life: to ways of sadness, solitude, and sorrow."[164]

Have you ever noticed that the verse says *walk* and not *run*? **Fear** (March 4) often causes panic and the instinct to run away from danger. But David doesn't say he *runs* through the valley to get out of it as quickly as possible. Rather he says he *walks* through it without fear of any **evil** (July 8) that might befall. While sheep have poor eyesight and are easily startled into fleeing by anything out of the ordinary, especially in the dark, we can do what is contrary to our nature—we can calmly walk through it—because the Shepherd is "with" us. What assurance and peace we have in Him!

Scriptures for Study: What is the cause of spiritual darkness in Psalm 107:10, 11? 🕮 What is the "great light" that shines on those who are in spiritual darkness in Isaiah 9:2 (also Matt. 4:16–17; John 8:12; 12:35–46)?

Rod [and] Staff

šēḇeṭ [and] miš‘eneṯ

Today we discover a twofold provision of the Shepherd that is rooted in the simplicity of ancient sheepherding. Psalm 23:4 assures us, "Thy rod and thy staff they comfort me."

While there are times when these two words are a little difficult to differentiate—in some contexts perhaps even interchangeable—there is little problem in the present context. **Rod** is *šēḇeṭ* (7626), which is used in a variety of ways in the OT: a crude weapon (2 Sam. 23:21, **staff**), a threshing tool (Isa. 28:27, **rod**), the shaft of a spear (2 Sam. 18:14, "darts"), and an instrument of discipline (Prov. 13:24; 22:15; 29:15, **rod**). It is also used to refer to a tool to collect and **count** sheep (Lev. 27:32; Ezek. 20:37).

Staff, then, is *miš‘eneṯ* (4938), which refers to a "staff, pole, or support," such as a cane or crutch (Exod. 21:19; Zech. 8:4). It is also a symbol of authority, such as a ruler's scepter (Num. 21:18) or the prophet's **staff** (2 Kings 4:29). Regarding the shepherd, this brings to mind the familiar **image** of the **staff** with a crook at the top used to rescue a sheep from a cliff or gully.

This provides us with the complete picture. As we journey through "the valley of the shadow of death," it is with the **rod** the Shepherd *protects* us from the predators that attack and it is with the **staff** He *rescues* us from other perils that befall. That is why **David** says, in short, it is in this there is complete "comfort." Just the sight of these "shepherd's tools," in fact, is a comfort; just knowing they are there ready for use is enough to calm our concerns. While much of the world's so-called "comfort" comes from syrupy sentimentality, psychobabble, and philosophical clichés—into which even many Christians have been lured—the Shepherd provides true comfort by His very presence though His **Word**.

Dear Christian **Friend**, are you trusting in the Shepherd and His "tools" to safely protect and rescue you as you walk daily through life's dangerous **valley**?

Scriptures for Study: What is the source of our comfort in Psalm 119:50 (also Rom. 15:4)?

Table

šulchān

There is yet another provision from the Shepherd in Psalm 23:5: "Thou preparest a table before me in the presence of mine enemies." Some expositors insist that **David** changes his metaphor here from the Shepherd taking care of his sheep in the field to the Host entertaining his guests at a banquet. We humbly submit, however, that such an assumption is unwarranted for two reasons: *First,* there is the context. The preceding verses are obviously about the Shepherd but so are the ones that follow. **Oil**, for example, as we will note **tomorrow**, was used in caring for the sheep.

Second, and more importantly, is the Hebrew behind **table**. This is *šulchān* (7979), which does not necessarily refer to what we normally think of as a **table**, whether the elaborate one in the banquet hall or even the tiny one for two in our breakfast nook. In the earliest OT times, in fact, a **table** was no more than an animal hide spread on a tent floor or the ground. One commentator, for example, observes that the words "prepare the table" in Isaiah 21:5 mean "spread rugs" and Bible historians consistently agree.[165] This is further supported in that Arabic and Syriac equivalents picture stripping hide off an animal.[166]

What, then, does David mean? Simply this: Even with enemies present, even as the battle rages, the meal is spread out. Spurgeon puts it beautifully: "When a soldier is in the presence of his enemies, if he eats at all he snatches a hasty meal, and away he hastens to the fight. But observe: 'Thou preparest a table,' just as a servant does when she unfolds the damask cloth and displays the ornaments of the feast on an ordinary peaceful occasion. Nothing is hurried, there is no confusion, no disturbance, the enemy is at the door and yet God prepares a table, and the Christian sits down and eats as if everything were in perfect peace. Oh! the peace which Jehovah gives to his people, even in the midst of the most trying circumstances!"[167]

In Psalm 78, Asaph reviews what God did for His people in the **wilderness**, reminding them how they doubted Him, even speaking against Him: "Can God furnish a table in the wilderness?" (v. 19; cf. Exod. 16:8–10; Num. 21:5). The **answer** to that, of course, as David attests, is, "Yes."

Scriptures for Study: Read the following verses and **rejoice** with the psalmist: Psalms 36:7, 8; 63:5.

Oil [and] Anoint (1)

šemen [and] dāšēn

Psalm 23:5 provides the believer with still another provision from the Shepherd: "Thou anointest my head with oil." "Anointest" is *dāšēn* (1878), which is not the **word** for ***anoint*** that we find in other contexts (see tomorrow's reading), rather a verb that literally means "to be or grow fat" and so figuratively "to anoint, to satisfy." Its first two occurrences, for example, refer to the "fatty ashes" that are left after a sacrificial animal is burned (Exod. 27:3; Num. 4:13). Additionally, since the fat of an animal was considered the best part, this led to the figurative idea of prosperous or rich. **David** is, therefore, saying that the blessing of God's **oil** "makes him fat," that is, spiritually rich and prosperous.

Oil, then, is *šemen* (8081), the general word used for olive **oil** in its various uses in the OT. A valuable trade item (Ezek. 27:17), it was used for ritual anointing of priests for **tabernacle** service (Exod. 29:7) and kings for ruling (1 Sam. 10:1; 16:1, 13; 1 Kings 1:39). **Oil** was also used for more ordinary things, such as preserving leather (2 Sam. 1:21), baking (Exod. 29:2), **lamp** fuel (Exod. 25:6), and as a medication (Isa. 1:6; Ezek. 16:9; Mark 6:13; Luke 10:34; James 5:14).

It is that latter use that is specifically in view in our text. As the sheep filed into the fold in the **evening**, a **good** shepherd would examine each one with an experienced eye, looking for cuts and other injuries, and would apply soothing, healing **oil** where needed. **Oil** was also used on the **head** and horns to help keep insects away.

All this fits the picture perfectly. It is inevitable that as we "walk through the valley of the shadow of death," unavoidably encountering "evil" as we go and facing the countless "enemies" that lurk, we are going to get some "cuts and bruises." We will endure weariness, discouragement, character attack, and all manner of suffering, for "all that will live godly in Christ Jesus shall suffer persecution" (2 Tim. 3:12). But as we come back to the fold each evening, our Shepherd is waiting to "look us over" and apply His healing **oil** where it is needed. What is that **oil**, then? **Oil** is a symbol of the anointing of the Holy Spirit (Ps. 45:7; 89:20; Zech. 4:12); it is He who comforts us, and He does that through the Word of God.

Scriptures for Study: What is the psalmist's confidence in Psalm 92:10?

Anoint (2)

māšach

Before continuing our meditations on Psalm 23, we should make mention of another **word** translated ***anoint*** in the OT. The Hebrew *māšach* (4886), in fact, is the most common word for anointing. Occurring about seventy times, its basic meaning is nothing special, simply to smear something, such as **oil** on a **shield** to prevent the leather from cracking (Isa. 21:5), paint on a **house** (Jer. 22:14), or oil on wafers as we might spread butter on **bread** (Exod. 29:2). Other nonreligious significance in the ancient Near East included anointing with oil to confirm such things as diplomatic agreements and business contracts.

It is the theological sense of *māšach*, however, that is crucial. Its primary significance is as a symbol of sanctification and service. In its first occurrence, for example, Jacob awakens from his dream of "the ladder," builds a monument to the event, consecrating it with oil, and even renaming the place "Bethel" (*bēyṯ-'ēl*, 1008, "the house of God," Gen. 31:13). We see this symbol often. Aaron and his sons were anointed to "consecrate them, and sanctify them" so they could "minister unto [God] in the priest's office" (Exod. 28:41), as were prophets (1 Kings 19:16; Isa. 61:1). The **tabernacle**, the **Ark**, and various vessels were anointed and thereby set apart unto **God** (Exod. 30:26–28). Even kings were anointed, such as Saul (1 Sam. 9:15, 16; 10:1; 2:10) and **David** (16:13; 2 Sam. 12:7), to set them apart for service to God and leading the people in sanctified obedience.

It is extremely significant that another form of *māšach*, namely *māšiyach* (4899), is the source of the word *Messiah.* While OT references to Jesus as this future anointed one are not numerous, conservative scholars agree that passages such as Daniel 9:24–26 and Psalm 2:2, with its context, could not be clearer. Additionally, the Septuagint almost always renders this *chriō* (5548G), "to daub, smear, anoint with oil," from which is derived *christos* (5547G), "Christ." *Chriō* appears, in fact, five times in the NT, four of which refer to the Father's anointing of Christ.[168]

The final appearance of *chriō* declares that all believers have been anointed by God (2 Cor. 1:21), demonstrating that we all are set apart, "sanctified, and meet for the master's use, and prepared unto every good work" (2 Tim. 2:21).

Scriptures for Study: The noun *chrisma* (5545G) also comes from *chriō* (5548G). Read its only two occurrences in 1 John 2:20 ("unction") and 27 ("anointing"), noting what we have in the Holy Spirit.

Cup (Runneth Over)

kôs [and] rewāyāh

Returning again to Psalm 23, another provision from the Shepherd is "my cup runneth over" (v. 5). The Hebrew *kôs* (3563) is the most common **word** translated **cup**, occurring about thirty times. The cups used by the Hebrews were probably modeled after those of Egypt (Gen. 40:11) or perhaps Phoenicia, both of which excelled in this craftsmanship. Whether made of ceramic, **gold**, or **silver**, Esther 1:7 indicates they were diverse and often elaborate.

Once again, however, it is the figurative use of the word that is the most important. It is used of the **cup** of (and therefore the drinking of) judgment (Jer. 25:15) and shame (Hab. 2:16) on the negative side, and **salvation**, deliverance, and blessing on the positive (Ps. 16:5; 116:13).

So **David** says that the blessings his Shepherd provides not only *fill* his **cup** but *overflow* it. **Runneth over** is *rewāyāh* (7310), a noun meaning "abundance, state of overflowing, or saturation." It appears only one other place, where the psalmist says that God brought His people "out into a [saturated, overflowing] place" (Ps. 66:12). This refers, of course, to the riches of Canaan, "a land flowing [that floweth] with milk and honey," a phrase we find some twenty times (e.g., Exod. 3:8, 17; 13:5; 33:3; Lev. 20:24; Josh. 5:6).

"A poor man may say this as well as those in higher circumstances," writes Charles Spurgeon. "'What, all this, and Jesus Christ too?' said a poor cottager as she broke a piece of bread and filled a glass with cold water. Whereas a man may be ever so wealthy, but if he be discontented his **cup** cannot run over; it is cracked and leaks." How many people today, both unbelievers and believers, have a "leaky cup"? Try as they might, the **cup** simply will not fill. Worse, they can't even find the leak.

No NT verse demonstrates all this better than Ephesians 3:20. The Greek construction of "exceeding abundantly" yields Paul's full thought: "Not only can God do *more than enough*, and *above and beyond* more than enough, but *even more* than above and beyond more than enough" (author's paraphrase). **God** can do infinitely more than that which any of us can "ask" or even "think" about asking.[169]

Dear Christian **Friend**, is your **cup** overflowing? "It reminds me," writes J. Vernon McGee, "of the little girl who said, 'Lord, fill up my cup. I can't hold very much, but I can run over a whole lot.'"[170]

Scriptures for Study: What is the "cup of blessing" in 1 Corinthians 10:16?

Good (1)

ṭôḇ

Psalm 23:6 declares, "Surely goodness and mercy shall follow me all the days of my life: and I will dwell in the house of the LORD for ever." We have studied **mercy** already (April 5); the Shepherd also provides **good**.

The noun (and adjective) *ṭôḇ* (2896), which also appears in Akkadian, Aramaic, Arabic, and Ugaritic, has a huge range of meanings: "good, pleasant, beneficial, precious, delightful, right, well-pleasing, fruitful, morally correct, proper, convenient." As one authority submits, the Creation narrative of Genesis 1 best expresses all these aspects of meaning when God declares each facet of His handiwork to be **good**.[171]

ṭôḇ appears in the OT more than 550 times. Something can be called **good** simply because it is beneficial (Gen. 2:18) or just because it is pleasant to look at, such as land (Num. 14:7) or a person (Esther 1:11). Something, such as eating and drinking, might be called **good** because it makes one happy (Eccles. 2:24) or just because it might look better than the alternative (Exod. 14:12, "better"). Other things are said to be **good** because they are of high quality, such as the **gold** in Eden (Gen. 2:12), Abraham's cattle (18:7), Abigail's intelligence (1 Sam. 25:3), and Canaan's fertility (Exod. 3:8; Num. 14:7). And those are just a few instances.

It is in the moral sense, however, that *ṭôḇ* is most significant. Genesis 2:17 and 3:5, for example, speak of **Adam** and **Eve** knowing the difference between moral **good** and **evil** because of the forbidden **fruit**. Translated "do good" five times in the AV, *ṭôḇ* emphasizes the critical nature of doing what is right and **good**. The first is in Psalm 34:14: "Depart from evil, and do good." The second is in Psalm 37:3: "Trust in the LORD, and do good." Of this verse, Spurgeon writes, "True faith is actively obedient."[172] Unlike the "easy-believism" of our **day**—regeneration without **repentance**, **salvation** without surrender, and **life** without Lordship—Spurgeon recognized that true **faith** involves obedience (April 9, 10).

We read again in Psalm 37:27: "Depart from evil, and do good." Spurgeon again is encouraging: "As Lot left Sodom without casting a look behind, so must we leave **sin**. No truce or parley is to be held with sin, we must **turn away** from it without hesitation, and set ourselves practically to **work** in the opposite direction. He who neglects to do good will soon fall into evil." We will continue these thoughts **tomorrow**.

Scriptures for Study: Read the following NT verses, noting how we are to "do good": Galatians 6:10; James 4:17; 1 Peter 3:10–11.

Good (2)

ṭôḇ

Continuing our thoughts on **good** as it is used in the OT, such verses as Psalms 136:1, 145:9, and others speak of God's goodness. How **good** God is! Theologians generally speak of God's goodness in five ways:[173]

First is God's goodness in general. "The LORD is good to all: and his tender mercies are over all his works. . . . The eyes of all wait upon thee; and thou givest them their meat in due season. Thou openest thine hand, and satisfiest the desire of every living thing" (Ps. 145:9, 15, 16). Also called "common grace," this simply means that God deals kindly and bountifully with every one of His creatures. He cares about *all* His creatures' welfare (Matt. 5:45), "preservest man and beast" (Ps. 36:6; 104:21; Matt. 6:26), and is even "kind unto the unthankful and to the evil" (Luke 6:35).

Second, God shows His goodness through His **love**. When God exercises His goodness toward men, it takes on the higher quality of love. This love can be defined as: *the perfection of God by which He is eternally moved to self-communication.* While the world's view of love is "feelings" and "warm fuzzies," God's love is not based upon emotional impulse, rather a rational and voluntary affection for His own sake and purpose. While He cannot love lost men to the fullest because their **sin** is an **abomination** to Him, He still shows them "common grace" because He made **man** in His own **image** (Matt. 5:44, 45).

Third and *fourth*, as we have noted in previous studies, God shows His goodness through His **mercy** (April 5) and through His **grace** (April 6).

Fifth, God shows His goodness through His longsuffering (Num. 14:18; Ps. 86:15; Jer. 15:15). Each of those verses contains an interesting Hebrew expression, *'arek 'aph* (750, see December 7), which literally means "long of face, long of nose" an idiom indicating "slow to anger." The Greek uses the **word** *makrothumia* (3115G), a compound word from *makro*, meaning "long," and *thumos*, meaning "temper." God is, indeed, *long*-tempered, not *short*-tempered, as was always the case with pagan gods. Part of God's love is to **bear** with sinful men in spite of their continual rebellion. Through the millennia God has been "long of face"—He has allowed men's sin and delayed the judgment that is to come. Again, what mercy!

"Surely," **David** declares, "[God's] goodness . . . shall follow me all the days of my life" (v. 6). In response, my **life** will be one of goodness.

Scriptures for Study: Read the verses cited today, rejoicing in God's goodness.

Good (3)

ṭôḇ

Before leaving this broad subject of **good**, we note what **David** writes in Psalm 119:68: "Thou art good, and doest good; teach me thy statutes." Since **God** *does* **good** because He *is* **good**, the psalmist wanted to be **good** because God is **good**. How could he do that? It is the **statutes** (February 19) and decrees of God engraved in stone that **teach** us how to *be* **good** and *do* **good**. While many today look to other things as a source of **good**, such as the ever-popular field of modern psychology and counseling, such things are usually futile and sometimes even destructive.

More futile still is the study of godless philosophy, one of the greatest controversies of which has always involved the problem of **good**, or "value." As one writer asks, "Does 'good' have an objective, absolute existence? Is there 'Good' with a capital 'G' so to speak, or is it always relative to the preference or satisfaction of some individual?"[174] Men invariably **answer** such foolish questions by clinging either to absolutism[175] or relativism.[176]

Worse, the discussion inevitably leads to the question, "But what is 'the highest good,' the *summum bonum*?" The most common and popular answer has been *pleasure,* or in more modern terms, "pleasant consciousness" or "pleasant feeling."[177] The **name** most typically given to this philosophy is "hedonism," from the Greek *hēdonē* (2237G), "sensual delight." To the hedonist **good** is identified with pleasant, and **evil** is identified with unpleasant. Not only is such a philosophy anti-biblical, but it can be (and has been) used for unthinkable immorality. Under the disguise of "utilitarianism" (the greatest **good** for the greatest **number**), Hitler murdered six million Jews for the "greater good" of Europe.

Worse still is how relativism has spilled over into the church. Long-established Christian doctrines are being challenged and "rethought" so they conform to modern thought, church ministry now involves what appeals to each person's wants and desires, and what people now call "Bible study" is nothing but people sharing what they *think* the Bible says or how it makes them *feel.*

Where, then, will **man** find **good**? Answer: *There are no ethics apart from revelation*. It is Christ alone who brings true knowledge, morality, and ethics to any society. A secular **book** written on "ethics" is an oxymoron, because apart from God's truth and standards, ethics are relative at best and impossible at worst. God is the only One who is **good** and only He reveals **good** through His statutes.

Scriptures for Study: Read the following verses (and there are many more), noting what each says about **good**: Psalms 4:6; 14:1; 34:8; 37:3, 85:12.

Evil

ra'

A study of **good** would not be complete without also considering its very opposite, **evil**. In fact, we find both words used together in some sixty-five verses, often within the same clause, such as: "good and evil" (Gen. 2:9), "evil for good" (44:4), "the evil and the good" (Prov. 15:3), "call evil good, and good evil" (Isa. 5:20), and so on.

The Hebrew generally used is *ra'* (7451, from the verb *rā'a'*, 7489), which appears about 650 times (*rā'a'* about 90 more). Its use in combination with *good* is the simplest **way** of **understanding** it. In light of *ṭôḇ*, whatever is not good, pleasant, beneficial, **precious**, delightful, right, well-pleasing, fruitful, morally correct, proper, or convenient is **evil**.

Like *ṭôḇ*, it is in the moral (and religious) sense that *ra'* takes on its greatest significance in that it "denotes activity that is contrary to God's will,"[178] as when **David** did something as seemingly innocent as taking the census but did it contrary to God's will (1 Chron. 21:17). **Evil** is all-encompassing: physical abuse (Num. 16:15; Ps. 22:16), slavery (Exod. 5:22, 23), dishonesty (Gen. 31:7), perverted sexual relations (Gen. 19:7), attempted murder (1 Samuel 26:21, "harm"), and the list continues.

Particularly striking to this writer is how often we see *ra'* in Judges and Kings in relation to idolatry. The repetition of the statement, "And the children of Israel did evil in the sight of the LORD" (or similar), which in "all the historical books . . . is the regular phrase for falling into idolatry,"[179] is striking (Judg. 2:11; 3:7, 12; 4:1; 6:1; 10:6; 13:1; 1 Kings 14:22; 16:30). God hates idolatry, and an **idol** can be anything from an **image** of stone to a desire for success.

If there is one thing the emphasis of good and **evil** demonstrates, it is the fallacy of the popular notion of "gray areas" of morality and behavior. Unlike the philosophy of our **day** that avoids distinctions between right and wrong, truth and error, good and **evil**, and moral and immoral, **Scripture** teaches no such ambiguities. In a day of vanishing absolutes, Christians have the responsibility to stand against **evil**. And how can we do that? Spurgeon is worth repeating (from February 23): "The surest way to abstain from evil, is to be fully occupied in doing good."[180]

Scriptures for Study: Where does **evil** begin, according to Isaiah 1:4 and Jeremiah 16:12? 📖 Why does the believer have no need to **fear evil** (Ps. 23:4)?

House (of the LORD)

bayiṯ

As we come to the end of David's great **psalm** of comfort, no ending could be more reassuring: "And I will dwell in the house of the LORD for ever" (Ps. 23:6).

House is *bayiṯ* (1004), which is common also to Aramaic, Arabic, Akkadian, and Ugaritic and appears, as one might expect, more than 2,000 times in the OT. Houses of the ancient world, in contrast to tents, were of higher quality than one might think, often made of stone, wood, and mortar (Lev. 14:45). Archaeology, in fact, has uncovered impressive homes with thick walls, such as Lot's **house**, as far back as 2000 BC. While usually one story, some houses still had an "upper room" (or similar) (1 Kings 17:19; cf. 2 Kings 4:10; Luke 22:12; Acts 1:13; 9:37; 20:8, 9), a separate room on top of the **house** used for favored guests.

It is with that familiar, homey, restful term, then, that David says he will "dwell in the house of the *LORD* forever." **LORD** (January 8), of course, is God's personal, **covenant name**. We find the phrase **house of the LORD**, in fact, some 230 times in the OT.[181] Here is the place of **worship**, the place of personal communion with God, the place of intimate fellowship with Him, the place where we are to **dwell**.

Significantly, this term **house of the LORD** appears nowhere in the NT. "God's house" is no longer a *place* where we *go*, but is in the *people* of *God*. Every believer is indwelt by the Holy Spirit (John 14:16–20; Rom. 8:9, 11, 23; 1 Cor. 6:19; 1 John 4:13). While the place we meet should certainly be one of reverent worship, it is the "body" of each believer that is now "the temple of the Holy Ghost which is in [us], which [we] have of God, and [we] are not [our] own" (1 Cor. 6:19).

David's thoughts, however, actually go beyond this realm into the heavenly ("for ever"). Once again, we appreciate Spurgeon: "While I am here I will be a child at home with my God; the whole world shall be his house to me; and when I ascend into the upper chamber I shall not change my company, nor even change the house; I shall only go to dwell in the upper [story] of the house of the Lord for ever."[182]

Scriptures for Study: Review our study of **heaven** on May 19 and 20 and **rejoice** that you will one **day** "dwell in the house of the LORD for ever."

Dwell

yāšaḇ

Going one step deeper into that **last** provision of the Shepherd in Psalm 23:6—"I will dwell in the house of the LORD for ever"—we conclude our study by considering the significance of that **word *dwell*.**

A common verb occurring about 1,090 times, *yāšaḇ* (3427) primarily means "to sit." This includes literally sitting down, such as sitting to eat (Gen. 27:19; Jer. 16:8), a **king** sitting on his **throne** (Exod. 11:5; 1 Kings 1:13), or a **judge** or other leader sitting in the **gate** of the city to carry out official duties (2 Sam. 19:8; Ps. 69:12; Prov. 31:23). **God** is also viewed as sitting on His throne, a metaphor for ruling (1 Kings 22:19; Ps. 2:4; 47:8). It also includes the metaphorical idea of "keeping company with," such as "[sitting] with the wicked" (Ps. 26:5; also 1:1).

Several other meanings are derived from *yāšaḇ*, including "to inhabit, endure, or stay," but the most common is "to dwell." Its first occurrence reflects this common meaning, as "Cain went out from the presence of the LORD, and dwelt [settled, inhabited, stayed] in the land of Nod, on the east of Eden" (Gen. 4:16). Similarly, Judah told his daughter-in-law, "Remain a widow at thy father's house, till Shelah my son be grown" (Gen. 38:11), and Jeremiah declared of God, "Thou, O Lord, remainest for ever; thy throne from generation to generation" (Lam. 5:19).

Significantly, the Septuagint renders *yāšaḇ* here, and elsewhere, as the Greek *katoikeō* (2730G), "to inhabit a house." In other places (e.g., Ps. 102:12), *yāšaḇ* is translated *menō* (3306G), which denotes "remaining in one place, keeping an agreement, and remaining valid, as in a law." The clear truth in all this, then, is permanence, continually dwelling in one place.

Does not **David**, therefore, **teach** us about attendance in corporate **worship**? David is speaking about spending the rest of his **life** worshipping God at the **tabernacle**. Does that not encourage us again (March 9) to faithful attendance in our local church for the rest of our days? As Hebrews 10:25 declares: "Not forsaking the assembling of ourselves together, as the manner of some is; but exhorting one another: and so much the more, as ye see the day approaching."

Indeed, we shall **dwell** with our **Lord** forever, and even now "sit together in heavenly places in Christ Jesus" (Eph. 2:6).

Scriptures for Study: Read the following verses, noting the gathering together of God's people: Acts 1:14; 2:1, 42; 20:7; 1 Cor. 5:4; 16:2.

Deceit

tarmiyṯ

While the Hebrew *tarmiyṯ* (8649) appears only six times in the OT, each is significant. Always translated either **deceit** or "deceitful" in the AV, *tarmiyṯ* means "to do something undercover, underhandedly, with **evil** or trickery in mind."

This is the **word** Jeremiah uses, for example, when he asks, "Why then is this people of Jerusalem slidden back by a perpetual backsliding? they hold fast deceit, they refuse to return" (Jer. 8:5). Here God's people *inwardly* deceive themselves and turn from **God**. Jeremiah uses this word later, where **deceit** is now *outward*, as with false teachers; after they themselves have been *deceived*, they become *deceivers* of others (14:14).

Paul paints the same picture in his final **counsel** to Timothy: "Evil men and seducers shall wax worse and worse, deceiving, and being deceived" (2 Tim. 3:13). Six verses later, Paul then charges Timothy with what he should do in the **face** of such deceitful teachers. He did not tell Timothy to be "seeker-sensitive" or to meet the "felt needs of the unchurched." Rather he told him, "Preach the word; be instant in season, out of season; reprove, rebuke, exhort with all longsuffering and doctrine. For the time will come when they will not endure sound doctrine; but after their own lusts shall they heap to themselves teachers, having itching ears; And they shall turn away *their* ears from the truth, and shall be turned unto fables" (4:2–4).

If any verses characterize our **day**, those do. "Endure" is *anechomai* (430G), which literally means "to hold one's self upright." In modern English, we would say, "They just won't put up with it," and, indeed, many today will not put up with authoritative **preaching**. As a result, they look for teachers who will tickle them behind the ear, make them "feel good about themselves," **keep** them laughing, and tell them what they *want* to hear instead of what they *need* to hear. What many *want* are anecdotes, comedy, pop psychology, motivational lectures, positive thinking, devotional thoughts, and small talk, when what they *need* is Truth.

While that is a strong statement and will be criticized by some, Christian leaders who provide the things we just mentioned have been deceived and have themselves become deceivers, whether or not they are aware of it. Mark it down: *If we are not giving people the Truth, we are deceiving them into believing that something else is adequate*. Oh, let us desire Truth!

Scriptures for Study: Note the other appearances of *tarmiyṯ*: Judges 9:31 ("privily"); Psalm 119:118; Jeremiah 23:26; Zephaniah 3:13. 🕮 In Psalm 119:118, what is in store for the deceiver?

Wonderful (1)

pele'

With no pun intended, we look today at a ***wonderful* word**. We first mentioned the Hebrew *pele'* (6382) back on January 30 but only briefly in reference to the coming Messiah in Isaiah 9:6. Today we go deeper.

While the noun *pele'* appears about thirteen times in the OT, the verb from which it is derived (*pālā'*, 6381) occurs about seventy times. This word presents a problem, however, caused by the limitations of language. As one authority puts it, while the word means "to be marvelous, be extraordinary, be beyond one's power to do, do wonderful acts," it is easy to see from those "suggested meanings [that] this verb is not easy to define."[183]

How can human language possibly describe the marvel of Creation, as in "the heavens [*šāmayim*, May 19] shall praise thy wonders" (Ps. 89:5)? Or how can words fully express the great "wonders" He did in delivering His people from Egypt (Exod. 3:20)? How, in fact, could we possibly **count** all the wonders He has done? As the psalmist again declares, "Many, O LORD my God, are thy wonderful works which thou hast done" (Ps. 40:5). Significantly, as the Psalms are permeated by **praise** of **God**, of the more than eighty OT instances of *pālā'/pele'*, thirty-seven of them are in the Psalms.

In the final analysis, it is really God alone who can do anything truly **wonderful**. As the psalmist once again declares, "Blessed be the LORD God, the God of Israel, who only doeth wondrous things" (72:18). As the beloved Puritan Matthew Henry comments, "Men's works are little, common, trifling things, and even these they could not do without him. But God does all by his own power, and they are wondrous things which he does, and such as will be the eternal admiration of saints and angels."

How tragic it is when God's people forget what He has done! "The children of Ephraim . . . kept not the covenant of God, and refused to walk in his law; And forgat his works, and his wonders that he had shewed them" (Ps. 78:9–11). That passage goes on to recount the wonders God did in delivering them from Egypt but how they sinned against Him unimaginably and how He had to **judge** them to bring them back to Him (vv. 12–34).

Let us not forget the **wonderful** things God has done (Ps. 105:5)!

Scriptures for Study: Based upon God's "wondrous works," what did the psalmist do in Psalm 71:17 (also 96:3)? 📖 What else should we do in 107:8, 15, 21, 24, and 31?

Wonderful (2)

pele'

Before we leave *pālā'* and *pele'*, **David** uses these words three times in that great **psalm** of **praise** to God's **Word**. He refers first to the "wondrous things" of God's **law** (Ps. 119:18), then to God's "wondrous works" that he can understand only through God's **precepts** (v. 27), and finally to God's **wonderful testimonies** (v. 129). There is, indeed, no better word that sums up the Word of God than **wonderful.** Ponder briefly ten wonders of the Bible:

First, its *unique authorship*, as it was written over a 1,600-year **time** span, by some forty authors from every walk of **life**, in different locations, and in different languages. *Second* is its *complete unity* of thought and teaching, presenting only one view of God, one view of sin, one method of **salvation**, and one program for the ages. *Third* is its *central theme*, the **Lord** Jesus Christ. The OT *points* to Him, the Gospels *present* Him, and the Epistles *propagate* Him. *Fourth,* it was *written in superior languages*. Hebrew is a pictorial, personal language that graphically recorded God's mighty acts. Aramaic was the local language of Palestine and served to link the OT and NT through the Lord Jesus and His apostles. The exactness of the Greek then precisely expressed the theological truths of the NT. *Fifth,* it is *unmatched in sale and circulation*, passing the two-billion-copies-in-print mark long ago and is still selling twenty-five million copies a year.

Sixth, its *prophetic accuracy* is astounding, with many ancient prophecies fulfilled to the letter, such as: the returning of the Jews to their own land (Ezek. 36), the utter destruction of Tyre and that it would never again be inhabited or rebuilt (Ezek. 26), and, of course, the many Messianic prophecies fulfilled by Jesus. *Seventh,* its *archeological authentication* is equally astonishing; in response to the denial of the biblical record by critics, the existence of many biblical cities has been **proved** by the archeologist's spade, such as: Ur of the Chaldees, Megiddo, and Jericho. *Eighth,* its *scientific accuracy* is also without flaw, providing us with absolutely accurate facts about Creation, astronomy, and even diet. *Ninth,* its *agelessness*—it is as up-to-date now as when it was penned. *Tenth,* its *indestructibility* is established by the thousands of manuscripts that have survived the ravages of time and that its truth has survived the violence of both direct attack (physical destruction) and critical attack (historical and textual challenge).

Oh, the wonders of God's Word!

Scriptures for Study: In Psalm 119:129, what should our response be to knowing the **wonderful testimonies** of God's Word?

Panted

šā'ap̱

In **light** of our study **yesterday**, when we truly see the **wonder** of **Scripture**, we cannot help but desire and long for it. A graphic Hebrew **word** that pictures this is the verb *šā'ap̱* (7602). Appearing fourteen times in the OT, its primary meaning[184] is "to gasp, pant, wait eagerly for, or hurry for," and therefore pictures desiring, longing for, or seeking something. In a negative sense, for example, in view of Job's unimaginable sufferings, Elihu told him to "desire not the night," that is, **death**, to deliver him from his agony (Job 36:20). Job himself had used it earlier, when he looks forward to future reward for his faithfulness by picturing a weary, hard-breathing laborer who is earnestly looking for some shade (7:2).

Most notably, it is right on the heels of **writing** about God's **wonderful testimonies** in Psalm 119:129 that **David** adds, "I opened my mouth, and panted: for I longed for thy commandments" (v. 131). Just as that laborer longs for a little shade, or just as a traveler in the desert pants for the cooling breeze, or just like "a stag that has been hunted in the chase, and is hard pressed, and therefore pants for breath" (Spurgeon), or just as the climber of Mount Everest pants harder for oxygen with each step higher, that is how David longed for the Word of God. What a picture! And oh, how we should pant, **plead**, and **pray** for God's Word!

We are reminded here again of Job: "Neither have I gone back from the commandment of his lips; I have esteemed the words of his mouth more than my necessary food" (Job 23:12). Jeremiah concurs, "Thy words were found, and I did eat them; and thy word was unto me the joy and rejoicing of mine heart: for I am called by thy name, O Lord God of hosts" (Jer. 15:16). And so did our **Lord** Himself: "My meat is to do the will of him that sent me, and to finish his work" (John 4:34). As we will detail tomorrow, Peter also encourages, "As newborn babes, desire the sincere milk of the word, that ye may grow thereby" (1 Pet. 2:2).

Dear Christian **Friend**, do you truly long for God's Word? Is it the cool breeze that refreshes you in the desert of this world? Is it the very air you breathe? We will meditate on this again **tomorrow**.

Scriptures for Study: How valuable was God's Word to the psalmist in Psalms 19:10 and 119:72?

Longed After

tā'aḇ

Concluding yesterday's thoughts, another Hebrew **word** that portrays a strong desire for something is *tā'aḇ* (8373), which appears only twice in the OT, both, in fact, in Psalm 119, where it is translated **longed after**. It "is used figuratively of a person's inherent desire for God's ethical and moral precepts."[185] In other words, why does the believer long for the Word of **God**? Because such longing is now "inherent," that is, natural, inborn, and intrinsic to the believer's nature.

David declares in verse 40, "Behold, I have longed after thy precepts," and then in verse 174, "I have longed for thy salvation, O LORD; and thy law is my delight." A derivative (*ta'aḇāh*, 8375) occurs one additional time back in verse 20: "My soul breaketh for the longing that it hath unto thy judgments at all times." This word speaks of an intense hunger; David was broken-hearted when deprived of God's Word. How many of us are broken-hearted when we can't be under the **preaching** and teaching of the Word? Mark it down: *The true Christian is one who has an insatiable appetite for God's Word.*

A **deep burden** on my **heart** for many years has been the ambivalence common **among** many who **call** themselves Christians, a lack of longing for God's Word. While some don't want it at all and seek the many user-friendly characteristics of the modern church, others don't make it a priority when their church *does* have the Word as the central emphasis. Other activities easily and often replace church attendance. While I do not wish to seem harsh, I have seen countless things come before church attendance, proving that God's Word is not the priority.

Peter graphically illustrates what the believer's attitude should be toward God's Word: "As newborn babes, desire the sincere milk of the word, that ye may grow thereby" (1 Pet. 2:2). Basic to the very nature of a baby is the desire for milk. Have we not all seen a baby when he or she knows milk is on the **way**? Often the mouth is already moving, the hands reaching for it, and even the legs moving as if they could run to it. Would we not think something wrong if that baby were lethargic and indifferent as to whether the milk came? Likewise, we had better take a closer look if we do not **long after** the Word of God.

Scriptures for Study: Read the following verses, noting what each encourages us to do: Acts 6:7, 12:24, and 19:20.

Refrained [and] Restrained

kālā'

The Hebrew *kālā'* (3607) is rendered several ways in our beloved AV translation: **restrained**, withheld, forbade, shut up, kept, and **refrained**, among a few others. This verb means "to close, hinder, restrain, or even restrict the flow of something." The basic idea "seems to indicate the interruption of what is in progress or would naturally be in progress."[186] It's used, for example, in Genesis 8:2 when **God restrained** the rain after the Flood. Likewise, the calves of the cows used to pull the cart on which the **Ark of the Covenant** was disobediently carried had to be "shut up" (enclosed) at home (1 Sam. 6:10).

First Samuel 25 is a graphic example. After protecting Nabal's sheep, **David**, according to the custom of the **day**, sent some young men to ask Nabal for a gift in **return**. Nabal answered them with so much contempt, however, that David was enraged and took about four hundred men with him to punish Nabal. Learning of her husband's folly and David's intention, Abigail gathered a large amount of food and intercepted David, pleading for **forgiveness**. David's response in verse 33 was, "Blessed be thy advice, and blessed be thou, which hast kept [*kālā'*] me this day from coming to shed blood, and from avenging myself with mine own hand." This **word**, then, demonstrates the holding back of strong intentions and drives.

Once again significant is the appearance of our word for the day in Psalm 119: "I have **refrained** my feet from every evil way, that I might keep thy word" (v. 101). What quality, more than any other, differentiates the Christian from the non-Christian? *Holiness*. Through the ages such separation from the world and its evils has characterized the true believer. Spurgeon says it well: "There is no treasuring up the holy word unless there is a casting out of all unholiness."[187] If we may say it this **way**: We do not **love** the *Word* if we live like the *world*.

David adds, in fact, that holiness of **life** is precisely how we "keep [God's] word" (Ps.119:101). The two greatest evidences of true conversion are *obedience to God's Word* (John 14:15, 23; 1 John 2:1–5) and *holiness of life* (Eph. 4:24; 1 Thess. 4:3, 4, 7). Moses, for example, **proved** his holy lifestyle by refusing the things of Egypt (Heb. 11:24, 25). Let us **strive** this day to "keep [God's] word" by living in a holy manner.

Scriptures for Study: What does David **pray** in Psalm 40:11 ("withhold")? 📖 How did Jeremiah prove his holiness (Jer. 9:2; cf. 1 Cor. 5:11)?

Portion

chēleq

The Hebrew *chēleq* (2506) is a rich **word** from Jewish history that refers to a share or piece of territory and is used in several ways. It is used for a part of the spoils of **war** (Gen. 14:24) or a **portion** of food (Lev. 6:17). Its most common use, however, was to refer to a share in an **inheritance**, as in a **portion** of land (Josh. 19:9). **God** gave the Promised Land to His people according to His **covenant** promise. This makes the term, in fact, a parallel of *nāchal* ("inheritance," May 25).

Psalm 119 once again provides a striking example of a word's use in poetry: "Thou art my portion, O **LORD**" (v. 57). The clear figurative use here is that while the world seeks happiness in **wealth**, property, and other earthly **spoil**, having "their portion in this life" only (Ps. 17:14), the true child of God seeks only God Himself and desires only what is found in Him. Profoundly struck by this truth, **David** writes again in Psalm 142:5, "I cried unto thee, O LORD: I said, Thou art my refuge and my portion in the land of the living." Another psalmist, Asaph, David's chief musician, probably picked it up from David and writes, "My flesh and my heart faileth: but God is the strength of my heart, and my portion for ever" (73:26).

Commenting on Psalm 16:5—"The LORD is the portion of mine inheritance and of my cup: thou maintainest my lot"—perhaps Spurgeon puts it best: "He is our portion, supplying all our necessities, and our cup yielding royal luxuries; our cup in this life, and our inheritance in the life to come. As children of the Father who is in heaven, we inherit, by virtue of our joint heirship with Jesus, all the riches . . . of grace; and the portion which falls to us sets upon our table the bread of heaven and the new wine of the kingdom."[188]

Abraham knew this truth. While Lot wanted the well-watered plain of Jordan and **pitched his tent** toward the advantages of **Sodom**, Abraham was satisfied with what God would provide *in the desert*. This picture was vividly painted for me when I drove across western Utah and then Nevada only to see hundreds of miles of desolation. What could anyone possibly find there that would satisfy? But Abraham was satisfied. Let us also be satisfied with the **portion** God chooses to give.

Scriptures for Study: What truth did Paul learn in Philippians 4:11–13? 📖 What is Peter's encouragement (2 Pet. 1:3)?

Famine

rā'āḇ

Have you ever been *really* hungry? We don't mean you missed lunch and were "starving" by suppertime. Rather, have you ever been without adequate food for days, weeks, months, or even years, perhaps to the point of **death**? Images that come to mind here are the countless pictures of the Jewish Holocaust, of the walking skeletons created by the Nazis. To prove this **horror** was not propaganda, and to **answer** those he knew would one **day** deny it even happened, General Eisenhower ordered all civilian news media, military camera units, and even regular GIs to take as many pictures as possible. Incredulously, some still deny it.

The Hebrew *rā'āḇ* (7458) appears some one hundred times in the OT and is usually translated **famine** (also "hunger, dearth, and famished"). Both Abraham and Isaac, for example, experienced **famine** in Canaan (Gen. 12:10; 26:1), and it is mentioned fifteen times in the story about Joseph and the **famine** in Egypt (Gen. 41–47).

The theological significance of *rā'āḇ* is particularly striking. **God** is clearly sovereign over hunger and **famine** (Deut. 8:3) and provides for His people who are hungry (Prov. 10:3). Jeremiah is especially dramatic in his use of this **word** some thirty-two times, most of which refer to the judgment that is to come upon Judah (by way of the Babylonians) because of her headlong plunge into idolatry.

It is Amos, however, who pictures a **famine** far worse than any physical one: "Behold, the days come, saith the Lord GOD, that I will send a famine in the land, not a famine of bread, nor a thirst for water, but of hearing the words of the LORD" (8:11). While Amos (a contemporary of Jonah, Hosea, and Isaiah) was a Judean **prophet**, God wanted him to speak to the northern tribes (Amos 7:15). During a time of great prosperity and security, God told the people the day was coming when because of their moral decay and rejection of truth, *they would no longer hear the Word of God read or preached*. This soon happened with the Assyrian captivity, and such "deafness" continues to this day.

What could possibly be worse than such a **famine**? And what of our own day? Amos does, indeed, have "a word for any nation in Israel's condition," one writer observes. "Put his descriptions in [modern] dress and they will strike home."[189] In a very real sense, some aspects of contemporary Christianity are causing a holocaust. Is the day coming when we will no longer hear the Word at all?

Scriptures for Study: Notice the further details of Amos' prophecy in 8:12, 13.

Vanity

heb̲el

Writing to young people around 900 BC, Solomon warns his readers in the **book** of Ecclesiastes not to live **life** according to human **wisdom**. He graphically paints the picture of life "under the sun" (e.g., 1:3, 9, 14) and dogmatically declares that without the presupposition of **God**, man's life is meaningless, empty, and futile. The second and third verses of the book declare its theme: "Vanity of vanities, saith the Preacher, vanity of vanities; all is vanity. What profit hath a man of all his labour which he taketh under the sun?"

The key **word**, of course, is **vanity**, which appears (along with "vanities") thirty-seven times in Ecclesiastes and is a translation of the Hebrew *heb̲el* (1892), which in turn literally refers to "breath, vapor, or mist." We noted this word back on February 12 (**Abel**) but consider it here in its deeper context. Job, for example, says his "days are vanity," that is, his life is a vapor (Job 7:16; also James 4:14). As the vapor we exhale on a cold **morning** is gone in an instant, our life is here one moment and gone the next.

Solomon's message is, therefore, clear and sobering. No matter what we pursue in this life, whether it be pleasure, possessions, **power**, popularity, or prestige, all of it is nothing more than vapor. Such a thought is depressing, indeed, until we realize the other half of the truth—God makes life meaningful, and everything we have is "from the hand of God" (Eccles. 2:24). What is the "conclusion of the whole matter?" Solomon goes on to **write**. "Fear God, and keep his commandments: for this is the whole duty of man. For God shall bring every work into judgment, with every secret thing, whether it be good, or whether it be evil" (12:13, 14).

How sad it is that most people go through life scratching and clawing as they chase the illusive (and elusive) dream of happiness and fulfillment while all the while having no idea that it will never come because they **know** not God. As God's people did in Isaiah's **day**, they "[provoke God] to anger with their graven images, and with strange vanities" (Jer. 8:19), for "the customs of the people are vain" (10:3). No matter what each person adopts as an **idol**, every one is empty.

Sadder still is when Christians are drawn into such philosophies as materialism, secularism, and pragmatism, and seek the things the world offers instead of God's Word alone.

Scriptures for Study: Read Ecclesiastes 3:10–15, 5:18–20, and 9:7–10, noting each aspect of life in which God alone brings true **joy**.

JUNE 29

Stranger

gēr

Have you ever been in a place where you were a **stranger**, perhaps a country where the language and culture were totally unfamiliar? Then again, there are even places in America where we might feel like an alien.

The Hebrew **word** that carries the narrowest meaning in regard to a **stranger** is *gēr* (1616), which appears ninety-two times in the OT. One authority tells us it refers to "anyone who is not native to a given land or among a given people. . . . those living in a strange land among strange people. Their stay was temporary or they did not identify with the group among whom they were living, no matter how long they stayed."[190]

Its first occurrence is in Genesis 15:13, where **God** tells Abram of Israel's future bondage in Egypt: "Thy seed shall be a stranger in a land that is not theirs, and shall serve them; and they shall afflict them four hundred years" (also Exod. 12:40, 430 years to be exact). Moses even used this word to **name** his son Gershom ("a stranger there") to demonstrate that he (Moses) was a **stranger** in Midian (Exod. 2:22).

A striking occurrence of *gēr* appears in Psalm 119:19: "I am a stranger in the earth." Oh, that we would realize the significance of David's statement! Here he was a native of the land and even **king** of that land. Still he says that he is *not* a native, rather a **stranger**, an alien. The apostle Paul realized the same truth. Referring to the Jews in Egypt but extending that to the Christian, he preached to those in Antioch that the people were "strangers in the land of Egypt" (Acts 13:17). Christians are, indeed, not a part of this world, just passing through, no matter how long we live here. "For our conversation [literally, "citizenship," *politeuma*, 4175G] is in heaven; from whence also we look for the Saviour, the Lord Jesus Christ" (Phil. 3:20; cf. Eph. 2:19).

What, then, is our map and survival guide to make it through this alien world in which we live? In a note on Psalm 119:19, the 1599 *Geneva Bible* encourages, "Seeing man's life in this world is only a passage, what should become of him, if your word were not his guide?" As David then adds in verse 54, "Thy statutes have been my songs in the house of my pilgrimage."

Scriptures for Study: Read Hebrews 11:13–16. Who is the subject of the passage? What is the "better country" it talks about? What does Peter add in 1 Peter 1:1 and 2:11?

Melteth [and] Heaviness

dālap̱ [and] tûg̱āh

As we saw **yesterday**, being a **stranger** can be almost unbearably lonely. Finding oneself in a country with different language, customs, and even currency is an isolation like no other.

David felt this **way**. As noted yesterday, he writes, "I am a stranger in the earth" (Ps. 119:19). Nine verses later he expresses his utter despair by adding, "My soul melteth for heaviness: strengthen thou me according unto thy word." Two words underscore David's anguish:

First, the word **melteth** is the Hebrew *dālap̱* (1811), which appears only two other places in the OT and literally means "to pour out or to leak." It refers to a leaking roof in Ecclesiastes 10:18 ("droppeth through"). Job also used it when his friends criticized him, causing him to "[pour] out tears unto God" (Job 16:20).

Second, added to this was the **heaviness** David felt. The Hebrew *tûg̱āh* (8424) is derived from a root verb (*yāg̱āh*, 3013) that means "to suffer and grieve in emotional despair as a result of a specific act or condition." The noun appears only three other times in the OT, all of them in Proverbs. A foolish son causes his parents great grief (10:1; 17:21), and in the end, after all the laughter in sinful pleasure fades away, all that remains is grief (14:13).

We now have the complete picture. David's grief, sorrow, and anguish weighed upon him, which brought about **deep** depression and weeping. Spurgeon, who like other great men of **God** suffered from depression from time to time, put it beautifully: "He was dissolving away in tears." Are there times when you, too, "leak" and feel you are dissolving away?

Because true persecution is virtually nonexistent in America at present, it is difficult to identify with believers who suffer for their **faith**, such as those in communist and Islamic countries. In this **psalm** alone, David repeatedly mentions that he is suffering for his commitment to God's Word (Ps. 119:28, 50, 67, 71, 75, 83, 92, 107, 109, 143, 153).

For what, then, does David **pray**? Does he pray that God will **destroy** his attackers, pray for their misfortune, or pray that he will be vindicated? No. He was, in fact, burdened and sorrowful for them (v. 136). He simply prayed, "Strengthen thou me according unto thy word" (v. 28).

Dear Christian **Friend**, the Word of God is always the **answer**. Only *it* will give you the **strength** to meet each **day** head-on and every attacker face-to-face.

Scriptures for Study: Read the verses in Psalm 119 listed above, noting both the problem and the solution in each (we will examine verse 83 **tomorrow**).

A Bottle in the Smoke

nō'd̲ [and] qiyṭōr

Today's study centers on a Hebrew idiom. As mentioned **yesterday**, David's **deep** grief, sorrow, and anguish are emphasized several times in Psalm 119. Particularly striking is verse 83: "For I am become like a bottle in the smoke." What in the world does David mean by this odd statement?

First, we note the individual words. **Bottle** is *nō'd̲* (4997), which refers to a wineskin, that is, a container made of animal skin in such a way as to hold liquid, such as wine (Josh. 9:4, 13) or milk (Judg. 4:19), without leaking. Jesus' metaphor of putting **new** wine in old bottles (Matt. 9:17) refers to this practice. **Smoke** is *qiyṭōr* (7008), which can refer to dense smoke, such as rises from a burning city (Gen. 19:28) or a **camp** fire in our text.

Various customs have been cited by commentators to explain our idiom. Some, for example, point out that the skins were sometimes hung up in the smoke to dry before the wine was actually put in them. If not done properly, however, such as hanging them in a tent where the smoke could not easily escape, they would be tainted. Others say that such bottles, when empty, were hung in the owner's tent and could be spoiled by smoke.

Whatever the cause, the outcome is the same.[191] The skins would now be useless. They would reek with smoke and become **black**, sooty, wrinkled, and shriveled. *That* is how David felt. One commentator paints an accurate picture for us: "David . . . was in the throes of despondency. Everything had gone against him. He was in the thick of the battle. There was a haze about him, like smoke rising from a smoldering fire. He could not see or think clearly. He appeared to be in the midst of the conflict, so that he considered that he was hanging above the fire, and likened himself unto a bottle in the smoke. His face was lined, his skin was wrinkled and shriveled, his countenance was blackened by the soot; he had about reached the place of despair."[192]

Thankfully, however, David adds, "Yet do I not forget thy statutes" (Ps. 119:83). We might be as low as is possible for a person to be, but it's always the **Word** of **God** that delivers us from despondency, despair, and depression. Yes, we will **know** distress and difficulties in faithful Christian living, but our **hope** is always in God and His Word.

Scriptures for Study: What is the content of the rest of David's **prayer** in Psalm 119:84–88?

Incline

nāṭāh (1)

The Hebrew *nāṭāh* (5186) appears 215 times in the OT and literally means "to extend, stretch out," that is, extending something outward and toward, as one would extend his **arm** (Exod. 7:5) or point a **staff** (Exod. 7:19) or a spear (Josh. 8:18). It is used also for stretching out, that is, pitching, a tent (Gen. 12:8; Exod. 33:7) and as the idiom for stretching out one's **hand** against something in a hostile manner (Job 15:25).

This **word** is often used, however, in a figurative **way**, such as inclining or leaning toward something. As the psalmist Asaph writes, for example, we are to "incline [our] ears to the words of [God's] mouth" (Ps. 78:1). Of special note is Psalms 119:36: "Incline my heart unto thy testimonies, and not to covetousness." The godly believer is not inclined or reaching toward covetousness ("which is idolatry," Col. 3:5), not "[inclined] . . . to any evil thing, to practise wicked works" (Ps. 141:4). Rather he or she is inclined toward God's **testimonies** (February 17), that is, the solemn testimonies of His will, the serious expressions of His standards for human behavior.

This pictures the same truth that Paul declares in Philippians 3:13, 14: "Brethren, I count not myself to have apprehended: but this one thing I do, forgetting those things which are behind, and reaching forth unto those things which are before, I press toward the mark for the prize of the high calling of God in Christ Jesus." In spite of being trained by our **Lord** Himself (implied in Gal. 1:16–18) and thirty years of Christian growth and ministry, Paul says (in effect), "I haven't arrived yet. I haven't reached the prize. I don't even fully comprehend the prize. I therefore continue to reach forth, to press toward, to pursue, to go after the prize of the knowledge of Christ." "That I may know him," was his driving motive (3:10).

Therefore, an essential part of a consistent Christian **life** is that we are always "reaching forth." Sadly, many Christians, and even Christian *leaders*, get to a point in their lives where they become complacent and satisfied. They might say, "Well, I think I'm okay. I know the basic truths of Christianity, I know what I believe, and I love the Lord. That's all I need." Such an attitude shows we have already failed! If we are not *always reaching*, we begin to stagnate and even **slide** back.

Dear Christian **Friend**, are you *always reaching*?

Scriptures for Study: Read the following verses, noting what each encourages us to do: 1 Kings 8:58; Psalms 119:51; 141:4; and Proverbs 2:2.

Declined

nāṭāh **(2)**

Before leaving *nāṭāh,* we are compelled to note another usage of it in Psalm 119:51: "The proud have had me greatly in derision: yet have I not declined from thy law." **Proud** is *zēḏ* (2086, March 19), which refers to exaggerated self-importance that includes defiance and rebelliousness. "Derision" is *liyṣ* (3887, February 27), a strong word for scorn and mockery, expressing utter contempt.

Sadly, a prominent philosophy in the church today is that we must actually appeal to the world, make the "unchurched" feel comfortable in our church services by giving them whatever they want. **David** says quite the opposite, however—the world will mock and scorn God's people as they stand for truth. Indeed, we will be held in contempt by the rationalist, scorned by the relativist, and even hated by the religionist.

Like David, however, this should never cause us to "[decline] from [God's] law." He says, in effect, "No matter what they say, I will lean *on* nothing else but God's Word and never lean *away* from it." While many Christians in the days when the theory of evolution was gaining prominence, for example, leaned away from God's Word so as not to be scorned and mocked for their "simple-mindedness" (February 26), we must never be so cowardly. The godly believer never leans away from God's Word, regardless of what attacks may come. He is absolutely confident in God's Word.

To further apply this, should we ever be worried when someone approaches us with a supposed "contradiction in Scripture," or asks, "Well, what about this problem? How do you reconcile this with that other thing over there?" Should we ever fretfully ask, "Oh, no, what I am going to do now? How am I going to answer this?" Such thoughts should never even occur to us because of our absolute confidence in God's Word. Since we **know** God's Word is right, we know the **answer** is there. If the answer is not immediately forthcoming, we have the unshakeable confidence that God will show it to us. Our confidence must never be shaken by the childishness, foolishness, and wickedness of men.

Scriptures for Study: What does Psalm 119:21 say about the proud? 🕮 What did they do to David in verse 69, and what was his response?

Turn Away

'āḇar

The Hebrew *'āḇar* (5674) is a particularly interesting word. In Psalm 119:37, for example, we read, "Turn away mine eyes from beholding vanity." **Vanity** here is a different **word** than we have previously noted (June 28). This word (*šāw'*, 7723) speaks of **deceit**, lie, or falsehood. It also carries several other meanings: emptiness, **evil**, ruin, uselessness, worthlessness, and lack of result.

David, therefore, prays that **God** would **turn away** his eyes from looking at such things. One authority describes *'āḇar*, which appears about 550 times, especially well: "The verb refers primarily to spatial movement, to 'moving over, through, or away from.' This basic meaning can be used of 'going over or through' a particular location to get to the other side, as when Jacob 'crossed over' the Euphrates to escape Laban (Gen. 31:21)."[193] Other usages of this word include passing through, by, or over something, as when "God made a wind to pass over the earth, and the waters assuaged" after the Flood (Gen. 8:1).

All this paints a vivid, poetic picture. David prays that his eyes would simply pass through, pass over, move away from all the evils of falsehood and emptiness. That is, indeed, an essential element of a consistent Christian **life**. We must be always watching out for the evils of this world and look past them and move away from them.

David uses the same word again in Psalm 119:39: "Turn away my reproach." This has been taken two ways by expositors. Some think it speaks of the reproach that will come against the writer from others as he stands for God. Others believe that it refers to the reproach and shame brought on by God because of the writer's **sin**. The latter was my own first impression as I examined the verse and does seem to better fit the idea of the rest of verse, "For thy judgments are good," as well as verse 37. Puritan Charles Bridges puts it well: "It was the reproach of bringing dishonour upon the name of his God, that David feared. . . . The fear of this reproach is a practical principle of tender watchfulness and circumspection, and of habitual dependence upon Almighty God."[194]

Whichever idea is correct, however, the point is the same: Whether because of the attacks of other people or our own sin, we must constantly be watching and examining our lives, always ready to **turn away** from evil.

Scriptures for Study: What is the **counsel** of Proverbs 4:14,15 ("pass"), 22:3 ("pass on"), and 24:30 ("went")?

Horror

zal'āpāh

While the Hebrew noun *zal'āpāh* (2152) appears only three times in the OT, it captures our attention. Its first occurrence is in Psalm 11:6: "Upon the wicked [the LORD] shall rain snares, fire and brimstone, and an horrible tempest: this shall be the portion of their cup." Translated "horrible" here, *zal'āpāh* refers to a burning or raging heat. As several commentators submit, it seems to refer to the Arab *simoom*, a hot, dry, violent, dust-laden wind that occurs in Asian and African deserts.[195] **David**, therefore, recognized the approach of the horrible, devastating "storm of burning wind and sand" of God's judgment upon the wicked. Anyone who has ever been in a sandstorm understands the metaphor all too well. Blowing sand cuts the skin, blinds the eyes, and can easily choke a person to death. The words "fire and brimstone" are undoubtedly an allusion to the destruction of **Sodom** and Gomorrah and make the **image** all the more frightening.

We see the same idea in the second occurrence of *zal'āpāh*, where we find its most graphic rendering, which is lost in modern translations: "Horror hath taken hold upon me because of the wicked that forsake thy law" (Ps. 119:53). David is struck again by the destructive nature of sin, specifically, when men "forsake [God's] law." We see the same picture in the final occurrence of *zal'āpāh*, where Jeremiah writes, "Our skin was black like an oven because of the terrible [*zal'āpāh*] famine" (Lam. 5:10). The **prophet** records the people's suffering under the hands of the Babylonians because of their repeated idolatry and disobedience to God's **Word**.

Here is a challenge to every Christian to be as horrified at **sin** as David was, to recognize what happens to every person exposed to the terrible storm due to one's rejection of God's Word. Such **horror**, in fact, should drive us to our knees in **prayer** for ourselves first and then for others. Obedience to God's Word must be our chief concern, else will we be caught in the horrible storm that is to come. The only safety, the only confidence that exists, lies in obeying the Word of God.

Scriptures for Study: What was David's further reaction to those who did not **keep** God's Word (Ps. 119:136, 158)? 🕮 What was Ezra's response (Ezra 9:3, 14; 10:6)?

Idol [and] Graven Image

'eliyl [and] šiqqûṣ [and] pesel

The English word **idol** is a translation of no fewer than twelve Hebrew words. Some of those words simply give the physical description of the **idol**, others describe the worshipper's terror of the god (e.g., *'ēymāh*, 367, Jer. 50:38) or the True God's **anger** with it (e.g., *šiqqûṣ*, 8251, 1 Kings 11:5–10). Still others speak of the **idol** as a thing of naught, a worthless and empty object (e.g., *'eliyl*, 457, Lev. 19:4; 26:1; Ps. 96:5).[196]

The latter two words especially stand out. The word *'eliyl* appears twenty times and literally means "worthless," as the **idol**, a false shepherd who leaves the flock, is worthless (Zech. 11:17). Most of its occurrences refer to vain, empty, worthless **worship**, usually of idols. Its first appearance sets the precedent: "Turn ye not unto idols, nor make to yourselves molten gods: I am the LORD your God" (Lev. 19:4). The word *šiqqûṣ* appears about twenty-nine times and refers to something filthy and detestable, as was Nineveh (Nah. 3:6), and an abhorrent, blasphemous object. That is, indeed, the true nature of idols (Deut. 29:17; 2 Kings 23:13, 24; 2 Chron. 15:8; Jer. 7:30, 31).

We should also note the term **graven image**, first used in Exodus 20:4 in God's command to make no such object. The Hebrew is *pesel* (6459), which means "to hew or to cut in creating an idol." At the very foundation of God's **Law** was that **man** was not to make any **image** whatsoever to represent deity for the purpose of worship.

Renowned Hebrew scholar Robert Girdlestone provides us with a pointed application: "Man is essentially an image-maker. . . . he seeks to make a visible representation even of God Himself, and gradually to transfer to the work of his own hands that reverence and dependence that properly belongs to the one living and true God. There is a strange fascination in exaggerated religious symbolism. It engrosses and excites the mind, but is by no means of a healthy character. It tends little by little to supplant the simplicity of spiritual worship, and to turn man into an idolater."[197]

How careful we must be in our churches, and personal lives, about such symbolism! Nothing *material* must be allowed to be lifted to the level of *spiritual*. "True worshippers . . . worship the Father in spirit and in truth: for the Father seeketh such to worship him" (John 4:23; also v. 24).

Scriptures for Study: Read the verses cited in today's study and guard against idolatry. 📖 In preparation for tomorrow's study, read Isaiah 21:9.

Break (Broken)

šāḇar

Yesterday's "Scriptures for Study" encouraged you to read Isaiah 21:9, where the **prophet** foresees the fall of Babylon and declares, "Babylon is fallen, is fallen; and all the graven images of her gods he hath broken unto the ground." The word **Broken** is *šāḇar* (7665), which appears some 147 times in the OT and means "to break, burst, break in pieces, break down, break up, smash, or shatter."

Its first occurrence is a good illustration, where the **evil** men of **Sodom** threatened to **break** down Lot's door to get at his guests (Gen. 19:9). It is actually a common **word** for breaking things, such as Gideon's 300 men terrifying the Midianites with the noise of breaking their pitchers and revealing their torches (Judg. 7:20; other examples include: Exod. 12:46; Jer. 19:10; 28:10, 12, 13; Hosea 1:5; 2:18). It is also used figuratively for the intense mental suffering we call a "broken heart" (Ps. 69:20).

Our text, therefore, is just one of several instances that speak of the tearing down, the shattering of idols (2 Kings 11:18; 18:4; 23:14; 2 Chron. 34:4; 14:3; Jer. 43:13). But Babylon is where it all started, where formalized idolatry began. From the **worship** of Semiramis descended the "mother and child" pairs of Ishtar and Tammuz to both the Babylonians and the Assyrians (e.g., Ezek. 8:13,14), Astarte and Baal to the Canaanites (e.g., 2 Kings 11:18; Asteroth is the Hebrew **name** in Jer. 7:18 and 44:17–19, 25), Aphrodite and Adonis to the Greeks, Venus and Cupid to the Romans, and Isis and Osiris to the Egyptians.

Idolatry distressed Moses so deeply he broke the tablets of God's **commandments** (Exod. 32:19). Far more serious, God's **heart** was broken by such spiritual whoredom (Ezek. 6:9), into which His people repeatedly fell and which ultimately led to their captivity in Assyria and Babylon.

How vital it is, therefore, that we identify any idols we might erect in our lives, and then **break** them down and **destroy** them. Significantly, upon their **return** from their decades of captivity in those pagan lands, not once did God's people ever fall into pagan idolatry again. They had had enough. What will it take for us?

Scriptures for Study: What else is spoken of in Leviticus 26:19 as needing to be broken?

Abomination

tô'ēḇāh

What is an **abomination**? The Hebrew is *tô'ēḇāh* (8441), which appears about seventy times in the OT, referring to something loathsome or detestable to another person. Here is something repugnant, repulsive, and revolting, something vile, villainous, and vain. Do we get the picture? Its first occurrence is in Genesis 43:32, where the Egyptians were repulsed at the thought of eating with Hebrews because of their diverse cultures. Proverbs 29:27 declares the axiom, "An unjust man is an abomination to the just: and he that is upright in the way is abomination to the wicked."

Most notably, many things are spoken of in **Scripture** that are loathsome to **God** because they **break** His **law**, such as: sexual perversions, including prostitution (Deut. 23:18) and homosexuality (Lev. 18:22–30; 20:13; 1 Kings 14:24), adopting occult practices (Deut. 18:9–14), eating unclean animals (Deut. 14:3–8), and even dishonest business dealings (Deut. 25:13–16). As one might expect, the most common use of *tô'ēḇāh* (about fifty times) is in reference to idolatry (e.g., Deut. 7:25, 26).

Besides these "dramatic" sins, *tô'ēḇāh* "is used in the sphere of jurisprudence and of family or tribal relationships."[198] In other words, anything that destroys the underpinnings of society or affects the harmony of relationships is abhorrent to God. There is no better summation of such abominations than in Proverbs 6:16–19: "These six things doth the LORD hate: yea, seven are an abomination unto him: A proud look, a lying tongue, and hands that shed innocent blood, An heart that deviseth wicked imaginations, feet that be swift in running to mischief, A false witness that speaketh lies, and he that soweth discord among brethren."

Some Christians today find "abhorrent" the idea that God actually hates anything. Many prefer to believe that God is "all love" and unconditionally pardons any "shortcomings," "mistakes," or "weaknesses" we might have. But that is not the God of the Bible. Yes, **love** is one aspect of His nature (1 John 4:8, 16), but so are holiness (January 25) and justice. He abhors and judges **evil**.

This instructs us that to love God, we must **hate** evil (Ps. 97:10). To help us understand that we must hate (August 28) what God hates, we will examine the list of abhorrent sins in Proverbs 6:16–19 starting tomorrow.

Scriptures for Study: Read the following verses, noting that love and hate can (and must) coexist in the believer: Amos 5:14, 15; Psalm 45:7; and Romans 12:9.

Proud Look

rûm

How significant it is that **pride** is the first **sin** mentioned in a list of sins that **God** abhors (Prov. 6:17)! Is not pride at the root of the problem?

We considered the words pride and **proud** on March 19, but we encounter a different **word** here. While *gā'āh* (1342) means "to rise, exalt, or lift up" and *zēḏ* (2086) carries the idea of an exaggerated self-importance, *rûm* (7311) is similar to *gā'āh* but seems to have the subtle difference of "great height," that is, the "state of being on a higher plane."[199]

That idea is certainly evident in the first occurrence of *rûm*, where the waters of the Flood "increased, and bare up the ark, and it was [*lifted*] *up* above the earth" (Gen. 7:17; emphasis added). Likewise, "The stormy wind . . . lifteth up the waves" (Ps. 107:25). Sadly, God's people were intimidated by the "taller" people of Canaan (Deut. 1:28), and used figuratively, **David** rejoices that God will "set [him] up upon a rock" so he would be high above any danger (Ps. 27:5).

The meaning in our text, then, is that God abhors those with a **proud look**, that highly exalted appearance that says, "I'm better than everyone else; I'm a cut above the rest." Solomon echoes, "O how *lofty* are their eyes! and their eyelids are lifted up" (Prov. 30:13, emphasis added). We have all seen this kind of person, the **man** (or **woman**) who acts as if they are on a higher plane than everyone else. Lucifer thought he was on a higher plane than God (Isa.14:13, 14, "exalt") and told **Eve** she and Adam, too, would be gods (Gen. 3:5). J. Oswald Sanders recounts the emperor's valet who said, "I cannot deny that my master was vain. He had to be the central figure in everything. If he went to a christening, he wanted to be the baby. If he went to a wedding, he wanted to be the bride. If he went to a funeral, he wanted to be the corpse."[200]

Let us be constantly on guard against exalting ourselves, lifting ourselves to a higher plane than others. Instead, "Let the God of [our] salvation be exalted" (Ps. 18:46), "and let us exalt his name together" (34:3).

Scriptures for Study: What will happen to those with "high looks" (Ps. 18:27)? 📖 What is "too high" for a **fool** and therefore out of reach (Prov. 24:7)?

Lying Tongue

lāšôn šeqer

The second abominable thing to **God** is a **lying tongue** (Prov. 6:17). **Tongue** is *lāšôn* (3956), which first refers to the physical organ, whether human (Lam. 4:4) or animal (Exod. 11:7). More often it refers to speech, as Moses was "slow of speech, and of a slow tongue" (Exod. 4:10), probably indicating both that he had trouble finding the right words to say and then trouble saying them.

The **word *lying***, then, is *šeqer* (8267), meaning lie or falsehood, occurring about 113 times, the first of which is in Exodus 5:9, where Moses' words about deliverance and liberty seemed false because of the increasing severity of the Egyptian bondage. We see this concept of deceptive speech often (Isa. 9:15; 59:3; Jer. 14:14), which is simply "a way of life that goes contrary to the **law** of God."[201]

It is significant that we find this word no fewer than seven times in Psalm 119, the great **psalm** that is devoted to praising the virtues, merits, and sufficiency of the Word of God and demonstrates the author's total commitment to it. Any lie was repugnant to him. He passionately hated any untruth (vv. 104, 128, 163), wanted it removed from his own **life** (v. 29), and prayed that the **proud** who lied about him would be brought to shame (vv. 78, 86, 118). Indeed, anything that goes contrary to **Scripture** is a lie.

Sadly, deception and **lies** are prominent in our **day**, even in the church. No truer words have been written that reflect our own day than those by one Hebrew authority: "Micah 2:11 portrays this attitude of Israel by saying that if a man whose way of life is 'wind and falsehood (*šeqer*)' were to come to them with lies, that is the one they would choose as their prophet."[202] Likewise, today it is the prosperity teacher, the self-esteem guru, the seeker-sensitive marketer of the **new** gospel, and a plethora of others who are the "prophets" of choice. Such false teachers are deceiving millions with "another gospel: which is not another," rather a "[perversion of] the gospel of Christ" (Gal. 1:6, 7).

The Septuagint often renders *šeqer* as *pseudē* (e.g., Prov. 6:19; 14:5; 17:4; Isa. 28:15; *pseudos*, 5579G), from which is derived our English word *pseudonym* (a false **name**) and means "the exact opposite of truth."[203] So as mentioned on January 26, let **truth** be our sole desire.

Scriptures for Study: Read the following verses in Proverbs, noting the challenge in each: 11:18 ("deceitful"); 14:5 ("false"); 17:7 (**lying**); 19:5 ("false"); 29:12 (**lies**).

(Hands That Shed) Innocent Blood

nāqiy dām

A boy once asked, "Dad, how do wars begin?" "Well, take the First World War," his **father** replied. "That got started when Germany invaded Belgium." Immediately his wife interrupted him. "Tell the boy the truth. It began because somebody was murdered." (She was right, of course; it was ignited as a result of the assassination of Austrian Crown Prince Franz Ferdinand in Sarajevo, Bosnia, on June 28, 1914.) The husband drew himself up with an air of superiority and snapped back, "Are you answering the question or am I?" Turning her back on him in a huff, the wife **walked** out of the room, slamming the door as hard as she could. When the dishes stopped rattling in the cupboard, an uneasy silence followed, broken finally by the son: "Dad, you don't have to tell me how wars begin; I know now!"

The cost of **war** in human **life** is mind-numbing. In World War I alone, the cost was almost eight and a half million. That almost pales in significance to World War II, the most costly of all, in which the total **number** of fatalities, including battle deaths and civilians of all countries, is estimated at fifty-five million, *plus* another six million in the Holocaust. Many millions of those deaths, of course, were not combat-related at all, rather the murder of innocents.

That is the point of the idiom "hands that shed innocent blood," the third abomination to God listed in Proverbs 6:17. **Innocent** is *nāqiy* (5355), an adjective that means "clean, free from, or exempt." It is often attached to **blood**, as it is here,[204] which is the Hebrew *dām* (1818) and refers to literal **blood**, whether animal or human, and is synonymous with "life" (Gen. 9:4). This paints the picture in our text, therefore, of an innocent person, a life that is **clean** and free from guilt, but which is taken by another. The reason murder is an **abomination** to **God** is that **man** is made in God's **image**, making murder an attack upon Him. So heinous is this that God instituted capital punishment (Gen. 9:6; cf. Matt. 26:52; Rom. 13:4; Rev. 13:10).

We can commit murder, however, even without anyone physically dying. Our **Lord** applied and extended the sixth **commandment** in Matthew 5:21, 22 by saying that "rash anger is heart-murder" (Matthew Henry). As with the other principles in the surrounding context, our Lord was concerned more with *attitude* than He was with *action*. Let us each carefully guard our attitudes.

Scriptures for Study: Review our February 16 reading about how our Lord's **Law** is far superior to the old law.

Wicked Imaginations

machašāḇāh

A fourth **abomination** to **God** is, "An heart that deviseth wicked imaginations" (Prov. 6:18). The noun **imaginations** is *machašāḇāh* (4284), which is derived from the verb *chāšaḇ* (2803), "to think, devise, reckon, regard, or invent." The most common idea in this **word** is "to plan and devise." The noun, therefore, denotes thought, plan, or invention. To show the nature of these **imaginations**, the word **wicked** (*'āwen*, 205) is added. "The primary meaning of the word seems to have two facets: a stress on trouble which moves on to wickedness, and an emphasis on emptiness which moves on to idolatry."[205] God, therefore, abhors "a heart devising thoughts of vanity" or that "imagineth wicked enterprises" or "plots evil plans."[206]

The first OT occurrence of *machašāḇāh* illustrates well this same idea: "And GOD saw that the wickedness of man was great in the earth, and that every imagination of the thoughts of his heart was only evil continually" (Gen. 6:5). I am profoundly struck by that verse every time I read it. So **deep** was **man** in **sin** that every thought he had, every idea he entertained, every plan he made, was **evil**.

The applications are many here, but the beloved Harry Ironside makes an unlikely one. He recalls how a few years before the turn of the twentieth century a well-known American **pulpit** orator stated that "expository preaching is the poorest type of preaching in the world because it leaves so little scope for the imagination." I suspect Ironside was referring to Henry Ward Beecher (1813–87), whose philosophy of **preaching** (March 15) changed the pulpit forever. Beecher was an orator and a showman, and ad-libbed most of his sermons. Oh, yes, he was enormously popular and drew large crowds, but he said little that was biblical. Not surprisingly, his theology grew progressively more liberal until ultimately he accepted evolution and higher criticism and even rejected eternal punishment and verbal inspiration. That is exactly what we are seeing today.

Ironside was correct when he wrote, "Thank God for any kind of preaching that leaves little scope for man's **imagination**, for the Word of God says, 'And God saw that the wickedness of man was great in the earth, and that every imagination of the thoughts of his heart was only evil continually.'"[207] Let us thank God for and commit ourselves to preaching that leaves man out of it.

Scriptures for Study: What does God do to men's "devices" (Ps. 33:10), and how does that compare with His "thoughts" (v. 11)? 🕮 What does Psalm 92:5 say about God's "thoughts"? (We will examine this verse **tomorrow**.)

Deep (1)

'āmaq

We interrupt our study of the "abominations" to **God** to consider a verse mentioned yesterday. One of the those truly captivating words of the Bible appears in Psalm 92:5: "O LORD, how great are thy works! and thy thoughts are very deep." **Deep** is *'āmaq* (6009), which, while occurring only nine times in the OT, refers to something truly profound. One can fall **deep** into apostasy and other **sin** (Isa. 31:6; Hosea 5:2; 9:9), and one might then **bury** that sin as **deep** as possible to try to hide it from **God** (Isa. 29:15; Jer. 49:8).

It is our text, however, that captures our attention (cf. Isa. 7:11). Interestingly, the equivalents of *'āmaq* are the Arabic *'amuqa*, "to be deep," and the Akkadian *emēqu*, "to be (deep) wise." How **deep** is God? "O the depth of the riches both of the wisdom and knowledge of God!" Paul writes, "how unsearchable are his judgments, and his ways past finding out!" (Rom. 11:33).

First, consider the depth of His *person*. In light of our study of God's names back in January, can we even begin to fathom the depth of who He is?

Second, consider the depth of God's ***power***, as He quite literally spoke all things into existence (February 25).

Third, consider the depth of God's *preservation*, as He continuously maintains in existence all the things He has made and maintains their original forms and functions (Ps. 36:6; Acts 17:28; Col. 1:17; Heb. 1:3). Even though God has *established* natural forces in nature and man, He still exercises a special and continuous *upholding* of these forces. Think of the atom and all its subatomic particles. What holds it all together? What would happen if God stopped thinking of His Creation for even a nanosecond? Everything would cease to exist!

Fourth, consider the depth of God's *providence*, as He continuously fulfills His original plan and design through all the tens of trillions (and more!) of events that occur in the universe. He reigns "over all" (1 Chron. 29:11, 12). Think of it! He controls the physical universe (Job 9:5–7)[208] including the animal world (Ps. 147:9),[209] and even the **nations** of the world (Ps. 22:28).[210] "There's a special providence in the fall of a sparrow," Shakespeare wrote. "If it be now, 'tis not to come; if it be not to come, it will be now; if it be not now, yet it will come. The readiness is all."[211]

Scriptures for Study: Read the following verses, noting how Job marveled at God: Job 5:9; 9:10–12; 11:7–9; 26:14; 37:23, 24.

Deep (2)

'āmaq

Yesterday we considered four of the **deep** things of **God** (Psalm 92:5). While we could mention several others, let us consider just one more.

Fifth, consider the depth of God's *paradoxes*. A paradox is a seeming contradiction that is nonetheless true.[212] One of the hardest things for any Bible student to live with is the paradoxes of **Scripture**, things we simply cannot comprehend but that are still true. We vainly **try** to explain them, which sometimes results in a distortion of one or more truths. "The secret things belong unto the LORD our God" (Deut. 29:29).

For example, was Jesus God or man? Yes. He was both 100 percent God from before the beginning (John 1:1) but was also 100 percent **man** in His incarnation (John 1:14). Can we comprehend this? No, but we believe it anyway.

Another question is, "Do *I* live my Christian life or does *Christ* live my Christian life?" Yes. Paul states both principles in Galatians 2:20. He also says in one place that *he* constantly struggled to discipline His body to **keep** it in submission (1 Cor. 9:27) but then says in another that "we are *his* workmanship, created in Christ Jesus unto good works, which *God hath before ordained* that we should walk in them" (Eph. 2:10, emphasis added). Which is true? Both. Can we comprehend it? No, but we believe it.

Of course the "really big one" is, "Is God sovereign, or is man free to choose?" Yes. Does Acts 4:27, 28 say that God decreed the suffering and **death** of our Savior at the hands of these wicked men? Indeed, it does. But does it say that these men were coerced or even forced to do what they did? No. While God knew and decreed the actions of Herod and Pilate, they still did them of their own accord. As theologian A. A. Hodge so ably put it: "We have the fact distinctly revealed that God has decreed the free acts of men, and yet that the actors were none the less responsible, and consequently none the less free in their acts."[213] While man is free to ***choose***, God is sovereign in *control*.

Perhaps we can think of our **understanding** of the **deep** things of God as standing between a set of railroad tracks and looking toward the horizon. Where we are standing, they are separate, but only in eternity do they converge.

Scriptures for Study: What will the Holy Spirit help us do (1 Cor. 2:10)? 📖 Take some **time** today to meditate on and **rejoice** in Romans 11:33–36.

Running (to Mischief)

rûṣ

The fifth **abomination** to **God** is "feet that be swift in running to mischief" (Prov. 6:18). **Mischief** is *ra'* (7451), which we considered back on June 17 (**evil**) and speaks of anything that is not **good** (June 16–18), pleasant, beneficial, **precious**, delightful, right, well-pleasing, fruitful, morally correct, proper, or convenient.

It is, of course, the modifier that is the main point, for the sinner is one who is ***running*** to evil. This is *rûṣ* (7323), which has equivalents in Ethiopic, Aramaic, and Akkadian, and appears about eighty times in the OT. It first occurs in Genesis 18:2, where our **Lord**, in pre-incarnate form, along with two angels, visited Abraham, who in his excitement ran to meet them. He excitedly ran again to get a calf and dress it for a meal (v. 7). One might also run in **fear** (Judg. 7:21), run to bring important news (2 Sam. 18:22; Esther 8:10, 14, "posts"), and run aggressively in battle (Nah. 2:4).

The metaphorical sense, then, of rushing to something is obvious. Besides our text, we read elsewhere that men's "feet run to evil" (Prov. 1:16). Isaiah 59:7 repeats that refrain and then adds that men "make haste to shed innocent blood: their thoughts are thoughts of iniquity; wasting and destruction are in their paths." With "vigour and diligence in the prosecution of sin," writes Puritan Matthew Henry on our text, men's feet "are swift in running to mischief, as if they were afraid of losing time or were impatient of delay in a thing they are so greedy of. The policy and vigilance, the eagerness and industry, of sinners, in their sinful pursuits, may shame us who go about that which is good so awkwardly and so coldly." While the world runs to evil, let us "run the way of [God's] commandments" (Ps. 119:32).

Psalm 147:15 declares, "He sendeth forth his commandment upon earth: his word runneth very swiftly [in communication]." The ancient world, of course, did not have the instant communications we have today, so rulers communicated by sending runners with important messages. We are reminded of the Pony Express in our own country, which while short-lived (April 1860–October 1861), being replaced by the telegraph, amazingly covered the 1,966 miles from St. Joseph, Missouri, to Sacramento, California, in ten days. As those riders of old risked their very lives to carry important communications, let us commit ourselves to proclaiming God's truth.

Scriptures for Study: What is the promise of Isaiah 40:31? 📖 Read about and recommit yourself to the Christian "race" in 1 Corinthians 9:24–26.

(False) Witness [and] Lies

'ēḏ [and] kāzaḇ

The sixth in Solomon's list of abominations to **God** is "a false witness that speaketh lies" (Prov. 6:19). Does it not strike us that this is the second reference to lying in this list? Why? Undoubtedly because lying is the most prominent **sin** of mankind and manifests itself in uncounted ways and situations.

While the **lying** of verse 16 is *šeqer* (8267), meaning "lie or falsehood," and seems to speak of everyday situations, the picture painted by **false witness** is that of the courtroom or other formal situation. **Witness** is *'ēḏ* (5707), "a person who has firsthand knowledge of an event or one who can testify on the basis of a report which he has heard (Lev. 5:1)."[214] This is reflected in verses that refer to the court system under the Mosaic **Law**, which stated that at least two witnesses were needed to convict someone of a crime (Num. 35:30; Deut. 17:6; 19:15). This is further seen in the fact that the Hebrew behind the **word *lies*** (*kāzaḇ*, 3576) appears four times in the **book** of Job (6:28; 24:25; 34:6; 41:9, "vain"), which is "filled with courtroom rhetoric, debating the trustworthiness of the speakers' accounts."[215] **David** wrote as well, "The proud have forged a lie against me" (Ps. 119:69; cf. Ps. 35:11; 109:2), indicating a well-thought-out lie that they swore to.

I am reminded here of the famous Nuremberg Trials after World **War** II, where several Nazis, including Hermann Goering—the organizer of the Storm Troopers and the Gestapo and commander of the Luftwaffe (air force)—were tried for crimes against **peace**, war crimes, and crimes against humanity. Despite the mountain of irrefutable evidence against them, they blatantly and arrogantly lied by denying complicity, most maintaining they were only "following orders." Of the twenty-four war criminals convicted, Albert Speer—the architect who built Nuremberg Stadium and other Nazi monuments and became Hitler's minister of armaments and directed war production using slave **labor**—was the only one to admit his guilt and spent twenty years in Spandau Prison. How many people have lied in courtrooms before and since?

Lying is an **abomination** to God. The words we speak are of the utmost importance. Let them, therefore, be words that are true (Prov. 12:17, 19, 22), wise (10:31; 16:23), carefully **chosen** (15:28; 21:23), helpful (10:21; 12:18), and appropriate (10:32; 25:11).[216]

Scriptures for Study: In addition to the verses above, read Matthew 5:11, 12. What are Jesus' encouraging words here?

Soweth Discord

šālach medān

The seventh and final **abomination** to **God** in the list of sins in Proverbs 6:16–19 is "he that soweth discord among brethren." The Hebrew idiom back in verse 16, "six things . . . yea, seven," can be taken a couple of ways. It might mean that the seventh is worst of all, as seven represents completeness. More likely, as one commentator submits, "The purpose of this kind of numerical pattern (x and x + 1) is not to give a complete list. Instead it is to stress the final (x + 1) item as the culmination or product of its preceding items."[217] We see a similar pattern of 3 +1 elsewhere in Proverbs (30:15, 16, 18, 19, 21–31) and the same pattern in Amos in his exposing of Israel's **sin** (1:3, 6, 9, 11, 13; 2:1, 4, 6). Another commentator calls this the "the *non plus ultra* of all that is hated by God,"[218] that is, the uttermost point, the point at which there is nothing further.

Do not **pride**, lying, murder, wicked thinking, hurried **evil**, and more **lies** culminate in **discord**? This is the Hebrew *medān* (4090), the plural of *māḏôn* (4066), and refers to strife and dissension. Its full force seems to be that once such conflict begins it is virtually impossible to stop, as indicated in Proverbs 17:14: "The beginning of strife is as when one letteth out water," and 18:19, "A brother offended is harder to be won than a strong city: and their contentions are like the bars of a castle."

This is further demonstrated by *šālach* (7971), which is translated **soweth** here but literally means "to send, send away, let loose, spread, or stretch out." It is used of the roots of a **tree** spreading out (Jer. 17:8) and of God sending a fire of judgment (Hosea 8:14). The more precise idea in our text then is "one sending forth contentions between brethren" (*Young's Literal Translation*).

What an abomination to God it is to spread dissension! It discourages, demoralizes, and destroys. Even in our churches we find such behavior. Gossip, backbiting, and other sins of the **tongue** can **destroy** God's **work** as quickly, if not quicker, than open immorality. While Paul addressed a case of incest going on within the Corinthian church (1 Cor. 5), for example, he dealt with the problem of **discord** and disunity first (3:1–8). The Christian must guard the tongue above everything else.

Scriptures for Study: Read the classic passage on the tongue in James 1:19, 26, and 3:2–12 and allow the Holy Spirit to guard your own tongue.

Spoil(s)

šālāl

One of the greatest benefits of battle and conquest in the ancient world was the **spoils** they brought. The same is true in more modern times. Why did Adolf Hitler want Russia? Yes, he hated the Bolsheviks, but what he really wanted were the oilfields of the Caucasus Mountains in the south. They would also open a gateway farther south to the oilfields of the Middle East. What was the whole **war** about for the Japanese? Again, raw materials, such as the coveted oilfields of the Dutch East Indies. The reason for their attack on Pearl Harbor, of course, was retaliation for the American embargo against sending them such raw materials.

The primary **word** translated **spoil** in the OT is *šālāl* (7998). Appearing some seventy-five times, it literally means "prey," as in an animal tracking and killing its prey (Gen. 49:27). It referred also to what was taken in military conquest (Deut. 20:14; Josh. 7:21).

Being a military man, **David** knew about the value of the **spoils** of war, having taken great **spoil**, in fact, at Ziklag (1 Sam. 30:16, 19; 26–31) and from the children of Ammon (2 Sam. 12:30). He, therefore, draws a comparison in Psalm 119:162: "I rejoice at thy word, as one that findeth great spoil." **Spoil** increases one's **wealth**, **power**, satisfaction, influence, and happiness; **rejoice** (*śûś*, 7797) pictures jubilant celebration. This portrays soldiers cheering after the battle as they raise the **spoils** above their **head** for all to see.

Unlike physical **spoil**, however, which never totally satisfies, God's Word does. Hitler, for example, was not satisfied with Russia—which he ultimately did not take anyway—but he wanted all of Europe and even planned to invade America; he wanted to capture the world. Only "spiritual spoil" satisfies.

We should also note that as the **spoils** of war do not come easily—they must be fought for—so the "spoils" of the Word of God do not come without conflict. We must **labor** in it and at times fight our own rebellion against it. We then even fight *for* it and defend it with our lives.

Scriptures for Study: What is the **counsel** of Proverbs 16:19? 🕮 What is a trait of the **Virtuous Woman** in 31:11?

Hiding Place

sitrāh

Perhaps you have read *The Hiding Place*, in which Corrie ten Boom tells the story of how she and her Dutch family, all devout Christians, felt compelled to hide Jews from the Nazis. They constructed a false **wall** in Corrie's bedroom, thereby creating a secret room, the **hiding place**, in the event the Nazis raided the **house**. So well-concealed was that room, in fact, that even though the ten Boom family was betrayed, arrested, and sent to concentration camps, the hidden Jews escaped detection even though the Gestapo virtually tore the house apart.

Infinitely more secure, however, no matter what trouble might come or who might betray us, is **God** Himself. **David** writes in Psalm 119:114: "Thou art my hiding place and my shield: I hope in thy word." **Hiding place** is the Hebrew noun *siṯrāh* (5643), which is derived from the verb *sāṯar* (5641), "to hide, conceal." Unlike a synonym such as *'ālam* (5956), *sāṯar* includes the additional concept of protection. This is vividly seen in Deuteronomy 32:38, for example, where God mocks the whole idea that pagan gods can be one's "protection."

David, therefore, viewed God as his **hiding place**, his **place** of refuge and protection from all dangers. Is this an isolated thought? Hardly. Of the some eighty occurrences of *sāṯar*, several of them speak of God. It is David again who writes in Psalm 17:8, "Keep me as the apple of the eye, hide [*siṯrāh*] me under the shadow of thy wings" (cf. 91:1). What a beautiful picture! "Even as the parent bird completely shields her brood from evil," Spurgeon writes, "and meanwhile cherishes them with the warmth of her own heart, by covering them with her wings, so do thou with me, most condescending God, for I am thine offspring, and thou hast a parent's love in perfection."[219] David again rejoices in Psalm 27:5 that "in the time of trouble [the LORD] shall hide me in his pavilion [or, 'shepherd's tent'[220], *sōḵ*, 5520]." Still again, he prays with absolute confidence, "Thou art my hiding place; thou shalt preserve me from trouble; thou shalt compass me about with songs of deliverance. Selah" (32:7).

Whether you have **time** to go into a secret room or are just driving down the highway, take some time today to **rejoice** that God is your **hiding place**.

Scriptures for Study: What does the prudent **man** do in Proverbs 22:3? 📖 What does God hide us from in Psalm 64:2?

Shield

māgēn

Not only does Psalm 119:114 tell us that **God** is our **hiding place**, but it also declares, even more graphically, that He is our **shield**. The Hebrew *māgēn* (4043) refers to the small, common type of round **shield** carried by **light** infantry and officers of David's **day** for defense. Several of its sixty occurrences refer to that literal sense (e.g., Judg. 5:8; 1 Kings 10:17; Isa. 22:6)

In far more verses, however, we find the figurative idea that God is our **shield**, our defense in battle. Its very first occurrence, in fact, is as early as Genesis 15:1, where God promises Abram, "Fear not, Abram: I am thy shield, and thy exceeding great reward." These words come on the heels of Abram's rescuing Lot from the kings of the east, likely causing Abram to **fear** reprisal. God's promise, therefore, assured him of *protection* and *provision.* Likewise, in his blessing upon Israel in Deuteronomy 33 before his **death**, Moses declares in the final verse, "Happy art thou, O Israel: who is like unto thee, O people saved by the LORD, the shield of thy help, and who is the sword of thy excellency! and thine enemies shall be found liars unto thee; and thou shalt tread upon their high places" (v. 29).

This truth is repeated in verse after verse: 2 Samuel 22:3, 36; Psalms 3:3; 7:10; 18:2; 28:7; 33:20; and the list goes on. "Oh what a shield is God for his people!" writes Spurgeon of Psalm 3:3. "He wards off the fiery darts of Satan from beneath, and the storms of trials from above, while, at the same instant, he speaks peace to the tempest within the breast." It is again **David writing** here; while a military **man** who knew the **power** of armor and armies, he knew that his real **strength** came from God.

What a striking parallel all this is to Ephesians 6:16, where the Christian warrior is told to "[take] the shield of faith, wherewith [we] shall be able to quench all the fiery darts of the wicked." While the **shield** here is the much larger one carried by the Romans, the parallel is not diminished. It is, indeed, our ***hope***, as David says (Ps. 119:114), and our ***faith***, as Paul says, in God's truth that protect us.

Scriptures for Study: There is a prerequisite for God's protection. To whom is God a **shield**, according to verses such as Proverbs 2:7, 30:5, and 2 Samuel 22:31?

Sword

chereḇ

We cannot mention the **shield** without the **sword** immediately coming to mind, an item with a long history indeed. Before the process of smelting metal was developed, swords were made of stone, **bone**, or wood. The first metal swords (bronze) were probably known to the Egyptians around 2000 BC (about the time of Abraham). These were followed later by iron and then steel.

With equivalents in several other Semitic languages, *chereḇ* (2719) appears 407 times in the OT and refers to a **sword** or "dagger" (also, but rarely, to a "knife or chisel"). The first occurrence of *chereḇ* is in Genesis 3:24, where a flaming **sword** guards the **Tree** of **Life**; we can only imagine its shape and substance. We then see the short "sickle sword" (Gen. 34:26)—the Egyptian *khopesh*—which was about twenty inches long with a curved blade in the last several inches that resembled the letter "C," with the outer edge as the cutting blade. This was probably the primary weapon of the Israelites during the conquest of Canaan. It seems it was the Philistines who then introduced a revolutionary weapon, the long two-edged iron **sword**, first mentioned in 1 Samuel 17:51.

The **sword** consistently gives pictures of warfare and conflict, including military conquest (Gen. 31:26; Num. 21:24; Isa. 3:25) and even personal trouble, as "the sword [would] never depart from [David's] house" because of his **sin** with Bathsheba (2 Sam. 12:10). The **sword** is also used often to represent God's punishment of His erring people (e.g., Lev. 26:25, 33; Isa. 1:20; Jer. 19:7), as well as His enemies (e.g., Jer. 44:13; Ezek. 25:13).

One of the Greek words used some 165 times in the Septuagint to render *chereḇ* is *machaira* (3162G), which is also used in Ephesians 6:17 for "the sword of the Spirit, which is the word of God." This was not the *rhomphaia* (4501G), the heavy broadsword that required only brute **strength**, rather the quick, deadly short **sword** used by the skilled, highly disciplined warrior. A well-trained soldier could cut and thrust from any position, even while lying on the ground.

It is, therefore, the **Word** of God that is the Christian's **sword**, for we are indeed in a violent, no-holds-barred **war**. Each of us must be well-trained in its use and then use it precisely against the attack of **Satan**. As the "whole armour of God" passage indicates, it is the only offensive weapon we need.

Scriptures for Study: How many principles can you note about the Word of God in Hebrews 4:12?[221]

Satan

Śāṭān

Some twenty-four times in the OT we encounter the Hebrew **word** *śāṭān* (7854), which is obviously the source of our transliterated English word ***Satan***. Derived from the verb *śaṭan* (7853), "to accuse or slander," the noun, therefore, means an "adversary, accuser, or one who devises means for opposing another."[222] It is used at times in a general way to refer to one's adversary, as did **David**: "They also that render evil for good are mine adversaries; because I follow the thing that good is" (Ps. 38:20; cf. 109:4, 20; 71:13).

It is with the definite article ("the"), however, that the word takes on a far deeper and more dangerous significance.[223] Its meaning is particularly dramatic in Job, where fourteen of its twenty-seven occurrences appear, all in the prologue (chapters 1 and 2) and all with the definite article indicating *the* slanderer. Satan's slandering of Job and plotting against him is vividly introduced in Job 1:9, where **Satan** asks God, "Doth Job fear God for nought?" How reminiscent this is of Satan's tactic of questioning in Genesis 3! He is always plotting, always seeking ways of sowing doubt.

An especially interesting occurrence of *śaṭan* is in Ezekiel 28:12–16, where we read of the condemnation of the **king** of Tyre (Tyrus), who is likened to someone who was perfect in "Eden the garden of God." While some students view this as referring to **Adam**, the description and parallelism seem much more reminiscent of **Satan**.

Significantly, the Greek equivalent of *śaṭan* is *diabolos* (1228G), which appears in both the Septuagint and the NT and also means "accuser or slanderer." Because *diabolos* appears more than any other title for **Satan** (about thirty-three times), we must conclude that one of his chief activities is slander and accusation. Again, he slanders **God** to men (Gen. 3:1–7) and men to God (Job 1:9; 2:4).

Satan is, indeed, our adversary. He is the slanderer, the accuser who will, either himself or through one of his minions, do all he can to **destroy** your **faith** and faithfulness. As Peter warns, "Be sober, be vigilant; because your adversary the [*diabolos*], as a roaring lion, walketh about, seeking whom he may devour" (1 Pet. 5:8). What is our defense? As noted yesterday, "Put on the whole armour of God, that ye may be able to stand against the wiles of the [*diabolos*]" (Eph. 6:11).

Scriptures for Study: Read Ephesians 6:10–20 and get ready for battle.

Try (Proved, Temptation) (1)

bāchan

As one Hebrew authority observes, **Scripture** declares that "men are beset by tempters who try to make men as much as possible like themselves."[224] Indeed, not only is **man** in himself inclined toward sin, but there are other forces at **work** to draw him even further into **evil**.

So what tool does **Satan** use to draw us into sin? **Among** several others, he uses **temptation**. The Hebrew verb *bāchan* (974) appears about thirty times and means to **try** or **prove** and refers to any kind of **test**, as when Joseph tested his brothers (Gen. 42:15, 16). A particularly interesting use of this **word** is in Job 12:11—"Doth not the ear try words? and the mouth taste his meat?"—which we will examine **tomorrow**.

Most significantly, however, this word usually refers to God's testing of men. Not only does **David** declare that "The LORD trieth the righteous" (Ps. 11:5) but goes on to request that God do so: "Search me, O God, and know my heart: try me, and know my thoughts" (Ps. 139:23). How many of us **pray** that way? Proverbs goes on to liken such testing to the refining of **precious** metals (Prov. 17:3; cf. Ps. 66:10; Job. 23:10; Zech. 13:9).

How, then, does this correlate with what we usually mean when referring to Satan's **temptation**? As the Hebrew authority quoted above well says, such trials and tests "are ordered by God as part of the great system of probation or testings to which every child of **Adam** is being subjected. The agency of the Evil One is permitted for the purpose of bringing a man into that sort of contact with evil that will serve to test his real principles."[225] As someone has wisely said, while Satan tempts us to bring out the worst in us, God tests us to bring out the best. As the smelting process draws out the impurities, leaving behind only what has genuine value, trials and tests prove what is genuine in our lives. As another Hebrew authority writes, "Unlike the Egyptian doctrine [and much modern thought, we would add] where the heart is weighed after death, Yahweh continually assays the hearts of his people that in the end they may come forth as gold (Zech. 13:9; Job 23:10)."[226]

Scriptures for Study: Read Psalm 11:4, 5, noting three principles: God's place ("his holy temple" sovereignly ruling), His presence (with "the children of men"), and His purpose (to "[try] the righteous").

Try (2)

bāchan

Today we consider a particularly significant occurrence of the Hebrew verb *bāchan* (974), which as mentioned **yesterday** means to **try** or **prove** and refers to any kind of **test**. Job 12:11 is part of Job's response to the arrogance of his critics. This response begins, of course, back in verse 2, where in biting sarcasm Job says, in effect, "You are, no doubt, the only wise people on earth, and when you die all wisdom will die with you." In view of what Job had been through and considering the self-righteousness of his "friends," we can hardly condemn Job for his response.

Job then adds in verse 3, "I have understanding as well as you; I am not inferior to you: yea, who knoweth not such things as these?" In the next few verses, he goes on to challenge them for their lack of concern and insensitivity to his plight. Additionally, while Zophar argues that men cannot **know** true **wisdom**, Job counters with the truth that God's creatures could actually tell men things they need to know.

This brings us to verse 11: "Doth not the ear try words? and the mouth taste his meat?" **Try** is *bāchan*, so Job is telling his critics they didn't really listen and **discern** what he was saying; they merely uttered ancient platitudes and opinions. The application for us is clear: Just as our ears test and prove words that are true, and just as the mouth determines **good** taste from bad, God has given each of us the *responsibility* and the *resource* to listen, taste, and discern all things. What is that resource? As always, it is the **Word** of God alone.

One commentator well writes on our text: "Man is endowed with the faculty of distinguishing what is wholesome from what is unwholesome, and he should, in like manner, exercise the faculty which God has given him of distinguishing the true from the false on moral subjects. He should not suppose that all that has been said, or that could be said, must necessarily be true. He should not suppose that merely to string together proverbs, and to utter common-place suggestions, was a mark of true wisdom. He should separate the valuable from the worthless, the true from the false, and the wholesome from the injurious."[227]

Amen!

Scriptures for Study: Review our March 25 reading on **discern** (*biyn,* 995).

Nations [and] Gentiles

gôy

The words "heathen," **Gentiles**, and **nations** appear several hundred times in the OT and always (except for a few instances of **nations**) are a translation of the Hebrew *gôy* (1471, plurals *gôyim* and *hāggôyim*). In eleven other instances, it is rendered "people." It speaks of **nations** or particular peoples in various settings and usually with the added concept of a "territorial or governmental unity/identity."[228] In other words, a nation is a group of individuals united around common **heritage**, land, customs, language, and government.

The first occurrence of *gôy* is in Genesis 10, where we read of the many **nations** that arose after the Flood (vv. 5, 20, 31, 32). We next see it in Genesis 12:2, where **God** promises Abram, "I will make of thee a great nation, and I will bless thee, and make thy name great; and thou shalt be a blessing." What is interesting about this **word** is that it is used not only to refer to Israel (and Judah) as a nation (Exod. 19:6; Ezek. 37:22), but also to the **nations** that would **arise** from Hagar (Gen. 21:13), and even to pagan, Gentile, and heathen **nations** (Exod. 9:24; 34:10; Ezek. 5:6–8), since all the earth, and therefore all its **nations**, belong to God (Exod. 19:5).

Israel, of course, was unique and was to remain so in God's plan. She was to be unique in every possible way a nation could be: land, language, government, religion, morality, and all else. She was to ever be a "holy nation" (Exod. 19:6), to **keep** herself separate and **pure** from all other **nations**, who would be judged for their abominations and idolatry (Deut. 9:4, 5; 18:9; 2 Chron. 33:2; 2 Kings 17:29; Ps. 9:8; 10:16). Further, Israel was warned repeatedly that if she lived and worshipped as other **nations** did, she would share in their judgment (Deut. 32:28; Isa. 1:4; Mal. 3:9).

The applications of all this are numerous. God turned to the **Gentiles** (*ethnos*, 1484G) "to take out of them a people for his name" (Acts 15:14), which is the church. While **Gentiles** were once "aliens from the commonwealth of Israel, and strangers from the covenants of promise, having no hope, and without God in the world" (Eph. 2:12), Christ has brought them **peace** and fellowship (vv. 13–19). The church, then, is unique and is to remain pure and separate from the world (2 Cor. 6:14–7:1; 1 John 5:21).

Scriptures for Study: Read Psalm 2, noting three principles: the **nations** *rebelling* (vv. 1–3), God *revealing* (vv. 4–7), and the **King** *ruling* (vv. 8–12).

Anger

chārāh

Appearing about ninety times, the Hebrew *chārāh* (2734) is related to both "a rare Aramaic root meaning 'to cause fire,' and to an Arabic root meaning 'burning sensation' in the throat."[229] Further, unlike other words for **anger**, this one speaks of the original stirring up of the **anger**, as one would kindle a fire, and the heat that results from it. This is seen, for example, in Potiphar's **anger** being "kindled" against Joseph (Gen. 39:19), and what he then did.

Truly significant is the first occurrence of *chārāh*, where **Cain** was angry at **Abel** (Gen. 4:4, 5), painting the vivid picture of a fire being ignited in his **heart**, and the utter devastation that resulted. Pitifully, Jonah was "very angry" with **God** because God wanted to be merciful to the unimaginably wicked and savage Assyrians in Nineveh (Jonah 4:1), as if some people are *less* deserving and others *more* deserving of **mercy**.

The things at which we get angry actually reveal much about our level of spiritual maturity. **Anger** at the wrong things, for example, reveals the absence of patience and lack of **trust** in God: "Rest in the LORD, and wait patiently for him: fret (*chārâ*) not thyself because of him who prospereth in his way, because of the man who bringeth wicked devices to pass" (Ps. 37:7).

Is **anger** ever justified? Indeed it is, but it must be aimed at the right things. God was angry with His people because of their murmuring (Num. 11:1) and breaking of His **law** (Josh. 23:16), and Moses was no less than enraged ("waxed hot") at Israel's idolatry (Exod. 32:19). We find this same principle in Ephesians 4:26, where Paul commands that while we can get angry, we must not **sin** in that **anger**: "Be ye angry, and sin not." The words "and sin not" are a check and a restraint, a **test** to show whether our **anger** is truly righteous. When does **anger** become sin? When it is not directed at things that are sin against God. In short, sinful **anger** is when our **anger** is motivated by personal reasons, that is, when someone has offended *us,* not God. Are we enraged at idolatry and sin against God's **Word**, or do we get mad only because someone "hurts our feelings"?[230]

Scriptures for Study: Read the following verses from Proverbs, noting what each says about **anger** and **wrath**: 14:17, 29, 35; 15:18; 16:32; 19:11, 19; 25:28.

Arise (1)

qûm

The Hebrew *qûm* (6965) is included in virtually every Semitic language, and appears more than 600 times in the OT. Its basic meaning is simply the physical act of rising up (Gen. 19:33, 35; Ruth 3:14) or the resulting position of that act, standing (Josh. 7:12, 13). Its first occurrence is in Genesis 4:8, where we can easily picture **Cain** (February 11) jumping up in a rage and killing his **brother Abel** (February 12).

It is from that literal idea, then, that a whole host of figurative (and encouraging) meanings are derived: "to endure, continue, establish, strengthen, perform, and be victorious." We see it in Exodus 33:10, where God's "people rose up and worshipped," encouraging us to demonstrate honor and respect. Likewise, as Balaam told Balak to "rise up" and "hearken" unto the **Word** of God (Num. 23:18), we should do the same. Just the simple act of standing during the public reading of **Scripture** expresses our honor of it, as the people did in Nehemiah 9:1–5, where we see *qûm* three times: "stood up" (vv. 3, 4), "stand up" (v. 5).

My personal **love** and fascination with Psalm 119 grows almost daily, where *qûm* appears four times (both literally and figuratively). Verse 28 declares, "My soul melteth for heaviness: *strengthen* thou me according unto thy word." In other words, "By the power of Your Word, Lord, help me to arise and stand against those who attack." Verse 38 goes on, "[Establish] thy word unto thy servant." It is God's **Word** again that must continue in us if we are going to truly stand. Verse 62 adds, "At midnight I will rise to give thanks unto thee because of thy righteous judgments." How important was the Word of God to **David**? So important he got up in the **middle** of the **night** to commune with God.

Finally, David declares, in view of God's Word being his **light** (May 22) and **lamp** (May 23), "I have sworn, and I will perform it, that I will keep thy righteous judgments" (vv. 105, 106). Here is his tenacious, resolute **vow** that he will stay loyal to the Word of God. Oh, how we need such a vow today! How often we are loyal only to our changing feelings, childish thoughts, and humanistic ideas. We compromise truth, capitulate to error, even contradict God's very words. As ***sworn*** indicates (see tomorrow's reading), we each need "to take an oath" of our loyalty to the Word of God as our *only* authority.

Scriptures for Study: Note David's use of *qûm* when he speaks of his enemies rising up against him (Ps. 3:1; 18:48), but then he calls on God to rise up and **save** him (3:7; 7:6), which God does indeed do (12:5).

Arise (2)

qûm

A verse that immediately comes to mind when we think of the **word** ***arise*** is Psalm 68:1. Many Bible students believe that **David** wrote this **psalm** to commemorate and reenact the **return** of the **Ark of the Covenant** (August 1) to Mount Zion after its capture by the Philistines (2 Sam. 6:2–18). We can almost hear the people shout, "Let God arise!" as the Ark is raised up. These words are virtually identical to those in Numbers 10:35, where the Ark started out from Sinai, where God's enemies are again in view.

Verses 1 and 2 reveal three characteristics of God's enemies: *First,* His enemies are *dedicated.* The word "enemies" is *'ōyēḇ* (341), used many times to refer to the **sworn** enemies of God and His people, such as Egypt (Exod. 15:9), the Canaanites (Lev. 26:34), the Philistines (1 Sam. 14:24), and others. *Second,* God's enemies are *deluded* in their abject hatred for God. This is *śānē'* (8130, August 28), a hatred so **deep** it blinds men to reason. *Third,* God's enemies are *depraved.* "Wicked" is *rāšā'* (7563, February 27), which refers to the criminal, the transgressor of **law**, morality, and all things decent.

It is, therefore, essential that we, as did the ancient people of God, beseech Him in **prayer** to rise up. How self-directed we have become, and how self-sufficient we think we are! As the Ark portrayed God's presence, we, too, need a **new** presence of God in our lives. We **face** exactly the same enemies of God, and it is only when He rises up that we will **know** victory; only then will the "enemies be scattered."

What do we specifically need from God's presence? *First,* we need to *commune* with Him. It was the **mercy** seat that represented a kind of **throne** of God, where He would commune with His people "from between the two cherubims" (Exod. 25:22), hearing their prayers and speaking His words. *Second,* we need the *commands* of God. The original tablets were kept in the Ark—and it is always God's Word we must **obey**. *Third,* we need the *control* of God. As the Ark guided the people then, God's Word controls our every thought and action now.

Oh, that we would "let God arise!"

Scriptures for Study: Read Psalm 68, where we see: the *cry* to battle (vv. 1–3), the ***call*** to **praise** (vv. 4–6), the *commemoration* of God's faithfulness (vv. 7–18), the *commendation* of His victory (vv. 19–31), and the *continuation* of praise (vv. 32–35).

Swear (Sworn) (1)

šaḇa

As mentioned yesterday, **David** unwaveringly vows of God's **Word**: "I have sworn, and I will perform it, that I will keep thy righteous judgments" (Ps. 119:106). **Sworn** is *šaḇa* (7650), an important Hebrew word that appears about 180 times in the OT and means in most contexts to **swear** or "take an oath."

An interesting fact about this word is that it is also the word for the **number** "seven" in Hebrew. While the relationship between the two meanings is uncertain, there is the possibility that since seven is the number of perfection in **Scripture**, then to **swear** is to (what we might call) "seven oneself," that is, to bind oneself with seven things. Abraham, for example, sealed an oath to Abimelech by giving him seven lambs (Gen. 21:23–31), and Jacob vowed to give Laban seven years for Rachel and for Leah (29:18–28). We also see two examples of being "bound by seven" in Samson's foolish behavior (Judg. 16:7, 13).

We, therefore, see this word often in making strong promises. Joshua instructed the Jericho spies to **swear** to Rahab they would bring her safely out (Josh. 6:22). The friendship of David and Jonathan was confirmed by such a strong promise (1 Sam. 20:17). Most significant of all, of course, on several occasions God swore promises by His own **name** and nature (Gen. 22:16, 17; Ps. 89:3, 35; Isa. 45:23; Jer. 22:5; Amos 4:2). On the negative side, David's enemies hated him so much they swore against him, or as it might be worded today, "I swear I'll get him if it's the last thing I ever do." Finally, in the end God says that **among** those He will **judge** are the "false swearers" (Mal. 3:5).

It is no wonder, then, that David swore to **keep** God's Word. "Under the influence of the clear light of knowledge," Spurgeon writes, "he had firmly made up his mind and solemnly declared his resolve in the sight of God. Perhaps mistrusting his own fickle mind, he had pledged himself in sacred form to abide faithful to the determinations and decisions of his God. Whatever path might open before him, he was sworn to follow that only upon which the lamp of the word was shining."[231]

Dear Christian **Friend**, have you made such a **vow**?

Scriptures for Study: Let us take to **heart** the many verses that speak of God's solemn vow to punish sin, and therefore live holy lives by His **grace** (Deut. 1:35; 1 Sam. 3:14; Ps. 95:11; Isa. 62:8; Jer. 22:5; Amos 4:2; 6:8).

Swear (Sworn) (2)

šaḇa

Before leaving this **word**, we are compelled to mention a notable negative occurrence. Titus 1:12 is a fascinating verse that actually refers to Greek culture 200 years before Menander (ca. 342–291 BC): "One of themselves, even a prophet of their own, said, The Cretians are alway[s] liars." Paul quotes the Cretan poet and reputed **prophet** Epimenides. One ancient proverb said, "To act the Cretan, is a proverb for to lie."[232] Just as to be "Corinthianized" meant that one had stooped to the grossest immorality and drunken debauchery (common in Corinth), to be called a "Cretan" was the same as being called a liar, a term used even in the literature of the **day**. The word "always" indicates that this was not the *exception* but the *rule*, the general moral character, "the national sin" of the Cretans.

Even before the days of Epimenides, however, Jeremiah labored in another nation of liars. Jeremiah 5 is perhaps the most graphic biblical example of what exists in our present society, a nation of liars. Historically, the northern **kingdom**, Israel, has already been taken into captivity by the Assyrians (722 BC). While Judah, the southern kingdom, remains, **God** has been telling them that they, too, will be judged harshly for their **sin** unless they **repent**.

So in verse 1, God sends Jeremiah scurrying through Jerusalem seeking anyone who "executeth judgment, that seeketh the truth," and promises to "pardon" the sins of the entire nation if Jeremiah can find *a single person*. But there was not one. Think of it! Not one person, whether rich or poor, whether citizen or leader (vv. 4, 5), told the truth. "Though they say, The LORD liveth," Jeremiah writes, "surely they swear falsely" (v. 2), where **swear** is *šaḇa* and falsely is *šeqer* (July 10).

Verses 11 and 12 go on to say they "dealt very treacherously against [God]" and lied to Him. Verse 27 paints the picture, "As a cage is full of birds, so are their houses full of deceit." Verse 31 records that even the "prophets [prophesied] falsely" and that the people loved it. Like today, people loved what was preached even though it was not true! Honesty, **integrity**, veracity, genuineness, and truthfulness were not virtues to be encouraged, but weaknesses to be avoided. They are not only bad for business but even bad for "ministry." While most people do not want to hear the **truth**, let us desire it with all passion.

Scriptures for Study: What does Paul go on to instruct Pastor Titus to do (Titus 1:13–16)?

Bear

nāśā'

The Hebrew *nāśā'* (5375), which appears some 650 times in the OT and has equivalents in other Semitic languages, carries important theological significance. Meaning "first the lifting up, secondly, the carrying away, and thirdly, the taking away of a burden,"[233] its second OT occurrence underscores all three ideas, as "the waters [of the Flood] increased, and bare up the ark, and it was lift up above the earth" (Gen. 7:17).

Among many other literal uses, the Israelites lifted up, bore, and carried away the **Ark of the Covenant** (Exod. 37:5; Josh. 3:8–17), an armor bearer was described by this **word** (1 Sam. 14:7–17; 16:21), as he lifted up, bore, and carried his **trust**, and **David** and his men "burned" the abandoned Philistine idols, that is, lifted them up, bore them, and carried them away to a place of burning (2 Sam. 5:21).

These meanings take on a truly special figurative sense when we read about someone bearing **sin** or guilt. In its first occurrence, in fact, **Cain** cries, "My punishment is greater than I can bear [lift up, and carry]" (Gen. 4:13). We also read often of the sinner having to **bear** his iniquity (e.g., Lev. 5:17; 19:8; 20:17, 19, 20; 24:15). It is this very truth that leads to something else, such as "the sin offering in the holy place," that could "bear the iniquity" of man's sin for him and "make atonement for [him] before the LORD" (Lev. 10:17). Like Cain, no one can lift up, **bear**, and carry his sin, for it is too great. Like the **scapegoat**, which symbolically carried away the people's sin forever into the **wilderness** (Lev. 16:22), **man** needs something outside of himself to lift, **bear**, and carry away the impossible weight of sin.

Who, then, is the one who has met that need for us? The **Lord** Jesus Christ. One Greek word used in the Septuagint to render *nāśā'* is *lambanō* (2983G), "to take, take up, take away," and appears in Matthew 8:17, where Jesus is He who "took our infirmities, and bare our sicknesses." This is taken right from Isaiah 53:4, which foreshadows "he [who] hath borne [*nāśā'*] our griefs, and carried our sorrows." Another Greek word is *airō* (142G), "to take up, lift, or raise," which we see in John the Baptist's famous words, "Behold the Lamb of God, which taketh away the sin of the world" (John 1:29).

Take some **time** today to **rejoice** in your Sin Bearer.

Scriptures for Study: The Greek *anapherō* (399G) is one other word used in the Septuagint to render *nāśā'*. Read Isaiah 53:11 ("bear" is *nāśā'*) and compare it with *anapherō* in Hebrews 7:27 ("offer up"), 13:15 ("offer"), and 1 Peter 2:5 ("offer up").

Ark (of the Covenant)

'arôn

Of the some 200 occurrences of the Hebrew *'arôn* (727), the first is in reference to Joseph's burial "in a coffin in Egypt" (Gen. 50:26). The basic idea in this **word**, then, is a box or chest. The latter idea appears in verses that refer to a chest that was used for collecting money to make repairs to the **temple** (2 Kings 12:10, 11; 2 Chron. 24:8, 10, 11).

Most occurrences of *'arôn*, however, refer to the **Ark of the Covenant**, which was a very special box. Modestly measuring about forty-five inches long and about twenty-seven inches both wide and high, it was built out of expensive acacia wood and overlaid both inside and out with **gold**. On top was the **mercy** seat, next to which sat two cherubim with outstretched wings covering it. There were also gold rings on the four corners through which wooden poles, also overlaid with gold, were inserted for carrying the **Ark** (Exod. 25:10–21; 37:1–9).

Far more important than its *construction*, however, were its *contents*. In it were kept the tables of stone with the **Law** (Deut. 10:1–5; Exod. 40:20), a pot of **manna**, and Aaron's **rod** that budded (Heb. 9:4). More important still was the Ark's *connotation*. It represented the very presence of **God** on earth, for immediately upon its completion (Exod. 40:33), the **cloud** of God's glory descended upon the **tabernacle** (vv. 34–38; Lev. 16:2).

Is there any NT significance in the **Ark**? In a sense, yes, but only as far as fulfillment is concerned. It is mentioned only twice, first in Hebrews 9:4, 5, where the following verses make it clear that Christ fulfilled and replaced it all. No longer do we need a tabernacle or **Ark**—God is present as a Tabernacle **among** us by way of Jesus Christ. As John 1:14 declares, "The Word [Jesus Christ] was made flesh, and dwelt among us, (and we beheld his glory, the glory as of the only begotten of the Father,) full of grace and truth." "Dwelt" here is the Greek *skēnoō* (4637G), which means "to pitch a tent or encamp" and is a beautiful allusion to the OT tabernacle. No longer do we see God's glory in an **ark** or a building, but in the person of Jesus Christ.

Additionally, while the **Ark** was where divine revelation was received (Lev. 16:2; Num. 7:89), we need no such place today. God's Word is complete; nothing more needs to be added.

Scriptures for Study: Review other references to the **Ark of the Covenant** on February 17, March 29, May 3 and 5, and June 25.

Cloud

'ānān

The Hebrew *'ānān* (6051) is translated as **cloud** (or cloudy) in its some eighty-six occurrences in the AV. At times it refers to the meteorological phenomenon, as when men knew that a **cloud** rising from the sea forecasts rain (1 Kings 18:44; cf. Isa. 5:6). **God** put a **rainbow** in the clouds to confirm His **new** relationship with **man** (Gen. 9:13, 14, 16). But even such references as that point to God, as does Nahum 1:3: "The LORD hath his way in the whirlwind and in the storm, and the clouds are the dust of his feet."

More significantly, "In the ancient world, clouds were often seen as the pedestal or shroud of the divine presence," and the same is true in the Hebrew Bible.[234] In the very next appearance of *'ānān*, God's presence was symbolized by a **cloud** leading the people away from their Egyptian bondage (Exod. 13:21, 22).

One of the most dramatic events in the history of Israel took place at Sinai, where God's "glory cloud," accompanied by thunder and lightning, displayed His presence, **power**, and permanence (Exod. 19:9, 16; 24:15, 16, 18; Deut. 4:11). It was also at that **time** God communicated His **Word** to Moses like never before (Deut. 5:22).

Perhaps most striking of all, as noted yesterday, the **cloud** of God's glory descended upon and filled the **tabernacle** (Exod. 40:34–38), and His presence there is mentioned some thirty times in Exodus through Deuteronomy (e.g., Lev. 16:2; Num. 16:42; Deut. 31:15). That same glory later "filled the house of the LORD," that is, the **temple** in Jerusalem (1 Kings 8:10, 11; 2 Chron. 5:13, 14).

What a glorious history of God's presence with His people! But does that speak to us today? Indeed it does. As the Greek *nephelē* (3507G) is used in the Septuagint to render *'ānān*, so it appears in the NT, first at Jesus' baptism, where God speaks from a **cloud**: "This is my beloved Son, in whom I am well pleased; hear ye him." It was at His ascension that our **Lord** "was taken up; and a cloud received him" and the promise given that He would **return** "in like manner" (Acts 1:9, 11; cf. Rev. 1:7).

Oh, how we look forward to that **day** when we will meet our Lord in the clouds (1 Thess. 4:17)! He came the first time in *faithful* ***grace***; He will come the second time in *full glory*.

Scriptures for Study: Who is being referred to as "clouds . . . without water" in Jude 12? What is the promise that is then given in verses 14 and 15?

Clean [and] Pure (1)

ṭāhôr

The Hebrew verb *ṭāhēr* (2891) means "to be or make **clean**, to be or make **pure**." Nearly half its occurrences appear in Leviticus alone, where it refers to the ritual cleansing outlined in the OT system, but virtually all its some ninety-five appearances speak of ritual (and therefore moral) cleansing. Back on June 2 we mentioned the derivative *ṭāhôr* (2889), which appears about ninety-five times and speaks of the absence of impurity, filthiness, defilement, or imperfection, such as "pure gold" (Exod. 37:11) or "pure words" (Ps. 12:6). **David** used it in his **repentance**, for he needed refinement (Ps. 51:7).

Everywhere we look in the OT, we see the need for purity, as symbolized by purified **gold**: the **Ark of the Covenant** (Exod. 25:11), the **mercy** seat (v. 17), various utensils (v. 29), the lamp stand (v. 31), the plate (28:36), the **altar** of incense (30:3), Aaron's clothing, (39:15), various **temple** furnishings and decorations (1 Chron. 28:17; 2 Chron. 3:4), and even Solomon's **throne** (2 Chron. 9:17). All such symbols demonstrate that **God** is **pure** and holy and that we must be **pure** and holy to come into His presence (Lev. 16:19, 30).

In himself, then, **man** has not an ounce of purity. Proverbs 20:9 asks the rhetorical question, "Who can say, I have made my heart clean, I am pure from my sin?" As purification rituals had to be performed for several things, such as cleansing from leprosy (Lev. 14:9), after touching a dead body (Num. 19:11), a **woman** after childbirth and menstrual flow (Lev. 12 and 15), and both men and women after sexual relations (15:18), so it is that God must "create in [us] a clean heart" (Ps. 51:10).

The Septuagint usually renders *ṭāhēr* and its derivatives as *katharízō* (2511G), *katharos* (2513G), or some other form, which speaks of cleansing or pruning, making free from any improper mixture (English *catharsis* and *cathartic*). As Hebrews 9:13, 14 declares, if the OT sacrifices could, to a certain extent, "[sanctify] to the purifying of the flesh: How much more shall the blood of Christ . . . purge [*katharizō*] your conscience from dead works to serve the living God?" While the true gospel continues to be diluted, denied, and even disdained in our **day**, it is, indeed, only "the blood of Jesus Christ his Son [that] cleanseth us from all sin" (1 John 1:7).

Take some **time** to today to rejoice in the purity you have in Christ.

Scriptures for Study: Read Hebrews 9:19–28, noting the blessed difference between the Old and **New** Testaments ("purged" in v. 22 and "purified" in v. 23 are *katharízō*).

Pure (2)

ṭāhôr

Yesterday we made reference to Psalm 12:6: "The words of the LORD are pure [*ṭāhôr*, 2889] words: as silver tried in a furnace of earth, purified seven times" (February 22). I am drawn often to this **wonderful** verse, and no one is more profound in his observations of it than the writer of the following:

"What a contrast between the vain words of man, and the pure words of Jehovah. Man's words are yea and nay, but the Lord's promises are yea and amen. For truth, certainty, holiness, faithfulness, the words of the Lord are pure as well-refined silver. In the original there is an allusion to the most severely-purifying process known to the ancients, through which silver was passed when the greatest possible purity was desired; the dross was all consumed, and only the bright and precious metal remained; so clear and free from all alloy of error or unfaithfulness is the book of the words of the Lord. The Bible has passed through the furnace of persecution, literary criticism, philosophic doubt, and scientific discovery, and has lost nothing but those human interpretations which clung to it as alloy to precious ore. The experience of saints has tried it in every conceivable manner, but not a single doctrine or promise has been consumed in the most excessive heat. What God's words are, the words of his children should be. If we would be Godlike in conversation, we must watch our language, and maintain the strictest purity of integrity and holiness in all our communications."

While that could have been written today, it was actually penned by Charles Spurgeon around 1860.[235] Many of the various "furnaces" Spurgeon lists began in his **day** and have continued to appear not only in greater **number** but in more sophisticated models. The Bible today is attacked from every possible direction using every conceivable tactic. Sadly, some of the worst, in fact, come from within Evangelicalism itself. Still, God's Word has lost nothing.

We must, therefore, as Spurgeon challenges, be God-like in our living, our language, and our loyalty. God's **pure**, unmingled words must be desired, defended, and declared.

Scriptures for Study: Review our February 22 reading, noting especially *'imrâ* (565), and compare it with today's reading's emphasis on God's **pure**, unmingled words.

Very Pure (3)

me'ōḏ ṣārap̱

Concluding our **meditation** on the concept of **pure**, we find a similar, though still deeper, verse in Psalm 119:140: "Thy word is very pure: therefore thy servant loveth it." Here is the only time in this **psalm** that **David** speaks of God's **Word** as being **pure**, but it's a different Hebrew word than those we have been examining.

Appearing also in Akkadian, Phoenician, and Syriac, *ṣārap̱* (6884) means "to refine, smelt," or **test** and "describes the purifying process of a refiner, who heats metal, takes away the dross, and is left with a pure substance."[236] So again, the Word of God is absolutely **pure**, with no dross of error, inconsistency, or obsolescence. (We will examine *ṣārap̱* further **tomorrow**.)

It was not enough, however, for David to say that God's word is **pure**; he adds the word **very**. The Hebrew is *me'ōḏ* (3966), a modifier that means "very, greatly, abundantly, exceedingly." Its **power** is seen in its first occurrence: "And God saw every thing that he had made, and, behold, it was very good" (Gen. 1:31). God's Word, then, is even *purer than* ***pure***, "pure-plus." What a description! Not only is there no *dross*, but there is not even the *possibility* of dross, just the absolutely **pure** truth of God. Is there any **wonder** David loved it? Do we?

Ṣārap̱ provides us with a great challenge. Used in a figurative way, God's Word speaks of God refining His people to make them **pure**. Its first OT appearance, in fact, provides such a picture, as God whittles down an army of 10,000 to a mere 300 by trying them—to get only the best (Judges 7:4, **try**). Likewise did David **pray**, "Thou hast proved mine heart; thou hast visited me in the night; thou hast tried me" (Ps. 17:3) and then even requested, "Examine me, O LORD, and prove me; try my reins and my heart" (26:2). How does God go about this? What is the furnace that tries us? As God revealed through Isaiah, "Behold, I have refined thee, but not with silver; I have chosen thee in the furnace of affliction" (Isa. 48:10). Contrary to modern thought, it's not *prosperity* that refines us, rather *problems*. Riches don't *produce* character; they *reveal* it.

What, then, will be the final result? "Take away the dross from the silver, and there shall come forth a vessel for the finer" (Prov. 25:4). Only the *valiant* become the *victors*.

Scriptures for Study: How much of God's Word is **pure** (Prov. 30:5)? 🕮 What is Peter's encouraging **counsel** (1 Pet. 1:7)?

Try (Refine, Test)

ṣārap̱

Before leaving this **word** *ṣārap̱* (6884), we should go a little deeper. As mentioned yesterday, this word means "to refine, smelt," or **test** and "describes the purifying process of a refiner, who heats metal, takes away the dross, and is left with a pure substance." In addition to Psalm 119:140, we find it about thirty times, mostly in Psalms and the prophets. (See July 23 for another word translated **try**.)

A derivative of this root (*ṣōrp̱iy*, 6885) refers to the actual tradesman, the **silver** or goldsmith, who does this **work**. While that word actually appears only once (Neh. 3:31), it is obviously often implied in *ṣārap̱*, which itself (as a participle) is sometimes translated "goldsmith(s)" (e.g., vv. 8, 32). One of the major applications of this man's skill was that of fashioning idols (Judg. 17:4; Isa. 40:19; 46:6). Idols were often first carved out of wood and then overlaid with silver or **gold**, which the smith would first smelt and then hammer and roll into sheets (41:7). Sadly, while the idols people fashion today are much more sophisticated, they are dead idols nonetheless and will eventually, with their makers, just **wither** away (Jer. 10:14, "confounded" is *yāḇēš*, 3001, "to be dried up").

The first occurrence of *ṣārap* captures our attention (Judg. 7:4). Gideon started out with 10,000 soldiers, but that was "too many" for **God** to display His **power** against 135,000 Midianites (January 13). So God said, "I will try them," and in the end only 300 were fit for battle. As an avid student of military history, I am often reminded of the demands made upon men who want to become U.S. Navy SEALs. I have sat in rapt amazement as I read books about what they suffer just to *qualify*, not to mention the training and then actual operational deployment that follow. Like those in Gideon's day, very few "make the grade."

As also mentioned yesterday, Isaiah 48:10 declares, "Behold, I have refined [*ṣārap̱*] thee, but not with silver; I have chosen thee in the furnace of affliction" (also 1:25, "purge"). While that speaks specifically of God purifying His people from their repeated rebellion and idolatry by means of the Babylonian captivity, it applies to us today just as strongly. Let us **keep** ourselves **pure**. Let us **pray** with the psalmist, "Examine me, O LORD, and prove me; try my reins and my heart" (Ps. 26:2).

Scriptures for Study: Why do Psalms 12:6 and 18:30 instill confidence?

Repent (Repentance)

nācham

The issue of **repentance** continues to be a controversy. The Hebrew verb *nācham* (5162) is an interesting one and is actually the source of the **name** of the **prophet** Nahum. The original idea in this root **word** "is generally understood to be to draw a deep breath," which pictures the "physical mode of giving expression to a deep feeling, either relief or sorrow."[237] Most of its some 100 occurrences actually refer to **God**. In that latter idea, for example, "It repented the LORD that he had made man on the earth, and it grieved him at his heart" (Gen. 6:6). God was deeply sorry and grieved because of man's sin.

Similarly, God was sorrowful that He had set up Saul as **king** (1 Sam. 15:11), but a few verses later we read that "the Strength of Israel [God] will not lie nor repent: for he is not a man, that he should repent" (v. 29). There is no contradiction here. While the first speaks of God's *conduct* in being sorrowful, the second addresses His *character* as being unchangeable. On the other **hand**, God also declared that if the people would "turn from their evil, I will repent of the evil that I thought to do unto them" (Jer. 18:8), that is, if they would turn from **evil**, He would (*from the human perspective*) change His course of action without violating His sovereign purpose.

For man, then, **repentance** is a realization of and sorrow for his **sin** (Jer. 8:6) and a turning from it (31:19). We see the same principle in the Septuagint and the NT. *Metanoeō* (3340G) means "to turn around, change one's mind, relent," and in the theological sense involves "regret or sorrow, accompanied by a true change of heart toward God."[238]

The *Westminster Confession of Faith* (1646) well says, "By [repentance] a sinner, out of the sight and sense, not only of the danger, but also of the filthiness and odiousness of his sins, as contrary to the holy nature and righteous law of God, and upon the apprehension of his mercy in Christ to such as are penitent, so grieves for, and hates his sins, as to turn from them all unto God, purposing and endeavoring to walk with him in all the ways of his commandments."[239]

It is puzzling, indeed, although sadly common nowadays, how anyone can deny the necessity for **repentance** and still think he is proclaiming the gospel.

Scriptures for Study: Read these NT verses (all containing metanoeō), noting the crucial principle of **repentance**: Matthew 9:13; Acts 2:38; 3:19; Revelation 2:5, 16, 21, 22; 3:3, 19.

Brother

'āch

The idea of a **brother** has a wide range of meanings in the Hebrew *'āch* (251), including: "brother, relative, fellow countryman, or even friend." Occurring some 630 times, the first refers to a full **brother**, that is, one who comes from the same mother and **father**, such as **Cain** and **Abel** (Gen. 4:2). It also refers several times to a half-brother, such as Joseph and his half-brothers (Gen. 37:2–5), as well as Abraham being Sarah's half-brother (Gen. 20:12).

Still another shade of meaning in *'āch* is simply a male **blood** relative. Abram referred to his nephew Lot as his **brother** (Gen. 14:16), Laban called his cousin Jacob a **brother** (29:15), and "Jacob told Rachel that he was her father's brother" (Gen. 29:12). Even a close **friend** who was not a relative could be called a **brother**, as illustrated in the friendship of **David** and Jonathan (2 Sam. 1:26).

Perhaps most significant of all is that even those of common ancestry in general are called brothers. All the children of Israel, descendants of Abraham and Jacob, were called brothers (Lev. 25:46, Deut. 3:18). This is graphically illustrated in Moses' enslaved countrymen being referred to as "his brethren" (Exod. 2:11; 4:18).

There can be little doubt that this "common ancestry" concept formed the basis for the NT idea of using "brothers" when referring to fellow believers. After all, we are all of the same "blood line" in Christ, who is, in fact, our **elder brother** (Rom. 8:29). Further, the Greek *adelphos* (80G) is commonly used in the Septuagint to render *'āch* and in most of the same ways. What is the significance of being "a brother or a sister" (1 Cor. 7:15) in Christ? It means we have the same parentage, proves a family relationship, shows closeness, and implies a future **inheritance**.[240]

Cain asked, "Am I my brother's keeper?" (Gen. 4:9). In a **word**, "Yes!" While "no man is the absolute keeper of his brother, so as to be responsible for his safety when he is not present," writes one commentator, "every man is his brother's keeper so far that he is not himself to lay the **hand** of violence on him, nor suffer another to do so if he can hinder it."[241] A **brother** is one we ***love***, not *loathe*. He is one we *cherish*, not *chafe*. He is one we *protect*, not *provoke*.

Scriptures for Study: What does Romans 14:14, 15 say about how we treat a **brother** in Christ? 📖 Read the apostle John's emphasis on the attitudes and actions of true Christian brothers and sisters: 1 John 2:9–11; 3:10–17; 4:20, 21.

Angel

mal'āḵ

The primary **word** used for **angel** in the OT is *mal'āḵ* (4397), which simply means "messenger," although its some 212 occurrences go far beyond what we think of as a messenger today.

First, *mal'āḵ* is used to refer to the "angel of the LORD," as in its first occurrence (four times), where this "angel" appeared to Hagar and told her she would have many descendants (Gen. 16:7–11). **Among** other instances, the **angel** of the **Lord** appeared to Abraham and **prevented** him from sacrificing Isaac (22:11–13). While there has been some debate, most conservative scholars and expositors agree that in this instance the term is actually a christophany, an OT appearance of the pre-incarnate Christ.

Second, *mal'āḵ* is used for heavenly messengers. In its second OT occurrence, "two angels" came to Lot in **Sodom** (Gen. 19:1) for the purpose of deliverance. Such appearances accomplish several other purposes, including: protection (Exod. 23:20), guidance (Gen. 24:40; Zech. 1:9), and executing judgment (2 Sam. 24:17).

Third, human messengers are also referred to as *mal'āḵ*: "Jacob sent messengers before him to Esau" (Gen. 32:3), Rahab "hid the messengers" sent to her (Josh. 6:17; cf. James 2:25), and "Saul sent messengers unto Jesse" ordering him to send **David** (1 Sam. 16:19). Especially important is the fact that prophets were called "messenger(s)," as they were God's official representatives (2 Chron. 36:15, 16; Isa.44:26; Mal. 2:7; 3:1).

Also significant is that *mal'āḵ* is rendered *angelos* (32G) in the Septuagint and the NT. It, too, means "messenger(s)," often a human messenger (Luke 7:24; cf. 19, 27; James 2:25).[242] While there is debate about the identity of the "angels" of the seven churches (e.g., Rev. 1:20; 2:1), it seems best to view them not as literal angels, but rather as the pastors of those churches. Literal angels are never the "authorities" in churches, are never spoken of as having to **repent**, and God has never spoken to angels through men (in this case, *to* angels *through* John). God is speaking here about earthly matters to earthly messengers, who will in turn pass on those matters to earthly listeners. Why bring heavenly beings into such a discussion? Further, the responsible parties in these letters are earthly, not heavenly beings.

Oh, how responsible God's messengers are today as they **lead** God's people! That is why the qualifications and requirements for leadership in the church are extremely high (1 Tim. 3:1–7; Titus 1:5–9). Take **time** today to **pray** for your leaders.

Scriptures for Study: What else do God's "heavenly messengers" accomplish (Ps. 103:20)?

Bread (1)

lechem

While the diet in the Near East included olives, **oil**, buttermilk cheese, fruits, vegetables, and occasionally meat, the principal food was (and still is) **bread**. So central was **bread**, that the expression "eat bread" was the same as saying "eat a meal" (Gen. 43:31, 32; Exod. 2:20). Appearing almost 300 times, then, *lechem* (3899) could refer not only to **bread** itself but also to a meal, as in a "morsel of bread," a modest meal (Gen. 18:4, 5), or a time of "meat," a full meal (1 Sam. 20:27). Additionally, *lechem* is used to refer to "food" in general (Deut. 10:18; Prov. 27:27) and even to the grain used to make **bread** (Isa. 28:28).

We should note here once again that unique substance called **manna** (May 14, 15). While the children of Israel complained about the shortage of food in the **wilderness** of Sin and wished they were back in Egypt where they could "eat bread to the full" (Exod. 16:3), **God** graciously told Moses, "I will rain bread from heaven for you" (v. 4; cf. vv. 8, 12, 22, 29, 32). While *lechem* is translated "bread," it was very special **bread**, a "heavenly bread" (cf. Neh. 9:15; John 6:30–33), the miraculous provision of God for which there was no **name**, just the puzzled question, "What is it?"

It is this picture, then, that underscores the deeper significance of **bread** (and food in general) in **Scripture**. From where does it all come? While part of the curse in Eden was that **man** would now have to do hard **labor** in order to "eat bread" (Gen. 3:19, the first occurrence of *lechem*), it is still God alone who is the provider of every morsel of food both man and beast eat (Ps. 78:25; 136:25; 147:9).

Still deeper is that **bread** goes beyond physical food, for "man doth not live by bread only, but by every word that proceedeth out of the mouth of the LORD doth man live" (Deut. 8:3). Is it not hugely significant that our **Lord**, after forty days of fasting, quoted these very words during His **temptation** by **Satan** (Matt. 4:4)? Isaiah likens just listening to the **Word** of God as eating **bread** (Isa. 55:2) and **Wisdom** invites the wise, "Come, eat of my bread" (Prov. 9:5).

Dear Christian **Friend**, as I **write** these words, I think of readers like you, whom I will never meet, but still **pray** that you will always hunger for the Word of God.

Scriptures for Study: Can you locate some precedents in Scripture for giving thanks before eating a meal?[243]

Bread (2)

lechem

We simply cannot leave the subject of **bread** as used in **Scripture** without at least briefly meditating on the true **Bread** of **Life**, the **Lord** Jesus Christ. In John 6, as is true in our **day**, many followed Jesus only to get something (v. 26), such as the meal He had just miraculously provided (vv. 1–15). The gospel is often marketed today simply as something that will meet "felt needs," make life easier, or even make one prosperous. On that note, Jesus said, "Labour not for the meat which perisheth, but for that meat which endureth unto everlasting life" (v. 27). With the provision of God's giving His people "bread from heaven to eat" (v. 31), we see five principles concerning Jesus as the *Ultimate* Provision:

First, the *provider* of this **Bread** is the **Father** (v. 32). Neither Moses nor anyone else could provide what the children of Israel needed in the **wilderness**, much less could anyone provide "true bread from heaven" that "giveth life unto the world" (vv. 32, 33).

Second, the *person* of this **Bread** is, of course, the Lord Jesus. "I am the bread of life: he that cometh to me shall never hunger" (v. 35), a statement that proclaims divinity ("I am," cf. Exod. 3:14), **salvation** ("life"), and security ("never hunger").

Third, the *particulars* of this **Bread** are at least threefold. This is the *true* **Bread** (v. 32). There are countless counterfeits, promising nourishment, growth, and satisfaction, but they are all false. In the end, each is **proved** to contain poisonous ingredients. This is also *divine* **Bread**. Others claim to be philosophical, mystical, even spiritual, but only this one is truly divine, truly of God. This is also *living* **Bread** (v. 35). Others claim to bring enlightenment, self-awareness, or personal fulfillment, but only this one gives life.

Fourth, the *purpose* of this **Bread** is to "[give] life unto the world" (v. 33). Without this **bread**, we are "dead in trespasses and sins" (Eph. 2:1), hopelessly and helplessly lost in a world that appears plenteous but is in truth empty.

Fifth, the *partaking* of this **Bread** is in simply believing upon it (vv. 35, 40). To believe, to have **faith** (April 10), is more than just mental assent; rather it is to **trust** fully, be firmly persuaded in, and to **obey**. Each of us goes on from there, everyday feasting on that **Bread** (cf. Jer. 15:16) and "[esteeming] the words of his mouth more than [our] necessary food" (Job 23:12).

Scriptures for Study: What do Psalm 119:103 and 1 Peter 2:2 say our **love** for God's **Word** should be?

Camp (1)

machaneh

The noun *machaneh* (4264) means a **camp**, an army, or a company. It is derived from the verb *chānāh* (2583), which not only means "to encamp," but also "to bend or curve" (ancient Semitic camps in general, not just the Hebrews', were basically circular).[244] About half the 143 occurrences of the verb and a fourth of the 214 occurrences of the noun are in the **book** of Numbers alone, which stands to reason since it deals with the nomadic travels of the children of Israel. Three observations (and their applications) stand out:

First, the **camp** demonstrates a unified body, a collection of *individuals* who now make up a *congregation*. The nation of Israel was just that. While she had many problems in her history, she remained (and still remains) a distinct nation. The Greek *parembolē* (3925G) provides a powerful parallel, as it is a rendering of *machaneh* in the Septuagint. It also refers to the church in Revelation 20:9 ("the camp of the saints"), picturing the **saints** of every age encamped around "the beloved city" of Jerusalem, the location of Messiah's **throne** and center of His millennial reign (cf. Isa. 24:23; Zech. 14:9–11). Does this not encourage us to church unity today?

Second, the selecting of a campsite was based upon two major concerns. One chief concern, of course, was water, which was often a spring or oasis (Josh. 11:5; Judg. 7:1). Without forcing any typology, a chief concern of the church today should be the "washing of water by the word [of God]" (Eph. 5:26; Heb. 10:22).

The other major concern for a campsite was that it provide a defensible position. Often the **camp** was set up on a higher spot than the surrounding terrain (1 Sam. 17:3; 26:3), a basic tenet of warfare still with us today. Other defenses were also set up, such as an actual "trench," into which the enemy might fall, or more likely a fortification made of earth or wagons (1 Sam. 17:20; 26:5–7). Likewise, each church today should be a place of fortification that will stand against the attacks that will come.

Third, the **camp** was built around the **tabernacle**, thereby demonstrating that God's presence was at its center. The **camp** was to remain **clean**—the dead were removed (Lev. 10:4, 5), lepers exiled (13:46), and criminals executed (24:23). How rare it is today to see the church at the center of Christians' lives, having been replaced by job, school, and sports. Further, how many Christians are **pure**, and how many churches practice church discipline?

Scriptures for Study: In preparation for tomorrow's study, read 1 Samuel 4:1–22.

Camp (2)

machaneh

The 3,500-plus sermons of Charles Spurgeon that compose *The Metropolitan Tabernacle Pulpit* are one of the church's greatest treasures, providing every Christian a lifetime of **meditation**. I was profoundly struck by one of those messages years ago, "Is God in the Camp?" based upon 1 Samuel 4:7. I dare to briefly, and humbly, adapt it here. (Quotations below are Spurgeon's.)[245]

As she often did, the Israelites had abandoned **God**, so He permitted pagans, the Philistines in this case, to humiliate them in battle and even enslave them. Instead of repenting, they made four mistakes we NT Christians still make today:

First, they looked to a *symbol* instead of their *Savior*. Instead of looking on God, they went to Shiloh to get the **Ark of the Covenant** (v. 4), considering it a "good luck charm" that would bring victory. We often hold on to some ceremony, ritual, or other such symbol. In the words of Spurgeon, "We lay hold of something beautiful that will charm the eye and produce a kind of sensuous feeling, and straightway we mistake our transient emotion for spiritual worship and true reverence."

Second, they preferred man's *position* over God's *presence*. Thinking that outward ritual was central, they called upon priests instead of God. Worse, these priests, Hophni and Phinehas (v. 4), had **proved** themselves immoral and unfit for their position (2:12–17, 22). Oh, how we must guard leadership today! "If the leader of the church be not one who walks with God, where will he lead you?" We again see the high standards of leadership that Paul outlines (1 Tim. 3:1–7; Titus 1:5–9).

Third, they confused *fervor* with ***faith***. Oh, how they shouted with zeal when they saw the Ark (1 Sam. 4:5), "but there was nothing in their noise"! If there is one thing many churches today do not lack it is excitement, but that is far from evidence of orthodoxy.

Fourth, they valued human *originality* above Scriptural *order*, "fixing their hope on this new method of fighting the Philistines." Indeed, one of the mantras of modern ministry is, "Be innovative, try the untried." There are more "ministries" and "programs" today than one would think possible, but what place do they give the principles, **precepts**, and precedents of the **Word** of God?

So, while the Philistines thought, "God is come into the camp" (v. 7), we today need to ask, *Is He really there?*

Scriptures for Study: Read the "odyssey of the ark" in 1 Samuel 4–7, noting its *capture* (chapter 4), the *calamity* it wrought (chapters 5, 6), and the *communion* with God that was finally restored (chapter 7).

Draw Near

nāgaš [and] qārab̲

The very first occurrence of the Hebrew *nāgaš* (5066) immediately sets the stage for its profound application: "Abraham drew near [unto the LORD]," as he pleads for **Sodom** to be spared (Gen. 18:23). After the giving of the Ten **Commandments**, and as the people "saw the thunderings, and the lightnings, and the noise of the trumpet, and the mountain smoking" (Exod. 20:18), Moses told them, "Fear not: for God is come to prove you" (v. 20), and he then "drew near unto the thick darkness where God was" (v. 21).

The picture painted by *nāgaš* is one of coming into close proximity to something. It is used in many ordinary ways, such as one person coming near to another (Gen. 27:21, 22, 25–27; 43:19; 48:10), respectfully approaching a person of exalted position (Gen. 43:18, 19), and even armies coming near each other in battle, as warfare in that **day** was truly up close and personal (1 Chron. 19:14).

We are drawn, however, to the instances of *nāgaš* that speak of men drawing near to **God**. Besides the verses noted above, it is often used of the priests coming into God's presence (Exod. 28:43; 30:20; Ezek. 44:13). A synonym of *nāgaš,* used interchangeably with it, is *qārab̲* (7126, April 17),[246] as when Moses drew near to God (Exod. 3:5). The Septuagint, in turn, usually renders *qārab̲* as *proserchomai* (4334G), "to approach, accede to."[247] How, then, can we **draw near** to God?

First, we **draw near** to God by ***prayer***. Unlike the lost of this world, who "pray unto a god that cannot save," God's people "draw near [*nāgaš*] together, [they] that are escaped of the nations" (Isa. 45:20; cf. Eph. 2:12, 16, 17). How much do we commune with our **Lord** each day?

Second, we **draw near** to God by *penitence*. "The LORD is nigh [*qārab̲*] unto them that are of a broken heart; and saveth such as be of a contrite spirit" (Ps. 34:18; cf. 51:17; Matt. 5:3; Luke 18:11–14). Are we truly *beaten, burdened,* and *broken* about our sin?

Third, we **draw near** to God through the *proclamation* of His **Word**. "And Joshua said unto the children of Israel, Come hither [*nāgaš*], and hear the words of the LORD your God" (Josh. 3:9). Is the **preaching** and teaching of God's Word a driving priority in your **life**?

Scriptures for Study: Read the Scriptures cited today, examining your own **heart**.

Precious

yāqār

Most of us have gazed upon a newborn baby and said, "Oh, isn't he (or she) precious!" We also refer to gems as "precious stones." The Hebrew Bible also speaks of **precious things**. Appearing some thirty-five times, the adjective *yāqār* (3368) "comes from a Semitic root which conveys the idea of 'heavy,' 'honor,' 'dignity,'" so "an object is considered precious or valuable either because of its intrinsic worth or its rarity."[248]

We find *yāqār* used, of course, in the same ways we use our English **word** *precious*. Upon the defeat of the city of Rabbah, that king's crown—the "weight whereof was a talent of gold with the precious stones"—was placed on David's **head** (2 Sam. 12:30). The foundation of Solomon's **temple** was laid with large, "costly stones" (1 Kings 5:17). Arriving with her huge caravan, the queen of Sheba brought "spices, and gold in abundance, and precious stones" to Solomon (2 Chron. 9:1). All those things, however, pale to insignificance compared with several far more **precious** commodities.

First, the Word of **God** is **precious**. This is the emphasis, in fact, of the very first occurrence of *yāqār*: "And the word of the LORD was precious in those days; there was no open vision" (1 Sam. 3:1). This is actually the negative side. Because of apostasy and the spiritual condition of Eli's **house**, the Word of God was a rarity, only two prophets having appeared during the entire **time** of the judges (Judg. 4:4; 6:8). Indeed, "where there is no vision [i.e., prophetic vision, divine revelation], the people perish" (Prov. 29:18).

Second, **wisdom** is "more precious than rubies" (Prov. 3:15) and cannot be traded for **gold**, **silver**, or **precious** stones (Job 28:15, 16), for its source is the Word of God.

Third, "the lips of knowledge are a precious jewel" (Prov. 20:15), once again emphasizing the Word of God as the source of true value. In our **day** the values of society are rooted in material things, rather than the knowledge God gives of Himself and His Creation.

Fourth, and amazingly, "Precious in the sight of the LORD is the death of his saints" (Ps. 116:15). Could any verse be more comforting? "The Lord watches over their dying beds," Spurgeon writes, "smoothes their pillows, sustains their hearts, and receives their souls."[249]

Oh, that we would value the valuable!

Scriptures for Study: What is the **precious** commodity of Psalm 139:17? 📖 What are the challenges of Matthew 6:19–24?

Power [and] Strength

kōach

The Hebrew *kōach* (3581) is a poetic **word** that appears about 124 times and means **power**, **strength**, "might," or "the ability to do something." A vivid example of this word's usage appears in Judges 16, where it appears seven times in reference to Samson's **strength**. The lords of the Philistines employ Delilah to find out the source of his **strength** (v. 5), she begs him to reveal it (vv. 6, 15), he finally tells her the truth (v. 17), his **strength** leaves him when she implements his confession (v. 19), but it is restored one last time in his **death** (v. 30, "might").

Many things are spoken of as having **power** or **strength**. Work animals, such as the ox, have **strength** (Prov. 14:4), **nations** have political, social, and economic power (Josh. 17:17; Dan. 8:24), and humans have **strength** to **labor** in the fields, although sometimes that labor yields no results (Gen. 4:12, the first occurrence of *kōach;* Lev. 26:20).

Infinitely greater, of course, is God's **strength** and **power**. It was by that alone He delivered His people from Egypt (Exod. 32:11, **power**), and can we even measure the **power** it took to part and hold back the waters of the Red Sea and then use them to **destroy** the enemy (15:6)? (That verse also speaks of the **power** in His **right hand**, which we will examine tomorrow.) Even His voice alone is powerful (Ps. 29:4), which is certainly evident at Creation (Jer. 10:12; 27:5; 51:15), as He spoke it all into being (e.g., Gen. 1:3, 6, 9). How does God's **power** apply to us?

First, God's **power** *prevents conceit*. What a self-reliant and self-sufficient **day** in which we live! But that is not really **new**. The **king** of Assyria arrogantly claimed his self-sufficiency in his conquests (Isa. 10:12–14). Isaiah even adds, in effect, "Does the axe glorify itself over the man who swings it?" (v. 15). The children of Israel also tended to **trust** in their own might to conqueror Canaan, prompting God to remind them, "Remember the LORD thy God: for it is he that giveth thee power to get wealth" (Deut.8:18).

Second, God's **power** *provides courage*. What a testimony Daniel and his three friends maintained even though surrounded by pagans! They had the "ability" to preserve and **teach** the truth though encompassed by error (Dan. 1:4).

Let us depend upon God's **power** for everything, for we have none of our own (Ps. 22:15; 31:10; 38:10).

Scriptures for Study: In Proverbs 24:5, what increases our **strength**? 📖 What is the challenge of Ecclesiastes 9:10?

Right Hand

yāmiyn

Yesterday we mentioned Exodus 15:6 in the context of God's **power**: "Thy right hand, O LORD, is become glorious in power: thy right hand, O LORD, hath dashed in pieces the enemy." But there is another significant **word** here, *yāmiyn* (3225), which refers, of course, to someone's literal **right hand**, as when the walls of water stood on the people's **right hand** and left as they crossed the Red Sea on dry land (Exod. 14:29).

While that literal sense is also present in Genesis 48:13, 14, 18, where Jacob blesses Joseph's two sons Ephraim and Manasseh, there is the deeper metaphorical meaning of bestowing favor and **strength** through the **right hand**. God does the same. Speaking anthropomorphically, of course, our text speaks of God's power flowing through His **right hand**. We read again that the Israelites "got not the [promised] land in possession by their own sword," but by God's **right hand** (Ps. 44:3). What, then, does God's **right hand** do for His people?

First, it gives ***salvation***. **David** declares that God "saveth his anointed . . . with the saving strength of his right hand" (Ps. 20:6) and then exults, "Though I walk in the midst of trouble, thou wilt revive me: thou shalt stretch forth thine hand against the wrath of mine enemies, and thy right hand shall save me" (138:7).

Second, God's **right hand** provides *strength*. God not only gives us strength *by His* **right hand** (Ps. 80:17), He gives it *through our* **right hand**. As God promised through Isaiah, "For I the LORD thy God will hold thy right hand, saying unto thee, Fear not; I will help thee" (Isa. 41:13). A **wonderful** picture of that appears in Peter's healing of a beggar, where "he took him by the right hand, and lifted him up: and immediately his feet and ankle bones received strength" (Acts 3:7).

Third, God's **right hand** supplies *stamina*. Once again David writes, "My soul followeth hard after thee: thy right hand upholdeth me" (Ps. 63:8). "Upholdeth" is *tāmaḵ* (8551), which means "to grasp, hold, or support" (cf. 139:10; 73:23).

Fourth, God's **right hand** promises *security*. Psalm 110:1 is quoted or alluded to in the NT more often than any other verse: "The LORD said unto my Lord, Sit thou at my right hand, until I make thine enemies thy footstool."[250] While messianic in its reference, in application we will be glorified with Him (Rom. 8:17) and rule with Him (2 Tim. 2:12; Rev. 2:26, 3:21).

Scriptures for Study: What was David's confidence in Psalm 16:8? 🕮 What else will we find at God's **right hand** (Ps. 16:11)?

Wonder [and] Sign

môp̱ēṯ

Appearing thirty-six times in the OT, the Hebrew *môp̱ēṯ* (4159) refers to a **wonder**, "marvel," **sign**, or "token." Its emphasis is twofold. It first displays *who **God** is* by manifesting an act of divine **power**. This is evident in its first occurrence, where "the LORD said unto Moses, When thou goest to return into Egypt, see that thou do all those wonders before Pharaoh, which I have put in thine hand" (Exod. 4:21), followed by other occurrences during the ten plagues (7:3, 9; 11:9, 10).

The next instances are in Deuteronomy, most of which point back to the wonders of those earlier days. (e.g., 4:34; 6:22). One exception is 28:45–46, where because of her disobedience, Israel was cursed and herself actually became a **sign** and **wonder** to future generations of the high price of such rebellion.

The other significant exception in Deuteronomy is where the subject is false prophets (13:1, 2). The issue was not whether their predictions came true, for even if they did the **prophet** was to be condemned if he was leading the people away from God. What an application that is for us today! Countless "prophets" and teachers make predictions, some of which even come true, but their teachings are far from biblical and their message is even farther from the true gospel.

The second aspect of *môp̱ēṯ* is to demonstrate *what God is doing* by using a **sign** for authentication or prediction. God gave a **sign** to authenticate the prediction of the coming of **King** Josiah 250 years before the fact (1 Kings 13:3, 5). Even more significant, the OT priests were a prophetic **sign** pointing to the priesthood of the "Branch," that is, the coming Messiah (Zech. 3:8; cf. 6:12, 13; Isa. 4:2–6; 11:1–5; Jer. 23:5–8; Acts 2:22; Heb. 8:1). "Branch" is *ṣemach* (6780), which refers to a budding, sprouting plant and pictures Messiah coming like a fresh plant out of the desert.

While signs and wonders were a necessity in those days, that is no longer the case. For one thing, signs and wonders were always for the sake of Jews, as "Jews require a sign" (1 Cor. 1:22). Sadly, some Christians today, though thoroughly Gentile, seek things that were never meant for them. For another, such signs and wonders are no longer needed today because we have the Scriptures, God's completed revelation (1 Cor. 13:10).[251] That alone is our authority, and we **rejoice** in it.

Scriptures for Study: Read Matthew 24:5, 11, 24 and 2 Peter 2:1–3, noting their warnings about false teachers.

Yesterday

temôl

Shakespeare expressed what most of us have thought at one **time** or another: "O! call back yesterday. Bid time return."[252] Another playwright of that day, Thomas Heywood, put it even more dramatically: "O God! O God! That it were possible to undo things done; to call back yesterday! That Time could turn up his swift sandy glass, to untell the days, and redeem these hours."[253] Indeed, if only we could get back a **yesterday** or two.

Most of the twenty-four OT occurrences of the Hebrew *temôl* (8543), as well as the few occurrences of its derivatives, are unremarkable, referring simply to **yesterday** or a time beforehand. At least one, however, stands out: "We are but of yesterday, and know nothing, because our days upon earth are a shadow" (Job 8:9). One of Job's three critics, Bildad, rightly observes that unlike the times when men lived several centuries, they live only a fraction of that now, and as a result **know** very little by comparison. Is it any **wonder** that the Latin phrase *Umbrae Sumus!* ("We are shadows!") used to appear on sundials, even stained glass sundials?

As expositor John Gill notes of this text, "Man's time is rather measured by days than by months and years, being so short." We should be constantly reminded that time is fleeting and our days are short. As **David** prayed: "For we are strangers before thee, and sojourners, as were all our fathers: our days on the earth are as a shadow, and there is none abiding" (1 Chron. 29:15). He repeated the same thought in Psalm 144:4: "Man is like to vanity: his days are as a shadow that passeth away."

Now, we certainly do *not* want to be *morose* here. In his poem "Calmly We Walk through This April's Day," Delmore Schwartz (1913–66), whose later **life** ended in alcoholism and finally insanity, wrote: "Time is the school in which we learn. / Time is the fire in which we burn." We *do* want to be *motivated*, however, that in the short time we are on this earth, our days should be filled with our **Lord**. As one other poet (unknown) puts it: "Two little lines I heard one day, / Traveling along life's busy way; / Bringing conviction to my heart, / And from my mind would not depart; Only one life, 'twill soon be past, / only what's done for Christ will last."

Scriptures for Study: Read 1 Corinthians 3:11–15. How does this passage underscore that "only what's done for Christ will last"?

Time

'ē̱t

The Hebrew *'ē̱t* (6256) occurs almost 300 times in the OT and is used to express several aspects, or kinds, of time:

First, it is used of normal, usual events, such as: seasons of the year, as in the season for harvest (Job 5:26; Jer. 50:16), animal migration (Jer. 8:7), mating seasons (Gen. 31:10), and even a woman's monthly "time" (Lev. 15:25).

Second, *'ē̱t* refers to an appropriate **time** for some specific event, such as one's appointed time for **death** (Eccles. 7:17) or God's appointed time for judgment (Ps. 21:9; 119:126). That latter idea underscores God's sovereignty, as does His control over nature (Lev. 26:4; Job 38:32; Ps. 104:27; Eccles. 3:11).

Third, *'ē̱t* refers to a fixed or set time. Such times are known only by God (Jer. 8:12), although the "wise men" (astrologers) claimed to **know** such times (Esther 1:13).

Oh, how this **word** encourages us in many ways! It challenges us to godliness of **life** and a **love** for the Word of God. As the psalmist writes, it is this believer, who strives for godliness and loves the Word, who spiritually prospers, who "bringeth forth his fruit in his season" (Ps. 1:3). It also comforts us, for "The LORD also will be a refuge for the oppressed, a refuge in times of trouble" (9:9). Still more it reminds us of His sovereignty, for "[our] times are in [His] hand" (31:15). It then drives us to **prayer** and confession of **sin**, "For this shall every one that is godly pray unto [Him] in a time when [He] mayest be found" (32:6). It especially reminds us to "bless the LORD at all times," that "his praise shall continually be in [our] mouth" (34:1). In the same vein, we "trust in him at all times" (62:8), having perfect confidence He will "cast me not off in the time of old age" (71:9), and will provide for us "in due season" (145:15).

Finally, it is significant that *'ē̱t* is often rendered *kairos* (2540G) in the Septuagint, which refers to a decisive or crucial place or point, such as a date. Of special note, then, is Paul's **counsel**, "Redeeming the time, because the days are evil" (Eph. 5:16), literally meaning to buy up all our time, every single moment, and devote it to God in growth and service, for it is sorely necessary in the depraved world in which we live.[254]

Scriptures for Study: What is the promise of Psalm 106:3? 📖 What is the command of Galatians 6:9, 10 ("season" and "opportunity" are *kairos*).

Tomorrow

māchār

Having considered the concepts of **time**, **yesterday**, and even **day** (way back on February 26), there remains one other important **word** that humans **face** in linear time: **tomorrow**. Like *temôl* (yesterday), most occurrences of *māchār* (4279), which number about fifty, are mundane, referring simply to the day that follows the present day (e.g., Exod. 16:23; Prov. 3:28).

The exceptions, however, are most noteworthy, especially those that anticipate divine action. Several "tomorrows" were, indeed, memorable days for Pharaoh. One **tomorrow** brought a swarm of flies (Exod. 8:23, 24), another brought the **death** of cattle (9:4, 5), another brought hail (9:18), and still another brought locusts (10:4). **Tomorrow** was surely greatly anticipated the day that "Joshua said unto the people, Sanctify yourselves: for tomorrow the LORD will do wonders among you" (Josh. 3:5). And how significant was the **tomorrow** that anticipated God's revelation of His **Law** at Mount Sinai (Exod. 19:10)!

Isaiah 22:12, 13 also captures our attention. Even as God was calling His people to "weeping, and to mourning," their philosophy was to "eat and drink; for to morrow we shall die." While God was calling them to ***repentance***, they were living in *riotousness*. That has always been (and still is) the sentiment of pagans (also 1 Cor. 15:32).

I was reminded here of the bleak despair of Shakespeare's Macbeth: "To-morrow, and to-morrow, and to-morrow creeps in this petty pace from day to day to the last syllable of recorded time, and all our yesterdays have lighted fools the way to dusty death. Out, out, brief candle! Life's but a walking shadow, a poor player that struts and frets his hour upon the stage and then is heard no more: it is a tale told by an idiot, full of sound and fury, signifying nothing."[255] It's interesting that "a tale told" is actually a reference to Psalm 90:9, which again speaks of life's brevity: "We spend our years as a tale that is told," or more literally, "We finish our years like a murmur," that is, it is over like a passing sigh.[256]

One other verse that immediately comes to mind when we think of the word **tomorrow** is Proverbs 27:1: "Boast not thyself of tomorrow; for thou knowest not what a day may bring forth." Let us be reminded today, **tomorrow**, and every day thereafter that "a man's heart deviseth his way: but the LORD directeth his steps" (Prov. 16:9).

Scriptures for Study: What is James' **counsel** regarding boasting about **tomorrow** (James 4:13–16)?

Companion [and] Friend [and] Neighbor

rēa'

Occuring not only in Hebrew but also in Akkadian, Ugaritic, and Aramaic, *rēa'* (7453) carries both broad and narrow meanings. In the narrow sense, which is actually the basic meaning of the **word**, *rēa'* denotes a close, personal **friend**, one who is virtually a **brother** (Ps. 122:8; Deut. 13:6). Note particularly Exodus 32:27, where **companion** (*rēa'*) and "brother" (*'āch*, 251, August 8) appear together.

This narrow sense of *rēa'* is especially seen in referring to one's spouse. In Song of Solomon 5:16, the **Shulamite maiden** speaks of Solomon as both her "beloved" (*dôḏ*, 1730, which speaks strongly of sexual affection [cf. 1:2, 4; 7:12; Prov. 7:18]) and her **friend**. This ever serves as an encouragement to every Christian that our spouse is both lover and **friend**, closer than anyone else on this earth ever could be (or should be).

Still another instance of *rēa'* encourages us: "The LORD spake unto Moses face to face, as a man speaketh unto his friend" (Exod. 33:11). How does one speak to a **friend**? He speaks "freely, familiarly, plainly, cordially, openly, without any reserve or show of authority, or causing dread and fear."[257] How comforting to **know** we can speak with our **God** "mouth to mouth" (Num.12:8)!

There is also the broad sense of *rēa'*, however, which is perhaps even more challenging than the narrow. This aspect of the word carries much the same idea as our English word **neighbor**, a person with whom we have a casual but not close relationship. Our concept of **neighbor** doesn't really demand much. Oh, we might take in the neighbor's mail while he is on vacation or we might lend him a hand when he needs to move some furniture, but that's about as far as it goes.

God's concept, on the other hand, is a bit different. He commands, "Thou shalt love thy neighbour [*rēa'*] as thyself" (Lev. 19:18), which means you don't steal from him, deceive him, cheat him, lie to him, ridicule him, slander him, or treat him better or worse than anyone else (vv. 13–17). So important is this principle that our **Lord** combined it with Deuteronomy 6:4, 5 (the "Shema," May 30) to summarize "all the law and the prophets" in only two commands: first, "Love the Lord thy God with all thy heart, and with all thy soul, and with all thy mind" and then, "Love thy neighbour as thyself" (Matt. 22:37–40).

Scriptures for Study: What is the danger of slandering your **neighbor** (Ps. 101:5)? 📖 Read these other verses about your **neighbor**: Proverbs 6:29; 11:9, 12; 14:21; 25:18.

Shulamite

Šûlammiyṯ

Mentioning Solomon's Song[258] even in passing, as we did **yesterday**, always brings to my mind that beautiful **love** story. The two principal characters, of course, are Solomon, who is referred to as "the Beloved" (*dôḏ*, 1730, June 1 and August 22) thirty-two times in the AV,[259] and the **Shulamite maiden**. While her identity is uncertain, three possibilities stand out. One is that she was an unknown maiden from Shulam, but there is no other mention of Shulam in the Bible or the known extra-Biblical literature. Other interpreters say it is simply another **name** for Shulem, located in lower Galilee, but that seems conjectural.

The third possibility makes more sense. **Shulamite** is a transliteration of *Šûlammiyṯ* (7759), which is actually the feminine form of Solomon (*Šelōmōh*, 8010). As scholar Augustus Strong points out, because the definite article is present, the term is "a pet name." In other words, having become Solomon's wife, she took his name, a common practice then that was instituted in Genesis 5:2, as **God** called "*their* name Adam," not just *his* name.

Solomon's Song has been variously interpreted. Neither the allegorical nor the typological view approaches it literally, making the characters and events, in one **way** or another, something not stated in the text. The most common opinion is that the story depicts God's love either for Israel or the church. But the church cannot possibly be in view because it was a mystery in OT times, hidden from the foundation of the world and not revealed until the NT apostles and prophets (Rom. 16:25, 26; Eph. 3:9). Even more basic than that, nowhere in the **book** is *God's* love the subject, rather the love of a **man** and **woman**.

By spiritualizing Solomon's Song, then, we totally miss its literal, **deep**, and vitally important message. There is no justification whatsoever for taking the book in any other way than at face value.

So why put "a love story" in the Bible? *To exalt human love and **marriage**.* If marriage is the very foundation of society, of living, of having and training children, of all human relationships, doesn't it make sense that God would devote an entire book of Holy **Scripture** to it? If Scripture is authoritative and solely sufficient in every area, would not the subject of marital love be treated in a practical, straightforward, even tastefully graphic manner?

Every Christian couple should read, reflect on, and **rejoice** in this striking love story.

Scriptures for Study: Over the next three days, read Solomon's Song with your spouse and enjoy its vivid imagery. Read chapters 1 and 2 today.

[Word Images in Solomon's Song] (1)

[Selected Words]

Even the briefest examination of Solomon's Song is beyond the scope of this book, but we can at the very least mention a few of its beautiful **word** images, metaphors that will be a blessing to every godly married couple.

In Song of Solomon 1:5–8, the **maiden** speaks of herself as being **black**. The Hebrew is *šāchōr* (7838), which refers here to "skin that is swarthy, darkened, in context because of the sun's rays."[260] She, therefore, feels that the **sun** has marred her complexion because she worked so much outdoors, in contrast to the ladies in the palace. But here is, in fact, a key to her character—she's not afraid to **work**. Nonetheless, in her insecurity, she needs the Beloved's reassurance.

Another key to her character is: "Why should I be as one that turneth aside?" (1:7). This is *'āṭāh* (5844), "to wrap around, to cover." In this context, the idea is literally "as one who is veiled." Unlike Tamar (Gen. 38:14–16), this girl values purity and rejects the veil (or any appearance) of the wandering prostitute. Propriety is primary.

In Song of Solomon 1:9 (and repeating eight more times: v. 15; 2:2, 10, 13; 4:1, 7; 5:2; 6:4), Solomon calls her **my love**, which is *ra'yāh* (7474), a form of *rēa'* (August 22) that means "lover, darling, or female companion." He also compares her "to a company of horses in Pharaoh's chariots," a "filly," we might say today. While most girls today wouldn't appreciate such a comparison, girls of that **day** would, because no animal was considered more beautiful and graceful. Being poor, she doesn't have jewelry, but he compliments her further that her "cheeks are comely with rows of jewels, [and her] neck with chains of gold." In other words, "You don't need jewelry. You are already adorned with natural jewels."

In verse 15, we see the couple looking into each other's eyes and talking, a key to intimacy. He compliments her eyes, calling them "doves' eyes," as doves are known for their tranquility and purity. Verses 16 and 17 reveal they are lying beside each other on the grass with the forest surrounding them. What a romantic setting! "The Bible actually talks about romance?" we might ask. Indeed, it does.

Husbands, when was the last time you complimented your wife and just told her you **love** her? Billy Sunday is quoted as saying, "Try praising your wife, even if it frightens her at first."

Scriptures for Study: Continue your reading of Solomon's Song with chapters 3 and 4.

[Word Images in Solomon's Song] (2)

[Selected Words]

Continuing our brief look at some of the vivid imagery in Solomon's Song, in chapter 2, verse 1, the **maiden** thinks of herself as only common flowers, a **rose** (*chabaṣṣeleṯ*, 2261) and a **lily** (*šûšan*, 7799). What a contrast that is to today's **vanity** and immodesty! In verse 2, however, as far as he is concerned, the **king** views all other women as **thorns** (*chôach*, 2336, also "briars" and "thistles") and her as the **lily** among them all.

Staying with a nature metaphor, in verses 3 through 6 she likens him to the **apple tree**. The Hebrew *tappûach* (8598) refers to the tree itself, or the **fruit** being round, firm, and fleshy. The imagery is in Technicolor, picturing three aspects of **love** that are important to a **woman**:

First, she says, "I sat down under his shadow with great delight" (v. 3), a picture of *protection*. In contrast to her working in the brutal **sun** (1:6), in him she finds rest.

Second, she says, "His fruit was sweet to my taste" (2:3), picturing *provision*. At the very foundation of a **marriage** is the husband's providing for his wife's needs, and she is totally secure in that.

Third, she says, "He brought me to the banqueting house, and his banner over me was love" (v. 4), which pictures *proclamation*. I love this imagery! He took her to the banquet hall to "show her off." In essence, he put a **banner** (*degel*, 1714) over her, proclaiming that he was not ashamed of her or embarrassed by his love for her.

The maiden further describes Solomon in verses 8 through 14 as either a **roe** (*ṣeḇiy*, 6643), which refers to a gazelle, or a young **hart** (*'ayyāl*, 354) (v. 9), which refers to a deer. As both these animals were **clean** according to the Mosaic **Law** (Deut. 12:15, 22; 1 Kings 4:23), he, too, was clean, attractive, strong, and agile, and is moving quickly because he can't wait to see her.

Verse 14 is very special. "O my dove, that art in the clefts of the rock, in the secret places of the stairs, let me see thy countenance, let me hear thy voice; for sweet is thy voice, and thy countenance is comely." What beautiful poetry! A **dove** (*yônāh*, 3123) would hide in the clefts of the hills to avoid detection, so Solomon requests that she come out and show her entire self to him and hold back nothing. "I want to know you," he says, "I want to know everything about you."

Scriptures for Study: Continue your reading of Solomon's Song with chapters 5 and 6.

[Word Images in Solomon's Song] (3)

[Selected Words]

Concluding our look at the beautiful imagery in Solomon's Song, after mentioning the **dove** in 2:14, Solomon mentions the **foxes** in verse 15, which are critical to the rest of the story.

Foxes is *šû'āl* (7776), which appears only seven times in the OT, four of which refer to the literal animals common to Palestine (Judg. 15:4; Neh. 4:3; Ps. 63:10; Lam. 5:18). They often inhabited ruins, preying on whatever they could find. It is also used figuratively in reference to false teachers, **foxes** who slyly prey on God's people (Ezek. 13:4).

The other two occurrences are here in our text. Using the literal idea that **foxes** are destructive to the vineyards, Solomon figuratively applies this to the "little foxes" that creep into a **marriage**, little problems that can **spoil** the relationship. These must be dealt with quickly, flushed out into the open and addressed. How important the "doves" and "foxes" are in a relationship! And how vital it is that couples receive detailed, biblical premarital **counsel**, which sadly is greatly lacking in churches today.

Continuing the narrative, 2:15–17 declares the very foundation of marriage, that each owns the other; 3:1–4 record the maiden's dream brought on by a **fear** of losing her Beloved; verses 6–11 describe the wedding procession; and 4:1—5:1 records the explicit details of the wedding **night**.

Beginning in 5:2 and going through the rest of **book**, we see the maturing of the marriage. At first, however, we see a problem (vv. 2–16). While intimacy, **joy**, and physical desire did not fade between the couple, the "little foxes" of 2:15 silently crept in—but thankfully are driven away. Moving to the end of the story, 8:5–7 explain the nature of true **love**; it is a *seal*, *strong*, *singular*, *stirring* (v. 6), and *supreme* (v. 7).

William Jennings Bryan (1860–1925), the great American lecturer, political leader, and devoted Christian and defender of the **faith**, was asked one **day**, "Why do you wear your hair over your ears?" Bryan responded, "There is a romance connected with that. When I began courting Mrs. Bryan, she objected to the way my ears stood out. So to please her, I let my hair grow to cover them." "But that was many years ago," the inquirer pointed out. "Why don't you have your hair cut now?" Bryan winked and answered, "Because the romance is still going on."[261]

Let us **pray** that our marriages will have continued romance.

Scriptures for Study: Conclude your reading of Solomon's Song with chapters 7 and 8.

Despise

mā'as

Today we encounter one of those "sad words" of **Scripture**, tragically occurring some seventy-five times. The Hebrew *mā'as* (3988) is a strong **word** that means "to reject, despise, or abhor"—in short, "to reject or treat as loathsome."[262] Its primary use describes people rejecting God's Word, treating it as something despicable and refusing to regard it.

Its first occurrence sets the stage for the norm: "And if ye shall despise [*mā'as*] my statutes, or if your soul abhor my judgments, so that ye will not do all my commandments, but that ye break my covenant" (Lev. 26:15). The very next verse actually demonstrates its other primary use, namely, God's own rejection of those who **despise** Him: "I also will do this unto you."

Throughout Scripture we see this pattern repeated. We see men's loathing of God's Word, as "they rejected his statutes" (2 Kings 17:15), and then see that "the LORD rejected all [their] seed" (v. 20). It is because men "despised the word of the Holy One of Israel" that "therefore as the fire devoureth the stubble, and the flame consumeth the chaff, so their root shall be as rottenness, and their blossom shall go up as dust" (Isa. 5:24). Again, "because they have not hearkened unto [His] words, nor to [His] law, but rejected it," He "will bring evil upon this people, even the fruit of their thoughts" (Jer. 6:19; cf. 8:9; Ezek. 5:6; 20:16).

Here is one of those words that truly reflect our own **day**, a day when the despising of God's Word is apparently at an all-time high. The philosopher rejects the "philosophy" of God's Word and turns to the wholly irrational concept of relativism. The evolutionist loathes God's Word so much he insists on the nonsensical idea that the universe sprang from nothing. The religionist despises God's Word when it speaks of **sin** and judgment, trusting rather in human merit and "man's inherent goodness." The liberationist "abhorreth [*mā'as*] not evil," rather condones the grossest, most unspeakable sins known to humanity. Even professing believers actually **despise** God's Word as they *redefine* God, *reinvent* the gospel, and *redesign* ministry.

Never do men stop to think that if God "greatly abhorred [*mā'as*] Israel" (Ps. 78:59), His own **chosen** people, and judged her sin severely, how much more will He **judge** the world? Let us go forth and boldly proclaim God's Word.

Scriptures for Study: Compare Psalm 118:22 ("refused" is *mā'as*) with Matthew 21:42, Ephesians 2:20–22, and 1 Peter 2:4–8. Who is the subject of these verses, and what is their point?

Hate

śānē'

If yesterday's **word** is tragic, today's is utterly dark. The Hebrew *śānē'* (8130) is an antonym of *'āhab̲* (157, April 12), it is the opposite of **love** and affection. Appearing some 145 times, "It expresses an emotional attitude toward persons and things which are opposed, detested, despised and with which one wishes to have no contact or relationship."[263] This meaning is apparent in the hatred Joseph's brothers had for him, described using this word three times (Gen. 37:4, 5, 8).

Just as those ungodly men hated godly Joseph, ungodly men have hated **God** through the centuries (Exod. 20:5; Deut. 5:9; 32:41; 33:11; Ps. 21:8), and it continues today. Using every outlet of our day—radio, television, newspaper, Internet—people spew forth their hatred of God in every possible way. Further, they "hate the good, and love the evil" (Mic. 3:2), having no idea that "all they that hate [God] love death" (Prov. 8:36).

This leads us to the fact that God Himself hates, a notion that is very unpopular in modern thought. While people prefer to picture God as the grandfather-type who is all **love** and "warm-fuzzies," that is not the God of the Bible. As we studied from July 8 through 17, there are seven things God hates and abhors (Prov. 6:16–19). It's not that He just "dislikes" these things, or that He "likes them less" than other things, as some teachers try to soften *śānē',* rather He loathes such things because they are **evil** and contrary to His holiness.

More unpopular still is the truth that God actually hates certain men. While the common teaching is that "God loves everyone" and that He hates only the **sin** but not the sinner, **Scripture** clearly declares that He "hatest all workers of iniquity" (Ps. 5:5; "iniquity" is *'āwen,* 205, July 12). Likewise, "the wicked and him that loveth violence [God's] soul hateth" (11:5), and He "abhorreth" (*nā'aṣ,* 5006, "to revile, scorn, reject") the covetous (10:3). Of some He adds, in fact, "I will love them no more" (Hosea 9:15). While **love** is at the root of God's *election* (Deut. 7:7, 8; Eph. 1:4), a holy hatred of sin is at the root of His *condemnation.*

The instruction to us in all this is that we are to "love the Lord [and] hate evil" (Ps. 97:10), and we are to "hate the evil, and love the good" (Amos 5:15). To truly **love** the **Lord** is to love what He loves and **hate** what He hates.

Scriptures for Study: Read the following, noting what we should **hate**: Psalm 101:3; 119:104, 163; Proverbs 8:13; Romans 12:9.

Destroy

šāmad

Unlike other Hebrew words that take on a meaning other than **destroy** in various contexts, *šāmad* (8045) always means "to destroy or annihilate" in its some ninety occurrences. It is "always used in passages dealing with vengeance or with the judgment of God."[264]

The **word** is used at times to refer to men destroying men, such as the reference in 2 Samuel 14:7 to the total extinction of a family line, which in that **day** was considered a terrible misfortune. It's also used of Haman's plot to **destroy** the entire Jewish nation (Esther 3:6, 13), as well as the Jews' planned revenge against the whole of the Persian Empire (Esther 8:11).

The predominant use of *šāmad*, however, focuses on God's judgment, which results because of man's actions and attitudes. While they are all interrelated, destruction comes upon **man** for at least three reasons:

First, there is man's *insolence*. In His condemnation of the Ammonites, God said, "Because thou saidst, Aha, against my sanctuary, when it was profaned . . . I will destroy thee" (Ezek. 25:3, 7). "Aha" is a rough transliteration of *he'āch* (1889), an expression of **joy** or excitement, but in this context is one of malicious contempt. Oh, the insolence and impudence of men against God!

Second, there is man's *insurrection*. Deuteronomy 9 recounts many instances of the Israelites' **sin** and rebellion. In one way or another and to one extent or another God brought destruction, as we see *šāmad* no fewer than six times (vv. 3, 8, 14, 19, 20, 25; cf. 28:20ff).

Third, and perhaps most significantly, there is man's *idolatry*. **Scripture** repeatedly warns about the consequences of idolatry. In Leviticus 26:1–13, we see promises for keeping God's **precepts**, but then in verses 14–39 see destruction for disobedience. "I will destroy your high places [pagan altars built on hills], and cut down your images [pagan idols], and cast your carcases upon the carcases of your idols, and my soul shall abhor you" (v. 30). Before his **death**, Joshua warned the people about forsaking God, and the destruction that would result if they disobeyed His Word and followed other gods (Josh. 23:15, 16). Such warnings are frequent (Deut. 7:4; Ezek. 6:3–6; Hosea 10:8), for God will not tolerate idolatry.

Instead of having to do it Himself and bringing on the resulting judgment, God would rather His people "destroy all their pictures, and destroy all their molten images, and quite pluck down all their high places" (Num. 33:52; cf. Josh. 7:12).

Scriptures for Study: In addition to the Scriptures cited today, review our July 6 and 7 readings.

Joy (Rejoice)

śāmach

The noun behind **joy** (*śimchāh*, 8057) is derived from the verb *śāmach* (8055), which means "to be joyful, to rejoice, or to be glad." It "usually refers to a spontaneous emotion or extreme happiness which is expressed in some visible and/or external manner."[265] The verb appears about 155 times in the OT and the noun some ninety more. What makes this **word** significant is the event, situation, circumstance, or experience that elicits the **joy**.

Practically anything can bring exuberant **joy**, such as a wedding (Jer. 25:10) or other festival (Gen. 31:27), wine (Ps.104:15), reuniting with a loved one (Exod. 4:14), a kind word (Prov. 12:25), a friend's **counsel** (27:9), or simply one's own foolish behavior or belief (15:30). Even others' tragedy makes some people happy, as the Babylonians are described as leaping for **joy** and dancing around at the rape and pillage of Israel (Jer. 50:11; Ps. 35:15; cf. Prov. 24:17). We cannot help but be reminded here of the sad pictures of Muslims shouting for **joy** and celebrating over the September 11, 2001, terrorist attacks on the World Trade Center and Pentagon. How fallen man's **heart** is!

Thankfully, however, **salvation** and the things of **God** are most often declared to be the grounds for **joy**. "Let all those that put their trust in thee rejoice [*śāmach*]: let them ever shout for joy, because thou defendest them: let them also that love thy name be joyful in thee" (Ps. 5:11). As one might expect, the Psalms continue to resound with such proclamations (9:2; 16:9; 32:11; 40:16; 63:11; 64:10; 86:4; 90:15; 92:4).

Of special note is Psalm 19:8: "The statutes of the LORD are right, rejoicing the heart: the commandment of the LORD is pure, enlightening the eyes." What could possibly make us more joyful than the Word of God? Ancient philosophers sought for what was **good** and right. Men today talk of what is "good for society" or what is "right for each person." But there is true and lasting **joy** *only* in the revealed truth of God's Word. Commenting on this verse, Spurgeon writes, "Earthborn mirth dwells on the lip, and flushes the bodily powers; but heavenly delights satisfy the inner nature, and fill the mental faculties to the brim. There is no cordial of comfort like that which is poured from the bottle of Scripture."

What brings you **joy** in **life**?

Scriptures for Study: What is the contrast in Proverbs 13:9? 🕮 What is the cause of **joy** in 23:15?

Void

rēyqām

One of my favorite verses is Isaiah 55:11: "So shall my word be that goeth forth out of my mouth: it shall not return unto me void, but it shall accomplish that which I please." The key **word** here, of course, is ***void***. The Hebrew is *rēyqām* (7387), which means "empty or empty-handed." Several of its sixteen occurrences describe someone who is (or is not) without something, such as money (Deut. 15:13), other **wealth** (Gen. 31:42; Exod. 3:21), or a **sacrifice** (Exod. 23:15; Deut. 16:16).

Our text, therefore, declares that God's Word will never **return** empty-handed. Verse 10 illustrates using the **image** of rain and snow, which might seem to us to accomplish nothing, such as when it falls on the desert. But it nonetheless brings forth vegetation, however small the amount. We see in this at least three principles:

First, and foremost, there is the *sovereignty* of God. It is not some mystical or magical **power** that accomplishes the **work**, and it certainly is not the efforts of **man**. Rather it is God Himself who accomplishes precisely what He pleases. Whether it be "the conversion of sinners" or the "comfort of saints" (John Gill),[266] it is the Sovereign God of the universe who plans, presents, and perfects His work.

Second, we see here the ***strength*** of God's Word. How powerful God's Word is! No verse is clearer than Hebrews 4:12: "For the word of God is quick, and powerful, and sharper than any twoedged sword, piercing even to the dividing asunder of soul and spirit, and of the joints and marrow, and is a discerner of the thoughts and intents of the heart."

Third, we see the *stamina* of the laborer. Contrary to modern thought, God does not **bless** methods, rather faithfulness. He doesn't want simply our physical *activity*, nor does He need our mental *productivity*—rather, He demands our total *reliability*. He wants to use us, but He wants to do it His way, which is outlined in His Word. We have inundated His church with gimmicks, gadgets, and games just to get results, but such results are temporary at best and totally false at worst. Only when we follow the Word will God bring about *His* results. "I have planted, Apollos watered; but God gave the increase," Paul wrote to the humanistic Corinthians. "So then neither is he that planteth any thing, neither he that watereth; but God that giveth the increase" (1 Cor. 3:6, 7).

Scriptures for Study: What does Jesus' parable of the vine imply about self-effort in Christian service (John 15:4, 5)?

Rock

sela'

Psalm 18 is to me an especially **wonderful psalm**. Its occasion is when **God** "delivered [David] from the hand of all his enemies, and from the hand of Saul" (from the Psalm 18 title) and is virtually identical to 2 Samuel 22. While it is a **song** of victory and **joy**, it opens with resounding **praise** in verses 1 through 3, for it is God alone who is the source of the victory and joy. These three verses extol the very character of God by using several metaphors on which we will meditate for the next few days. While we examined many of God's names back in January, it is a theme we should **return** to often.

Note that **David** says, "The LORD is my rock," a metaphor found about twenty times in the Psalms. **Rock** is *sela'* (5553), which refers not just to a rock but also a cliff. This metaphor provides several applications:

First, the Rock is our *security*. David writes elsewhere, "Be thou my strong rock, for an house of defence to save me" (Ps. 31:2), and an aged, unnamed psalmist adds, "Be thou my strong habitation, whereunto I may continually resort . . . for thou art my rock" (71:3). God is our refuge, our place of habitation; He is where we live.

Second, the Rock is our *stability*. Again it is David who declares, "He brought me up also out of an horrible pit, out of the miry clay, and set my feet upon a rock, and established my goings" (40:2). It is that lifesaving miracle, in fact, that prompts David to add in verse 3: "And he hath put a new song [January 1] in my mouth, even praise unto our God." Let us **rejoice** with David, as he prays for the Rock to "hold up [our] goings in [His] paths, that [our] footsteps slip not" (17:5; cf. 18:36). Even our very "steps . . . are ordered by the LORD" (37:23). As the old hymn well puts it: "On Christ the Solid Rock, I stand; / All other ground is sinking sand."

Third, the Rock is our *sustenance*. It was that "rock" in the **wilderness** that miraculously yielded water for God's people: "He brought streams also out of the rock, and caused waters to run down like rivers" (Ps. 78:16; cf. Num. 20:8–12; Neh. 9:15). Why do we ever doubt God's promised provision (Matt. 6:25–34)?

Scriptures for Study: Read the parable of the two builders in Luke 6:46–49. Can you think of some "sandy soils" on which people **build** their lives today?

Fortress

meṣûḏāh

Next to Jerusalem, the **fortress** stronghold Masada (*meṣûḏāh*, 4686) is the most popular destination of Jewish tourists visiting the Holy Land. The capture of Jerusalem and the destruction of the **temple** by the Roman general Titus in AD 70 practically ended the "Great Revolt" led by the Zealots. The remaining few fled to Masada, a fortress on top of an enormous rock plateau near the Dead Sea. Only three narrow, difficult **paths** lead to the top, and anyone climbing them was an easy target. The Roman Tenth Legion had to settle for a siege that lasted several months. Then, rather than be captured, all 960 defenders committed suicide (except for two women and five children who had hidden themselves). So important is Masada as a focal point of Jewish survival, Israeli soldiers take an oath there: "Masada shall not fall again."[267]

Unlike that **fortress**, however, we have one that will *never* be breached. While *meṣûḏāh* is used to refer to literal fortresses, such as David's capture of Zion (Jerusalem) from the Jebusites (2 Sam. 5:6, 7, "strong hold"), many of its occurrences are figurative references to **God** and His acts of **salvation**. Psalm 91:2 stands out: "I will say of the LORD, He is my refuge and my fortress: my God; in him will I trust." Spurgeon observes here: "Let us, when we are secure in the Lord, rejoice that our position is unassailable, for he is our fortress as well as our refuge. No moat, portcullis, drawbridge, wall, battlement and donjon, could make us so secure as we are when the attributes of the Lord of Hosts environ us around."[268]

Coupling **rock** and **fortress**, David again writes: "Thou art my rock and my fortress; therefore for thy name's sake lead me, and guide me" (31:3). If we may also repeat from yesterday, "Be thou my strong habitation, whereunto I may continually resort: thou hast given commandment to save me; for thou art my rock and my fortress" (71:3). It is this perfect pair of words that bring to our minds the third stanza and refrain of that great hymn:

> How oft in the conflict, when pressed by the foe,
> I have fled to my Refuge and breathed out my woe;
> How often, when trials like sea billows roll,
> Have I hidden in Thee, O Thou Rock of my soul.
>
> Hiding in Thee, hiding in Thee,
> Thou blest Rock of Ages, I'm hiding in Thee.

Scriptures for Study: Read Psalm 91, noting the source of security (God's character, vv. 1, 2, and care, vv. 3–8), and the support of security (God's continual protection, vv. 9–13, and comforting compassion, vv. 14–16).

Deliverer

pālaṯ

Continuing our look at Psalm 18:2, it is not surprising that out of some twenty-six occurrences of *pālaṯ* (6403) in the OT, nineteen of them are in the Psalms. There, **praise** is expressed like no other place in **Scripture** and praise is, indeed, appropriate when it comes to this **word**.

The verb *pālaṯ* depicts a **deliverer**, one who helps to escape and bring to safety. Psalm 71:2 is especially noteworthy: "Deliver me in thy righteousness, and cause me to escape [*pālaṭ*]" (*pālaṭ* again appears in v. 4, "deliver"). As one reads that **psalm**, it is easy to notice first the unknown psalmist's *roar* for help (vv. 1–3), second his *request* for God's deliverance based upon his confidence in Him (vv. 4–13), and third his *resolve* to continue praising God always (vv. 14–24).

A verse that immediately comes to our minds here is 1 Corinthians 10:13: "There hath no temptation taken you but such as is common to man: but God is faithful, who will not suffer you to be tempted above that ye are able; but will with the temptation also make a way to escape, that ye may be able to bear it."

Here is one of the greatest promises to the Christian when it comes to living a sanctified **life**. First, there is the challenge that there are no excuses. We can never say, "The temptation was just too strong; I couldn't help myself," for God will not allow us to be tempted beyond our capacity to resist. Second, there is the encouragement that He will provide deliverance.

We would submit that the key phrase in this verse is "a way to escape," which is a single word in the Greek, *ekbasis* (1545G), meaning "to go out." The focus, however, is the article "a," which is actually *tēs*, the *definite* article "the." God, therefore, doesn't make just *a* way to escape **temptation**, rather it is always *the same way—the Word of God*. In all three areas in which our **Lord** was tempted (Matt. 4:1–11)—the lust of the flesh (vv. 2, 3), the **pride** of life (vv. 5, 6), and the lust of the eyes (vv. 8, 9)—*our Lord had victory because He quoted the Word of God* (v. 4, Deut. 8:3; v. 7, Deut. 6:16; v. 10, Deut. 6:13, 14). The real **test** in temptation, therefore, is *to see if God's Word will rule*. (See also our July 23 and 24 readings.)

Scriptures for Study: From what is the psalmist being delivered in the following verses: 18:43, 48; 37:40; 43:1?

Strength

ṣûr

The fourth metaphor for **God** that we notice in Psalm 18:2 is **strength**. (Note: God here is *'ēl*, 410, January 23.) While we studied another **word** translated **strength** back on August 16, the Hebrew here is *ṣûr* (6697), which is actually a synonym for *sela'* (5553, September 1), referring again to such objects as a boulder (Judg. 6:21; 13:19), a cliff or rock **wall** (Exod. 17:6; 33:21, 22), and even "the top of the rocks," that is, a **mountain** (Num. 23:9). The fact that **David** uses two similar words underscores the critical importance of having the right foundation.

Also like *sela'*, *ṣûr* is often used to figuratively picture God's support and defense of His people (e.g., Deut. 32:4, 15). In a dramatic contrast, in fact, it appears in Deuteronomy 32:31 to differentiate the true God from pagan gods: "For their rock is not as our Rock." The lost person only *thinks* he has a rock, only *imagines* he has **salvation**, only *reasons* he has **hope**. It is the true believer who has all that and infinitely more.

Another verse that strikes us is Psalm 73:26: "My flesh and my heart faileth: but God is the strength of my heart, and my portion for ever." Calvin writes of this verse, "There is here a contrast between the failing which David felt in himself and the strength with which he was divinely supplied; as if he had said, 'Separated from God I am nothing, and all that I attempt to do ends in nothing; but when I come to him, I find an abundant supply of strength.'"[269] Indeed, in ourselves, we are nothing. The world declares, "We are each our own person," and pop psychology says, "We each have our own self-worth and self-esteem." But David declares that in ourselves we will fail, that we need God's **strength**.

Finally, we should **observe** in our text a subtle difference between this metaphor for God and the others: This is the only one to which David adds an amplifying thought—"in whom I will trust." A rock foundation can accomplish nothing in our lives unless we **trust** in it and utilize its **strength**. As we will examine tomorrow, "trust" is *chāsāh* (2620), "to rely on, take refuge in," and demands an act of the will.

Dear Christian **Friend**, wherein does your **strength** lie?

Scriptures for Study: Rejoice in the following occurrences of *ṣûr*: Psalms 19:14; 27:5 ("rock"); 73:26; 95:1 ("rock"); 144:1.

Trust

chāsāh

Before moving on to the next metaphor **David** uses for **God** in Psalm 18:2, we should first meditate on the word ***trust***. As noted yesterday, **strength** is the only metaphor to which David adds an amplifying thought: "in whom I will trust."

Trust is *chāsāh* (2620). Appearing about thirty-five times, its primary meaning is to seek a refuge but also implies the underlying idea of putting one's **trust** in something,[270] the object in which one takes refuge. It is used in the literal sense of one taking refuge in the shade of a **tree** (Judg. 9:15) or taking shelter in a storm (Isa. 4:6; 25:4; Job 24:8).

It's predominantly a poetic word, however, appearing often in the figurative sense of seeking refuge and, therefore, trusting in one's God. In keeping with yesterday's mention of Deuteronomy 32:31—"For their rock is not as our Rock"—we then read in verses 37 and 38, "Where are their gods, their rock in whom they trusted...?" again underscoring the incalculable difference between the true God and pagan gods. While fallen men seek refuge where there is none, the believer can confidently **trust** in the True Refuge.

Consider for a moment where men take shelter in our **day**. Some **trust** in the god of *science*, but how foolish that is, for its theories change often, and sometimes a **new** discovery challenges even some foundational **law**. Others take refuge in the god of *philosophy*, but if there is anything that changes more than science, it's philosophy. While its goal is to explain the universe and the meaning of man's place in it, how can one find shelter in hundreds (if not thousands) of uncertain ideas, opinions, and nebulous concepts? Still others take refuge in the god of *religion*, which is really nothing more than philosophy in a different wrapper. The irony here is that religion *itself* is many people's refuge, as if a non-entity could provide shelter instead of the Person on whom the focus should be. Many **trust** in some nebulous "faith in faith" with no object (April 10), while others **trust** in their **good** works or even their own "inherent goodness."

Those, of course, are not the only gods. There are the gods of money, popularity, position, success, and the list goes on. But there is no Refuge to **trust** in other than the One, True God who has provided it all in Jesus Christ.

Scriptures for Study: Turning again to Psalms, **rejoice** in the following occurrences of *chāsāh*: 2:12; 5:11; 11:1; 34:22; 36:7; 71:1; 118:8.

Horn (of My Salvation)

qeren

The next metaphor **David** uses to describe **God** in Psalm 18:2 is "my buckler," the Hebrew *māgēn* (4043, **shield**), which we examined back on July 20. God truly is our shield, our defense in battle.

That brings us, therefore, to the fascinating metaphor **horn**. This is *qeren* (7161), which like many words has a literal and figurative meaning. Literally, of course, it refers to the horns of animals, as the ram that was caught in the thicket by its horns and became the substitute for Isaac (Gen. 22:13). Another literal reference is the *šôp̄ār* (7782), the ceremonial trumpetlike ram's **horn** used to **call** the people together (Exod. 19:16; Josh. 6:5). Hollowed-out horns were also used to store anointing **oil** (1 Sam. 16:1; 1 Kings 1:39).

An interesting mistranslation concerning this **word** appears in the inherently weak Latin Vulgate in Exodus 34:29, where Moses' **face** "shone" after His encounter with God. The Hebrew is *qāran* (7160), "to radiate light," but by misreading it as the similar *qeren*, the translators rendered it as the Latin *cornuta*, **horn**. It is because of this horrible error that several pieces of classical art, most notably Michelangelo's famous sculpture, depict Moses as having horns!

Qeren is also used to refer to the hornlike projections on the corners of altars (April 23), figuratively picturing **strength** and **power** as some scholars believe the **sacrifice** was bound to these horns, and that was where **blood** was applied (Exod. 29:12). It is no doubt this picture that leads to the idea of God Himself being referred to as a **horn**. It is His strength and power alone, David adds, that is our **salvation** (*yēša'*, 3468, see April 3). Such divine power is pictured elsewhere, as in Psalm 112:9: "He hath dispersed, he hath given to the poor; his righteousness endureth for ever; his horn shall be exalted with honour." Deeper, this is nowhere more evident than in 132:17: "There will I make the horn of David to bud: I have ordained a lamp for mine anointed" (cf. Ezek. 29:21). Here is a messianic prophecy (cited in Luke 1:69) declaring that a great Ruler and Redeemer will come.

Our text, then, provides not only the **wonderful salvation** we have *positionally* in God but also *practically*. As the strength and defense of many animals is in their horns, God "[enables us] to push down [our] foes, and to triumph over them with holy exultation."[271]

Scriptures for Study: What is the promise and application of Psalm 75:10?

High Tower

miśgāḇ

David's final metaphor for **God** in Psalm 18:2 is a **high tower**. What a picture we have here! This is a single **word** in the Hebrew, *miśgāḇ* (4869), which refers to a stronghold on elevated ground, either a natural one or one made by **man**. An example of the former is in Isaiah 33:16, where God's righteous people will be victorious against His enemies. The righteous man "shall dwell on high: his place of defence [*miśgāḇ*] shall be the munitions of rocks: bread shall be given him; his waters shall be sure." "Munitions" is *meṣāḏ* (4679), another form of *meṣûḏāh* (4686, September 2), so natural defenses themselves can be a **good** fortress.

Miśgāḇ is then used to refer to a manmade fortification, such as a fort with **high** walls (Isa. 25:12, "high fort") or a city with a "high wall" (Prov. 18:11; Isa. 30:13); **wall** in those **last** two verses is *śagaḇ* (7682), the root of *miśgāḇ, which* means "to be inaccessibly high," implying walls that are insurmountable.

All this, therefore, provides peaceful assurance to the believer for, "The LORD also will be a refuge for the oppressed, a refuge in times of trouble" (Ps. 9:9, both instances of "refuge" are *miśgāḇ*). So sure can we be of this fact that we should say, "Because of his strength will I wait upon thee: for God is my defence [*miśgāḇ*]" (59:9), and then we should "sing of [His] power; yea, I will sing aloud of [His] mercy in the morning: for [He] hast been my defence [*miśgāḇ*] and refuge in the day of my trouble" (v. 16).

What comfort there is in knowing that God is our **high tower**, "a citadel high planted on a rocky eminence beyond the reach of my enemies, from the heights of which I look down upon their fury without alarm, and survey a wide landscape of mercy reaching even unto the goodly land beyond Jordan."[272]

John Gill well sums up these great metaphors: "These various epithets show the fulness of safety in Jehovah, the various ways he has to deliver his people from their enemies, and secure them from danger; and the psalmist beholding and claiming his interest in him under all these characters, rendered him exceeding lovely and delightful to him; and each of them contain a reason why he loved him, and why, in the strength of grace, he determined to love him. God may be regarded in all these characters by Christ as man."[273]

Scriptures for Study: What is our further assurance in the following verses: Psalms 46:7; 62:2?

Circumcision

mûl

The Hebrew *mûl* (4135) simply means "to cut short, to cut off." All its some thirty-six occurrences, most in the Pentateuch (seventeen of those in Genesis alone), refer to **circumcision**, the surgical procedure of removing the foreskin from the male organ. This practice actually existed not only **among** the Israelites but also among several of the **nations** surrounding Israel, including Egypt prior to Abraham; it is even depicted in Egyptian hieroglyphics. The difference comes, of course, in the symbolism of the practice.

While there is uncertainty, many scholars believe that to the Egyptians and Semitic people other than the Israelites (Moabites, Ammonites, and Edomites) **circumcision** was probably a rite that initiated one into puberty, being perhaps a symbolic sacrificing of one's reproductive powers to the gods or perhaps even a symbol of human **sacrifice**.

To the Israelites, however, the meaning was quite different, as prescribed and defined by **God** Himself. The first occurrence of *mûl* is in Genesis 17:10, where God designates **circumcision** to be the **sign** of His **covenant** (February 9) with Abraham. It was first a symbol of the peoples' submission to God. More importantly, it was a symbol of the impurity of nature and, therefore, the laying aside of that impurity and a commitment to cleanness and separation from defilement. Interestingly, a byproduct of physical **circumcision**, as many modern medical authorities agree, is that its cleanliness lowers the risk of certain forms of cancer in both husband and wife.

Tragically, by the time of Christ, Judaism had degenerated into little more than a works-oriented religion, **circumcision** having become the ultimate sign of one's acceptance by God. But Paul made clear that both "Circumcision . . . and uncircumcision [are] nothing," that is, meaningless and worthless; rather what matters is the "keeping of the commandments of God" (1 Cor. 7:19).[274]

More specifically, as Colossians 2:11 declares, "In whom also ye are circumcised with the circumcision made without hands, in putting off the body of the sins of the flesh by the circumcision of Christ." It is Christ, by His **death** on Calvary, who is the true **circumcision**, and it is through Him believers are circumcised. It is through Him we now submit to God, lay aside the impurity of the flesh, and commit ourselves to cleanness and separation from defilement (Col. 3:5; Phil. 3:3).

Scriptures for Study: Read Romans 4:1–12. How was Abraham justified? Which verse clearly excludes works as a means to **salvation**? For whom is the gospel intended?

Fury (Wrath)

chēmāh

It is actually a NT verse that sets the stage for today's OT **word**: "For the wrath of God is revealed from heaven against all ungodliness and unrighteousness of men, who [suppress] the truth in unrighteousness" (Rom. 1:18). The word ***wrath*** here is the Greek *orgē* (3709G), which is in contrast to *thumos* (2372G); while *thumos* is passionate and temporary, *orgē* indicates "a more enduring state of mind."[275] From Romans 1:18 through 3:20 we read God's indictment of the world, first illustrating man's sinfulness and then revealing man's need for righteousness.

We mention those Greek words because they both are utilized in the Septuagint as translations of the Hebrew *chēmāh* (2534): *orgē* (e.g., Isa. 34:2; 63:6; Jer. 21:5) and *thumos* (e.g., Isa. 51:17; 63:3; Jer. 4:4). The translations **fury** or "furious" (71 times) and **wrath** or "wrathful" (35 times) well define *chēmāh*, which also includes the ideas of rage and heat.

Man's rage is sometimes the subject of this word, such as Esau's **anger** at Jacob (Gen. 27:44, the first occurrence of *chēmāh*). The dangerous character of such rage is also addressed (Prov. 6:34; 15:18; 27:4).

Most of its some 120 occurrences, however, speak of God's **wrath**. Its severity is often pictured as being poured out from a **cup** (Isa. 42:25; 51:17). While many today try to downplay God's **wrath**, preferring to speak always about His **love** and **forgiveness**, we need to understand that His **wrath** is actually a **good** thing. Why? Because it demonstrates His *hatred of sin*, which in turn flows from His *holiness of character*.

We could also consider this in another **way**. Would a God who just winks at **sin** be worthy of **worship**? Would a God who is tolerant of **evil** be deserving of **praise**? Indeed not. Like all God's attributes, we should thank and praise Him for His **wrath** against sin because it proves His holy character. We also thank Him because while we "*were* by nature the children of wrath, even as others" (Eph. 2:3, emphasis added), we have *now* been "delivered . . . from the wrath to come" (1 Thess. 1:10) and "reconciled to God by the death of his Son" (Rom. 5:10).

What is the practical application for us today? The sobering reality of God's **wrath** against sin and sinners should motivate us to evangelism, to *proclaim* with our *lips* and *prove* with our *lives* the coming **wrath** of God and the only **salvation** from it.

Scriptures for Study: What **counsel** is given concerning **wrath** in the following verses: Proverbs 15:1; 22:24; 29:22?

Wealth

hôn

Roman poet Horace (65–8 BC) wrote, "Make money, money by fair means if you can, if not, by any means money."[276] In his *Imitations of Horace*, famous English poet Alexander Pope (1688–1744), best known for his satirical verse and his translation of Homer, parroted that philosophy: "Get place and wealth, if possible with grace; / if not, by any means get wealth and place."[277] Those sentiments pretty much sum up the world's outlook on **life**.

God says something a little different. Appearing twenty-six times in the OT (all but four in the **Wisdom** books and eighteen in Proverbs alone), the Hebrew *hôn* (1952) means **wealth**, "substance, riches, possessions, or enough." That last meaning, in fact, graphically describes the **heart** of man, as illustrated in Proverbs 30:15, 16, where like a leech's insatiable appetite for **blood** and a fire's unquenchable consumption of everything in its path, men continually cry for more, but more is never enough.

While **wealth** and riches are at times a **sign** of blessing in the OT (Ps. 112:3), more often we see it as a sign of ungodliness: "He that hasteth to be rich hath an evil eye" (Prov. 28:22). While the godly **man** trusts in God as his "strong tower . . . and is safe," the rich man imagines in his "conceit" that his riches are "his strong city, and . . . high wall" (Prov. 18:10, 11; cf. 10:15). Sadly, this man deceives himself, for "there is that maketh himself rich, yet hath nothing: there is that maketh himself poor, yet hath great riches" (13:7). This can be true even of the believer, as was the case in the church at Laodicea: "Because thou sayest, I am rich, and increased with goods, and have need of nothing; and knowest not that thou art wretched, and miserable, and poor, and blind, and naked" (Rev. 3:17).

The words of the psalmist again capture our attention, declaring that the **Word** of God gives more cause for rejoicing than material riches: "I have rejoiced in the way of thy testimonies, as much as in all riches" (Ps. 119:14). It literally reads, "as over all riches." If **David** was the writer of this **psalm**, and this verse is strong evidence of that, he was a **king** with incalculable **wealth**, but his rejoicing was in the **wealth** of the Word.

Dear Christian **Friend**, is that *your* view as well?

Scriptures for Study: What was Job's view of **wealth** (Job 28:18)? 🕮 What is the **counsel** of Proverbs 3:9?

Work

'āśāh

The principal ideas in the Hebrew *'āśāh* (6213; February 25) are "to do, to make, to accomplish." It appears an enormous number of times (about 2,630), which immediately underscores the importance of this fundamental concept. **Work** is basic to existence itself.

This is seen first and foremost in the **work** of **God**. The one, true God is pictured as constantly working. This is seen primarily, of course, in His **work** of Creation (we find *'āśāh* eleven times in the Creation account (Gen. 1:7, 11, 12, 16, 25, 26, 31; 2:2–4, 18; cf. Ps. 96:5). God's **work** can be summed up as being: *powerful* ("God said," Gen. 1:3, 6, 9, 11, 14, 20, 24, 26), *productive* ("fruitful," vv. 22, 28), and *positive* (**good**, vv. 4, 10, 12, 18, 21, 25, 31). God's **work** is also apparent in the countless things He has done for His people (e.g., "done" in Josh. 23:3; Ps. 98:1; and "did" in Ps. 78:12).

This **word** also occurs in reference to **man** and his **work**, such as his constructing something (note "made" in Gen. 8:6; 13:4, 33:17; Ps. 106:19), growing crops (Ps. 107:37, "yield"), making **war** (Gen. 14:2; Josh. 11:18), and doing **evil** (Ps. 15:3; 34:16; 51:4). Of the latter, in fact, Romans 3:10 is a foundational verse concerning the **salvation** message and is taken from Psalm 14:1: "There is none that doeth good" (cf. 53:1, 3).

Most importantly, then, man is told to "do" what God commands. Leviticus 19:37, for example, declares, "Therefore shall ye observe all my statutes, and all my judgments, and do them: I am the LORD." Other verses add that obedience brings God's blessing: "And thou shalt do that which is right and good in the sight of the LORD: that it may be well with thee, and that thou mayest go in and possess the good land which the LORD sware unto thy fathers" (Deut. 6:18; also Exod. 23:22). "The numerous contexts in which this concept occurs," writes one Hebrew authority, "attest to the importance of an ethical response to God which goes beyond mere mental abstraction and which is translatable into obedience which is evidenced in demonstrable act."[278]

Such an "ethical response" is repeatedly emphasized, as in Psalm 34:14: "Depart from evil, and do good." Let that encourage us to **pray** with the psalmist, "I delight to do thy will, O my God: yea, thy law is within my heart" (40:8).

Scriptures for Study: Read the following verses, noting the promise in each: Psalms 37:3; 103:17, 18; 106:3.

Harlot

zānāh

Today's **word** might seem an odd one on which to base a devotional thought, but it is actually an extremely important word in OT spirituality. The Hebrew verb *zānāh* (2181) literally means "to go whoring, play a harlot, be a prostitute." It is the usual term for prostitution throughout Hebrew history, appearing about 100 times in the OT.

Its most important use was a figurative one, to picture spiritual harlotry, the turning away from **God** to false gods. Whether it be fame, fortune, fun, or false teaching, anything can be elevated to god status. Let us note four parallels:

First, the *action* of the prostitute, of course, is illicit sexual relations, perverting what God designed to be between only husband and wife. Israel, both literally and figuratively, had relations with gods other than the One, True God (Deut. 31:16). This was literally true because the fertility cults of the **day** included **temple** prostitution, a practice which was believed to increase the fertility of flocks and crops. It was (and still is) figuratively true in people's illicit relations with the false gods listed above.

Second, the *attitudes* of the prostitute are obviously those of rebellion, greed, and shamelessness. Inexplicably, the children of Israel turned to idolatry soon after their deliverance from Egypt (Exod. 32), even after the Mosaic **Law** had been given (Exod. 20). Likewise, all false teachers are rebellious and greedy and are shameless in their ways of acquiring money. A driving force and an earmark of false teachers, in fact, is the greed for money, as they "make merchandise" of people (2 Pet. 2:3, *emporeuomai*, 1710G).[279]

Third, there is the *attire* of the prostitute, which was recognizable (Prov. 7:10). Common practices were a veiled **face** to hide one's identity (Gen. 38:15), seductive clothing, and excessive jewelry. Oh, how false gods hide their true identity and camouflage their real character! That leads to one other parallel.

Fourth, the *allure* of the prostitute is instant gratification with seemingly no consequences; she is subtle and deceptive (Prov. 6:24–26). False gods likewise promise everything but in the end deliver nothing. Philosophy always looks interesting, religion always looks compelling, and **sin** always looks pleasing. Again, we should be reminded often of false teaching; countless people are lured into cults and religions by all kinds of promises: belonging, unity, harmony, paradise, and even divinity.

Let us beware of the **harlot** (Exod. 34:14–17).

Scriptures for Study: What metaphor is used in Proverbs 23:27 for the **harlot**? 📖 What is the end for the **harlot** and those who follow her (Prov. 6:32; Hosea 5:3–6)?

Tree (1)

'ēṣ

Back on August 25, we mentioned the **apple tree**, but any **tree** in the Middle East was a great blessing. The Hebrew *'ēṣ* (6086), which has equivalents in Akkadian and other Semitic languages, appears some 325 times in the OT. This might **lead** one to assume that trees were common, but just the opposite was (and still is) true in some areas. While trees were abundant in some locations (e.g., the Jordan **Valley**), they were very scarce in others because of the arid climate (e.g., the Negev Desert). That *scarcity*, however, perhaps intensifies the *symbolism* surrounding trees.

The first occurrence of *'ēṣ* is in Genesis 1:11, followed by fifteen more in the accounts of Creation and the Fall. That first mention declares, "And God said, Let the earth bring forth grass, the herb yielding seed, and the fruit tree yielding fruit after his kind, whose seed is in itself, upon the earth: and it was so," which demonstrates that the **tree** stands as a symbol of **life** and nature. One **tree**, in fact, was called "the tree of life" and stood "in the midst of the garden" of Eden (Gen. 2:9; cf. 3:22, 24; Rev. 22:2). In the same verse is mentioned another, "the tree of knowledge of good and evil," which was instrumental in introducing **death** into the world.

Of all the trees mentioned in **Scripture**, none is of more importance than the one referred to in Galatians 3:13: "Christ hath redeemed us from the curse of the law, being made a curse for us: for it is written, Cursed is every one that hangeth on a tree." Paul refers here to an ancient Jewish tradition recorded in Deuteronomy 21:22, 23 that God's curse was upon an executed person who is hung on a **tree**. Paul therefore declares that Jesus became just such a curse for us, a curse rooted in the **Law** itself. The *Law* cannot **save**, rather only the ***Lord*** can save. Peter picked up on the same theme and wrote: "Who his own self bare our sins in his own body on the tree, that we, being dead to sins, should live unto righteousness: by whose stripes ye were healed" (1 Pet. 2:24).

Is there any doubt as to why **tree** is a symbol of life, **joy**, and well-being? It is all because our Lord hung on that **tree** for us. We will go a little deeper into this **tomorrow**, but **rejoice** today in the life you have because of the cross.

Scriptures for Study: In preparation for tomorrow's study, read the following verses in Proverbs: 3:18; 11:30; 13:12; 15:4.

Tree (2)

'ēṣ

As noted **yesterday**, the **tree** in **Scripture** (*'ēṣ*, 6086) stands as a symbol of **life** and nature. There is a particularly fascinating metaphorical use of **tree** in Proverbs; in four places we encounter the term *tree of life.* Picturing the **tree** of the same **name** in Genesis 2:9, each of these verses provides a **wonderful** metaphor of what should be true in the believer's life.

First, we read, "[Wisdom] is a tree of life to them that lay hold upon her: and happy is every one that retaineth her" (Prov. 3:18). This verse comes at the end of a passage concerning the spiritual **wealth** that comes from **wisdom** (vv. 13–18). It is *pleasing* (v. 13), it is ***precious*** (vv. 14, 15), it is *prevailing* (v. 16), and it is *pleasant* (vv. 17, 18). There truly is life in wisdom.

Second, we discover that "the fruit of the righteous is a tree of life; and he that winneth souls is wise" (11:30). Here wisdom (March 22) and righteous living have two results: a ***blessed*** life (February 27), pictured by **fruit**, and a *bountiful* life, indicated by "winneth souls." While this verse has been used many times as a picture of evangelism, that does not seem to be the precise meaning. The Hebrew behind "winneth" is *lāqach* (3947), a broad term that appears about 960 times and whose "exact meaning must be discerned from its context."[280] With the context being about wisdom (March 22), then, and with the primary meaning of *lāqach* being "to take or grasp," the idea is that he who is wise takes others to wisdom, that is, imparts it to them. While this certainly can include evangelism, it goes deeper in imparting to people the fuller truths of Scripture knowledge.

Third, we should note that "hope deferred maketh the heart sick: but when the desire cometh, it is a tree of life" (13:12). There is nothing wrong with wanting things as long as they are **good** and wholesome and within God's will, so when such things are "deferred" (drawn out or delayed) in fulfillment there is disappointment. But when they finally come, they are a **joy** and a blessing.

Fourth and finally, we are challenged that "a wholesome tongue is a tree of life: but perverseness therein is a breach in the spirit" (15:4). "Wholesome" is *marpē'* (4832), which speaks of "health or healing." Oh, how vital it is that our tongues be a source of *healing*, not *hurting*.

Scriptures for Study: Read the following verses, noting what they say about the **tongue**: Proverbs 12:18; 16:24; James 3:1–8.

Tree (3)

'ēṣ

Before leaving this **word** *'ēṣ*, we would mention the **Tree** of **Life** one final time. Our **Lord** ends His Revelation letter to the Ephesians with this statement: "To him that overcometh will I give to eat of the tree of life, which is in the midst of the paradise of God" (2:7). Had **Adam** and **Eve** been permitted to eat of this **tree** while in their sinful condition, they would have forever remained sinful (Gen. 3:22). Our text, then, and Revelation 22:2, speak of us eating the **fruit**, and the leaves being used to heal the **nations**.

More specifically, believers will partake of the fruit as a symbol of eternal life. Then, since it is through the nation of Israel that all nations will be **blessed** (Gen. 18:18), the leaves (and perhaps the fruit also) will be used to "heal" the nations, that is, make them acceptable in God's sight. We say this since the **number** twelve is symbolic of the twelve tribes of Israel and because the twelve is then used in reference to the **Tree** of Life. All this points to the fact that all men, regardless of nationality, are accepted by God because of Jesus Christ. It doesn't mean all men are accepted no matter what they believe—rather that they are accepted if they have trusted in the merits of Christ.

Most importantly, however, *obedience brings God's blessing*, and that blessing will take place in "the paradise of God," that is, **heaven** and the **New** Jerusalem. As Jesus said to the thief on the cross, "To day shalt thou be with me in paradise" (Luke 23:43). Likewise, Paul recounted how he had been "caught up into paradise, and heard unspeakable words, which it is not lawful for a man to utter" (2 Cor. 12:4). What does Paul mean? We don't **know**! It was beyond the limits of what language can explain. And as the apostle John declares later, "And I John saw the holy city, new Jerusalem, coming down from God out of heaven, prepared as a bride adorned for her husband" (Rev. 21:2).

Dear Christian **Friend**, have you fallen out of **love** with the Savior, as did the Ephesians believers? Have you "left [your] first love" behind (Rev. 2:4)? Have you abandoned your basic devotion to Christ and His Word? Christian Pastor, have you left behind the Truth of the Word of God alone? If so, it is **time** to ***remember***, ***repent***, and ***return*** (v. 5).

Scriptures for Study: Read the tragedy of the church at Ephesus (Rev. 2:1–7) and be challenged to never allow this to happen to you.

Leaf

'āleh

Not only do we see great significance in the **word *tree*** in **Scripture**, but so it is with **leaf** as well. The Hebrew is *'āleh* (5929), which is used, of course, both literally and figuratively. In the literal sense, for example, it was the **leaf** of an olive tree, an extremely hardy tree, that the **dove** brought back to the **ark**, demonstrating that vegetation was returning to the purged earth (Gen. 8:11).

What makes *'āleh* particularly interesting in its figurative sense is that it is both positive and negative. On the negative side, it pictures spiritual degeneration as a fading or withering **leaf**, which we see in several OT occurrences. In a key verse concerning the depravity of **man** and the failure of human works, Isaiah writes, "But we are all as an unclean thing, and all our righteousnesses are as filthy rags; and we all do fade as a leaf; and our iniquities, like the wind, have taken us away" (Isa. 64:6; cf. 1:30; 34:4; Jer. 8:13; see also **filthy rags**, April 4).

But **praise** be to **God**, the matter does not end there. On the positive side, a "green" **leaf** or a **leaf** that does "not wither" serves as a vivid picture of a healthy spiritual condition. There is no healthier believer than he who is described in Psalm 1:1–3, where verse 3 declares: "He shall be like a tree planted by the rivers of water, that bringeth forth his fruit in his season; his leaf also shall not wither; and whatsoever he doeth shall prosper" (see February 27). No matter what comes, whether drought, disease, or other distress, the believer is "ever green," for "the inward man is renewed day by day" (2 Cor. 4:16; cf. Jer. 17:8). And what is the result? "The righteous shall flourish as a branch [*'āleh*]" (Prov. 11:28).

Perhaps most significant of all is the prophet's description of the restoration of the millennial land and **temple** in Ezekiel 47 and 48. On those trees will be leaves that will in some way provide healing (v. 12). This imagery is vivid, as leaves were often used for medicinal purposes—blackberry leaves were applied to burns, olive leaves were used for an astringent, and sycamore and walnut leaves were applied to wounds.[281] John borrowed this imagery in his description of the **New** Jerusalem in Revelation 22:2, as noted **yesterday**.

Take some **time** today to praise God for the healing you have in Christ.

Scriptures for Study: Read Isaiah 53:1–5. How is Messiah described in verse 2? What, then, did He accomplish?

Fruit

periy

Continuing the imagery surrounding **tree** as used in **Scripture**, we look today at one other crucial aspect—the **fruit** it produces. Like *'āleh* (**leaf**), the Hebrew for ***fruit*** (*periy*, 6529) is used both literally and figuratively. Literally, of course, it refers to the **fruit** of a tree (Gen. 1:12), a vine (Zech. 8:12), or even the womb (Gen. 30:2). Of that latter use, Psalm 127:3 is especially **blessed**: "Lo, children are an heritage of the LORD: and the fruit of the womb is his reward." How sad it is that many Christians today **choose** voluntary sterilization, for they are missing part of their **inheritance** and reward (cf. Gen. 1:28; 8:17).

Also like "leaf," the figurative use of **fruit** is both positive and negative. Not only did our **Lord** Himself declare this—"Every good tree bringeth forth good fruit; but a corrupt tree bringeth forth evil fruit" (Matt. 7:17)—but it was true, of course, in the Garden of Eden (cf. Gen. 1:29; 2:16, 17). Bad **fruit**, therefore, will come from the ungodly person (Prov. 1:31; Jer. 6:19; 21:14; Hosea 10:13; Mic. 7:13), while **good fruit** will come from the godly (Prov. 31:31; Isa. 3:10).

Psalm 1:3 is once again a pivotal verse here, declaring that the godly **man** "bringeth forth his fruit in his season." The NT parallel here is one of the most important truths of the Christian **life**. Just as **fruit** automatically comes from a plant or tree because it is its nature to do so, spiritual **fruit** is automatic in the Christian. The irrefutable proof of a person's **salvation** is that he *will* **bear fruit**.

What constitutes **fruit** in the Christian life? The NT declares there are no less than five types of **fruit**: *First,* there is *witnessing for Christ* (John 4:36; Rom. 1:13; 1 Cor. 16:15; Mark 1:17). While some **teach** that only *winning* people is **fruit**, just the *witnessing* itself is **fruit**. *Second,* there is ***worship of God*** (Heb. 13:15; Hosea 14:2, where "calves" is *par*, 6499, used figuratively for "fruit"). *Third,* there is *wholesome conduct* (Rom. 6:22; Col. 1:10; Phil. 1:10, 11). *Fourth,* there is *winsome character* (Gal. 5:22, 23), which is proof positive of true conversion. *Fifth,* there is *wealth-sharing with other Christians* (Rom. 15:28, 29; Phil. 4:16, 17).[282]

Let us each ask ourselves, What fruit is evident in my life?

Scriptures for Study: Read the many verses cited above, examining your own **heart** and life for **fruit**.

Leaven

chāmēṣ

The primary Hebrew **word** for **leaven** in the OT is *chāmēṣ* (2557), which specifically refers to the yeast that causes **bread** to rise or the process of rising itself. Its first occurrence is in Exodus 12:15: "Seven days shall ye eat unleavened bread; even the first day ye shall put away leaven out of your houses: for whosoever eateth leavened bread from the first day until the seventh day, that soul shall be cut off from Israel" (cf. vv. 19, 20; 13:7).

The scene here, of course, is the first **Passover** (April 26) and the Feast of Unleavened Bread. To commemorate their hasty exodus from Egypt, which was mounted so quickly that there was not enough time to **leaven** the bread for the journey (vv. 34, 39), the Israelites did not eat any leavened bread for seven days or even have it in their homes. This act reminded them that God's people should leave **sin** and the world behind and should do so as quickly as possible.

The believer's separation from the world is a recurring theme in **Scripture**, with the Israelites as the quintessential example. A particularly dramatic example is when the Israelites are urged to leave Babylon quickly after the exile and **return** to Jerusalem. The repetition of "Depart ye, depart ye" demonstrates the urgency of the need to "go ye out from thence, touch no unclean thing; go ye out of the midst of her" (Isa. 52:11).

Another aspect of the use of **leaven** in Scripture is its permeating character and influence. While some teachers insist that **leaven** *always* represents **evil**, that is not the case. In Matthew 13:33, it represents the ***good*** influence of the **kingdom** of **heaven**. Galatians 5:9 is an example of this meaning: "A little leaven leaveneth the whole lump." In a context on false teaching, one of the reasons for the terrible danger of such teaching is its permeating influence. If allowed to continue, it will take over the entire church. The same was true of the sexual sin Paul addressed in 1 Corinthians 5; such sin had to be "purge[d] out" (*ekkathairō*, 1571G, to cleanse thoroughly) before it permeated the whole (v. 7).

Oh, how we must guard against the permeating nature of sin and depart even from its appearance (1 Thess. 5:22).

Scriptures for Study: Read 2 Corinthians 6:14–7:1, a picture taken from Deuteronomy 22:10 (cf. Lev. 19:19), which commanded not to yoke together an ox and a donkey in plowing because their step and pull is uneven. Note Paul's increasingly graphic and even more contradictory comparisons.

Throne (1)

kissē

Occurring in most other Semitic languages, *kissē* (3678) refers to a place of honor or a seat of authority and **power**, what we call a **throne**. What makes this **word** noteworthy is that it is used to refer to the thrones of both **God** and men. Concerning men, we read of the thrones of Pharaoh (Exod. 11:5; 12:29), Solomon (1 Kings 2:19), Jehoshaphat (22:10), Ahasuerus (Esther 1:2), and others.

When speaking of men, however, the vast majority of occurrences refer to David's **throne**. Second Samuel 7:4–17 is the full statement of the **covenant** (February 9) God made with David, the essence of which is in verse 16: "And thine house and thy kingdom shall be established for ever before thee: thy throne shall be established for ever." God's unconditional promise to David was that his son (Solomon) would **build** the **temple**, sit on David's **throne**, and that David's **house** and **throne** would last forever. So important is this covenant that it lays the foundation for Messiah, who would be in the line of David and literally sit on that very **throne**. Since Solomon's **throne** was a literal, political **throne**, the ultimate fulfillment through Messiah will also be literal and political. This is the basis for the premillennial view of Christ's **return**.

While some dear Christian brethren today hold to a view other than premillennialism (see also January 21 and June 4), the OT is brimming with references to a *literal* **kingdom** on earth.[283] Any nonliteral view runs into problems. A single case in point is Luke 1:31–33. Since Jesus was *literally* conceived in Mary's womb, *literally* named "JESUS," *literally* became "great," was *literally* "the Son of the Highest," how is it that He will not literally reign on David's **throne** over Israel? To try to view this passage as literal *and* figurative is questionable hermeneutics at best.

Premillennialism was, in fact, the prominent position of the early church from the first to the third century.[284] Sadly, the drift away from this view came as a result of Origen (ca. 185–254) being influenced by pagan philosophy, especially dualism,[285] and his new "allegorical approach" to biblical interpretation. This approach looks at words as symbols of something besides the normal meaning of the words, the result of which is that words can be made to say anything the interpreter chooses.

Oh, what blessings we miss if we deny David's perpetual **throne**!

Scriptures for Study: Read and **rejoice** in what Isaiah says will occur during the reign of Messiah on the earth: 2:4; 11:6–9; 19:23–25; 32:1; 35:1–7; 51:3; 65:20–22.

Throne (2)

kissē

No **throne**, of course, is more important, or more prominent in **Scripture**, than God's. More than half the 135 occurrences of *kissē*, in fact, refer to God's **throne**, in which we see three principles:

First, and foremost, God's **throne** *proclaims sovereign rule*. While we have mentioned God's sovereignty several times (January 24, August 20, 31), it cannot be overemphasized. In a sense, sovereignty itself is the very definition of God. If God is not absolutely sovereign, He is not God at all, and it is that **image** of **throne** that declares that fact: "The LORD hath prepared his throne in the heavens; and his kingdom ruleth over all" (Ps. 103:19). "[God] is an autocrat," Spurgeon writes, "and His dominion arises from himself and is sustained by his own innate power. . . . Over the whole universe he stretches his scepter."[286]

Second, God's **throne** *provides saving righteousness*. "God sitteth upon the throne of his holiness" (Ps. 47:8). Unlike human rulers who are motivated by their *humanness*, God is motivated by His *holiness*. Moreover, such *inherent* holiness in God demands *imparted* holiness to **man**. In his sin, man cannot come to God, so God must decree to impart holiness to man. "Justice and judgment are the habitation of [His] throne," writes the psalmist, but also from that **throne** "mercy and truth shall go before [His] face" (Ps. 89:14; also Prov. 20:28).

Third, God's **throne** *produces strengthening resources*. Psalm 132:11, 12 declares: "The LORD hath sworn in truth unto David; he will not turn from it; Of the fruit of thy body will I set upon thy throne. If thy children will keep my covenant and my testimony that I shall teach them, their children shall also sit upon thy throne for evermore." These verses again refer to the Davidic **covenant**, stating that if God's people had remained obedient, David's **throne** would not have been vacated from the fall of Jerusalem until Jesus sits on it in the Millennium. So while these verses apply directly to that time, there is still a practical application today, namely, to **obey** God for truth, blessing, and **power**.

Spurgeon again writes, "We have no hereditary right to the divine favour: . . . grace does not run in the blood, and we are filled with holy fear lest in any of our seed there should be an evil heart of unbelief in departing from the living God."[287]

Scriptures for Study: Read the following verses, noting what they declare about God's **throne**: Psalms 9:4, 7; 11:4; 103:19; 115:3.

Noah (1)

Nōach

Noah is near the top of my "favorites list" of Bible characters. So important is **Noah** that he is mentioned some fifty times in nine books of **Scripture**. Here is a **man** who did *what* **God** said, the *way* God said to do it, and *when* God said to do it. I think his **name** gives us a clue into why that is true.

Lamech named his son **Noah** (*Nōach*, 5146), hoping this son would "comfort us concerning our work and toil of our hands, because of the ground which the LORD hath cursed" (Gen. 5:29; cf. Matt. 11:28). This name is, in fact, related either to *nācham* (5162, "comfort" in this verse), "to comfort or repent" (August 7), or *nûach* (5118), which appears only four times in the OT and refers to rest or a resting place (2 Chron. 6:41; Esther 9:16–18).

Lamech's **hope** was realized in his son. **Noah** did, indeed, bring comfort and rest to a troubled world, although it came after the most cataclysmic event in the earth's history, the universal Flood. But to be able to *instill* that kind of comfort and rest in others, those attitudes would first have had to be *inherent* in him.

So where did **Noah** get such attitudes? Like all the other examples in that great "Hall of Faith" in Hebrews 11, "By faith Noah, being warned of God of things not seen as yet, moved with fear . . . and became heir of the righteousness which is by faith" (v. 7). He just believed God and rested in that; he simply did "according to all that God commanded him" (Gen. 6:22). For 120 years (v. 3), he went on building the **ark** and **preaching** the **Word** (2 Pet. 2:5).

It often strikes me that if **Noah** had been successful by modern standards, he would have had to **build** several boats and then done anything to get people on one of them. He probably would have run an attendance contest, given away balloons with dinosaur pictures on them, put on a stage play, made people feel comfortable by appealing to their "felt needs," and then had a celebrity give his testimony. But Noah's ministry was not a pragmatic one. He just did it God's way, and it is only by doing the same that we, too, find comfort and rest. If we will just do that, we will see God's blessing like never before.

Scriptures for Study: In preparation for tomorrow's study, read about **Noah** in Genesis 6:8–22.

Walked [and] Noah (2)

hālaḵ [and] Nōach

As noted yesterday, **Noah** demonstrates the comfort and rest one can **know** by simply believing in and doing what **God** says. Before leaving this pivotal character, we would do well to note a few other aspects of Noah's **life**.

Theologian Charles Ryrie's book *Balancing the Christian Life* deals with spirituality and basic Christian living.[288] That term "balancing" is an excellent one for describing what the believer's life includes, and **Noah** is one of the greatest models in **Scripture**. We see in him five aspects of a balanced life:

First, we discover that "Noah *walked with* God" (Gen. 6:9). **Walked** is *hālaḵ* (1980), which in the literal sense means "to go or walk." In this literal **way** it refers simply to movement, whether it be a **man** walking (Gen. 12:9, "going"; 2 Sam. 15:30, "went"), an animal crawling or slithering (Lev. 11:27, "goeth," and 42, "go"), and even the flowing of a **river** (Gen. 2:14, "goeth", first occurrence), the tossing of the sea (Jonah 1:11, 13, "wrought"), and the receding water of the Flood (Gen. 8:3, 5, "continually"). Speaking anthropomorphically, of course, God is spoken of as walking on the wind (Ps.104:3) and in the heavens (Job 22:14).

The figurative idea in *hālaḵ*, then, is how a man "walks" in life, that is, how he conducts himself, how he lives. Psalm 1:1 tells us, "Blessed is the man who walketh not in the counsel of the ungodly," that is, not taking the advice, adopting the philosophies, and living by the standards of wickedness. Those who do also "walk . . . after the imagination [*šeriyrûṯ*, 8307] of their evil heart," that is, according to their own hardness and obstinacy, their refusal to listen to God (Jer. 3:17, "walk" is the variant of *hālaḵ*: *yālaḵ,* 3212).

In stark contrast, there was **Noah** (as well as Enoch, who also "walked with God," Gen. 5:24). What does it mean to "walk with God"? The main characteristic, as noted yesterday, is obeying what God says. In fact, this principle is emphasized in several verses that couple walking with God with obeying His **Word**. One of the clearest is Judges 2:17, where God's people "went a whoring after other gods, and bowed themselves unto them: they turned quickly out of the way which their fathers walked in, obeying the commandments of the LORD; but they did not so."

Oh, that we today would walk with God!

Scriptures for Study: Read the following verses and note how each couples walking with God with keeping His Word: Deuteronomy 28:9; Psalm 26:3; Isaiah 38:3; Ezekiel 18:17.

Noah (3)

Nōach

Concluding our observations of Noah's "balanced life," not only do we see he ***walked*** *with* **God**, but *second,* he *worked for* God.

What a job God gave **Noah**! Assuming the "cubit" **Noah** used was the standard eighteen inches, which most conservative Bible scholars believe, the **ark** was 450 feet long, 75 feet wide, and 45 feet high. To put it in perspective, that is one-and-a-half football fields in length, roughly one-fourth of that field in width, and about the height of a four-story building. Those dimensions yielded a volume of more than 1,500,000 cubic feet, or about 550 standard railroad livestock cars.[289] Indeed, true **faith** always includes obedience, and **Noah** certainly **proved** his.

Third, **Noah** *witnessed* for God. Second Peter 2:5 declares, "[God] spared not the old world, but saved **Noah** the eighth person, a preacher of righteousness, bringing in the flood upon the world of the ungodly." For 120 years, both Noah's ***life*** and his *lips* were constant proclamations of what was coming to an ungodly world. But with the exception of his family, **Noah** reminds us of Jeremiah, who preached for forty years without a single convert. How many today are **preaching** the **pure**, undiluted gospel regardless of the "results"?

Fourth, **Noah** *waited* on God. A quick reading of the Flood account can easily miss the fact that **Noah** didn't immediately exit the ark when he saw that the ground was dry but rather waited on God to tell him (Gen. 8:13–19). How often do we think we **know** best? We may think that all the circumstances point to a certain act or that we have all the facts we need to make our decision, but we get ahead of God. We need to be reminded each **day** that we might "[devise our] way: but the LORD directeth [our] steps" (Prov. 16:9).

Fifth, **Noah** *worshipped* God. Genesis 8:20 indicates that the very first thing **Noah** did after leaving the ark was **build** an **altar** and offer the most **precious** objects on the ark in sacrificial **worship**. The total number of animals in **sacrifice** amounted to one-fourteenth of his flock and herds. What thanksgiving! And Noah's sacrifice was "a sweet savour" to God (v. 21; cf. Eph. 5:2), that is, it was pleasing to Him. How much, therefore, are we pleasing Him in giving our **time**, talents, and treasures?

Scriptures for Study: Combining today's study with yesterday's on **walk**, what does Isaiah 40:31 **teach** us?

Imagination

yēṣer

One of the many fascinating (and entertaining) aspects of children is watching them use their **imagination**. Any object—a stick, a rock, a box, whatever—can become anything they **choose**. Like virtually anything else, however, **imagination** can be used for **good** or bad.

One **word** translated **imagination** is *šeriyrûṯ* (8307, September 22), but we look today at *yēṣer* (3336), which appears only nine times but with profound implications, both positive and negative. Its basic meaning is "to form, frame, or fashion, the shaping or forming of the object involved."[290] An **image** that immediately comes to our mind is that of the potter fashioning a **vessel**, an image we find, in fact, in Isaiah 29:16, where a rebellious people switch the roles of the potter (**God**) and the clay (themselves) and turn "things upside down" by thinking they are in control (also Jer. 18:1–6; Rom. 9:20, 21). We do well to **remember** who is the Potter and who is the clay.

This word is also used in the context of making idols, as in Habakkuk 2:18, where the **prophet** asks rhetorically, "What profiteth the graven image that the maker thereof hath graven it; the molten image, and a teacher of lies, that the maker of his work trusteth therein, to make dumb idols?" Here *yēṣer* is translated **work**, but we could translate it "imaginative work," for every **idol** is, indeed, a work of the **imagination**.

The first appearance of *yēṣer* is the strongest image of all: "And God saw that the wickedness of man was great in the earth, and that every imagination of the thoughts of his heart was only evil continually" (Gen. 6:5). That was man's depraved condition at the **time** of the Flood. Think of it! Except for **Noah** and his family, there was not a single action, thought, motive, purpose, or desire that was good (June 14–16). Society today is closing in on that condition, and as Jesus Himself declares, "As the days of [Noah] were, so shall also the coming of the Son of man be" (Matt. 24:37).

There has been controversy over the depravity of **man** throughout church history. But after the Flood was over, we read God's words about man's basically unchanged nature: "The imagination of man's heart is evil from his youth" (Gen. 8:21; cf. Ps. 14:1–4; Rom. 1:28–30; Eph. 2:1–3). **Praise** be to God that He has saved us from ourselves!

Scriptures for Study: What is the encouragement of 1 Chronicles 28:9? 📖 What is the promise of Isaiah 26:3 ("mind" is *yēṣer*)? 📖 You might also review **wicked imaginations** (July 12).

Counsel

'ēṣāh [and] tachbulāh

Appearing some eighty-eight times in the OT, and almost always translated **counsel** in the AV, the noun *'ēṣāh* (6098) means "advice or counsel," with the extended idea of plan and purpose in some contexts. The verb form (*yā'aṣ*, 3289) appears about eighty more times. The first occurrence of the verb (Exod. 18:19) sets the tone of this **word** group as Jethro encourages his son-in-law Moses to listen to his **counsel** about his plan for the enormous task of leading God's people.

This theme is repeated frequently throughout the OT, whether the **counsel** is **good** or bad, or whether the **counsel** is received or rejected. In contrast to Jethro and Moses, we see Ahithophel's good **counsel** to Absalom, which he rejects, and then see Hushai's **evil counsel** that Absalom accepts (2 Sam. 17). Several occurrences of this word encourage us in three ways:

First, we must *receive* the **counsel** of God. While the **counsel** of worldly men is empty—"The LORD bringeth the counsel of the heathen to nought: he maketh the devices of the people of none effect" (Ps. 33:10)—God's **counsel** is true and timeless: "The counsel of the LORD standeth for ever, the thoughts of his heart to all generations" (v. 11). If we will, therefore, allow Him to "guide [us] with [His] counsel," He will "afterward receive [us] to glory" (73:24).

Second, we should *regard* the **counsel** of godly people. There is no blessing or benefit to "the counsel of the ungodly" (Ps. 1:1), and, "Where no counsel is, the people fall: but in the multitude of counsellors [*yā'as*] there is safety" (Prov. 11:14; also 15:22; 24:6). As long as our friends and fellow believers are offering us godly **counsel**, we should listen to and consider it. We should also note that the word **counsel** in this verse is *tachbulāh* (8458), a nautical term used of steering a ship (cf. 1:5; 11:14; 20:18; 24:6). Indeed, godly, biblically accurate **counsel** will steer us in the right direction.

Third, we can then be a *resource* of **counsel** to others. Once we have received God's **counsel**, both from Him and from godly believers, we can then claim it as our own: "Counsel is mine, and sound wisdom: I am understanding; I have strength" (Prov. 8:14). We are now equipped to lovingly and prayerfully become a part of that "multitude of counsellors" and **minister** to others.

Scriptures for Study: What specifically should be our "counsellors" (*'ēṣāh*), according to Psalms 119:24? 🕮 How does 2 Timothy 3:15–17 apply?

I Will (1)

(Grammatical)

Today's "word" is not our typical study. While English constructs a statement such as "I will make" (Gen. 2:18) using three words, the Hebrew construction of a verb includes the words **I will**, just as it could be modified to express other thoughts, such as "I made." We mention this only because of the significance of **I will** when used of **God**: "I will destroy" (6:13), "I will shew" (12:1), "I will establish" (17:19), "I will spare" (18:26), and so on.

In short, the words **I will** are the words of sovereignty. They express the autonomous, independent, self-sufficient God of the universe acting unilaterally according to His will and purpose. These words appear hundreds of times in the OT, but there is no better representative passage than Exodus 6:6–8. Not only do we see the word **LORD** (*Yāhweh*, January 8) three times and **God** (*'Elōhiym*, January 7) twice, but we also observe that twelve of the twenty-three personal pronouns in these verses refer to God. This powerful passage proclaims seven "I wills" of *Yāhweh*.

First, there is the **I will** of *deliverance*: "I will bring you out from under the burdens of the Egyptians" (v. 6). "Burdens" is *seḇālāh* (5450), which speaks of burden-bearing, compulsory service, even forced **labor**. It appears only six times in the OT, all of which refer to the forced labor of the Israelites in Egypt (Exod. 1:11; 2:11; 6:6, 7). It is derived from the root *sāḇal* (5445), which appears another ten times and means "to carry a load as a slave or laborer." It is *sāḇal*, in fact, that appears twice in Isaiah 53 in reference to the Suffering Savior who has "borne our griefs, and carried [*sāḇal*] our sorrows" (v. 4), and will "bear [our] **iniquities**" (v. 11, April 2). So important is this truth that Matthew cited this very prophecy: "That it might be fulfilled which was spoken by Esaias the prophet, saying, Himself took our infirmities, and bare our sicknesses" (Matt. 8:17).

How sobering this thought is! By sovereign decree, our Savior took upon Himself all our sin, guilt, grief, burdens, sorrows, regrets, and all else, and "was once offered to bear the sins of many" (Heb. 9:28). What is the practical result for the believer? His "yoke is easy, and [His] burden is light" (Matt. 11:30), and we can "[cast] all [our] care upon him; for he careth for [us]" (1 Pet. 5:7).

Scriptures for Study: What was the purpose of Christ bearing "our sins in his own body on the tree" (1 Pet. 2:24)? 🕮 What was the reason this had to occur (3:18)?

I Will (2)

(Grammatical)

Yesterday we considered the significance of God's sovereignty as demonstrated in the words **I will**. Continuing with the seven "I wills" of Exodus 6:6–8, we see the *second* **I will**, that of *liberty*. "I will rid you out of their bondage" (v. 6). This, of course, is related to the first **I will** (*deliverance*), but it goes further. Delivering His people would not have been all that glorious if they had not been truly free after that. If they still wore Egyptian shackles, would that be freedom? But they were, indeed, free. Likewise, God not only lifted the ***burden*** of **sin** from us through Christ, but He also released us from its *bondage*.

Let us go a little deeper on this point because of its critical application to Christian living. "Knowing this," Paul writes, "that our old man is crucified with him, that the body of sin might be destroyed, that henceforth we should not serve sin" (Rom. 6:6). The shackles are gone! Based on the fact that *every* verb tense in Romans 6 that refers to our identification with Christ is a past tense (aorist or perfect), Paul's point is clear: It is not by our experiential effort that sin is defeated in our lives (which is a common teaching), rather it was by the sovereign judicial act of God through Christ in the past.

As J. Sidlow Baxter masterfully summarizes, here is the meaning of Romans 6:6 according to the language of the text: *Our old* ***man*** (all that we were in position and relation to **Adam**, with all our culpability and condemnation), *was crucified with Him* (was judged and executed in the once-for-all **death** of Christ), *that the body of sin* (the whole Adam humanity as guilty before God), *might be destroyed* (completely done away with in the judicial reckoning of God), *that we should no longer be in bondage to sin* (that is, no longer in *legal* bondage through *judicial* guilt).[291]

Does that mean we *never* sin again? No, because the flesh is still present (Rom. 7). But it *does* mean we no longer *have* to sin (6:1, 2), that we are no longer dominated and controlled by sin (v. 14), that we are free from the shackles of sin (v. 7). While we are not yet *sinless*, we do sin *less*.[292] How do we have victory over the sin that remains? That is why Paul wrote Romans 8 (more later).

Scriptures for Study: Read Romans 6:1–14, rejoicing in your release from the shackles of sin.

I Will (3)

(Grammatical)

As we have been studying, Exodus 6:6–8 is an example of the hundreds of God's sovereign "I wills" in **Scripture**. *First,* there is the **I will** of *deliverance* (v. 6), and *second,* there is the **I will** of *liberty* (v. 6).

Third, there is the **I will** of ***redemption,*** "I will redeem you" (v. 6). Again in Exodus we read Moses' words to the people of God: "And it came to pass, when Pharaoh would hardly let us go, that the LORD slew all the firstborn in the land of Egypt, both the firstborn of man, and the firstborn of beast: therefore I sacrifice to the LORD all that openeth the matrix, being males; but all the firstborn of my children I redeem" (Exod. 13:15). By sovereign act, God redeemed His people miraculously. We, too, have been miraculously redeemed (Eph. 1:7, 14; 4:30; Heb. 9:12, 15; April 8).

Fourth, there is the **I will** of *election,* "I will take you to me for a people" (Exod. 6:7). As noted back on April 14, the doctrine of election is one that is sadly controversial. There is no reason for such debate, however, for this doctrine is taught in Scripture with unambiguous clarity. "Take" is the Hebrew *lāqach* (3947), a broad term for taking or seizing something. It is used figuratively here for election, just as it is when it refers to God taking Abraham from his father's **house** (Gen. 24:7) for His sovereign purpose. Note also that back in Genesis 12:1–3 we see **I will** five times to emphasize the sovereign, unilateral, unconditional election of Abraham by God. We see *lāqach* again for God's "[taking] him a nation [Israel] from the midst of another nation" (Deut. 4:34; cf. 7:7, 8). So just as God sovereignly chose Israel, He has also sovereignly **chosen** us. As He chose Israel from **among** the **nations**, He "did visit the Gentiles, to take out of them a people for his name" (Acts 15:14; cf. Eph. 1:4–6, 9, 11, 12).

Fifth, there is the **I will** of *rule,* "I will be to you a God" (Exod. 6:7). Because of God's sovereignty, He is the ruler, we are the subjects. And why does He have such a right? Because He is **God** (*'Elōhiym*, January 7). He is our **King** (January 28), our Sovereign Ruler. Let us meditate today on submitting to His rule.

Scriptures for Study: What does Deuteronomy 7:6 declare? 🕮 What, then, are we called in 1 Peter 2:10?

I Will (4)

(Grammatical)

What a passage is Exodus 6:6–8! These seven "I wills" of **God** are representative of all His "I wills" in **Scripture**, loudly proclaiming His sovereignty. We conclude today with the final two, which are, in fact, wondrously related.

Sixth, there is the **I will** of *promise,* "I will bring you in unto the land" (v. 8). While there is not a specific Hebrew **word** for "promise," the concept is nonetheless encapsulated in the use of words such as *dāḇār* and *'imrāh* (February 22), which refer to words and speech, as well as *beriyṯ* (**covenant**, February 9).

The most outstanding **among** the hundreds of God's sovereign promises include: the promise of a needed Redeemer (Gen. 3:15; cf. Isa. 53), which theologians **call** the *proto-evangelium* (the first gospel, or first **good** news); the perpetual promise to **Noah** (8:21, 22; 9:11–17); the promise to Abraham concerning a nation and land (e.g., 12:1–7; 15:18); the promise to **David** concerning his perpetual **throne** (e.g., 2 Sam. 7:12, 13, 18); the promise of Israel's restoration, as well as the coming of Messiah, the Holy Spirit, the **Kingdom**, and the New Covenant (e.g., Isa. 2:2–5; 4:2; 55:5; 66:13; Jer. 31:31–34; 32:37–42; 33:14; Ezek. 36:22–31; 39:25–29). The NT then not only reiterates the above, but also expands on such subjects as the gift of the Holy Spirit (e.g., John 14:16; Luke 24:49; Acts 1:4; Eph. 1:13), and adds others. "Doth his promise fail for evermore?" the psalmist asks (Ps. 77:8), and we can rest in the fact that not one ever will.

Seventh, there is the **I will** of ***inheritance,*** "I will give it you for an heritage" (Exod. 6:8). Right in line with the promises we have *from* God, there is the inheritance we have *in* God. As noted back on May 25, what a **heritage** we have in God!

In addition to the "I wills" here in our text, we read a plethora of others: "I will give" (Gen. 17:8), "I will deal well" (32:9), "I will be with thee" (Exod. 3:12), "I will dwell" (29:45), "I will cast out the nations before thee, and enlarge thy borders" (34:24), "I will walk among you" (Lev. 26:12), "them that honour me I will honour" (1 Sam. 2:30), "I will heal thee" (2 Kings 20:5), "I will fill [your mouth with words]" (Ps. 81:10), and the list goes on and on. Oh, let us **rejoice** in God's sovereign "I wills"!

Scriptures for Study: What is the prerequisite for receiving God's promises (Gal. 3:14, 22)? 🕮 Can you find some additional "I wills" of God?

Arm

zerôa'

The **prophet** Isaiah declares in his great messianic chapter 53, "Who hath believed our report? and to whom is the arm of the LORD revealed?" (v. 1). **Arm** is a translation of the Hebrew *zerôa'* (2220), which appears about ninety times and has equivalents in several Semitic languages. A unique characteristic of this **word** is that its literal meaning of someone's physical **arm** is actually the rarity, such as in reference to Samson's arms being tied (Judg. 15:14; 16:12) and a few other instances (e.g., Gen. 49:24, first occurrence; 2 Sam. 1:10; Isa. 17:5).

The figurative meaning of *zerôa'*, which appears more often, is "power, strength, and help." Men's military and political **power** is spoken of as an **arm**, or the plural "arms" (Dan. 11:15, 22, 31), as is their **strength** in general (whether positive or negative: 1 Sam. 2:31; Job 22:9; Ps. 10:15; Jer. 48:25; Ezek. 30:24, 25).

Most often, however, and most significantly, this word represents God's power. We repeatedly find it in references to God bringing Israel out of Egypt (Exod. 6:6, first occurrence; Deut. 4:34; 5:15; 7:19; 9:29; Ps. 136:12). We encounter it several more times referring to His protection, provision, and preservation of His people (Deut. 33:27; Ps. 89:13; Isa. 33:2; 40:11; 51:5). It also shows His power leveled against His enemies in judgment (Isa. 30:30; Jer. 21:5). In short, it is an image of His omnipotence: "Ah Lord GOD! behold, thou hast made the heaven and the earth by thy great power and stretched out arm, and there is nothing too hard for thee" (Jer. 32:17).

All this makes our text all the more significant. It is Messiah, Isaiah declares in the messianic chapter 53, who will be the greatest manifestation of God's power. It is, indeed, in that **arm** there is the strength to **save** the members of a spiritually dead race and help them in their infirmities. The psalmist likewise exults, "Thou hast with thine arm redeemed thy people" (Ps. 77:15).

This is further underscored by the Greek word used in the Septuagint for **arm**. It is *brachiōn* (1023G), which literally refers to the **arm** from the elbow to the shoulder and also, like *zerôa'*, figuratively represents the strength and power of God. It is not at all surprising, then, when we read John's quotation of our text in John 12:38.

Let us **rejoice** this **day** in the **salvation** God has brought by His mighty **arm**!

Scriptures for Study: What is and is not the source of our strength (Ps. 44:3)?

Bow (Rainbow) (1)

qešeṯ

Of the seventy-seven occurrences of *qešeṯ* (7198) in the OT, virtually all of them refer to the familiar weapon that shoots arrows (2 Kings 9:24) used by the hunter (Gen. 27:3) and the warrior (1 Sam. 31:3).

The **bow** is a truly ancient weapon, mentioned first in Genesis 21:20 (about 2000 BC) as being the weapon of choice of Ishmael, the son of Abraham and the Egyptian **woman** Hagar, but unquestionably existing before him. It was the common long-distance weapon (300–400 yards) of the Egyptians, Syrians (1 Kings 22:34), Philistines (1 Sam. 31:3), Elamites (Isa. 22:6), Lydians (Jer. 46:9), and ultimately the Hebrews (2 Sam. 1:18), of the which the Benjamites were experts (1 Chron. 8:40). The Septuagint uses the equivalent *toxon* (5115G, Rev. 6:2).

Used figuratively, the **bow** symbolized victory (Ps. 7:12), as well as falsehood and **deceit** (Ps. 64:3, 4; Hosea 7:16; Jer. 9:3). It also pictured disease or calamity sent by **God** (Job 6:4; Ps. 38:2), which leads us to the other use of *qešeṯ*.

In contrast to the weapon, the three appearances of *qešeṯ* in Genesis 9:13–16 refer to a very different **bow**, "God's bow," which He hung in the sky as a picture of **peace** after using the "bow" to bring the calamity of the Flood, God's "battle with a wicked world." Here was the **sign** of God's **covenant** with **Noah**, and all subsequent mankind, that He would never again **destroy** the earth with a universal flood.

The **rainbow** is an amazing and beautiful phenomenon, one that mesmerizes us every **time** it appears. Rain did not occur before the Flood, rather a mist watered the earth (Gen. 2:5, 6). The Flood brought a drastic atmospheric change, allowing falling water droplets to form, each of which acts as a prism, dividing sunlight into the varied colors of the optical spectrum, most commonly listed in Newton's sevenfold order—red, orange, yellow, **green**, blue, indigo, and violet—and remembered by the popular mnemonics "Roy G. Biv" and "Richard Of York Gave Battle In Vain."

As we continue **tomorrow**, we will meditate on the three rainbows mentioned in **Scripture** and how they will help us through the storms of **life**. For today, let us simply be reminded of the faithfulness of God's promises, not to mention His **grace** (April 6) in saving Noah and his family (Gen. 6:8). Even in **wrath** there is **mercy**.

Scriptures for Study: We find the phrase "found grace" eighteen times in the OT. **Rejoice** today in the following examples: Genesis 19:19; 33:10; 39:4; Exodus 33:12, 13, 16, 17.

Bow (Rainbow) (2)

qešeṯ

Rainbow appears three more times in **Scripture**, once in the OT and twice in the NT. When we compare all these occurrences, we see a threefold significance that applies to the storms of **life** the believer will encounter:

First, **Noah** saw the **rainbow** *after* the storm. While a storm rages, it is difficult to think about anything else. Our foremost thoughts are simply about finding shelter and hoping the storm doesn't do serious damage. Like Noah, we must wait until it's all over before seeing the **sun** again. It is then the **rainbow** reassures us every storm is temporary and that no matter how much damage it does, it could always have been worse.

Second, the **prophet** Ezekiel saw the **rainbow** *during* the storm. Ezekiel 1–3 records the prophet's **call**, first describing the *visions* he saw (ch. 1) and then the *voice* he heard (chapters 2 and 3). No Scripture writer ever tried to describe **God** directly but did so only using images the human mind could grasp.

Ezekiel's visions of God began with a violent storm of horrendous wind and fiery lightning, demonstrating God's judgment **power** and blazing glory (1:4). Then came four "living creatures" (vv. 5–14), undoubtedly cherubs (9:3; 10:5, 15, 20), which are always symbolic of God's holy presence and unapproachability, as in their guarding God's glory in the Holy of Holies (Exod. 25:10–22; Ps. 80:1). Next, beside each cherub was a wheel within a wheel (vv. 15–21), which seems to portray a chariot-throne that is in motion and moving toward judgment upon Jerusalem.

Finally, Ezekiel's fourth **vision** (Ezek. 1:22–28) included a "firmament" (an expanse) over the heads of the cherubs that dazzled like crystal, "the likeness of a throne," and the "likeness . . . of a man" on that **throne**, undoubtedly the pre-incarnate Son of God. It was then a **rainbow** appeared, "the brightness" of which shown not in the semicircle of a normal **rainbow**, rather "round about" (*sāḇiyḇ*, 5439, "surrounding, all around"), a complete eternal circle all around in "the likeness of the glory of the LORD" (v. 28).

Indeed, Ezekiel saw the **rainbow** *during* the storm, one unlike any other, and "fell upon [his] face" in humble submission. Let us be reminded during the storms that come—God is on the **throne** and we are to submit to all He is doing.

Scriptures for Study: What is the promise of Romans 8:28? 🕮 Go on to read God's "Golden Chain of Salvation" in verses 29 and 30 and then those great verses of encouragement that follow, 31 through 39.

Bow (Rainbow) (3)

qešeṯ [and] iris

Not only do we see its occurrences in **Scripture** *after* the storm (**Noah**) and *during* the storm (Ezekiel), but we also see it *before* the storm, as revealed in the NT.

Third, like Ezekiel, the apostle John had a **vision** of the **throne** of **God** in **heaven** and wrote, "And he that sat [on the throne] was to look upon like a jasper and a sardine stone: and there was a rainbow round about the throne, in sight like unto an emerald" (Rev. 4:3).

The Greek for **rainbow** is *iris* (2463G), which appears only here and in Revelation 10:1, and was used from the **time** of Homer for **rainbow**. In classical Greek it refers to any bright halo surrounding an object, including the iris of the eye and the circle around the "eyes" of the peacock's feathers.[293]

Again like Ezekiel, John sees a **rainbow** *encircling* God's throne, announcing the completeness and perfection of God. This multicolored **bow** is dominated by a soothing emerald **green**. As a symbol, then, of **peace** and God's faithfulness to His promises, this **bow** assures John *before* the coming horrendous judgments even start that there will be peace when it is all over.

It continues to amaze and baffle this writer that some Bible students can read Revelation and deny its future significance, casually dismissing it as a description of the events of 70 AD, when the Roman general Titus sacked Jerusalem. Our **Lord** Himself said of the coming Tribulation period described in such graphic detail in chapters 4 through 19, "For then shall be great tribulation, such as was not since the beginning of the world to this time, no, nor ever shall be" (Matt. 24:21). Nothing in history comes remotely close to the incomprehensible events that are to come upon this rebellious world. That is precisely why God reassures John that no matter what happens, peace will come, God's people will be delivered, and God will be glorified (a further reminder comes later in Revelation 10:1).

Dear Christian **Friend**, all this reminds us that God is always faithful to His promises. Whether we see the **rainbow** *before*, *during*, or *after* the storm of trial, we are always assured of "the peace of God, which passeth all understanding, [which] shall keep [our] hearts and minds through Christ Jesus" (Phil. 4:7).

Scriptures for Study: Read the following verses, noting what each declares about the "storms" of **life** you will encounter: Romans 8:18; 2 Timothy 3:12; 1 Peter 1:7, 8; 4:12, 13. 📖 In your study, can you identify some other Scriptures before we note them tomorrow?

Bow (Rainbow) (4)

qešet̲

Can any of us fully fathom the solemnity of that moment when the first **rainbow** appeared? **Noah** and his family's first response upon exiting the **ark** was **worship** (Gen. 8:20), praising **God** for their deliverance from the incomprehensible destruction that had just occurred. On the heels of that worship God gave His promise and hung His assuring **sign** in the sky. Such solemnity provides us with at least three additional principles:

First, the **rainbow** is a *remembrance* of God's ***power***. Every **time** we look at a **rainbow**, we **remember** the Flood. And what is it that we remember, or at least *should* remember? That in His omnipotence, God destroyed the earth because of **sin**. Because of His holy nature, God cannot tolerate sin. As in those days of Noah, God "shall not always strive with man" (Gen. 6:3).

But we also should remember not only God's power to execute **wrath**, but also His power to ***save***. As He saved Noah and his family because they believed and obeyed what He said (cf. Heb. 11:7), He saves those today who receive Him as Savior and **Lord**.

Second, the **rainbow** is a *reminder* of God's *purpose*. Noah, Ezekiel, and the apostle John are all powerful reminders that God always has a purpose, even in the storms. Just as our ***salvation*** is by God's sovereign purpose (Rom. 8:29, 30), all the *storms* that come our **way** are also by His sovereign purpose (8:28). But even at that, "The sufferings of this present time are not worthy to be compared with the glory which shall be revealed in us" (8:18). That leads us to one other comforting principle.

Third, the **rainbow** is a *reassurance* of God's ***peace***. As the **rainbow** assured Noah, it now reassures us that God is always faithful to His promises. God will "keep him in perfect peace, whose mind is stayed on [Him]: because he trusteth in [Him]" (Isa. 26:3). Most important of all, our Lord assures us: "Peace I leave with you, my peace I give unto you: not as the world giveth, give I unto you. Let not your heart be troubled, neither let it be afraid" (John 14:27).

Dear Christian **Friend**, the next time you look at a **rainbow**, may you *remember* God's power, be *reminded* of His purpose, and be *reassured* of His peace—in other words, who God is and what He is doing.

Scriptures for Study: Read these additional verses concerning the storms **life** will bring but also the **rainbow** you can see: Romans 5:2–5; 2 Corinthians 4:15–17; Hebrews 10:36; 12:1 (cf. 11:1–40); James 1:3, 4.

Voice (1)

qôl

As we continue with our thoughts on the **rainbow**, Psalm 29 comes to mind. It is significant because **David** penned it as he observed a particularly violent and frightening thunderstorm. The **psalm** can easily be divided into three sections: the *duty* of giving **praise** and glory to **God** (vv. 1, 2), the *description* of the storm (vv. 3–9), and the ***deep** impression* this made on David (vv. 10, 11).

It is that middle section that captures our attention, for in it David uses the **word *voice*** seven times, likening the sounds of the storm to the very **voice** of God. The Hebrew here is *qôl* (6963), which appears more than 500 times in the OT and refers primarily to a sound made with vocal cords, as in speech (Gen. 27:22), **singing** (Exod. 32:18), and even laughter (Jer. 30:19), but also to other sounds (e.g., Jer. 47:3; Exod. 19:16; 1 Kings 14:6; Nah. 3:2).

We will examine **voice** in Psalm 29 tomorrow, but let us meditate a moment on the general significance of *qôl* as it refers to the **voice** of God. Its first occurrence helps us understand this idea. In Genesis 3:8, the now fallen **Adam** and **Eve** "heard the voice of the LORD God walking in the garden in the cool of the day." One of the ancient Targums—these were oral Aramaic "interpretive renderings"[294] (not translations) of the OT made from the second century to about the seven century AD—paraphrases: "the voice of the Word of the Lord God."[295] While there has been some debate concerning what Adam and Eve heard in the garden,[296] it seems quite obvious—they heard the Word of the pre-incarnate **Lord** Jesus Himself as He **walked** in the Garden. In His incarnation, He was "the Word [who] was made flesh, and dwelt among us" (John 1:14), and it appears He communed with our first parents in that perfect world.

Oh, how crucial it is that we listen to God's **voice**! At times that **voice** will be as a roar of thunder (Exod. 19:16–19; Ps. 18:13), for God needs to get our attention. More often it will be "a still small voice" (or, "a sound of soft stillness," 1 Kings 19:12), requiring us to be absolutely silent and listen. God's voice also comes through the men of God who **preach** and proclaim His Word (Exod. 3:18; Deut. 18:16–19; Jonah 3:2; Rom. 10:14, 15; 2 Tim. 4:1–4; see also March 15–17).

Scriptures for Study: What are the tragedy and challenge of Psalm 81:10–12? 🕮 What, then, is the command of Psalms 95:7–9 and 103:20?

Majesty [and] Voice (2)

hādār [and] qôl

What is particularly striking about Psalm 29 is that in the **midst** of this terrifying storm, **David** is at perfect **peace** and writes one of the most majestic of all the psalms. As he listens to God's **voice** and writes down his impressions, he provides us with two principles:

First, we see the *splendor* of God's **voice**. As the storm begins "upon the waters" of the Mediterranean Sea, "the God of glory thundereth" (v. 3). "Glory" is *kāḇôḏ* (3519), which is derived from the verb *kāḇēḏ* (3513, January 31), "to be heavy or weighty." To speak of God's glory, then, is to speak of His "weight," His quality, and therefore His **majesty** and splendor.

Verse 4 further adds: "The voice of the LORD is full of majesty." **Majesty** is *hāḏār* (1926), the thirty OT appearances of which are all in poetic passages, and means "glory, majesty, and honor." It refers, for example, to "goodly trees," that is, "trees of splendor and beauty" (Lev. 23:40, first occurrence), as well as His countless "wondrous works" (Ps. 145:5, "honor"). These two words appear together in Isaiah 35:2, where we read that in the Millennium people "shall see the glory [*kāḇôḏ*] of the LORD, and the excellency [*hāḏār*] of our God."

Second, we see the ***strength*** of God's voice. To say this storm was "powerful" (Ps. 29:4) was an understatement, so David expounds. As it moved inland to the mountains of Lebanon and Sirion (Mount Hermon, Deut. 3:8, 9), he saw the wind knock down some cedar trees—the cedar is a strong, hardy evergreen—and then shake and bend the others, making them appear to "skip" (*rāqaḏ*, 7540, Ps. 29:5, 6). He also saw the lightning, which perhaps split trees or even started brush fires (v. 7). Continuing on, the storm "[shook] the wilderness [or desert] of Kadesh" (v. 8; this seems to refer to the town about seventy-five miles north of Damascus, not Kadesh 200 miles to the south). There it caused the deer to prematurely give birth to their young due to **fear**, and stripped the leaves from the trees (v. 9, "discovereth" is *chāśap̄*, 2834, "to make bare, or strip off").

All this should, indeed, cause "every one [to] speak of his glory" (v. 9). We do not **serve** a *syrupy*, *sentimental*, and virtually *spineless* God, as some teach today, rather the God of *splendor* and *strength* who rules the universe. *Soli deo gloria*!

Scriptures for Study: Read the following verses, and give God glory throughout the **day**: Psalms 90:16 ("glory" is *hāḏār*); 96:6 (**majesty**); 104:1 (majesty).

Mourning [and] Discouraged (1)

qāḏar [and] māsas

Have you ever been **discouraged**? I doubt there is a single Christian throughout history who would not **answer** that question with a resounding "Yes!" Even in **Scripture** we see great men such as Moses, **David**, Elijah, Jeremiah, Habakkuk, and others who had times of discouragement, despair, and depression.

The psalmist who penned Psalms 42 and 43 was certainly **discouraged**. **Among** other places, we encounter there the **word *mourning*** (42:9; 43:2) This is the Hebrew *qāḏar* (6937), a verb that means "to be dark." Used literally, it refers to the darkening of the sky due to a storm (1 Kings 18:45) or the total absence of **light**, as in Ezekiel's prophecy against Pharaoh (Ezek. 32:7, 8).

Used figuratively, then, *qāḏar* speaks of **mourning** over the loss of a loved one (Ps. 35:14) or other such sadness, but also of what we would call "discouragement," a despair and melancholy that can cripple us. This is the scene here in our text; the psalmist is **discouraged** in the face of persecution by his enemies.

Another word that expresses this concept is *māsas* (4549), which means "to melt or dissolve." Used literally, it refers to the melting of wax (Ps. 68:2) and the evaporating of **manna** (Exod. 16:21). It is used several times, however, in the figurative sense of a person's **heart** "melting," that is, losing courage and just sitting down and wallowing in despair.

Significantly, the figurative occurrence of *māsas* is the most graphic. Returning from their reconnaissance of the land of Canaan (Num. 13), ten of the twelve spies gave a negative report. I once heard it put that these spies were impressed by four "Gs": *grapes* (v. 23), *giants* (v. 33), and *great cities* (v. 28), which made them feel like *grasshoppers* (v. 33). As a result, according to the account in Deuteronomy, they became **discouraged** (*māsas*, 1:28). Why? Because they forgot about the fifth "G"—***God***. They simply did not really believe that God could bring them into the land.

How inconceivable! Even though the omnipotent Sovereign God of the universe had promised them the land, and even though He had miraculously delivered them from bondage, they still didn't believe. There they stood, as it were, at the very gates of the Promised Land, but they would not go in.

What is the real cause, then, of discouragement? Unbelief. As we continue these thoughts **tomorrow**, let us resolve to overcome discouragement by believing what God says.

Scriptures for Study: Whose heart was melting in Joshua 2:11 and why? 📖 Note David's discouragement: "My heart . . . is melted" (Ps. 22:14). How did he overcome it in the verses that follow?

Mourning [and] Discouraged (2)

qāḏar [and] māsas

Why did the apostle Paul **write** to the Galatians, and by extension to us, the words, "Let us not be weary in well doing" (Gal. 6:9)? The reason is obvious: because we tend to get *weary in well doing*, tend toward discouragement and surrender.

One of the most vivid illustrations of discouragement is found in the Epistle to the Hebrews. The Christian Jews there were being persecuted by fellow Jews, and there was a strong possibility such persecution was going to intensify (10:32–39; 12:4). They were, therefore, tempted to look back to that old religion and **return** to its now meaningless symbols and rituals. They were even tempted to compromise certain truths of Christianity, such as demoting Christ to being a mere **angel** (as implied in 1:4–13). In short, in their discouragement they were tempted not just to give up a single battle but to surrender the whole **war**!

As mentioned **yesterday**, discouragement is actually a result of unbelief, a doubting of God's principles, **precepts**, and promises. Moses, Elijah, Jeremiah, Habakkuk, and others had times of discouragement, but thankfully didn't stay in that condition. To have victory over discouragement, we must embrace three principles:

First, we must stop looking at *ourselves* and start looking at *God*. Considering again Psalms 42 and 43, they contain fifty-two personal pronouns: "I" is used fourteen times, "me" sixteen times, and "my" twenty-two times. In contrast, God is referred to only twenty-one times. The writer's problem, then, was that he was self-occupied; he was concerned only with *his* feelings, *his* plans, *his* questions.

Such preoccupation with self will sooner or later bring discouragement. We live in an age of unprecedented "self-awareness" and "self-consciousness," and sadly this philosophy has become embedded in Christianity. Many want to speak of "self-esteem" and "self-image," but what happens when that gets bruised? We fall like we've been hit by a truck, because "self" is not enough.

Our confidence must lie not in *self* but in *God*. Let us not speak of *self*-esteem—the buzzword of modern "psychology" that is found nowhere in **Scripture**—but rather demonstrate a *Christ*-esteem. Let us not **teach** our children the humanistic philosophy of *self*-image, rather the biblical truth of *Christ*-image. Let us be challenged: We cannot become **discouraged** as long as we are leaning upon the **Lord** and are becoming "conformed to [His] image" (Rom. 8:29).

Scriptures for Study: Read the following verses, noting what they indicate about "esteem": 2 Corinthians 3:4, 5; Philippians 2:3. 🕮 What trait did Paul say would characterize men in the **last** days (2 Tim. 3:2)?

Mourning [and] Discouraged (3)

qāḏar [and] māsas

How can we have victory over discouragement? *First*, as we discussed **yesterday**, we must stop looking at *ourselves* and start looking at ***God***.

Second, we must stop looking at the *past* and start looking at the *future*. While we can and should look at the past for lessons and challenges, we must not live there and be defeated by it. **Satan** will try to bring to our memory past failures and try to convince us we can never have victory because of them. God wants us to live in the future; that is, He wants us to live according to **hope**, live according to certainty. The writer of Psalms 42 and 43 finally knew God would defeat the enemy (43:1), would give him **strength** (v. 2), would direct him (v. 3), and would give him **joy** (v. 4). Dear Christian, look to what God is going to do *in* you and *through* you.

Third, we must *stop searching for reasons* and *start resting on promises*. Ten times the writer of Psalms 42 and 43 asked, "Why?" But there is no record whatsoever that God ever told him why. In contrast, Habakkuk asked God several questions that God *did* **answer**. Why the difference? Because Habakkuk asked with *submissive concern* instead of *self-centered complaint*.

Oh, how often we ask God, "Why?"! More often than not, however, if God told us why at the moment we ask, we still wouldn't understand. God told Habakkuk when the time was right and He does the same with us. We must **trust** Him and patiently wait for **understanding**. The key verse of Habakkuk, in fact, is 2:4: "The just shall live by his faith." Don't trust feelings, "inner urgings," or your own thoughts, ideas, and opinions. Trust what God says. Isn't it **wonderful** that a verse from one of the so-called *Minor* Prophets is quoted three times in the NT (Rom. 1:17; Gal. 3:11; Heb. 10:38)? Just trust what God says.

When we are spiritually ready to understand the workings of God, He will then reveal them. I **pray** that the following statement will be read, memorized, and quoted often by us all: *We do not live by explanations; we live by promises*. Has God reneged on even one promise? No! Why then is it so hard for us to simply trust in His promises? The world says, "We must have proof." God says, "Trust me."

Scriptures for Study: What kind of **faith** does God want from us (Mark 10:15)? If you are a parent, ponder the application of that in light of "explanations" and "promises."

Build (1)

bānāh

We have all seen those signs that say, "Under Construction," whether it be for a building, a bridge, a road, or some other project. I've even seen a few expectant mothers wearing a maternity top with those words, along with an arrow pointing to the "construction zone."

We likewise see a lot of construction going on in **Scripture**, the Hebrew *bānāh* (1129) appearing some 375 times. In its literal sense, as one would expect, it means "to build or construct something physical." Its first occurrence, in fact, describes the first "building project," where **God** took a rib from **Adam** and "made he a woman, and brought her unto the man" (Gen. 2:22; some might consider this a figurative use). Its second occurrence refers to **Cain** building a city (4:17), and its third occurrence refers to **Noah** building the **ark** (8:20). Many other physical structures are mentioned, including: a **house** (33:17), an **altar** (Exod. 20:25; Deut. 27:5), the **temple** (1 Kings 3:1; 5:18; 6:2), and the city of Jerusalem (Ps. 147:2), as well as some twenty references in Nehemiah for the rebuilding the walls of Jerusalem (e.g., 2:5, 18, 20; 3:1).

Of special significance is *bānāh's* reference to *God* building something. Literally, although using metaphorical terms, He built the universe, laying its foundation and cornerstone with His hands (Isa. 48:13; Ps. 102:25; 104:3; Job 38:4–6), and even used measuring tools (Isa. 40:12).

It is when we find *bānāh* used figuratively of God, however, that we see His full **power** as the Master Builder. God's greatest "building project" is **salvation** itself. "I will praise thee," the psalmist exults, "for thou hast heard me, and art become my salvation. The stone which the builders refused is become the head stone of the corner" (Ps. 118:21, 22). That messianic prophecy is quoted either fully or partially in no less than five NT passages and alluded to in one other (see today's "Scriptures for Study"). The entire **work** of salvation is based upon that Cornerstone, God's Son. God's salvation is further described as "a strong city," complete with "walls and bulwarks" (Isa. 26:1, 2).

Additionally, it is in His sovereignty God builds up some **nations** and tears down others (Jer. 1:10; 18:7–10; 42:10), and it was by His **grace** that He rebuilt Israel (Jer. 31:4; 24:6; 33:7). Oh, what a Master Builder is He! We all, with Abraham, "[look] for a city which hath foundations, whose builder and maker is God" (Heb. 11:10).

Scriptures for Study: Read the following passages, rejoicing in the Cornerstone: Matthew 21:42; Mark 12:10, 11; Luke 20:17; Acts 4:11; Ephesians 2:20; 1 Peter 2:7.[297]

Build (2)

bānāh

Before leaving this important OT concept, we should consider another aspect of building described in **Scripture**, namely, how it relates to **man**. Used literally, of course, as noted **yesterday**, the OT refers to men building various physical structures. But far more important is how we **build** *non*-physical structures. Psalm 127 talks about three things we each should **build**, all of which depend upon the providence of **God**:

First, we should **build** a *home*: "Except the LORD build [*bānāh*] the house, they labour in vain that build [*bānāh*] it: except the LORD keep the city, the watchman waketh but in vain" (v. 1). No matter how elaborate, comfortable, or accommodating a **house** (June 18) might be, if God is not in the **labor**, the whole structure is empty and meaningless.

This has an even deeper application when we recognize it is one thing to **build** the *structure* of a ***house***, but quite another to **build** the *spirit* of a *home*. Of what value is a *palace* without ***peace***? A home is a place of rest, security, warmth, and **joy**. Many people today lack such a place because the **LORD** is not there.

Second, we should **build** a ***hope***: "It is vain for you to rise up early, to sit up late, to eat the bread of sorrows: for so he giveth his beloved sleep" (v. 2). Many people get up in the **morning**, eat breakfast, go to **work**, eat lunch, work some more, come home, eat dinner, go to bed, and then do it all over again the next **day**. Many just live for the money they can then spend on the weekend. All such existence is vain and without hope. Not so the godly Christian, who knows true rest and contentment in Christ.

Third, we should **build** a ***heritage*** (vv. 3–5). The remainder of this **psalm** is about children, that they are actually part of our heritage (*nachalāh*, 5159, a derivative of *nāchal*, 5157, May 25), that is, our **inheritance**. While many people today (sadly even Christians) look upon children as a ***burden***, God means them for a *blessing*. He gives them as a *"reward,"* the psalmist adds, while some people consider them to be *retribution*. Not wanting children in Solomon's day was unheard of and abortion was unthinkable. How things have changed! What soldier in his right mind wants an empty quiver (v. 5)? Oh, that we would **build** families today for God's glory!

Scriptures for Study: Read Paul's analogies in 1 Corinthians 3:9–15 and Ephesians 2:10, 20–22 and reflect on the kind of "structure" you are.

Bone

'eṣem

Most of us have at one **time** or another said, "Oh, I just feel it in my bones." That actually expresses a figurative concept included in the Hebrew *'eṣem* (6106). Literally, it refers to the physical bones, as when **Adam** declared of **Eve**, "This is now bone of my bones, and flesh of my flesh: she shall be called Woman, because she was taken out of Man" (Gen. 2:23, first occurrence). The **woman** was taken from a literal **bone** of the **man**. Job knew basic anatomy when he commented, "Thou hast clothed me with skin and flesh, and hast fenced me with bones and sinews" (Job. 10:11). This of course included the idea of human remains (Gen. 50:25; Num. 19:16).

But it is the figurative idea that captures our attention. **David** laments, "Have mercy upon me, O LORD; for I am weak: O LORD, heal me; for my bones are vexed" (Ps. 6:2). Bones here picture the whole person, the sum total of all that one is, the core of one's being. "Vexed" is *bāhal* (926), "to be troubled, dismayed, anguished, or even terrified." **Sin** troubled the psalmist, deeply dismayed him, brought anguish to the core of his being. David writes again in Psalm 38:3, "There is no soundness in my flesh because of thine anger; neither is there any rest in my bones because of my sin." Is that how sin affects us?

In contrast, the verse that should perhaps strike us most is Jeremiah 20:9: "Then I said, I will not make mention of him, nor speak any more in his name. But his word was in mine heart as a burning fire shut up in my bones, and I was weary with forbearing, and I could not stay." In his **discouraged** state, Jeremiah was tempted to remain silent, to stop **preaching** God's Word because of persecution. But he simply could not be silent. So deeply was the Word of God embedded in him, so much a part of his very being, that he could not contain it, could not help but proclaim it.

Can we, therefore, say with Peter and John, "For we cannot but speak the things which we have seen and heard" (Acts 4:20), and can we say with Paul, "Necessity is laid upon me; yea, woe is unto me, if I preach not the gospel!" (1 Cor. 9:16)?

Scriptures for Study: What is spoken of as being "marrow to [our] bones" in Proverbs 3:7, 8)? 🕮 What **counsel** did God give Jeremiah concerning proclaiming the truth (Jer. 1:17–19)?

Bury

qāḇar

The Hebrew *qāḇar* (6912), which is also found in most of the other Semitic languages, appears some 130 times in the OT, the vast majority of which are in the Pentateuch and historical books. It means "to bury or entomb" and in every instance except one (Jer. 22:19) refers to human burial.

This fact immediately and fundamentally underscores that burial was important in Hebrew thinking. "A proper burial was a sign of special kindness and divine blessing," writes one authority.[298] Not to be properly buried, in fact, was considered great misfortune, calamity, and even judgment (1 Kings 13:22; 14:11; 2 Kings 9:37; Ps. 79:3; Jer. 7:33; 8:1; Ezek. 29:5; Rev. 11:9). In accordance with Genesis 3:19, burial was the accepted method for disposal of the dead. We repeatedly see God's people buried throughout **Scripture**, often in a family tomb, as with Sarah (Gen. 23:19), Abraham (25:9), Isaac, Rebekah, and Leah (49:31), and Jacob (50:13).[299]

All this provides an **answer** to an increasingly common question **among** Christians: "What about cremation?" There is no doubt whatsoever that cremation was predominantly practiced among pagans, such as the Greeks and Romans. First-century Roman senator and historian Tacitus observed that in contrast to the Romans, it was a serious matter of piety with the Jews "to bury rather than to burn dead bodies."[300]

Cremation was, in fact, rare among the Hebrews: "According to the Mosaic law burning was reserved, either for the living who had been found guilty of unnatural sins (Lev. 21:9; also 20:14; Gen. 38:24; 2 Kings 23:16, 20), or for those who died under a curse, as in the case of Achan and his family."[301] It was also used to prevent epidemics in the case of mass **death** (Amos 6:10).

As a rule, then, burning was considered the ultimate desecration of the dead (1 Kings 13:2; 2 Kings 23:16, 20). Note that even though the bodies of Saul and his sons were burned, undoubtedly because the bodies were badly mutilated and/or decayed, the bones were still buried (1 Sam. 31:11–13), not crushed into powder as in modern cremation.[302] It should also be noted that there is not a single instance of cremation in the NT, and that the body is always treated with respect, the burial of our **Lord**, of course, being the greatest example. Throughout Scripture, therefore, we see that it is *burial*, not *burning*, that honors the body.

Scriptures for Study: Read 1 Corinthians 15:35–46, noting not only the obvious precedent of burial, but also rejoicing in the resurrection that is to come.

Calamity

'ēyḏ

Floods, hurricanes, tornadoes, and other such devastating incidents well illustrate our **word** for today. **Calamity** is a translation of *'ēyḏ* (343), which is also rendered "destruction" in seven of its twenty-four occurrences, all of which are in poetic contexts.

This word first appears in Deuteronomy 32:35, the text on which Jonathan Edwards based his famous sermon *Sinners in the Hands of an Angry God*: "To me belongeth vengeance, and recompence; their foot shall slide in due time: for the day of their calamity is at hand, and the things that shall come upon them make haste." This verse is a reminder that **God** does bring **wrath** for disobedience (Rom. 12:19; 13:4; Heb. 10:30) and is also a warning repeated elsewhere: "Wherefore let him that thinketh he standeth take heed lest he fall" (1 Cor. 10:12).

There are, indeed, several sobering occurrences of *'ēyḏ*. Job asks, "Is not destruction to the wicked? and a strange punishment to the workers of iniquity?" (Job 31:3). Using the concept of **wisdom** as His voice, God declares, "I also will laugh at your calamity; I will mock when your fear cometh" (Prov. 1:26; also Ps. 2:4).[303] While we are tempted to think this rather severe, the reason is stated in the previous verse: "But ye have set at nought all my counsel, and would none of my reproof." In his arrogance, **man** scorns the Word of God, but that very scorn will come back to haunt him.

Introducing those seven abominations that God hates in Proverbs 6:16–19 (see July 8–17), verses 14 and 15 declare: "Frowardness [perversity] is in [the wicked man's] heart . . . Therefore shall his calamity come suddenly; suddenly shall he be broken without remedy" (also Prov. 29:1; 1 Thess. 5:3). Those who reject God and go their own **way** will fall without warning and will be without **hope**.

Such a sobering truth encourages us not only to *practice* obedience and submission but also to *proclaim* it to others. In a day of unprecedented tolerance and relativism, where even some Christian leaders never warn of **sin** and wrath, there is a critical need to warn a lost world of the calamity that will come upon those who *deny* God, *disregard* His Word, and ***descend*** further into the abyss of **sin**.

Scriptures for Study: Read 1 Thessalonians 5:1–11. How does Paul describe the **return** of Christ? 📖 What are the contrasts between the believer and unbeliever?

Froward (Perverse)

tahpuḵāh

Froward is one of those odd Old English words in the AV that puzzle us when we encounter them. A modern equivalent is **perverse**, which also appears in the AV for today's Hebrew **word**. The idea in both these translations is "turning away from what is right or good, unyielding and obstinate opposition."

All those ideas are found in the Hebrew *tahpuḵāh* (8419), which appears ten times in the OT, all except once in Proverbs. It is derived from the verb *hāp̱aḵ* (2015), which appears almost 100 times and means "to turn around, change, throw down, overturn, pervert, destroy, be turned against, turn here and there, or wander." All this paints a graphic picture, indeed. There is nothing redeeming about the **froward** person. He or she not only turns away and wanders from the truth, but deliberately tries to overturn, pervert, and **destroy** it by action and attitude, by word and deed.

Proverbs 2:12 sets the stage for this word's usage in that **book**. With the theme of **wisdom** established in the surrounding context, one of the benefits of wisdom is that it will "deliver [us] from the way of the evil man, from the man that speaketh froward things." Error surrounds us these days. From false religions, to subtle cults, even to diluted, perverted Christianity, false teaching is everywhere. Listening to truth is absolutely essential if we are to **discern** the **froward** speech that inundates us.

Verse 13 further describes the **froward** person as one "who [leaves] the paths of uprightness, to walk in the ways of darkness," clearly indicating a deliberate, calculated act. Verse 14 then adds, "Who rejoice to do evil, and delight in the frowardness of the wicked," demonstrating that such people not only **delight** in their own **sin** but also the sin of others.

The first occurrence of *tahpuḵāh* is perhaps the strongest of all. It describes not a single person or even the circle of friends in which he revels, but rather an entire generation who had turned their backs on **God** (Deut. 32:20), a whole nation who had perverted the truth. Does that not remind us of our own **day**? Ours is a nation who removed God from our schools in the early 1960s, legalized the murdering of babies in 1973, and have more recently banished God's moral commandments from the civil courtroom.

Dear Christian **Friend**, let us separate ourselves from the **froward** person.

Scriptures for Study: Read the other occurrences of *tahpuḵāh* and note each characteristic of the **froward** person: Proverbs 6:14; 8:13; 10:31, 32; 16:28, 30; 23:33 (**perverse**).

Clothe

lābaš

The Hebrew *lābaš* (3847) is another example of a common **word** that is given **deep** theological significance through figurative use. Occurring some 110 times, it literally means "to clothe or put on clothing." It appears many times for the simple act of getting dressed ("put on" in Gen. 38:19, Exod. 29:30, and 1 Sam. 28:8; "apparelled" in 2 Sam. 13:18; **clothe** in Hag. 1:6). Saul also tried to **clothe** young **David** with armor (1 Sam. 17:38, "armed").

The first appearance of *lābaš* is in Genesis 3:21, which while used literally to refer to **God** clothing **Adam** and **Eve** with animal hides, also sets the stage for its figurative use in **Scripture**. That sad scene provides us with three principles:

First, we see the *inadequacy* of man's clothing. As a result of their sin, Adam and Eve realized their nakedness and tried to cover their shame by making crude aprons out of fig leaves (3:7). What a picture of man's futile effort to cover himself! Just as those leaves would quickly dry up and disintegrate, all man's "righteousnesses are as filthy rags; and we all do fade as a leaf; and our iniquities, like the wind, have taken us away" (Isa. 64:6, April 4).

Second, we observe the *intervention* of God. Only God could provide them with suitable clothing. Have you ever thought about that scene? Yes, God could have simply created clothing out of nothing, but He didn't. **Blood** had to be shed for **sin** (Heb. 9:22). Did He perhaps even slay an animal(s) in front of Adam and Eve so they could see the consequences of sin? What **horror** such slaughter surely would have been to once-innocent eyes! **Death** had never occurred before, but now "by one man sin entered into the world, and death by sin; and death passed upon all men, for that all have sinned" (Rom. 5:12). Praise be to God that we can now "greatly rejoice in the LORD . . . for he hath clothed [us] with the garments of salvation, he hath covered [us] with the robe of righteousness" (Isa. 61:10; cf. Gal. 3:27; Phil. 3:9; Rev. 7:9–14).

Third, we note the *instruction* of modesty. While modern society continues to wear less and less clothing in public, that sad scene in the garden underscores the shame that should be *sensed* instead of *suppressed* (cf. Rom. 1:18). The simple rule of dress is "Be modest" (1 Tim. 2:9; Titus 2:5; cf. Prov. 7:10).

Scriptures for Study: Read Ephesians 4:22–32. "Put on" (v. 24) is *enduō* (1746G), which not only means "dressing oneself," but, figuratively, "assuming qualities or virtues." What, then, does the believer take off and put on?[304]

Firstborn

beḵôr

What **joy** there is when the first baby is born from a marital union! This certainly does not mean that baby will be better or more loved than others who might follow. Rather that first little one is special in the sense of being the first physical **fruit** to spring from that sacred union, the "first installment," so to speak, of the **inheritance** that children are (Ps. 127:3–5, September 17, October 11).

That **image** is graphically drawn in **Scripture**. **Firstborn** in the OT is *beḵôr* (1060), which appears about 115 times and is probably derived from the Arabic root *bakara*, "to arise, to be first, to come early."[305] Used literally, it refers simply to the ordinary physical birth of the first offspring, whether animal (Exod. 11:5) or human (Gen. 25:13).

It is the figurative use, however, that is of great theological significance. "The 'oldest' or 'firstborn' son (Exod. 6:14; [Gen. 27:19–36; 43:33; Deut. 25:5, 6]) had special privileges within the family. He received the special family blessing, which meant spiritual and social leadership and a double portion of the father's possessions, or twice what all the other sons received (Deut. 21:17)."[306]

That principle is carried over into the NT in a wonderful way. The Greek equivalent of *beḵôr* in the Septuagint is *prōtotokos* (4416G), "firstborn one." Messiah was to be the "firstborn," as in Psalm 89:27, and was, indeed, the "firstborn son" of the Virgin Mary (Matt. 1:25; Luke 2:7) by the Holy Spirit, after which she gave birth to other children by Joseph (Matt. 13:55, 56). Romans 8:29 then declares that Jesus was "the firstborn among many brethren." Those "many brethren" are not the aforementioned half-brothers and half-sisters of Jesus, rather those who have been born again by the Holy Spirit (John 3:5–7) by receiving Jesus Christ as Savior and **Lord** (vv. 15–18; Rom. 10:9, 10). Think of it! We are Jesus' "spiritual siblings."

The greatest blessing appears when we go to the **book** of Hebrews. While in 1:6 Jesus is again called the "firstbegotten" who will come again,[307] we then read in 12:23 of the "church of the firstborn [literally, "firstborn ones"], which are written in heaven." This refers to all Christians of all time, those who are members of the church, those whose inheritance is already secured and waiting for them. What a wonderful paradox! While He is the "first firstborn," we are the "second firstborns."[308]

Scriptures for Study: Read Colossians 1:15–18, where *prōtotokos* appears twice. What observations can you make here?

Firstfruits

bikkûriym [and] rē'šiyṯ

There is another "first" that captures our attention in the OT: **firstfruits**, which is a translation of two Hebrew words. The first, *bikkûriym* (1061), actually comes from the same root (*bāḵar*, 1069, "to be born first") as yesterday's **word**, *beḵôr* (1060). This plural noun (note the *-iym*) occurs about twenty times and refers not only to literal **fruit**, such as grapes (Num. 13:20) and figs (Nah. 3:12), but also to raw grain (Lev. 23:10, 11), baked **bread** (v. 20), and even sheep's wool (Deut. 18:4). All these were the first parts of the harvest that were given to the **Lord** as an **offering** of thanks.

The second word is *rē'šiyṯ* (7225), "beginning, first, or choicest." This is actually the first word in the Bible, where it is translated "In the beginning" (Gen. 1:1), that is, "In the first moment of time." Other things that have a beginning at a certain point in **time** include: a king's reign (Jer. 26:1), a kingdom's founding (Gen. 10:10), and even something abstract, such as strife (Prov. 17:14). In fact, the most notable example of that latter sense is in Proverbs 1:7, which we could paraphrase, "The point in time at which knowledge begins is the moment we fear the LORD."

About one-third of the some fifty occurrences of *rē'šiyṯ* refer to **firstfruits**. While mostly synonymous with *bikkûriym*, *rē'šiyṯ* seems to add the subtle idea of "choicest," that is, the very best of the first (Num. 18:12).[309] This entire concept comes from Creation itself. Since **God** made all things, all things belong to Him (Ps. 24:1), and that motivates us to give Him the first and best.

The Septuagint again ties together the OT and NT. The Greek *aparchē* (536G) appears in eight NT verses, one of which declares, "Of his own will begat he us with the word of truth, that we should be a kind of firstfruits of his creatures" (James 1:18). Think of it! While the primary idea here is that James' readers were **among** the first converts to Christ with a promise of more to come, the wider application is that all believers everywhere are the "choicest" of God's Creation, the greatest testimony to the saving **power** of God.

Does this not also challenge us in our Christian living? Since we are "fruit," we should likewise be fruitful (September 17).

Scriptures for Study: Read 1 Corinthians 15:20–23. Of what does this passage assure us?

Rebel

mārāh

In a letter to James Madison dated January 30, 1787, Thomas Jefferson wrote: "I hold it that a little rebellion now and then is a good thing, and as necessary in the political world as storms in the physical." While we might debate such an idea as either **good** or bad *politically*, there can be no argument that rebellion is never good *spiritually*.

The Hebrew *mārāh* (4784) means "to rebel or be rebellious." Of its some forty-five OT appearances, all but five refer to rebellion against **God**. Those five refer to: rebellious children and their fate if that rebellion is perpetual (Deut. 21:18–20), Job's "friends" who derided him (Job 17:2, "provocation"), Job himself in his own bitterness (23:2, *meriy,* 4805, a derivative of *mārāh*), and the **evil man** who "seeketh only rebellion" (Prov. 17:11). (We might also wonder about the attitudes of Meraiah, the **head** of one of the priestly clans under the **priest** Joiakim [Neh. 12:12], for his **name** is derived from *mārāh.*)

Again, everywhere else *mārāh* pictures man's perpetual rebellion against God. It began when Moses called the children of Israel "rebels" in their complaint over what they think is a lack of water (Num. 20:10; also v. 24; 27:14). It culminated in God's refusal to allow them to enter Canaan and their resulting **wilderness** wandering (Deut. 1:26–40; also 9:7, 23, 24). The prophets repeatedly warned of the consequences of the people's rebellion (Isa. 1:20; 63:10; Jer. 4:17; 5:23; Ezek. 20:8, 21; Hosea 13:16). Even the poetry of the Psalms recounts such rebellion (Ps. 78:17; 40, 56; 106:7, 33, 43; 107:11).

There was **hope**, however: "That the generation to come might know [God's laws], even the children which should be born; who should arise and declare them to their children: That they might set their hope in God, and not forget the works of God, but keep his commandments: *And might not be as their fathers, a stubborn and rebellious generation*; a generation that set not their heart aright, and whose spirit was not stedfast with God" (Ps. 78:6–8, emphasis added).

As George Santayana's often-quoted line warns, "Those who cannot remember the past are condemned to repeat it."[310] To underscore that warning, historian William Shirer used it as one of the epigraphs for his monumental (and shocking) 1959 **book**, *The Rise and Fall of the Third Reich.*

Let us, therefore, not repeat the past. Let us ***obey,*** instead of ***rebelling***.

Scriptures for Study: Read the verses cited today and be challenged to obey, not rebel.

Book

sēp̱er

How many of us take pleasure in sitting down, enjoying a **cup** of coffee, and engrossing ourselves in a **good book**? The Hebrew *sēp̱er* (5612), however, actually refers to anything written. It is one of those words "on loan"[311] from Akkadian, coming from "*šipru*, **writing**, 'message' (itself from *šapāru*, 'to send,' 'write')."[312]

It is significant that the first occurrence of *sēp̱er* is in Genesis 5:1, which declares, "This is the book of the generations of Adam," testifying to the fact that writing was, contrary to Bible critics, a well-established practice in Moses' time (February 19). The some 186 occurrences of *sēp̱er* refer to a wide range of documents: letters (2 Sam. 11:14; Esther 1:22; Jer. 29:1), legal documents—such as a "bill" of divorce (Deut. 24:1) or "evidence" of a purchase (Jer. 32:10, 12, 14, 16)—genealogies (Gen. 5:1; Neh. 7:50), and of course books—that is, scrolls (Num. 5:23; Ps. 40:7).

The earliest "books" were actually clay tablets. Those that followed included animal skins sewn together to form rolls, and the stems of papyrus plants split and sewn together to form scrolls. What we now call a **book** was called a "codex," but did not appear until about the second century after Christ. Several "books" are named in the OT, including: prophetic histories, such as the "book of Samuel the seer" and the "book of Nathan" (1 Chron. 29:29); "the book of the wars of the LORD" (Num. 21:14, an ancient **book** lost to posterity); "a book of remembrance" (Mal. 3:16); and others.

One occurrence of *sēp̱er* (*biblos* [976G] in the Septuagint and NT[313]) that strikes us profoundly is in Nehemiah (March 16), where God's people cried, "Bring the book," and stood for hours listening to the reading and exposition of "the book of the law of God" (8:1, 3, 5, 8, 18; 9:3; also Exod. 24:7; Deut. 31:24). It was that **book** that meant everything to them, the **book** they longed for and needed after years of captivity in pagan lands.

Dear Christian **Friend**, if I may, I would encourage you to read the **Word** of God. Whether you do so in **book** order, chronological order, or selected passages, it is a crucial task. Read good Christian books, as well, ones that are *solely* Scripture-based, ones that expound the text of **Scripture**, drawing truth from that *alone*. In a day of opinion-driven relativism, let us say with the people of God, "Bring the book."

Scriptures for Study: What is the command of Isaiah 34:16? 🕮 Why should we do so (John 5:39)? 🕮 What assurance do we have concerning all this (Matt. 5:18)?

Wall

chômāh

Joshua 5:13 through 6:27, one of the most exciting military accounts in the OT, tells the story of Israel conquering Jericho, how the **wall** fell down simply as a result of the people marching around the city in obedience to **God** (vv. 5, 20).[314] *chômāh* (2346) is also used to refer to the walls around other cities (Lev. 25:29, 30; Deut. 3:5; 2 Kings 14:13; 2 Chron. 36:19). Such walls were essential in ancient times for protection against invaders. This is graphically seen in the **book** of Nehemiah, where "the wall of Jerusalem also [was] broken down, and the gates thereof [were] burned with fire" (1:3), prompting heart-broken Nehemiah to **lead** the needed rebuilding project.

A beautiful picture of two other physical walls is in the first occurrence of *chômāh*, where the Israelites crossed "the [Red Sea] upon the dry ground: and the waters were a wall unto them on their right hand, and on their left" (Exod. 14:22).

There is also, however, a figurative sense in which **wall** is used in **Scripture**. Figuratively, *chômāh* denotes a "surrounding protection and fortification." What do people rely upon for their "walls" of protection and security? For many it is **wealth** and/or their own **pride** and attitude of self-sufficiency: "The rich man's wealth is his strong city, and as an high wall in his own conceit" (Prov. 18:11). Worse, some never learn to discipline their lives in any way and are defenseless against the inevitable disaster: "He that hath no rule over his own spirit is like a city that is broken down, and without walls" (25:28).

What, then should be our walls? Isaiah 26:1, 2 answers: "In that day shall this song be sung in the land of Judah; We have a strong city; salvation will God appoint for walls and bulwarks. Open ye the gates, that the righteous nation which keepeth the truth may enter in." While that is the beginning of a hymn to be sung for redeemed Israel, it no less portrays the very **redemption** we have in Christ. As a city has walls, barricades, parapets, and other such fortifications to protect its occupants, it is our salvation in Christ that is our **wall** of safety and security. Take some **time** today to **rejoice** in the **wall** that surrounds you (Ps. 31:21).

Scriptures for Study: How is God portrayed in Zechariah 2:5? 📖 Read and rejoice in the **New** Jerusalem that is coming (Rev. 21:10–27).

Gate (1)

ša'ar

On March 9 we briefly mentioned the **word** *gates* in a study of Psalm 100:4, one of some 370 occurrences of the Hebrew *ša'ar* (8179). Its first occurrence demonstrates its ordinary meaning, that of the strong, fortified gate(s) of a walled city, including the open area on either side of it; in this case, it is the city of **Sodom** (Gen. 19:1; cf. 2 Chron. 26:9; Ps. 107:16).

Depending upon the size of a city, there were often several gates that served the obvious function of allowing access to the city. There was usually a main **gate** that was a central part of ancient city **life**. It was the place where the civil court would gather. In fact, the statement in Genesis 19 that Lot was in the city **gate** indicates he was a **judge** in the city (vv. 1, 9; cf. Deut. 21:19; Josh. 20:4). It was also a place for legal transactions (Ruth 4:1) and the public marketplace (2 Kings 7:1). *Ša'ar* is also used to indicate the **gate** of a **camp** (Exod. 32:26), the **gate** of the **tabernacle** (Exod. 27:16), and the gates of the **temple** (2 Chron. 23:19).

Since a city's main **gate** was a place where people naturally congregated, prophets often spoke to the people from there (2 Kings 7:1; Jer. 17:19, 20; 36:10). Of special note once again is Nehemiah 8:1 and 3, where we read that "all the people gathered . . . before the water gate; and they spake unto Ezra the scribe to bring the book of the law of Moses, which the LORD had commanded to Israel. . . . And he read therein . . . from the morning until midday." Since Jerusalem was not built on a **river**, water had to be drawn from wells and springs. The *Water **Gate*** was so named because it led to the Gihon Spring in the Kidron **Valley**. It is significant that while other gates needed repair during Nehemiah's reconstruction project, this one did not, only the walls adjacent to it (3:26, 27). **Among** several figurative uses of *water* in **Scripture**, one is a picture of the Word of **God** (John 15:3; Eph. 5:26; cf. Ps.119:9; John 17:17), and it is the *water **gate*** (figuratively speaking) that reminds us that God's Word never needs repair. While many "higher critics" challenge its historical accuracy and "lower (or textual) critics" continue to question (and "rebuild") the "authentic text," God's Word remains solid and in no need of reconstruction.

Soli deo Gloria!

Scriptures for Study: In preparation for tomorrow's study, read about the other gates mentioned in Nehemiah 3.

Gate (2)

šaʿar

Nehemiah 3 recounts those who participated in rebuilding the walls and gates of Jerusalem after the Israelites' **return** from Babylonian captivity, and the **gate** on which each labored. While we must be very careful not to become "hyper-typers" (those who abuse "typology" to force biblical objects to portray ideas not directly supported by the text[315]), the gates of Jerusalem do graphically illustrate and figuratively remind us of several truths taught clearly elsewhere in **Scripture**:

First, we begin at the *Sheep **Gate*** (vv. 1, 2) on the north **wall**, very near the **temple**. This was the **gate** through which sacrificial animals were brought into the city, washed in the pool of Bethesda, and then taken to the temple for **sacrifice**. Note that Nehemiah began (and ended) the tour at this **gate**. Perhaps he did so to direct attention to the Ultimate Sacrifice, "the Lamb of God, which taketh away the sin of the world" (John 1:29; cf. v. 36; 5:2).

There were two other important features of this **gate**. One is that, unlike other gates (Neh. 3:3, 6, etc.), this one had no "locks" or "bars." We can use this to illustrate that the **way** to **redemption** is open to anyone who believes. Another feature is that this was the only **gate** that was "sanctified" (v. 1, *qāḏaš*, 6942, January 20), set aside for **God**, consecrated, made sacred. Likewise, all those who entered there were sanctified.

Second, walking west along the wall and angling a little south, we arrive at the *Fish **Gate*** (v. 3). Fish were a staple of **life** in ancient times, and it was through this **gate** that fish were brought from the Mediterranean and the Jordan to be sold at the market. Merchants brought fish from as far away, in fact, as the coastal city of Tyre (100 miles to the north) to sell in Jerusalem (13:16).

This **gate** reminds us of the words of our **Lord**, "Follow me, and I will make you fishers of men" (Matt. 4:19). Wherever we go, wherever people are, we are to proclaim the gospel (Acts 1:8). Evangelism is "a staple" of Christianity. Vance Havner well said: "Evangelism is to Christianity what veins are to our bodies. You can cut Christianity anywhere and it will bleed evangelism. Evangelism is vascular; it's our business. Talk about majoring on evangelism, you might as well talk about a doctor majoring on healing. That's our business."[316]

Scriptures for Study: What does evangelism involve, according to Matthew 28:19, 20? 📖 If you would like to explore further, read the **book** of Acts, noting how the program in 1:8 was followed: chapters 1–7 (Jerusalem); 8–12 (Judea and Samaria); 13–28 ("the uttermost part of the earth").

Gate (3)

šaʿar

We continue our "tour" of the gates of Jerusalem, rebuilt under the leadership of Nehemiah.

Third, leaving the Fish **Gate**, and again walking westerly along the **wall**, we arrive at the northwest corner of the city and the *Old* ***Gate*** (Neh. 3:6), perhaps also called the *Corner* ***Gate*** (Jer. 31:38). This probably refers to the **gate** that led to the old city of Salem, first built by **Melchizedek**, and reminds us we shouldn't forget what is old. Things change rapidly, radically, and often regrettably. Many of the changes are just as Jeremiah wrote: "Thus saith the LORD, Stand ye in the ways, and see, and ask for the old paths, where is the good way, and walk therein, and ye shall find rest for your souls. But they said, We will not walk therein" (Jer. 6:16).

Even many Christians and Christian leaders today refuse to follow what they regard as "old-fashioned," constantly seeking something **new**, exciting, or "socially relevant." Many have gone so far as to throw off the "old gospel," replacing it with a new, more palatable, man-centered message. Quoting Vance Havner again, "We don't need to be in the novelty shop, as much as we need to be in the antique shop, where we find the old truths of God's Word. We don't need something new today half as much as we need something so old that it would be new if anybody tried it."[317]

Fourth, turning south and walking the longest distance between gates, we finally arrive at the ***Valley Gate*** (v. 13), so named because it opened into the Valley of Hinnom. As we have previously studied, it is in the valleys, not on the mountaintops, that we learn the lessons of **life** (April 29–May 2). The *trials* that seem the longest are the ones that bring the greatest *triumphs*.

Fifth, walking further south brings us to the *Dung* ***Gate*** (vv. 13, 14) at the very opposite end of the city from the Sheep **Gate**. It was through this **gate** that refuse was taken and dumped into the Valley of Hinnom (*hinnōm*, 2011, May 17). This vividly reminds us of Paul considering all else in life as nothing but "dung" in contrast to Christ (Phil. 3:8). It further encourages us to throw out whatever might defile us (2 Cor. 7:1), for such things are the polar opposite of the new, transformed life that appeared at conversion (2 Cor. 5:17).

Scriptures for Study: What is the admonition of Deuteronomy 32:7? 🕮 Read 2 Corinthians 6:14—7:1 again (September 18) and consider what might be a defilement in your life.

Ophel [and] Gate (4)

'ōpel [and] ša'ar

Our tour of the gates of Jerusalem in Nehemiah's **day** (Neh. 3) continues.

Sixth, as we gratefully leave the smell of the Dung **Gate** behind, we round the corner at the sharp tip of the city and head back north along the **wall** until we come to the *Fountain **Gate*** (v. 15). This **gate** was near the Pool of Siloam, which was fed by the Spring of Gihon outside the Water **Gate** by **way** of Solomon's water tunnel (2 Kings 20:20). Water is **life**, and this water system was essential to the city.

While water for *cleansing* gives a picture of the ***Word*** of **God**, as we noted on October 22, water for *consuming* portrays the *Holy Spirit* of God. As our **Lord** Himself promised the **woman** at the well, "But whosoever drinketh of the water that I shall give him shall never thirst; but the water that I shall give him shall be in him a well of water springing up into everlasting life" (John 4:14). On the "last day" of the Feast of the Tabernacles He also "cried": "If any man thirst, let him come unto me, and drink. He that believeth on me, as the scripture hath said, out of his belly shall flow rivers of living water. (But this spake he of the Spirit, which they that believe on him should receive)" (7:37–39). This indwelling of the Holy Spirit is a major emphasis in Romans 8.

Seventh, having now been refreshed at the Fountain **Gate**, we walk north again to the *Water **Gate*** (v. 26). We have discussed this **gate** already, but we look on it with great thanksgiving as we pass by. We can never visit this **gate** too often.

Then something captures our attention just north of the Water **Gate**. It is the "Ophel" (Neh. 3:26). This proper **name** is a transliteration of the Hebrew *'ōpel* (6077), which means "mound or knoll," but also speaks of a "fortress or stronghold." The Ophel in Jerusalem is a hill just south of the **temple** area on which a fortified tower sits. This was the perfect location for the home of the temple servants, placing them not only close to the temple but also close to water.

While we do not have servants of the temple today, we certainly have servants of the cross and servants of the Word of God. In a day when preaching is shallow and few people give much mind to Scripture authority, how we need men who will live *near it* and *attend to* it!

Scriptures for Study: Read Romans 8:1–9. Why are we no longer condemned? How did we used to walk, and how do we walk now? What is the evidence of conversion?

Gate (5)

šaʿar

Today we end our tour with the last three gates of Jerusalem (Neh. 3). *Eighth*, continuing north from our "side trip" to Ophel, we come to the ***Horse Gate*** (v. 28). It is believed this was the **gate** by which horses came and left the old palace of **David**. Additionally, during Solomon's time, many horses were brought in from Egypt (2 Chron. 1:16, 17) and became, along with chariots, critical to national defense (Isa. 2:7, December 13).

This reminds me of Paul's even more vivid imagery, that of the individual Roman soldier in full battle armor (Eph. 6:10–20). With this scene he depicts the Christian **life** as an all-out **war**, also adding in his letter to Timothy that pastors are the "generals" who are to **lead** and **teach** others how to carry on the battle (2 Tim. 2:1–4). When our battle is over, will we be able to say with Paul, "I have fought a good fight, I have finished my course, I have kept the faith" (2 Tim. 4:7)?

Ninth, still continuing north we arrive at the *East* ***Gate*** (v. 29). While sealed with large stones in AD 1530 by Muslim conquerors (the Ottoman Turks), it was originally the first **gate** opened each **morning**, as it faced the rising ***sun***, reminding us of the *Son*. Although not stated in **Scripture**, many believe it was this **gate** through which the **Lord** Jesus entered Jerusalem at His triumphal entry. In any event, we do **know** that while the glory of **God** *left* the **temple** at the East **Gate** (Ezek. 10:16–22), our Lord will ***return*** the same **way** (43:1–5). Let us, therefore, be "looking for that blessed hope, and the glorious appearing of the great God and our Saviour Jesus Christ" (Titus 2:13).

Tenth, a few yards farther on we come to the ***Gate*** *Miphkad* in the northeast corner of the city (v. 31). The **name** comes from *mip̱qāḏ* (4663), a "numbering or census," allowing us to translate the name as "Muster **Gate**" or "Inspection **Gate**," as in the gathering of troops for review. This **image** reminds us that upon His return, our Lord will "gather the troops" for review at His Judgment Seat and reward them accordingly (2 Cor. 5:10; Rev. 22:12).

Well, our tour has come to an end. We turn left, walk a few paces east, and find ourselves back at the exact point where we started, the Sheep **Gate** (v. 32). Everything begins and ends right there!

Scriptures for Study: Read 1 Corinthians 3:10–15 and Romans 14:10–12. What do these passages teach us about what is to come?

Vineyard [and] Wild Grapes

kerem [and] be'ush

A **vineyard** is a beautiful sight. A drive through California's Napa **Valley**, for example, is well worth the time. Vineyards in the Near East were, and still are, a vital part of **life**. They are mentioned in the OT more than ninety times using the Hebrew *kerem* (3754), the first of which is in Genesis 9:20, where **Noah** "planted a vineyard," although he tragically abused the wine he got from it. Several other literal vineyards are mentioned (e.g., Exod. 22:5; Lev. 25:3; Judg. 21:20; Ps. 107:37; Prov. 31:16).

Vineyard is also used metaphorically. One graphic example is the treading of the winepress, which foretells divine judgment (Isa. 63:3; Rev. 14:19). Of special significance is Isaiah 5, where Israel is likened to God's **vineyard**. Using the exact terms one would for a real **vineyard**, each of which has a figurative meaning, God describes all He has done for His people. He planted His **vineyard** on a "fruitful hill" (Jerusalem), "fenced it" (with walls), cleared "out the stones" (the Canaanites) so it could be planted, used "the choicest vine" for planting (the **Law**), and "built a tower in the midst of it" (the priests and the prophets) so the watchman could see in all directions and protect it (vv. 1, 2). So thorough had He been that He even asks, "What could have been done more to my vineyard, that I have not done in it?" (v. 4).

In spite of all that patient **labor**, this **vineyard** was not a beautiful one, bringing forth instead **wild grapes** (v. 2). This is a single **word** in the Hebrew (*bā'uš*, 891), which comes from the root *bā'as̱h* (887), "to stench, be repulsive." This root is used to describe rotting fish (Exod. 7:18, 21), the stink of millions of dead frogs during the plagues in Egypt (8:13, 14), and spoiled, worm-ridden **manna** (16:20).

The grapes of this **vineyard**, then, were pungent, putrid, and poisonous. At this point, pruning, hoeing, or other **work** was futile. The **vineyard** was beyond salvage. Judgment was inevitable and imminent. God pronounced and carried out six "woes" upon Israel, which we will examine **tomorrow**.

This OT parable provides us with a sobering warning. Just as the **Lord** stood outside the door of the church at Laodicea, knocking to ask permission to enter (Rev. 3:20), He is knocking at the door of the church today. Oh, that we would "open the door" and bring Him back in!

Scriptures for Study: Read Revelation 3:14–22, noting the following in this letter: the lack of any *regard* (**praise**), and then the *rebuke* (vv. 15–17), *requirement* (vv. 18, 19), and *reassurance* (vv. 20–22).

Woe (1)

hôy

Appearing fifty times in the OT, all but one of which are in the Prophets, *hôy* (1945) is an interjection. While it is used a few times for **mourning** (1 Kings 13:30) as well as expectant **joy** (Zech. 2:6, "Ho, ho"), it is used most often for the sad lament of coming judgment, often translated **woe**. There is no better example of this usage than Isaiah 5. As a result of the **wild grapes** that came from God's **vineyard**, Israel, He pronounced "six woes" upon the nation, six philosophies that are still with us today:

First, there was the **woe** upon Israel for their *materialism* (vv. 8–10). These verses describe greed in general and land-grabbing in particular. The rich cheated the poor and sought monopolies on the land, in blatant disregard for God's property laws (Lev. 25:23–28; cf. 1 Kings 21:13; Num. 36:7). The judgment would be that a mere six gallons (a "bath") of wine would come from ten acres of grapevines and only half a bushel (an "ephah") of grain would be the yield from six bushels (a "homer") of **seed**.

We live in a **day** of unprecedented materialism. Many grab for all they can get, thinking that such things are the only things worth living for and the only things that will last. But just the opposite is true, for "moth and rust doth corrupt" these things and "thieves break through and steal" them (Matt. 6:19). How careful Christians need to be to not get caught up in the process of amassing things; rather, we should "lay up for [ourselves] treasures in heaven" (6:20) and "set [our] affection on things above, not on things on the earth" (Col. 3:2).

Second, there was the **woe** for *hedonism* (Isa. 5:11–17). Here we read that pleasure and revelry were the *manner* of **life**, and alcohol was the chief *means* to that end. From dawn to dark, pleasure was the philosophy of life. Here was, in fact, a chief reason for the Babylonian captivity that was to come. This sin, too, is one in which even the Christian can be caught up. The church itself, in fact, is a place where many people seek pleasure and entertainment, practically "getting drunk" on excitement. Let us do what the Israelites did not: Desire "knowledge" (v. 13), seek holiness, and **glorify God** (v. 16).

Scriptures for Study: What do Proverbs 11:4, 16:16, and 23:5 say about riches? 🕮 What does Luke 17:26–29 declare about hedonism?

Woe (2)

hôy

We conclude today our sobering look at the "six woes" **God** declares against Israel in Isaiah 5 in his parable of the **vineyard**.

Third, there was the **woe** upon Israel for their *skepticism* (vv. 18, 19). The defiant attitude of verse 19 demonstrates the skeptic. To paraphrase, "If God really is working, really in control, let's see it." Such God-defiers even challenge God to bring on His judgment if He really can. While living in their blatant sin, they don't expect God to respond to them. How many today openly defy God and think He will not respond!

Fourth, there was the **woe** due to Israel's *relativism* (v. 20). Nothing defines "modern morality" better than this verse. Society "[calls] evil good, and good evil." In today's moral relativism, *adultery* is called "an affair," abortion is called "terminating a pregnancy" or "a choice," *lying* is called "spin," *stealing* is called "an entitlement," ***pride*** is called "self-esteem," ***sin*** (if acknowledged at all) is called "a mistake" or "a weakness," and the list goes on. No longer are there moral standards. Rather, each person decides what is right or wrong for himself. This has even invaded the church. People can interpret the Bible in any way that pleases them. The old adage, "Well, that's just your interpretation," is the fruit that has sprung from the seed of relativism.

Fifth, there was the **woe** for *egotism* (v. 21). "Wise in their own eyes" also describes many people in our **day**. Pride (March 19), a perception of self-sufficiency, and self-determination rule the day. But while "professing themselves to be wise, they became fools" (Rom. 1:22).

Sixth, there was the **woe** as a result of *elitism* (Isa. 5:22, 23). This philosophy advocates rule by an elite class, a select group who possess certain abilities, **wealth**, or other distinctions that supposedly qualify them to rule. These verses describe the worst kind of elitism, rule by corrupt, even drunken, magistrates who were bribed. The injustice of these "leaders" reminds us of our own day of corrupt, elitist politicians driven by personal ambition, not to mention influences by lobbyists who will fund their campaigns, cutting their deals at cocktail parties.

It is in verse 24 we read the root of Judah's disintegration. It was all "because they have cast away the law of the LORD of hosts, and despised the word of the Holy One of Israel." Let us be on guard, for we, too, can fall into such philosophies.

Scriptures for Study: Read the following verses, noting the **woe** pronounced in each: Jeremiah 23:1; Ezekiel 13:3; 34:2. How are they related?

Wither

yāḇēš

Like countless Hebrew words, *yāḇēš* (3001) immediately paints a picture for us. Its literal sense is the drying up of land (Gen. 8:7, first occurrence; Amos 1:2, "Carmel" means "garden land"; 4:7), or the withering of plant **life** (Isa. 42:15) for lack of moisture. Most of its seventy occurrences, however, are figurative, and carry **deep** theological significance.

First, it *depicts the fullness* of **God**. Amazingly, this **word** is used to depict no less than three of God's attributes. His immutability (unchangeableness) is seen in the fact that just as He **dried up** the Red Sea, He also dried up the Jordan River (Josh. 4:23). His sovereignty is demonstrated by the drying up of the "green tree" solely because "the LORD [has] spoken and [has] done it" (Ezek. 17:24). His omnipotence, therefore, is displayed in all these incidents along with many more in **Scripture**. As Job summarizes, "Behold, he withholdeth the waters, and they dry up: also he sendeth them out, and they overturn the earth" (Job 12:15).

Second, it *describes the frailty* of **man**. Psalm 90:4–6 compares man's fleeting life span with God's eternality. While man might live a thousand years (as Methuselah almost did), that is no more than a single four-hour "watch in the night" (*'ašmûrāh* March 13) from God's perspective (v. 4; cf. 2 Pet. 3:8). Man's lifespan is, indeed, little more than withering grass and a fading flower (Isa. 40:7, 8).

Third, it *declares the forecast* of judgment. This word is repeatedly used to foretell God's judgment on various peoples through drought: Moab ("Nimrim," Isa. 15:6), Egypt (19:4–7), Assyria (Zech. 10:11), Babylon (Jer. 50:35-38), and Israel and Judah (Jer. 12:4; Isa. 42:15; Joel 1:20). Similar judgment will also be part of the Great Tribulation (Rev. 16:12).

Fourth, it *demonstrates the finality* of God's Word. In stark contrast to man's *frailty* is the Word's *finality* and enduring character. While the grass (people) withers away, "the word of our God shall stand for ever" (Isa. 40:8). As our **Lord** Himself declared, "Heaven and earth shall pass away, but my words shall not pass away" (Matt. 24:35; cf. 5:18), and as Peter reiterates, "The word of the Lord endureth for ever" (1 Pet. 1:25). What a blessing and comfort to **know** that God's Word endures! Take some **time** today to give God **praise** and thanks for His enduring Word.

Scriptures for Study: To what does James liken man's life (James 4:14)? 🕮 Read Ezekiel 37:1–14 (*yāḇēš* occurs in v. 11, "dried"). What is the **image** used here and what does it predict (cf. Rom. 11:26)? 🕮 Read and meditate on Psalm 119:89–96.

Dried Up

chārēḇ

The Hebrew *chārēḇ* (2717) is "almost equivalent to *yāḇēš,* though *chārēḇ* is employed more frequently to indicate bodies of water becoming dry. *yāḇēš* is employed more often to portray dryness of vegetation."[318]

The first occurrence of *chārēḇ*, which is right on the heels of *yāḇēš* in Genesis 8:7, is in verse 13, where "the waters were *dried up* from off the earth," and "the face of the ground was *dry*" (emphasis added, the adjective *chārēḇ*, 2720, "dry, desolate"). We can only imagine how truly desolate the earth looked after the Flood. Perhaps it was close to Apollo 11 astronaut Buzz Aldrin's description of the lunar landscape—"a magnificent desolation." Likewise, perhaps you have seen a dry lake or riverbed with its cracks and fissures.

Those are the images in *chārēḇ*. Another derivative is translated "deserts" in Isaiah 48:21 (*chorbāh*, 2723). Its equivalents in Akkadian (*charābu*, "be desolate") and Arabic (*chariba*, "be void of water and vegetation") further underscore the desolation inherent in this **word**, and describe vividly how dry the ground was as God's people **walked** across the Red Sea (Ps. 106:9; Isa. 51:10), which should forever silence the critic who says the water was just knee-deep.

Like *yāḇēš*, *chārēḇ* and its derivatives are used, especially by Jeremiah, to describe judgment (Jer. 26:9, "desolate"), and Ezekiel (Ezek. 6:6, "laid waste"). They both declared the terrifying desolation to come when God sent the Assyrians and Babylonians in judgment upon Israel and Judah (respectively). The prophets also wrote of the desolation that would come to the enemies of God, such as Edom (Isa. 34:10), Tyre (Ezek. 26:19), and Egypt (29:12).

Especially devastated was Tyre, which stood on an island a half-mile out to sea. It was to be so utterly destroyed that it would never again be rebuilt, even scraped **clean** like the top of a rock, and its stones, timbers, and its very dust cast into the sea (26:4, 5, 12–14). About 260 years later, Alexander fulfilled this to the letter, using the walls of the old city (destroyed by the Babylonians) as material to **build** a causeway (which still exists) out to the island. Just as verse 5 declares, fishermen today use the island as a place to spread their nets for drying and repair.

Such fulfilled prophecy is not only a *blessing* to us, but a ***burden*** as well, as we declare such a warning to a lost world.

Scriptures for Study: What was the purpose of such judgment (Ezek. 12:20; Jer. 33:10; Zeph. 3:6, 7)? 🕮 What will God one day do for His people (Isa. 51:3; 52:9; "waste places" is *chorbâ*)?

Earthen Vessel

chereś keliy

Today we consider a truly humbling and encouraging truth. The Hebrew *keliy* (3627) is a broad term that includes many useful items, including a ship (Isa. 18:2), clothing (Deut. 22:5), various utensils (Ezek. 40:42, "instruments"), even "instruments of war" (1 Sam. 8:12) and "instruments of musick" (2 Chron. 5:13). Many of its some 320 occurrences refer to various containers or vessels for storing or carrying things. Such vessels were made of wood (Lev. 11:32), various metals (Josh. 6:19), or clay (Lev. 6:28), and were used to store just about anything.

Especially significant for our **meditation** today are references to an **earthen vessel** (Lev. 6:28; 11:33; 14:45, 50; Num. 5:17; 2 Sam. 17:28; Jer. 32:14). The qualifying word **earthen** (*chereś*, 2789) refers to clay pottery. Clay pots were easily and inexpensively made and were common in ancient times for storage. They were also used to transport waste and garbage and for storing valuables that were then buried (Matt. 13:44). Even documents were stored in clay pots, as Jeremiah 32:14 states, and as illustrated by the Dead Sea Scrolls discovered in 1947 in pots left in caves about a mile inland from the north shore of the Dead Sea.

We find precisely the same **image** in 2 Corinthians 4:7: "We have this treasure in earthen [*ostrakinos*, 3749G] vessels [*skeuos*, 4632G], that the excellency of the power may be of God, and not of us." Paul was relentlessly attacked by false teachers in Corinth, who tried to undermine him as being without oratorical skills, without **good** looks, and just plain common. How could such a person, they insisted, have any credibility in what he teaches?

As the adage goes, Paul was "between a rock and a hard place." He needed to defend the gospel, which these Judaizers were undermining (February 15), but how could he defend himself without appearing **proud**? His **answer** was, in effect, "You are quite correct. I am nothing but a common, cheap, clay pot, with no value of my own, but I contain the most priceless message on earth, the gospel of Jesus Christ. The value is not in me, but in God." Contrary to today's attitude, **God** doesn't use our rhetoric or arguments, rather He uses the gospel, which *itself* is "the power of God unto salvation" (Rom. 1:16).

What a blessing it is to be a clay pot!

Scriptures for Study: Read 1 Corinthians 1:23–29 and 2:1–5. What does Paul tell the philosophically oriented Greeks about **preaching** the gospel in contrast to debate and argument?

Answer

'ānāh

Appearing about 320 times, the Hebrew *'ānāh* (6030) carries two predominant meanings. The first is "to respond nonverbally." An example appears in Deuteronomy 20:11, 12, where **God** says that when demanding a city's surrender in **war**, if the city will "make thee [an] answer of peace," that is, respond peaceably by opening their gates, then **peace** will be established; otherwise, siege would be laid upon it.

The second predominant meaning of *'ānāh* is to respond verbally. This is illustrated in its first OT occurrence, where after God had spoken to him, Abraham humbly and incredulously "answered and said, Behold now, I have taken upon me to speak unto the Lord, which am but dust and ashes" (Gen. 18:27). Other examples include when Moses verbally "answered" God with his objections to God's calling him to service (Exod. 4:1); **Satan** "answered" God concerning the **temptation** of Job (Job 1:7, 9); God "answered" Job (38:1; 40:1) and Job "answered" God (42:1); and God's people "answered" Joshua by saying they would **obey** all he commanded (Josh. 1:16).

Many of the some forty occurrences of *'ānāh* in the Psalms are particularly striking. The first is Psalm 3:4, where David prays, "I cried unto the LORD with my voice, and he heard me out of his holy hill. Selah." The **word** *heard* indicates that God responded to David. Several other instances **plead** for God to respond: "Hear me when I call" (4:1; cf. 13:3; 27:7), and thankfully still others tell us again that God did (and will do) so: "I have called upon thee, for thou wilt hear me" (17:6; cf. 20:1; 20:6). Men should be warned, however, that while God's enemies will cry out to Him, "there [is] none to save them: even unto the LORD, but he answer[s] them not" (18:41).

How comforting it is to **know** that God responds to His people: "I sought the LORD, and he heard me" (34:4). But not only does God respond to us, we are to respond to Him: "Sing [*'ānāh*] unto the LORD with thanksgiving; sing praise upon the harp unto our God" (147:7). Further, we are to respond to others with the Word of God: "My tongue shall speak of thy word" (119:172), that we may "be ready always to give an answer to every man that asketh [us] a reason of the hope that is in [us] with meekness and fear" (1 Pet. 3:15).

Scriptures for Study: What is the promise of Psalm 86:7? 🕮 What are the blessings listed in 91:11–15 (**answer** in v. 15 is *'ānāh*)?

Youth (Young Man) (1)

na'ar

The Hebrew *na'ar* (5288) is variously translated in our AV with the words ***youth, lad, young man,*** and a few others. Its some 240 occurrences range from an infant (Exod. 2:6; 2 Sam. 12:16) to **young** men of various ages (e.g., Gen. 21:12; Exod. 24:5; Num. 11:27; 1 Sam. 2:17; 2 Sam. 14:21; Isa. 40:30, "youths" and "young men"). It also refers to servants, as those were often **young** men, such as an armor-bearer (1 Sam. 14:1) and a king's personal attendant (Esther 2:2). Various **young** men in **Scripture teach** us much. While we could look at many, we will consider just a few—two that teach a negative lesson and two that provide some positives:

First, in Samson we see an *arrogant* **youth**. We find *na'ar* five times in reference to Samson (Judg. 13:5, 7, 8, 12, 24). As his story unfolds in the next three chapters, we discover that while "the LORD blessed him" and the Spirit empowered him (vv. 24, 25), also present was an arrogance and self-reliance, seen in his marrying a pagan (14:1–10), his killing out of personal revenge (15:9–20), his foolish game-playing (16:1–14), and his attitude of invincibility (vv. 15–17). It was such **pride** and an air of self-sufficiency that destroyed him (Prov. 16:18). Samson stands as a great warning to **young** men everywhere to be humble and attentive to teaching (Prov. 1:8; 4:1; 23:22; cf. 17:25; 19:26; 29:3).

Second, in Absalom we see an *angry* **youth** (2 Sam. 13–18; *na'ar* appears in 14:21 and 18:5[319]). We see his seething (also calculating) nature early on, in his murder of his own **brother** Amnon (13:20–33; **David** as civil authority should have executed Amnon, Lev. 20:17). We see it in his burning of Joab's field to force him to arrange a meeting with David (14:30–33). We see his **anger** culminate in his plotting a coup against his **father** (15:1–12).

"Anger is momentary insanity," wrote first-century BC Roman poet Horace (*Epistolae*). Benjamin Franklin added, "Whatever is begun in anger ends in shame" (*Poor Richard's Almanack*). Absalom is proof of both. The biblical injunctions are numerous: "Cease from anger, and forsake wrath" (Ps. 37:8); "Be not hasty in thy spirit to be angry: for anger resteth in the bosom of fools" (Eccles. 7:9); "Be ye angry, and sin not: let not the sun go down upon your wrath" (Eph. 4:26).

Young men, beware of arrogance and anger.

Scriptures for Study: Read the Proverbs listed above in the paragraph about Samson, as well as the following verses concerning anger: Proverbs 14:29; 19:11; Romans 12:19–21.

Youth (Young Man) (2)

na'ar

Having considered two examples of *wayward* **youth**, let us conclude by considering two examples of *well-behaved* **youth**, two **young** men whose outstanding character stands out in **Scripture**.

Third, in Isaac we see an *agreeable* **youth**. The incident of Abraham being willing to **sacrifice** his **precious** son Isaac (Gen. 22; *na'ar* appears in v. 12, "lad"), that miracle child of promise, has been addressed many times by expositors. Every parent can imagine such a situation. My wife and I certainly could, as our only child, a son, was conceived after fourteen years of trying and after doctors said it would never happen.

But while Abraham is considered often, Isaac is just as often overlooked. While Abraham's **faith** is lauded (and rightly so), what about Isaac's? Have you ever first noticed Isaac's *perception*? In verse 7, he asks, "Behold the fire and the wood: but where is the lamb for a burnt offering?" Abraham answers, "God will provide" (v. 8, January 10). More importantly, have you ever then noticed Isaac's *submission*? After Abraham built the **altar**, laid the wood on it, and then "bound Isaac his son, and laid him on the altar" (v. 9), we hear not a word from Isaac. There was no questioning, no argument, no protest, just submissive faith. How different that is from today when children argue with, challenge, and **rebel** against the leadership **God** has put over them.

Fourth, we look at **David**, and see an *authentic* **youth**. Every Christian parent will agree when we say how fun and fascinating it is to watch children. And watching the differences between girls and boys is especially entertaining. Most of us have said at one **time** or another, "He's *all* boy," or, "She's *all* girl." Well, **young** David was indeed all boy. We see him first as a "ruddy" and handsome **youth** tending the sheep (1 Sam. 16:11, 12), and we see him become an expert with a sling (17:40, 49, 50).

It is then that we see the true character of this **young man**, his courage in taking on not only a **lion** and a bear that were killing sheep (1 Sam. 17:33–35, *na'ar* appears in v. 33), but then in unthinkably taking on Goliath. From where did such character and authenticity come? David's confidence was always, "The LORD . . . will deliver me" (v. 37).

Young men, if I may encourage you, be agreeable and authentic.

Scriptures for Study: Read the following verses, noting how that early **trust** in the **LORD** permeated David's **life**: Psalms 11:1; 18:16, 17; 63:7; 138:3, 7, 8.

Maiden (Young Woman)

na'arāh

It might be considered *unfair* if we mentioned **young** men without also mentioning **young** women; it would certainly be *unwise,* because they also **teach** us much. Both **maiden** and **young woman** are translations of *na'arāh* (5291), the feminine form of *na'ar*. It refers to a little girl (2 Kings 5:2), as well as a girl of marriageable age and those who attend her (as we will see below). It also often emphasizes the girl's virginity (Deut. 22:15, 16, 23, 29, "damsel"; Judg. 21:12; 1 Kings 1:2). Three **young** ladies of whom *na'arāh* is used stand out as wonderful examples for **young** ladies today:

First, in Rebekah we see *purity*. The first OT occurrence of *na'arāh* is in Genesis 24:14 and then in five verses that follow (16, 28, 55, 57, 61). The scene is Abraham sending Eliezer (cf. 15:2; 24:2) to find a bride for his bachelor son Isaac. Verse 16 is very clear on the fact that "the damsel" Rebekah "was very fair to look upon, a virgin, neither had any man known her." There is, indeed, nothing in a **young** girl's **life** more important than this, to remain **pure** until that one "special day," the one when she weds the **man God** has provided for her.

Second, in Ruth we see *pleasantness*. *Na'arāh* is used of Ruth in 2:5, 6, so while not a virgin, since she was a widow, she must still have been **young** and of marriageable age. One who reads this beautiful love story is struck by the unselfishness, faithfulness, and general pleasantness of this amazing **woman**. She is the only **woman** in **Scripture** who is referred to, in fact, as "a virtuous woman" (3:11; cf. Prov. 31:10–31; February 6). It is no wonder Boaz obviously loved her and wanted to marry her. There could not be a better model for **young** women today than Ruth.

Third, in Esther we see *perceptiveness*. Esther, whose Persian **name** means "star" and Hebrew name Hadassah means "myrtle" (a flowering shrub), was also a *na'arāh* (2:7). In a **book** that dramatically illustrates the sovereignty and providence of God (although God is not mentioned directly[320]), the beautiful **maiden** Esther stands out as perceptive, wise, and courageous. While apparent sexual indiscretions indicated in Esther 2:12–14 certainly tarnish her reputation a bit, her other qualities are noteworthy.

Instead of the feminists, glamour magazine models, and music stars who are sadly elevated as role models, let us desire more Rebekahs, Ruths, and Esthers.

Scriptures for Study: At your leisure, read the stories mentioned today. 🕮 You might also **want** to review our February 6 reading on the **Virtuous Woman**.

Integrity (1)

tōm

Integrity. What a critical **word** this is for our times! Even the origin of the English word itself is instructive and fascinating. It comes from the Latin *integer*, also an English word, and literally means "whole or complete," as a whole **number** in mathematics; its figurative idea, then, is "sound, virtuous, and upright," as in the expression *integer vitae*, "blameless of life."

An interesting contrast to this word, along with *unus* ("one," as in "unity," "unison," etc.), is *duo*, "two." It was the Greek philosopher/mathematician Pythagoras who, out of superstition, viewed this word as reflecting **evil**, an idea that is actually embedded in hundreds of English words (duplicity, dualism, doubt, etc.).[321]

The Hebrew *tōm* (8537), then, means "whole, complete, free of duplicity, and therefore possessing integrity of character." The first of its some twenty-five occurrences refers to the Philistine **king** Abimelech (Gen. 20:4-6), who in honest "integrity of [his] heart and innocency" took Sarah only because of Abraham's own duplicity in calling her his sister, a half-truth. Here is a sad picture of more **integrity** in a pagan than in a believer.

The essence of **integrity**, therefore, is allegiance, standing firm for what is right without duplicity, double-mindedness, or divided allegiance. Consider the contrast between Joshua and **Achan**. Achan had a double allegiance; he tried to **serve** two masters: **God** and material possessions. This divided allegiance cost him everything; he and his entire family were stoned and burned along with everything they owned. Joshua, on the other **hand**, was a **man** of **integrity**. Not recognizing a visitor, Joshua asked, "Art thou for us, or for our adversaries?" (Josh. 5:13), emphasizing that one must be on one side or the other, that there is no middle ground, no "gray areas." To stand for what is right takes **integrity**. Later, just before his **death**, Joshua said, "Now, therefore, fear the LORD, and serve him in sincerity [*tāmiym,* 8549, from the same root as *tōm,* February 28] and in truth" (24:14). *That* is a man of **integrity**!

Consider also Saul and **David**. While a mighty warrior and king, Saul had not an ounce of **integrity**. He tried to serve the **Lord** while at the same time being totally self-directed; never was he dependent upon God. But David was a man of great personal **integrity**. In fact, Psalm 78:70–72 tells us God chose David to replace Saul because of the "integrity [*tōm*] of his heart."

Let us each be a man or **woman** of **integrity**.

Scriptures for Study: How did David want to be judged (Ps. 7:8)? 📖 What else did **integrity** do for him (25:21)?

Integrity (2)

tōm

One of the many threads woven through the fabric of **Scripture** is the essential quality of **integrity**. The twenty-five occurrences of *tōm* (8537), coupled with other Scriptures, provide us with three basic principles about **integrity**:

First, we see the *weight* of **integrity**. As noted **yesterday**, men such as Joshua and **David** were men of **integrity**. Considering David further, **God** appeared to Solomon and used his **father** David as an object lesson of the importance of this quality and challenged him by telling him the **man** he should be: "If thou wilt walk before me, as David thy father walked, in integrity [*tōm*] of heart, and in uprightness, to do according to all that I have commanded thee, and wilt keep my statutes and my judgments: Then I will establish the throne of thy kingdom upon Israel for ever" (1 Kings 9:4, 5).

Job, too, was a man of **integrity** (Job 2:3). **Satan** knew this, which is why he wanted to attack Job. What a victory it would be to uncover duplicity in a man like Job! Even Job's friends recognized this quality—"Is not this thy fear, thy confidence, thy hope, and the uprightness [*tōm*] of thy ways?" (4:6)—making their criticisms all the more reprehensible. Job never succumbed to such criticism, declaring, "Till I die I will not remove mine integrity [derivative *tummāh*, 8538] from me" (27:5) and, "Let me be weighed in an even balance, that God may know mine integrity" (31:6).

Second, there is the *worth* of **integrity**. In stark contrast to those who have **integrity**, some of our Lord's most scathing condemnations were against those without this quality, those who were duplicitous and hypocritical (Matt. 6:2, 5, 16; 15:7; 22:18; Luke 12:1, 56; 13:15). The apostle Paul followed suit by clearly condemning Peter and Barnabas in their being "carried away with their dissimulation [i.e., hypocrisy, *hupokrisis*, 5272G]" because of their unthinkable duplicity with the Judaizers (Gal. 2:11–13). Paul also told Timothy that in the latter days there would be many false teachers who would "[speak] lies in hypocrisy; having their conscience seared with a hot iron" (1 Tim. 4:2). **Among** eight traits of godly **wisdom**, James writes that one of them is being "without hypocrisy" (James 3:17). Peter (having learned his lesson) declares there is no place for hypocrisy in the believer's **life** (1 Pet. 2:1).

Scriptures for Study: How did David **lead** God's people (Ps. 78:70–72)? 📖 Read Matthew 23, noting each of our Lord's criticisms of the scribes and Pharisees for their lack of **integrity**.

Integrity (3)

tōm

Concluding our thoughts on the crucial need for **integrity**, we have noted its *weight* and *worth*, but there is one more principle in **Scripture** concerning this essential character quality.

Third, there is the ***wealth*** of **integrity**. The riches and blessings of **integrity** are enormous: **God** is "a buckler [i.e., **shield**, *māgēn*, July 20] to them that walk uprightly [*tōm*]" (Prov. 2:7); "He that walketh uprightly [*tōm*] walketh surely [i.e., securely, assuredly, *beṭach*, 983, November 12]" (10:9); "The way of the LORD is strength to the upright [*tōm*]" (10:29); "The integrity [derivative *tummāh*, 8538] of the upright shall guide them" (11:3); and the blessings go on.

Whenever I think of the word **integrity**, I am immediately reminded of the Huguenots of sixteenth-century France. They held strong morals and possessed high **integrity**. To be "honest as a Huguenot" was said to have been the highest **praise** of one's **integrity**. Put simply, what the Puritan was in England, the Huguenot was in France. A conservative estimate says that by 1561 one-sixth of France was strong in the foundational doctrines of Christianity, which were reasserted in the Reformation, and blameless moral character; other estimates say one-fourth.

But history then reveals that the Huguenots were forced to leave France in 1685 and hence settled in England, Prussia, Holland, South Africa, and the Carolinas and other colonies here in America. (I had the **joy** of once visiting a Huguenot Church in Charleston, South Carolina.[322]) What's especially significant about that exodus is that it was a terrible economic blow to France, since most Huguenots were skilled artisans and professional men of the middle class (paralleled by the taxpaying middle class in America). Does that not explain the intellectual emptiness and moral debauchery that permeates France to this very day? Does that not explain the virtually incomprehensible ramblings of French philosophers such as Voltaire (1694–1778), André Maurois (1885–1967), and especially Jean Paul Sartre (1905–1980)?

In a day when there is little **integrity among** politicians, businessmen, and sadly even some religious (and "Christian") leaders, the need for **integrity** cannot be overemphasized. While society today places virtually no value on personal **integrity**, it is a trait that is at the very **heart** of a true believer.

Scriptures for Study: What is the contrast drawn in Proverbs 19:1 and 28:6? 📖 What is another blessing of the **man** who walks with **integrity** (20:7)?

Vow

nēḏer

Appearing sixty times in the OT, the Hebrew *nēḏer* (5088) refers either to "the solemn promise one makes to **God** or the thing that is promised." Making a **vow** was an extremely important act and was not done lightly. There were three basic features of a **vow**:

First, it was always made to God, never between men. This is evident in its first occurrence (Gen. 28:20–22), where we read about "the most frank and open utterance of newborn spiritual liberty from the heart of man that has yet appeared in the divine record."[323] In response to all that God has done, Jacob vows that since God is with him and will watch over him, he will **build** a memorial to God and give Him a tenth of his substance as a symbol of devotion.

Second, a **vow** was always voluntary. Any concept of a mandatory vow associated with religious piety, as taught by some today, is foreign to Scripture. Even one of the most sacred vows, the Nazirite **vow** (Num. 6:2–21), was voluntary, issued from a **heart** totally committed to God.

Third, a **vow** was binding; once made, it had to be kept. "When thou vowest a vow unto God, defer not to pay it . . . Better is it that thou shouldest not vow, than that thou shouldest vow and not pay. . . . Neither say . . . that it was an error" (Eccles. 5:4–6).

Without question the greatest **vow** ever made was by Messiah. As **David** records in that great messianic Psalm 22, "I will pay my vows before them that fear [the LORD]" (Ps. 22:25). And what was our Lord's **vow**? To offer Himself as the only sufficient Savior and **sacrifice** for **sin**. As one poet writes of verse 1: "Deserted! God could separate from His own essence rather; / And Adam's sins have swept between the righteous Son and Father; / Yea, once, Immanuel's orphaned cry His universe hath shaken — / It went up single, echoless, 'My God, I am forsaken!' / It went up from the Holy's lips amid His lost creation, / That, of the lost, no son should use those words of desolation!"[324]

What of today? Vows, along with the sacrifices that often accompanied them (e.g., Lev. 7:16; 22:18; Deut. 12:6), are no longer needed. The Christian's conversation is as sacred and binding as any **vow**. While not Scripture, the adage "My word is my bond" should be true of every believer.

Scriptures for Study: Read the following verses, noting that "our words are our bond": Matthew 5:34–37; Colossians 3:17; James 1:22; 5:12; 1 John 3:18.

War (1)

milchāmāh

Plato wrote, "Only the dead have seen the end of war." Sadly, there is much truth in that. The Hebrew *milchāmāh* (4421) occurs about 320 times, demonstrating how **war** permeates human history.

The first occurrence of *milchāmāh*, in fact, is as early as Genesis 14:2, where we read about a major "international" **war** around 2000 BC between the five city-states of the Jordan plain (including **Sodom** and Gomorrah) and the four eastern city-states (including Sumeria and early Persia). Because of his foolish involvement with Sodom, Lot was captured in that **war**, compelling Abraham to rescue his nephew.

There are, of course, numerous other references to **war** (e.g., Exod. 17:16; Num. 31:14–24, "battle"; Deut. 20:1–4; Judg. 3:1–4; 1 Sam. 14:20–23; Eccles. 3:8). Such references, especially many in Joshua about the seemingly merciless destruction of the Canaanites, including men, women, and even children (e.g., 4:13; 6:3; 8:1–3; 10:24–26; 11:18–23), appall some Christians. "How could a loving God be so bloodthirsty?" they ask.

Deuteronomy 13:12–17 explains that **God** simply used His people to **judge** willing idolaters. Even the briefest study of the Canaanites reveals an unimaginably wicked, idolatrous people who did things so vile in the **name** of their "gods" that destruction was the only possible purging.

This, then, has led to such questions as, "What is the Christian's place in war?" or, "Is there such a thing as a 'just' war?" Referring to our Revolutionary **War** (or the "War of Independence," since the colonies had already been forced out of the empire by an act of Parliament and were a free nation[325]), Thomas Paine wrote, "If there was ever a just war since the world began, it is this in which America is now engaged."[326] He, as well as Puritans of that day, spoke not of *revolt* against an established government but *resistance* against invasion.[327]

Likewise, despite a few critics in that era, how could any honest person say World **War** II, waged against incomprehensible **evil**, was not just? A generation before, Sergeant Alvin York, a devout Christian, struggled with going to **war**, but ultimately did so (and won the Congressional Medal of Honor), because he felt that fighting evil was just.

Certainly, no godly person *wants* **war**, but there *is* "a time of war, and a time of peace" (Eccles. 3:8), and evil—whether personified by **King** George III or Adolf Hitler—calls for a **time** of **war**.

Scriptures for Study: In preparation for tomorrow's study, read what **David** said about his spiritual warfare: Psalms 18:35–42; 27:1–3; 144:1, 2.

War (2)

milchāmāh

Far more important than the terrifying reality of *physical* **war** is the need to recognize the existence of a *spiritual* **war**. While some Christians might register as "conscientious objectors" there is no such alternative for the spiritual **war** that has existed since the Garden of Eden. Every Christian is a soldier in God's army. The question that remains is, "Am I a good one?"

Yesterday's "Scriptures for Study" revealed a few of David's battles. The Greek commonly used to translate *milchāmāh* in the Septuagint is *polemos* (4171G), which usually refers to physical **war**, as in its first NT occurrence about "wars and rumours of wars" in the last days (Matt. 24:6). In contrast, *strateia* (4752G), which refers to military service, warfare, or military campaign, is used of this spiritual **war**, as Paul declares, "For the weapons of our warfare are not carnal, but mighty through God to the pulling down of strong holds" (2 Cor. 10:4), and also warns Timothy, "war a good warfare; Holding faith" (1 Tim. 1:18, 19).

The most graphic passage on the Christian's spiritual warfare, of course, is Ephesians 6:10–20 (compare in Isa. 59:17 some identical terms in reference to God). While neither the Hebrew or Greek word above appears there, the **image** is no less clear and graphic. How critical it is that we understand the **war** in which we are engaged! While President Harry Truman called the Korean **War** a "police action," it was no such thing, and neither is the Christian **life**. Nor is it a "border dispute," "pacification," or any such euphemism. It is an all-out **war** to the **death**. Satan's desire is to **destroy** you, so you must "put on the whole armour of God" (Eph. 6:11). "Whole armour" is *panoplian* (3833G), from *pas* (3956G), "all or whole," and *hoplon* (3606G), "weapon," so we are to take "all the weapons," both offensive and defensive, employed by the heavily armed Roman soldier.[328]

As mentioned yesterday, Plato wrote, "Only the dead have seen the end of war," but he did not **know** what is to come. Eventually "wars [will] cease" (Ps. 46:9) and the trappings of **war** will be destroyed (Ps. 46:9; Isa. 2:1–5; Mic. 4:1–5). Nevertheless, until then let us, with Paul, "[fight] a good fight . . . [finish our] course . . . [and keep] the faith" (2 Tim. 4:7).

Scriptures for Study: How is God referred to in Exodus 15:3 and 1 Samuel 17:26, 45? 🕮 What does 1 Samuel 17:47 add? 🕮 Does all this encourage you, and if so, how?

Safety (1)
beṭach

David wonderfully pictures the meaning of our **word** for today: "I will both lay me down in peace, and sleep: for thou, LORD, only makest me dwell in safety" (Ps. 4:8). **Safety** is *beṭach* (983), which when used as a noun, as it is here, indicates security and calm assurance.

The first occurrence of *beṭach* is actually a tragic one. Genesis 34 records Dinah's rape and her brothers' revenge. Because of their cruel deception and even blasphemous misuse of the **covenant sign** (**circumcision**), Simeon and Levi were able to enter the Canaanite city "boldly" (that is, securely, without being intercepted) and kill all the incapacitated males (v. 25). While the provocation was certainly great, such ruthlessness cannot honor **God**, and as a result their descendants were dispersed throughout the nation of Israel (49:5–7).

How much more sanctified, then, is David's use of this word! His security was not in treachery and pragmatic plotting, rather simply in God's presence in his **life**. Our text, of course, is the last verse in this **psalm**, but the rest of it demands our attention. Let us note three principles that demonstrate the difference **prayer** makes:

First, David *prays* to God for *defense*: ". . . thou hast enlarged me when I was in distress; have mercy upon me, and hear my prayer" (Ps. 4:1). We should note here that the NIV mistranslates the Hebrew. It reads, "Give me relief" (which would be a Hebrew *imperative* [command]) instead of, "Thou hast enlarged me," which is a Hebrew *perfect*. Very simply stated, the term "perfective" is the preferred description, which expresses the totality, completeness, even the perfection, of an action. David is not *commanding* God to **enlarge** (*rāchab*, May 26) him, rather *acknowledging* that God has already done so and prays that God will continue to do so by His **mercy**.

Second, David *pleads* with his enemies about their *danger* (vv. 2–5). Coupled with Psalm 3, most commentators **observe** that the historical setting is David's flight from his son Absalom (2 Sam. 15:1–18:33). "How long will you continue in your sin?" he asks, in effect. "How long will you continue in your vanity [or 'delusion', *riyq*, 7385] and lies ['leasing' is *kāzāḇ*, 3577]? God is on my side, and you will be defeated and judged unless you stop your sin and 'commune' with God."

We will conclude tomorrow, but let us be encouraged that our **safety** is in God's hands.

Scriptures for Study: What is David's testimony in Psalm 16:9 (**hope** is *beṭach*)? 🕮 What is the background of 78:53 ("safely")?

Safety (2)

beṭach

Concluding our **meditation** on *beṭach* in Psalm 4:8, we see *third* that **David** *praises* **God** for *discernment* (vv. 6–8). He understood the great difference between knowing ***good*** and knowing *God.* Like the rendering of verse 7 in the modern *Tanakh*[329] (Jewish Bible)—"Oh, for good days!"—countless people want the *blessings* God gives but want nothing to do with the *Benefactor* Himself. Oh, yes, they want the *harvest,* but they don't want the *Husbandman* (John 15:1). David knew the difference and rejoiced in His **heart** that He had both.

In reading Charles Spurgeon's exposition of this **psalm** in his *The Treasury of David,* one cannot help but be struck by his quotation of Robert Stephen Hawker's (1803–75) reflections on it:

"Reader! let us never lose sight of the Lord Jesus while reading this psalm. He is the Lord our righteousness; and therefore, in all our approaches to the mercy seat, let us go there in a language corresponding to this which calls Jesus the Lord our righteousness. While men of the world, from the world are seeking their chief good, let us desire his favour which infinitely transcends corn and wine, and all the good things which perish in the using. Yes, Lord, *thy favour is better than **life** itself.* Thou causest them that love thee to inherit substance, and fillest all their treasure.

"Oh! thou gracious God and Father, hast thou in such a wonderful manner set apart one in our nature for thyself? Hast thou indeed chosen one out of the people? Hast thou beheld him in the purity of his nature,—as one in every point godly? Hast thou given him as the covenant of the people? And hast thou declared thyself well pleased in him? Oh I then, well may my soul be well pleased in him also. Now do I know that my God and Father will hear me when I call upon him in Jesus' name, and when I look up to him for acceptance for Jesus' sake.

"Yes, my heart is fixed, O Lord, my heart is fixed; Jesus is my hope and righteousness, the Lord will hear me when I call. And henceforth will I both lay me down in peace and sleep securely in Jesus, accepted in the Beloved; for *this is the rest wherewith the Lord causeth the weary to rest, and this is the refreshing.*"

Scriptures for Study: What are God's promises in Proverbs 1:33 ("safely" is *beṭach*) and 10:9 ("surely")?

Awake

'ûr

One pastime I enjoy is bird watching, especially hummingbirds, which I have studied at some length. If there is one thing that is true of birds, it is that when they are **awake** they are busy. That is the **image**, in fact, of the first occurrence of the Hebrew *'ûr* (5782), which means "to stir, arouse, or awaken": "As an eagle stirreth up her nest, fluttereth over her young, spreadeth abroad her wings, taketh them, beareth them on her wings: So the LORD alone did lead him, and there was no strange god with him" (Deut. 32:11, 12). As a mother eagle is **awake** and alert, so was **God** as He led and preserved His people after leaving Egypt.

This is a recurring theme in the OT use of *'ûr*, in fact. God is not the detached God of the deist, the anemic God of Arminianism, or the clueless God of Open Theism. Rather, God is all-knowing and is actively involved with His Creation. He is, indeed, sovereign, working out all things after the **counsel** of His own will. He "stirred up" the **king** of Assyria against the Transjordan tribes (1 Chron. 5:26), "[raised] up" the Babylonians against Jerusalem (Ezek. 23:22), and in turn "[stirred] up" the Medes against the Babylonians (Isa. 13:17; cf. Jer. 50:9, 11; 51:11). Further, on behalf of His people, God "stirred up" King Cyrus' **heart** to make his historic proclamation (2 Chron. 36:22, 23; Ezra 1:1, 2), and He "stirred up the spirit of Zerubbabel . . . [the] governor of Judah" to complete the construction of the second **temple** (Hag. 1:14).

While from our impatient viewpoint God seems to be sleeping, as the psalmist thought several times (7:6; 35:23; 44:23), He "shall neither slumber [briefly] nor sleep [soundly at length]" (Ps. 121:4). It is we who must **awake**. Three times **David** uses *'ûr* in Psalm 57:8: "Awake up, my glory; awake, psaltery and harp: I myself will awake early" (cf. 108:2). "No sleepy verses and weary notes shall be heard from," Spurgeon writes. "Three times the Psalmist calls upon himself to awake. Do we need so much arousing, and for such work? Then let us not spare it, for the engagement is too honourable, too needful to be left undone or ill done for want of arousing ourselves."[330] How important it is to start the **day** with the **Lord**!

Scriptures for Study: Read Matthew 26:36–41 and ponder the challenge it gives us. 🕮 What should we be doing instead of sleeping (1 Thess. 5:6)?

Sow [and] Seed (1)

zāraʻ [and] zeraʻ

Occurring fifty-six times and with equivalents in Akkadian and other Semitic languages, the verb *zāraʻ* (2232) means "to sow, scatter seed, or make pregnant." Its first occurrence graphically depicts its literal use, where we find both verb and noun side by side: "God said, Let the earth bring forth grass, the herb yielding [verb *zāraʻ*] **seed** [noun *zeraʻ*, 2233, occurring about 230 times], and the fruit tree yielding fruit after his kind, whose **seed** [*zeraʻ*] is in itself, upon the earth" (Gen. 1:11).

These were, of course, important words in the agrarian economy of the ancient Near East, and we find many references to the sowing of crops (e.g., 26:12; Exod. 23:10; Lev. 25:3; Isa. 37:30; Jer. 12:13). We see it also in reference to human conception, as in Numbers 5:28, where a **woman** "shall conceive [*zāraʻ*] seed [*zeraʻ*]," as well as in the concept of the **seed** of human posterity (Gen. 4:25; 9:9; 21:13; Deut. 1:8; Ps. 89:4).

It is the metaphorical use of these words, however, that are particularly striking. **God** is said to have sowed Israel in the land (Hosea 2:23) and even in her present dispersion (Zech. 10:9). Because the basic concept of sowing **seed** speaks of reproduction and growth, moral **good** and **evil** are also pictured in this way, such as the positives of justice (Prov. 11:18) and righteousness (Hosea 10:12), and the negatives of iniquity (Prov. 22:8), wickedness (Job 4:8), and idolatry (Isa. 17:10, "set").

It is that latter thought that leads to our application—the **law** of sowing and reaping. The Septuagint and NT equivalents of these words are *sperma* ("sperm," 4690G) and *speirō* (4687G). We find them together, for example, in the parable of the wheat and tares, where the "kingdom of heaven is likened unto a man which sowed [*speirō*] good seed [*sperma*] in his field" (Matt. 13:24).

It is then Galatians 6:7, 8 (*speirō*) that declares that foundational law (rooted in the OT—Job 4:8; Prov. 11:18; Hosea 10:12–13): "Be not deceived; God is not mocked: for whatsoever a man soweth, that shall he also reap. For he that soweth to his flesh shall of the flesh reap corruption; but he that soweth to the Spirit shall of the Spirit reap life everlasting." Sadly, society—driven by humanistic and behaviorist psychology—denies this law. **Man** thinks he can live the way he wants with no consequences, but he deceives himself and mocks God. We will go a little deeper **tomorrow**.

Scriptures for Study: What is the contrast and promise in Proverbs 11:18? 📖 What is the warning of Hosea 8:7?

Sow [and] Seed (2)

zāra‘ [and] zera‘

The Akkadian equivalent of today's words is *zēru*, which means "cultivated land," for that is where all this sowing and reaping take place. "Thus," as one authority sums up, "the whole agricultural cycle is practically summed up in the word *zera‘*; from the act of sowing to the seed planted, to the harvest taken."[331]

It is that thought that captures our attention. While the world recognizes this reality in the physical realm, it ignores it in the spiritual. With Galatians 6:7, 8 as the backdrop, let us consider five laws of sowing and reaping that apply to both realms:

First, there is the **law** of *perpetuity*. Throughout the ages, the law has been that you **sow** what you reap and reap what you **sow**. This is impossible to alter and inescapable in consequence.

Second, there is the law of *posterity*. As the offspring of a progenitor will continue to be the same to the furthest generation, each of us will reap the same in kind as what we **sow**. This is true not only physically (Gen. 1:11, 12, 24, 25) but spiritually. If we **sow** to the flesh (*sarx*, 4561G)—that is, our selfish inclinations, self-centered perversity and propensity, and the desire for self-gratification and self-satisfaction that are inherent in our moral nature (Rom. 7:18–25)—we will reap more of the same.

Third, there is the law of *proliferation*. We always reap far more than what we **sow**. As the expression goes, "Anyone can count the seeds in an apple, but only God can count the apples in a seed." While the *reward* for *service* is great, so is the *recompense* for ***sin***. As Proverbs 22:8 declares, "He that soweth iniquity [*‘ewel*, 5766] shall reap vanity [*'āwen*, July 12]." If we may paraphrase the translation: "He that sows what is contrary to right reaps trouble and wickedness."

Fourth, there is the law of *proportion*. As Paul explains, "He which soweth sparingly shall reap also sparingly; and he which soweth bountifully shall reap also bountifully" (2 Cor. 9:6).

Fifth, there is the law of *postponement*. We reap in a different season than we **sow**. As the farmer must wait awhile for the harvest, so must we, but the wait is worth it (cf. Prov. 11:18). For the sinner, **God** in His **mercy** postpones judgment, but let no one think that it will never come (cf. Num. 32:23).

Scriptures for Study: What is the promise of Psalm 97:11? 🕮 Review May 22 (**light**, *'ôr*) and March 7 (**joy**, *śimchāh,*) for more insight into this verse.

Sow [and] Seed (3)

zāra' [and] zera'

Two verses that simply cannot be passed by when thinking on this subject of sowing and reaping are Psalm 126:5, 6: "They that sow in tears shall reap in joy. He that goeth forth and weepeth, bearing precious seed, shall doubtless come again with rejoicing, bringing his sheaves with him." It is generally believed that this **psalm** was penned by Ezra (or perhaps Haggai and/or Zechariah) upon the nation's **return** from the Babylonian captivity. Naturally, upon their return there were no crops to harvest; it would take trouble, toil, and tears to replant and wait for the yield.

As most Bible students intuitively recognize, there is a **wonderful** spiritual application here. In light of the parable of the sower and the **seed** in Matthew 13, the **Word** of **God** is the **seed** we are all to spread everywhere we go, which in turn falls on four types of soil. This verse, therefore, reveals two principles about our going forth to **sow** the most "precious seed" of all:

First, there is a time for *weeping*. Why would the farmer weep as he went into the field? There could have been several reasons. Perhaps the soil was bad or the weather too severe at times. Past disappointments, such as poor harvest in previous years, would also promote frustration and discouragement. Perhaps there were even enemies who attacked workers or poisoned water sources. Spiritually speaking, all those troubles will plague all Christian workers in their **witness** for Christ.

While there is a certainly a danger of emotionalism and sentimentality, we must not lose sight of the need to weep over souls. Our **Lord** wept over a single **man** (Lazarus, John 11:35), a nation (Israel, Luke 19:41), and the entire world (22:41–44), and there is certainly cause for us to do the same today.

Second, there is a time for *reaping*. Reaping cannot come without the weeping. It is here, then, we see the promise that we "shall *doubtless* come again with rejoicing, bringing" the harvest (Ps. 126:6, emphasis added). This does not imply that it is our methods of evangelism or even our efforts in general that "get results." All we can do is plant and water, while it is God who gives the increase (1 Cor. 3:6, 7). What it does ensure, however, is that God *will* give His sovereign increase to those who **labor** and weep. What rejoicing there will be!

Scriptures for Study: Read the parable of the sower (Matt. 13:1–8; 18–23) and prepare yourself to go forth and **bear precious seed**.

Strive (Plead)

riyb̲

The Hebrew verb *riyb̲* (7378; noun, 7379) is a fascinating one. Occurring about sixty-five times, its primary meaning is "to strive physically in combat (Exod. 21:18; Judg. 11:25) but also means "to plead or make a charge in a legal case." Its first appearance, in fact, portrays this, where "the herdmen of Gerar did strive with [or brought charges against] Isaac's herdmen" (Gen. 26:20, also "strove" in 21, 22). Likewise, our own legal system is often referred to as an "adversarial process." This **word** is also used several times to indicate God's "case" against His rebellious people (e.g., Isa. 3:13; Mic. 6:1).

A wonderfully striking verse here is Psalm 119:154, where **David** asks the **Lord**, "Plead my cause, and deliver me." He used this word again in the same way in reference to his conflict with Saul, and Saul's pursuit of him: "The LORD therefore be judge, and judge between me and thee, and see, and *plead my cause*, and deliver me out of thine hand" (1 Sam. 24:15, emphasis added). He uses it still again in Psalm 35:1: "*Plead my cause*, O LORD, with them that strive with me: fight against them that fight against me" (emphasis added). David says, in effect, using legal phrasing heard today, "Lord, please take my case. No one else will defend me. No one else will even touch this case."

Here is a clear OT illustration of a NT truth. The **wonderful** Greek word *paraklētos* (3875G) appears five times, all in John's **writing**. Four of its appearances refer to the Holy Spirit as our "Comforter" (John 14:16, 26; 15:26; 16:7, 8), and the final one refers to the Lord Jesus as our "Advocate" (1 John 2:1). The prefix *para* means "alongside" and is used in such English words as *parallel* (lines that are alongside one another). The root *klētos* (from *kaleō*, "to call") speaks of "one who is called." In Classical Greek, *paraklētos* literally means "one who is called alongside to aid" and was originally used in the court of justice to show legal assistance. Our English word *paraclete* carries much the same idea. The Comforter pleads our case *inwardly on earth* by teaching (John 14:26), empowering for **witness** (15:26, 27), and convicting (16:7, 8), and the Advocate pleads our case *outwardly in* ***heaven*** by declaring that He died for those acts of **sin** we still commit.[332]

Scriptures for Study: Note the following occurrences of *riyb̲* and **rejoice** that God has "taken your case": Psalm 43:1; Proverbs 23:10, 11.

Sodom [and] Sodomite

sed̲ōm [and] qād̲ēš

The **name** of the infamous city **Sodom** derives directly from the Hebrew *sed̲ōm* (5467), which, as Augustus Strong tells us, is "from an unused root meaning to scorch" and describes a "burnt (i.e., volcanic *or* bituminous) district." Once thought to have existed at the north end of the Dead Sea, most scholars now believe that it (along with the other four cities of the plain: Gomorrah, Admah, Zeboiim, and Zoar) were actually located at the southern end in the **Valley** of Siddim (Gen. 14:2, 3). As a result of their destruction, the area now is nothing but a burnt-out wasteland of **oil** and asphalt (v. 10). Visible until about first century AD, the rising water of the Dead Sea has claimed the whole area, although bitumen deposits can still be found today.

Even to many nonreaders of the Bible, the city of **Sodom** is infamous. It was destroyed because of its unspeakable sins, although the same sins rage today with hardly an outcry from society. The **word *sodomite,*** in fact, is *qād̲ēš* (6945, a derivative of *qād̲aš*, January 20), which while denoting something "holy or consecrated," the question is, Consecrated to what? In the context of the pagan **temple**, the word was used of a **man** who was set apart for temple service, that is, a male prostitute (Deut. 23:17; 1 Kings 14:24; 15:12; 22:46). In light of the homosexual **sin** of **Sodom** (Gen. 19:4, 5; also Lev. 18:22, 29; 20:13; Rom. 1:24, 26, 28; 1 Cor. 6:9; 1 Tim. 1:10), it seems clear that such men were homosexual, or at least bisexual, prostitutes.

It is because of such sin, as well as the tremendous prosperity of **Sodom** to which Lot was drawn (Ezek. 16:49), as we will see tomorrow, that **Sodom** serves as the quintessential **image** of the world and all that is a part of it. **Sodom**, in fact, is practically synonymous with a whole catalog of sins: idolatry, fornication, homosexuality, materialism, hedonism, secularism, and the list goes on.

Sodom stands, therefore, as one of the most graphic warnings in **Scripture**. As **God** "[turned] the cities of Sodom and Gomorrha into ashes . . . making them an ensample [example] unto those that after should live ungodly" (2 Pet. 2:6), "suffering the vengeance of eternal fire"(Jude 7), He will do the same to those who follow. We must not only **preach** the gospel to the world, but also be careful that we do not become tainted.

Scriptures for Study: How are **Sodom** and Gomorrah used as an analogy in Mark 6:7–13?

Pitched [His] Tent

'āhal

The Hebrew *'ōhel* (168, May 3) means "tent" and is used in this literal sense as the home of nomadic peoples, such as the Genesis patriarchs (Gen. 4:20; 9:21; 13:5; 25:27) and soldiers (1 Sam. 17:54). The **word** *'āhal* (167) is a verb that simply means "pitch one's tent." While the word is rare in the OT, appearing only three times (Gen. 13:12, 18; Isa. 13:20), one of those occurrences is extremely significant and serves as a solemn warning.

Lot is one of the most graphic examples in **Scripture** of a **man** who *loved* the world and *longed* for its wonders. He had spent time in Egypt, and he liked what he saw. As he entered the land of Canaan with his uncle Abraham, who in turn allowed his nephew the choice of what land to take, "Lot lifted up his eyes, and beheld all the plain of Jordan, that it was well watered every where . . . *like the land of Egypt* (Gen.13:10, emphasis added; cf. 1 John 2:16). We can just picture Lot standing there gazing on that breathtaking land, reminiscing about the beauty and plenty of Egypt, and then saying, "Ah, I want *that*!" Mark it down: What the **heart** *loves*, the eyes *lust* for.

Sadly, that is hardly the end of the story, for it is just two verses later we read, "Lot dwelled in the cities of the plain, and pitched his tent toward Sodom." Indeed, while Abraham could take Lot out of Egypt, he could not take Egypt out of Lot. Steadily, step after step, and oblivious to what was to come, Lot moved gradually toward disaster. His journey, in fact, appears to be one that had not even a moment's hesitation: He *looked* toward **Sodom** (Gen. 13:10), he *moved* toward Sodom (v. 12), he *arrived* in Sodom (14:12), and finally even became *part* of Sodom as a city official (19:1, October 22).

Dear Christian **Friend**, Lot's journey into disaster was not unique. On the contrary, it simply **proved** an axiom: *Complicity* with the world *courts* disaster. Note that even what Abraham acquired in Egypt caused problems. His (and Lot's) **wealth** divided the family (13:5, 6), and the Egyptian servant Hagar and her son Ishmael brought incalculable misery (16:1–16) that rages to this **day** with the Arab **nations**.

Oh, let us never pitch our tent toward Sodom!

Scriptures for Study: What does James say about the world (James 4:4; cf. Rom. 8:7)? 📖 What is John's **counsel** on this matter (1 John 2:15–17)?

Descend (Go Down)

yāraḏ

Used literally, the Hebrew *yāraḏ* (3381) simply speaks of the mundane ideas of coming down a **mountain** (Exod. 19:14), birds descending from the air (Hosea 7:12), moving from any higher point to a lower one, as when Rachel "went down unto the well" (Gen. 24:45), and so forth. Most of its some 350 occurrences, in fact, refer to such literal movement, including **God** descending onto Mount Sinai to give His revelation (Exod. 19:11–25; 34:5), and to the tabernacle to be with His people (Num. 12:5).

The figurative idea of descending, however, is of great significance. This is probably due partly to the general human perception that "up" is **good** and "down" is bad (e.g., going down into a pit or up out of it; Ps. 28:1; 30:3). How graphic this is with Sampson and his **father**, *yāraḏ* appearing five times of their going down to Timnah to secure Samson's **marriage** to a pagan (Judg. 14:1, 5, 7, 10, 19).

One of the most striking (and sad) instances of this figurative use of *yāraḏ* appears in Genesis 12:10: "And there was a famine in the land: and Abram went down into Egypt to sojourn there." Even though Jerusalem was elevated, requiring one to literally "go up" to get there, going up to Jerusalem also pictured going up to God's presence and blessing. In contrast, to **go down** to Egypt was to **descend** once again into the world (note the warnings of Isa. 30:1, 2 and 31:1). But sadly, that is what we read of Abraham. Instead of trusting in God's promises, he runs to the world for help. How often we do the same!

First, like Abraham, we run to Egypt for *provision*. Instead of waiting on God, being satisfied with what He gives, we take that second job, live beyond our means, and do whatever it takes to "get ahead." But such bait hides the trap.

Second, we run to Egypt for *prosperity*. Mark it down: If you rely on the world, you will never be satisfied; you will always **want** more. There are many "prosperity teachers" in the church today, but as noted yesterday, the prosperity Abraham acquired in Egypt accomplished nothing good.

Third, we run to Egypt but find only *paganism*. Like many ancient lands, Egypt was one with the vilest of pagan **worship**. But we must never be complicit with idolatry (July 7). We are only "*strangers* in the land of Egypt" (Acts 13:17, emphasis added)—not *citizens* (June 29).

Scriptures for Study: What is the big difference between Abraham's going down to Egypt and Jacob's doing so (Gen. 46:1–4)?[333]

Gold

zāhāḇ

An interesting, if not even paradoxical, feature of the **word *gold*** in **Scripture** is that while it is a rare commodity, therefore difficult to obtain, it is also one of the most frequently mentioned, occurring some 420 times. The vast majority of these occurrences (about 390) are in the OT and are translations of the Hebrew *zāhāḇ* (2091).

In the literal sense, of course, *zāhāḇ* refers to the **precious** metal (usually the raw ore), which we find scores of times (e.g., Gen. 2:11, 12, first occurrence; 13:2; 24:35; Josh. 7:21; Job 28:17; Jer. 10:9; Ezek. 27:22). But the figurative meanings of *zāhāḇ* are the key to **understanding** its profound biblical significance:

First, and most obviously, **gold** implies **wealth** and **power**. Several powerful individuals are referred to as possessors of **gold**, including: Abraham (Gen. 13:2), Joseph (41:42), Xerxes (Esther 4:11), and Mordecai (8:15). It is also significant that because the wise men sought the "king of the Jews," one of the gifts they brought was **gold** (Matt. 2:2, 11; the Greek equivalent of *zāhāḇ* is *chrusos*, 5557G).

Second, **gold** suggests superiority. Whenever a writer wanted to suggest superiority, in fact, he used **gold**. The **Shulamite maiden** used **gold** in her description of her beloved (Song of Sol. 5:11, 14, 15), and **gold** is used in calculating the value of **wisdom** (Job 28:15). But most significantly, as valuable as **gold** is, it does not compare with the value of God's Word (Ps. 19:10; 119:72). Psalm 119:127 is especially significant. **David**, a **man** of enormous wealth, writes, "I love thy commandments above gold; yea, above fine gold." While **gold** (*zāhāb*) refers to **gold** ore, "fine gold" (*paz*, 6337) refers to **pure**, refined **gold**, an even scarcer commodity. Indeed, true wealth is not in the *world*, rather it is in the *Word*.

Third, **gold** suggests permanence and indestructibility. One reason wealth is dangerous is because the natural tendency is to look to it for security (cf. Matt. 19:23, 24). Job recognized that **gold** was neither his **hope** nor his "confidence" (31:24), and Ezekiel warned that **gold** could not satisfy (7:19). In contrast, true indestructibility is found in **heaven**, which is made of pure transparent **gold** (Rev. 21:18, 21), and real treasure is in the spiritual riches of Christ (1 Cor. 3:11–15).

Take some time today to examine your **life** and determine where your treasure is (Matt. 6:19–21; Col. 3:2).

Scriptures for Study: What commodity does Peter say is more important than **gold** (1 Pet. 1:7)? 🕮 Note how this worked out in the lives of the following Bible characters: Job 23:10; Zechariah 13:9; Malachi 3:3.

Silver

kesep̱

Second only to **gold**, **silver** is another graphic **image** of value and **wealth** in **Scripture**. In its literal use, *kesep̱* (3701)—which appears about 400 times and has equivalents in several other Semitic languages, including Akkadian and Aramaic—refers to **silver** ore (Job 28:1; Prov. 2:4) or that which was made from it. The latter included vessels (1 Kings 10:21), jewelry (Gen. 24:53), and currency (Gen. 20:16; Exod. 21:32).

Again, while not as rare (and therefore **precious**) as gold, **silver** was still valuable and was often used to refer to someone's wealth. Its first occurrence, for example, describes Abram as being "very rich in cattle, in silver, and in gold" (Gen. 13:2; cf. 42:25).

This leads to another crucial symbol in **silver** (as well as in gold), namely, the ***temptation*** *to greed*. Being somewhat more easily obtained than gold, **silver** was an ideal commodity for building wealth. Selling Joseph to Midianite traders for twenty pieces of **silver** was easy money for his twelve brothers (Gen. 37:28), not to mention Judas' similar act concerning our **Lord** (Matt. 26:15). Likewise, **Achan** yielded to the temptation of quick wealth, **silver** playing a major part (Josh. 7:21, 22, 24, see April 29, 30).

To go one step deeper, such acts also illustrate the inseparable link between man's *insatiable lust* for wealth and his *innate leaning* toward idolatry. Idols were often made of **silver** (Deut. 29:16, 17; Ps. 135:15; Hosea 8:4; Acts 19:24). In their conquest of the Promised Land, **God** commanded the people to burn every **idol** they found and not to "desire the silver or gold that [was] on them, nor take it unto [them], lest [they] be snared therein" (Deut. 7:25). Omri, one of the most wicked kings in Israel's history, used **silver** to buy the city of Samaria, which he immediately dedicated to idolatrous **worship** (1 Kings 16:24, 25, 32; cf. Hosea 8:5, 6; Mic. 1:5–7).

Centuries later, nothing has changed. **Man** still worships chiefly at the **altar** of wealth: "For the love of money is the root of all evil" (1 Tim. 6:10). Take any issue, any practice, and just start tracing it back. As you peel back the layers, you will ultimately uncover greed. Colossians 3:5 declares that covetousness is actually idolatry, the worship of a false god.

In stark contrast, "Happy is the man that findeth wisdom, and the man that getteth understanding. For the merchandise of it is better than the merchandise of silver, and the gain thereof than fine gold" (Prov. 3:13, 14).

Scriptures for Study: What commodities are far more important than wealth in Proverbs 8:10, 10:20, and 22:1?

Tithe

ma'aśēr

For the Christian, any discussion of money must inevitably **lead** to talk of stewardship. At the foundation of OT stewardship, of course, was the **tithe**. The Hebrew *ma'aśēr* (4643), which occurs about thirty times, means "tenth part" and is believed to be a derivative of the root *'sr*, which in turn is related to the Arabic verb *'ashara*, "to form a group." Perhaps it is then because the basic group (or collection) of all is the ten fingers of the **hand**, the essential idea in the word group became "ten."[334]

Tithing, then, is the giving of ten percent of one's income and goods for religious purpose. This practice was not unique to the Mosaic **Law**. In fact, it not only predates the Law—Abraham paid tithes to **Melchizedek** (Gen. 14:17–20, May 11), and Jacob tithed his property to **God** after his **vision** at Luz (28:22)—but it even existed in other peoples, such as the Egyptians and Mesopotamians.

With the coming of the Mosaic Law, then, several tithes were prescribed, which, when totaled, amounted to about twenty-three percent. Ten percent was given for the Levites (Lev. 27:30) because they received no land **inheritance** or other means of support, another 10 percent was set aside to sustain the national feasts and holidays (Deut. 14), and an additional **tithe** was collected each third year for a benevolence fund (14:28, 29). In reality, these were not freewill offerings, but rather taxes to operate the government, just as Christians are required to pay their taxes (Rom. 13:6).

So what about the Christian's giving? Some Bible teachers insist that tithing is a **good** place to start. The NT standard for giving is far superior and is summarized in 1 Corinthians 16:2: "Upon the first day of the week let every one of you lay by him in store, as God hath prospered him." The word "prospered" in this verse comes from the Greek *euodoō* (2137G), which literally means "to prosper, make good one's journey." What, then, is at the root of our giving? It is based upon the **wonderful** journey God has provided in Christ. Such giving transcends a "cut and dried" percentage. It flows from a thankful **heart** for all God has done.[335]

Scriptures for Study: Read the definitive NT passage on Christian giving, 2 Corinthians 8 and 9. How many principles of Christian giving can you **discern** there?

Jealous (1)

qānā'

The Hebrew verb *qānā'* (7065), and the noun *qin'āh* (7068), and two other derivatives, appear eighty-seven times in the OT. The verb expresses "a very strong emotion whereby some quality or possession of the object is desired by the subject." These words are actually used not only in negative tones ("hostile and disruptive passions," Prov. 27:4), as one would think, but also in positives ones ("consuming zeal focused on one that is loved," Psalm 69:9).[336] While we will consider the positive **tomorrow**, let us today examine the negative.

The first occurrence of our root is where the Philistines "envied" Isaac because of his prosperity and forced him to leave their territory (Gen. 26:14–17). More profound was barren Rachel's envy of her sister Leah's fertility (Gen. 30:1). Such **sin** drove Rachel to sin more by her sending her maid Bilhah in to Jacob. Sadly, instead of following the example of his **father** Isaac (25:21), Jacob followed that of his grandfather Abraham (16:1–16). While this was the legal custom of the day, it was never God's design for **marriage**. It is also significant that no polygamous marriage recorded in **Scripture** is shown to be a happy one. Worse still was how jealousy drove Joseph's brothers to contemplate killing him, but then to commit the less drastic, though still unthinkable, act of selling him into slavery (37:11–36).

Such jealousy and envy, therefore, are deeply embedded, powerfully motivating, and patently destructive emotions. They can certainly never be allowed to rule in the believer's **life**. Besides destroying others, it destroys the envious person as well. Shakespeare put it well: "O, beware, my lord, of jealousy! It is the green-eyed monster which doth mock the meat it feeds on."[337]

A very special warning is also given to the believer not to be envious of sinners, who seem to *flourish* while the believer seems to *flounder*. "Envy thou not the oppressor, and choose none of his ways. For the froward is abomination to the LORD: but [God's] secret is with the righteous" (Prov. 3:31, 32; cf. 23:17). **David** adds, "Fret not thyself because of evildoers, neither be thou envious against the workers of iniquity. For they shall soon be cut down like the grass, and wither as the green herb" (Ps. 37:1, 2). Spurgeon well says: "Who envies the fat bullock the ribbons and garlands which decorate him as he is led to the shambles [slaughterhouse]?"[338]

Scriptures for Study: Read Proverbs 24:1, 2, 19, 20. What do these verses have to say about today's subject ("envious" is *qānā'*)?

Jealous (2)

qānā'

As noted **yesterday**, while there is a negative aspect of the Hebrew *qānā'*, there is also a positive, namely, a "to be filled with a consuming righteous zeal, a passionate enthusiasm, focused on one who is loved."

A key OT example of this was a husband's legitimate "jealousy" (that is, *zeal*) for his **marriage** in light of his wife's suspected adultery (Num. 5:12–31), which in turn was punishable by **death** if **proved** true (Lev. 20:10; Deut. 22:22).

All this helps us understand the many verses that speak of **God** being a **Jealous God** (*qannā'* [7067] appears in Exod. 20:5; Deut. 4:24; 5:9; and 6:15; while *qannô'* [7072] is used in Josh. 24:19 and Nah. 1:2). Since idolatry was no less than spiritual adultery (Ezek. 16:38), God repeatedly warned His people of judgment (Josh. 24:19; Ezek. 5:13; 8:3, 5; 16:38). While in His perfection God is not contaminated by the **sin** of *jealousy*, in His holiness He possesses a holy *zeal* that cannot tolerate another **love**. Like the betrayed husband, God acts from a righteous zeal.

Turning finally to the believer, we, too, can practice a righteous zeal. Elijah, in light of Israel forsaking God, testified, "I have been very jealous for the LORD God of hosts . . . I, even I only, am left" (1 Kings 19:10). Likewise, **David** wrote, "My zeal hath consumed me, because mine enemies have forgotten thy words" (Ps. 119:139). In contrast to a world much of which hates God's **Word**, how many of us can say His Word consumes everything about us, consumes our thinking and our living?

It is Psalm 69:9, however, that should captivate us: "For the zeal of thine house hath eaten me up." David is once again consumed, "eaten up," by the things of God, especially by the thought of God's **house** (that is, the **temple**), for which he had the plans and was gathering the building materials. It is extremely significant that Jesus' disciples remembered this verse during His **first** cleansing of the temple from the money changers (John 2:17).

Sadly, what can be said of churches today? Many have been defiled, having become merely places that market Jesus like any other commodity and appeal to people in whatever **way** pleases them. Oh, that Christians (and their leaders) would have a true zeal for the things of God!

Scriptures for Study: Jesus repeated the act of driving the money changers from the temple at the close of His ministry. What did He say that time (Matt. 21:13; Mark 11:17)? 📖 Read Acts 19:24–27, noting how pagans also try to make money off religion.

Kingdom

mamlāḵāh

Back on September 19 we focused on the **word *throne*** with a specific reference to 2 Samuel 7:4–17, where **God** makes His perpetual **covenant** with **David**: "And thine house and thy kingdom shall be established for ever before thee: thy throne shall be established for ever" (v. 16; cf. 2 Sam. 5:12). We return to this verse by emphasizing the word **kingdom**.

The Hebrew is *mamlāḵāh* (4467), a noun derived from the verb *mālaḵ* (4427), "to rule, be king, or make king," and noun *meleḵ* (4428), **king** (January 28), and means "the area and people that constitute a kingdom."[339] Appearing about 116 times (three of which are in our text; vv. 12, 13, and 16), it is used to refer to many kingdoms: Babel under Nimrod (Gen. 10:10, first occurrence), the Amorites under Sihon and Bashan under Og (Num. 32:33), Israel (1 Sam. 24:20), and others.

In light, then, of David's throne and **kingdom**, we consider again that God's covenant promised an *earthly* **kingdom**. It is important to note that every occurrence of *mamlāḵāh* refers to a *literal* earthly **kingdom**, not some mystical or spiritual **kingdom** that supposedly "reigns in men's hearts." It is that latter idea that is oddly held by many today concerning Christ's **kingdom**, thereby rejecting the whole idea of the literal reign of Jesus Christ on the earth during the Millennium. With a wave of an allegorical **hand**, some teachers dismiss numerous prophecies that speak of that literal **Kingdom**.

Inexplicably, for example, the literal language of Revelation 20:1–7 is arbitrarily chosen to be symbolic instead of literal. Totally ignored is that every **number** that is used in Revelation, *without exception*, is literal, not symbolic: the seven churches (chapters 2, 3); the 144,000 (the product of 12,000 times twelve, 7:1–8; 14:1); the 200,000,000 ("two hundred thousand thousand," 9:16); the "ten thousand times ten thousand, and thousands of thousands," that is, an incalculably large number (5:11; 7:9); the seven seals, the seven trumpets, and the seven bowls; the three unclean spirits of 16:13; the three angels connected with the three **last** woes (8:13); the two witnesses (11:3); the equivalency of 1,260 days and three-and-a-half years; and the twelve apostles and twelve tribes of Israel (21:12–14).

It is puzzling, indeed, why some teachers reject the very event that will result in the culmination of human history—the return of Jesus Christ to the earth to reign for a thousand years. *Soli deo Gloria!*

Scriptures for Study: Review our September 19 reading (and endnotes) and **rejoice** in the **Kingdom** that is to come.

Labor

'āmāl

While the Hebrew *'āśāh* (**work**, September 11) is a general **word** for **man** at work, *'āmāl* (5999) goes deeper to portray the hardship and drudgery of **labor** and toil. Each of its some fifty occurrences expresses the "other side" of work: its severity and grinding monotony.

Jeremiah paints in broad strokes when he writes that the toils, hardships, and sorrows of **life** start the moment we come "forth out of the womb" (Jer. 20:18). Eliphaz, one of Job's "counselors," at least was right on this point as he recognized man's inherent curse: "Man is born unto trouble, as the sparks fly upward" (Job 5:7; this is actually a beautiful Hebrew expression that literally means "the sons of flame fly up"). Moses likewise laments that life is full of **labor**, toil, and **burden**, and then life ends (Ps. 90:10). My dear, late father-in-law received many a strange look because of a bumper sticker he had on his van; it read, "Cheer up, you'll soon be dead!"

In the ultimate statement of futility, Solomon also mourns, "What profit hath a man of all his labour which he taketh under the sun?" (Eccles. 1:3), for as he looked "on the labour that [he] had laboured to do," he realized that it "all was vanity and vexation of spirit, and there was no profit under the sun" (2:11). This is further underscored by the fact that *'āmāl* appears twenty-one times in this **book** alone.

Perhaps sensing the discouragement this word could bring throughout history, Moses uses it for the first time in Genesis 41:51, and it is this first occurrence that is actually one of great encouragement. Here Joseph named his **firstborn** son Manasseh because the **joy** of that son made him forget all his toil in Egypt. The transliterated Hebrew *menaššeh* (4519), in fact, literally means "one who causes to forget," being derived from *nāšāh* (5382), "to not call to mind or to not let something dominate one's thinking."[340]

What, then, overcomes the toils of life? What will encourage you when the hardship and drudgery of the daily grind are about to overwhelm you? What gives you **peace** and joy in the midst of adversity and suffering? *God's gracious gifts and His glorious presence.* While modern psychology recommends wallowing in self-pity while blaming the past for the problems of the present, we **know** that God is "[our] defence and refuge in the day of [our] trouble [*miśgāḇ*]" (Ps. 59:16, September 7).

Scriptures for Study: What does Habakkuk say about God's character (Hab. 1:13; "iniquity" is *'āmāl*)? 🕮 Read John 16:17–28. How does it encourage you?

First

ri'šôn

Back on October 18, we noted the **word** *rē'šiyṯ*, meaning "beginning, first, or choicest." Today we consider another word (*ri'šôn*, 7223) that comes from the same root, *rō'š* (7218, **head**).

Appearing some 180 times, the primary idea in this adjective is "first in a series," such as the **first** child born, as was Esau (Gen. 25:25, note another word, *bekôr*, used specifically for **firstborn**, October 17). Another meaning in this word is "former," implying importance, such as: Joseph's former position (Gen. 40:13), "ancestors" (Lev. 26:45), the patriarchs (Deut. 19:14, "they of old times"), and "former prophets" (Zech. 1:4).

Still another concept in this word is "most prominent in a series," such as prominent people at a feast (Esther 1:14). Particularly noteworthy here is Isaiah 43:27: "Thy first father hath sinned, and thy teachers have transgressed against me." While some interpreters take this all the way back to **Adam** and others say it refers to Abraham (which is more likely), the application is the same either way. The **prophet** underscores the sad truth that Israel's beginning (if not man's in general) started with rebellion, and that fact has not changed either in Isaiah's day or our own. (Isaiah also speaks of God's prominence [44:6; 48:12], but we will examine this tomorrow.)

A verse that stands out, however, is Genesis 13:4, the second OT occurrence of *ri'šôn*: "Unto the place of the altar, which he had made there at the first: and there Abram called on the name of the LORD." Is not Abraham a little enigmatic? After all, he *forsook* Ur by God's command, had ***faith*** in God's promises, but seriously *faltered* by going to Egypt. He was trusting God one moment but self-reliant the next. But, of course, we are no less enigmatic, for we do the same.

What, then, is the **answer**? What must we do? How significant it is that upon returning from Egypt Abraham came back to the **first altar** he had built in the land of promise (12:7)! It was there he was renewed. We must do the same. Like Abraham, we live **among** pagans and can easily be drawn away from the **Lord** in attitude and action. While we have no altar as such today (see April 23), the application is no less clear: *We must come back to where we left the Lord.* As did the Prodigal Son, we will find the **Father** waiting in the same spot where we left Him.

Scriptures for Study: Read the story of young Jesus in the **temple** (Luke 2:41–50). How does it illustrate the lesson we learned today?

Last

'acharôn

Like *ri'šôn* (**first**), the Hebrew behind **last** (*'acharôn*, 314) has several shades of meaning when used in the temporal, or sequential, sense.

One such nuance is "latter of two things," as when **God**, during Moses' reluctance to **lead** the people, gave him a "first" **sign** and then a "latter" sign to convince him He would be with him (Exod. 4:8). Another idea is "last of a series of things," as when Ezra publicly read the **Law** to the people "day by day, from the first day unto the last day" (Neh. 8:18). The **word** is also used to emphasize the finality of something, as illustrated by "the last words of David . . . the sweet psalmist of Israel" (2 Sam. 23:1).

That latter idea leads right to the most important use of *'acharôn*. When used in conjunction with *ri'šôn*, as in "the first and the last," it forms an idiom of completeness. Solomon's entire history, for example—"the acts of Solomon, first and last"—are documented by the meticulous Chronicler, based on several historical authorities of that day, including the records of "Nathan the prophet" (2 Chron. 9:29).[341]

By far, the most important use of this idiom is in reference to God. It is Isaiah who emphasizes this in three places, the strongest of which declares, "Thus saith the LORD the King of Israel, and his redeemer the LORD of hosts; I am the first, and I am the last; and beside me there is no God" (Isa. 44:6; cf. 41:4; 48:12). The great John Gill well says, He is "the first cause and last end, of all things in nature, and providence, and grace; all things are of him, through him, and from him."[342]

Further, the **LORD** (*Yāhweh*) **God** (*'Elōhiym*) declares that there is no True God other than He. Whether it be the Allah of Islam, the indefinable, impersonal Brahman of Hinduism, or **man** himself in humanism, every god other than the One, True God of the Bible is false. Yes, there are many gods by ***name***, but none by *nature*, many by *claim* but none by *character*, many *replicas* but none that is *real*. All others are damning, satanic **lies**.

Is it not a blessing to **know** that **God** is the **first and the last**? Is there not indescribable assurance in knowing that He is the beginning and the end and everything in between?

Scriptures for Study: Read Isaiah's other references to the **first and the last** (41:4; 48:12). 🕮 Now read Revelation 1:8, 11; 21:6; and 22:13. What do these verses declare?[343]

Hand

yāḏ

As is true of **right hand** (August 17), the **word *hand*** (*yāḏ*, 3027), which appears some 1,600 times, also has both a literal and a deeper, metaphorical meaning. Its literal reference, of course, is to the **hand** at the end of one's **arm** that is used to perform whatever action one chooses (right or wrong). What is then significant is that the very versatility of the physical **hand** yields several theological meanings (through a plethora of idioms), which can be summarized by three principles:

First, the **hand** signifies *sovereignty*. **God** gave **man** dominion over the animals after the Flood with the phrase, "Into your hand are they delivered" (Gen. 9:2). The same basic phrase expresses Joseph overseeing Potiphar's **house** (39:3) and Moses' and Aaron's leadership of Israel (Num. 33:1), to **name** only two more examples. Most importantly, we should testify with **David** as to God's sovereign authority over us: "Into thine hand I commit my spirit: thou hast redeemed me, O LORD God of truth" (Ps. 31:5; cf. v. 15).

Second, the **hand** signifies ***strength***. In that dramatic confrontation with Pharaoh, we read twice that God told Moses to "stretch out [his] hand" to bring plagues on Egypt. But most significant again is how often this idea is used to illustrate God's strength and **power**. His **hand** created all things (Ps. 8:6; 95:5), delivered His people from Egypt (Exod. 13:3), and upholds and strengthens each of us (Ps. 37:24). We should never doubt that, as that old **song** declares, "He's got the whole world in His hands."

Third, the **hand** signifies *sanctification*. The idiom "laying on of hands," or similar wording, was a symbol first of blessing, as when Jacob put his **hand** on Ephraim's **head** (Gen. 48:17–20). This laying on of hands also indicated a commission to service, as when Moses passed leadership on to Joshua (Num. 27:18). This same symbol was passed on to the church, as called, qualified, and trained men (1 Tim. 3:1–7; 2 Tim. 2:2) are then ordained for ministry (Acts 13:1–3; 1 Tim. 4:14; 5:22).

All in all, the challenge here for us is, "Whatsoever thy hand findeth to do, do it with thy might" (Eccles. 9:10; Col. 3:23), and "Whether therefore ye eat, or drink, or whatsoever ye do, do all to the glory of God" (1 Cor. 10:31).

Scriptures for Study: Read Nehemiah 3, noting the words "next unto" (or "next to"), which appear ten times. This is *yāḏ* with the preposition *'al* (5921), so literally, "at (or by) his hand." Coupled with Nehemiah 4:6, what lessons can we learn from this?

Head

rō'š

As already noted (November 29), *rē'šiyṯ* ("beginning, first, or choicest") and *ri'šôn*, (**first**) are derived from the root *rō'š* (7218), which has equivalents in almost all Semitic languages. Besides meaning **head**, other concepts include "chief, beginning, or top." Its first of some 600 occurrences, for example, is in Genesis 2:10, where the **river** that went out of Eden separated to form the "heads" (beginnings) of four rivers. It is also used in the geographical sense to refer to the top of a hill or **mountain** (Exod. 17:9), or the top of a building (Gen. 11:4).

One of the more significant ideas in *rō'š* is to indicate the superlative, since Hebrew words themselves do not have such forms as do English words (e.g., "fast, faster, fastest," or "good, better, best"). Anointing **oil**, for instance, was made of "principal [the best, choicest, finest] spices" (Exod. 30:23).

This leads to a dominant concept in *rō'š*, namely, leadership and ruling authority. Just as the physical **head** rules the body, so metaphorically a **head** indicates such dominance. Wanting Jephthah to **lead** them, "the elders of Gilead" said, "Be our head" (Judg. 11:8). In Psalm 18:43, **David** wrote that **God** not only had "delivered [him] from the strivings of the people" in civil **war** (2 Sam. 3:1), but had also "made [him] the head of the heathen [i.e., ruler of many **nations**, 2 Sam. 8]." Likewise, tribal leaders **among** the Israelites were referred to as "heads over the people" (Exod. 18:25).

The NT adopts this same concept with the Greek *kephalē* (2776G), "the head, top, that which is uppermost in relation to something." "The head of Christ," for example, is God the **Father** (1 Cor.11:3). In other words, while there is no difference in essence, there is in order and function, so Christ submits to the Father. In the same verse, the husband is the **head** of the wife. Again, he is not superior in essence but is in authority of leadership (Eph. 5:23). Further, again in the same verse, every **man** is under the authority of Christ; Jesus is the **Head**. Further still, our **Lord** is "the head over all things to the church" (Eph. 1:22).

This principle demands that we constantly and consistently examine ourselves to ensure that we are submitted to Christ as our **Head**, both in our homes and our churches.

Scriptures for Study: In light of today's study, review our October 10 reading concerning Psalm 118:22: "The stone which the builders refused is become the head stone of the corner."

Foot (1)

regel

In the vast majority of its OT occurrences, *regel* (7272) refers to the literal, physical **foot** (or feet), whether human (e.g., Gen. 18:4; 2 Sam. 4:4) or animal (Gen. 8:9, first occurrence; Ezek. 32:13), even including insects (Lev. 11:42).

Among several metaphorical uses of *regel*, a prominent one is that of rule and dominion. Using the poetic line, "put all things under his feet," **David** portrays how **God** gave **man** "dominion over the works of" Creation (Ps. 8:6). Putting one's **foot** on the neck of a conquered enemy was also such a picture (Josh. 10:24), and such ceremonies were often depicted on Egyptian monuments. That very **image** points to God's own treading underfoot His enemies (Isa. 41:2; Lam. 3:34).

That latter image is again underscored in Psalm 47, where the psalmist celebrates the reign of the **Lord** over all the earth. In a statement that looks forward to the millennial reign of Messiah (September 19), verse 3 declares, "He shall subdue the people under us, and the nations under our feet."

Another metaphor in **foot**, and one that is of great application, is that of a journey or pilgrimage, a common image in Israel's history (e.g., Ps. 91:12; 94:18; 121:3). That image has the corollary of picturing a person's "walk," that is, his moral conduct in **life** (73:2; Job 23:11; 31:5). Especially significant in one's journey is the responsibility to spread the gospel. As Romans 10:15 declares, "How beautiful are the feet of them that preach the gospel of peace, and bring glad tidings of good things!" which quotes and fulfills the promise of Isaiah 52:7. After all, feet are not particularly attractive in themselves but become so, spiritually speaking, when they go forth proclaiming Christ.

Another wonderfully practical metaphor is that to sit at one's feet was to assume the place of student, as when God's **saints** "sat down at [His] feet" and "[received His] words" (Deut. 33:3). We see the same image in the NT, where in his training, Saul of Tarsus learned "at the feet of Gamaliel," one of the greatest of the rabbis (Acts 22:3).

It is then Luke 10:39 that provides us with the greatest illustration, where Martha's sister Mary "sat at Jesus' feet, and heard his word." Is there any place in the universe that is equal to that place?

Dear Christian **Friend**, it is there you sit every time you open God's **Word**, so take care never to neglect that opportunity.

Scriptures for Study: What are the challenges of Psalm 119:59, 101, and 105? 🕮 In preparation for tomorrow's **meditation**, read Deuteronomy 32:35.

Slide (Slip) [and] Foot (2)

môṭ [and] regel

One other significant metaphorical concept in **foot** is the danger of its slipping or sliding. While *môṭ* (4131) is most often translated "moved" in the AV, it is also rendered **slip** three times and **slide** once. Meaning "to totter, shake, or slip," it is used literally of something shaking or wavering, such as the world *not* being "removed" because **God** laid its foundations (Ps. 104:5). On the other hand, in preparation for the Millennium, Isaiah declares that "the earth is moved exceedingly" and will "reel to and fro like a drunkard" (Isa. 24:19, 20).

Of its thirty-eight occurrences, however, most of which are in Psalms and Proverbs, *môt* is most often used figuratively to denote insecurity and calamity. Calamity is especially emphasized when *môt* is used in conjunction with *regel* (**foot**). How easy it is to **slip** and fall in our spiritual walk, even when we are walking in the right path. "Hold up my goings in thy paths," **David** prayed, "that my footsteps slip not" (Ps. 17:5).

Spurgeon writes of that verse, "What! Slip in God's ways? Yes, the road is **good**, but our feet are **evil**, and therefore **slip**, even on the King's highway. Who wonders if carnal men **slide** and fall in ways of their own choosing, which, like the vale of Siddim, are full of deadly slime-pits? One may trip over an ordinance as well as over a **temptation**. Jesus Christ himself is a stumbling-block to some, and the doctrines of grace have been the occasion of offence to many. Grace alone can hold up our goings in the paths of truth."[344]

How careful we must be in our Christian walk (see also September 22)! The world, in fact, will "rejoice over [us] when [our] foot slippeth" (Ps. 38:16). "The least flaw in a saint is sure to be noticed," Spurgeon writes again; "long before it comes to a fall the enemy begins to rail, the merest trip of the foot sets all the dogs of hell barking. How careful ought we to be, and how importunate in prayer for upholding grace!"[345]

What, then, will **keep** us from slipping? One of the many reasons to "make the voice of [God's] praise to be heard" is because He allows "not our feet to be moved" (Ps. 66:8, 9). So as we each "trust in the LORD with all [our] heart; and lean not unto [our] own understanding. In all [our] ways acknowledge him, and he shall direct [our] paths" (Prov. 3:5, 6).

Scriptures for Study: What is the promise of Psalm 94:18?

Slide (Slip) [and] Foot (3)

môṭ [and] regel

Before leaving these words, we are compelled to mention one more verse. In a day when many of the facts surrounding America's founding have been obscured or rewritten, it is critical for us to be reminded of her Christian roots. As made clear in the Mayflower Compact (1620), as well as in later founding documents, America was without argument founded by godly men and upon biblical morality.

Sadly, however, a serious spiritual decline developed in New England. The city of Enfield, Connecticut, remained unmoved by revival and was perhaps the most wicked of all. To aid the ministers there, Jonathan Edwards went to Enfield and preached his now-famous sermon *Sinners in the Hands of an Angry God* during the afternoon session on Wednesday, July 8, 1741. It was a message he had actually preached a month before in his own church in Massachusetts and would **preach** again several times after Enfield.

While expositors today commonly construct a message using three or more points, Edwards had only one, namely: His listeners were not in **hell** at that very moment only because of God's "pleasure," that is, His **grace**. As has been well documented, the response was staggering. Even though Edwards spoke in a virtual monotone, demonstrating that it wasn't oratory that affected the people, they began to weep and wail in terror, some grabbing the pillars of the church in **fear** of slipping into hell. It continued through the **night**, as people throughout the city cried out to God for **mercy**, with some 400 coming to Christ. It was that event, along with the **preaching** of Whitefield, that ignited the Great Awakening.

Edwards' text was from the Song of Moses (Deut. 31:30–32:43): "To [God] belongeth vengeance, and recompence; their foot shall slide in due time: for the day of their calamity is at hand, and the things that shall come upon them make haste" (32:35). Referring to His vengeance upon the **evil** of Israel's enemies, God is saying, in effect, "At the appointed time, they will slip and fall quickly into their own doom."

While many today think such "hellfire and brimstone" preaching out of date, even cruel and damaging to people's "self-esteem," **Scripture** declares, "It is a fearful thing to fall into the hands of the living God" (Heb. 10:31), "for our God is a consuming fire" (12:29; cf. Deut. 4:24; 9:3). Let us go forth and share the gospel with those who without it will one day **slip**.

Scriptures for Study: Edwards' sermon is readily available in print and even audio. We would encourage you to read or listen to its **power**.

Hid [and] Heart

ṣāpan [and] lēḇ

In one of the most poignant and powerful verses in all of God's **Word**, **David** writes, "Thy word have I hid in mine heart, that I might not sin against thee" (Ps. 119:11). **Hid** is *ṣāpan* (6845), "to hide, keep secret." It is used of concealing something, often of great value, such as that **precious** picture of when the baby Moses was hidden (Exod. 2:2, 3) and when Rahab **hid** the spies (Josh. 2:4). Figuratively, it means "laying up in the heart, putting back that which we value." The Word of God is, indeed, priceless, the most valuable thing we can own.

Heart, then, is *lēḇ* (3820). While it refers to the physical organ, most of its some 600 occurrences refer to one's inner self and nature, including the intellect, emotions, and will—that is, the personality. So where do we hide God's Word? *In our whole personality!* The Word of God must govern all of us, our entire being.

In a sense, this verse is the key to Psalm 119 as a whole. To hide the Word of God in our hearts is to be totally *captivated by* it, *committed to* it, and *controlled through* it. To hide God's Word in one's **heart** is to recognize that it alone is sufficient to fill that **heart** with all that is needed for living.

Spurgeon well said of the psalmist: "He did not *wear* a text on his heart as a *charm*, but he *hid* it in his heart as a *rule*."[346] While many today wear a cross around their neck, some religious symbol on a charm bracelet, or other outward symbolism, the psalmist says he **hid** God's **word** in his **heart**—that is, his whole self. *Symbolism* is one thing; *substance* is quite another.

This challenges us to ask, "How much Scripture do I know? How much have I committed to memory?" The things we commit to memory will control our thoughts, values, and actions. We, therefore, need to memorize **Scripture**. There have been many methods offered to do this, although they can sometimes be either artificial or have the wrong motive behind them. Another method is simply to memorize the Scripture that God lays on your **heart**, those verses (or passages) that make the greatest impact on your **heart**—that is, your whole self.

Dear Christian **Friend**, are you hiding God's Word in your **heart**?

Scriptures for Study: Read Genesis 6:5. What is the antithesis there of hiding God's Word in our **heart**? 🕮 What does the **fool** do (Ps. 14:1, March 27)? 🕮 What does God cause us to do (Ps. 19:8)?

Nose

'ap̱

At first thought, few of us would think the **word *nose*** is of much significance. After all, it's just used for smelling, and everybody has one (whatever shape it might be). The Hebrew is *'ap̱* (639), which does refer to the literal **nose**, as in Psalm 115:6 in reference to dead, powerless idols.

The first of its some 275 occurrences is also basically literal, as **God** "breathed into [man's] nostrils the breath of life" (Gen. 2:7), a life, in fact, unique to **man** over any other creature.

The most graphic metaphorical idea in *'ap̱* is that of indicating **anger**. One fascinating verse declares, "The LORD is merciful and gracious, slow to anger, and plenteous in mercy" (Ps. 103:8; cf. Neh. 9:17). "Slow to anger" is actually *'ārēḵ* (750, "long or slow") *'ap*, an idiom that literally means "long of nose." The idiom comes from the picture of flared nostrils as a characteristic of anger. These two words are also translated "longsuffering" in several places (Exod. 34:6; Num. 14:18; Ps. 86:15). Are you not thankful that God is "long of nose"?

In stark contrast, we also read, "He that is soon angry dealeth foolishly" (Prov. 14:17). "Soon angry" is another Hebrew idiom. "Soon" is *qāṣār* (7116), which literally means "short of something," such as **power** (Isa. 37:27, "small") or days, as in "short-lived" (Job 14:1, "few"). The idiom then is "short-nosed" (short-tempered). How foolish, it is to be short-tempered because this disposition can bring disaster in an instant.

Have you ever noticed, in fact, that with very few exceptions human anger is almost always viewed in **Scripture** as bad? One notable exception appears in Exodus 32:19, where Moses' "anger" (*'ap*) "waxed hot" (*chārāh*, 2734, "to be kindled, glow with anger"). It appears that Saul, too, was justified in his righteous indignation (1 Sam. 11:6).

Paul also speaks of such "righteous anger" in Ephesians 4:26: "Be ye angry, and sin not." What is "righteous anger"? It is a settled state of mind in which there is an indignation and hatred of that which is offensive to and sinful against God, and a desire for God's justice.[347] In contrast, sinful anger is when our anger is motivated by personal anger—that is, when someone has offended us, not God.

Let us beware of what makes us "glow with anger."

Scriptures for Study: In contrast to Proverbs 14:17 (mentioned above), what does verse 29 encourage (**wrath** is *'ap*)? 🕮 What is the command and **counsel** of both Paul and James (Rom. 12:19; James 1:19, 20)?

Breath (1)

rûach [and] nešāmāh

Yesterday we touched on Genesis 2:7: "And the LORD **God** formed **man** of the dust of the ground, and breathed into his nostrils the breath of life; and man became a living soul." There is another **word** here that captures our attention. **Breath** is *nešāmāh* (5397), which refers to "breath, wind, or spirit." Along with our text, it often generally signifies the **breath** of **life** (Gen. 7:22; Job 33:4; Isa. 42:5).

Similarly, *rûach* (7307) basically means "air in motion" and appears some 387 times. While generally parallel to *nešāmāh*, there seems to be a subtle difference, namely, the former suggests "a gentler blowing," the latter often "a blast." Examples include the "blast" of a storm (Isa. 25:4) and "the four winds from the four quarters of heaven," that is, the four directions of the earth (Jer. 49:36; cf. Ezek. 37:9). Particularly striking is the blast of "wind" that assuaged the flood waters (Gen. 8:1, the details of which appear in Ps. 104:6–9), as well as the "wind" that rolled back the waters of the Red Sea (Exod. 14:21) and then rolled them back in place again (15:10; cf. Isa. 11:15; Gen. 1:2, "Spirit," first occurrence).

The contrast between these two words, especially in the figurative sense, is evident from verses where they appear together, such as, "By the blast [*nešāmāh*, "breath"] of God they perish, and by the breath [*rûach*, "blast"] of his nostrils are they consumed" (Job 4:9) and, "All the while my breath [*nešāmāh*] is in me, and the spirit [*rûach*] of God is in my nostrils" (27:3; cf. 33:4).

Isaiah 42:5 is especially notable: "Thus saith God the LORD, he that created the heavens, and stretched them out; he that spread forth the earth, and that which cometh out of it; he that giveth breath [*nešāmāh*] unto the people upon it, and spirit [*rûach*] to them that walk therein." As John Gill wrote, "Not only breath in common with the beasts of the field, and other creatures, but a rational spirit, or a reasonable soul, an intellective faculty, a capacity of understanding things."[348] (Note also how Nebuchadnezzar's "mind" [*rûach*] was "hardened in pride," Dan. 5:20.)

To whom do we owe the living, breathing spirit within us? To whom do we raise our voices in **praise** for the gift of cognitive reason? To whom do we give all the glory for the ability to **know** and understand truth? God alone, for it all comes as a blast from His sovereign **power** and glory.

Scriptures for Study: Read and meditate on the following verses: Psalms 33:6 (**breath**); 139:7 ("spirit"); 147:18 ("wind").

Breath (2)

rûach

One of the most pivotal aspects of *rûach* is its reference to **God** moving men to utter and **write** His **Word**. Ezekiel testified, "And the spirit [*rûach*] entered into me when he spake unto me, and set me upon my feet, that I heard him that spake unto me" (Ezek. 2:2). **David** also declared, "The Spirit of the LORD spake by me, and his word was in my tongue" (2 Sam. 23:2). Even the likes of a deficient **prophet** like Balaam—"the spirit of God came upon him" and controlled the message (Num. 24:2; cf. 2 Pet. 2:15; Jude 11; Rev. 2:14).

Here we encounter the doctrine of *inspiration*, one of the key doctrines in the study of **Scripture**, in fact, for without it we have no authoritative Bible. It is the very Spirit of God, His "blasting breath," that uttered His truth to men.

To those of us who believe in the inspiration of Scripture, then, it comes as no surprise that the Greek equivalent for *rûach* is *pneuma* (4151G). The Septuagint, in fact, renders *rûach* as *pneuma* in more than 260 of its 387 occurrences. To demonstrate the uncanny parallel, *pneuma* comes from the verb *pneō* (4154G). While the Greek *psuchō* (5594G), means "to breathe naturally," *pneō* is a forceful expiration of air; in the NT, in fact, it's "used only of the 'blowing' of a dangerous wind or of the south wind which brings heat (Matt. 7:25, 27; Luke 12:55; John 6:18) or the destructive winds in Revelation 7:1."[349] Additionally, while the Greek *aēr* (109G) means "to breathe unconsciously," *pneō* refers to conscious breathing.

What, then, is inspiration? *It is the forceful and conscious exhaling of God into the Scripture writers*. That is, indeed, the meaning of "God-breathed" (*theopneustos*, 2315G, 2 Tim. 3:16). It is actually the *expiration* of God, to be precise, since the word "inspiration" ("breathing *in*") comes from the corrupted Latin Vulgate (*divinitus inspirata*).

Think of it! God consciously, forcefully "blew" His very words into the Scripture writers. Does this imply that He simply "dictated" Scripture, as to a stenographer who takes down the words of the speaker? No, because every Scripture writer's own style is clearly evident. Rather, God, while allowing the writers their own style, controlled in such a **way** that the result of their **writing** was *exactly*, word for word, what He wanted written. That, in fact, is a far greater miracle.[350]

Oh, let us thank God for His inspired Word!

Scriptures for Study: Read 2 Timothy 3:1–15. Why is inspiration in verses 16 and 17 needed?

Count (Number)

sāpar

In its simplest form, *sāpar* (5608) speaks of the mundane activity of counting something, such as money (Ezra 1:8), houses (Isa. 22:10), stars (as innumerable, Gen. 15:5, first occurrence, "tell" and **number**; cf. 32:12; 41:49), and even people (2 Sam. 24:10).

In light of that last reference—David's numbering the people against God's will—we cannot help but be reminded of today's reliance upon numbers as the gauge of success. Almost prophetically, A. W. Tozer wrote about such pragmatism decades ago: "Fiction, films, fun, frolic, religious entertainment, Hollywood ideals, big business techniques, and cheap, worldly philosophies now overrun the sanctuary. The grieved Holy Spirit broods over the chaos but no light breaks forth."[351]

More significantly, another form of *sāpar* conveys the idea of "recounting," that is, declaring and telling something. Most striking here are verses that command the believer to recount (declare and tell) the great deeds of God. First Chronicles 16:24 is a prime example: "Declare [*sāpar*] his glory among the heathen; his marvellous works among all nations." The clear idea is that of recounting, even listing, the marvelous deeds God has done. As noted early in our study (January 5), one of the greatest acts of **worship** is to **remember** the things God has done. What better **way** to do that than to ***count*** them, to make a list? As the old hymn encourages, "Count your many blessings / Name them one by one / And it will surprise you / What the Lord has done."

David declares this truth in no uncertain terms: "That I may publish with the voice of thanksgiving, and tell [*sāpar*] of all thy wondrous works" (Ps. 26:7). "God's people should not be tongue-tied," Spurgeon writes. "The wonders of divine grace are enough to make the tongue of the dumb sing. . . . so the saints rejoice to tell of the great things which the Lord hath done for them."[352]

How vital it is that we then pass on such testimony to each subsequent generation, as the psalmist again challenges concerning God's **Word**, "Which we have heard and known, and our fathers have told [*sāpar*] us. We will not hide them from their children, shewing [*sāpar*] to the generation to come the praises of the LORD, and his strength, and his wonderful works that he hath done" (Ps. 78:3, 4).

Scriptures for Study: What does Psalm 139:17, 18 encourage? 📖 What, then, does 119:26 challenge ("declared" is *sāpar*)?

Lion

'ariy

Of the approximately eighty occurrences of *'ariy* (738) in the OT, only a handful refer to a literal **lion**, such as those killed by Samson (Judg. 14:5), **David** (1 Sam. 17:34, 35), and Benaiah (2 Sam. 23:20). Other instances include the **lion** that killed a disobedient **prophet** (1 Kings 13:24; 20:36), those the **Lord** sent **among** the settlers in Samaria (2 Kings 17:25), and of course those who spent the **night** with Daniel (Dan. 6:7, 12, 16, 19, 20, 22, 24, 27, Aramaic *'aryēh*, 744). These were probably of the Asiatic variety, which while smaller than the African was still quite formidable.

The remaining references to a **lion** are generally metaphorical, highlighting its various characteristics: **strength** (Judg. 14:18), boldness (2 Sam. 17:10), ferocity (Ps. 7:2), stealth (10:9; Lam. 3:10), and virtual unstoppability (Ps. 7:2; cf. 22:21). Such images prompted the prophets to describe Israel's enemies as predatory lions (Jer. 4:7; 5:6; 50:17; Ezek. 32:2; Joel 1:6). Wicked men in general are also depicted as lions (Ps. 7:1, 2; 10:9; 17:12; 22:13, 21; 57:4; 58:6).

We cannot help but mention 1 Peter 5:8 here: "Be sober, be vigilant; because your adversary the devil, as a roaring lion [*leōn*, 3023G], walketh about, seeking whom he may devour." Like a **lion**, **Satan** stalks his prey, lurks in the shadows, blends in with the tall grass, and just waits for the precise moment to pounce with the frightening savagery we've all watched on nature programs. How vital it is that we remain vigilant!

God Himself, however, is also likened to a **lion** in His sudden destructive **wrath** (Isa. 31:4; 38:13; Jer. 49:19; Hosea 5:14; 11:10; 13:7; Amos 3:8). In a day when God is viewed as "all love and no wrath," we need to be reminded (and remind others) that God is both, one who saves believers but condemns unbelievers (e.g., John 3:18).

In the same vein, we are reminded of Revelation 5:5: "Behold, the Lion of the tribe of Juda, the Root of David, hath prevailed to open the book, and to loose the seven seals thereof" (cf. Gen. 49:8–10). Occurring before the judgments of chapters 6 through 18, this verse underscores that while Christ came the first time as a *Lamb* to the *slaughter*, He will come the second time as a ***Lion*** to *devour*. Let us proclaim the coming **Lion**!

Scriptures for Study: Read the many verses cited today and meditate on their applications.

Dog

keleb̲

According to one survey, almost forty-five million American households own a **dog** as a pet.[353] Indeed, dogs are very dear to the **heart** of Western society. Sayings such as "a boy and his dog" and "man's best friend" demonstrate that dogs are far more than just pets. Very often they are like a member of the family, and to lose one to **death** brings more tears than one could imagine shedding for a mere animal.

The attitude in Eastern thought, however, couldn't be more opposite. The Hebrew *keleb̲* (3611) appears thirty-two times in the OT, but not one instance is positive and many indicate open contempt. Why?

In that day dogs were not the sweet, lovable pets of various adorable breeds we value today. Most were wild, savage scavengers (Exod. 22:31; Ps. 59:14, 15; Mark 7:27) that not only ate what is repulsive to humans (Prov. 26:11), but were one of the few animals that would even feed on human corpses (1 Kings 14:11; 21:23, 24; 2 Kings 9:10). Similarly, pigs also were wild, vicious scavengers, the quintessential picture of filth and uncleanness. Significantly, in fact, dogs and pigs are mentioned together several times (Isa. 66:3; Matt. 7:6; 2 Pet. 2:22).

To call someone a **dog**, therefore, was the height of insult. It was used as a general term for the wicked (Isa. 56:10, 11) and specifically for people who engaged in despicable acts, such as male **temple** prostitutes (Deut. 23:18; cf. Rev. 22:15) and cruel and savage enemies (Ps. 22:16, 20). This explains Paul's use of **dog** in referring to the Judaizers (Phil. 3:2); nothing is more despicable than a false mixing of **law** and **grace** (February 15).

This also explains Jesus' words, "Give not that which is holy unto the dogs, neither cast ye your pearls before swine, lest they trample them under their feet" (Matt. 7:6). As unthinkable as it would be to cast anything of value to such animals—they would just trample them into the filth—it is equally unimaginable to continue sharing the gospel or other holy truths with people who do nothing but mock, malign, and molest such spiritual riches. People do enough of this without our giving them more opportunity and even an open forum.

Heartrending as it might be, then, there will be times when you will lovingly **witness** to someone who reacts with abject scorn (Matt. 10:5–15), from whom you should **turn away** and "shake off the dust of your feet" (v. 14).

Scriptures for Study: Read Matthew 13:10–15, 34 (Ps. 78:2; cf. Isa. 6:9, 10). Why did Jesus begin speaking exclusively in parables?

Horse

sûs

One other prominent animal in **Scripture** is the **horse**, the Hebrew *sûs* (5483, see "**Horse Gate**," October 26), which appears about 140 times with equivalents in Akkadian and other Semitic languages.

There is, indeed, something special about horses. For some people, the bond between them and their **horse** is almost mystical. This goes back a long way. Believed to have been domesticated at least 4,000 years ago by nomads in Central Asia, horses demonstrate a level of cognitive skill, learning ability, and even social development. They quickly came to be used for a wide range of purposes and activities.

The chief use of horses as recorded in Scripture, of course, was **war**, and they became the primary indicator of military might. Both the Egyptians (Exod. 14:9, 23) and the Babylonians (Jer. 4:13) had many horses and chariots, as did the Syrians (1 Kings 20:20), the Philistines (2 Sam. 1:6), and the Medes and Persians (Jer. 50:42). There was no more powerful weapon or terrifying sight than charging horses and chariots.

There is, however, a striking contrast here between those **nations** and Israel. While the first mention of horses is when Joseph takes some in trade for **bread** (Gen. 47:17), we never see horses in widespread use in Israel until **David**. While he destroyed most of the Syrians' horses and chariots, and even hamstrung the 100 horses he kept, he still compromised by introducing their use (1 Chron. 18:4; cf. 2 Sam. 8:4). Worse, Solomon built this up by the thousands (1 Kings 4:26; 10:26), even building whole cities as staging areas for his chariots (9:19).

But all this was disobedience to **God**. Why? Because the Mosaic **Law** actually forbade the breeding of horses (Deut. 17:16, "multiply" is *rāḇāh* [7235], the **word** used in Gen. 1:22 and 9:1 for populating the earth). Solomon got around this by *importing* his horses from Egypt (2 Chron. 1:16, 17), but he missed the whole point.

So what *was* God's point? *He wanted His people to **trust*** Him, *not military might*. Did He not annihilate Pharaoh's horses and chariots in the Red Sea (Exod. 14:23–30)? Did He not give the victory over the Canaanite confederacy, with its mass of horses and chariots, and command Joshua to hamstring the horses and burn the chariots (Josh. 11:4–11)? Did He not cause the Kishon River to flood and sweep away Sisera's chariots and horses (Judg. 4:15; 5:4, 5, 19–22)?

It is God who is our **shield** and **sword**. We need only trust in Him.

Scriptures for Study: What is the warning of Isaiah 31:1–3 (cf. Ezek. 17:15)?

Morning

bōqer

In one of the greatest hymns of the Christian **faith**, Reginald Heber (1783–1826) wrote, "Holy, holy, holy! Lord God Almighty! / Early in the morning our song shall rise to Thee. / Holy, holy, holy, merciful and mighty! / God in Three Persons, blessed Trinity!" While most of the some 200 occurrences of *bōqer* (1242) are mundane, simply indicating **morning** as the first part of the **day** (e.g., Gen. 1:5, first occurrence), many of these are significant.

Heber's words, for example, express the biblical truth that **morning** was a time of **prayer** and **praise**. As **David** testified, "My voice shalt thou hear in the morning, O LORD; in the morning will I direct my prayer unto thee, and will look up" (Ps. 5:3; cf. 88:13). "This is the fittest time for [communication] with God," Spurgeon wrote. "An hour in the morning is worth two in the evening. While the dew is on the grass, let grace drop upon the soul. Let us give to God the mornings of our days and the morning of our lives. Prayer should be the key of the day and the lock of the **night**. Devotion should be both the morning star and the evening star."[354]

Morning was also a time of **worship**, as when barren Hannah, after vowing that if **God** would give her a male child (Samuel, "heard of God") she would dedicate him to God's service (1 Sam. 1:11–18), then "rose up in the morning early, and worshipped before the LORD" (v. 19). Likewise, **morning** was a time of **sacrifice** (Lev. 6:12; 2 Kings 3:20; 16:15; Job 1:5).

Is there any doubt that **morning** should be a very special time for the believer? It is then we are reminded "of the LORD'S mercies," that "they are new every morning," and are reminded that "great is [His] faithfulness" (Lam. 3:22, 23). The **morning** is a time to "sing of [God's] power" (Ps. 59:16) and "hear [His] lovingkindness" (143:8). As the children of Israel saw "the glory of the LORD" in the **morning** (Exod. 16:7) and saw the **manna** that came with the **morning** dew (vv. 13–15), let us be reminded each **morning** of "the bread which the LORD hath given [us] to eat" (v. 15).

Finally, every **morning** brings a **new day** and therefore renewed **hope**. Whatever we might suffer, even if it be God's chastisement, "Weeping may endure for a night, but joy cometh in the morning" (Ps. 30:5).

Scriptures for Study: Meditate on the verses cited today, and then read them again ***tomorrow*** **morning**.

Evening

'ereḇ

Evening is a beautiful **time** of the **day**. Who doesn't enjoy gazing upon a colorful sunset or perhaps watching the planets and stars "pop out" one by one? Like *bōqer* (**morning**), while the Hebrew *'ereḇ* (6153) most often speaks of **evening** as the ordinary transition between day and **night**, even those instances are significant.

One such **image** is that **evening** constitutes the end of the day's **labor** and the beginning of the night's rest: "Man goeth forth unto his work and to his labour until the evening" (Ps. 104:23). One application here is that all of us are to **work**. So foundational is the concept of work that Paul told the Thessalonians "if any would not work, neither should he eat" (2 Thess. 3:10). Such socialistic theories as "entitlements," "welfare," "redistribution of wealth," and others have destroyed every society in which they have been adopted. Karl Marx's maxim, "From each according to his abilities, to each according to his needs," is one of the most subtly destructive political dicta ever stated.

Another principle here is that while many people make their living in "shift work" and often find themselves on the "graveyard shift," this is sadly not the ideal. "Night work should . . . be avoided as much as possible," Spurgeon encouraged. "There are twelve hours in which a man ought to work: the night is meant for rest and sleep."[355] While *'ereb* itself is not used, the picture is still vivid in Genesis 3:8, where we read of the practice of our pre-incarnate **Lord** "walking in the garden in the cool of the day" with **Adam** and **Eve**.[356]

Another practical image in **evening** is provided by references to sacrificial acts and ceremonial meals, **Passover**, of course, being the most important (Exod. 12:6, 18), as well as general references to eating in the **evening** (16:8, 12, 13). In the Near East there were two meals a day, a **light** midday lunch and the main meal in the **evening** after work, *and every family member was present.* It was a vital time of relaxation and family unity.

Tragically, one survey reports that only 40 percent of American families eat meals together and even then no more than two or three times a week.[357] Worse, that **number** is decreasing. In a day of vanishing values and beliefs, the family **evening** meal is a time for sharing **life** and imparting truth as well as eating.

Scriptures for Study: Read Matthew 20:1–8, noting the best pattern for labor.

Night

laylāh

As is true of *bōqer* (**morning**) and *'ereḇ* (**evening**), *laylāh* (3915) also carries both literal and figurative meanings in its 233 occurrences. While it is used in the ordinary sense of **night** in contrast to **day** (e.g., Gen. 1:5, 14, 16, 18; Ps. 1:2), its figurative meanings are truly profound.

On the negative side, **night** is sometimes associated with trouble, turmoil, and even terror. "I am weary with my groaning," **David** wrote; "all the night make I my bed to swim; I water my couch with my tears" (Ps. 6:6; cf. 42:3; 77:2). Job likewise wrote, "Wearisome nights are appointed to me. When I lie down, I say, When shall I arise, and the night be gone? and I am full of tossings to and fro unto the dawning of the day" (Job 7:3, 4; 30:17).

On the positive side, however, and in **answer** to the negative, **night** is also a **time** of *consolation*. Even in distress, Job wrote of "God my maker, who giveth songs in the night" (Job 35:10), and the psalmist mused, "In the night his song shall be with me, and my prayer unto the God of my life" (Ps. 42:8).

Another positive is that of ***counsel***. **God** not only guided His people during the day "in a pillar of a cloud," but also during the night "in a pillar of fire" (Exod. 13:21; cf. Ps. 78:14; Isa. 4:5). God's guidance is *always* present if we but look for it. And how does He guide us today? As "the word of God came to Nathan" at **night** (1 Chron. 17:3; cf. 2 Sam. 7:4), so it should be for us as we open its pages.

One more encouraging significance of **night** is that it is a time for *communion*. Asaph wrote of his communion with the **Lord**, "I call to remembrance my song in the night: I commune with mine own heart: and my spirit made diligent search" (Ps. 77:6). David likewise communed with God at **night**, with God's **Word** at the core: "I have remembered thy name, O LORD, in the night, and have kept thy law" (119:55). A few verses later, he adds, "At midnight [i.e., middle of *laylāh*"] I will rise to give thanks unto thee because of thy righteous judgments" (v. 62).

Indeed, **night** can certainly be a time of *trouble*, but in God it is a time for *truth*.

Scriptures for Study: What are the encouragements of Psalms 91:5 and 92:2? 🕮 Note also the use of **night** in regard to the **Virtuous Woman** (Prov. 31:15, 18, February 6).

Image [and] Likeness

ṣelem [and] demûṯ

We consider two words today because of their inseparable connection. Our first **word**, ***image,*** is the Hebrew *ṣelem* (6754). It refers essentially to a representation of something. Most of its eighteen appearances refer to a literal statue that represents a god—that is, an **idol** (Exod. 20:4; 2 Kings 11:18). But it's also used in the more metaphorical sense of something having the essential nature of what it represents, as when **Adam** "begat a son in his own likeness, after his image; and called his name Seth" (Gen. 5:3).

It is that latter sense that we find in the very first occurrence of *ṣelem*, where "God said, Let us make man in our image, after our likeness" (Gen. 1:26; cf. 5:3). It is also here that *ṣelem* is coupled with our second word, **likeness**, the Hebrew *demûṯ* (1823). Appearing about twenty-five times, this word refers to something being the same pattern, shape, or form of something else (e.g., 2 Kings 16:10, "fashion"; 2 Chron. 4:3, "similitude"; Ezek. 1:10).

It has been debated whether these two words are synonymous or clearly distinct. Some early church fathers, for example, thought that while **image** pictured the physical aspect of **likeness** to **God**, **likeness** pictured the ethical.[358] It is generally accepted, however, that the words are synonymous, being used elsewhere interchangeably (*ṣelem* alone is used in Gen. 1:27, while *demûṯ* is used alone in 5:1), and are therefore used together for the sake of emphasis.

So what does it mean that **man** is made in God's essential nature, pattern, and form? For one thing, it is certainly unique from the animals. In the face of the evolutionist, humanist, and other such ilk of pseudo-truth, Bible teacher and commentator John Phillips wonderfully writes, "God does not begin with man's body and relate man to the beasts. He begins with man's moral and spiritual nature, and relates man to God. Indeed, reference to the creation of man's body is relegated to a footnote at the end of the creation story (2:7)."[359]

Think of it! Man was originally created in the moral and spiritual pattern of God. Man's entire personality—intellect, emotion, and will—was a reflection of the divine essence of the Creator. Yes, the entrance of **sin** seriously marred that **image**, but Jesus Christ restored it. No, we are not "gods" as some **teach**, but we are in *God's* ***image.***

Soli deo gloria!

Scriptures for Study: Read Colossians 3:10 and Ephesians 4:24, noting what Christ accomplished. 🕮 Review our July 11 reading. Why is murder such a terrible sin?

Burden (Load)

maśśā'

The **word** *maśśā'* (4853) is one of the many fascinating words in Hebrew. Appearing about sixty times, its basic meaning in about half of those occurrences is the literal idea of carrying a **burden**, as would a donkey (Exod. 23:5, first occurrence) or other animal (2 Kings 5:17; 8:9).

Another noted use refers to various Levite clans who were given the responsibility of carrying parts of the **tabernacle** (Num. 4:15, 19, 24, 27, 31, 32, 47, 49). Special attention is also paid to the prohibition of carrying any **burden** on the **Sabbath** (Jer. 17:21–27), which included such activities as carrying harvested crops or packing a donkey (Neh. 13:15, 19).

Among the more figurative uses of *maśśā'* is "carrying a load of despair or hardship." We can only imagine Moses' burdens of leadership as he asked **God**, "Wherefore have I not found favor in thy sight, that thou layest the burden of all this people upon me?" (Num. 11:11). And **David** writes of his sin, "For mine iniquities are gone over mine head: as an heavy burden they are too heavy for me" (Ps. 38:4).

The chief metaphor in this word, however, is the idea of a burdensome message that must be delivered, which we find in roughly the other half of its occurrences. The word occurs repeatedly in the Prophets to introduce the message of judgment each is about to deliver. Lamenting the invasion of Jerusalem by the Persians, Isaiah speaks of "the burden of the valley of vision" (Isa. 22:1, May 2). Elsewhere he introduces various messages with "the burden of Babylon" (13:1), "Moab" (15:1), "Damascus" (17:1), "Egypt" (19:1), and others. Nahum likewise announced "the burden of Nineveh" (1:1).

Other prophets used the same word in a slightly different and even more significant way. Both Zechariah (9:1; 12:1) and Malachi (1:1) spoke of "the burden of the word of the LORD," and Habakkuk spoke of "the burden which [he] did see" (1:1).

All this underscores the very real **burden** it is to the **man** of God as he delivers God's message. Whether that message be one of exposing sin, proclaiming the gospel, teaching doctrine, refuting error, or any other message, the true preacher is a man who carries a heavy **burden**. In a day when we see fewer and fewer such men, the need is all the more acute. **Pray** for God to raise up more.

Scriptures for Study: Read Jeremiah 23:33–38, noting how the people scoffed at the message the **prophet** delivered. The same is often true today.

Sun

šemeš

As one might expect, in most of its some 130 occurrences, the Hebrew **word** for **sun** (*šemeš*, 8121) refers to the literal object that is the source of **light**. Such references, of course, refer to the **sun** rising (Num. 21:11; Isa. 45:6) and setting (Gen. 15:12, first occurrence; Deut. 11:30; cf. Gen. 1:14–16). Another **time** indicated by this word was about 9 a.m., the time the **sun** became hot (1 Sam. 11:9; Neh. 7:3). Of several figurative uses of *šemeš*, three stand out:

First, there is the picture of *supremacy and sovereignty*. **Sun** worship is **among** the oldest pagan religious practices (Job 31:26, 27, **sun** here is *'ôr,* May 22). It was common among the Egyptians, Chaldeans, and others. The compound *Bēyṯ Šemeš* (1053, "house of the sun"), in fact, appears several times in reference to a sanctuary dedicated to **sun** worship (Josh. 15:10; 19:22). Another compound, *Iyr Šemeš* (5905, "city of the sun") not only appears in **Scripture** (19:41) but was also common to many cities in antiquity.

Of special note here was Egypt, where the god Ra was worshipped (note *Bēyṯ Šemeš* again in Jer. 43:13). It is therefore extremely significant that the ninth plague upon Egypt, the plague of darkness (Exod. 10:21–29), was aimed at the very **heart** of Egypt's **sun** worship. Ra was shown to be no match for the sovereign **power** of Yahweh.

Second, the **sun** provides us with a picture of *Scripture*. Oh, how glorious Psalm 19 is! While we see "natural revelation" in verses 1–6 (cf. Rom. 1:20), these verses lead right to the "special revelation" of God's Word in Psalm 19:7–13: "The law of the LORD is perfect, converting the soul: the testimony of the LORD is sure, making wise the simple" (v. 7; cf. 2 Tim. 3:15–17). Oh, the blazing brightness of God's Word, and nothing escapes its "heat"!

Third, the **sun** also provides us with a picture of *surety*. The psalmist declares, "His name shall endure for ever: his name shall be continued as long as the sun: and men shall be blessed in him: all nations shall call him blessed" (Ps. 72:17; cf. v. 5). It is estimated that there is enough fuel in our **sun** (see **star**) to keep it burning for another few billion years, and God is even surer than that.

Scriptures for Study: The Jews were repeatedly warned against **sun** and other nature worship (Deut. 4:15–19;[360] cf. 17:3–7; Jer. 7:18; 10:3–5). Is the scene today really all that different, or have we simply renamed it "the environment"? (See July 6.)

Moon [and] New Moon

yārēach [and] chōḏeš

As **God** made "the sun to rule by day," He likewise made "the **moon** [*yārēach*, 3394] and stars to rule by night" (Ps. 136:8, 9; cf. Gen. 1:14–18; Jer. 31:35). That latter picture took on a more practical application in the Near East than it does in the West. Its especially great brilliance in that part of the world, aided further by the reflective quality of the sands there, enabled people to carry on many tasks at **night**; a full **moon**, in fact, even allowed people to travel.

Because the Hebrew calendar is a lunar one, the chief application of the moon's movement was the marking out of **time** in the monthly cycle, that is, the seasons (Ps. 104:19). Added to this was the term **new moon**, *chōḏeš* (2320), which appears about 280 times and is derived from the root verb *chāḏaš* (2318), "to renew, restore, or repair" (e.g., 1 Sam. 11:14; Ps. 51:10; Isa. 61:4). A **new moon**, then, was basically "an equivalent to our **word** *month* because the month began when the thin crescent of the **new moon** was first visible at sunset."[361] Each month of the Hebrew calendar is referred to either by **name** or **number** (e.g., all twelve are listed by number in 1 Chron. 27:1–15).

As with the **sun** in Psalm 19:5, 6, the overarching practical application the **moon** provides is that of *regularity and consistency*. Have you ever watched the **moon** for an entire month? It is truly fascinating to **observe** its phases, notice that it rises about fifty minutes later each night, and then marvel at its dazzling glow when full. And it's been doing that month after month, century after century, since Creation.

Such consistency prompted the psalmist to **write** in reference to David's eternal lineage, "It shall be established for ever as the moon, and as a faithful witness in heaven. Selah" (Ps. 89:37). Likewise, **writing** directly about his son Solomon's reign but with clear overtones of the coming Messiah and *His* **kingdom**, David declares, "In his days shall the righteous flourish; and abundance of peace so long as the moon endureth" (72:7).

Should not all this motivate us to **praise**? As the "sun" and **moon** and "all [the] stars of light" praise Him (148:3), should not that also be our greatest desire?

Scriptures for Study: Read Numbers 28:11–15 and Psalm 81:3 ("time appointed" is *kese'* [3677], literally, "full moon"), noting that the **new moon** and full **moon** were special days of praise and celebration. Let those days still encourage us to praise.

Soft Answer

raḵ ma'aneh

Our focus today is Proverbs 15:1: "A soft answer turneth away wrath: but grievous words stir up anger." First we must understand the two operative words.

Answer *ma'aneh* (4617) appears only eight times but is derived from the root *'ānāh* (6030), which appears about 320 times. We considered this root back on November 2, where we noted that it means "to answer or respond," either verbally, as when Abraham answered **God** with words (Gen. 18:27, first occurrence), or non-verbally, as when Israel proclaimed **peace** to a city to "make [the inhabitants] answer of peace," in order to avoid a siege (Deut. 20:10–12).

Soft is *raḵ* (7390), which appears about fifteen times; on occasion it means "weak" (Gen. 33:13; Deut. 20:8; 2 Sam. 3:39), but it primarily means "gentle, soft, or tender." When our pre-incarnate **Lord** visited Abraham, the latter ran into his herd and found a tender calf to prepare for a meal (Gen. 18:7, first occurrence). The coming Messiah is called a tender twig of a cedar **tree** in Ezekiel 17:22.

Turning now to our text, we should also briefly mention again the **word *wrath*** (*chēmāh*, September 9), which expresses the ideas of rage and heat. What, then, will **turn away** heat and **anger** in a conflict? An equally heated response certainly won't do it. Neither will a harsh remark or "telling them off." In either case, in fact, the rest of Proverbs 15:1 tells us what the result will be: "Grievous words stir up anger" ("grievous" is *'eṣeḇ*, 6089, "pain, hurt, toil"). Such responses will only make the situation worse.

Rather what Solomon counsels is the use of a **soft answer**, a calm response that consists of mild, gentle words that flow from a humble **heart**. Does this mean we never speak directly, or imply we should compromise truth? Certainly not. This is the very contrast Paul addresses in Ephesians 4:14, 15; as serious as false teaching is, and must, therefore, be addressed, we still must "[speak] the truth in love." While Paul wrote many strong, sometimes even scathing, rebukes to the believers in Corinth, for example, no one there could have accused him of being unkind or unloving.

So, as Gideon's **soft answer** turned away the wrath of the Ephraimites (Judg. 8:1–3) and Abigail's **soft answer** turned away David's wrath (1 Sam. 25:21–33), let us offer the same when conflicts threaten.

Scriptures for Study: What else does Solomon **counsel** about the **tongue** in Proverbs 15:2–7?

Lot (1)

gôrāl

Assumed to be derived from the Arabic *garwal* (pebble), the Hebrew *gôrāl* (1486) refers to a small stone used in determining God's will. Lots were tossed or allowed to fall to determine a choice or make a selection. Its first of some eighty occurrences, for instance, was "Aaron shall cast lots upon the two goats; one lot for the LORD, and the other lot for the scapegoat" (Lev. 16:8).

One reason for casting lots was the dividing of land (1 Chron. 6:54–81) for **inheritance** (May 25), but it was used in several ways for decision making (Judg. 20:9; 1 Chron. 24:5, 31; 25:8; 26:13; Neh. 10:34; 11:1; Joel 3:3). We don't **know**, though, exactly how the procedure was carried out.

What we *do* know, however, is significant, namely, that God was still in control of the outcome: "The lot is cast into the lap; but the whole disposing thereof is of the LORD" (Prov. 16:33). We have all heard the adage, one's "lot in life," that is, one's way of life or worldly fate, but as **David** assures the believer, "The LORD is the portion of mine inheritance and of my cup: thou maintainest my lot" (Ps. 16:5).

There is a crucial lesson to be learned in all this. Tragically, many today seek guidance and make decisions based upon feelings, impressions, circumstances, burdens, and even visions and dreams. But **Scripture** nowhere says that such things are to be used to dictate decision making. In fact, the concept of God's "individual will" as another aspect of God's will that is apart from His *sovereign* will and *moral* will is not a biblical concept.[362]

How, then, does God **lead** today? By His **Word**, of course. A common approach to "finding God's will" nowadays is "putting out a fleece," using Gideon as a model. Some say, "Lord, if You do this, then I'll know I should do that." But Gideon is actually a quintessential example of how *not* to find God's will. God's *clear word* to Gideon was that he would win the battle, that God would use him to deliver Israel from the Midianites (Judg. 6:16), but that wasn't **good** enough for Gideon, so in his unbelief he asked for a **sign** (vv. 36–40). Gideon simply did not believe what God told him.

Let us not *toss lots*; let us *trust* the ***Lord***!

Scriptures for Study: What is God's will according to each of the following verses and passages: Ephesians 5:17, 18; 1 Thessalonians 4:3–7; 5:18; Romans 12:2; 1 Timothy 2:8; 1 Peter 2:13–15; 3:17; 4:19?

Lot (2)

gôrāl

While no thinking person makes an important decision by "flipping a coin" or "rolling the dice," that is actually what many do who depend upon subjective criteria such as feelings or urges. While lots were necessary in ancient times, **God** has provided us with no less than four tools for making decisions:

First, He has given us His ***Word***. As noted yesterday, many verses tell us exactly, word-for-word, what God's will is. This is always the starting point, and more times than not it is the only guideline we will need. I have heard some people say, for example, "I'm looking for a sign not to marry that unbeliever," when God has stated categorically that a Christian should *never* do that (2 Cor. 6:14–7:1). "[God's] Word is a lamp unto [our] feet, and a light unto [our] path" (Ps. 119:105), and it will show us each step we need to take and the decision we need to make.

Second, inseparably linked to His *Word*, God also gives us ***wisdom***. We need only ask Him for it (James 1:5). Wisdom is the ability to make the right choices at the opportune times (March 22), and so it is the ability to apply God's Word to *any* situation, even those not specifically addressed. Solomon is our example. Already having the written **Law**, he did not ask for more revelation, but asked God for discernment (March 25) to apply what he already had (1 Kings 3:5–12). God answered that request, and the verses that follow illustrate how he used that gift (vv. 16–28).

Third, God also allows us our *wishes,* if they are godly. Desire does have something to do with our decisions. The most important aspect of desire, of course, is found in James 4:3: "Ye ask, and receive not, because ye ask amiss, that ye may consume it upon your lusts." Be sure your desire is not just lust, but a godly, biblical desire. With that established, what do you want to do? As **David** assures us, "Delight thyself also in the LORD; and he shall give thee the desires of thine heart" (Ps. 37:4).

Fourth and finally, God also gives us *warning*. As the last "safety valve," God provides us with the godly **counsel** of others. This can be a godly **friend**, a parent, or a pastor who might see something we don't or might give encouragement we didn't consider.

Scriptures for Study: Read the following verses for each of our four points: Word (Ps. 119:89, 97–100, 129, 30; 2 Tim. 3:16, 17; 2 Pet. 1:3); wisdom (Prov. 1:20–23; 2:1–6); wishes (Eccles. 9:9–17; 11:9); warning (Prov. 12:15; 15:22; 19:20; 27:9).

Midst (Middle, Among)

tāwek̲

The literal idea in about 215 of the some 400 occurrences of the Hebrew *tāwek̲* (8432) is "in the **middle** (or **midst**)" or "at the heart." Its very first appearance is one of the most graphic: "And God said, Let there be a firmament in the midst of the waters, and let it divide the waters from the waters" (Gen. 1:6; cf. vv. 7, 8). The "firmament" (*rāqiya'*, 7549), the great atmospheric expanse above the earth, divided the waters below on earth's surface from the waters above in the canopy that surrounded the earth.

Another dramatic scene is when "the children of Israel walked upon dry land in the midst of the sea; and the waters were a wall unto them on their right hand, and on their left" (Exod. 14:29). Still another was Samson's final act of pulling down "the two middle pillars" that were the main supports of the roof of Dagon's **temple** (Judg. 16:29).

In about 140 places, however, *tāwek̲* is rendered as **among** in our beloved AV translation. **God** "brought out Israel from among [the nations]," for instance (Ps. 136:11), and **David** testified, "I will greatly praise the LORD with my mouth; yea, I will praise him among the multitude" (109:30).

A verse that stands out in this regard is Exodus 25:8: "And let them make me a sanctuary; that I may dwell among them." The scene, of course, was the building of the **tabernacle** (May 3), the purpose of which was to provide a dwelling place for God **among** His people. This provides us with no less than three pictures (or "types"):

First, it pictures *Christ*. When our **Lord walked** this earth, "in him [dwelt] all the fulness of the Godhead bodily" (Col. 2:9). He was "a greater and more perfect tabernacle, not made with hands" (Heb. 9:11).

Second, it pictures the *Christian*. Every Christian's body is "the temple of the Holy Ghost which is in [us], which [we] have of God, and . . . [we] are not [our] own." This is because we have been "bought with a price" and as a result are to "glorify God in [our] body" (1 Cor. 6:19, 20).

Third, it pictures the *church*. Even in the context of church discipline, a church is a church "where two or three are gathered together in [His] name," for He is "in the midst of them" (Matt. 18:20; cf. 1 Tim. 3:15; Heb. 10:21).

Scriptures for Study: What is David's testimony in Psalms 22:22 and 109:30? 🕮 *Tāwek̲* is also translated "within" several times. Note these examples: Ps. 40:8, 10; 143:4–6.

Prince (of Peace)

Śar (Šālôm)

Oh, what a verse we read in Isaiah 9:6! Describing the coming Messiah, the **prophet** declares, "For unto us a child is born, unto us a son is given: and the government shall be upon his shoulder: and his name shall be called Wonderful, Counsellor, The mighty God, The everlasting Father, The Prince of Peace." After the "Hallelujah Chorus" the next most well-known aria of Handel's *Messiah* is based upon this verse.

Having considered the words **Counsellor** (January 30; **counsel**, September 25) and **wonderful** (June 21, 22), we are drawn here to our Lord's title of **Prince of Peace**. **Peace**, of course, is *Šālôm* (January 13), "completeness, wholeness, harmony, or fulfillment."

Prince, then, is *śar* (8269), which appears more than 400 times and refers not only to a **prince** but also a chief, captain, ruler, governor, or other such official. Its first occurrence, for example, recounts that Pharaoh's "princes" (officials, courtiers) noticed Sarah's beauty and "commended" her to Pharaoh (Gen. 12:15). Phichol, the commander of Abimelech's forces, is referred to as "the chief captain" (21:22), and Potiphar was Pharaoh's "captain of the guard" (Gen. 37:36; 39:1). Tribal leaders and chieftains of various peoples are also called *śar* (Num. 21:18; 1 Sam. 29:3, 4; Jer. 48:7; Amos 1:15).

Does all this not dramatically illustrate the title **Prince of Peace**? While human officials rule over their insignificant little corners of the earth, our Lord is the **Prince**, Captain, Chief, Magistrate over the whole realm, the entire **kingdom**, of **peace**. As Paul stated it, Christ "*is* Himself our peace" (Eph. 2:14, literal translation and emphasis added). Paul did not call Christ a "peace*maker*" (which would be the Greek *eirēnopoios*), rather he called Him ***peace*** itself. Men have sought **peace** through the ages, but it is nowhere to be found outside of Christ.

While this is the traditional **day** of commemorating Christ's birth, He is far more than the seasonal cliché "Peace on earth, good will to men." He *is* **Peace**. But infinitely even more important than Jesus' *birth*—which actually is never specified in **Scripture** as being a "holiday" (literally, "holy day"), and since we don't actually know what day it was—is His *resurrection*. That day is, indeed, specified as a day to **remember** and celebrate, which is what we do every Lord's Day. Better still, not only was He born, not only did He die, and not only did He rise from the dead, *but He is coming again*!

Scriptures for Study: Read Ephesians 2:14–18, noting the blessings of **peace** Christ has provided. 🕮 Read also Isaiah 9:7 and 11:1–9, rejoicing in the millennial **peace** to come.

Face (Countenance) (1)

pāniym

Author, naturalist, philosopher, and naval commander Pliny the Elder (AD 23–79) long ago wrote, "The human features and countenance, although composed of but some ten parts or little more, are so fashioned that among so many thousands of men there are no two in existence who cannot be distinguished from one another."[363]

While that fact is amazingly true, as even identical twins still have subtle differences, it is equally true that every person's **face**, that is, his **countenance** (facial expression) displays his or her true attitudes and sentiments. To put it succinctly, as we will explore more **tomorrow**, what the **heart** *feels*, the **face** *reveals*.

Perhaps reflecting the same observation that Pliny made—that of the face's many varied features—all the some 2,100 occurrences of *pāniym* (6440) are in the plural (note the *-iym*). While some of those occurrences are simply ordinary references to the **face**, as when Joseph "washed his face" (Gen. 43:31; cf. Lev. 13:41; 1 Kings 19:13), most are strongly figurative.

We see this figurative use first of **God** Himself. To come before God's **face** simply means to come into His presence. God promised Moses, "My presence [*pāniym*] shall go with thee, and I will give thee rest" (Exod. 33:14). Some 500 years later, **David** wrote, "When thou saidst, Seek ye my face; my heart said unto thee, Thy face, LORD, will I seek," (Ps. 27:8); or, how about this metrical rearrangement according to the *Scottish Psalter of 1650*?—"When thou didst say, seek ye my face, / then unto thee reply / Thus did my heart, above all things / thy face, Lord, seek will I."

Again we read in Psalm 119:58: "I entreated thy favour [*pāniym*] with my whole heart: be merciful unto me according to thy word" (cf. vv. 169, 170, "before"). Because of his weakness, David appeals to God alone, seeking His **face** and coming into His presence for healing and rest. Why? Because there is nowhere else to go. As the *Psalter* expresses this verse: "With my whole heart I did entreat / thy face and favor free: / According to thy gracious word / be merciful to me." David declares still later, "Make thy face to shine upon thy servant; and teach me thy statutes" (v. 135).

Tragic, indeed, is today's trend toward mysticism, new revelation, and the like, for where do we find truth? We find it only "before God's face," and He reveals His **face** only in His **Word**.

Scriptures for Study: Read the following verses, noting each command: Psalms 95:2 ("presence"), v. 6 ("before"); 100:2 ("presence"); 105:4 (**face**).

Face (Countenance) (2)

pāniym

"Your face . . . is as a book, where men may read strange matters," said Lady Macbeth to her husband.[364] How true it is that people can often read our faces like a **book**. As noted yesterday, what the **heart** *feels*, the **face** *reveals*. Let us each ask ourselves, then, what does my **countenance** tell others?

First, a "hard face" is the **face** of *rebellion*. As **God** sent Jeremiah through Jerusalem seeking a single person who "executeth judgment, that seeketh the truth" (Jer. 5:1, July 30), we also read that "they [had] made their faces harder than a rock" and "refused to return" (v. 3). Every parent has seen this **face** on their child, the **face** of defiance and revolt.

Sadly, most pastors have also seen this **face**. When the **Word** of God is preached, people often **rebel**, preferring to continue in **sin** rather than submit to truth. This is precisely why God told Jeremiah earlier, "Be not afraid of their faces: for I am with thee to deliver thee, saith the LORD" (1: 8). Some will frown, fuss, and fume, so God needs men who will not **fear** the people's faces.

Second, a "fallen countenance" is the **face** of *rage*. **Cain** is our example here (Gen. 4:5, 6). Spewing forth from offended **pride**, Cain's **anger** exploded, being *intended* for God, whom he could not hurt, but *aimed* at **Abel**, whom he could hurt. Likewise, rebellion and rage are always a reaction against God's revealed truth, whether or not we are even aware of it.

Third, a "fierce countenance" is the **face** of *ruthlessness*. Babylon itself is the model here, "a nation of fierce countenance" (Deut. 28:50) that swooped down on Israel because of her rebellion. How we need to realize that God will not long tolerate rebellion!

Fourth, in stark contrast, is not the **face** of *rejoicing* to be much preferred? As Solomon encourages, "A merry heart maketh a cheerful countenance" (Prov. 15:13) and, "God giveth to a man that is good in his sight [*pāniym*] wisdom, and knowledge, and joy" (Eccles. 2:26), and still again, "A man's wisdom maketh his face to shine, and the boldness of his face shall be changed" (8:1). And finally, the psalmist declares, "Why art thou cast down, O my soul? and why art thou disquieted within me? hope thou in God: for I shall yet praise him, who is the health of my countenance, and my God" (Ps. 42:11).

Scriptures for Study: What does the hardened face indicate (Prov. 21:29)? 🕮 What can godly friends do for one another (27:17)?

River

nāhār

A **river** invokes images **among** the most serene in nature. Humans are irresistibly drawn to rivers, a source of refreshment and even **life** itself.

The Hebrew *nāhār* (5104), which is found in several Semitic languages, appears about 120 times in the OT. The first is when "a river went out of Eden to water the garden; and from thence it was parted, and became into four heads" (Gen. 2:10). Think of it! Flowing through the perfection of Eden was a **river**, undoubtedly a quite large one, for it fed four others. That **river** probably made the "Mighty Mississippi" look like a creek.

Several other great rivers are mentioned in **Scripture**, including the Euphrates (Gen. 15:18; 31:21), the Nile (15:18, "river of Egypt"), and the Tigris (Dan. 10:4, "Hiddekel"). *Nāhār* also refers to ocean currents, as Jonah was tossed about by the "floods . . . billows . . . and . . . waves" (Jonah 2:3).

At least one major reason rivers were so significant in Jewish thinking was because there were so few of them in their territory. Unlike the rich, fertile lands of Egypt and Mesopotamia, which existed solely because of their rivers, Israel was "a land of hills and valleys, and drinketh water of the rain of heaven: A land which the LORD thy God careth for" (Deut. 11:11, 12).

Psalm 46 is a case in point. Why is **God** "our refuge and strength, a very present help in trouble" (v. 1)? Because in the **midst** of raging, cataclysmic chaos (vv. 2, 3), "There is a **river**, the streams whereof shall make glad the city of God, the holy place of the tabernacles of the most High" (v. 4). While Jerusalem, of course, has no **river** (cf. October 22), God Himself is the **river** and brings it many blessings. This verse looks forward to the millennial Jerusalem and was obviously in John's mind as he penned the **book** of Revelation (22:1, 2; cf. Zech.14:8–11).

We defer to Spurgeon in closing today: "Divine grace like a smoothly flowing, fertilizing, full, and never-failing river, yields refreshment and consolation to believers. . . . It is no boisterous ocean, but a placid stream, it is not stayed in its course by earthquakes or crumbling mountains, it follows its serene course without disturbance. Happy are they who know from their own experience that there is such a river of God."

Scriptures for Study: Psalm 46 (January 14) is one of thanksgiving and **trust**. Read it through prayerfully, noting that God is our *refuge* (vv. 1–3), our *resources* (vv. 4–7), and our *ruler* (vv. 8–11).

Beerlahairoi

be'ēr lachay rō'iy

This interesting place **name** before us today, *be'ēr lachay rō'iy* (883), is a somewhat complex compound. To get at its meaning, we must examine each part. The noun *'be'er* (875) means "a well or pit," whether natural or man-made. Because of the arid climate, a well became a symbol of **life** and value (Gen. 21:25, 30; 26:15, 18; Exod. 2:15; Num. 21:16–18).

The noun *chay* (2416) refers to a living thing and is most commonly translated "animals" or "beasts" (e.g., Gen. 1:24, 25, 28, "living"; 8:9; 1 Sam. 17:46; Ezek. 29:5). Finally, *rō'eh* (7203) speaks of a seer or the prophetic **vision** he sees. The former is seen in reference to Samuel the seer (1 Chron. 9:22; 26:28; 29:29). In the latter sense, Isaiah refers to the **sin** and debauchery of Judah by declaring that even the visions of the prophets are flawed and aimless (28:7).

Putting it all together, *be'ēr lachay rō'iy* appears only three times in the OT, the first being the key. Genesis 16 records the sin of impatience, as Sarah persuades Abraham to **father** a child by her maid Hagar. While culturally acceptable in that **day**, such behavior was never sanctioned by **God**. The conflict that followed was inevitable, and Hagar fled into the desert. The pre-incarnate Christ appeared to her beside a well, commanded her to **return** and submit to Sarah, and promised He would "multiply [her] seed exceedingly."

We then read in verse 14 that Hagar named the well **Beerlahairoi**. The Hebrew compound has been rendered several ways—"The Well of a Living One, My Seer"; "The Well of Him That Liveth and Seeth Me"; and "The Well of the Vision of Life"—but the most likely seems to be "The Well of the Living One Seeing Me" (or "The Well of the Living One Who Sees Me"). We also note that Isaac passed there as he went to meet and wed Rebekah (24:62), and Isaac lived there after his father died (25:11). This had become a noted, even *holy*, spot in the desert.

While the exact location of this well today is unknown—some believe it is about fifty miles southwest of Beersheba and about twelve miles west of Kadesh-barnea—that really doesn't matter. What matters is God's promise to always see and hear His people, to provide for their needs. That promise is still good today.

Scriptures for Study: Review our January 10 (**Jehovah-Jireh**) and May 15 (**Manna**) readings and **rejoice** in God's never-failing provision.

The Word of the LORD Came

dābār Yāhweh hāyāh

Today we consider a phrase that actually builds on several words we have already examined. We do so because of the powerful application that appears when these words are combined. It is a fitting phrase to consider as our year together comes to a close.

The first **word** is *dābār* (1697, February 22), which means "a **word** or speech" and is a general term for God's revelation. The second **word** is *Yāhweh* (3068, January 8), God's "covenant name" **LORD**, the **name** He most often used when making covenants and giving promises to His people. The third is *hāyāh* (1961, January 8), "to be or exist," and is here translated **came**.

Genesis 15 records God's promise to Abraham concerning a son. Verse 1 contains the phrase **the word of the LORD came**. This is the first of more than ninety instances of this phrase in the OT (e.g., 2 Sam. 7:4; 1 Kings 6:11; Jer. 1:2, 4, 11; Ezek. 1:3). And what a phrase it is!

Even the **word** of man, that is *language* itself, is a marvel beyond comprehension. In fact, even if there were no other proofs, language alone would be enough to show the folly of evolution. How **man** developed the nuances of words, the complexities of syntax, the rules of grammar, and even the subtleties of tonality, where animals did not, simply cannot be rationally explained without God as Creator.

Far above even that, however, is **the word of the LORD**. *Yāhweh*, in His covenant-making relationship, reveals Himself. And how does He go about doing that?—through words, speech, language. "As a matter of fact," one expositor writes, "the very purpose of language is that God might communicate His will to man and man might respond in praise to God. Since man was created for fellowship with God, and since fellowship requires communication, it is essential that the Creator somehow speak to man."[365] Oh, how foolish it is to reject so basic a truth!

We should note here that this is also the first occurrence of the instructions "Fear not" in **Scripture**, a phrase God repeated to Isaac (Gen. 26:24) and Jacob (46:3). And what exactly brought such deliverance from **fear**, and imparted **peace** of mind? **The word of the LORD**. That is always our comfort (cf. Isa. 41:10, 13, 14; 43:1, 5; 44:2, 8).

Oh, that we would never lose sight of the truth that God's written **Word** is His revelation to us! We need nothing else.

Scriptures for Study: How high has God elevated His **Word** (Ps. 138:2)? Is it possible, therefore, to elevate it too high?[366]

Selah

selāh

As we close our study of the rich vocabulary of the OT, we could not consider a more appropriate final **word** than *selāh* (5542).[367] It appears seventy-one times in the Psalms and three times in a **prayer** by Habakkuk (3:3, 9, 13), which was set to a tune and directed to the chief singer. It is not surprising it is omitted in the corrupt Latin Vulgate, but does appear in the Septuagint and is translated as *diapsalma*, which refers to some variation or modulation of the voice in **singing**.

While the precise meaning is not known for sure, several possibilities have been offered. Some think it derives from a root (*sal*) that means "to raise, elevate, lift up" and suppose that it directs an elevation in the voice, to sing louder, or to pitch the tune up to a higher key, because there is nobler matter to come. Others view it as an affirmation of the truth of something, whether **good** or bad, and render it "verily" or "truly," corresponding to the idea of "Amen," that is, "so be it," "so shall it be."

The most common view, however, is that this is a musical notation that means a pause and musical interlude and is derived from the word *salah*, "to strew or spread out," implying that the subject should be spread out, meditated upon, strewn out in front of us that we might attentively consider it. It often follows a noteworthy statement, good or bad, and likely indicates a pause for reflection while the instruments play an interlude. This seems to be the most probable meaning.

When we read this word, then, we are encouraged to pause, reflect, meditate, and consider carefully what has been said. This meaning is made all the more probable by its use in Psalm 9:16: "The LORD is known by the judgment which he executeth: the wicked is snared in the work of his own hands. Higgaion. Selah." As noted at the beginning of our study (January 6), the transliterated word *Higgaion* (*higgāyôn*, 1902) means **meditation** (January 6), musing, and thinking in the **heart**. How we should, indeed, reflect and meditate on verses such as Psalm 66:4: "All the earth shall worship thee, and shall sing unto thee; they shall sing to thy name. Selah."

Dear Christian Friend, the author and publisher of this book pray that *selāh* will become an important word in your Christian walk. May God richly bless you.

Scriptures for Study: Read the following occurrences of *selāh*: Psalms 24:10; 44:8; 50:6; 59:13; 62:8; 66:4; 68:19, 32; 143:6.

Soli deo Gloria – To God alone be the glory.

Chronological Bible Reading Schedule

Reading your Bible straight through, that is, in *book order*, is of course a wonderful and rewarding exercise. Schedules for doing so in one year are typical and plentiful. Reading it through *chronologically*, however—that is, in the order of the events—has an obvious advantage. This enables you to see it all "as it happened" and better understand the sweep of biblical history.

The following schedule, therefore, will take you through Scripture in chronological order. You will see the following: the Book of Job is integrated with Genesis because Job lived before Abraham; prophetic passages appear within the historical setting in which they occurred; individual Psalms follow their appropriate historical event; Proverbs appear at the time in which they were penned; the Gospels are ordered to tell Jesus' story from beginning to end; and Paul's Epistles are integrated into the book of Acts.

JANUARY

Date	Passage
The Beginning	
1	Genesis 1–3
2	Genesis 4–7
3	Genesis 8–11
The Patriarchs	
4	Job 1–5
5	Job 6–9
6	Job 10–13
7	Job 14–16
8	Job 17–20
9	Job 21–23
10	Job 24–28
11	Job 29–31
12	Job 32–34
13	Job 35–37
14	Job 38–39
15	Job 40–42
16	Genesis 12–15
17	Genesis 16–18
18	Genesis 19–21
19	Genesis 22–24
20	Genesis 25–26
21	Genesis 27–29
22	Genesis 30–31
23	Genesis 32–34
24	Genesis 35–37
25	Genesis 38–40
26	Genesis 41–42
27	Genesis 43–45
28	Genesis 46–47
29	Genesis 48–50
Exodus and Law	
30	Exodus 1–3
31	Exodus 4–6

FEBRUARY

Date	Passage
1	Exodus 7–9
2	Exodus 10–12
3	Exodus 13–15
4	Exodus 16–18
5	Exodus 19–21
6	Exodus 22–24
7	Exodus 25–27
8	Exodus 28–29
9	Exodus 30–32
10	Exodus 33–35
11	Exodus 36–38
12	Exodus 39–40
13	Leviticus 1–4
14	Leviticus 5–7
15	Leviticus 8–10
16	Leviticus 11–13
17	Leviticus 14–15
18	Leviticus 16–18
19	Leviticus 19–21

20	Leviticus 22–23
21	Leviticus 24–25
22	Leviticus 26–27
23	Numbers 1–2
24	Numbers 3–4
25	Numbers 5–6
26	Numbers 7
27	Numbers 8–10
28	Numbers 11–13

MARCH

Date	Passage
1	Numbers 14–15; Ps. 90
2	Numbers 16–17
3	Numbers 18–20
4	Numbers 21–22
5	Numbers 23–25
6	Numbers 26–27
7	Numbers 28–30
8	Numbers 31–32
9	Numbers 33–34
10	Numbers 35–36
11	Deuteronomy 1–2
12	Deuteronomy 3–4
13	Deuteronomy 5–7
14	Deuteronomy 8–10
15	Deuteronomy 11–13
16	Deuteronomy 14–16
17	Deuteronomy 17–20
18	Deuteronomy 21–23
19	Deuteronomy 24–27
20	Deuteronomy 28–29
21	Deuteronomy 30–31
22	Deuteronomy 32–34; Psalms 91
Israel in Canaan	
23	Joshua 1–4
24	Joshua 5–8
25	Joshua 9–11
26	Joshua 12–15
27	Joshua 16–18
28	Joshua 19–21
29	Joshua 22–24
30	Judges 1–2
31	Judges 3–5

APRIL

Date	**Passage**
1	Judges 6–7
2	Judges 8–9
3	Judges 10–12
4	Judges 13–15
5	Judges 16–18
6	Judges 19–21
7	Ruth
Monarchy Begins (Saul)	
8	1 Samuel 1–3
9	1 Samuel 4–8
10	1 Samuel 9–12
11	1 Samuel 13–14
King David	
12	1 Samuel 15–17
13	1 Samuel 18–20; Ps. 11; Ps. 59
14	1 Samuel 21–24
15	Ps. 7; Ps. 27; Ps. 31; Ps. 34; Ps. 52
16	Ps. 56; Ps. 120; Ps. 140–142
17	1 Samuel 25–27
18	Ps. 17; Ps. 35; Ps. 54; Ps. 63
19	1 Samuel 28–31; Ps. 18; 1 Chron. 10
20	Ps. 121; Ps. 123–125; Ps. 128–130
21	2 Samuel 1–4
22	Ps. 6; Ps. 8–10; Ps. 14; Ps. 16; Ps. 19; Ps. 21
23	1 Chronicles 1–2
24	Ps. 43–45; Ps. 49; Ps. 84–85; Ps. 87
25	1 Chronicles 3–5
26	Ps. 73; Ps. 77–78
27	1 Chronicles 6
28	Ps. 81; Ps. 88; Ps. 92–93
29	1 Chronicles 7–10
30	Ps. 102–104

MAY

Date	**Passage**
1	2 Sam. 5:1–10; 1 Chron. 11–12
2	Ps. 133
3	Ps. 106–107
4	2 Sam. 5:11–6:23; 1 Chron. 13–16
5	Ps. 1–2; 15; 22–24; 47; 68
6	Ps. 89; 96; 100; 101; 105; 132
7	2 Samuel 7; 1 Chron. 17
8	Ps. 25; Ps. 29; Ps. 33; Ps. 36; Ps. 39
9	2 Samuel 8–9; 1 Chron. 18
10	Ps. 50; Ps. 53; Ps. 60; Ps. 75
11	2 Sam. 10; 1 Chron. 19; Ps. 20
12	Ps. 65–67; Ps. 69–70
13	2 Sam. 11–12; 1 Chron. 20
14	Ps. 32; 51; 86; 122
15	2 Samuel 13–15
16	Ps. 3–4; 12–13; 28; 55
17	2 Samuel 16–18
18	Ps. 26; 40; 58; 61–62; 64
19	2 Samuel 19–21
20	Ps. 5; Ps. 38; Ps. 41–42
21	2 Samuel 22–23; Ps. 57
22	Ps. 95; Ps. 97–99
23	2 Samuel 24; 1 Chron. 21–22; Ps. 30
24	Ps. 108–110
25	1 Chronicles 23–25
26	Ps. 131; 138–139; 143–145
27	1 Chron. 26–29; Ps. 127
28	Ps. 111–118

29	1 Kings 1–2; Ps. 37; 71; 94
30	Ps. 119:1–88

King Solomon

31	1 Kings 3–4; 2 Chronicles 1; Ps. 72

JUNE

Date	Passage
1	Ps. 119:89–176
2	Song of Solomon
3	Proverbs 1–3
4	Proverbs 4–6
5	Proverbs 7–9
6	Proverbs 10–12
7	Proverbs 13–15
8	Proverbs 16–18
9	Proverbs 19–21
10	Proverbs 22–24
11	1 Kings 5–6; 2 Chronicles 2–3
12	1 Kings 7; 2 Chronicles 4
13	1 Kings 8; 2 Chronicles 5
14	2 Chronicles 6–7; Psalms 136
15	Psalms 134; Psalms 146–150
16	1 Kings 9; 2 Chronicles 8
17	Proverbs 25–26
18	Proverbs 27–29
19	Ecclesiastes 1–6
20	Ecclesiastes 7–12
21	1 Kings 10–11; 2 Chron. 9
22	Proverbs 30–31

The Divided Kingdom

23	1 Kings 12–14
24	2 Chronicles 10–12
25	1 Kings 15:1–24; 2 Chron. 13–16
26	1 Kings 15:25–16:34; 2 Chronicles 17
27	1 Kings 17–19
28	1 Kings 20–21
29	1 Kings 22; 2 Chronicles 18
30	2 Chronicles 19–23

JULY

Date	Passage
1	Obadiah; Ps. 82–83
2	2 Kings 1–4
3	2 Kings 5–8
4	2 Kings 9–11
5	2 Kings 12–13; 2 Chron. 24
6	2 Kings 14; 2 Chron. 25
7	Jonah
8	2 Kings 15; 2 Chron. 26
9	Isaiah 1–4
10	Isaiah 5–8
11	Amos 1–5
12	Amos 6–9
13	2 Chron. 27; Isaiah 9–12
14	Micah
15	2 Chron. 28; 2 Kings 16–17
16	Isaiah 13–17
17	Isaiah 18–22
18	Isaiah 23–27
19	2 Kings 18:1–8; 2 Chron. 29–31; Ps. 48
20	Hosea 1–7
21	Hosea 8–14
22	Isaiah 28–30
23	Isaiah 31–34
24	Isaiah 35–36
25	Isaiah 37–39; Ps. 76
26	Isaiah 40–43
27	Isaiah 44–48
28	2 Kings 18:9–19:37; Ps. 46; 80; 135
29	Isaiah 49–53
30	Isaiah 54–58
31	Isaiah 59–63

AUGUST

Date	Passage
1	Isaiah 64–66
2	2 Kings 20–21
3	2 Chronicles 32–33
4	Nah.
5	2 Kings 22–23; 2 Chronicles 34–35
6	Zephaniah
7	Jeremiah 1–3
8	Jeremiah 4–6
9	Jeremiah 7–9
10	Jeremiah 10–13
11	Jeremiah 14–17
12	Jeremiah 18–22
13	Jeremiah 23–25
14	Jeremiah 26–29
15	Jeremiah 30–31
16	Jeremiah 32–34
17	Jeremiah 35–37
18	Jer. 38–40; Ps. 74; 79

The Exile

19	2 Kings 24–25; 2 Chronicles 36
20	Habakkuk
21	Jeremiah 41–45
22	Jeremiah 46–48
23	Jeremiah 49–50
24	Jeremiah 51–52
25	Lamentations 1:1–3:36
26	Lamentations 3:37–5:22
27	Ezekiel 1–4
28	Ezekiel 5–8
29	Ezekiel 9–12
30	Ezekiel 13–15
31	Ezekiel 16–17

SEPTEMBER

Date	Passage
1	Ezekiel 18–19

2	Ezekiel 20–21
3	Ezekiel 22–23
4	Ezekiel 24–27
5	Ezekiel 28–31
6	Ezekiel 32–34
7	Ezekiel 35–37
8	Ezekiel 38–39
9	Ezekiel 40–41
10	Ezekiel 42–43
11	Ezekiel 44–45
12	Ezekiel 46–48
13	Joel
14	Daniel 1–3
15	Daniel 4–6
16	Daniel 7–9
17	Daniel 10–12

Return From Exile

18	Ezra 1–3
19	Ezra 4–6; Psalms 137
20	Haggai
21	Zechariah 1–7
22	Zechariah 8–14
23	Esther 1–5
24	Esther 6–10
25	Ezra 7–10
26	Nehemiah 1–5
27	Nehemiah 6–7
28	Nehemiah 8–10
29	Nehemiah 11–13; Psalms 126
30	Malachi

OCTOBER

Date	Passage

The Gospel Story

1	Luke 1; John 1:1–14
2	Matthew 1; Luke 2:1–38
3	Matt. 2; Luke 2:39–52
4	Matt. 3; Mark 1; Luke 3
5	Matt. 4; Luke 4–5; John 1:15–51
6	John 2–4
7	Matthew 8–9; Mark 2
8	John 5
9	Matt. 12:1–21; Mark 3; Luke 6
10	Matthew 5–7
11	Matthew 8:1–13; Luke 7
12	Matthew 11
13	Matthew 12:22–50; Luke 11
14	Matthew 13; Luke 8
15	Matthew 8:14–34; Mark 4–5
16	Matthew 9–10
17	Matt. 14; Mark 6; Luke 9:1–17
18	John 6
19	Matt. 15; Mark 7
20	Matt. 16; Mark 8; Luke 9:18–27
21	Matt. 17; Mark 9; Luke 9:28–62
22	Matthew 18
23	John 7–8
24	John 9:1–10:21
25	Luke 10–11; John 10:22–42
26	Luke 12–13
27	Luke 14–15
28	Luke 16–17:10
29	John 11
30	Luke 17:11–18:14
31	Matthew 19; Mark 10

NOVEMBER

Date	Passage
1	Matt. 20–21
2	Luke 18:15–19:48
3	Mark 11; John 12
4	Matt. 22; Mark12
5	Matt. 23; Luke 20–21
6	Mark 13
7	Matthew 24
8	Matthew 25
9	Matthew 26; Mark 14
10	Luke 22; John 13
11	John 14–17
12	Matthew 27; Mark 15
13	Luke 23; John 18–19
14	Matthew 28; Mark 16
15	Luke 24; John 20–21

The Church and Epistles

16	Acts 1–3
17	Acts 4–6
18	Acts 7–8
19	Acts 9–10
20	Acts 11–12
21	Acts 13–14
22	James
23	Acts 15–16
24	Galatians 1–3
25	Galatians 4–6
26	Acts 17–18:18
27	1 Thessalonians; 2 Thessalonians
28	Acts 18:19–19:41
29	1 Corinthians 1–4
30	1 Corinthians 5–8

DECEMBER

Date	Passage
1	1 Corinthians 9–11
2	1 Corinthians 12–14
3	1 Corinthians 15–16
4	2 Corinthians 1–4
5	2 Corinthians 5–9
6	2 Corinthians 10–13
7	Acts 20:1–3; Romans 1–3
8	Romans 4–7
9	Romans 8–10
10	Romans 11–13

11	Romans 14–16
12	Acts 20:4–23:35
13	Acts 24–26
14	Acts 27–28
15	Colossians; Philemon
16	Ephesians
17	Philippians
18	1 Timothy
19	Titus
20	1 Peter
21	Hebrews 1–6
22	Hebrews 7–10
23	Hebrews 11–13
24	2 Timothy
25	2 Peter; Jude
26	1 John
27	2 John; 3 John

Christ's Return

28	Revelation 1–5
29	Revelation 6–11
30	Revelation 12–18
31	Revelation 19–22

Mining Bible Word Riches

While the studies in this book cover many OT words, it is certainly not exhaustive; there are countless more jewels to mine. The student might even want to go a little deeper into some of the words covered in this book. This chapter, therefore, presents some principles and procedures, as well as some language tools, that will equip the student to examine OT Hebrew words.

Basic Study

For many students, the following basic tools for studying OT words will be enough.

First, the foundational tool is a concordance. One such concordance, of course, is the universally known *Strong's Exhaustive Concordance of the Bible*. It's available not only in book form, but virtually every computer Bible program includes it. It gives each word as it is used in the AV followed by a listing of the Scripture references, and a short portion of the verse where that word appears, along with a number that Baptist minister and theologian Augustus Strong (1836–1921) assigned to that word. This number can then be used to look up the word in the dictionary in the back of the book. Here is an example listing for the word **love** as the lines actually appear:

word

Ps	119:	11 Thy *w* have I hid in mine heart	565
		16 statutes: I will not forget thy *w*	1697

The corresponding dictionary definitions, then, are as follows. Normal print numbers are for Hebrew words, while numbers in italics are for Greek words. Also note the helpful phonetic spelling for each word.

565. הרמא, *'imrâ, im-raw'*; or הרמא, *'emrâh*, em-raw' feminine of 561, and meaning the same: commandment, speech, word.

1697. דבר *dâbâr, daw-bawr'*; from 1696; a *word*; by implication a *matter* (as *spoken* of) of thing; adverbially a *cause*:—act, advice, affair, answer, X any such (thing), + because of, book, business, care, case, cause, certain rate, + chronicles, commandment, X commune (-ication), + concern [-ing], + confer, counsel, + dearth, decree, deed, X disease, due, duty, effect, + eloquent, errand, [evil favoured-] ness, + glory, + harm, hurt, + iniquity, + judgment, language, + lying, manner, matter, message, [no] thing, oracle, X ought, X parts, + pertaining, + please, portion, + power, promise, provision, purpose, question, rate, reason, report, request, X (as hast) said, sake, saying, sentence, + sign, + so, some [uncleanness], somewhat to say, + song, speech, X spoken, talk, task, + that, X there done, thing (concerning), thought, + thus, tidings, what [-soever], + wherewith, which, word, work.

Strong's definitions and numbers are, therefore, extremely helpful to the student. The numbers are, in fact, so universally used that most Hebrew tools available today are keyed to those numbers, enabling the student to quickly find what he needs. Every Bible student is deeply indebted to Strong's efforts.

On the other hand, while *Strong's* is very useful, *Young's Analytical Concordance to the Bible*, written by Scottish Free Church theologian Robert Young (1822–1888), uses a little different approach and is in some ways superior in analyzing Hebrew words. Here are two entries for the same words mentioned above:

WORD—

3. *A saying, speech,* הרמא *'emrâh.*
Lam. 2.17 he hath fulfilled his word that he had co.

4. *A saying, speech,* הרמא, *'imrâ.*
Psa. 12: 6 The words of the LORD (are) pure words
119: 11 Thy *w* have I hid in mine heart, that

5. *A word, matter, thing,* דבר *dâbâr.*
Gen. 15: 1 After these things the word of the LORD
Psa. 119: 105 Thy word (is) a lamp unto my feet, and

This approach is a little "cleaner" than Strong's, listing all the references for a particular Hebrew word in its own separate section, instead of having numbers intermingled in one long list. While *Strong's* provides longer definitions, *Young's*, though short, are right in front of you. Especially helpful is *Young's* "Index-Lexicon" in the back of the book. This lists each Hebrew word along with the different ways that word is translated in the AV and the number of instances that translation appears. Here is the entry for one of the words for **word** we've been using:

IMRAH אמרה,

commandment 1
Pass. pt. speech 7
word 28

Some entries reveal that a particular word is actually translated in several ways. The reason for this is usually the context in which the word appears; the context will often give a word a little different shade of meaning. A good example is the other word for **word** we have been using, which we examined in our February 22 reading. Here are just a few of the ways it is translated and listed:

DABAR דבר

act 52
answer 15
commandment 20
matter 63
message 3
speech 10
word 770

So, when it comes to a concordance, *Young's* is the most useful (in the author's opinion). *Strong's* is really needed only for its numbering system since the many other tools available today are keyed to its numbers and provide more in-depth explanations. It actually can be replaced totally, in fact, with *The Complete Word Study Old Testament*, which we'll examine next.

Second, we recommend *The Complete Word Study Old Testament* (AMG Publishers) by Dr. Spiros Zodhiates and Dr. Warren Baker (general editors). Like its predecessor on the NT, it contains the entire OT text (AV) with a *Strong's* number above each word. Numbers in normal type correspond to the *Strong's* dictionary included in the back of the book, while numbers in bold face *also* correspond to the "Lexical Aids" section, which provides more detailed definitions. Also appearing above each word are letters that refer to the grammatical construction of a word, which are then explained in the "Grammatical Notations" section (one each for Hebrew and Aramaic). The letters "qpf," for example, appear above the word "created" in Genesis 1:1, which refers to the Hebrew Qal perfect, which in turn "indicates in the active voice, simple, effective action, viewed as a whole" (note 100 in "Grammatical Notations").

Third, the Hebrew dictionary of choice for basic study (in this writer's opinion) is *The Complete Word Study Dictionary: Old Testament* by Dr. Warren Baker and Dr. Eugene Carpenter. Once again, like its predecessor on the NT, it is keyed to *Strong's* numbers and defines and explains every OT word. Another indispensable tool (though not exhaustive) is the classic *Vine's Expository Dictionary of Old & New Testament Words* (Nelson). Several computer software companies provide these titles in electronic form.

Deeper Study

The following works are for the student who wants to go a little deeper into OT words:

First, the classic *Girdlestone's Synonyms of the Old Testament* (coded to *Strong's*) by Robert Baker Girdlestone is really between basic and advanced. If one is comfortable with *Vine's* mentioned above, Girdlestone should present no problem. It is a wonderful work whose subtitle, *Their Bearing on Christian Doctrine*, accurately describes what it accomplishes.

Second, another must-have classic for the more serious student is the *Theological Wordbook of the Old Testament* by Gleason Archer, Laird Harris, and Bruce Waltke. In this writer's opinion, this work is without equal. Once again coded to *Strong's*, it explores the meaning and use of every theologically significant OT word. It, too, is available in electronic form from various software companies.

Third and finally, for the student who wants to actually learn Hebrew, there are various choices. One I like is *Learn Biblical Hebrew*, 2nd edition, by John H. Dobson (Baker Academic), which offers an easy method of learning this beautiful biblical language.

A Word of Caution on "Interpretation"

Let it be clearly stated, *word study is only one aspect* of "rightly dividing the word of truth" (2 Tim. 2:15). Basing interpretation solely on a word's etymology, isolating a word from the verse in which it appears, or separating it from the whole of Scripture are all dangerous, to say the least. Besides the "Grammatical Principle," which we outlined earlier, there are several other principles of correct biblical interpretation that must *always* be followed. Here is a very brief summary of the most important ones.

First, there is the "Plain Principle." To interpret "plainly" (or "literally") is to explain the original sense of the speaker or writer according to normal, customary, and proper usage of words and language. Some of the most heinous heresies in history have come by "allegorizing" or "spiritualizing" Scripture. The Bible, therefore, is to be taken in its plain meaning unless it makes it clear that it is to be taken otherwise. When Scripture is speaking figuratively, it makes it plain that it is doing so either in the immediate context, the larger context of Scripture, or through historical reference.

Second, there is the "Contextual Principle." Probably the most violated principle of biblical interpretation is the ripping of verses from their context. This principle, therefore, involves examining the words that surround the word in question, the verses that surround that verse, and the basic theme of the book where the verse appears. I don't know whom to credit for this thought, but it has been well said: "A text without a context is pretext."

Third, there is the "Comparison Principle." No Scripture verse stands by itself. Comparing Scripture with Scripture is absolutely essential to arriving at the proper interpretation of a given text. This principle is called *analogia scripturae*, "the analogy of Scripture," that is, comparing Scripture with Scripture.[1] In other words, we allow Scripture to interpret itself.

Fourth, there is the "Historical Principle." It is vitally important to understand the social customs, historical names and events, political climate and rulers, and even geographical references that might be pertinent to a given text. No study of Scripture is complete (or honest) without the historical context.

Fifth, there is the "Illumination Principle." As we study the Word of God, we must ever remember that what we are doing is not some intellectual exercise. Our ultimate purpose is not intellectual, but spiritual. Therefore, no matter how much we study the Word, no matter what tools we use, no matter how many principles we employ, nothing can substitute for the illumination of the Holy Spirit.

Sixth and finally, there is the "Practical Principle." By this we don't mean that we sit back and say, "What is the Bible saying to me?" That is practiced quite often in the church today, even to the extent of people supposedly "receiving new revelation." What we mean here is that we simply ask, "In light of my diligent study of what the Bible *says*, what does it now *demand* of me?" There is nothing mysterious about this, for once we go through the interpretation process, the application reveals itself. We don't have to *look* for the application; it becomes self-evident.

May God richly bless you as you mine the infinite riches of His Word.

---

1. This is further explained by the principle: *Scripturam ex Scriptura explicandam esse* ("Scripture is to be explained by Scripture"). This principle is related to another: *Analogia Fide* ("Analogy of Faith"), i.e., Bible doctrine is to be interpreted in relation to the basic message of the Bible, which is the Gospel, the content of faith, or simply "The Faith" (cf. 1 Cor. 2:13; 15:1–4; Jude 3).

Notes

1 Dr. J. D. Watson, *A Word for the Day: Key Words from the New Testament* (Chattanooga, TN: AMG Publishers, 2006. (Hereafter abbreviated *AWFTD*.)

2 From "To the Councilmen of All Cities in Germany That They Establish and Maintain Christian Schools" (1524).

3 Adapted from Charles Earle Funk, *Heavens to Betsy and Other Curious Sayings* (New York: HarperCollins, 1955, 1983), 103.

4 Warren Baker and Eugene Carpenter, *The Complete Word Study Dictionary: Old Testament* (Chattanooga ,Tennessee: AMG Publishers 2003) 317.

5 See the author's *AWFTD*, p. 1.

6 Gleason Archer, Laird Harris, Bruce Waltke, *Theological Wordbook of the OT* (Chicago: Moody Bible Institute, 1980), #2378. (Hereafter abbreviated TWOT.)

7 *TWOT*, #2378.

8 *TWOT*, #2405.

9 Willem A.VanGemeren, ed., *New International Dictionary of Old Testament Theology and Exegesis* (Grand Rapids: Zondervan, 1997), #H9005. (Hereafter abbreviated NIDOTTE.)

10 *Zākar* is at times used of God (e.g., Jer. 23:36). This, of course, does not mean he can forget as would we and must consciously try to remember. Rather it refers to fulfilling His word, acting in a fashion consistent with His promise.

11 While that latter view has been especially popular, other Old Testament deities are referred to using *'elōhiym* (e.g., Baal in Judg. 6:31, "a god"; and Ashtoreth, 1 Kings 11:33, "goddess"). The fact of *elohim* being plural is not needed to prove the clear teaching of the Trinity in the Old Testament. (See also next note).

12 Dr. William Barrick writes: "Too many evangelicals even are soft on seeing the Trinity in the Old Testament, where it is clearly present. Within the first nineteen chapters of Genesis there are already at least three Persons referred to in the Godhead. In a couple of chapters of Isaiah there are even three different Persons named together with their respective works (e.g., Isa. 63:7–10 where the LORD in vv. 7–8 is the Father, the angel of His presence in v. 9 is the Son, and the Spirit is mentioned in v. 10)."

13 Ibid.

14 Kittle, III, 1067.

15 Isa. 6:1; Jer. 1:11, 12, 13; Ezek. 1:1, 4, 15, 27, 28; 2:9; 8:2, 6, 7, 10, 15; 10:1, 9; 11:1.

16 *TWOT*, #2401.

17 *Keil & Delitzsch Commentary on the Old Testament.*

18 Colin Brown (General Editor), The New International Dictioanry of NT Theology (Grand Rapids, MIchigan: Zondervan, 1975) Vol. 3, 564 (Hereafter abbreviated: NIDNTT).

19 *Vine's*, "Sanctify (To)" entry.

20 *TWOT*, #93.

21 Ibid: "This leads A. B. Davidson to conclude that these qualifications both elevate the concept of *'ēl* in Scripture and distinguish the term as used biblically from others who might be so named (A. B. Davidson, *Theology of the Old Testament*, 61)."

22 Baker and Carpenter, #7706.

23 Thomas Watson, *A Body Of Divinity* (London: The Banner of Truth Trust, 1965), 82.

24 Stephen Charnock, *The Existence And Attributes Of God*. Grand Rapids: Baker Book House, 1979 (from the 1853 edition), Vol. II, 112–13.

25 *TWOT*, #116.

26 Kittle, Vol. I, 238.

27 Baker and Carpenter, #1419.

28 Latin, *consuetudinarius*.

29 *John Gill's Exposition of the Entire Bible* (electronic edition).

30 **Father** is predominantly New Testament, but besides the two Old Testament references cited in the text, there are others: Deut. 32:6; Isa. 63:16; 64:8; Jer. 31:9. Fatherhood is also clearly implied in verses such as Exod. 4:22 and Ps. 89:27.

31 *TWOT*, #4.

32 For more on *abba* and the concept of **Father** in general, see the author's *AWFTD*, p. 4.

33 *Hamlet*, II.2.311

34 For more on *kainos anthropos*, see the author's *AWFTD*, p. 1.

35 Girdlestone, 64–65. He goes on to support strongly the view that *'enôš* is derived from *'ānaš* (p. 66).

36 Girdlestone, 67.

37 Dr. William Barrick, and Baker and Carpenter, #582.

38 Dr. William Barrick: "This reading is actually more fitting on Mother's Day. The totality of the book of Ruth demonstrates that Ruth, indeed, had a total commitment to God (*Yahweh*), but this particular statement is focused more on her relationship to Naomi."

39 From Paul Lee Tan, *Encyclopedia of 7,700 Illustrations*, electronic edition.

40 Douglas Wilson, *Reforming Marriage* (Moscow, ID: Canon Press, 1995), 19 (emphasis in the original).

41 Some Bible teachers call this "the gift of singleness," and view it as another of God's "spiritual gifts," along with those of Romans 12:6–8, etc. We submit, however, two problems. First, no text ever *says* this is a "spiritual gift." Second, every spiritual gift is given *plentifully* to Christians, but celibacy is rare. While it is certainly a very special empowerment, it doesn't appear correct to include it with the general spiritual gifts.

We would also interject, that celibacy is never mandated in Scripture for any leader. Paul warned, in fact, that such "forbidding to marry" was an indication of false teachers (1 Tim. 4:1–3). Suppressing the normal drives that God has given will inevitably lead to perversion. God's norm, therefore, God's rule that has few exceptions, is marriage.

42 While the text deliberately states the matter simply, "Something else to be emphasized in the biblical concept of covenants (*beriyṯ*) is that they define relationships—the relationship between God and the individual or group with whom He made the covenant. Both sides of the *beriyṯ* have responsibilities in that relationship. Whereas man often proves to be unfaithful or in breach of the covenant, God is never unfaithful (cf. 2 Tim. 2:13; Heb. 6:13–14). Covenants involve stipulations—rules, standards, obligations, and promises. Sometimes the covenant is unilateral—as in most biblical covenants—meaning that God is the one who establishes the covenant and who fulfills the stipulations of the covenant. Covenants are also witnessed and call upon witnesses in some situations. When God entered the covenant with Abram, Abram was asleep. Who witnessed the covenant? Obviously, the witnesses have to be either the multiple Persons of the Godhead, the angels, or the inanimate creation (cf. Isa. 1:2 and Mic.

6:1—in which inanimate creation is called upon to witness God's actions and/or words)." (Dr. William Barrick)

43 See the previous note. Many of those facets come across to this covenant relationship (e.g., mutual accountability and responsibility to fulfill the stipulations of the covenant relationship).

44 Henry M. Morris, *The Genesis Record* (San Diego: Creation-Life Publishers, 1976), 135.

45 *Vine's*, "Testimony" entry.

46 Baker and Carpenter, #6490.

47 "Many commentators believe that *'imrāh* might also, in at least some of its usages, be the equivalent of 'promise.'" (Dr. William Barrick)

48 For more on *rhēma*, see the author's *AWFTD*, p. 261.

49 *The Treasury of David* (comment on Ps. 119:3).

50 Baker and Carpenter, #734.

51 Scripture contains no less than thirteen specific references to this: Gen. 19:5; Lev. 18:22; 20:13; Deut. 23:17–18; 1 Kings 14:24; 15:12; 22:46; 2 Kings 23:7; Rom. 1:26, 27; 1 Cor. 6:9; 1 Tim. 1:10; Jude 7 (which actually refers back to the first).

52 The word **Scripture** appears thirty-one times in the NT, always *graphē* (1124G).

53 John Gill, *John Gill's Exposition of the Entire Bible* (electronic edition).

54 *Vine's*, "Write (To)" entry.

55 Baker and Carpenter, #835.

56 For more on *makarios*, see the author's *AWFTD*, p. 12.

57 Baker and Carpenter, #8549.

58 The view of Davidic authorship of Psalm 119 is strengthened by three points. *First*, it is clealy Davidic in tone. *Second*, it matches David's personal experiences. As Adam Clarke writes, "Several of the ancients, particularly the Greek fathers, have considered it as an abridgement of David's life; in which he expresses all the states through which he had passed; the trials, persecutions, succours, and encouragements he had received." *Third*, and most significant, it parallels David's own words concerning the Word of God in Psalm 19. While John Calvin, for example, was not dogmatic, he did lean toward Davidic authorship. Others, such as Mathew Poole and Charles Spurgeon were far more insistent.

59 *TWOT*, #712.

60 J. Vernon McGee's *Thru The Bible* (WORDSearch Software electronic edition).

61 Ps. 102:18; 104:35; 105:45; 106:1, 48; 111:1; 112:1; 113:1, 9; 115:17, 18; 117:2; 135:1, 3, 21; 146:1, 10; 147:1, 20; 148:1, 14; 149:1, 9; 150:1, 6 (twice).

62 Zodhiates, #239.

63 Girdlestone, 242, n3. Lehman Strauss offers, "Allelujah, without the initial 'h,' is a misspelling, having been robbed of its initial aspirate" (*The Book of Revelation* [Neptune, NJ: Loizeaux Brothers, 1964], 315).

64 *TWOT*, #499.

65 For more on *doxa*, see the author's *AWFTD*, p. 224.

66 *TWOT*, #847.

67 *TWOT*, #285.

68 Adapted from *TWOT*, #1776.

69 This is called the reflective, or reciprocal, form, which simply means the action points back to the subject.

70 Girdlestone, 241.

71 *The Treasury of David* (comment on Ps. 64:1).

72 *TWOT*, #2303.

73 *Vines*, under the "Call (To)" entry.

74 In contrast, in NT times, the Jews were forced to adopt the Roman division of four watches of three hours each (Matt. 14:25; Mark 13:35).

75 For more on *adialeiptōs*, see the author's *AWFTD*, p. 151.

76 For more on *euangelizō* and *kērussō*, see the author's *AWFTD*, pp. 138–39.

77 *The Ante-Nicene Fathers*, Vol. 1; Ages Digital Library, "The First Apology Of Justin," Chapter 67.

78 James Montgomery Boice, *Psalms: An Expositional Commentary* (Grand Rapids: Baker Books, 2005), 1028.

79 Alister Begg, *Preaching for God's Glory* (Wheaton, IL: Crossway Books, 1999), 9.

80 *TWOT*, #547.

81 Louis Sperry Chafer, *Systematic Theology* (Dallas: Dallas Seminary Press, 1947–48), Vol. IV, 254.

82 *The Epistle of Barnabas* 15:8–9 (AD 100): "Finally, [the Lord] says to them: 'I cannot bear your new moons and Sabbaths' [Isa. 1:13]. . . . This is why we spend the eighth day in celebration, the day on which Jesus both rose from the dead and, after appearing again, ascended into heaven." (J. B. Lightfoot and J. R. Harmer [translators], *The Apostolic Fathers*, Second Edition [Grand Rapids: Baker Books, 1989], p. 183.) *The Letters of Ignatius: To Magnesians* 8:1–9:1 (107): "Do not be deceived by strange doctrines or antiquated myths, since they are worthless. For if we continue to live in accordance with Judaism, we admit that we have not received grace. . . . If, then, those who had lived in antiquated practices came to newness of hope, no longer keeping the Sabbath but living in accordance to the Lord's Day, on which our life also arose through him and his death." (Lightfoot, 95). It is incontrovertible fact that the early church met on the first day of the week.

83 Chafer, Vol. IV, 110.

84 *TWOT*, #647.

85 *Biblical Theology of the Old Testament* (Chicago: Moody, 1991), 232.

86 *TWOT*, #239.

87 "Interestingly, what the AV (and other translations) give as 'an understanding heart' is really 'a listening heart.' The listening heart prepares one for proper discernment—listening first to God and then carefully listening to others who might be involved in the situation about which we are to have discernment." (William Barrick)

88 For a deeper study of discernment, see the author's *AWFTD*, pp. 197–204.

89 *TWOT*, #44.

90 *TWOT*, #1011.

91 Brown-Driver-Briggs, Strong's number 3642.

92 Stephen D. Renn (Editor), Expository Dictionary of Bible Words (Peabody, MA: Hedrickson Publishers, Inc.) 2005, "Turn" entry.

93 *Vine's*, "Return (To)" entry.

94 Girdlestone, 91.

95 Joel Osteen on CNN, *Larry King Live* (10/16/2007). When then asked who will go to heaven, whether an atheist, Muslim, or Jew, Osteen demonstrated his inclusivism by answering, "I don't know; I just think only God can judge a person's heart . . . I've spent a lot of time in

India with my father and I don't know everything about their religion, but I know they love God. I don't know, I've seen their sincerity. I don't know."

96 Baker and Carpenter, #7686.

97 *Vine's*, "Transgress (To)" entry.

98 For more on *sarx* and Rom. 7—8, see the author's *AWFTD*, pp. 70–71, and for "confess" (*homologeō*, 3670) in 1 John 1:9, see p. 31.

99 Baker and Carpenter, #3467.

100 Charles Spurgeon, *The New Park Street Pulpit* (Grand Rapids: Baker Book House, 1990 reprint), Volume 3, 195.

101 *Vine's*, "Loving-kindness" entry.

102 "Even stronger, *chesed̲* speaks of 'loyal love' or 'steadfast love' associated with a covenant relationship. All kindness associated with this word is conditioned by loyalty and some kind of commitment. This is the loyal love shown by Ruth to her mother-in-law Naomi. Likewise, David's loyalty to Jonathan caused him to be kind to Mephibosheth. The mercy that God shows (described by *chesed̲*) is due to His commitment to His promises, His covenant. *Chesed̲*'s meaning is demonstrated in the use of the root as a name for the Hasidic Jews. They call themselves 'Hasidic' because they are the ones who are 'loyal' to God, 'committed' to Him." (William Barrick)

103 Thayer, #1656. For a deeper study of *eleos*, see the author's *AWFTD*, p. 86 (March 26).

104 *TWOT*, #694.

105 Ibid: "The verb *chānan* and its derivatives are components of the names of fifty-one persons. These include: Baalhanan, Elhanan, Hananel, Hanani, Hananiah, Hannah, Hanun, Henadad, Jehohanan, Johanan, Tehinnah. Cf. the Punic names Hanno and Hannibal. The woman's name Hannah has given us Anna, Ann, Nan, Nancy, Anita (Spanish) and Annette (French). Johanan has given us the name John: Jean (French), Giovanni (Italian), Juan (Spanish), Johann, and Hans (German), Jan (Dutch), and Ivan (Russian)."

106 *Vine's*, "Gracious (To Be)" entry.

107 For a deeper study of *charis*, see the author's *AWFTD*, p. 44.

108 Girdlestone, 135.

109 *Vine's*, "Redeem (To)" entry.

110 "The only cognate being an Amorite proper name" (*Vine's*, "Redeem (To)" entry).

111 It is the author's view that Paul was, indeed, the author of Hebrews. Read his defense of this position ("Does the Authorship of Hebrews Matter?") at: http://www.thescripturealone.com/TOTT-11.htm and http://www.thescripturealone.com/TOTT-12.htm.

112 Helena Matheopoulos, *Maestro: Encounters With Conductors of Today* (Harper & Row, 1982), 7.

113 As one Greek authority points out, *pisteuō* implicitly and indisputably carries the idea "to obey": "The fact that 'to obey,' as in the Old Testament, is particularly emphasized in Heb. 11. Here the *pisteuein* [faith] of Old Testament characters has in some instances the more or less explicit sense of obedience. . . . Paul in particular stresses the element of obedience in faith. For him *pistis* [faith] is indeed *hupakon* [obey] as comparison of Rom. 1:5, 8; I Thes. 1:8 with Rom. 15:18; 16:19, or 2 Cor. 10:5 with 10:15 shows. Faith is for Paul to *hupakouein tō euangeilō* [literally, "obedient to the good news"], Rom. 10:16. To refuse to believe is not to obey the righteousness which the Gospel offers by faith, Rom. 10:3. . . . He coins the combination *hupakon pisteuō* [literally, 'obedience of faith], Rom. 1:5" (Kittel, Vol. VI, p. 205).

114 Session 6, canon 9.

115 *Vine's*, "Love (To)" entry.

116 *TWOT*, #29.

117 For a deeper study of these words, see the author's *AWFTD*, pp. 19–21.

118 "Treating the words individually is not at odds with seeing that they also address every area of a person's existence. Likewise, seeing them as a reference to man as a whole is not necessarily contrary to considering the words individually. Both approaches are correct, if they both occur at the same time—it is not an either/or option." (William Barrick)

119 The Greek verb behind "chosen" in Ephesians 1:4, for example, is in the middle voice, indicating the subject acting in its own interest, that is, receiving the benefit of the action. God, therefore, did the choosing independently in the past and did so *primarily* for His own interest, that is, His glory.

120 Baker and Carpenter, #977.

121 *TWOT*, #231.

122 For a deeper study of *elpizō*, see the author's *AWFTD*, p. 13.

123 *TWOT*, #859.

124 Robert Leighton, *A Practical Commentary upon the First Epistle of Peter*.

125 Girdlestone, 206.

126 Technical note: *Apo* is here attached to "God" (*theos*), which is in the genitive case (*apo theou*). The genitive is the case of description.

127 Technical note: *Pros* is here attached to the definite article ("the") and the noun "God" (*theos*), which are in the accusative case (*pros ton theon*). The accusative is the case of limitation, marking the limit or end of an action. When used with the accusative, then, *pros* marks the object toward or to which something moves or is directed.

128 Technical note: The text reads *hē eirēnē tou theou*, "the peace of the God." *Tou theou* is again in the genitive case, describing to whom the peace belongs.

129 Girdlestone, 99. He elaborates in comparing *'āšām* with *chāṭā'* (2398, April 1) and the differences of opinion on these.

130 Baker and Carpenter, #3722.

131 Henry M. Morris, *The Genesis Record* (San Diego: Creation-Life Publishers, 1976), 182.

132 "The relationship of the noun for Passover to this particular verb root is extremely disputed. As in many Hebrew words, there could have been a homonymous root (a word sounding the same) having a totally different meaning. Or, the verb never did exist, only the noun. Not every Hebrew word has a verbal root." (William Barrick)

133 *TWOT*, #1786.

134 "Fellowship" is *koinōnia* (2842G), which speaks of a partnership, close union, and brotherly bond. For a deeper study of *koinōnia*, see the author's *AWFTD*, pp. 303–4.

135 *TWOT*, #285b.

136 John Walvoord, *The Holy Spirit* (Grand Rapids: Zondervan, 1954, 1958, 1979], 198.

137 *TWOT*, #1277, summarizes: "Actually the views of the derivation are four. 1) From an Arabic root, *naba'a*, "to announce," hence "spokesman" (Cornill, Koenig, Eiselen, G. A. Smith). 2) From a Hebrew root, *nābā'*, softened from *nāba'* "to bubble up," hence pour forth words (Gesenius, von Orelli, Kuenen, Girdlestone, Oehler). 3) From an Akkadian root *nabû* "to call," hence one who is called [by God] (Albright, Rowley, Meek, Scott), hence one who felt called of God; 4) From an unknown Semitic root (A. B. Davidson, Koehler and Baumgartner, BDB, E. J. Young, Heinisch.) The latter view is favored by Hobart E. Freeman in his excellent book (*An Introduction to the Old Testament Prophets*, Moody, 1968, 37–39). This paragraph is a very brief summary of Freeman's treatment."

138 Zodhiates writes, "In the New Testament *prophētēs* corresponds to the person who in the Old Testament spoke under divine influence and inspiration. This included the foretelling future events or the exhorting, reproving, and threatening of individuals or nations as the ambassador of God and the interpreter of His will to men (Ezek. 2). Hence the prophet spoke not his own thoughts but what he received from God, retaining, however, his own consciousness and self–possession (Exod. 7:1; 2 Pet. 1:20, 21; especially 1 Cor. 14:32). . . . In Eph. 2:20; 3:5, the prophets, named side by side with the Apostles (meaning the Eleven and those who were commissioned by Jesus directly) as the foundation of the New Testament church, are to be understood as exclusively New Testament prophets. They are listed in Eph. 4:11 between apostles and evangelists (see 1 Cor. 12:28). New Testament prophets were for the Christian church what Old Testament prophets were for Israel. They maintained intact the immediate connection between the church and the God of their salvation. They were messengers or communicators. Such prophets were not ordained in local churches nor do they have successors" (#4396, 1244–46).

139 For a deeper study of the NT "apostle," "prophet," "evangelist," and "pastor-teacher," see the author's *AWFTD*, pp. 179–83.

140 *Vine's*, "Priesthood" entry.

141 Rome maintains, according to the Council of Trent, that Jesus Himself "constituted [the apostles as] priests of the New Testament; and by those words, Do this in commemoration of me [Luke 22:19; 1 Cor. 11:24, 25], He commanded them and their successors in the priesthood to offer" Jesus' "body and blood under the species of bread and wine" (Session 22, Chapter 1), while Scripture, of course, says no such thing.

142 For a deeper study of the New Testament "pastor-teacher," "elder," and "bishop," see the author's *AWFTD*, pp. 182–85.

143 *Young's Literal Translation.*

144 Girdlestone, 306.

145 John Gill writes on this verse, for example: "Some render it, 'shall return to the grave,' to the earth, the original dust from whence they came; but this is common to all men, to the righteous as well as the wicked; rather *še'ôl* here signifies the place of torment, commonly called hell, where devils and damned spirits are; hither the souls of the wicked go immediately upon their departure from their bodies, Luke16:23" (*John Gill's Exposition of the Entire Bible*, electronic edition).

146 *TWOT*, #2303. See that in-depth discussion for the differing opinions on the meaning of this word.

147 William Dyrness, *Themes in Old Testament Theology* (Downers Grove: InterVarsity Press, 1979), 239, 240.

148 Baker and Carpenter, #216.

149 The first four types adapted from an outline in *Handfuls On Purpose* (Peabody, MA: Hendrickson Publishers, 2004), Series VIII, 305.

150 For a deeper study of *klēros*, *arrabōn*, and *sphragizō*, see the author's *AWFTD*, pp. 27, 29, and 30, respectively.

151 *TWOT*, #2143.

152 Two of these, for example, we have previously mentioned: *yāḏa'* (3045; March 8) and *biyn* (995, March 24).

153 *TWOT*, #1116.

154 Ibid., #910. "It is also used of 'casting the finger or hand' in the sense of pointing the way by gesturing with the hand with the forefinger extended, especially to point out a route or way. This is explained about the cognate *tôrāh* in Koehler and Baumgartner's *Hebrew and Aramaic Lexicon of the Old Testament*." (William Barrick)

155 For a deeper study of *akouō*, see the author's *AWFTD*, p. 119.

156 Baker and Carpenter, #5588.

157 *The Treasury of David* (comment on Ps. 119:113, emphasis in the original).

158 George Zemek, *Road Maps for the Psalms* (Valencia: CA: The Master's Academy International, 2006), Psalm 23 (no page numbers).

159 *The Treasury of David* (comment on Ps. 23:1, emphasis in the original).

160 Renn, under the entry "Soul."

161 Strong's: soul (475); life (117); person (29); mind (5); heart (15); creature (9); body (8); himself (8); yourselves (6); dead (5); will (4); desire (4); man (3); themselves (3); any (3); appetite (2); miscellaneous (47).

162 *Vine's*, "Life" entry.

163 Renn, under the entry "Soul."

164 *Albert Barnes Notes on the Bible*, electronic edition.

165 John H. Walton, Victor H. Matthews and Mark W. Chavalas, *The IVP Bible Background Commentary: Old Testament* (InterVarsity Press, 2000), electronic edition, Isa. 21:5. Further, as one Bible historian, for example, observes: "In many cases the Arab custom would seem to indicate to the Westerner that they use no table at all, when serving a meal. Actually, a mat spread upon the ground serves the purpose of a table. This is especially true of the tent Arab. This was the early Semitic table of Old Testament times, for the Hebrew word 'Shool-khawn,' [7979], usually translated 'table,' has as its root meaning, 'a skin or leather mat spread on the ground.' With this sort of a table in view, the Psalmist can be understood when he said concerning his enemies, 'Let their table become a snare before them' [Ps. 69:22]. David's meaning would be, 'Let their feet become entangled in it, as it is spread on the ground.' If the Arabs use more of a table than this mat, then it is likely to be a polygon stool, no higher than about fourteen inches, and those eating would sit on the floor around this Stool." (Fred Wight, *Manners and Customs of Bible Lands* [WORDsearch Corporation, originally published in 1953, electronic edition]).

166 *TWOT*, #2395.

167 *The Treasury of David* (comment on Ps. 23:5).

168 Luke 4:18, quoting Isa. 61:1; Heb. 1:9, quoting Psalm 45:7; Acts 4:27, referring back to the quotation of Ps. 2 that precedes it; and Acts 10:38.

169 For a deeper study of this phrase, see the author's *AWFTD*, p. 61.

170 J. Vernon McGee, *Thru the Bible Commentary* (Nashville: Thomas Nelson, 1981), electronic version on Ps. 23:5.

171 Baker and Carpenter, #2896.

172 *The Treasury of David* (comment on Ps. 37:3).

173 Based on the discussion in Louis Berkof, *Systematic Theology* (Grand Rapids: Eerdmans Publishing Company, 1993 reprint), 71–72.

174 The complete quotation is: "Does 'good' have an objective, absolute existence? Is there 'Good' with a capital 'G' so to speak, or is it always relative to the preference or satisfaction of some individual? Are there value judgments which are universal, valid for all men everywhere? Is there anything which all human beings regardless of time, place, race, or culture unite to call 'good'? Or does each person, in the final analysis, have an individual and perhaps unique system of values? Each person appears to decide, consciously or unconsciously, what he considers of value in the world and what he will spend his life trying to attain. Are there any objective standards by which we can judge this system of values that his actions imply? Or is his bald statement, 'I find X to be good,' the last word that can be said on the matter?" (Hunter

Mead, *Types and Problems of Philosophy* [New York: Holt, Rinehart, Winston, 1946, 1953, 1959], 256.]

175 The absolutist believes that there is only one standard or code for morality that is valid for all mankind and for all time. Now, while that sounds right, absolutism does not imply moral conservatism; in other words, the absolutist can be either a moral conservative or a moral radical. He is not required to either praise or condemn any specific moral act. All absolutism means is that *whatever* is right or wrong holds true for all men.

176 On the other hand, relativism is a revolt against absolutism, and is the prevailing view of our day in every area of human endeavor: science, politics, morals, and religion. Instead of *one* "Good," there are *many* "goods." What might be good or right for one group might not be good or right for another. All value is relative to the time, place, and civilization in which one finds himself.

177 Mead, op. cit, 274.

178 *TWOT*, #2191.

179 Albert Barnes, *Barnes' Notes on the Bible* (electronic version), note on Judg. 2:11.

180 *The Treasury of David* (comment on Ps. 119:3).

181 "This phrase is used of the Tabernacle, so we need not deny David the authorship of Psalm 23 the way some liberal scholars do. Compare Exod. 23:19; Josh. 6:24; 1 Sam. 1:7, 24; 2 Sam. 12:20." (William Barrick)

182 *The Treasury of David* (comment on Ps. 23:6).

183 *Vine's*, "Marvelous (To Be)" entry.

184 Other meanings include (Baker and Carpenter, #7602): "to pursue, chase, swallow, devour" (Job. 5:5; Ps. 56:1; Ps. 57:3; Isa. 42:14; Ezek. 36:3); and "to trample on, to crush" ("swallow" again in Ps. 56:1; 57:3; Ezek. 36:3).

185 Baker and Carpenter, #8373.

186 *TWOT*, #980.

187 *The Treasury of David* (comment on Ps. 119:101).

188 *The Treasury of David* (comment on Ps. 16:5). While **portion** here is actually a different Hebrew word (*mānāh*, 4490), Spurgeon's comment is not diminished.

189 David and Pat Alexander (editors) *Eerdmans Concise Bible Handbook* (Minneapolis: WorldWide, 1981), 237.

190 Baker and Carpenter, #1616.

191 Another commentator (Rosenmuller in *Biblical Illustrator*) says: "For it was a custom of the ancients to hang wineskins in the smoke of a fire for very much the same reason that we sometimes stand a claret bottle on the hearth, in order to mellow the wine by a gradual and moderate warmth, and to bring it to an earlier perfection. In that custom the psalmist finds an illustration of the meaning, and of the mercy of the afflictions to which he has been exposed. They have been sent to act on him like the warm smoke on the wine, to refine, mellow, and ripen his character; and because, under them all, he has refused to part with his faith in God and duty, because he has been true to God and God's statutes, they have had their intended and proper effect upon him." This doesn't seem to fit the context, however, as Keil and Delitzsch agree.

192 Erling C. Olson, *Meditations in the Book of Psalms* (Neptune, NJ: Loizeaux, 1939, 1941), 851.

193 *Vine's*, "Pass over" entry.

194 Charles Bridges, Psalm 119 (Carlisle, Pennsylvania: Banner of Truth Trust, 1974), 95.

195 Albert Barnes, *Barnes Notes on the Bible* (electronic edition), comment on Ps. 119:53, Adam Clark on 11:6 and 119:53 (*Adam Clark's Commentary on the Bible*, electronic edition), and John Gill on Lam. 5:10.

196 Adapted from a discussion by Girdlestone, 329.

197 Girdlestone, 328.

198 *Vine's*, "Abomination" entry.

199 *Vine's*, "Exalted (To Be)" entry.

200 Cited by William MacDonald, *Believer's Bible Commentary* (Nashville: Thomas Nelson, 1995), 806.

201 *Vine's*, "Falsehood" entry.

202 *TWOT*, #2461.

203 For a deeper study of *pseudos*, see the author's *AWFTD*, p. 73.

204 Also: Deut. 19:10, 13; 21:8, 9; 1 Sam. 19:5; 2 Kings 21:16; 24:4; Ps. 94:21; 106:38; Prov. 6:17; Isa. 59:7; Jer. 7:6; 22:3, 17.

205 *TWOT*, #48.

206 Respectively, *Young's Literal Translation*, *Geneva Bible*, Jay Green's *Literal Translation of the Holy Bible*).

207 Harry Ironside, *1 Corinthians* (New York: Loizeaux, 1938), 407–8.

208 See also Gen. 41:32; Job 38:12–15; Ps. 104:14, 147:16–18; Amos 4:7; Nah. 1:3; Matt. 5:45, 46; Acts 14:17.

209 See also Ps. 104:21; Dan. 6:22; Matt. 6:26; 10:29.

210 See also Dan. 2:21; Rom. 13:1; 1 Chron. 16:31; Job 12:23; Ps. 47:7, 66:7; Is. 10:5–7, 15; Dan. 2:38, 39; 4:25, 35; Acts 17:26.

211 *Hamlet*, 5.2.218–222.

212 "Paradox" comes from the Latin word *paradoxum*, which in turn comes from the Greek *paradoxos* (3861G). The root *doxa* means "opinion, expectation, or glory," and the prefix *para* means "beyond." In Greek, then, a paradox was something that was beyond expectation, something that surpassed all the opinions and anticipations of men. This word appears only once in the NT: "And they were all amazed, and they glorified God, and were filled with fear, saying, We have seen *strange things* to day" (Luke 5:28). The scene was the healing of the paralytic. When Jesus healed him, and he got up and walked, the people were amazed and said that they had seen "strange things" (*paradoxa*), that is, something that was beyond expectation, something that surpassed all the opinions and anticipations of men. Applying this to Biblical interpretation, there will be times when we will encounter things that are simply beyond our expectations, our opinions, and our anticipations. To put it simply, there will be things that we simply cannot comprehend, just as those spectators could not comprehend Jesus' miracle.

213 A. A Hodge, *Outlines of Theology* (Carlisle, PA: Banner of Truth Trust, 1991 reprint), 210.

214 *TWOT*, #1576.

215 Baker and Carpenter, #3576.

216 Note the following table: *Copyright 1985 Cook Communications Ministries.* ***The Bible Knowledge Commentary: Old Testament*** *by Walvoord and Zuck. Reprinted with permission. May not be further reproduced. All rights reserved.*

Words and Speaking in Proverbs	
I. Wrong Uses of Words	II. Right Uses of Words
A. Lying 6:16–17; 10:18; 12:19, 12:22; 17:4, 17:7; 19:5, 19:9, 19:22; 21:6; 26:28	A. Words that help and encourage 10:11, 10:20, 10:21; 12:14, 12:18; 15:4; 18:4, 18:20–21
B. Slandering 10:18; 30:10	B. Words that express wisdom 10:13, 10:31; 14:3; 15:1, Pro_15:7; 16:10, 16:21, 16:23; 20:15
C. Gossiping 11:13; 16:28; 17:9; 18:8; 20:19; 26:20, 26:22	C. Words that are few 10:19; 11:12; 13:3; 17:27
D. Constant talking 10:8, 10:10, 10:19; 17:28; 18:2; 20:19	D. Words that are fitting (kind, appropriate, pleasant) 10:32; 12:25; 15:1, 15:4, 15:23; 16:24; 25:11, 25:15
E. False witnessing 12:17; 14:5, 14:25; 19:5, 19:28; 21:28; 25:18	E. Words that are true 12:17, 12:19, 12:22; 14:5, 14:25
F. Mocking 13:1; 14:6; 15:12; 17:5; 19:29; 21:11; 22:10; 24:9; 30:17	F. Words that are carefully chosen 13:3; 15:28; 16:23; 21:23
G. Harsh talking (perverse, reckless, harsh, evil, sly words) 10:31–32; 12:18; 13:3; Pro_14:3; 15:1, 15:28; 17:4; 19:1, 19:28	

217 *The Bible Knowledge Commentary*, comment on Prov. 6:16.

218 *Keil & Delitzsch Commentary on the Old Testament.*

219 *The Treasury of David* (comment on Ps. 17:8).

220 John Gill, *John Gill's Exposition of the Entire Bible* (electronic edition).

221 Scripture is: of God, alive, sharp, piercing, divisive and offensive, and discerning.

222 Girdlestone, 313.

223 See discussion in *TWOT*, #2252.

224 Girdlestone, 312.

225 Girdlestone, 317.

226 *TWOT*, #230.

227 Albert Barnes, *Barnes Notes on the Bible* (electronic edition), comment on Job 12:11.

228 *Vine's*, "Nation" entry.

229 *TWOT*, #736.

230 For a deeper study of the related words in Eph. 4:26, see the author's *AWFTD*, 74.

231 *The Treasury of David* (comment on Ps. 119:106).

232 Albert Barnes, *Barnes Notes* (electronic edition): "Thus the scholiast says, *paroimia esti to kretizein epi tou pseudesthai*, to act the Cretan, is a proverb for to lie."

233 Girdlestone, 155.

234 Baker and Carpenter, #6051.

235 Charles Spurgeon, *The Treasury of David* (comment on Ps. 12:6). This work was first published in weekly installments over a twenty-year span in the London Metropolitan Tabernacle's periodical, *The Sword and the Trowel.* Completed sections were released volume by volume, until the seventh and final volume was released in 1885.

236 Baker and Carpenter, #6884.

237 Girdlestone, 103–104.

238 Zodhiates, #3340.

239 Chapter XV, Section II. Likewise, *The London Baptist Confession of Faith of 1689* declares: "God in [the elect's] effectual calling gives them repentance to life. . . . This saving repentance is an evangelical grace (Chapter 15, Sections 1, 3)

240 For a deeper study of *adelphos* and details about these four ideas, see the author's *AWFTD*, p. 333.

241 Albert Barnes, *Barnes' Notes on the Bible* (electronic version), note on Gen. 4:9.

242 For a deeper study of *angelos*, as well as such issues as their ministry and "guardian angels," see the author's *AWFTD*, p. 320.

243 John 6:11; Luke 24:30; Acts 27:35; Rom. 14:6; 1 Thess. 5:18.

244 *TWOT*, #690.

245 Sermon #2239; January 17, 1892.

246 *TWOT*, #1297.

247 For a deeper study of *proserchomai*, as well as a study of four principles concerning what it means to draw near to God, see the author's *AWFTD*, pp. 115–16.

248 *TWOT*, #905.

249 Charles Spurgeon, *The Treasury of David* (comment on Ps. 116:15).

250 Cf. cf. Matt. 22:44; 26:64; Mark 12:36; 16:19; Luke 20:42, 43; 22:69; Acts 2:34, 35; 7:55; Rom. 8:34; Eph. 1:20–22; Col. 3:1; Heb. 1:3, 13; 8:1; 10:12, 13; 12:2; 1 Pet. 3:22.

251 While this has long been a subject of debate, the only view that fits the context is that the "perfect" (*teleio*, mature, full-grown, complete thing) can refer only to *the completed New Testament Scriptures*. Throughout his letter Paul has been emphasizing preaching, teaching, and knowledge. In verses 11 and 12 he speaks of immature and incomplete knowledge, but when the New Testament Scriptures were completed, there was then mature, full-grown, knowledge. Instead of being children, they would then be adults. Spiros Zodhiatus puts it well: "The phrase 'when that which is perfect is come' refers to the written revelation of Scripture. When this revelation was completed, there was no need for the temporary gifts (e.g., tongues, prophecies, and knowledge) which were given in order to substantiate the message that the apostles were preaching" (*Hebrew-Greek Key Study Bible* [Chattanooga: AMG Publishers, 1984, 1991], 1436).

252 *King Richard II* (III.2.69).

253 *A Woman Killed with Kindness*, scene 6.

254 For a deeper study of *kairos*, including its use in Eph. 5:16, see the author's *AWFTD*, pp. 240–41.

255 *Macbeth*, 5.5.19–28

256 The Hebrew here is *hegeh* (1899), a muttering, rumbling, growling, moaning, or sighing sound.

257 John Gill, *John Gill's Exposition of the Entire Bible* (electronic edition).

258 The title "Song of Solomon" that appears in several English translations comes from verse 1, which states that the book was written by Solomon. The ancient Hebrew versions, however, call it "Song of Songs." This title translates the superlative in the Hebrew (*Shir Hash-Shirim*) as does "Holy of Holies," for example (Exod. 26:33, 34). In other words, of the 1,005 songs Solomon wrote, this is *the* song, Solomon's best.

259 Inexplicably, the margin in the NIV refers to Solomon as "Lover" and the maiden as "the Beloved." Why such a total reversal of what has been recognized through the ages?

260 Baker and Carpenter, #7838.

261 Dennis J. DeHaan, *Windows on the Word: Illustrations from "Our Daily Bread"* (Grand Rapids: Radio Bible Class, 1984), 99.

262 Baker and Carpenter, #3988.

263 *TWOT*, #2272.

264 See *TWOT*, #2406.

265 *Vine's*, "Rejoice, To" entry.

266 *John Gill's Exposition of the Entire Bible* (electronic edition), comment on Isaiah 55:11.

267 Interestingly, it appears that Israeli textbooks mix heroic myth with fact concerning the Masada incident. In his book, *The Masada Myth:Collective Memory and Mythmaking in Israel* (University of Wisconsin Press, 1995), Jewish author Nachman Ben-Yehuda attempts to differentiate what was fact and what was fiction. (William Barrick)

268 Charles Spurgeon, *The Treasury of David* (comment on Ps. 91:2).

269 *Calvin's Commentaries* (Psalms).

270 Renn, under the "Trust" entry.

271 Charles Spurgeon, *The Treasury of David* (comment on Ps. 18:2).

272 Ibid.

273 *John Gill's Exposition of the Entire Bible* (electronic edition).

274 "Which is in keeping with the teaching of the Old Testament regarding having a circumcised heart in Deut. 10:16 and 30:6, as well as Jer. 4:4 and 9:25–26 and Ezek. 44:7 and 9. The New Testament did not come up with this concept—the New Testament writers took it from the Old Testament. We see again, as emphasized in the Introduction, that most New Testament doctrine is rooted in Old Testament doctrine." (William Barrick)

275 Zodhiates, #2372.

276 *Epistles*, Book 1, Epistle I, 1ine 66.

277 *Imitations of Horace*, Epistle I, Book 1, line 103.

278 *TWOT*, #1708.

279 For a study of *emporeuomai* (1710G) and its use in 2 Peter 2:3, see the author's *AWFTD*, p. 165.

280 Baker and Carpenter, #3947.

281 Leland Ryken, James C. Wilhoit, and Tremper Longman III (General Editors), *Dictionary of Biblical Imagery* (InterVarsity Christian Fellowship, 1998, electronic edition), "Leaf" entry.

282 For a more detailed discussion of each of these principles, see the author's *AWFTD*, pp. 231–35.

283 Renald E. Showers wonderfully summarizes both OT and NT references to the Millennium (*There Really Is a Difference* [Bellmawr NJ: The Friends of Israel Gospel Ministry, Inc., 1990]).

- Nature will be restored to its prefall condition (Matt. 19:28; Acts 3:19–21; Rom. 8:18–23).

- The climate and natural elements will be controlled perfectly for the good of man (Isa. 30:23–26; Ezek. 47:1–2; Joel 2:21–26; Zech. 14:8).
- There will be unprecedented growth and fruitage of trees (Isa. 41:19–20; Ezek. 36:8–11, 29–30; 47:6–7, 12; Joel 2:21–26).
- Animals will experience great productivity (Ezek. 36:11; 47:8–10).
- Food will be abundant (Ps. 72:16; Isa. 30:23–24; Jer. 31:10–14; Ezek. 34:25–30; 36:29–30; Joel 2:21–26; Zech. 8:11–12).
- All animals will be tame and vegetarian in diet (Isa. 11:6–9; 65:25).
- Diseases and deformities will be abolished (Isa. 29:18; 33:24; 35:5–6).
- Human life will experience great longevity (Isa. 65:20–22).
- War will be abolished (Isa. 2:4; Mic. 4:3).
- Satan will not be able to instigate any activity on the earth (Rev. 20:1–3).

284 As the renowned ninetieth century Church historian Philip Schaff wrote, and as can be demonstrated by reading the listed writers: "The most striking point in the eschatology of the ante-Nicene age is the prominent chiliasm, or millennarianism, that is the belief of a visible reign of Christ in glory on earth with the risen saints for a thousand years, before the general resurrection and judgment. It was indeed not the doctrine of the church embodied in any creed or form of devotion, but a widely current opinion of distinguished teachers, such as Barnabas, Papias, Justin Martyr, Irenaeus, Tertullian, Methodius, and Lactantius" (*History of the Christian Church*, Vol. II [Grand Rapids: Eerdmans Publishing Company, 1973], 614) .

285 Dualism teaches that matter is evil and only the nonphysical is good. This resulted in Origen viewing a literal, physical kingdom with physical blessings as evil and prompted him to develop the idea of a spiritual kingdom where Christ simply rules presently in the hearts of believers, which is actually the definition of Amillennialism.

286 Charles Spurgeon, *The Treasury of David* (comment on Ps. 103:19).

287 Charles Spurgeon, *The Treasury of David* (comment on Ps. 132:12).

288 While we do like most of this book, we do not agree with the author's view that salvation demands no turning from sin, no resulting change in lifestyle, no commitment, or even a willingness to yield to Christ's lordship (*Balancing the Christian Life* [Chicago: Moody, 1969], 169–70).

289 For the inquisitive reader, we would recommend Ken Ham and Tim Lovett, "Was There Really a Noah's Ark & Flood?" in *The New Answers Book: 25 Top Questions on Creation/ Evolution and the Bible*, ed. by Ken Ham (Green Forest, AR: Master Books, 2006), 125–40.

290 *TWOT*, #898.

291 In my humble opinion, Baxter's trilogy on the Christian doctrine of sanctification is unequalled: *A New Call To Holiness*, *His Deeper Work In Us*, and *Our High Calling* (Zondervan).

292 For a deeper study of the "old man" and the "flesh," see the author's *AWFTD*, pp. 69–71.

293 This is, of course, the origin of our English word "iris" because of the numerous colors found among this family's 200–300 species of flowers.

294 Bruce M. Metzger, "Important Early Translations of the Bible," *Bibliotheca Sacra* 150 (Jan. 93), pp. 35. He goes on to explain: "The Targums are interpretive renderings of the books of the Hebrew Scriptures (with the exception of Ezra, Nehemiah, and Daniel) into Aramaic. Such versions were needed when Hebrew ceased to be the normal medium of communication among the Jews. In synagogue services the reading of the Scriptures was followed by a translation into the Aramaic vernacular of the populace. For a reading from the Pentateuch the Aramaic translation followed each verse of the Hebrew; for a reading from the Prophets three verses were followed by the Aramaic translation. At first the oral Targum was a simple paraphrase in

Aramaic, but eventually it became more elaborate and incorporated explanatory details inserted here and there into the translation of the Hebrew text. To make the rendering more authoritative as an interpretation, it was finally reduced to writing."

295 *The Targums of Onkelos and Jonathan*, cited in John Gill, *John Gill's Exposition of the Entire Bible* (electronic edition). As Metger (previous note) explains, these were "two officially sanctioned Targums, produced first in Palestine and later revised in Babylonia . . . both of which were in use in the third century of the Christian era."

296 "We could very well translate *qôl* as 'sound' in Gen. 3:8 and 10. This would, in fact, be consistent with the theophanies of the Old Testament, which involved earthquake, wind, lightning, and thunder. A similar incident is recorded in 2 Samuel 5:24. The implication, then, is that God regularly met with Adam during the 'wind of the day.' The purpose of theophanies in the Old Testament is to give revelation. These meetings were indeed intended to be times of God speaking to Adam and giving him revelation. He would do so 'face to face'—not at a distance from somewhere else in the garden. While the Targums catch the significance of the usual purpose (previous note), his time, Adam was not ready to receive the revelation, because of his disobedience. What a lesson that is to us! As soon as he heard the sounds of the theophany, he and Eve hid themselves out of guilt." (William Barrick)

297 For a deeper study of "Cornerstone," see the author's *AWFTD*, p. 191.

298 *Vine's*, "Bury (To)" entry.

299 Just a few more include: Moses (Deut. 34), Gideon (Judg. 8:32), Samson (16:31), Samuel (1 Sam. 25:1), David (1 Kings 2:10–12; 1 Chron. 29:26–28), Solomon (1 Kings 11:41–43), and the long list goes on.

300 Tacitus (ca. 56–ca. 117 AD), *The Histories*, Book V (ca. AD 110).

301 James Orr (General Editor), *International Standard Bible Encyclopedia* (electronic edition), "Burial" entry.

302 Question is sometimes raised over Asa, but he was unquestionably buried, but then was honored by "a very great burning," that is, a fire of incense and spices (2 Chron. 16:14). In contrast, Jehoram did not receive the honoring spice burning because of his shameful reign (21:19).

303 While Proverbs 8:22–31 has been interpreted as representing a picture of Christ, there is really no justification for doing so. The context is about the eternal character of *wisdom*, and there is no merit to the idea that it is Messianic. Yes, Christ is the Word (John 1:1, 14), He is the revelation of God's wisdom (1 Cor. 1:24), and He possesses all wisdom and knowledge (Col. 2:3), but this passage is not prophetic. One glaring reason that it is not a reference to Christ is that we are forced to conclude that He was "brought forth," that is, created, which is apostasy (cf. John 1:2–4). Sadly, the Septuagint implies this, which is what Arius used to teach his apostate doctrine that Jesus was not coequal with God but was a created being (Arianism).

304 The believer is to: take off lying and put on truth (v. 25); take off unrighteous vengeance and put on righteous anger (vv. 26–27); take off stealing and put on laboring (v. 28); take off corrupt speech and put on good speech (v. 29); take off natural reactions to put on spiritual actions (vv. 30–32).

305 *TWOT*, #244.

306 *Vine's*, "Firstborn" entry.

307 Most evangelical commentators agree that Hebrews 1:6 is, indeed, a reference to the Second Coming. For example, the *Bible Knowledge Commentary* states: "The prerogatives of the One who bears this superlative title are set forth beginning with this verse. Instead of the NIV's **And again, when God brings His Firstborn into the world**, it would be preferable to translate, 'and when He again brings the Firstborn into the world.' The reference is to the Second Advent when the kingly prerogatives of the Son will be recognized with open angelic worship (cf. Psa. 97:7 where the Septuagint rendering 'angels' correctly renders the text)."

308 “The concept of God’s people being **firstborn** is not new to the New Testament. It was already applied to Israel in Exodus 4:22 and Jeremiah 31:9 (in the context of the New Covenant!).” (William Barrick)

309 Another possible distinction is that *rē'šiyṯ* refers “generally to what is prepared by human labor,” while *bikkûriym* indicates “the direct product of Nature” (*International Standard Bible Encyclopedia*, “First-fruits” entry).

310 *The Life of Reason* (1905–06), Vol. 1, *Reason in Common Sense,* 284.

311 A “loan word” (also spelled “loanword”) is a word taken directly from one language into another with little or no translation. English, for example, is saturated with such words. The following estimates have been made: French, including Old French and early Anglo-French (28.3%); Latin, including modern scientific and technical Latin (28.24%); Germanic languages, including Old and Middle English (25%); Greek (5.32%); no etymology given (4.03%); derived from proper names (3.28%); all other languages contributed (less than 1%). (Source: Thomas Finkenstaedt and Dieter Wolff, *Ordered Profusion* [C. Winter, 1973]).

312 *TWOT*, #1540.

313 For a study of *biblos* and more on ancient writing, see the author’s *AWFTD*, pp. 354–55.

314 I still recall a certain preacher who used that incident to counsel a young man that if he wanted to win his girl, all he need do was march around her seven times and the “walls of her heart” would fall down. Such nonsensical spiritualizing would be funny if it were not so tragic. The need for proper interpretation of Scripture has never been greater than it is in our modern times.

315 A “type” (Greek *tupos*, “figure, form, impression,” 5179G), is a picture or object lesson of some truth. A valid example of a person being a type is Isaac (a picture of Christ), or a valid event that is a type is the deliverance of the Israelites from Egypt (a picture of redemption). Forcing types into virtual allegory was the practice of early Church Fathers Origen, Ambrose, and Jerome. Examples include reading significance into the cords and pins of the tabernacle, each pillar of the temple, and even the 153 fish that the disciples caught on the night the risen Lord appeared to them.

316 Preaching at the Moody Bible Institute’s Founder’s Week in 1974.

317 Interview with Vance Havner by Dennis Hester; October 1982.

318 *TWOT*, #837.

319 We also note in Absalom’s case that *na'ar* can cover even a married man who had three sons and a daughter (2 Sam. 14:27).

320 Some interpreters see the Hebrew tetragrammaton YHWH (January 8) “acrostically hidden” in four verses (1:20; 5:4, 13; 7:7). It is insisted that in some manuscripts these Hebrew letters appear larger at the beginning (or end) of consecutive words and therefore spell out YHWH. While intriguing, this idea remains unsubstantiated for lack of evidence.

321 Wilfred Funk, *Word Origins: An Exploration and History of Words and Language* (New York: Wings Books, 1950, and Random House, 1998), 323.

322 Charleston, South Carolina became a chief Huguenot settlement. The French Huguenot Church of Charleston—founded in 1685 and pastored by Rev. Elie Prioleau from the town of Pons in France—remains independent to this day and is the oldest continuously active Huguenot congregation in the United States.

323 *Albert Barnes Notes on the Bible* (electronic edition).

324 Elizabeth Barrett Browning, “Cowper’s Grave,” *The Poetical Works of Elizabeth Barrett Browning* (London: John Murray, 1914), p. 143. In tears she penned this in her grief over William Cowper’s loneliness and lack of salvation assurance.

325 The reader might enjoy Gene Fisher and Glen Chambers, *The Revolution Myth* (Greenville, SC: Bob Jones University Press, 1981).

326 Thomas Paine, *The American Crisis*, No. 21, March 21, 1778.

327 Another fascinating and accurate book of American history records the Puritans' view: "Our fathers . . . did not initiate a rebellion against an established Constitution; they stood simply for their hereditary English rights, their legal and chartered rights; and when those rights were assailed with armed invasion, they stood in arms for the defense of their inheritance and their political existence. They did not begin the war, rushing to take up arms before any demonstration in arms had been made against them: they waited in the hope that justice would prevail in the councils of the king; they offered no resistance, but by remonstrance and petition, till their king made war on them. They did not commence with an act of secession from the British Empire, nor with renunciation of their allegiance to the British crown. Their declaration of independence was not made till after the king and Parliament had begun the attempt to establish, by military power, new methods of government over them" (Benjamin Morris, *The Christian Life and Character of the Civil Institutions of the United States* (Powder Springs, Georgia: American Vision, Inc., 2007), 334.

328 For a deeper study of the words in Eph. 6:10–20 and related verses, see the author's *AWFTD*, pp. 274–82.

329 *Tanakh* is an acronym (***TaNaKah***) formed from the initial Hebrew letters of the three traditional subdivisions of the Old Testament Scriptures: Tora (the Law or Teaching), Nevi'im (the Prophets) and Ketuvim (the Writings).

330 *The Treasury of David* (comment on Ps. 57:8).

331 *TWOT*, #582.

332 For a deeper study of *paraklētos*, see the author's *AWFTD*, pp. 157–59.

333 God commanded Jacob to do so, went with him, and brought him back up.

334 *TWOT*, #1711.

335 For a deeper study of the principles for Christian giving according to 1 Cor. 16:2, see the author's *AWFTD*, pp. 331–32.

336 *TWOT*, #2038.

337 *Othello* (III, 3,192–94)

338 *The Treasury of David* (comment on Ps. 37:1).

339 *Vine's*, "Kingdom" entry (usage number 2).

340 Baker and Carpenter, #5382.

341 Fascinatingly, 1 and 2 Chronicles include their own documentation, specifying many contemporary sources used in recording the chronicled events: "the account of the chronicles of king David" (1 Chron. 27:24); "the book of the kings of Israel and Judah" (2 Chron. 27:7; 35:27; 36:8); "the book of the kings of Judah and Israel" (16:11; 25:26; 28:26; 32:32); "the story of the book of the kings (24:27); "the records of Samuel the seer" (1 Chron. 29:29); "the records of Nathan the prophet" (2 Chron. 29:29; 9:29); "the records of Gad the seer" (1 Chron. 29:29); the prophecy of Ahijah the Shilonite (2 Chron. 9:29); the visions of Iddo the seer (9:29); the book of Shemaiah the prophet (12:15); the book of Iddo the seer (12:15); the annals of the prophet Iddo (13:22); the vision of Isaiah the prophet (26:22; 32:32).

342 John Gill, *John Gill's Exposition of the Entire Bible* (electronic edition).

343 For a deeper study of these verses and their reference to "The Alpha and the Omega," see the author's *AWFTD*, p. 102.

344 *The Treasury of David* (comment on Ps. 17:5).

345 Ibid (comment on 38:16).

346 *The Treasury of David* (comment on Ps. 119:11, emphasis added).

347 For a deeper study of Eph. 4:26 and "anger" as it is used there, see the author's *AWFTD*, p. 74.

348 John Gill, *John Gill's Exposition of the Entire Bible* (electronic edition), comment on Isa. 42:5. Matthew Henry concurs: God gives "not only air to breathe in, but the breath of life itself and organs to breathe with; nay, he gives spirit, the powers and faculties of a rational soul, to those that walk therein." More specifically, *TWOT* (#2131) makes these distinctions: "*rûaḥ* is the principle of man's rational and immortal life, and possesses reason, will, and conscience. It imparts the divine image to man, and constitutes the animating dynamic which results in man's *nepesh* as the subject of personal life. The distinctive personality of the individual inheres in his *nepesh*, the seat of his emotions and desires. *rûach̦* is life-power, having the ground of its vitality in itself; the *nepesh* has a more subjective and conditioned life. The New Testament seems to make a clear and substantive distinction between *pneuma* (*rûach*) and *psuchē* (*nep̱eš*)."

349 Kittel, Vol. VI, 452.

350 For a deeper study of the Greek words mentioned today, as well a study of 2 Tim. 3:16–17 and the related 2 Peter 1:19–20, see the author's *AWFTD*, pp. 311–14.

351 A. W. Tozer, *God Tells the Man Who Cares* (Harrisburg: Christian Publications, 1970), 145.

352 *The Treasury of David* (comment on Ps. 26:7).

353 "Industry Statistics & Trends." American Pet Products Manufacturers Association, Inc., 2007–08.

354 *The Treasury of David* (comment on Ps. 5:3).

355 *The Treasury of David* (comment on Ps. 104:23).

356 While some think that "cool of the day" refers to the morning, that is not necessarily true. Adam Clarke, for example, argues: "It is very likely that God used to converse with them in the garden, and that the usual time was the decline of the day . . . in the evening breeze [*rûach*, Dec. 8]; and probably this was the time that our first parents employed in the more solemn acts of their religious worship, at which God was ever present." Likewise, Keil & Delitzsch submit: "In the cool of the day (lit., in the wind of the day), i.e., towards the evening, when a cooling wind generally blows." There are others.

357 Food Marketing Institute.

358 A good summary appears in the *International Standard Bible Encyclopedia* (electronic edition; "Image" entry): "Is there any distinction to be understood between 'image' and 'likeness'? Most of the Fathers, and some later theologians, attempt to distinguish between them. (a) Some have referred 'image' to man's bodily form, and 'likeness' to his spiritual nature (Justin Martyr, Irenaeus). (b) Others, especially the Alexandrian Fathers, understood by the 'image' the mental and moral endowments native to man, and by the 'likeness' the Divine perfections which man can only gradually acquire by free development and moral conflict (Clement of Alexandria and Origen), or which is conferred on man as a gift of grace. (c) This became the basis of the later Roman Catholic distinction between the natural gifts of rationality and freedom (= the image), and the supernatural endowments of grace which God bestowed on man after He had created him (the likeness = *donum superadditum*). The former remained after the Fall, though in an enfeebled state; the latter was lost through sin, but restored by Christ. The early Protestants rejected this distinction, maintaining that supernatural righteousness was part of the true nature and idea of man, i.e., was included in the 'image,' and not merely externally superadded. Whatever truth these distinctions may or may not contain theologically, they cannot be exegetically inferred from Genesis 1:26, where (as is now generally admitted) no real difference is intended. We have here simply a 'duplication of synonyms' (Driver) for the sake of emphasis. The two terms are elsewhere used interchangeably."

359 *Exploring Genesis: An Expository Commentary* (Kregel Academic. 2001), p. 45.

360 "Among the Egyptians, almost everything in nature was the object of their idolatry; among beasts were oxen, heifers, sheep, goats, lions, dogs, monkeys, and cats; among birds, the ibis, crane, and hawk; among reptiles, the crocodile, serpents, frogs, flies, and beetles; all the fish of the Nile, and the Nile itself; besides the sun, moon, planets, stars, fire, light, air, darkness, and night. These are all included in the very circumstantial prohibition in the text, and very forcibly

in the general terms of Exod. 20:4, the reason of which prohibition becomes self-evident, when the various objects of Egyptian idolatry are considered" (*The Treasury of Scriptural Knowledge*, electronic edition, comment on Deut. 4:17).

361 *TWOT*, #613.

362 God's *sovereign will* is His predetermined plan and purpose. This has also been called God's "decretive will" or His "hidden will" (Latin *deus absconditus*). This is what He has determined will come to pass. In contrast, God's *moral will* involves what He has spoken in His Word and what is therefore absolute. This is also called His "perceptive will" or His "revealed will" (Latin *deus revelatus*). God's *will*, therefore, is revealed in His *Word*. Both of these aspects of God's will are referred to in Deut. 29:29: "The secret things belong unto the LORD our God: but those things which are revealed belong unto us and to our children for ever, that we may do all the words of this law."

In contrast to those, one writer puts the matter well concerning the supposed *individual will*: "The phrase 'will of God' is simply not used in this sense of idealized personal plan that forms a pattern of decision making. This supposed 'individual will' is not God's sovereign will, which is behind providences, nor is it the revealed will of God in Scripture. It is something in between these two and separate from them. The passages that are cited [to prove such an idea] (Col 1:9; 4:12; Rom. 12:2; Eph. 5:17; 6:6), all actually refer to God's will as revealed in his commandments and applies to our lives. So advocates of this view are using a category that is not introduced in Scripture—a big problem!" (James Petty, *Step By Step: Divine Guidance for Ordinary Christians* [Phillipsburg, NJ: P&R Publishing, 199]). Cited in Dave Swavely, *Decisions, Decisions* [Phillipsburg, NJ: P&R Publishing, 2003], 55–56.)

363 Pliny the Elder (Editors: John Bostock, H.T. Riley, Esq.), *The Natural History* (London: Taylor and Francis, Red Lion Court, Fleet Street, 1855), Book vii. Chap 1.

364 William Shakespeare, *Macbeth*, I. v. 62–63.

365 Henry M. Morris, *The Genesis Record* (San Diego: Creation-Life Publishers, 1976), 322.

366 Henry Morris again says it well: "It is impossible to place the inspired, inerrant Word of God on too high a pedestal, for God Himself honors it above His name! The Word is not greater than God, for He wrote it by His Spirit, but it is greater than His "name," which represents Him, and all that He is and does. His Word, however, represents Him more fully than His name alone can do: in His Word His name is revealed" (*The Defender's Study Bible*, comment on Ps. 138:2).

367 Another important word here is *āmēn* (543). See the author's *AWFTD*, p. 366.

Bibliography

Notes are keyed to this Bibliography.

Archer, Gleason. Harris, Laird; Waltke, Bruce. *Theological Wordbook of the OT*. Chicago: Moody Bible Institute, 1980. (Abbreviated TWOT in the notes.)

Baker, Warren and Carpenter, Eugene. *The Complete Word Study Dictionary: OT*. Chattanooga: AMG Publishers, 2003.

Brown, Colin (General Editor). *The New International Dictionary of NT Theology* (3 Vol.). Grand Rapids: Zondervan, 1975. (Abbreviated NIDNTT in the notes.)

Brown, Francis; Driver, R.; and Briggs, Charles. *Brown-Driver-Briggs Hebrew-English Lexicon*. Electronic edition by WORDsearch Corporation.

Renn, Stephen D. (Editor). *Expository Dictionary of Bible Words*. Peabody: MA: Hendrickson Publishers, Inc., 2005.

Girdlestone, Robert Baker. *Girdlestone's Synonyms of the OT*. Reprint; Grand Rapids: Baker Book House, 1983.

Kittle, Gerhard (Editor). *Theological Dictionary of the NT (10 Vol.)*. Grand Rapids: Eerdmans, 1964; reprinted 2006).

Strong, James. *Strong's Exhaustive Concordance*. Updated electronic version by The Online Bible.

VanGemeren, Willem A., ed. *New International Dictionary of Old Testament Theology and Exegesis. 5 vols*. Grand Rapids: Zondervan, 1997. (Abbreviated NIDOTTE in the notes.)

Vine, William E., Merrill F. Unger, and William White, Jr. *Vine's Expository Dictionary of Biblical Words*. Nashville: Thomas Nelson, 1992.

Scripture Index

Exodus

Leviticus

Numbers

Deuteronomy

Joshua

Judges

Ruth

1 Samuel

2 Samuel

1 Kings

Job

Psalms

Proverbs

Ecclesiastes

Song of Solomon

Isaiah

Jeremiah

Lamentations

Ezekiel

Daniel

Hosea

Mark

Luke

John

Acts

Romans

1 Corinthians

2 Corinthians

Galatians

Ephesians

James

1 Peter

2 Peter

1 John

Jude

Revelation

English Word Index

Hebrew and Greek Word Index

(Greek words are followed by a "G")

Strong's Number Index

(Greek numbers are followed by a "G")